D0169285

SOLVING PROBLEMS THROUGH TECHNICAL AND PROFESSIONAL WRITING

SOLVING PROBLEMS THROUGH TECHNICAL AND PROFESSIONAL WRITING

George E. Kennedy
Washington State University

Tracy T. Montgomery
Idaho State University

McGRAW-HILL, INC.

New York St. Louis San Francisco Auckland Bogotá Caracas
Lisbon London Madrid Mexico Milan Montreal New Delhi
Paris San Juan Singapore Sydney Tokyo Toronto

This book was developed by STEVEN PENSINGER, Inc.

This book was set in Caslon by Better Graphics, Inc.
The editors were Steve Pensinger and Jean Akers;
the designer was Joan Greenfield;
the production supervisor was Louise Karam.
The cover art was by Hera Marashian.
R. R. Donnelley & Sons Company was printer and binder.

Credits

Engineering Feasibility of a 150-kW Irrigation Pumping Plant Using Shallow Solar Ponds, by E. A. Platt and R. L. Wood, reprinted by permission of the University of California, Lawrence Livermore National Laboratory, and the Department of Energy under whose auspices the work was performed.

"Lives of a Cell," copyright (c) 1971 by the Massachusetts Medical Society, from *The Lives of a Cell* by Lewis Thomas. Used by permission of Viking Penquin, a division of Penguin Books USA Inc.

Excerpt from a review of the year's activities of a regional Planned Parenthood agency reprinted with permission by Planned Parenthood of Spokane and Whitman Counties.

Figure reprinted with permission from Sandia National Laboratories, "Unattended Video Surveillance System for Nuclear Facilities," in *Sandia Engineering and Science Accomplishments*, December 1990, p. 36.

Figure reprinted with permission from Sandia National Laboratories, "The Use of Advanced Diagnostics and Computer Modeling to Examine Energetic Material Ignition and Combustion," in *Sandia Technology*, August 1989, p. 26.

SOLVING PROBLEMS THROUGH TECHNICAL AND PROFESSIONAL WRITING

1 2 3 4 5 6 7 8 9 0 DOC DOC 9 0 9 8 7 6 5 4 3 2

ISBN 0-07-034056-0

Library of Congress Cataloging-in-Publication Data

Kennedy, George E.
    Solving problems through technical and professional writing /
  George E. Kennedy, Tracy T. Montgomery.
        p.   cm.
    Includes bibliographical references and index.
    ISBN 0-07-034056-0
        1. English language—Technical English.   2. English language—
  Business English.   3. English language—Rhetoric.   4. Technical
  writing.   5. Business writing.   I. Montgomery, Tracy T.   II. Title.
  PE1475.K46   1993
  808'.066—dc20   92-26674

ABOUT THE AUTHORS

George E. Kennedy is an associate professor of English at Washington State University. He has a Ph.D. in English from New York University and has taught nineteenth century British literature, humanities, composition, and technical and professional writing since 1973 at several places: Herbert H. Lehman College (CUNY), Southern College of Technology (Marietta, GA), and currently at Washington State University (Pullman). Kennedy has been principal investigator or associate investigator on grants from the National Institute of Education and the National Endowment for the Humanities. His publications include articles on Dickens, Gissing, and the theory and pedagogy of technical and professional writing. He is currently working on an interdisciplinary text on language and culture, called LANGUAGE IN CULTURE, designed for students in linguistics, anthropology, communication, education, and English composition.

Tracy T. Montgomery is an assistant professor of English at Idaho State University. She earned her D.A. (Doctor of Arts) degree in English from Idaho State, one of about 25 universities in the country that offer this pedagogical doctorate. From 1985 to 1988, she worked as a technical writer, an in-house writing teacher, and, subsequently, Publications Manager at Westinghouse Electric Corporation, under contract to the U.S. Department of Energy, at the WIPP Project in Carlsbad, NM. She then taught technical writing at Washington State University before coming back to Idaho State in 1990. She has presented several papers at professional technical communication conferences and published in *The Technical Writing Teacher* and *Rendezvous*.

To Nancy and Hannah
  G.E.K.

To my students
  T.T.M.

CONTENTS

Preface   xvii

1   PROFESSIONALISM AND PROBLEM SOLVING   1

Case Study: Susan James   2
Professionals and Professionalism   3
    Examples of Professionalism   4
    Professional Activity   5
Profiles of Professionals   7
    The Problems They Solve and the Documents They Write   7
    Highlights of the Professional Profiles   15
Solving Problems by Asking and Answering Questions   16
Exercises   18
Assignment   18
    Term Project Option   18

2   TECHNICAL PROBLEM SOLVING   21

Case Study: Susan James   22
An Overview of Technical Problem Solving   23

Definition   23

   Defining Multiple Problems   25

   Techniques of the Definition Process   27

   Summary of the Definition Process   32

Research   32

   Straightforward Primary Research   33

   Complex Primary Research with Fieldwork   33

   Acquiring and Evaluating Secondary Research Materials   35

   Summary of the Research Process   38

Analysis   38

Resolution and Synthesis   41

Implementation   44

Conclusions   46

Exercises   46

Assignments   47

   Term Project Options   47

3   RHETORİCAL PROBLEM SOLVING   49

Case Study: Mary Anne Cox   50

An Overview of Rhetorical Problem Solving   51

Purpose   56

   Primary Purposes   57

   Secondary Purposes   57

Audience   58

   First Level of Audience Analysis   59

   Second Level of Audience Analysis   60

Context   65

Ethical Stance   66

Rhetorical Problem Solving as a Recursive Process   66

Writing for Someone Else's Signature   70

Conclusions   71

Exercises   72

Assignments   78

   Term Project Option   81

4 SOLVING PROBLEMS THROUGH PROPOSALS 83

Case Study: Patricia Wynjenek　84

Fundamentals of a Proposal　85

　Purpose and Rationale　85

　Kinds of Proposals　85

Analyzing the Process of Proposal Writing　88

　Statement of the Problem　88

　Analysis of the Audiences　91

　Statement of the Objectives of the Work Proposed　94

　Review of the Literature and Previous Work　95

　Methods for Doing the Work　96

　Facilities　98

　Personnel　98

　Budget and Schedule　99

　Expected Results and Evaluation Plan　100

Format of a Proposal　100

　Basic Format　101

　Expanded Format　101

Conclusions　107

Exercises　107

Assignments　112

　Term Project Option　112

　Student Proposal 1　113

　Student Proposal 2　133

　Student Proposal 3　144

5 SOLVING PROBLEMS THROUGH PROGRESS (PERIODIC) REPORTS AND COMPLETION REPORTS 155

Case Study: Leah Feldstein　156

Fundamentals of a Periodic Report　157

　Purpose and Rationale　157

Questions That Periodic Reports Answer　158

　What Project or Work Is Being Reviewed in the Report?　158

What Period of Time Does the Report Cover?   159

In Summary, What Has Happened during This Period?   159

What Work Has Been Accomplished?   160

What Problems Arose While Doing the Work?   160

Is the Work on Schedule and within Budget?   161

What Work Has to Be Done in the Future?   162

Format and Substance of a Periodic Report   163

Sample Professional Periodic Report   163

Exercises   163

Assignments   169

Term Project Option   169

Case Study: Patricia Wynjenek   170

Fundamentals of a Completion Report   171

Purpose and Rationale   171

Questions That Completion Reports Answer   172

What Is the Problem? Why Does It Warrant Special Attention?   172

What Work Was Done? How Was It Done? What in General
Were the Results?   173

What Conclusions Can Be Drawn from the Work That Was Done?
How Can the Data Be Interpreted? What Decisions, If Any Are Necessary,
Can Be Made Given What Is Now Known?   174

Format and Substance of a Completion Report   175

Elements of the Format for a Nonacademic Audience   175

Elements of the Format for an Academic, Research-Oriented
Audience   181

Sample Professional Completion Report   185

Exercises   185

Assignments   207

Term Project Option   207

Student Completion Report   208

6 SOLVING PROBLEMS THROUGH TRIP REPORTS, FEASIBILITY STUDIES, AND LAB REPORTS   227

Case Study: Bruce Kennewick   228

Fundamentals of a Trip Report   229

Purpose and Rationale   229

Analyzing the Process of Writing a Trip Report   229
   Introduction   230
   Overall Assessment of the Work Done   230
   Problems and Solutions   231
   Conclusions and Recommendations   232
Format and Substance of a Trip Report   232
Sample Professional Trip Report   232
Exercises   232
Assignment   240
   Term Project Option   240

Case Study: Al Robinson   241
Fundamentals of a Feasibility Study   241
   Purpose and Rationale   241
Analyzing the Process of Writing a Feasibility Study   242
Sample Outline for a Feasibility Study   243
   Sample Engineering Feasibility Study   244
Exercises   272
Fundamentals of Scientific Writing   272
   Evolution of Scientific Writing   272
   The Professional Writing Continuum   273
Format and Substance of a Scientific Report   275
Sample Student-Authored Scientific Article   275
Exercises   276

7 SOLVING PROBLEMS THROUGH POLICY STATEMENTS, MANUALS, AND PROCEDURES   291

Case Studies: Ruth Warner, Bob Hanley, Rick Allen   292
Distinguishing among Policy Statements, Manuals, and Procedures   296
   Policy Statements   296
   Manuals   296
   Procedures   297
Rhetorical Problem Solving for Policy Statements, Manuals, and Procedures   298
Guidelines for Writing an Enforceable Policy Statement   299
Sample Policy Statement   300

Guidelines for Producing a Functional Manual   301

   Formatting   301

   Readability   302

   Organization   302

   Appendixes and Attachments   303

Sample Outline for a Manual   303

Guidelines for Writing a Logical Procedure   303

   Essential Characteristics of Procedures   305

   Model for Procedure Writing   307

Sample Administrative Procedure   309

Sample Operations Procedure   314

Analyzing an Administrative Procedure   317

Conclusions   317

Postscript   321

Exercises   321

Assignment   321

8 SOLVING PROBLEMS THROUGH LETTERS AND MEMORANDA   325

Case Study: Jay Dalton   326

Memos and Letters as Problem Solvers   327

   Documenting with Memos and Letters   327

   Distinguishing between Memos and Letters   328

Format of a Letter and a Memo   328

   Standard Letter Format   329

   Standard Memo Format   329

Conventions of Administrative Writing   329

   Structure and Content   333

   Length   333

Reading and Writing Professionally at Two Levels   334

   The Literal Level   334

   The Implicit Level   339

Analyzing the Administrative Writing Process   341

   Isolating the Main Problem   342

   Identifying Underlying Problems   342

   Applying the Principles of Rhetorical Problem Solving   343

Sample Professional Memo Written to Solve a Problem   344

Postscript   348

Transmittal Letters as Problem Solvers   348

   Functions of a Transmittal Letter   349

   Copy Notation for a Transmittal Letter   349

Sample Professional Transmittal Letters   350

Writing for Someone Else's Signature   350

   Considering the Audience   350

   Analyzing the Rest of the Rhetorical Situation   350

   Proofing the Document   353

Conclusions   353

Exercises   353

Assignments   354

   Term Project Option   356

9 SOLVING PROBLEMS IN THE PROFESSIONAL JOB SEARCH

357

Case Study: John Loomis   358

Fundamentals of the Job Search   359

   Appealing to Employers   359

   Common Job Application Errors   360

The Job Search Process   362

   Reactivate Placement File   363

   Approach Recommenders   364

   Research Possible Employers and Find Position Descriptions   365

   Update Résumé   365

   Sample College Résumé   366

   Sample Professional Résumé   369

   Write Cover Letters   372

   Sample Position Description   374

   Sample Cover Letter for an Advertised Position   374

   Submitting an Unsolicited Application   377

   Sample Cover Letter for an Unsolicited Application   378

Postscript   378

Shaping Up a Student Résumé   382

   First Draft of the Résumé   382

Revised Student Résumé   384

Fundamentals of the Interview Process   386

    The Interviewer   386

    Interview Guidelines   386

Conclusions   389

Exercises   390

Assignments   390

    Term Project Option   390

10 SOLVING PROBLEMS THROUGH COLLABORATION AND EDITING

393

Case Study: Alfred Gutierrez   394

An Overview of Professional Collaboration   395

    The Role of the Lead   395

The Collaboration Process   396

    Initial Planning, and Organization and Assignment of Tasks   397

    Establishment of a Tracking System   398

    Drafting   398

    Review and Comment   398

    Final Revision and Production Preparation   401

    Distribution and Document Control   401

Postscript   401

Conclusions   402

Exercises   402

Assignments   402

11 SOLVING PROBLEMS THROUGH DOCUMENT DESIGN

403

Case Study: Kevin Ersting   404

The Importance of Presentation   405

Elements of Document Design   407

    White Space   408

    Text   409

    Graphics   414

Sample Professional Document Design   421

Creativity versus Convention in Document Design   424

Conclusions   426

Exercise   426

Assignment   426

    Term Project Option   426

12 SOLVING PROBLEMS THROUGH ORAL PRESENTATIONS

427

Case Study: Leah Feldstein   428

The Naturalness of Oral Communication   429

    Practical Limitations Resulting from the Setting   429

Rhetorical Analysis of an Oral Presentation   430

    Purpose   431

    Audience   432

    Context   434

    Ethical Stance   434

Essential Elements in the Preparation of an Oral Presentation   435

    Knowing the Material   435

    Knowing What Is Important to Discuss   436

    Planning the Physical Aspects of the Presentation   437

    Practicing   438

Planning the Text for an Oral Presentation   439

    The Introduction (or the Appetizer)   439

    The Body (or the Main Course)   442

    The Conclusion (or the Dessert)   444

The Mechanics of Effective Public Speaking   447

    Relax   448

    Speak Loudly Enough to Be Heard   448

    Maintain Eye Contact with the Audience   448

    Keep the Body Poised and Vibrant   449

    Talk—Don't Read   450

    Don't Take the "Sleepers" Personally   450

Tips for Giving Oral Presentations to Specific Groups   451

    Committees   452

    Civic or Special Interest Groups   453

    Boards of Directors   455

Conclusions   456

Exercise   456

Assignment   457

    Term Project Option   457

APPENDIX 459

Selected Problems of Usage and Style   459

Problems with the Passive Voice   459

Identifying Passive Voice and Passive Constructions   459

Recognizing When It Is Appropriate to Use the Passive Voice   460

Variations of Passive Constructions   462

Exercises   462

Problems with Nominalization   463

Identifying Nominalizations   463

Recognizing When a Revision Will Alter Meaning   465

Exercises   466

Problems with Diction and Jargon   467

Some Questionable Nouns   468

Some Questionable Verbs and Verbals   469

Other Problems with Diction   472

Exercises   474

Problems with Embedded Prose   475

Identifying Embedded Prose   475

Why Embedded Prose Is a Common Problem   475

Why the Strategy of Embedding Is a Bad Policy   476

The Writer's Commitments to Avoid Embedded Prose   476

Exercises   479

Problems with Sentence Structure   479

Sentence Fragments   479

Run-On Sentences and Comma Splices   480

Fused Sentences   481

Exercises   481

Index   483

PREFACE

We based this book on two premises: that solving problems is the primary activity of all professionals and that the process of solving problems is always, in some way, reflected through writing. From the very beginning, and throughout our discussions, we try to support these premises. Readers are constantly reminded of the process of solving problems in all kinds of writing: from the planning of the briefest memo to the proofing of the longest completion report. And we try to show that the process is organic and multidimensional, that the demands of definition, research, analysis, resolution and synthesis, and implementation must be met at various stages or levels of investigation. The process is not simply flat and linear. It is instead recursive and thoroughly analytical, often flipping back on itself, requiring redefinition and reanalysis of the old in light of the new. It is a demanding process but, if fully engaged in, is also rewarding. And as we point out in Chapter 1, it is one that all professionals, if they are acting professionally, take part in.

This latter notion, that of acting professionally, has also informed our sense of purpose in writing this book. We think it is important that students who are educating and training themselves to join the professional working world know what that world expects of them. They need to understand, if they don't already, that the responsibilities they have to their families, friends, and themselves expand not only in number but also in kind when they become members of the professional world. Problems they will address, no matter how seemingly trivial at times, are part of a pantheon of problems that if left unaddressed or unsolved, will negatively affect the public and private lives of many. It is not too grand to claim, on the other hand, that professionals who meet their responsibilities conscientiously, energetically, and ethically do much to improve the quality of life for everyone.

In presenting the various problems that professionals have to address, we have chosen situations that are typical of the working world and, in every case, have either implicitly or explicitly pointed to the responsibilities the participants have to others and to themselves to address and solve those problems professionally. Through this, we hope we have revealed the inherent redundancy in the idea of *good* problem solving, since the result of bad problem solving is no solution at all.

One other important element we should mention has to do with the kinds of writing done in the professional world at large. Our notion, which we discuss specifically in Chapter 3, but which is implicit throughout the book, is that distinct rhetorical differences (dependent on purpose, audience, context, and ethics) exist among kinds of writing in the professions. And those differences, which help dictate content and format or presentation, are determined by the degree of professional objectivity writers feel they have to attain and demonstrate. On a continuum of objective to subjective, science writing is thought of as the most objective and most conventional; that is, it is dictated by rigid expectations, styles, and forms. Technical and professional writing falls in the middle, with varying expectations and ideas of the need for objectivity, styles, and forms. Administrative writing comes at the other end, the most fluid in many senses, displaying a good deal of variety of style, and not objectivity, but subjectivity. We offer this continuum because it helps lay out the realities of solving problems and writing in the professional world. Not all situations are alike, and they shouldn't be seen as such; each requires different approaches, different analyses, and different results. Knowing and understanding this makes the use and appreciation of writing in the professions much more pertinent and effective.

So much for the philosophical basis of the book. We turn now to a brief review of how we have structured the contents. The first three chapters on professionalism and the nature of solving problems, and the basics of solving both technical and rhetorical problems, we think of as more theoretical. They deal with the generic process of solving problems, which is essential to the purpose of the book. Still we have tried to discuss and reveal the process in real situations. Thus readers see in the cases of Susan James and Mary Anne Cox, among others, how problems arise, how they are defined, researched, analyzed, and ultimately resolved—and then written about. The ways these women go about their work and put theory into practice is clearly an important element of a book like this.

Chapters 4 through 8 and Chapter 10 discuss more specific kinds of writing that result from solving specific kinds of problems: proposals; periodic reports; policy statements, procedures, manuals; letters and memoranda; and collaboration and editing. Again, in almost every case, real working-world problems form the basis of the discussion and create practical examples—many examples, from formal proposals through letters and memoranda. We believe we have covered, in more or less detail, practically every writing situation professionals find themselves confronting (though we don't claim that every professional will have to write in every situation).

Chapters 9, 11, and 12 discuss different kinds of situations, some not immediately associated with specific writing products, though they are clearly related to writing and require the same kind of analysis that all professional writing requires. Chapter 9, which discusses the professional job search, presents strategies of applying for jobs: when and how to revise a résumé; the rhetorical needs for writing letters of application, both for first jobs straight out of college and for subsequent jobs; and some tips on preparing for interviews. Chapter 11 offers suggestions on the physical design of documents and use of graphics to meet rhetorical needs in writing. Chapter 12, on oral presentations, discusses the process of preparing oral presentations and shows how it is similar to the writing process. An Appendix offering a review of selected problems in usage and style completes the substance of the book.

Just a word on our intended readership. We have in mind students of technical and professional writing from a variety of fields who would benefit from approaching or solving a research problem in a sustained way over the course of a term or semester. The discussions of proposals and of periodic, trip, and completion reports would be particularly useful for completing the work of sustained projects. By no means are we excluding students who will be addressing shorter, more discrete projects and problems. Our discussions are set up in such a way that different emphases can be fully accommodated, both for students and teachers.

Solving problems in the professional world takes imagination, dedication, and energy. It is hard work, but its benefits are many. We think we demonstrate this effectively in the following pages.

Acknowledgments

For their help in technical matters, enthusiastic support, and patience, we would like to thank the following people: Susan Glasstetter, Dori Glennon, Kjierstie Gunther, Donald Hanley, Richard Haswell, Bruce K. Kennedy, Alison L. McKee, Nancy P. McKee, Peter H. D. McKee, Susan McLeod, Judy Oerkvitz, Robert Pedersen, Tom Pendergast, D. L. Plung, H. Perry Reynolds, Tom Samford, Barbara Sitko, and Scott Urstad.

McGraw-Hill and the authors would like to thank the following reviewers for their many helpful comments and suggestions: Santi Buscemi, Middlesex County College; Laura Casari, University of Nebraska, Lincoln; Dean Hall, University of Kansas; Polly Marshall, Hinds Junior College; Elray Pedersen, Brigham Young University; Nell Pickett, Hinds Junior College; Randall Popken, Tarleton State College; Richard Profozich, Prince George's Community College; Jack Selzer, Pennsylvania State University; and Sherry Southard, East Carolina University.

George E. Kennedy
Tracy T. Montgomery

PROFESSIONALISM

AND PROBLEM SOLVING

Preview of the Chapter

Professionals and Professionalism
> *Examples of Professionalism*
> *Professional Activity*

Profiles of Professionals
> *The Problems They Solve and the Documents They Write*
> *Highlights of the Professional Profiles*

Solving Problems by Asking and Answering Questions

March 15, 1992
1:30 P.M.
Susan James's office
ITE Industries, Inc.
Richmond, California

It may have been the lack of lunch hour, or maybe the lousy pastrami sandwich she had delivered from the corner deli, but Susan James felt particularly out of sorts as she stared at her computer, trying to complete the outline of her latest quarterly report. As head of Purchasing, Susan had been under fire recently. The Engineering Department had been pointing to her and her staff as the main reason for missing several deadlines and not meeting some of the objectives that had been set for Engineering. This was not an uncommon position to be in, however. Purchasing fit the description of the perfect scapegoat in a production facility: as an administrative function, as a support activity rather than a production activity, Purchasing often had to make up everyone else's lost schedules.

But further complicating Purchasing's existence these days were the reams of forms to be filled out to meet regulations for a federal government project ITE had recently landed, restrictions on placing certain percentages of company business with the most reliable suppliers in an effort to bring in untried minority-owned suppliers, and what seemed to be an unusual lack of engineering planning—or preplanning, as they now call it in the latest management jargon. In addition, Susan was currently shorthanded, since a couple of her key buyers defected to other departments in the company, giving as their reasons for leaving "undue pressure."

Despite all this, Susan had to report progress. She had to have something to say for the category "Extraordinary Achievement," and preferably, it should have something to do with Purchasing's support of Engineering. So she wrote this: "Purchasing supported Engineering's crane replacement project by finding an in-state supplier within 24 hours of Engineering's request." An impressive accomplishment and true as far as it went. But what Susan knew, as others did not yet, was that the in-state crane was actually inadequate for ITE's needs and that, furthermore, no firm decision to buy the crane could result without long negotiations with the supplier.

Susan also knew that if management read her report quickly, her statement would gain her points. But she suspected that when the rest of the story came out, her reports would never be read so casually again. She decided after some thought that she simply couldn't report an "extraordinary achievement" this quarter and left the category blank. She further decided that until she actually had something extraordinary to report, she would continue documenting all on-going efforts to support Engineering for her own file. Small consolation in the short run, but a sound strategy in the long run.

Having made this decision, Susan felt a little better and finished her outline rather easily. But she made one other decision before going on to her next chore: on days like this, instead of pastrami, she'd order roast beef.

PROFESSIONALS AND PROFESSIONALISM

The word *professional* has come to mean several things. People talk, for example, about the difference between amateur and professional sports. Amateur athletes may be the best in the world, winners of gold medals in the Olympics and world championships, but they are not considered professionals until they accept their first checks for what they do.

On the other hand, people often talk about amateurs as being truly professional, that is, acting in a way that commands the respect of others. They perform with singular effort, with practiced discipline and skill, and they win or lose with dignity and grace. But then some performances are called unprofessional. The participants may be highly skilled and perform with a singular effort, but they violate the conventions of professional behavior by disputing, arguing, and fighting about calls on their performance.

Sports is only one area where we hear the word *professional* used. Indeed, for many, it also brings to mind the traditional professions—theology, education, medicine, law. And those have been extended to include other areas of science, technology, and industry. To most people, however, professionals are those, in any field, who have special training or education to do specialized work that involves making decisions and solving problems. This work may require degrees ranging from the associate of arts to the Ph.D.

Susan James, in the situation described here, is just such a professional. In college, she majored in business with an emphasis in management systems. She worked for a couple of years as a purchasing agent for a small manufacturer of electrical novelty items—revolving pen displays, signs advertising beer, and the like. She has worked for ITE Industries for 3 years, the last 2 as head of Purchasing. The way she should report her department's quarterly activities is just one example of the problems she has to solve and the decisions she has to make. We will say more later about how professionally she solves those problems and makes those decisions.

Professionals, in general, are usually held in high esteem by other members of society, and much is expected of them. It is they who keep the society running well—effectively, efficiently, humanely—and who move it forward under the popular notion of progress.

Talking about professional versus unprofessional behavior touches on the idea of what it means to be a professional. Being a professional is a matter of attitude, or the way people think of themselves and their responsibilities in the context of their occupations. Professionalism is, then, a social notion. It is determined by the members of a group or, more loosely termed, the profession, and it has to do with the conventions of behavior within the group. Those conventions may differ from profession to profession, but the differences are less important than the similarities. Most will agree that professionalism means maintaining high standards of performance, accuracy, thoroughness, honesty, and integrity.

Examples of Professionalism

Although the definition of *professionalism* contains abstract terms, it can be made more concrete by looking back at Susan James's situation. Susan was under pressure from both the Engineering Department and upper management to support effectively and efficiently some of the vital operations of the company. But she had to do this under adverse circumstances: increased bureaucratic paperwork, restrictions on the kinds of suppliers she could use, and a decrease in the number of key departmental personnel. As she saw the need to report on her support activities, including a category that would cite "extraordinary achievement," she was tempted to report as extraordinary the fact that her group found a crane supplier within 24 hours of Engineering's request. She was also tempted to obscure the facts—that this crane would not actually serve Engineering's needs and that an agreement to buy the crane could not be reached until long negotiations with the supplier had taken place. To say that she had found a supplier in 24 hours would be true and accurate. To say, however, that the crane could do what it was needed to do and that it could be on site in a short time would simply be a lie—but one that she could embed in language that would not sound like a lie.

Susan's decision not to mention the possibility of buying the crane under the category of "extraordinary achievement" is an example of her intelligence, honesty, and high standards of professionalism. Tempted as she was to make something of almost nothing, she resisted, knew the truth of the situation would finally surface anyway, and decided in the end that no claim for "extraordinary achievement" would be better for all concerned than a bogus claim. Susan acted professionally.

The same abstract terms used above (high standards of performance, accuracy, thoroughness, honesty, and integrity) can be made more concrete by considering some instances where high standards were not maintained. The Wall Street insider trading scandals of several years ago are a good case. The people involved in those scandals, such as Ivan Boesky, were certainly thought of as professionals. They had performed for years with singular effort and were highly trained or educated. They did specialized work with good results, making decisions and solving problems, all supposedly for the benefit of their firms and clients. When it was discovered that they had made decisions based on confidential information, which would benefit only themselves and a few others, it was clear they had violated the trust that people had placed in them. They in turn had to forfeit their claims to professionalism, since they had ignored its standards of honesty and integrity.

Other examples are more dramatic, since they have to do with the loss of life, not just of money. Take the case of the space shuttle *Challenger* disaster in 1985. As the voluminous reports on the event show, Morton Thiokol, the engineering firm in charge of the design of the booster rockets, had been pressured by NASA to give the go-ahead to the launch even during weather that technically was too cold for certain vital functions to operate correctly. When the O-rings, part of the fuel supply system, failed, the booster rockets ignited, completely destroying the shuttle and all who were aboard.

This tragic event was also the result of breaches in professionalism. The launch, since it was to take the first schoolteacher into space, was a much-touted public relations venture, and America was waiting. Morton Thiokol felt pressure from NASA in two ways: to keep to a schedule that already had fallen behind and to win again the contract it had had with NASA, which had just gone up for new bid. Bowing to these pressures, executives at Morton Thiokol overrode the objections their engineers had to the launch and permitted it to happen. We all know the result of that decision: the loss of seven lives and a setback of 3 years in the space shuttle program—certainly a costly conclusion to breaches in professional integrity and ethics.

Professional Activity

Solving Technical and Rhetorical Problems

Professional activity—the kinds of things professionals do regularly—is broad and diverse. It can mean teaching, lawyering, preaching, curing. Depending on the field, it can involve basic research, research and development, production, quality control, marketing, sales, public relations, or any combination of these. But whatever is done, and in whatever field, a common activity has to take place: solving problems.

And the problems professionals face are many and varied. They may reflect the needs of a particular job (how to prevent failures in a computer system), or the needs of a professional-social situation (how to get Research and Development people to work more closely with Production people), or the needs of the problem solver (how to put oneself forward without seeming pushy). Throughout this text we will consider these problems as operational problems, political problems, and ethical problems. But it is also important to remember that we use the word *problem* in a broad sense to mean any unresolved situation. An unresolved situation may appear placid on the surface. For example, communications may be proceeding quite smoothly in an organization despite the lack of a style guide. Nevertheless, the quality of those communications is inconsistent and, therefore, much less efficient than it might be. So the lack of a style guide is still a problem, although it doesn't suggest the urgency of the more dramatic problems that catch the headlines every day.

It is also necessary to see that professional problems worthy of anyone's attention are composed of two basic elements: the technical and the rhetorical.

The *technical* elements have to do with the fundamental workings of one's profession or discipline. The *rhetorical* elements have to do with the communication of those workings—what's been done or will be done about them—to various people interested in them. The two elements are always present in any problem.

How to prevent failures in a computer system, for instance, will take a good deal of technical expertise and attention. Understanding the hardware and the software and how the two interface, and deciding how either needs to be altered to make the interface work better to prevent failures in the future clearly require that computer engineers draw on their education, training, and experience in computer science.

But that doesn't mean that they can ignore telling someone else about what they have found out. Their superiors will need to know what they have done to address or solve the problem so that they can make decisions about the conduct of future operations. Their peers will need to know what they have done in order to anticipate similar problems in their own work and be able to apply reasonable remedies. Certainly technicians will need instructions about how the system will be changed and operated in the future so that they can keep it on-line and functioning as it should.

All these situations call for written communications that require different rhetorical approaches. The superiors should get at least a memo report, telling them in summary why the failures in the system occurred and what will be done to correct them. They need to know how long it will take and how much it will cost to get the system back in good operating order. They also need to know what other decisions they will have to make to ensure that troubles with the system won't occur again.

The peers should get a copy of the report to the superiors, with a technical addendum that discusses in detail the causes of the failures and the remedies applied. They need this information to keep current, to know what troubles could turn up again and how to deal with them.

The technicians need new instructions. Although they may have some interest in the basics of the failures from a theoretical point of view, they are most interested in the mechanics of correcting the system and running it well in the future. If the changes will require new training for them, they will need to know how and when that will happen.

It is clear from this that even though computer engineers in this situation may spend much of their time dealing with the technical element of the problem, they still have compelling needs for rhetorical analysis and writing.

Writing in Response to Problems

In fact, attempts to solve or at least to address problems almost always require writing of some sort. The writing may include proposals, reports on data collection in the field or in the lab, explanations of designs for new production methods, suggestions for finding new markets, correspondence with present and future clients or customers, reports on projects in progress, or memoranda on possible implementation methods.

Simply scanning the ranks of professionals shows how much writing results from attempting to solve problems. Engineering firms, for instance, write proposals to prospective clients, both private and public, stating what they know about flood control, or traffic control, or the ways of automating inventory control, to suggest specifically how they might solve problems in those areas.

Professional researchers in the hard sciences or in the social sciences collect data, either in the field or in the lab, and write proposals to study and prove some hypothesis, for example, that drug abuse is increasing among those who profess a religious affiliation or that the presence of the AIDS virus is increasing and will continue to increase in all sectors of the society.

Production experts report on new ways of making production more efficient, and marketing experts construct surveys of consumers in different parts of the country and the world to see what consumers' tastes are and how they might be affected by new products. Teachers report to their school districts about how a change in curriculum has affected students' learning of a particular subject, while nutritionists report on how dietary habits have changed among people who have taken part in state-supported nutritional education programs.

PROFILES OF PROFESSIONALS

The Problems They Solve and the Documents They Write

Following are profiles of six professionals: an engineer, a chemist, a social worker, a museum director, a computer specialist, and a businessperson. The profiles describe the responsibilities these people have for solving problems in their day-to-day work, but especially they describe the kinds of documents they write in response to those problems. The writing tasks are divided into three kinds:

- **Technical and professional writing** tasks are those that require the specialized knowledge of professionals, depending on their fields.
- **Administrative writing** tasks are those that grow out of needs and demands of the positions these people have within their respective organizations.
- **Review and/or editing** tasks are those that require all professionals at some time to review and perhaps edit other people's writing. This includes anything they have specifically assigned others to write, or writing that others are normally responsible for, but that because of its importance to the work these people do, should be reviewed and/or edited before it is sent out.

The profiles that follow are typical, but they are not necessarily inclusive, and do not suggest all problems these professionals might face or all the documents they may have to write. They do suggest, however, a realistic and reasonable range of professional activity and the amount of time that each person usually spends on writing or on tasks related to writing.

Professional Profile 1

JOSEPH T. BROWN
Operations Engineer
(Working for a nuclear waste disposal site)

Primary Areas of Responsibility for Solving Problems
Design of the facilities for storage of nuclear waste. Supervision of other personnel, including other engineers, within his operations group. Liaison to other operations groups and to upper management.

Technical Writing Tasks
1. **Policy statements,** e.g., on training required to operate special equipment.

2. **Facility descriptions,** e.g., a full description of the low-level waste-handling room to be used for federal officials to plan and get authorization for funds.
3. **Technical procedures,** e.g., unplugging the borehole (storage sleeve) for high-level waste retrieval.
4. **Process descriptions,** e.g., a description for a lay audience of the facility's plan for handling low-level waste from receipt to emplacement.
5. **Instructions,** e.g., extremely detailed descriptions for operating unfamiliar equipment.
6. **Formal technical reports,** e.g., a report on the inadequacies in the waste transporter.
7. **Lesson plans** for the Training Department to use to train waste-handling operators.
8. **Proposals,** most likely as part of a team, adapting standardized (boilerplate) materials for specific purposes and audiences.
9. **Accident reports,** as part of a team, of significant accidents (such as a fire in a silicon-controlled rectifier [a motor that drives the waste hoist]).
10. **Responses** to quality assurance audits that detail fixes for complicated technical problems.
11. **Safety procedures** (particularly for Brown's own group), e.g., procedure for entering a hot cell (area where high-level waste is located).
12. **Papers and articles** on theoretical and practical issues and discoveries for professional meetings and journals.

Administrative Writing Tasks

1. **Periodic progress reports**—weekly, monthly, quarterly, semi-annually, annually—for various audiences (including the general public) who require separate reports.
2. **Justifications** written to upper management for more staff, more money, more equipment, more overtime. (Budget justifications are also often written to show the effects of proposed cuts on Brown's operation.)
3. **Personnel documents:** evaluations, e.g., of the manager who reports directly to him, and justifications, e.g., to hire a particular person or for raises, promotions, leaves, etc. (Included here would be letters of recommendation for people in his group applying for other jobs either inside or outside the organization.)
4. **Letters and memos** to upper management on particular problems, e.g., how the procedures of another group are slowing down the operation of his group.
5. **Reports** to upper management on the annual goals of his group (particularly required by management-by-objective organizations).
6. **Articles** for the in-house newspaper on the activities of his group.
7. **Documentation** for his own files on troublesome or potentially troublesome situations, e.g., plans for instituting new procedures over which he has little control.

Review and/or Editing Tasks

1. **Manual material:** lower-level procedures for performing a number of tasks within Brown's operation.

2. **Specifications** for particular operations within his operation, or from other operations that may involve his.
3. **Minor accident reports.**
4. **Procedures** from other departments that will affect his operation.
5. **Engineering drawings** and schematics.
6. **Planning documents** written by superiors that require his technical review before they can be published.

Total time spent writing or on writing-related tasks: 70% ■

Professional Profile 2   **ELIZABETH J. FREDERICKSON**
Chief Chemist, Assistant Manager; Department of Engineering Research (Working for a Pacific Coast utilities company)

Primary Areas of Responsibility for Solving Problems

Direction of the management of hazardous materials, including supervision of laboratory analysis, field work (soil sampling), training of new personnel, and continuing review of pertinent federal and state legislation. Liaison to the Legal Department and occasionally to lobbyists at the state legislature.

Technical Writing Tasks

1. **Policy statements,** e.g., on special training necessary for work with hazardous materials.
2. **Technical procedures,** e.g., methods of analysis of hazardous materials; methods of soil sampling.
3. **Safety procedures** for handling hazardous materials.
4. **Instructions,** e.g., extremely detailed descriptions for operating unfamiliar equipment.
5. **General training manuals** for new personnel.
6. **Formal technical reports** written about the progress of certain established projects.
7. **Field logs or notebooks.**
8. **Site reports** (emphasizing soil sampling and analysis) on new projects just getting started.
9. **Proposals,** most likely as part of a team, for changes in procedures.
10. **Critical analyses** of existing, new, and potential legislation pertinent to the use, handling, and disposal of hazardous wastes.
11. **Papers and articles** on theoretical and practical issues and discoveries for professional meetings and journals.

Administrative Writing Tasks

1. **Periodic progress reports**—weekly, monthly, quarterly, semi-annually, annually—for various audiences, depending on their needs for periodic reporting.
2. **Justifications** written to upper management for more staff, more money, more equipment, more overtime. (These would be passed through her manager to upper management.)

9

3. **Personnel documents:** first-level evaluations of staff written for her manager's review; new personnel training reports.
4. **Articles** for the in-house newspaper on the activities of the department.
5. **Documentation** for her own files on troublesome or potentially troublesome situations, e.g., plans for instituting new procedures over which she has little control.

Review and/or Editing Tasks
1. **Existing, new, and proposed laws** dealing with the use, handling, and disposal of hazardous materials.
2. **Site and laboratory reports** from staff personnel.
3. **Segments of proposals** written by staff personnel. (Frederickson would review these, but they would be discussed more fully in staff meetings.)
4. **Reports and position papers** written by her manager, for which Frederickson's particular knowledge and expertise are needed before they are published.

Total time spent writing or on writing-related tasks: 60% ■

Professional Profile 3

LEAH S. FELDSTEIN

Director of Client Relations
(Working in a drug education and rehabilitation program for youth ages 12 to 17)

Primary Areas of Responsibility for Solving Problems
Direction of general drug education program in the public schools; direction of outreach work to identify adolescents who are using drugs and should benefit from specific education and rehabilitation. Supervision of other social workers who work as counselors of adolescents inside and outside the public schools. Liaison to the director of the program, to the board of directors, and occasionally to the government agencies funding the project.

Technical Writing Tasks
1. **Informative pamphlets** written for teachers in the public schools on the kinds of drugs available, the psychological and physical effects they can have on people who use them, and how their use is viewed generally by their students.
2. **Informative manuals** written for outreach workers on how to identify adolescents who are using drugs, and on what drugs they are most likely using.
3. **Instructions,** which amount to detailed lesson plans, for teachers on what should be covered in classroom units on the use and abuse of drugs.
4. **Instructions to outreach workers** on the kinds of counseling that can take place both on and off the counseling site.
5. **Informative articles** written for the PTAs and local newspapers explaining exactly what drug education and rehabilitation have come to mean and how they are generally conducted.
6. **Proposals,** usually written with others, to various agencies—local, state, and national—for initial or continued funding.
7. **Persuasive/informative papers and articles** written for professional meetings and journals in the areas of social work and education.

Administrative Writing Tasks

1. **Periodic progress reports**—monthly, quarterly, and annually—to three audiences: the director, the board of directors, and the funding agencies, who require such reports at different times, depending on their needs.
2. **Requests to the director** for more staff and expansions of physical facilities for counseling.
3. **Numerous memos to outreach staff** answering particular queries, commenting on reports they have submitted on individual clients, suggesting new approaches in counseling. (These would probably be written in confirmation of suggestions discussed at staff meetings.)
4. **Letters to other agencies or programs** doing similar work in other places to request information on the structure of those programs and on their approaches to drug education and rehabilitation.
5. **Personnel documents:** evaluations of existing outreach personnel and of potential new hires for outreach work; informal evaluations, i.e., without direct administrative impact, of teachers in the public schools. (Also included here are letters of recommendation for people looking for jobs elsewhere, and letters of commendation of teachers who have done particularly well in discussing the units on drug use and abuse in their classrooms.)
6. **Formal annual report** to the director, but ultimately intended for the board of directors, on the workings of the Client Relations unit. This report would discuss how well the education and outreach efforts have worked, and how they have been evaluated, e.g., how many students were given information in school, how many students were identified as potential clients for rehabilitation, how many potential clients were identified outside the schools for education and/or rehabilitation. It would also discuss the results, as they could be determined, of educational and rehabilitation efforts: how many students cut down on or stopped taking drugs, when in the process of education and/or rehabilitation they did so, what general effects of those two conditions have been realized.

Review and/or Editing Tasks

1. **Reports from outreach staff** on initial client contacts, continued or ongoing client contact and counseling, and plans for new outreach efforts. (These reports come in monthly, more often if a situation demands immediate attention.)
2. **Proposals from outreach staff** for new procedures in the bureaucratic dealings with clients, or for new approaches to counseling of existing and prospective clients.
3. **Segments of proposals** written for funding agencies by various members of the outreach staff on areas in which they have particular interest or expertise. (Feldstein would review these, make editing suggestions, but would regularly bring together the contributors to discuss the questions or changes she has in mind.)
4. **Reports and position papers** written by the director, for which Feldstein's professional knowledge and expertise are needed before they are published.

Total time spent writing or on writing-related tasks: 65% ■

Professional Profile 4	VICTORIA P. WILSON

Director, University Art Museum
(Working in a small art museum in a public university in the northwest)

Primary Areas of Responsibility for Solving Problems

General planning and supervision of all museum activities, including conduct and timing of all exhibits (both permanent and temporary), tours, and other uses of the museum for activities related to the forwarding and preservation of the arts. Liaison to the university's Campus Arts Committee and Museum Advisory Sub- committee, to the Friends of the Museum, and to the office of the Dean of Humanities and Social Sciences, College of Arts and Sciences.

Professional Writing Tasks

1. **Correspondence** with museums, galleries, private lenders, exhibit touring services, and individual artists to arrange exhibits.
2. **Loan requests and loan agreements** with museums, galleries, private lend- ers, exhibit touring services, and individual artists.
3. **Requests for permission** to publish images, e.g., for posters if the museum does not have the copyright.
4. **Correspondence with co-curators,** i.e., people elsewhere who share cura- torial duties for exhibits being planned either on or off the museum premises, but nevertheless in cooperation with the museum.
5. **Invitations to prospective exhibit jurors,** i.e., in a competitive, or juried exhibit, people (jurors) are needed to assess the quality of the work to go into the exhibit.
6. **Proposals,** usually written with others, to state and federal agencies (such as the National Endowment for the Arts) for aid in developing the permanent collection, the showing of temporary exhibits, and generally for furthering the work of the museum.
7. **Correspondence with the Dean's office,** including proposals for art pro- grams, branch campus exhibits, security for paintings, plans for exhibit pro- gramming, plans for exhibit publications.
8. **Program planning,** including exhibition schedules and budgets.
9. **Replies to inquiries** from museums, galleries, exhibit touring services, and private individuals about certain works or works by certain artists in the museum's permanent collection; about traveling exhibits offered to the mu- seum; about art in general, artists, or certain works of art.
10. **Liability documents:** correspondence with lenders, insurance companies, lawyers, shipping companies about damage to works in transit or while at the museum.
11. **Development documents:** annual report to the Friends of the Museum of Art, letters to various committees of the Friends, letters to prospective donors of works to the museum.
12. **Thank-you letters** to lenders for exhibits, board members, museum docents, volunteers, donors of art, donors of funds, lecturers, people who host events for the museum, and musicians at receptions. (Wilson writes many of these herself, but she also reviews some that she has asked others to write for her; see "Review and/or Editing Tasks" below.)

Administrative Writing Tasks
1. **Funding requests** to the Dean of Humanities and Social Sciences for more equipment, minor capital improvement, transfer of funds, visiting lecturer funds. The museum's detailed annual budget is also included here.
2. **Personnel documents:** requests for sabbaticals or leaves without pay, annual reviews of faculty and staff, requests for additional faculty or staff positions, letters of recommendation for employees, faculty members, artists, museum professionals at other museums.
3. **Police services documents:** security procedures, reports on breaches of security, requests for police-record checks on security guards, requests for special police coverage.
4. **Periodic progress reports** on the use of private, state, or federal grant funds.
5. **Correspondence with the Department of Physical Plant** about fire protection, repairs, and general maintenance of the museum.
6. **Administrative planning documents:** biennial review, long-term (five-year) planning, statements of purpose for future operations.
7. **Professional organizations:** various documents related to membership in professional museum organizations.

Review and/or Editing Tasks
1. **Thank-you letters** (see "Professional Writing Tasks," item 12, above).
2. **Exhibition handouts.**
3. **Museum newsletter.**
4. **Press releases.**
5. **Postcards and exhibit posters.**
6. **Brochures** about museum programs.
7. **Segments of grant proposals** written by others.

Total time spent writing or on writing-related tasks: 75%   ■

Professional Profile 5

JAMES R. BROOKINGS

Director of Marketing
(Working for a third-party developer for a major computer company)

Primary Areas of Responsibility for Solving Problems
Determines corporate marketing policy and oversees domestic and international distribution of company products. Designs annual advertising campaigns, coordinates company participation in national and international industry trade shows. Oversees the creation of product packaging and the writing of hardware and software documentation; arranges cooperative sales ventures with compatible hardware and software manufacturers. Trains new marketing personnel and acts as liaison among sales personnel, technical support, and upper management.

Technical Writing Tasks
1. **Policy statements**, e.g., on special training necessary for work with on-site computer systems.
2. **Press releases** regarding the marketing of new products and product upgrades for circulation in industry magazines, newsletters, and other related literature.

13

3. **Promotional brochures** written for end-users describing company products and possible applications.
4. **Informational pamphlets** to be used in-house for customer service sales representatives, which describe company products, possible applications, and compatibility information.
5. **Product documentation**, including technical specifications for company products and hardware and software user's manuals.

Administrative Writing Tasks

1. **Periodic progress reports** to the president and vice-president assessing the effectiveness of existing marketing strategies and advertising campaigns.
2. **Long-range projections** of sales figures and marketing projects, submitted to the president and vice president on a biannual basis.
3. **Monthly financial reports** to the Business Officer accounting for expenditures in the marketing department.
4. **Requests to the General Manager** for more funding for additional staff and for the advertising budget.
5. **Letters** to other hardware and software computer companies negotiating cooperative promotional strategies and compatibility features for new products and to group end-users (such as churches, schools, and governmental agencies requesting discount bulk pricing).
6. **Personnel documents**, e.g., evaluations of marketing, customer service, and technical support staff members which inform in-house decisions regarding promotions and salaries.

Review and/or Editing Tasks

1. **Proofs from advertising agencies** of all print ads. (These proofs generally include graphics as well as text.)
2. **Drafts of hardware and software manuals** from in- or out-of-house technical writers.
3. **Promotional slide shows** on disks created by marketing staff members.
4. **Reports or memos** written by the Director of Sales which negotiate terms or affect dealings with domestic and overseas distributors.

Total time spent writing or on writing-related tasks: 75% ■

Professional Profile 6

BRUCE K. KENNEWICK

Director of Catering
(Currently working for a medium-size resort hotel in the midwest)

Primary Areas of Responsibility for Solving Problems

Scheduling and supervision of all catering services: setups for meetings, including refreshments, lunches, dinners, full-scale banquets; setups for private parties, including weddings, bar mitsvahs, anniversaries, retirements, etc.—all food and beverage planning and presentation. Some responsibility for sales of catering services to local organizations and individuals. Liaison to upper management, to other lateral department heads, and to clients (both existing and potential).

Professional Writing Tasks

1. **Local Standard Operating Procedures (LSOPs),** e.g., changes in Home Office SOPs for physical setup of meeting rooms or for presentation of food and beverages, as determined by local needs.
2. **Letters to clients** explaining and confirming arrangements for a meeting or party; frequent follow-up letters until all arrangements are understood and set.
3. **Sales letters** to prospective clients explaining the facilities and services of the Catering Department.
4. **Descriptions** of the Catering Department's services written for general sales brochures produced by the hotel.
5. **Brief proposals** written to upper management (usually Director of Sales) on new sales approaches to be attempted locally.

Administrative Writing Tasks

1. **Monthly memos** to the Director of Food and Beverages confirming arrangements and needs for catering services already booked.
2. **Memos to the Director of Sales** reporting on the results of local sales initiatives.
3. **Proposals to the Director of Food and Beverages** for changes in LSOPs.
4. **Personnel documents,** e.g., evaluations of the various managers who report to Kennewick, letters of recommendation for his managers.
5. **Formal annual report** on the performance of the Catering Department.
6. **Formal annual statement** outlining goals for the future as required by management-by-objectives organizations.

Review and/or Editing Tasks

1. **Reports on various operations** Kennewick has asked his managers to write.
2. **Segments of the formal annual reports** on performance and on goals his managers write.
3. **Evaluations of staff** reporting to his managers.
4. **Reports or memos** written by lateral heads of departments (directors) that speak of catering services, and that need his check for accuracy.
5. **Reports or memos** written by the Director of Food and Beverages that speak of catering services, and that need his check for accuracy.

Total time spent writing or on writing-related tasks: 40% ■

Highlights of the Professional Profiles

These profiles represent a reasonable cross-section of the professional world. They come from the pure and applied sciences, the social sciences, the humanities, and business.

They show that professional life presents a series of problems that should be solved and that require communication of some kind, either speaking or writing. We also chose these six people because they are in management or supervisory positions, which demand even more writing to help solve administrative problems.

Joseph Brown, for instance, had no idea, when he was promoted to Operations Engineer, that he would have to spend up to 70 percent of his time on writing or on tasks related to writing. As a staff engineer, he had spent a good deal of time writing—maybe 50 percent of his time—but with the added responsibilities of management, he assumed added responsibilities for writing.

The same is true of Bruce Kennewick, who is on the low end of the spectrum for time spent on writing. When we asked to interview him, he shrugged and said, "Oh, I don't really write very much. I mostly solve problems by talking—a lot of talking." But when we asked him to catalog the kinds of problems he had to solve, he realized that his position as Director of Catering—having to deal with managers under him, as well as those above him—meant a good deal more writing than he had first thought. Forty percent of his time spent on writing he acknowledged is substantial, and he admitted that with a promotion to Director of Food and Beverages, the percentage of time would increase.

The consensus among these six professionals was that as they progress upward through the middle ranks of management, more writing is required of them. They also agreed that the time spent on technical and professional writing will decrease, while the time spent on administrative and review and/or editing writing tasks will increase. Writing descriptions, procedures, instructions, accident reports, proposals, and the like will be assigned increasingly to people who work for them, and their own responsibilities will involve more statements of purpose and policy and review and editing of work they have assigned to others.

They agreed, finally, that if they were to reach the upper ranks of management, the time they would spend on writing would decrease overall. All the basic writing and much of the review and editing would be done by others, even though they would sign many of the final documents. The actual writing responsibilities of upper management are limited generally to major policy and planning statements, correspondence with lateral upper management, and reports to boards of directors or boards of trustees, and even these generally are written by others.

But there was no question in anyone's mind that progress through the ranks of any organization is realized only through effective problem solving, which in turn is expressed only through effective communication, both oral and written.

The end of the matter is that *good professionals solve problems effectively, and effective problem solving happens only through good communication.* There is no other way.

SOLVING PROBLEMS BY ASKING AND ANSWERING QUESTIONS

Although the problems professionals have to solve are many and diverse, in both their technical and rhetorical elements, the process of solving them always involves asking questions and attempting to find answers to them. Each step in problem solving can be developed fully only when the professional responds to the questions implied there. (Chapters 2 and 3 present detailed analyses of the questions that must be dealt with at each stage of technical and rhetorical problem solving.)

Before attempting to proceed along the stages of the problem-solving process, professionals must first determine whether a problem truly exists. The answer to this question can be determined by asking four basic questions:

1. What is wrong?
2. What is lacking?
3. What is unknown?
4. Who feels the need for and will benefit from a solution?

Some problems will present answers to all four questions; some will present answers to three; but all problems must present answers to at least two, the one constant being, Who feels the need for and will benefit from a solution? If no one can be identified as needing or benefiting from a solution, no problem exists.

To demonstrate, we suggest the problem of cancer, which provides answers to all four questions:

- *What is wrong?* People are dying in increasing numbers and in all segments of the population.
- *What is lacking?* A cure for the disease in its various forms is lacking.
- *What is unknown?* A clear cause of most forms of the disease is unknown.
- *Who feels the need for and will benefit from a solution?* The population in general, but in particular, those who are at risk or who already suffer from cancer feel the need for and will benefit from a solution.

If, however, we take the case of geologists studying the history of glacial movement in Antarctica, the problem is defined adequately by answering only two of the questions:

- *What is unknown?* The direction and speed of centuries old glacial movements is unknown.
- *Who feels the need for and will benefit from a solution?* Geologists and other environmental scientists interested in reconstructing the natural history of the earth in order to predict future environmental changes and conditions feel the need for and will benefit from a solution.

It is important to remember that a problem must be defined at least in terms of a felt need; that is, some segment of the population must feel the need of a solution. Cancer, in its many forms, is a problem felt by a much larger segment of the population, and by its nature is felt much more forcefully than is the problem of determining and understanding the history of glacial movements. Although perhaps only a small segment of the population feels the need of a solution in the latter case, the need is felt nevertheless, and therefore, understanding the history of glacial movements qualifies as a problem. This process of defining a problem is the first stage of technical problem solving, which is discussed in detail in Chapter 2.

The process of asking and answering questions suggests that all problems can be solved. But that is not true. Lack of knowledge and resources at times simply may render a problem insoluble—at least at the time it is first confronted, and perhaps for some time after that. That does not mean, however, that the problem should not be addressed, or that professionals should not continue to ask and attempt to answer questions to try to find out as much about the problem as they possibly can. For example, although no actual solution to the problem of cancer—a cure—has been found, procedures and treatments have been discovered that can control the spread of the disease or that can alleviate the symptoms. These steps along the way—the results of asking and attempting to answer questions—are important because they may lead to an ultimate solution.

Problem solving is a continuing process. Some problems are solved, some are not, and some are in the state of being solved. The process cannot be denied, ignored, or lightly undertaken: it is essential to the work of professionals. In Chapters 2 and 3 we present detailed analyses of both the technical and rhetorical aspects of problem solving.

EXERCISES

1. Conduct an interview with a professional in your major field of interest—an academic (on campus) or someone working in the field (off campus). Ask questions that will provide information about what this person does, how he or she works, what kinds of problems this person confronts and attempts to solve, and what he or she has to write in response to those problems. Ask the person you interview for some samples of the writing he or she has to do, and then return to class with your interview notes and the samples of writing for small group and general discussion.

2. Consider whether the following problems can be defended as problems, given the criteria on page 17 of this chapter.
   a. The wolf is losing habitat in the Yukon.
   b. Hearing aids aren't covered anymore on insurance plans.
   c. Ten large elms now surround the old mine shaft.
   d. Work in the office gets done with a typewriter.
   e. The local cable company wants to upgrade service to its customers.

ASSIGNMENT

1. Write a three-page memo report to the director of undergraduate studies of the department in which you are majoring telling her or him what you have learned from your interview (in Exercise 1 above) and suggesting that some kind of newsletter highlighting this kind of information be published for undergraduate majors. In your memo, emphasize the kinds of problems professionals in your field face, and the kinds of writing that result from addressing or solving those problems. You should refer specifically to the samples of writing you have obtained and attach them as exhibits to your memo.

TERM PROJECT OPTION

Students who decide to pursue a term project will be able to produce original research from their individual fields of study or from fields they have an interest in. These projects will take the form required by the problem to be solved—depending on students' judgments.

For example, students completing these projects can produce several kinds of products, such as technical reports, feasibility studies, articles for publication, and computer manuals, to name a few. Students will end the term with an oral presentation based on the completed written project.

The first thing to do is make a short list of problems you would consider exploring throughout the term. When asked, be sure to defend them as problems based on the criteria discussed in this chapter.

TECHNICAL

PROBLEM SOLVING

Preview of the Chapter

An Overview of Technical Problem Solving

Definition
Defining Multiple Problems
Techniques of the Definition Process
Summary of the Definition Process

Research
Straightforward Primary Research
Complex Primary Research with Fieldwork
Acquiring and Evaluating Secondary Research Materials
Summary of the Research Process

Analysis

Resolution and Synthesis

Implementation

Conclusions

March 16, 1990
6:30 P.M.
Susan James's office
ITE Industries, Inc.
Richmond, California

It was time to go home; Susan James was tired. The outline of her latest quarterly report, which she had worried about the day before, was harder to fill in than she had anticipated. Although she was still pleased with her decision not to report an "extraordinary achievement," she nevertheless had to show that her group had indeed made progress, especially in meeting the Engineering Department's needs. And that would still depend largely on Engineering's request for a new crane and Jones and Son's attractive bid—especially in terms of time—since this company could have the crane in place and operating in 48 hours.

Susan decided, therefore, to define the problem from a new perspective, the fact that Jones and Son's bid was unacceptable for two basic reasons: the available crane couldn't do the work required, and Jones and Son wouldn't qualify under the new push (initiated by the recent contract with the government) to hire minority contractors. In writing the report, she would have to keep in mind Engineering's priorities—the need for good equipment delivered in a timely manner—and upper management's priorities—efficient, timely, cost-effective delivery, preferably from a minority contractor.

When writing the report, she knew that she would have to depend on some research she had already done—indeed, research that went on in her department every day—on suppliers, the kinds and qualities of products they can supply, and their records of timely delivery and of acceptable performance. The only trouble was choosing the best, most useful, and pertinent information from that research. That in many ways took more defining, but it also took analysis—breaking up what she knew about the suppliers into its parts and seeing the relationships among them—in order to understand what ITE Industries ultimately needed to do to stay competitive.

Susan eventually figured this all out. She defined what her department's problems were, how they were affected by Engineering's problems, and how they were affected by ITE's problems in general. After she analyzed the various connections, she resolved to write the report. She decided that it would follow generally the outline she had written the day before, but that it would contain more information to indicate that she had done her homework—that she knew what the problems were and had some idea of how to solve them.

AN OVERVIEW OF TECHNICAL PROBLEM SOLVING

The process of technical problem solving can be divided into five basic stages: definition, research, analysis, resolution and synthesis, and implementation.

In the first stage, *definition* (from Latin *definere*, meaning "to set limits"), problem solvers establish the nature of the problem, its scope (or limits), who or what is affected by the problem, and what benefits would result from a solution to it.

The next stage, *research* (from French *rechercher*, meaning "to look for" or "to search again"), involves collecting data, or information, pertinent to the problem. The research can be primary, that is, firsthand, when problem solvers collect their own data through lab experiments, fieldwork, or surveys, or it can be secondary, when they collect data from other researchers who have published their findings for public review. Or it can be, and most often is, a combination of both.

Analysis (from Greek *ana lyein*, meaning "to break up") is the point at which problem solvers look at the data from various points of view to determine, even tentatively, what the data mean, given the problem as it has been defined.

Resolution and synthesis (from Latin *resolvere*, meaning "to loosen" and from Greek *synthesis*, meaning "to place or to put together") happens when problem solvers assemble all they know about a problem—from definition, research, and analysis—and suggest a solution or alternative solutions to the problem.

Finally, *implementation* (from Latin *implere*, *impletum*, meaning "to fill up" or "to finish") happens only when the other stages of the process are complete and when a solution, or steps toward achieving a solution, has been determined.

As noted in Chapter 1, each stage in problem solving can be developed fully only when the professional responds to the questions implied there. Note that for each stage there is one general question that can be answered by asking other related questions. The importance of asking good questions cannot be overstated. Figure 2.1 suggests the kinds of questions that need to be asked and answered within each stage.

DEFINITION

This first stage is a crucial part of the process. Without a clear definition of the problem, problem solvers cannot know the right directions to take in researching, analyzing, resolving and synthesizing, or finally implementing a solution to the problem. Although clear definition at the outset is essential, a problem may also be redefined on the basis of what happens in the research and analysis stages. Problem solving, then, at least in the first three stages, can be a recursive process, doubling back on itself, as information is uncovered and understood.

For example, computer engineers working for a large manufacturer concerned with protecting the firm's computer system from computer viruses may discover in the research stage and then again in the analysis stage that viruses attack with different magnitudes depending on the level of exposure to other computer

Figure 2.1
*Questions to ask
and answer in the
technical problem-
solving process*

QUESTIONS THAT TECHNICAL PROBLEM SOLVING ANSWERS

Definition of the Problem: What is the felt need?

- What is wrong?
- What is lacking?
- What is unknown?
- Who feels the need for and will benefit from a solution?

Research of the Problem: What information exists?

- What sources are available to provide data?
- Are they primary sources? Of what kind?
- Are they secondary sources? Of what kind?
- How can data be collected from these sources?

Analysis of the Problem: What do the data mean?

- Do the data address the problem as defined?
- Are there relationships among the data?
- Do they show cause and effect? How so?
- Are there patterns? trends? anomalies?

Resolution and Synthesis of the Problem: Are there solutions to the problem?

- What significance emerges from analysis?
- Does the significance suggest solutions?
- Are the possible solutions reasonable?
- Are some more resonable than others? Why?

**Implementation of the Solution: What is necessary to carry out the solution
(or steps toward solution)?**

- What steps are needed to carry out the solution(s)?
- How will the steps be performed?
- Who will perform them?
- What equipment or materials are needed?
- How much will the process cost?
- How long will the process take?

systems beyond the firm's own. They would do well, then, to return to the definition stage and redefine the problem as having to do with level of outside contact rather than with the simple fact of outside contact, something that may not have occurred to them when they first set out to define the problem. Such refining of the definition would help in further research and analysis, and ultimately, of course, in the resolution and synthesis stage. When defining and redefining a problem, problem solvers must remember that a problem must be able to be defined in terms of a felt need (see Chapter 1).

If the problem has been defined well, the research and analysis can be more specifically designed and carried out, and a reasonable, feasible resolution or synthesis is more apt to follow.

Defining Multiple Problems

Professionals often face situations having multiple problems to be defined. Susan James had three problems. The first, though for ITE in general not the most important, combined her own and her department's problems. She had to show progress in meeting other department's needs, in particular, Engineering's needs, since it most frequently complained about Purchasing's performance, often blaming its own missed deadlines on Purchasing's failure to provide necessary equipment on time. The definition of that problem, therefore, had to do with only Susan and her department. She knew *what was wrong*: Engineering was always pushed to produce and was likely to suggest Purchasing's performance as a reason for many of its failings, because Purchasing couldn't or didn't supply what Engineering needed on time. And since Purchasing is a support department, not a production department, upper management was likely to be sympathetic to Engineering's complaints. She knew also who would benefit from a solution to the problem: immediately, the Purchasing Department, and then, ITE in general.

The second problem needing definition was fulfilling Engineering's request for a crane quickly. *What was wrong* and *what was lacking* were essentially the same: the need of a new crane in place and operating in a short time. And it was ITE's production operation that immediately *felt the need* for and would benefit from a solution.

Embedded in this second problem was a third, and in some ways the most important, problem. Susan knew that Jones and Son could get ITE a crane in 48 hours, but she also knew they did not have the kind of equipment that ITE eventually would need. She knew further that the contractual agreements would not meet the government's regulations for the minority contractors program and so had to define what the obligations for program participants were and how they would affect Purchasing's activities, which in turn would affect ITE's activities, not only in this particular case but also in the long run.

This embedded problem points to something important in the whole process of defining and solving problems. Problems that on the surface seem simply and straightforwardly defined often contain other problems that also need to be defined, researched, and analyzed. The embedded problems ultimately may be more important for those who need to have them solved. If so, the writer needs to get this greater importance across to persuade the reader.

In this case, Susan knew the difference between getting a crane expediently and getting one that wouldn't meet specifications for its use or regulations of the minority contractors program. It was much more important that Engineering have a crane that fulfilled specifications than that it have the first one available. Likewise, it was more important for upper management to understand how the process of purchasing in general, which clearly affects production, would be affected by the minority contractors program than that Engineering's requests be fulfilled rapidly, or worse yet only for the short term or illegally.

In this case, the quality of the equipment and the need for understanding and meeting contractual obligations should supersede speed of delivery and installation.

Once Susan had decided that she could actually report some progress, the definition phase was crucial. She would have to say specifically why the crane supplier she had found in 24 hours and who could deliver the crane in another 24 was inadequate to serve the needs of the Engineering Department, and that further investigation into other suppliers' capabilities most likely would suggest a better supplier and a better product.

She decided she would give a physical description of the crane Jones and Son could supply—for example, the tonnage it could lift, the ranges of movement from one lift spot to another, and the time required for lifts and placements. These elements would then have to be compared with or contrasted to the capabilities of other cranes produced by other suppliers and to the needs of the Engineering Department to show that Jones and Son, although it could have the crane in place in a very short time, nevertheless would not be supplying ITE's needs appropriately.

The additional problem Susan had to define was having to seek minority contractors. Jones and Son did not qualify. Its owners are Anglo; the founder and still Chairman of the Board, Hershel T. Jones, and his son, Raymond L. Jones, Chief Executive Officer (CEO), run the family business. Though they hire minority workers, none has been hired in managerial positions. There are no women, Hispanics, Afro-Americans, Asians, or Native Americans in any policy-making or policy-reviewing positions. The government's minority contractors program requires that at least 22 percent of those positions, in lieu of direct ownership, be held by minorities. The government also requires that minorities in a range of 12 percent to 24 percent be employed in all other areas. And finally, the new guidelines require a more complicated process than would normally be required of an agreement with an old, trusted supplier like Jones and Son.

Though she knew that the Sales and Development Department was aware of these stipulations in its dealings with the government, and that upper management would have some idea of the resulting necessary contractual obligations between ITE and its suppliers, she was not sure that upper management knew how those obligations would affect purchasing agreements made by her department. She decided that she would define in the main text of her report the basics of how the minority contractors program affected purchasing, especially with regard to doing business with Jones and Son. She then would include as an appendix more detailed information about how purchasing from other suppliers would be affected.

In the appendix, she decided she would include some of the history of the minority contractors program and how other firms have dealt with the problems of purchasing. She could also use the experience of some firms she knew well, or could get information about, as an example of how purchasing is affected: what kinds of restrictions that purchasing agreements imposed, especially as to timely delivery. Finally, she could include a more detailed description of the process required in bidding for contracts: what the requests for bids (RFBs) or requests for quotes (RFQs) should include and how long the bidding process is supposed to take—something that presented a problem in the case of Jones and Son. (For more information on RFBs and RFQs and on proposals in general, see Chapter 4.)

Techniques of the Definition Process

Although it is essential to understand the process of definition, how to ask and answer the right questions so that the problem at hand is framed effectively, knowing how to fill in the frame—the techniques of defining—is also important.

Techniques to Use for a Well-Informed Audience

Because Susan's audience was relatively well informed—used to reading general descriptions of equipment used regularly in their operations and familiar with the bidding process—she used the following techniques to define her problems:

- Physical description
- Comparison and contrast
- Process description
- Example

Physical Description   Susan needed to describe specifically the various physical characteristics of the crane Jones and Son could supply—lift capability; range of movement; speed of lift, movement, and placement; and the like.

Comparison and Contrast   Susan needed to compare and contrast the qualities of Jones and Son's crane and other suppliers' cranes not only according to physical characteristics, but also according to contractual obligations for delivery and service. She had to point out how other cranes would serve the physical needs of the Engineering Department better, and also how other crane suppliers might meet ITE's contractual obligations having to do with minority contractors.

Process Description   In writing the appendix to her report on the minority contractors program and how it would affect purchasing, Susan had to write what amounted to a process description. A description of a process differs from a description of an object, or physical description, in that there is no tangible matter to be described—no height, weight, volume, energy consumed, and so forth. Rather, a series of related steps, considered both individually and in the ways they relate to one another, needs to be described. What needs to happen to make an individual step take place (cause)? How has that step caused or allowed another, subsequent step to take place (effect)? And finally, how does the process as a whole fit together to produce the intended result?

Susan needed to describe the purchasing or procuring process, which required three steps:

STEP 1   The first step was writing and sending to potential suppliers the request for quote (RFQ), which had to include exact specifications of the object to be purchased (all physical characteristics and operating capabilities); allowable times for delivery and installation (21 days was specified for the minority contractors program); and all stipulations and obligations on the parts of both parties for maintenance, service, and replacement. The minority contractors program also required that the RFQ be sent to all minority contractors qualifying to supply the necessary materials (Susan had a list of them), and that no more than the same number of RFQs be sent to nonminority contractors.

STEP 2   The second step was to receive and evaluate the quotes. The minority contractors program required that ITE allow 10 working days from the day suppliers received the RFQ for them to respond. No more could Susan rely on calling a well-known, trusted supplier and have something delivered in a few days. This was not allowed under the minority contractors program, except under emergency conditions, which had to be defined and documented fully. In fact, all this activity had to be defined—the time it takes to review quotes, how minority and nonminority contractors should be compared and contrasted, and finally, how to decide on a contractor.

STEP 3   The last step was awarding the contract. If, after the review of quotes, a minority contractor were awarded the contract, nothing more than a copy of the contract, including the delivery date and all stipulations regarding maintenance, service, and replacement, need be supplied. But if a nonminority contractor were chosen, then extensive documentation as to why it was chosen over a minority contractor had to be supplied. Susan would need to define more carefully the process of taking part in the program, and thereby remind upper management of the difficulties that will inevitably arise—difficulties that shouldn't be blamed solely on her or her department.

Example   The last method of definition Susan used is an example. She knew that Norgaard, Inc., was competitive in only some areas of ITE's operations and that it had a similar corporate structure. She also knew through contacts with people at her own managerial level that Norgaard had agreed to take part in the minority contractors program, and that Norgaard was generally encouraged by the possibilities of doing work with minority contractors.

But Susan also found out that Norgaard realized that the contractual obligations, starting with the bidding process, were fairly cumbersome and restricting.

Although it had thought this would probably be true when considering the change, Norgaard decided that participation in the minority contractors program ultimately would be more beneficial (due in large part to an increase in the number of government contracts it was apt to get) than troublesome. Susan's contact, Henry Caswell, voiced these concerns and problems, but he did not suggest that Norgaard, and certainly not ITE, pull out of the program.

Susan was able to use Norgaard's experience as an example of how participation in the minority contractors program actually works, something a thorough job of defining should include if at all possible.

Given Susan's audience, upper management of ITE, all these techniques were appropriate, and depending on the amount of detail she included and where she included it, they were also effective. Her audience certainly needed to know why the crane she had decided not to buy was inadequate to serve the needs of ITE (physical description), how it was similar to or different from other suppliers' cranes (comparison and contrast), how the minority contractors program worked and therefore influenced her decisions and activities (process description), and finally, how other firms like ITE had dealt with, or were dealing with, the stipulations of the minority contractors program (example).

Techniques to Use for a Lay Audience

When an audience is not well informed on the subject, other techniques of definition may be used. Techniques more appropriate for a lay audience include the following:

- Etymology
- Synonyms and antonyms
- Similes and metaphors
- Analogies
- History of discovery or development

Etymology   Etymology lays out the linguistic origins of the term in question. It tells what language(s) the term is derived from and how the origins make the derived term easier to understand. Determining the etymology of a word should operate in two ways. The *analytical* breaks up the whole into parts to see what the whole means. Earlier in this chapter, for example, the etymology of the word *analysis* showed that the word is made up of two Greek words, *ana*, a suffix meaning "up," and *lyein*, a verb meaning "to break." It is easier, then, to understand and remember that *analysis* is the process of breaking up a whole into its parts so that they can be considered and understood by themselves, and then in their relation to other parts.

The other way is *analogical*, that is, likening the essence, meaning, or function of a term to the same characteristics of another term. Thus the term *crane*, denoting a machine that does heavy lifting, moving, and placing by means of a long, swinging projection, gets its name analogically from the bird of the same name, which is noted for its long, swinging, projecting neck.

Etymology is useful only when the derived term is in fact more clearly defined by either analysis or analog. The origins of some terms in use today are either unknown or so far removed from present meaning that they are useless in extending a definition; also there may be no analogs in present knowledge or experience that can be used meaningfully or effectively. Using etymology in these cases is basically a waste of time.

In sum, using etymology is a good technique for extending a definition only under these general circumstances: the linguistic origins, either analytic or analogic, are relevant and vivid enough to enhance definition and understanding; and the audience for whom the definition is written needs such relevance and vividness to further its understanding of the term.

Synonyms and Antonyms   Synonyms and antonyms are words that mean either the same thing (synonyms) or the opposite thing (antonyms) as the term being defined. Thus for the word *hydroponics* a choice of synonym might be *soilless agriculture,* or *water gardening,* whereas its antonym might be *traditional horticulture,* or *agronomy.* Again, the whole point of extending a definition by using synonyms or antonyms is to enhance the understanding of the term being defined by suggesting other terms that might be more familiar to the intended audience. Such a technique would not normally be useful or necessary for an audience educated in the field of the problem.

Similes and Metaphors   Both are figures of speech that compare the term being defined to one that is already understood. Similes use the words *like* or *as* to form the comparison. Howard Ensign Evans, for instance, in his "In Defense of Magic: The Story of Fireflies" from *Life on a Little-Known Planet* (New York: Dutton, 1968) uses these similes to help define the flashing behavior of fireflies: "Not only would the synchrony of the flashes increase the brightness but the alteration of light and dark would also be eye-catching, *like . . . flashing neon signs*" [italics added] and "brilliant, synchronous flashes serve *as a beacon* to attract females from the surrounding forest" [italics added].

Metaphors, however, compare the known with the unknown by equating them, without signals such as *like* or *as.* In describing the South American "railroad worm" with its "eleven greenish lights down each side of the body [and] two red lights on the head," Evans suggests that the insect becomes *"a fully lighted railroad train"* [italics added] as it moves along the ground.

Although similes and metaphors are more often used to extend definitions for uninitiated or lay audiences, their use is by no means limited to such audiences. Writers for professional audiences often use similes and metaphors to define and explain problems at hand. Thus scientists talk about inexplicable voids in space as "black holes" or the structure of the DNA molecule in terms of "chains," "ribbons," and "backbones." In most scientific and technological discourse, there are times when situations and phenomena cannot be defined easily in anything other than familiar terms—terms that everyone, including experts, can understand immediately, because they share the common structures of language and culture.

Analogies   Analogies are similar to similes and metaphors, in that they compare unknowns to knowns, but they deal with larger concepts and situations, not with specific words. In creating analogies, writers may also use similes and metaphors, but this usually happens in cases where the writer is writing for uninitiated or lay audiences, not for expert audiences. Consider, for example, the following, an excerpt from Lewis Thomas's article "Germs" in his collection *Lives of a Cell* (New York: Viking Penguin, Inc., and London: Garnstone Press, 1974):

> The microorganisms that seem to have it in for us in the worst way—the ones that really appear to wish us ill—turn out on close examination to be rather more like bystanders, strays, strangers in from the cold. They will invade and replicate if given the chance, and some of them will get into our deepest tissues and set forth in the blood, but it is our response to the presence that makes the disease. Our arsenals for fighting off bacteria are so powerful, and involve so many different defense mechanisms, that we are in more danger from them than from the invaders. We live in the midst of explosive devices; we are mined.

Thomas constructs two analogies here. One likens microorganisms (which he calls *germs*, also an appeal to a lay audience) to the homeless. He anthropomorphizes them, giving them the human characteristic of willfulness. Once they find a place to live, they burrow in deep, they "invade." In keeping with that notion, the other analogy likens the body's reaction to a war, talking about "arsenals," "fighting," the "danger" from "invaders," and the fact that we "live in the midst of explosive devices; we are mined." Both analogies trigger recognition in readers: the activities of bacteria become better understood more quickly. Most people know about the homeless; they certainly know about invading, fighting, and living among explosive devices (being mined) in war times, because they hear about them regularly or have to live with them.

Though we find analogies useful in many situations for the expert audience, writers by and large limit their use to uninitiated or lay audiences.

History of Discovery or Development   When using this technique, the writer or speaker notes the background of the term, concept, or problem in question, and how it came into being. Often it is useful to know what has gone on in the past to see why a problem is pertinent today. In Susan James's case, for instance, she could have reviewed briefly the beginnings of the minority contractors program, what the government had in mind in promoting minority contractors, why it was necessary, what the government thought the private sector could gain from the program, and finally, how that might meet the notions of governmental and social mandates.

But again, the use of this kind of information is generally reserved for lay audiences, who require more basic information. If Susan were to include this information, she would do so only briefly in the appendix to her report as a reminder of the purposes and goals of the program and how ITE's participation helps meet them. For a less-informed audience, her treatment would be longer and more detailed, and might well need to appear in the body of the report instead of only in an appendix.

Summary of the Definition Process

Professionals must first clearly define a problem before they can attempt to solve it. If they don't know what the components and the limits of a problem are, attempts to research, analyze, and solve it will be simply hit or miss. That kind of approach is expensive in all terms: time, money, and effort. And even if they have spent much in these areas, there is never any guarantee that the problem ultimately will be solved. Although that may be true of any problem and of any attempt to solve it, it is most surely true of one that has not been clearly defined. Thus at this definition stage three things should be kept in mind:

1. The felt need must be clearly known and expressed.
2. The audience who will benefit from an address of or a solution to the problem must be clearly known and analyzed.
3. The techniques of definition to accommodate the felt need and the audience who will benefit from an ultimate address of or solution to the problem need to be understood and used appropriately.

RESEARCH

Once a problem has been defined, problem solvers need to collect information or data. They need to know what has already happened to create the problem, what is going on in the present, and what is likely to happen in the future. They need to know what sources of data are available, and whether they are primary in nature—providing data that the researcher needs to collect firsthand, or secondary—data provided through publications of research already performed. They also need to know how best to collect the data—which research design is most effective for the primary work, which sources are most useful and reputable for the secondary work. Most research is conducted using both methods, but depending on the nature of the problem, one method may dominate.

Primary research dominates when the problem has received little attention in the past, only recently has been defined, or perhaps needs to be redefined by discovering new elements through laboratory experimentation or fieldwork. Such problems center on the phenomenal world; they are tangible. Several examples are relevant: research in genetic engineering, nuclear fusion, drug therapies for the relief or cure of cancer or AIDS, or the research of social scientists about human behavior.

Cases in which secondary research dominates usually involve possibly significant changes in existing theory about intangible matters, such as philosophy, history, and the humanities in general. For example, a philosopher might reassess Thomas Kuhn's notion of scientific revolution, or a literature theorist might take on Derrida's idea of textual deconstruction.

Straightforward Primary Research

Susan James's case provides, as many problems do, a need for fairly straightforward primary research. To report on the problem of the inadequate Jones and Son crane, Susan would have to collect specifications on the proposed crane from Jones and Son, as well as specifications from other suppliers. Specifications, although published by individual suppliers, are not analyzed for the reader; they simply list capabilities or ranges of performance of the product in question. Researchers who collect the specifications have to analyze them themselves and must also determine how well they meet the needs of the problem in question. Culling that information takes what has been defined here as primary research.

Susan had to determine exactly which specifications were pertinent for purposes of comparison and contrast, for example, how the elements of lifting, shifting, lowering, and placement would meet the needs of the Engineering Department. Thus she had to review Engineering's specifications and perhaps clarify them by talking to members of that department. If time permitted, she might also have to observe the crane on site: watching it in actual operation to determine how the work progressed in terms of time and space provided, although she would probably have to have an engineer along to help her determine (and interpret) pertinent events. In other words, any collection of data that has not already been collected and analyzed qualifies as primary research.

Complex Primary Research with Fieldwork

As noted earlier, Susan James's need for primary research is fairly simple and straightforward. Other problems professionals address require more involved research designs and methods of collecting data. The two discussed below require fieldwork, something that Susan would not have to do unless she did site observations.

The first example is that of Elizabeth Frederickson, chief chemist for a Pacific Coast utilities company, whose professional profile appears in Chapter 1. Unlike the problems Susan James has to solve, those that Elizabeth Frederickson has to solve require a great deal more primary research. Determining how to manage hazardous materials that her company produces means two kinds of primary research: fieldwork, in the form of soil sampling, and laboratory work, which analyzes those soil samples.

When designing the fieldwork, Elizabeth must decide on the following:

- The sites for soil sampling, and why they are necessary or appropriate
- The methods and specifications for sampling: the size of areas, the amount of soil, and the depths from which soil should be sampled
- The necessary equipment and personnel to do the sampling

When designing the lab work, Elizabeth must make similar decisions, such as the following:

- How many soil samples need to be analyzed
- Which tests they will be subjected to, and why
- The amount of time needed for doing the analysis, which of course must be coordinated with time constraints the company has identified for optimum production

Good research design is the first and an essential step in carrying out good research, but design should not be confused with performance. Like any problem solver, Elizabeth must be sure that the mechanics, or performance, of the design are carried out well—that contingencies and variables are accounted for—and that the research will indeed provide the kind of data necessary for meaningful analysis and later synthesis. This requires, then, careful supervision of the methods of field and laboratory work, not only of others who may be working on the project, but also of oneself as a part of the research team.

A second example of primary research is the case of Patricia Wynjenek, a cultural anthropologist who wanted to study the economic survival strategies of low-income Mexican Americans living in an American-Mexican border city. (This case is discussed again in Chapters 4 and 5.) The problem, simply stated, was posed in this question: How do intact families whose incomes are far below the officially designated national poverty level manage to survive economically and to stay together? (The question presents an implicit contrast to other urban poor, whose families are not intact, and who survive by way of social economic programs like Aid to Dependent Children.) The answer to the question might suggest different approaches to and definitions of social and economic programs that all urban poor could benefit from.

The approach to this problem requires a good design for primary research, one that assures that all the necessary primary evidence will be collected. The first part of the design would require participant observation, whereby Patricia takes up residence in one of the poorer neighborhoods of the town, establishes contacts with some of the key individuals (those everyone seems to know, and who take some kind of leadership role) in the neighborhood, and generally takes part in the life of the community when it is possible and appropriate. By living this way, she can take notes—observations on how the community gets along—in the following areas:

- What and how social events, like parties, dances, and sports events, take place
- What and how religious or other cultural events, like holidays, elections, dedications of new civic facilities or programs, take place
- How the foregoing events are influenced by the interactions within, between, and among families
- How families deal with their private occasions of change: births, deaths, initiations, graduations, marriages, and the like

This kind of information is essential for research anthropologists to collect, but in this case it is just part of the work of primary research, because it relies on the ability of the researcher to get to places and situations where she can observe. The other part of the research means gathering information on a one-to-one basis, talking to specific people about how they live, and how they get along economically.

This approach requires work that most anthropologists cannot do on their own. Because they are foreign to the culture or subculture they are studying, specific people they need to interview are often shy about giving information about their lives. So the first task is to find members of the community who would be willing to conduct interviews that pose specific questions about family employment, education, medical care, and family life in general.

Patricia then needs to decide on several other essential elements of her research design:

- How many households should be interviewed to get a reasonable sample
- How many interviewers she will need
- How the households will be chosen—at random or by some means of stratification—and the reasons for choosing either method
- How the interviews will take place—whether questions and responses should be recorded by hand or be taped
- What kinds of questions and how many of them interviewers should ask
- How long the interviews should last

It is essential, then, that plans for primary research be made and justified before the work proceeds; without planning and clear ideas about the logic of the plans, the work will stumble and falter.

Acquiring and Evaluating Secondary Research Materials

As we suggested earlier, most problems require a mix of primary and secondary research. The examples above help illustrate that. In Susan James's case, most of the information she can get on the minority contractors program will come in the form of secondary materials: government publications on the history of the program, the provisions it has established for its operation, and reports of how the program has worked in specific instances. The source of these publications is usually the government itself, who will send information of this kind to anyone who asks for it. But they can also be found in full-service libraries, either public, corporate, or academic, that have large holdings in government documents.

Though this kind of information may be fairly easy to acquire, Susan, or any researcher like her, must remember that it is written with a certain amount of inevitable bias. The government, from whatever mandate it feels the most pressure, will publish documents that reflect well on its efforts. It may not knowingly alter information to suit its needs or the audience for which the information is intended, but it will certainly present, in the most positive light, the intent and accomplishments of its efforts. In other words, Susan, in reading government materials, would be likely to get only part of the story—and the most positive part at that.

In order to get a more impartial picture of how the minority contractors program is working, Susan might turn to reports from other firms participating in the program. These reports generally can be found in trade journals—publications written for particular audiences in various areas of interest, in Susan's case, those having to do with heavy industrial production, or with purchasing in particular. Since publications of this kind are designed to present up-to-date information on the workings of the trade—new ideas, new trends, recent accomplishments—they are apt to present fairly full and realistic assessments of what is going on. It is true that much of their reporting tends to be upbeat, but in fairness to their readers, they do not avoid reporting on the downside of things—and certainly would report it if the minority contractors program was not working well.

The important thing for Susan to remember is that secondary materials often have been written with bias, and so more than one source of information should be consulted to get a fuller picture.

Elizabeth Frederickson's need for secondary research is slightly different. Since her primary research is based on an established tradition and methods of soil sampling and laboratory analysis, she usually does not need to do secondary research to explain or substantiate that. In her education she has already consulted those sources; she knows how the methods she uses are supported by theory and testing. Only when new methods are introduced would she do well to consider the published material that explains and analyzes them.

The real job of secondary research for Elizabeth lies in review of federal and state legislation having to do with hazardous materials. She must be aware not only of the laws, but also of how they affect her firm's activities; she must also know about ideas and movements for future legislation. Her basic sources for information would be the *Congressional Record*, California's and Oregon's state legislative records, and of course, copies of the laws that have already been enacted. But beyond these, she would want to look at analyses of the laws in force and of those proposed, which are written by several groups: offices of legislators and members of Congress, lawyers representing industries in question, and environmental protectionists. She would find these various reports in a full-service library, but also, and more immediately, directly from the various offices that write and produce them.

Most of what she would have to read will be fairly straightforwardly written. The records of Congress and legislatures are themselves not interpretations: they are direct transcriptions of what went on and are biased only to the extent to which the authors of testimony are biased. The analyses of legislation written by other interested parties will inevitably bear the stamp of the interest that produces them. When the overall viewpoint of the interest group is known, there is little need to ferret out subtleties of analysis and presentation. For example, an analysis of an abortion bill by a right-to-life group would reflect in a very straightfoward way the group's stand against abortion.

The case of Patricia Wynjenek involves more of what is thought of as traditional academic secondary research. In designing her primary research, she would have to draw upon the methods others have used in similar situations. She would find those described in ethnographies published by other anthropologists. She would also have to reconsider anthropological theory, making sure that she understands how it has evolved and how it informs current practice. In addition to recognizing differences in schools of thought (or theoretical bias), she would want to be concerned with the currency of the secondary material and whether it reflects the best that is known presently.

The sources of these materials are almost exclusively academic libraries, the depositories of ethnographies, monographs, and journal articles that discuss a variety of issues and problems that anthropologists want to address and to solve. And since almost all large libraries, academic or otherwise, have automated access to their holdings, it is relatively simple and rapid to search the database, or to search other databases that a library may be connected to cooperatively, to locate pertinent materials. This kind of service is not limited to the anthropologist's needs; both Susan James and Elizabeth Frederickson could use similar search services in completing their secondary research.

The Annotated Bibliography: A Helpful Tool

Researchers doing secondary research often find the annotated bibliography a very helpful tool. The annotated bibliography (AB) is a list of pertinent secondary sources that includes the researcher's commentary (annotation) about each source. The AB can be adapted for any researcher's needs, but customarily includes brief statements about the thesis of a source, its scope, its particularly useful sections and why they are useful, and its strengths and weaknesses. The length of annotations can range from a couple of sentences to a paragraph, although it is clear that the thoroughness of an annotation can save much rework down the line. More complete ABs might even include significant quotations from the source, with page number noted, of course.

To generate the material for an AB, researchers need only peruse and skim the source. If it is a book, they may look at the preface to determine the author's theoretical or rhetorical position. They can skim the table of contents to see what topics are covered. They may want to read chapter summaries, introductions, or concluding paragraphs.

If the source is an article, they may use the article's abstract or summary, which if it is well written, will state what the article's thesis is, what the author's findings were, and, perhaps, why they are significant. In other words, the summary will be conclusive.

It is a good idea at this point to distinguish between abstracts and summaries (often called executive summaries). Abstracts are short, usually only a paragraph long, and appear separately at the beginning of articles. The purpose of an abstract is to identify the main point of the discussion, plus any other information required, such as topics covered or key words. But abstracts are not conclusive. They don't reveal important secondary points, conclusions, or recommendations. They don't tell the significance of the author's findings. That's the job of a summary. Obviously, in writing a useful annotated bibliography, researchers will find the job easier if they can read useful, conclusive summaries.

Armed with a conclusive AB, researchers can build a resource base that will communicate clearly to them even after they've not seen the original source for some time. A conclusive annotation will reveal the main point of the source; it will not simply list the topics within the source without telling what the author thinks about those topics. In other words, a conclusive annotation will tell "who done it"; it will give away the answer.

While it is tempting to resist being so explicit, explicitness is a trait to be cultivated in professionals' lives because it keeps them closer to the truth. It's good to remember that people don't read professional material for fun; they read it for answers.

A short but conclusive annotation of *Cinderella* might read like this: "A much put-upon stepsister finds her destiny to wed the kingdom's prince, after her fairy godmother helps her escape her hearth-bound existence." An inconclusive annotation might say something like this: "A young girl suffers under her stepmother and undergoes many trials." The inconclusive annotation reveals the general topic, but does not reveal the final outcome—marrying the prince—and that's what the conclusion of *Cinderella* is all about.

To take another example, we could imagine the following annotation: "This report takes on the cigarette industry to examine whether safety standards have been upheld." Such an annotation gives the topic of the report, but does not give the answer the report is supposed to reveal. A conclusive annotation would provide the answer: "This report of safety practices in the cigarette industry concludes that safety practices are not only keeping up to standards, but have, in fact, raised standards over the past five years." This annotation gives the answer, the conclusion. It is a conclusive piece of writing.

Summary of the Research Process

We can see from the examples of Susan James, Elizabeth Frederickson, and Patricia Wynjenek that the research stage of problem solving is very important. Figure 2.2 provides a checklist for the research process. If the research design is good, that is, if the researchers have asked intelligent questions about what they are seeking to know, and have devised the best means to collect information to answer those questions, then they will have supplied the requirements for the next stage of problem solving—analysis. The quality of the analysis depends to a large degree on the quality of the research. No matter how good the researchers' analytical skills are, if the body of data gleaned from research is incomplete, biased, irrelevant, out of date, or some combination of any of these, the analysis will yield very little of use in solving the problem.

ANALYSIS

As noted in Figure 2.1, the analysis stage answers the basic question, What do the data mean? Here researchers look carefully at the data to see how the various parts paint a picture or tell a story. Analysis requires discovering relationships—how one event or situation or fact brings about or affects another, how that connection may bring about another of its kind, but perhaps slightly different in its makeup. The

Figure 2.2
Checklist for the research process

Primary Research

____ 1. Be sure that the design for primary research includes all the areas and variables that need to be studied and considered.

____ 2. Consider, use, adapt, and/or reject methods used by other researchers. Know why you are using, adapting, and/or rejecting them.

____ 3. Once you decide on a course and method of research, follow it consistently and thoroughly.

Secondary Reseach

____ 1. Be sure to review thoroughly the literature on the problem you are researching. Use the automated search capabilities of a full service library to ensure thoroughness.

____ 2. Decide carefully, in reviewing the literature, which ideas agree or conflict with your ideas and analysis of the problem you are researching.

____ 3. Analyze the problem as you have defined it, and show what your analysis contributes to a general understanding of the problem within the field.

important thing to remember is that analysis in solving problems is not a discrete process that happens only after definition and research have taken place, or that does not have to take into account resolution and synthesis (the suggestion of a solution) and possibly implementation, the last steps in solving problems. Analysis goes on all the time in solving problems, as we have illustrated in Figure 2.3.

Analysis is a part of the process of definition: very few, if any, problems are made up of only one identifiable element. Knowing what the various elements are and how they contribute to the full definition of the problem requires analysis.

Analysis is a part of research. One has to know what research is necessary and why. Therefore, deciding on a research design—the needs and parts of both primary and secondary research—requires analysis.

Analysis is also a part of resolution or synthesis and of implementation. Solutions also have parts that depend on each other and influence each other; knowing and understanding the relationships among the parts, so that the solution as a whole seems sensible, also requires analysis.

Although analysis is not a discrete process, but rather a continuous one, it is important to understand that there are times when analysis will take center stage, and that happens after definition and research. Thus Susan James must go beyond the analysis of her needs for primary and secondary research and analyze fully the data she has collected. For example, from the primary data, she must actually compare and contrast, perhaps in tabular form, the specifications of cranes from other suppliers to those from Jones and Son and then to the specifications suggested by the Engineering Department. She then has to point out where the

Figure 2.3
*The role of
analysis in the
technical problem-
solving process*

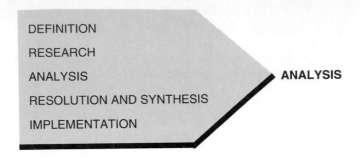

DEFINITION

RESEARCH

ANALYSIS   **ANALYSIS**

RESOLUTION AND SYNTHESIS

IMPLEMENTATION

specifications differ, to what degree, and how important the differences are for the proposed use and operation of the crane. For this she needs some advice from one of the staff engineers.

If she observed the operations on site, she would have to analyze her notes, perhaps again with some help from someone in the Engineering Department and decide how elements of the actual operation reflect the published specifications, and how that might influence the needs of the Engineering Department.

Her analysis of the secondary data would be essentially the same, involving comparing and contrasting. From her reading of government documents and trade journals on the history, provisions, and operation of the minority contractors program, Susan would compare how the program is intended to operate to how it actually operates in various situations. She would further compare or contrast those situations to her own to decide how the program most likely will affect her purchasing operation, and then how it will affect generally the operations of ITE. The result of her analysis of both primary and secondary data will form the substance of her resolution and synthesis of the problem.

Analysis of primary data for Elizabeth Frederickson is a highly technical affair. It involves exact laboratory procedure that will reveal the presence of hazardous materials and their type and concentration in the soil. It will also suggest the source of the hazardous material, since Elizabeth knows what the possible sources are, especially within the workings of her own firm.

As for analysis of secondary data, Elizabeth's job is similar to Susan's in that she has to do a certain amount of comparing and contrasting. She has to compare or contrast, for instance, how legislation on the control of hazardous materials has affected the operations of utility companies similar to the one she works for. She also has to predict the operations of her company as compared with others and how future legislation will affect the operations of her company.

But Elizabeth's other concern in analysis is what the impact of reviews of legislation written by environmental groups has already been or yet may be. She has to assess the importance of these groups in influencing public opinion and in bringing about legislation. She can do that by noting how often environmental groups have succeeded in getting measures they want passed, and what kinds of measures they are, how restrictive, how permissive, how expensive to those who must comply with them, and so forth.

Finally, Patricia Wynjenek's job of analyzing primary data also has to do with comparing and contrasting, though in a slightly different way. She must categorize the answers to the questions of the survey she conducted, which amounts to deciding which answers are alike, which are different, and of course, how alike or different they are. For example, in response to a question on birth control practices, she could get responses from women that fall into several possible categories—yes, they consciously control the size of their families, and by what means they do that; or no, they let whatever is to happen, happen; or they practice a combination of the two.

Patricia must then decide how the answers to her survey questions compare or contrast with what she knows about the community from her own participant observation. She must take into account how the answers she gets to questions from her survey are similar to or different from her own observations. She must consider the effect her interviewers have on the people they interview, people who are not used to formal questioning, or maybe to any questioning at all. She must consider the following kinds of questions:

- Are those interviewed shy or reticent? To what extent and why?
- Do they answer questions willingly?
- How fully do they answer them?
- Do they appear hostile? How do they appear so?
- What is the likelihood that they are giving false information?

She must decide, in general, what restraints the people she is observing feel about her presence, and how they feel in general about what she is trying to do, even with the help of people from the community.

The main job of analysis of secondary data comes for Patricia when she assesses the validity of the conclusions drawn in other ethnographic studies similar to her own. She must determine whether the means by which data were collected—kind and duration of participant observation, kind and method of execution of survey instruments, and so forth—can actually support the conclusions the ethnographer has drawn. She must then, once again, compare and contrast her own fieldwork methods to those of other ethnographers to see whether they have provided the kind of information she needs to draw valid conclusions. She would do this latter analysis to confirm the solidity of her research design, since in planning it initially, she had to consider the designs of other ethnographies. But it is always possible, even this late in her work, that Patricia could discover some defect in her methods and have to correct it. Even though that may delay her final step, the resolution and synthesis, she knows that it is better to find and correct that error now than to risk rendering invalid conclusions.

RESOLUTION AND SYNTHESIS

Throughout the problem-solving process, problem solvers have to make decisions—decisions about the nature and scope of the problem, about research design and methods of collecting data, and about what the data collected actually mean, given the problem as defined. But it is in the resolution and synthesis stage that decisions must be made about what may or ultimately will solve the problem. This means that the significance of the analysis of the preceding stage must be determined, and whether that significance suggests a solution or solutions to the problem.

It also means that decisions have to be made about how reasonable the solutions are, and why some are more reasonable than others. In other words, what are the general advantages and disadvantages of any one of the possible solutions? This involves general assessments of costs and time and the final effect of the solution in light of expected or possible results.

Many would think that resolution and synthesis should be the last step in technical problem solving, because it implies a solution to the problem. On the face of it, that is true, but it is important to remember that not all problems can be solved, or at least not readily solved, within the limitations of time and resources. The trouble we as a society have had in solving such problems as poverty and the plight of the homeless; finding cures for cancer, heart disease, and AIDS; and wiping out our international trade or national budget deficits is evidence enough that not all problems can readily be solved. It may take years, decades, even centuries before some problems are solved, and even then we have to be careful when deciding whether a solution is indeed a solution, and not just a diversion from the basics of the problem, or whether the solution creates other problems. A common example of this kind of situation is one that Rachel Carson talks about in "The Obligation to Endure" from *Silent Spring* (Boston: Houghton Mifflin, 1962). In our quest to improve agricultural production and to rid ourselves of the pests that attack our crops, we have come up with ever more powerful chemicals to spray on the pests (but also into the crops and into the environment). In so doing, we have added to already staggering conditions of pollution, risking, as Carson says, "the contamination of man's total environment [with] substances that accumulate in the tissues of plant and animals and even penetrate the germ cells to shatter or alter the very material of heredity upon which the shape of the future depends." What we have done is to find a short-term solution (killing the present pests) that in itself creates a much longer-term problem. In Carson's words, "It is ironic to think that man might determine his own future by something so seemingly trivial as the choice of an insect spray."

This notion should not be overstated and therefore misunderstood. Most problems professionals have to face on a day-to-day basis can be solved, at least in the short term, without the kind of damage Rachel Carson talks about. But it seems more realistic and useful to think about this step of the process as one by which the elements of the problem, after being defined, researched, and analyzed, are put back together and some decision is made, rather than think of it as absolutely the last step, where a solution for better or for worse is declared. This way we can account for both those problems that actually can be solved within limitations of time and resources, and those that require repeated addresses, and resolutions and syntheses along the way, before they ultimately can be solved.

Susan James's problem fits into the category of problems resolved or synthesized, but not actually solved. Although she was initially troubled and unsure about how to report on progress that showed no extraordinary achievement, she was satisfied, after she had defined the problem and collected and analyzed the data, that the decision she had made not to purchase the crane from Jones and Son was sound. She was sure that her recommendation to go through a more extensive bidding process, which now would meet the guidelines of the minority contractors program, would eventually turn up a supplier who could best meet ITE's needs. She was also sure that her decision and recommendation were unassailable, and that if she were to be criticized for making them, that would have to happen for reasons other than the good practical sense she had shown. But the fact is that she had not actually solved the original problem: finding and putting in place a crane to meet Engineering's needs in record time. The solution to that problem was yet to come.

It may seem obvious that the resolution and synthesis step involves making decisions, the kind of decisions that finally initiate action. But other decisions are usually made at various earlier steps in the process of technical problem solving, and they anticipate resolution and synthesis and the final step, if it is possible to carry out, implementation.

To illustrate this with Susan James's case, once she suspected that the Jones and Son crane probably would not serve ITE's needs, she decided to compare and contrast Jones and Son's specifications with those of other suppliers. And further, since she knew that Jones and Son would not qualify as a preferred supplier under the minority contractors program, she decided to research and explain more fully how the program affected purchasing and the other operations of ITE as she understood them. Both of these decisions were based on information Susan obtained before this resolution and synthesis step.

So we see that resolution and synthesis means putting back the pieces of the ongoing analysis, making things simpler to see as a whole, and confirming decisions that have already been made at least tentatively earlier in the process. The result of resolving and synthesizing a problem is seldom a surprise, and it shouldn't be. Good preparation, which means careful definition and thoughtful collection and analysis of data, will suggest how a problem is to be solved, or resolved and synthesized. Resolution and synthesis becomes, then, both a resting place and a spur to action.

For Susan James, it meant that she could see the sense in what she had decided, and that there should now be no barriers to acquiring a crane through acceptable means, given the findings of her research and analysis. This problem for Susan James is solved, at least for now. In her quarterly report she will explain why she did not contract Jones and Son; will recommend strongly that ITE seek other suppliers, in keeping with the guidelines of the minority contractors program; and will stress that in all future major acquisitions the same process be followed.

Elizabeth Frederickson's task of resolving and synthesizing is hard. It means deciding how her firm's hazardous materials affect the environment and how the impact as defined and dealt with coincides with concerns of environmental groups and with legislation. It becomes a balancing act, one that she has to perform to meet at least three demands: the needs of her employer, the needs of the public, and the needs dictated by her own position as a professional chemist.

Each situation poses problems of ethics. Elizabeth must exhibit loyalty to her employer and try to further the company's best interests, so that she can get along in the company; she must understand and have a certain sympathy with the public, because the public has a right to be heard and protected; and she must understand and stand up for the conduct and ethics of her own profession. Her suggestions, then, based upon her laboratory work and her library work have to take all these considerations into account. Absolute solutions, under these conditions, are not possible. But Elizabeth can suggest ways of proceeding that will address, if not exactly solve, all the problems each group perceives in an attempt to bring all three together in some kind of reasonable and responsible package. This is tricky, but not impossible.

Patricia Wynjenek's resolving and synthesizing situation is different from the preceding cases. She has to decide two things, which initially may not be seen as solutions to the problems that suggest them. First, she has to decide how the people she is studying actually survive economically, while keeping their family structures and their extra-familial social structures intact. She also has to decide what that information means for the way those people are perceived by others.

The first decision comes directly from the analysis of her research. This decision serves as a resolution and synthesis of the kind defined earlier—one that offers no solution. Economically speaking, the people she is studying survive on very little, but they are willing and able to do so as long as they can keep their families intact. Ironically, however, it is because they keep their families together that they are worse off economically than many of their counterparts in other poor urban areas of the United States.

These families have few material goods, and those they have are old, used, and in constant need of repair. Their housing is likewise old or cheaply constructed and small. Their nutrition is below standard, relying heavily on starches and other carbohydrates and less on animal protein and fruits and vegetables. They have limited access to medical care, though they do not avoid modern, "scientific" methods; neither do they throw over completely traditional means of healing; many do not have family doctors and rely largely on a handful of free clinics or hospital emergency rooms for necessary medical attention. Nevertheless, the population has a strong sense of community, family obligation, and self-worth. Although statistically, and in real terms, they are a part of the growing underclass of American citizens, they manifest few of the commonly understood signs of alienation and disaffection associated with other American populations suffering from economic deprivation.

Deciding what this means about the ways others, such as sociologists, social workers, and government bureaucrats, perceive these problems and phenomena and deal with them, and more important how they will deal with them in the future, is a problem Patricia Wynjenek has yet to solve. But having done her study, having resolved and synthesized many of the problems she had before doing her work, she is now in a much better position to attempt to solve that problem.

IMPLEMENTATION

Implementation grows directly out of the preceding stage, resolution and synthesis. In fact, ideas of implementation are rooted in that stage—that is where the possibilities and feasibilities of solutions are generated and first-level decisions are made.

Implementation deals with practicalities: the actual means by which solutions will be realized, who will bring them about, how they will be brought about, how much they will cost, and how long they will take. Decisions made at this level are practical rather than theoretical. If a certain route should be taken, how could it reasonably be taken, given the constraints of time and resources? Decisions made at this level may change the means of implementation, but they usually don't change the basic need for or structure of implementation.

Implementation requires four elements:

1. A clear organizational plan to realize the solution, that is, to see the solution over various structural hurdles inherent in any organization
2. A reasonable plan to employ resources, either internal or external, to bring about the solution
3. Specific knowledge of what it will cost and how long it will take to bring about the solution
4. A clear idea of what the results of implementing the solution will be

Implementation has to be systematic and careful. Once an organization has decided to take a certain path, even if it's only an interim path along the way to a final solution, it must take it confidently. To do otherwise means misfires, false starts, and ultimately time, money, and effort wasted.

Had Susan James actually solved her original technical problem and found a crane for the Engineering Department in 24 hours with delivery in another 48, she would have had to implement the solution quickly. She would need approval from the Vice President of Operations to spend $250,000 to buy the crane. That would probably mean a personal visit to him or to some significant subordinate to lay out the immediate need.

She would also have to make sure that Jones and Son would be able to deliver the crane in the 72 hours since the deal had been approved. This would probably require a trip to Jones and Son, but if not that, at least several telephone conversations with the production manager—maybe even with Hershel Jones himself. And, finally, she would need some assurance from the Engineering Department that the new crane would do what needed to be done. Engineering would need to look at performance specifications and judge them appropriate and effective for its operations.

Susan's position is a good one to illustrate implementation, because the nature of the problems she solves requires her direct involvement. But many other professionals seldom implement the problems they solve, simply because their work does not call for it. Elizabeth Frederickson and Patricia Wynjenek are two examples.

Although, as we pointed out earlier, Elizabeth's job of resolving and synthesizing is difficult because of the pressures on her ethical stance, once she has solved a problem and made a decision, she passes the implementation on to her superiors. If, for example, she decides that her firm must adopt a new method of disposing of hazardous materials at a particular location, she will recommend the new method, pointing out why it is necessary and suggesting the means of implementation. However, she herself will not be directly responsible for the process. But note that in her recommending a new method and suggesting a means of implementation, she lays the necessary groundwork for someone else to do the work. That means that she has to be aware of what implementation involves.

The same is true of Patricia Wynjenek. Although at some time she may be able to recommend new social programs based upon what she has found out about the economic survival strategies of the people she was studying, she is not in a position to implement them. Others in public or private agencies would be responsible for implementing the solutions that Patricia recommends. But again, Patricia's understanding of what implementation involves will make her recommendations more specific and therefore more likely to be carried out effectively.

CONCLUSIONS

The basics of technical problem solving—definition, research, analysis, resolution and synthesis, and implementation—are dynamic and demanding tasks. They require a commitment to understanding and willing participation in professionalism that most who seek meaningful work in their lives are willing to make. But if they are to work—if they are to be used successfully to solve problems— they require close attention to the process involved in using them.

It is not enough simply to define a problem. One then has to research it to find out the details of what has defined it. Once the details have been gathered, they have to be analyzed—looked at as discrete entities, then as parts of the whole to see how they fit into a larger picture. Then the whole process needs to be resolved and synthesized—to be bound up to decide ultimately what it might mean. And, if possible, a decision must be made as to how a solution will be implemented. At every stage the need for redefinition, further research, and reanalysis may present itself. Solving problems is not a clean and linear activity; it is often messy and frustrating, doubling back on itself; but once honestly and conscientiously taken on, it can render great rewards. It is not merely honorific to say that any job has been well done. The ability to say that with conviction is the ultimate test.

EXERCISES

1. In small groups use the definition techniques discussed in this chapter to try to convey the following concepts to the groups indicated:
    a. Shin splints to a nonexerciser
    b. Having a brother or sister to an only child
    c. A word processor to someone who has used only a typewriter
    d. The ocean to someone who has never been out of North Dakota
    e. An engine and generator to an English major
    f. The value of poetry to an engineering major

2. In small groups, or as a class, consider the problems listed below by answering the fundamental questions posed in defining a problem: What's wrong, what's lacking, what's unknown, and who will benefit from a solution to the problem? Remember that not all problems will have answers for all questions but all problems must have some group that will benefit from a solution.

a. Protection of the spotted owl in the Pacific northwest
b. Acid rain in the industrial midwest
c. Balance of international trade
d. Growing drug abuse among teenagers
e. Social and economic effects of an aging population
f. Automobiles powered by alternative fuels
g. The AIDS epidemic

3. In small groups, suggest the kinds of problems you already know professionals in your various fields of study have to face. Choose one of the problems and construct an outline of problem-solving stages around it. Be as specific as possible about the questions that would have to be answered and ways of answering them at each stage of the outline.

ASSIGNMENTS

1. Using an article your instructor has assigned, write first an abstract of the article and then a summary. Review the differences between the two on pages 47 and 48 of this chapter. Your reader should be able to see marked differences between the two.

2. Write a conclusive annotated bibliography of five sources on a topic your instructor has assigned.

TERM PROJECT OPTIONS

1. Write a memo to your instructor that fulfills the following requirements:
a. Uses standard memo format. (Memo formats are discussed in Chapter 8.)
b. Defines in detail the research problem you want to address or attempt to solve during the remainder of this term. Keep in mind the needs and techniques of defining problems discussed in this chapter.
c. Suggests the ways you will go about gathering information, both in primary and secondary research.

2. Write an annotated bibliography of ten secondary sources that you believe will be helpful in addressing or solving your research problem. On the title page of this assignment, be sure to state what your research problem is. At this point, you may have a problem clearly in mind or perhaps only a question you would like to pursue. This annotated bibliography will help you narrow your interests and focus on a problem.

Following the title page, present the bibliography, heading each annotation with the appropriate bibliographic information for the source (for example, Carson, Rachel. *Silent Spring*. New York: Houghton Mifflin, 1962.). Sources should be listed alphabetically by author's last name, or in lieu of an author's name, by the first substantive word of the title of the piece.

Your annotations should consist of two full paragraphs. In the first paragraph write a conclusive summary of the source. In the second paragraph explain how you think the source will be useful in your work. For example: Will it provide introductory material? Will it provide an interesting perspective on the problem as you understand it?

Note: You will be able to use this annotated bibliography to help you write your proposal to research the problem (proposals are discussed in Chapter 4).

3

RHETORICAL

PROBLEM SOLVING

Preview of the Chapter

An Overview of Rhetorical Problem Solving

Purpose
  Primary Purposes
  Secondary Purposes

Audience
  First Level of Audience Analysis
  Second Level of Audience Analysis

Context

Ethical Stance

Rhetorical Problem Solving as a Recursive Process

Writing for Someone Else's Signature

Conclusions

March 21, 1990
7:45 A.M.
Mary Anne Cox's office
Outerware, Inc.
17 D Street
Hartford, Connecticut

Mary Anne Cox got to her office at the usual time—7:45 A.M.—early for some people, late for others, but just about right for her. She went about the usual chores of making some coffee, sorting out yesterday's mess on her desk, and turning on her desktop computer, one of three in her office. When she did, she found a message from her immediate superior, Tim Sanford, saying that something had gone terribly wrong with the last test of the environmental control system Outerware had installed in late February in the capitol building, and that they'd need to discuss it as soon as possible. Mary Anne got a little nervous: to get a message like this from Tim meant that he was upset—he usually dropped in on her when he had something to talk about, and seldom left a message on her computer. It also meant that since she hadn't got the message until now, he'd either stayed late, later than she had stayed the day before, or that he had gotten in earlier this morning. She checked the time Tim had sent the message: 6:15 P.M., March 20. She had left at 5:30 that day, having put in a full day, and she began to relax, at least about the timing.

Mary Anne had worked for Outerware, Inc. for 3 ½ years. She had earned her B.S. in Computer Science from the University of Connecticut in 1987, had interviewed with several firms in the area, and was hired by Outerware as a systems engineer. Outerware was developing at the time an automated environmental control system, by which the ambient temperatures of many different offices in a complex could be controlled at a central location, thus eliminating the need for individual thermostats and yet keeping offices at comfortable temperatures throughout the year. Outerware had named the system ENCONTRO. One of Mary Anne's primary responsibilities was the programming of ENCONTRO— and working out any bugs that popped up in it. Tim, her superior, maintained a liaison position between research and program development and Outerware's clients. The two worked closely together, Tim providing Mary Anne with analyses of the needs of new clients, Mary Anne providing Tim with the technical analyses and answers to those needs.

Mary Anne met with Tim as soon as they could both manage it. Tim told her the capitol building's chief operations engineer, Janice Trippling, reported that ENCONTRO had rendered the capitol building basically unlivable on its last test run: in the mild late March weather, half the offices, mostly in the east wing, had been cooled to 62 degrees F (just about the outdoors' ambient temperature), while most of the west wing offices had been warmed to 78 degrees F, well over the usual 70 to 72 degree range. This had happened in the last couple of hours of the previous working day, and thus the late report. Mary Anne agreed to meet with Janice Trippling that day to discuss the problem and to report in writing her analysis of and proposed solutions to the problem.

The meeting with Trippling did not go particularly well. Trippling was annoyed, even a bit hostile, since, as she pointed out, she had had nothing to do with the decision to install ENCONTRO. That decision had been made somewhere up the line, and she, as Chief Operations Engineer, had to implement it and live with it, even though she had seen no particular advantages to using the system. Even given the hostility, Mary Anne learned that there was nothing intrinsically wrong with the system, but that the assistant operations engineer, Sonny Baker, who had responsibility with others for monitoring it, had misunderstood crucial procedures for using the control system software. They would have to be trained once again. The system was sound and would remain so, if only those who use it would use it properly.

Mary Anne went home that night with questions and worries. How should she write a report that Tim would read; that John Springer, Vice President of Program Development at Outerware would read; and finally, that Janice Trippling and several of her superiors and subordinates would also read? Mary Anne didn't sleep well, but she woke up with some ideas.

 ## AN OVERVIEW OF RHETORICAL PROBLEM SOLVING

Mary Anne Cox's story is typical of professional activity in all areas. In fact, it is in the nature of professional problem solving that a number of people with differing interests in a problem will be affected by a solution to it. This fact speaks of the complexity of professional life and of the need for careful analysis in the work professionals perform.

The ideas that Mary Anne woke up with had to do in part with the reality that literally hundreds of people had been affected by ENCONTRO's malfunctioning. She knew that she would have to deal with that technical problem first, which in fact she had already begun to do. In her meeting with Janice Trippling, Mary Anne discovered that Trippling, Sonny Baker, and others who were in charge of monitoring ENCONTRO did not fully understand some of the basic functions of the system. Mary Anne realized that the training she had given them had been inadequate, and that she would have to retrain them to meet their needs. She had already started to shape the contents and tone of those future training sessions, in which she was planning to emphasize the links between theory and implementation, whereas in the first training sessions, when ENCONTRO was first installed, she had taken shortcuts and had stressed implementation only.

She felt pretty good about her ability to solve the *technical* problem, but she was still a little worried about the *rhetorical* problem—the need to write a report about this situation. She realized that she would probably have to write two reports. The first would have to deal with ENCONTRO's malfunctioning and the reasons for it; a second would have to evaluate how the proposed solutions had worked. Both would have to be written to multiple audiences, even though there would perhaps be only one addressee, or specifically identified audience, Tim Sanford, Mary Anne's immediate superior. Mary Anne thought rightly that if she did a good job of analyzing and solving the rhetorical problem for the first report, which would be expected in a day or two, she would be in good shape for writing the second report, since the primary audiences would be the same.

Mary Anne's task, rhetorical problem solving, was one of effective communication through texts, words, and graphics, and also through oral means. The word *rhetoric* in everyday use has come to have negative connotations. People often say that a politician's speech, for example, is "just so much rhetoric," meaning that the speaker has used nice-sounding words that really have no content but contain only empty promises. These speakers seem to give "only rhetoric"—only what some may want to hear, but not necessarily the truth.

Rhetoric, however, has a more general, less negative meaning than its popular connotation suggests. Defined simply, it means "effective communication." These two words—*effective communication*—are loaded with implications that need to be fleshed out later. But the first point to remember about rhetorical problem solving is that it concerns effectively communicating the essentials of technical problem solving. Chapter 2 details the process of technical problem solving; this chapter details the process of rhetorical problem solving, that is, effectively communicating the pertinent matter of technical problems that already have been solved. The written and spoken products of rhetorical problem solving develop after technical problem solving has taken place. Even if the solution to a problem may not yet be clear, professionals generally still will be responsible for some written and oral communication about the technical work in progress.

So, as one concern in technical and professional writing, writers should remember two levels of problem solving:

1. *Technical*—defining, researching, analyzing, resolving and synthesizing, and implementing (if possible) feasible addresses and solutions to a problem.
2. *Rhetorical*—effectively communicating the results of that work. Technical problem solving is only as good as the ability to communicate it effectively. Many professionals get locked into a certain slot in the hierarchy of their organizations because of their inability to communicate effectively the technical problems they have solved.

It is now time to reconsider the phrase *effective communication*, to see what it means when writers try to accomplish it. Communication refers to activities ranging from writing formal technical reports to running a meeting. It encompasses both written and oral forms. The profiles of professionals in Chapter 1 show clearly that professional work requires constant written and oral communication.

The qualifier in the phrase *effective communication* is obviously the word *effective*. Professional and technical data must be transformed from their raw state into something that an audience—any audience—can understand and deal with significantly. Upper management, peer experts, subordinates, or members of the public outside the organization all need to have the results of technical problem solving explained to them clearly and significantly so that they can act upon what they learn in ways appropriate to their positions.

It is important for professionals to realize that good technical problem solving and effective communication of the results are important and intrinsically human activities. They require human responsibility. Computers cannot generate professional and technical writing that solves problems meaningfully, because computers cannot think. It's only through careful thinking and accepting one's responsiblity for good technical problem solving and effective communication that the world's work gets done well.

The elements of effective communication are purpose, audience, context, and ethical stance. Every writing or speaking task depends for its success on careful consideration of these four elements. As professionals tackle a communication task, they begin to think systematically, and that habit of mind helps establish the confidence needed to solve the rhetorical problem. A closer look at the elements shows how rhetorical problem solving works.

To establish the *purpose* of the task, writers or speakers ask themselves several questions. Why am I writing this, or why am I giving this talk? What do I hope to get accomplished? What do I want my readers or listeners to know, or to be able to do, or even to become as a result of my writing or speaking? It is helpful to think of the purpose of communicating in terms of actions that produce results, such as persuading, explaining, directing, teaching and informing.

The *audience* of a communication is the readers or listeners. Writers or speakers ask themselves whom they will be trying to reach with this communication. What are they like? What do they know? What don't they know? What do they want to know? What do they need to know? Basically, why are they reading or listening? Sometimes the answers are obvious and specific: I'm writing to my boss, Tim, whom I've known for 10 years, and who wants to know what went wrong in our service of the Cushing account.

But sometimes the audience is more difficult to define: for example, potential buyers of VCRs in the California bay area. This audience will be mixed, having in common, perhaps, only that they have discretionary money to spend and that they might like to watch films at home. It is hard, but not impossible, to appeal to such an audience; considering audience is one of those constants that has interesting twists.

Context in this discussion has to do with the environmental factors that must be taken into account. We use the word *environmental* broadly to include workplace realities that define place and time. For example, as far as place is concerned, writers and speakers need to remember organizational politics and hierarchical levels, whether they exist in two-tiered family-owned businesses or in multilevel, multinational corporations. It is important to consider the lines of communication and understand one's place in them. Are the lines direct and consecutively ordered? Or are there lateral detours that need to be taken, someone who should be aware of what is going on, though his or her position on the face of it wouldn't seem to demand such consideration? In other words, have writers and speakers considered all parties who, for whatever structural or political reasons, should be cognizant of the workings of the organization?

Addressing time constraints includes consideration of production schedules, past correspondence and agreements, and assignment due dates. It is important to remember to orient readers and listeners to constraints of time, especially so that contractual obligations can be met. But time constraints are also important in precontractual, planning stages so that opportunities for the effective conduct of business won't be missed. Because most readers and listeners have many demands on their attention, exigencies of time need to be clearly and directly laid out.

Ethical stance concerns the writers' or speakers' conscientiously considered ethical position on the subject of the writing or speaking task. In some cases one's ethical stance can be diametrically opposed to the context. Whereas the context considers the phenomenal world involved in the task, the political realities, and the organization's interests, the ethical stance considers the writers' or speakers' personal and professional opinions about the task. They ask questions such as: Is there anything about this subject that gives me a philosophical or an ethical problem? Can I live with myself for taking a position that I know my readers and listeners will agree with but that may not be my own? Am I telling the truth, or do I know what the truth is about this situation?

The important thing to remember is that it is part of professionals' responsibility to consider ethical stance just as carefully as they consider purpose, audience, and context. While professionals usually want to act to serve their employers, they must also remember to serve themselves as well, but only in ways that coincide with the accepted notions of professionalism (as discussed in Chapter 1). By taking their ethical responsibilities seriously, professionals save themselves from becoming mere cogs in a wheel, facing work as meaningless drudgery.

The four elements of rhetorical problem solving can be summarized as follows:

1. *Purpose* considers the communication task and answers the question of why it should be performed.
2. *Audience* considers the readers or listeners and answers the questions of who will be concerned, and why.
3. *Context* considers the environment of the problem and answers questions about where the message is being sent and when it needs to be acted upon.
4. *Ethical stance* considers the positions of individual writers or speakers and answers questions of where they stand on the issue at hand.

As they approach the task of rhetorical problem solving, professionals must continue to ask and answer questions, just as they did in the technical problem-solving process. Figure 3.1 presents the types of questions that must be considered during the rhetorical aspect of problem solving.

A short example of the rhetorical problem-solving process will help introduce the more complex case of Mary Anne Cox. In honor of National Engineering Week, Max Chen is assigned by his employer to give a short talk to twelve fifth-graders at Sunvale Bible School, a small fundamentalist Christian school, on any subject he chooses from his field of expertise, chemical engineering. Having received the directive, Max puts what he knows about the situation through the process of rhetorical problem solving.

1. *Purpose*: Why is Max giving this talk? There are a couple of answers to this question. First, he is to provide a public service for his company, from which both the community and the company will benefit. Second, he is to teach these students something about engineering and what engineers do, because it is National Engineering Week. But the most important purpose is to suggest to these children that engineering can be fun and interesting. He wants them to get a positive impression of chemical engineering.
2. *Audience*: What does Max know about these children? What do they already know about chemical engineering? What do they want and need to know? Why

Figure 3.1
*Questions to ask
and answer in the
rhetorical
problem-solving
process*

QUESTIONS THAT RHETORICAL PROBLEM SOLVING ANSWERS

Purpose: What do I hope to accomplish with this communication?

Primary Purposes

- Am I simply answering questions of fact? (record keeping)
- Do I need to communicate fully why something was done? (formal documentation)
- Am I simply providing information? (informing)
- Am I providing information so that others can act or make a decision? (enabling)

Secondary Purposes

- Am I creating, maintaining, or improving my professional image?
- Am I maintaining or improving interpersonal relations, either internally or externally, or both?
- Am I creating, maintaining, or improving a sense of trust or reliability?

Audience: Whom am I trying to reach with this communication?

First Level of Audience Analysis

- What are my audiences' backgrounds, levels of education, and technical expertise?
- What positions, biases, or attitudes are they likely to have on or toward my subject?
- What purposes do they have for reading or listening to what I am communicating?
- What do I want them to know or become after reading or listening to what I have to say?
- What do I want them to be able to do after reading or listening to my communication?

Second Level of Audience Analysis

- What do they already know about the problem?
- What do they want to know?
- What do they need to know?

Context: What environmental factors must I take into account?

Considerations of Place

- What is the environment of the problem?
- Are there physical, financial, political, or philosophical constraints?
- What are they, and how do they affect what I have to communicate?

Considerations of Time

- What are the constraints of time?
- Are there things I must know or do by a certain time?
- To what extent am I dependent on others to meet deadlines?

Ethical Stance: Have I considered my ethical position

- Does anything about this subject present an ethical problem?
- Am I writing or speaking only to please my audience, but not myself?
- Am I telling the truth as far I know and understand it?

will they be listening to him? Max knows that these students are about ten years old, come from conservative backgrounds, and have some basic notions and information about science, but probably know little or nothing about chemical engineering. Because they are ten and have been taught to respect school and learning, they will probably want to know whatever Max can tell them. What they need to know is slightly different. They will need to know that chemical engineers help provide many of the products that make their lives easier and better—from safer, more durable plastics their toys are made of to safer, more environmentally sound fertilizers and insecticides their parents use on their lawns and gardens.

3. *Context*: What about the environment of the speaking situation does Max need to remember? In this case, *where* is the important question, not *when*, since Max doesn't expect the students to respond specifically to what he says (except perhaps by way of their approval), as he would expect of professional readers or listeners. But *where* is significant, since he's to speak at this small, not particularly prosperous church-run school. Max figures that he will have to supply any visuals, models, or other tangibles for the children, but that he should also describe them at least to the principal and class teacher, accompanied by a brief outline of his talk, so that they will know that the topics of his talk and all supporting materials are appropriate, given the school's educational orientation.

4. *Ethical Stance*: Since Max believes both in religious and educational freedom, he decides he has no ethical problem with talking to this group. But he also decides that any topic he chooses to talk about should be as free of philosophical controversy as possible; he doesn't want to risk contradicting any of the school's premises.

Having put his task through the four basics of rhetorical problem solving, Max returns to his primary purpose: to inspire the children. He wants to breathe some life into what might seem to them a hopelessly technical field. So he resolves to take a "Mr. Wizard" approach. He will let the children work with him to break down several familiar substances into their chemical components. The children will enjoy the hands-on approach, and Max hopes they will get the message that chemicals are an important, but also everyday, part of life and that the work chemical engineers do enhances the quality of life for everyone.

PURPOSE

Mary Anne Cox's situation is a more complex demonstration of rhetorical problem solving. Since she had already solved the technical problem, she needed to move to solving the rhetorical problem—communicating the solution to those people vitally interested. She would have to ask and answer several questions about what she had to write. The first series of questions Mary Anne had to consider centered on her purposes—both primary and secondary—for writing.

Primary Purposes

In the case of primary purposes, Mary Anne could be writing simply to be able to answer questions of fact: what has happened in her work, what is happening now, or what is likely to happen? *Record keeping* is in fact an important part of a professional's work: documentation of work accomplished, or work in progress, or work yet to be done, written in the form of notes or logs is usually necessary to remind oneself and others of the directions a project may take, and how those involved may be affected by factors already known and predicted.

But since the malfunction of ENCONTRO demanded immediate attention, and since Outerware ultimately would have to shoulder the responsibility for what went wrong at the capitol building, Mary Anne knew the sometimes informal activity of keeping records was not enough. She would have to *document formally* what she had done and why she had done it. Although she may never have to show this documentation to anyone, she knew that at least it would be there in case questions arose, and she would also be able to use it to help her form the substance of the reports that would go to specified and directly concerned audiences.

She thought also that she should be writing to impart *information*. Clearly that is a function of any document: if it doesn't provide information, what good is it? But the difference here is whether the document is written for the sole purpose of defining, describing, or explaining—showing what ENCONTRO is, what it can do, and how it might be used—or whether it is written to exact a decision about how the system should work. In this latter case, the writer's purpose moves from simply informing to informing on matters of policy or value, so that readers can take action or make a decision. Mary Anne concluded rightly that her initial report to Tim would require some action from him, if nothing else than for him to say, yes, go ahead and retrain the operations personnel at the capitol building. Although she figured he would probably come to this decision anyway, she decided she would have to write her report in a way that would make the decision inevitable—and one that Tim, not she, had made, based on her advice. Figure 3.2 summarizes graphically Mary Anne's analysis of her purposes for writing to this point.

Having analyzed the technical problem, Mary Anne decided what she had to do to solve it: retrain operations personnel. She was then able to decide that her main purpose in writing about the problem was to bring about decisions in at least two quarters: Tim's liaison position and John Springer's program development position, both within her own firm. Decisions within the capitol building concerning this problem would certainly be influenced by the decisions that Mary Anne's superiors made.

Secondary Purposes

Because a purpose is deemed secondary, it is not necessarily of lesser importance. The distinction is simply that primary purposes are those that come immediately to the foreground in attempts to solve a problem. Secondary purposes lie perhaps

Figure 3.2
*Mary Anne Cox's
primary purposes
for writing*

in the background or are not immediately apparent. In Mary Anne's case, the primary purposes were the needs for formal documentation of the ENCONTRO malfunction and for Tim to make a decision about retraining the capitol building personnel. Her secondary purposes were to show Tim and his superior, John Springer, that she was on top of things, had analyzed the situation well, and was assuming responsibility for the initial inadequate training of capitol building personnel. In other words, she wanted to be perceived as acting in a fully professional way. This would be important later on when she was considered for new assignments, promotion, or a raise in her salary.

One could argue, of course, that secondary purposes for writing will always be the same for any professional. No one wants to be perceived as unprofessional, or as not caring about later promotions and raises. But this would make the notion of secondary purposes too simple. There may be other equally legitimate and compelling secondary purposes for writing. Mary Anne may want to help direct the decision to retrain and, as we said earlier, to make the decision inevitable and one that she would have to implement in her own way. Certainly, these are important purposes for writing, although they fall within the secondary category. Generally speaking, however, we can summarize the purposes for communicating as shown in Figure 3.3.

AUDIENCE

Realizing that a problem is not solved until others know about it and understand and approve it, Mary Anne began to analyze her audiences more fully. Mary Anne thought the question of who her audiences were seemed simple. After all, she

Figure 3.3
Summary of primary and secondary purposes for writing

What are the purposes for writing?

Primary Purposes
- Record Keeping
- Formal Documentation
- Supplying Information
- Changing Opinion (persuading)
- Moving to Action (persuading and enabling decision making)

Secondary Purposes
- Creating, maintaining, or improving image
- Maintaining or improving interpersonal relations, either internally or externally or both
- Creating, maintaining, or improving a sense of trust or reliability

could name her audiences easily enough: Tim Sanford, John Springer, Janice Trippling, and perhaps several other people at the capitol building who were in positions either superior or subordinate to Janice's but who were for some reason vitally interested. But as she began to think of who those audiences actually were—to think beyond names to the people themselves—she remembered that she had been in this situation before: she had had to solve problems that multiple audiences would be concerned with, in sometimes distinctly different or sometimes only subtly different ways. Those concerns she knew would be dependent in part on the audiences' backgrounds, education, experience, and positions in the structural setup. She knew she would have to take them all into account, which made the seemingly simple task something less than simple.

She began, then, the more detailed analysis of who her audiences were and what kind of information she had to give them by asking questions at two levels. The first level had to do with the purposes she had for writing; the second had to do with the specific knowledge that the audiences required about the situation.

First Level of Audience Analysis

To find the answers to who Mary Anne's audience was and what information it required, she had to ask herself questions very similar to those she asked when considering her purpose. Purpose and audience are closely related; one cannot be considered without the other. Some of the questions she asked are shown in Figure 3.1 under the heading "First Level of Audience Analysis."

This first level of audience analysis allowed Mary Anne to gain a general understanding of her readers and their needs. But this alone was not enough. The answers to these questions, while providing Mary Anne with important information on who her audiences were and what their backgrounds and roles in the rhetorical situation were, remained rather theoretical and unspecific. To understand what requirements her audiences had specifically, she had to look to a second level of analysis.

Second Level of Audience Analysis

Mary Anne was able to fill in the specifics lacking on the first level of questions by asking and answering questions on the second level:

- *What do the audiences already know about the problem?* Answers to this question will distinguish what can be assumed from what needs to be explained, laid out, or reiterated, at least at this initial stage.
- *What do the audiences want to know about the problem?* In most cases the information is specifically requested, either through oral or written communications, but in either situation, it is clear that some specific information must be supplied.
- *What do the audiences need to know about the problem?* Answers to this question reveal what information audiences should have to make informed decisions. Sometimes a fine line is drawn between what audiences want to know and what they need to know. But it is an important part of the writer's analysis to ask the question and to determine the difference if one exists. Audiences may have asked for information that would supply an answer to a problem they have to solve, but they may not realize that they need something else, some other kind of information, to solve the problem fully.

Once Mary Anne had asked these preliminary questions, she began to answer them for each of her audiences. And as she answered the questions, she began also to think about the problem of what her report should contain, the tone it should set, and the ethical limitations of the problem. She knew from other writing experiences that *tone*—the attitude of the writer toward her or his subject—is extremely important in producing an effective, successful document. A report, memo, or letter may contain all the technical information necessary to address the problem at hand, but if its tone is wrong, for example, aggressive or condescending, or if the writer has portrayed an attitude that is somehow inappropriate or offensive to the audiences in question, the problem will not have been adequately addressed, and the document will fail to do what it was intended to do. The following audience profiles show how Mary Anne analyzed her audiences individually.

Audience Profile 1	**TIM SANFORD**
	Projects Director, Outerware, Inc.

Tim was Mary Anne's primary audience, that is, the person who asked for the problem to be solved, and who will be the direct addressee of some written response to the request. Tim had a B.S. in electrical and computer engineering, also from the University of Connecticut, and had worked for Outerware for the past 5 years. He had started out in the job Mary Anne now had and had moved into his present position as Projects Director 2 years after he arrived. He was quite proud of his advancement and was ambitious to go further.

Mary Anne had known Tim for 10 years and had worked for him for the last 2. They got along well. Each understood the nature and pressures of the other's job; they respected each other for the way they met their responsibilities.

Mary Anne knew that Tim, as Projects Director, had to maintain informative and congenial relations between Outerware and its clients, and so would require information on the political context of the problem. She also knew that in her position as Systems Engineer, she had to know all the technical details of any system that she had worked on and Outerware had sold and installed. Further, she was expected to have contact with clients about any technical problems that arose, especially through any maintenance contract agreement.

What Did Tim Already Know?

Mary Anne was able to catalog the events and his knowledge of them fairly simply: on March 21, ENCONTRO had malfunctioned, causing extreme temperatures (both cold and hot) in both wings of the capitol building. Tim also knew that Janice Trippling was very upset and had demanded immediate technical aid. And finally, Tim knew that that aid had to come from Mary Anne, that she would have to be in touch with Janice Trippling, and that he was ultimately responsible for maintaining good relations between Outerware and the capitol building.

In determining the information that Tim already knew, Mary Anne could eliminate any mention of this kind of background information in her report. Tim knew all the background and would not want it fed back to him. Mary Anne, then, could get on to answering the next question.

What Did Tim Want to Know?

The answer to that question was straightforward: Tim wanted to know *what went wrong and how she proposed to fix it*. She would have to tell him, then, that Janice Trippling, Sonny Baker, and others who monitored ENCONTRO had misunderstood its operation on a day-to-day basis. He would also want to know what Mary Anne planned to do to correct that problem, and how she would bring the correction about. So she knew that she would have to talk about the need for more training of capitol building personnel, and that the training would have to emphasize more the links between the theory and actual operation of the system, something for which she was clearly responsible, but had not thought necessary to explain when the system was first installed.

Mary Anne turned then to the final question.

What Did Tim Need to Know?

She initially thought that this was one of those times when the distinction between what an audience wants to know and what it needs to know is so fine as to appear virtually nonexistent. Certainly, Tim would need to know what he also wanted to know: what went wrong and how Mary Anne proposed to fix it.

But as she gave the question more thought, she realized that Tim also *needed to know* that Janice Trippling and Sonny Baker did not presently have the theoretical understanding and technical expertise to run ENCONTRO efficiently. Mary

Anne had simply misread their needs at the initial training sessions and had not given them the right kind of training. Although she thought that through retraining, she could improve the situation and bring them to a reasonable, even effective, understanding and use of the system, Tim also needed to know that future dealings with the personnel at the capitol building might be troublesome. Trippling and Baker did not seem particularly amenable to help or advice from the outside, and this combined with their lack of technical knowledge might make for some rough going in the future. Again, she was willing to accept responsibility for at least part of the difficulty: had she read their needs more carefully at the beginning, perhaps the failure would not have happened, and they would not have been embarrassed and resentful.

Because of the delicate nature of this information, Mary Anne decided that it could not be included in the general report on ENCONTRO's malfunctioning. Instead, she would write a separate memo to Tim, who could then decide, perhaps with the help of John Springer, what to do about the problem. She thought that under the time constraints (Tim wanted her report "as soon as possible" after her meeting with Janice Trippling) a separate memo would be the best way to go, though she knew that she could also write two reports, one for in-house review, one for external review. The two of course would reflect the differences necessary in Mary Anne's approaches to her audiences.

Because Tim was Mary Anne's primary reader, her analysis of his needs had to be fairly detailed. She knew after answering these questions that she had essentially answered the questions on the first level: she would have brought Tim up to date on the nature of the problem (what do I want my audiences to know or become?) and would have given him enough information to decide what next had to be done, especially on the political front (what do I want my audiences to be able to do?). By spending time at this preliminary stage—before writing—to analyze her audience carefully, she would save time in the end because much of the content of her report and her approach to establish the appropriate tone would have been decided. Actual writing time then could be significantly reduced. Such detail about the primary audience usually meant that the time needed to analyze her other audiences could also be reduced.

| Audience Profile 2 | ## JOHN SPRINGER |

Vice President, Program Development, Outerware, Inc.

As Vice President of Program Development and as Tim Sanford's immediate superior, John Springer became in this situation Mary Anne's most direct *secondary* audience. Springer had a B.A. from Trinity College in political science and an M.B.A. from the University of Hartford. What he knew about computers he had picked up through special courses and his 7 years of experience at Outerware, the last 2 of which he had spent as Vice President of Program Development.

Since he had been responsible for landing the account at the capitol building, he took special interest in what Mary Anne had found out and was recommending, because:

1. He was responsible for developing new business, and the capitol building, which was still a new account, was thought to be valuable not only in itself, but

also as a means of generating more business elsewhere. It was entirely likely that he would have to make some kind of decision about the problem that Mary Anne or Tim could not make.

2. As Tim's superior, he also, of course, wanted to see how well Tim approached problems, and how well he attempted to solve them.

Springer would receive his own copy of the report. We should point out that not all secondary readers are this directly involved. Depending on the problem and the reader's position within the organization, secondary readers may take a more casual interest in documents written to address or solve a problem. They would read for information only, not expecting to have to take any action or make a decision. They would also probably not get their own copy of a document, but rather be included on a list of interested readers attached to a circulating copy.

Mary Anne knew all of this about John Springer, and therefore took some time to analyze his needs as a direct secondary audience.

What Did John Springer Already Know?

Mary Anne thought rightly that it would be about the same as what Tim knew. He may not know some of the details of ENCONTRO's malfunctioning that Tim knew, but she was sure that he would have the essential outline. She needn't add anything to what she would already provide Tim.

What Did John Springer Want to Know?

The answer to this question was also similar to what Tim wanted to know: what had gone wrong, why, and whether there was something that could be done to solve it to keep the client's good faith—and business. The answer to the last question was for Springer the most important, maybe even more important than for Tim, so that Mary Anne knew she would have to be very clear about what the retraining program would entail, what kind of time it would take out of the capitol building personnel's daily schedules, and, in general, what efforts Outerware was willing and able to make to bring matters back into line. Since that was the kind of detail Tim would expect anyway, Mary Anne did not worry that she would be too explicit. She also knew from her experience that it was better to include more detail than less: good readers realize at once a writer's attempt to provide what is wanted. They can always skip the particular details if they don't need them, but if the document is written without sufficient detail, the writer will just have to go back and rewrite what was already written.

Mary Anne went then to the last question.

What Did John Springer Need to Know?

This again presented some problems for her. Springer needed to know basically what Tim needed to know—that the capitol building personnel lacked certain technical knowledge and expertise that Mary Anne had not discerned, and that she therefore had not provided adequate training. Finally, he needed to know that maybe because of this, the capitol employees were reluctant to take help and advice from outsiders. But since Springer had struck the contract with superiors of Janice Trippling, it was through them that he would have to deal, if he were to deal at all. He would have to let those people know that ENCONTRO would work well, and that Trippling, Baker, and the others who would monitor the system would more willingly accept the system and would feel more comfortable using it, if they were to get some additional training—training provided by Mary Anne Cox.

As in Tim's case, Mary Anne decided that the nature of the information Springer needed to know was delicate enough to warrant its own internal memo; even allusions to the problems with Trippling and Baker in her general report might backfire. So she decided the most efficient way of dealing with the problem was to write the separate memo to Tim and show Springer as the direct recipient of his own copy. That way Mary Anne could keep the analysis of the problem at her level within Outerware, and Tim and Springer could decide how to approach Trippling's and Baker's superiors at the capitol building.

Again Mary Anne was doing for Springer very much the same as she was doing for Tim: providing him with policy-related information that would enable him to make a decision.

Audience Profile 3	JANICE TRIPPLING
	Chief Operations Engineer, Capitol Building, Hartford

Normally Trippling would have been considered a *tertiary* audience, two steps removed from Tim in the direct concerns of the report. Tertiary audiences almost always read only to gain information, seldom to make decisions, and therefore require a less thorough analysis on the writer's part. The decisions a writer makes about content and tone are almost always directed by the analysis of the primary and secondary readers, seldom of the tertiary readers. Mary Anne knew this, but she also knew that Trippling had specifically asked her for a copy of her report, something she certainly could not refuse to provide. And thus Trippling was brought into the position of a *secondary* audience, requiring at least as thorough an analysis as she had given Springer.

So Mary Anne reviewed what she knew about Trippling. She had a B.S. in mechanical engineering technology from the University of Massachusetts and had minored in computer science. She had worked for the capitol building as a systems engineer for 10 years, and only within the last 6 months had been promoted to Chief Operations Engineer, jumping ahead of several men who had been with the state for a combined 35 years. Trippling was ambitious, but also nervous in her new position, thus making her wary about anything that Mary Anne might do that could possibly throw her work into a bad light.

Once again Mary Anne asked and answered the pertinent questions.

What Did Janice Trippling Already Know?

Trippling already knew basically the same things that the other audiences knew. ENCONTRO had malfunctioned while she was in charge; the capitol building had gotten either too hot or too cold, depending on the locations of offices, and Outerware was going to have to do something to solve the problem. She also knew that the decision to install ENCONTRO had been made at levels above hers, and it was probably unlikely the decision would be reversed. This, Mary Anne noted, might have a dual effect on Janice's reading of the report: she might look for reason to take offense, since she had had nothing to do with making the decision, and she would be looking for any suggestion that she was perhaps to blame for the malfunction. Though Mary Anne had already decided, through her analysis of Tim and Springer as audiences, that the content and tone of the report would have to show that Outerware, particularly Mary Anne herself, was responsible for inadequate training of the capitol building personnel, this part of her analysis of Trippling as an audience confirmed that need.

What Did Janice Trippling Want to Know?

When she considered this question, Mary Anne again came up with similar answers to those she had already formed, though again colored a bit differently, given that this audience was a client and not in-house personnel. She obviously wanted to know what went wrong and what it would take to fix it, but she would also want to know what part she had had in the malfunctioning, assuming correctly that she, as the direct superior of the monitors of the system, would have had to have at least some part in it. Mary Anne would have to mention the inadequate training, but mainly as a problem she was responsible for. And, so as not to alienate Trippling, she would have to be very careful not to mention that the personnel seemed to lack the necessary theoretical background and technical expertise to run the system without more training—or perhaps training of a more fundamental kind. That problem should be discussed between Tim and her, and maybe John Springer, at a different time and in a different context.

What Did Janice Trippling Need to Know?

She needed to know just what everyone else needed to know—that Outerware had a workable solution to ENCONTRO's malfunction in the form of additional training, and that she and others who would monitor the system could come to use it comfortably and efficiently.

Whereas in Tim's and Springer's cases, Mary Anne knew that she was having to provide them with enough information about the problem to enable them to make decisions, this was not true for Janice Trippling. Trippling would not have to make a decision based on what Mary Anne had provided, but she would have to continue to use ENCONTRO, and Mary Anne knew that it was much better to have her become a willing user than an unwilling one. Unwillingness could only mean trouble for Outerware, and particularly for Tim and her, in the future. The tone and content of her report would indeed have to be carefully crafted to make all audiences into something Mary Anne wanted them to be: willing and efficient decision makers and users of the system.

CONTEXT

Having fully analyzed her audiences, Mary Anne next turned to the questions concerning the context of her problem. As for considerations of time and place, Mary Anne considered specifically a few issues. The significance of place was already somewhat analyzed in her consideration of John Springer as a secondary audience. The capitol building was a client, and a government client at that, so Mary Anne knew she couldn't assume much flexibility from this group when she scheduled her retraining sessions. Second, the capitol building was a very big account, so any of its problems took top priority. Also, because it was such a big account, the upper-level Outerware personnel needed to be involved in the solution. Mary Anne had taken care of this through her analysis of audiences.

The time consideration was a bit tricky. She first needed to make absolutely clear to Tim the date by which she needed replies so that she could implement her solution. Then she needed to suggest retraining times that would work well both for Outerware and for the capitol building employees. Assuming that Janice Trippling was cooperative, Mary Anne could start almost immediately. If Janice was not cooperative, however, because she saw the ENCONTRO malfunction as Outerware's problem and didn't want to put herself out to be capable with the system, then Mary Anne would have to negotiate.

ETHICAL STANCE

Thinking about the ethics of the situation, Mary Anne asked herself whether she was being as straightforward as possible with all concerned. Was she telling the truth she had come to after the technical problem solving? Yes. She had as evenhandedly as possible traced cause and effect, responsibility, and solution, so that the capitol employees' parts were clear, but not overstated. She accepted her own responsibility for underestimating the needs of the initial training program. She shaped a solution in the spirit of Outerware's maintenance agreement. Mary Anne had even extended herself to consider Janice Trippling's anxieties in her new position, and while she thought Janice's hostility was misplaced, she felt no need to retaliate.

Mary Anne's documents would acknowledge her own part, because it was part of her ethical code to do so, and because the last impression she wanted Tim and John to have of her was of someone who ducked her responsibilities. In short, the ENCONTRO problem did not present difficult ethical dimensions to Mary Anne. She was sympathetic to company policy on such problems. But she might have had trouble if Outerware insisted on shouldering either all the blame or none.

RHETORICAL PROBLEM SOLVING AS A RECURSIVE PROCESS

The discussion to this point has outlined an ideal process, one that works well, but one that needs to be qualified. The process implies linearity, that the steps need to be taken sequentially. But that is not in fact the way most of us think. Most of us, instead of thinking in a line, jump forward to ideas that ideally would occur to us only after we had considered others. Or, while we are presently formulating an idea, we may fall back to some idea we have already had and consider how that might influence what we are currently thinking about. The process then is recursive—jumping forward, falling back—fairly fluid until it is complete. And when it is complete, it presents another question: is it complete when writers and speakers are satisfied they have analyzed the problem as fully as they can or when they are required to have some answer—when they have to meet a deadline? It can be either or both, but there is always an end to the process—it cannot go on forever—and that end is almost always determined by the deadline. There is a point at which the product of work will be called for; it is then that it must be complete, for better or for worse, and submitted.

Mary Anne's situation once again is a good example. She asked and answered all the questions that we have spoken about, but she did not do so linearly. In fact, she did not have to. As she realized, several of the questions dealing with the audience's knowledge of the problem could probably be answered in basically the same way for each audience, with variations of course, but with variations that she could keep easily in mind.

She thought, for example, of what Tim, her primary audience, already knew about the problem and realized that her other audiences, John Springer and Janice Trippling, already knew the same. She also saw that what they wanted to know—what went wrong and how it could be fixed—was the same, though given their different positions, they would probably use that information differently. Tim could show Springer that he could reassure his contacts at the capitol building that matters were in hand, and Trippling could show that the fundamental problem had been generated by Outerware, not by her and her personnel, and that it was being corrected, with her cooperation of course.

What happened in this case shows that thinking about audiences does not have to take place linearly. The knowledge, wants, and needs of Tim Sanford, John Springer, and Janice Trippling clearly overlap, and Mary Anne thought of them in that way. She realized that she did not think of any one part of the problem in sequence: sometimes she would think of needs, sometimes of wants, sometimes of what her audiences already knew. Mary Anne also knew that she had to consider her audiences as part of the package, along with purpose, context, and ethical stance. At times it seemed she was dealing with all levels of the analysis at once. Janice knew she would have to sort them out soon, because Tim had called for her report "as soon as possible," which she understood to mean "within the next day or two" after her meeting with Janice Trippling. It was then that she sat down in front of her computer to write the actual documents.

Before we look at what Mary Anne wrote, there is another important idea to mention here. The audiences for whom people write in practically every professional environment are chosen for them; the writers or speakers themselves do not choose them. Mary Anne did not have to conjure up the audiences to solve the problem of ENCONTRO's malfunction: they were there, concrete, not abstract, and clearly defining themselves, demanding information and expecting help. Tim Sanford, John Springer, and Janice Trippling were all directly involved in the problem for different reasons, and with slightly different expectations for a solution, but they were not strangers to each other or to Mary Anne, which in the end makes the whole process of audience analysis basically easier than it seems. The information is there: a problem and people involved in the problem, and each has to be analyzed to produce a reasonable solution.

We should now look at the fruits of Mary Anne's analysis and analyze ourselves what she wrote. Figure 3.4 shows a memo report on Mary Anne's meeting with Janice Trippling at the capitol building, and Figure 3.5 shows Mary Anne's memo to Tim on the potential problems she sees with capitol building personnel.

Figure 3.4
Mary Anne Cox's
memo report

OUTERWARE, INC.

17 D STREET, HARTFORD, CONNECTICUT 06902   TEL: (609) 398-4701   FAX: 609-398-4700

Memorandum

To: Tim Sanford, Projects Director
From: Mary Anne Cox, Systems Engineer
Date: March 23, 1992
Subject: Meeting with Janice Trippling, March 21, Capitol Building

*The opening paragraph
reestablishes the context
of the problem, gives
the specifics of what Cox
did to meet with the cap-
itol building personnel,
and summarizes the
general outcome of the
meeting. Note the con-
ciliatory tone in the last
sentence. Note, too, its
conclusiveness.*

*The second paragraph
lays out for Sanford
exactly what went
wrong. Although it tells
of the monitors' part in
the malfunction, it does
not lay blame on them;
it suggests that the
mistakes they made are
understandable.*

*Cox, in the third
paragraph, assumes
the responsibility for
faulty training and
suggests that additional
training will probably
solve the problem. She
is specific as to what
the training would
cover and when it might
begin. She acknowledges
that Sanford is the one
to make the final deci-
sion. She closes in the
fourth paragraph with
a dignified apology and
an appeal for action.*

*She sends copies to her
secondary readers:
Springer, who is San-
ford's superior and has
special interest in the
problem, and Trippling,
who asked for a copy
of her report.*

Following our morning conversation on March 21, I met with Janice
Trippling in her office at the capitol building from 2:00 to 3:30 P.M. to
discuss ENCONTRO's malfunction of March 20. Sonny Baker and Jim Pierson,
of Ms. Trippling's staff and monitors of the system when it went down, were
also there. The meeting proved very helpful in establishing what actually
went wrong and in suggesting what we can do to prevent similar
malfunctions in the future.

From what we can determine, the malfunction was directly caused by a
communications lockup at one of the modules; this caused temperatures to
shift in both wings. Also, the monitors misread the data at the command
location, figuring that since one of the two chillers was shown as
operating, temperatures in both wings were being maintained at acceptable
levels. As you know, this is an area where mistakes can easily be made:
instead of looking for patterns in the data, monitors sometimes tend to
concentrate on individual characters, which in turn causes them to misread
the overall configuration.

We all agreed also that better training of the personnel when ENCONTRO was
first installed could have prevented this from happening. Had I spent more
time on the basics of the system, Ms. Trippling and her staff would have
been better prepared to monitor it effectively. So the best solution I can
suggest, and one that the people at the capitol building agree with, is for
me to offer some basic retraining. I think we can cover the necessary
material, such as a review of the system's diagnostic tools, and some dry
runs of troubleshooting techniques in two or three sessions of a couple
hours apiece. I propose to start the sessions as soon as I get your
approval, but my schedule and those of the people at the capitol building
could permit us to begin as soon as next Tuesday, March 27.

I'm sorry for the inconvenience of the event, but I hope you'll agree that
we are on a reasonable course for preventing similar troubles in the
future. I look forward to hearing from you.

cc: John Springer
    Janice Trippling, Capitol Building

Figure 3.5
Mary Anne Cox's memo

In the first paragraph Cox recognizes Sanford's need to know about the political context of the problem at the capitol building. She is candid and straightforward about the atmosphere of the meeting and about the attitudes of the people she met with, but she also concedes that they dealt with the malfunction better than might be expected.

Cox, in the second paragraph, addresses the first of two problems that she could not have mentioned in her first memo: the client's lack of technical expertise. She again acknowledges her responsibility for not recognizing this, and suggests specifically the kind of retraining that will help correct the problem.

The third paragraph deals straightforwardly with the attitude problem, but again Cox concedes that the capitol building personnel are in a difficult position, and that she contributed to that by misreading their needs for training. Again she suggests how she will correct that.

The last paragraph mentions the final element of the second problem—possible resistance to her training instruction—and suggests further political action.

She again sends a copy to Springer, who also may have to take part in the corrective action.

OUTERWARE, INC.

17 D STREET, HARTFORD, CONNECTICUT 06902   TEL: (609) 398-4701   FAX: 609-398-4700

Memorandum

To: Tim Sanford, Projects Director
From: Mary Anne Cox, Systems Engineer
Date: March 23, 1990
Subject: Future Dealings with Janice Trippling's Office, Capitol Building
Re: Memo of March 23 on Meeting with Janice Trippling

I have referred to my memo report on my meeting with Janice Trippling on March 21 to help provide the context of a problem beyond ENCONTRO's malfunction of March 20. I said there that the meeting was very helpful in determining what had gone wrong and how we might fix it, and that's true; the meeting was helpful. But it was not particularly congenial, and what I learned from it, beyond the technical aspects of the malfunction, is that Trippling and her staff are embarrassed and, therefore, angry that the system went down, thus making hundreds of people uncomfortable. That they got it back up and running, so that the last test run was not a complete failure, shows that they have a good deal of energy and some basic technical expertise to correct that kind of malfunction.

I am worried, however, about two things. The first is less important, but nevertheless worthy of my mention: the staff's technical knowledge of this kind of system is not what it might be. They don't understand the kinds of problems that can occur, and seem not to have been educated in some of the necessary theoretical bases of how a system like this operates, something I realize I should have known when I started training sessions in early February. This, I feel confident, I can correct with the right kind of retraining. It seems reasonable that I should concentrate on having them see patterns in the data that come across their screens and on diagnostic and troubleshooting techniques.

The other problem has to do with attitude. Trippling and her staff are put out by having to implement a system they were never really consulted about. Their questions to me were aggressive—what went wrong? why did it go wrong? how do we deal with it? what are we supposed to do about it now? I felt defensive, because I had helped implement the system and, as it turns out, had not trained them sufficiently. That certainly was a mistake, but I think that my plan of two or three retraining sessions of about two hours each will help correct it.

I wanted you to know, however, that the personnel at the capitol building system may be reluctant and resistant to taking to my instruction and suggestions. I don't think we have a permanent problem, but rather one that will crop up again without some correcting on all of our parts. I intend to extend Janice Trippling every courtesy, but thought I might take her and her staff to lunch as well to improve the atmosphere. Can we budget for this? If there is anything else I can do, let me know. I look forward to hearing from you.

cc: John Springer

WRITING FOR SOMEONE ELSE'S SIGNATURE

We have been speaking all along of Mary Anne Cox as a professional who solves problems with the help of writing. That is, she has been confronted with a problem and has either been assigned to report on a proposed solution in writing, or has herself seen the need to report; in the latter case, her writing comes from self-direction. In either case, however, writing comes about from direct or central involvement in the problem-solving process; the problems, in other words, pertain directly and naturally to her own work. But what we have not pointed out yet is that this kind of writing constitutes only a part of the writing that professionals do. There is another substantial amount of time spent on writing for others, or *ghost writing*, that is, writing documents that will show others as the authors.

It is true that ghostwriting is also assigned, but the difference is that it addresses other people's (always superiors') problems—technically not those that the actual author is involved in. In Mary Anne's case, for example, Tim is vitally interested in knowing how she assesses the problem at the capitol building and realizes the need to correspond with his contacts there, people in management positions superior to Janice Trippling's. But for a couple of possible reasons, lack of time and/or lack of knowledge or confidence in technical matters, he is unable to write the memo or letter to Anthony Capello, Director of Operations at the capitol building in Hartford, to explain what went wrong with ENCONTRO and what will be done to correct it. He, therefore, assigns the task to Mary Anne, saying, of course, that he will review and perhaps edit her work before he signs and sends it. That places Mary Anne in the position of having to analyze the problem, not only from her perspective and role, but also from Tim's—an uncomfortable and difficult situation sometimes, but one that cannot be avoided: it is a simple fact of professional life. Although writing for someone else involves all the same steps of analysis that we have been speaking about here, it also requires additional understanding of the relationship between the sender and the recipient of the document in light of the problem the document addresses. This means that Mary Anne has to draw on her knowledge of the nature of Tim's position and the demands it puts upon him, as well as her understanding of the relationship Tim has with Capello, something she may know about through observation, but may also need to strengthen and confirm through conversations with Tim.

The professional profiles in Chapter 1 show that ghostwriting is a common necessity for professionals in middle management, even though they, too, have occasion to assign writing tasks to those who work for them. This is evident by the number of documents they have to review and/or edit—a number of which they themselves have assigned to others to write. But again, as we indicated there, when professionals move up the ranks, the amount of writing they have to do in general decreases, but the amount of ghostwriting they have to do in particular decreases to almost nothing. Instead of being assigned to write someone else's document, they assign others to write for them. It is simply the way of any hierarchically structured organization.

CONCLUSIONS

What Mary Anne went through in preparing her documents—a report and a memo—is what should happen whenever a professional faces a rhetorical problem. It is important to remember that most rhetorical problems grow out of technical problems, and that the whole problem-solving process takes a combination of technical knowledge and expertise (the ability to solve the technical problem) and knowledge and expertise in communication (the ability to solve the rhetorical problem). Professionals can solve problems not only with the help of what they know about their various fields—computers, engineering, social work, geology, or some other field—but also with the help of what they know about writing and speaking.

The discussion of Mary Anne Cox's situation demonstrates that rhetorical problem solving is a specifically human activity requiring effective communication. To do this, writers and speakers must think systematically, though not necessarily linearly, touching the four essential bases of purpose, audience, context, and ethical stance. As we pointed out in Chapter 1, problems that professionals face cannot really be called problems unless there are people who feel the need of and will benefit from a solution. Thus, the malfunction of ENCONTRO at the capitol building in Hartford is not just some abstract, theoretical breakdown to be corrected by simple tinkerings and adjustments in the technology. Because people were made uncomfortable and were inconvenienced, the problem takes on the necessary human dimension. And because people—both at Outerware and at the capitol building—were directly responsible for the technological mishap, the problem demonstrates a greater level of human involvement.

What we see, then, is technology that works only if people make it work. And thus we have Mary Anne's analysis of the human element in the breakdown: her own misreading of the needs for training capitol building personnel; Janice Trippling's embarrassment and resulting resentment of the system and of those who put it in place; and Tim Sanford's and John Springer's needs to reestablish easy, congenial, and productive relations with their client.

We see, further, the kinds of documents that must be written to reflect the nature of the problem and what should be done about it, without putting off any of the audiences who will read them. Reports to Tim Sanford, with copies to John Springer and Janice Trippling in the first instance, and a memo, with a copy to Springer, in the second instance, both dealt with the same problem, but with different purposes and potential results in mind. We should also remember the memo that Tim has in mind for Mary Anne to write to Anthony Capello, but that will go out under Tim's signature.

In the end, the whole enterprise becomes basically human. People feel the effects of a technological breakdown; people are responsible for the technological breakdown; and people must clean up after themselves and correct the technological breakdown through human interaction. Careful and thoughtful writing and speaking, which are the results of careful and thoughtful analysis, are the means by which this can be done. They are, as far as we know, the best answer to solving problems in professional life.

EXERCISES

1. Following are four excerpts of technical and professional writing, taken from various fields. In small groups, read and consider at least two of the excerpts, and answer the following questions:

   a. What purpose does the writer have for writing? You may see both primary and secondary purposes.
   b. Who is the audience for the piece? Do you see more than one? What are their levels of education and technical expertise likely to be? What positions, attitudes, biases are they likely to have on the subject in question? How does the writer appeal to them (through emotion, authority, ethics)?
   c. What purpose does the reader have for reading?
   d. Do you pick up any clues about context—considerations of place and time?
   e. Does the excerpt suggest any ethical dilemma for the writer?

I. FROM A REVIEW OF THE YEAR'S ACTIVITIES OF A REGIONAL PLANNED PARENTHOOD AGENCY

A Message from the President and Executive Director

What a year we have had! Momentous and courageous decisions were made towards accomplishing the mission of Planned Parenthood. Resounding support was received from the community for Planned Parenthood's work.

- Acting on the news of the impending retirement of a local abortion provider, and on the final report of a study commissioned by our board, the Board of Directors (after 3 board meetings in the month of August) unanimously voted to begin offering first trimester abortion services in the summer of 1990.
- In the face of ultimatums by the local Catholic Diocese, the United Way Board of Directors voted to retain Planned Parenthood as a member. The 1989 United Way campaign met its adjusted goal for funding all the remaining agencies at the prior year's level.
- During 1989, direct contributions to Planned Parenthood increased by 30% and our donor base increased by 24%. United Way contributors specifically designating Planned Parenthood increased tenfold, to over $115,000.

- Notwithstanding the withdrawal of support by key sponsors, the Smith Commission brought Dr. James Ploski to Pleasantville to speak to over 1500 appreciative teens, parents, and professionals. A private reception was held for Dr. Ploski which included Planned Parenthood staff, President Circle donors, and board members.

We . . . you . . . are part of an organization considered to be one of the most credible non-profit agencies in America. We are doing more than just talking about the need for family planning; quality, objective sexuality education; preventing unwanted pregnancies; and treatment and education for sexually transmitted diseases. Planned Parenthood is providing those needed medical services, that needed education, that needed advocacy of people's right to make their own choices. The more polls and studies we see, the more we come to realize that we do, in fact, speak for the majority of the people in this country.

. . .

We need to continue to provide medical services, to educate and to advocate. We will need your help, your contributions of time, talent, and treasure. This coming year will require at least as much work as last year for us to accomplish our mission: making every child a wanted child.

II. FROM A RESEARCH MEMO WRITTEN BY A PARALEGAL WORKING FOR A LARGE EASTERN PUBLIC POWER SUPPLIER ON THE SUBJECT OF UNAUTHORIZED USE OF COMPUTER PROGRAMS

DATE: June 20, 1990

TO: James P. St. Pierre, Chief Counsel

FROM: Alison L. McKee, Paralegal I

SUBJECT: Copyright and Literary Property

REFERENCE: Unauthorized Use of Computer Programs

Query:

Assume that the Supply System is held liable for the unauthorized use of unlicensed software in Supply System P.C.s—explain the nature and extent of liability for punitive or exemplary damages or other damage measures beyond just payment of royalties.

Short Response:

According to 17 USCS #504, an infringer of copyright is liable for either (1) the copyright owner's actual damages and any additional profits of the infringer, or (2) statutory damages. "Punitive damages" per se are not available under the federal Copyright Act.

Discussion:

I. Background

The Supply System wants to develop agency standards for use of licensed software. The prime area of inquiry is what stance the agency should adopt when faced with situations where multiple copies are made of purchased software

II. Copyright Protection

The Copyright Act of 1976 (17 USCS #101 et. seq.) protects the exclusive right or privilege of authors or proprietors of literary property to print or otherwise multiply, publish, and vend copies of literary, artistic or intellectual productions, when secured by compliance with the copyright statute, 17 USCS #101. The definitional provisions of the Copyright Act of 1976 encompass computer programs and data bases in the definition of "literary works."

The Act was amended by the adoption in 1980 of the Computer Software Copyright Act. This amendment replaced former section 117, added a specific definition of "computer program" and provided for the lawful copying of a program in two instances: (1) by its rightful owner for use "in conjunction with a machine"; or (2) for "archival purposes."

The discussion proceeds for three single-spaced pages defining and talking about a variety of topics: the components of computer programs that are protected, successful court precedents, civil liability, and criminal liability. The author then concludes with the following:

V. Conclusion

The magnitude of the problem of trying to provide legal protection for computer programs is staggering; it has been estimated that some 15,000 computer programs are written each day in the United States and that the total value of this software is in the tens of billions of dollars. (See "Schmidt, Legal Proprietary Interest in Computer Programs: The American Experience" 21 Jurimetrics 345 (1981) as cited in Jostens, Inc. v. National Computers Systems, Inc., 318 NW2d 691, 214 U.S.P.Q. 918, 33 UCCRS

1642, 30 ALR4th 1229.) The Copyright Act provides the owner of a copyright with a variety of remedies, including injunction, the impoundment and destruction of all reproductions, recovery of actual damages and any additional profits realized by the infringer, or a recovery of statutory damages, and attorneys fees. But despite the fact that the Supreme Court speaks of a copyright owner's ''potent arsenal of remedies against an infringer,'' (see Sony Corp. of America v. Universal City Studios, Inc., 104 S Ct 774, 464 U.S. 417, 78 L.Ed.2d 574, 220 U.S.P.Q. 665 (1984)) a software firm which discovers that an individual has surreptitiously copied its computer program may have little to gain from filing a suit for copyright infringement since the recovery probably would not be enough to cover legal costs. This situation has been likened to piracy of phonorecords by individuals onto cassette tapes which has become so commonplace that the recording industry does not, as a practical matter, prosecute individuals. However, possible benefits from suing an individual for copyright infringement of a computer program would be publicity that might discourage potential customers from pirating programs instead of buying authorized copies.

Let me know if you need further research into this issue.

III. FROM A REPORT ON THE INSTALLATION OF TRANSMISSION LINES IN A WESTERN PUBLIC UTILITY DISTRICT

APPENDIX B
TRANSMISSION LINE SURVEY REQUIREMENTS
FOR
PUBLIC UTILITY DISTRICT NO. 2 OF GRANT COUNTY

I. General

    A. All work shall be completed under the direction of a professional land surveyor licensed by the state of Washington.

    B. All horizontal control surveys shall be a minimum of third order, Class II accuracy. Vertical control surveys shall be a minimum of third order accuracy. Third order and third or Class II shall be as defined in CLASSIFICATION, STANDARDS OF ACCURACY AND GENERAL SPECIFICATIONS OF GEODETIC CONTROL SURVEYS as reprinted in 1979 by N.O.A.A.

    C. All horizontal points shall be referenced to the Washington State Plane Coordinate System or as otherwise agreed to between the District and Contractor. When Washington State Plan Coordinates are used, provide Washington State grid factors on each drawing.

    D. All field and office work required for the project surveys shall be based on a closed traverse of triangulation network.

II. Survey Requirements

A. The survey shall locate all road, highway, railroad, pipeline, transmission line, canal and other utility right-of-ways which may affect the transmission line centerline. All right-of-ways shall be referenced to section corners and State Plane Coordinate System.

B. The work shall include locating all property lines, section corners, and quarter section corners. Property lines shall be tied down to section corners and quarter section corners. Section and quarter sections shall be located in the field and referenced to the State Plane Coordinate System.

C. The survey shall extend into private property to include the transmission line right-of-way as specified by the District engineer.

D. The survey shall locate all proposed transmission line P.I.'s in relation to the section corners and State Plane Coordinate System. P.I.'s shall be staked with nominal 2" × 2" × 8" hubs and tacks and flagged with lath and surveyors flagging.

E. Point-on-Tangents (P.O.T.) shall be staked on the transmission centerline with nominal 2" × 2" × 8" hubs and tacks placed at intervals not exceeding 2000 feet and flagged with lath and surveyors flagging. Surveyors hubs and tacks used in the control survey and on line of proposed centerline shall be left intact. If removal of the control survey hubs is desired or recommended, coordinate with Jim Smithson or the District engineer assigned to the project.

F. The survey shall locate other survey monuments in the area of the transmission right-of-way such as USGS triangulation stations and benchmarks. These monuments shall be referenced to the State Plane Coordinate System.

G. When specifically requested on the request for professional services for the specific project, the survey shall include a detailed plan and profile of the transmission line right-of-way. The plan and profile shall include the information listed below in addition to that information requested in paragraphs A to E above and in Section IV below.

IV. FROM LEWIS THOMAS'S ARTICLE "GERMS" IN *LIVES OF A CELL* (NEW YORK: VIKING PENGUIN, INC., AND LONDON: GARNSTONE PRESS, 1974)

It is the information carried by the bacteria that we cannot abide.

The gram-negative bacteria are the best examples of this. They display lipopolysaccharide endotoxin in their walls and these macromolecules are read by our tissues as the very worst of bad news. When we sense lipopolysaccharide, we are likely to turn on every defense at our disposal; we will bomb, defoliate, blockade, seal off, and destroy all the tissues in the area. Leukocytes become more actively phagocytic, release lysosomal enzymes, turn sticky, and aggregate together in dense masses, occluding capillaries and shutting off the blood supply. Complement is switched on at the right point in its sequence to release chemotactic signals, calling in leukocytes from everywhere. Vessels become hyperactive to epinephrine so that physiologic concentrations suddenly possess necrotizing properties. Pyrogen is released from leukocytes, adding fever to hemorrhage, necrosis, and shock. It is a shambles.

All of this seems unnecessary, panic-driven. There is nothing intrinsically poisonous about endotoxin, but it must look awful, or feel awful when sensed by cells. Cells believe that it signifies the presence of gram-negative bacteria, and they will stop at nothing to avoid this threat.

I used to think that only the most highly developed, civilized animals could be fooled in this way, but it is not so. The horse-shoe crab is a primitive fossil of a beast, ancient and uncitified, but he is just as vulnerable to disorganization by endotoxin as a rabbit or a man. Bang has shown that an injection of a very small dose into the body cavity will cause the aggregation of hemocytes in ponderous, immovable masses that block the vascular channels, and gelatinous clot brings the circulation to a standstill. It is now known that a limulus clotting system, perhaps ancestral to ours, is centrally involved in the reaction. Extracts of the hemocytes can be made to jell by adding extremely small amounts of endotoxin. The self-disintegration of the whole animal that follows a systemic injection can be interpreted as a well-intentioned but lethal error. The mechanism is itself quite a good one, when used with precision and restraint, admirably designed for coping with intrusion by a single bacterium: the hemocyte would be attracted to the site, extrude the coagulable protein, the micro-organism would be entrapped and immobilized, and the thing would be finished. It is when confronted by the overwhelming signal of free molecules of endotoxin, evoking memories of vibrios in great numbers, that the limulus flies into panic, launches all his defenses at once, and destroys himself.

It is, basically, a response to propaganda, something like the panic-producing pheromones that slave-taking ants release to disorganize the colonies of their prey.

I think it likely that many of our diseases work in this way. Sometimes, the mechanisms used for overkill are immunologic, but often, as in the limulus models, they are more primitive kinds of memory. We tear ourselves to pieces because of symbols, and we are more vulnerable to this than to any host of predators. We are, in effect, at the mercy of our own Pentagons, most of the time.

2. Using the questions asked above, analyze two of the documents obtained from your interviews of professionals in Chapter 1.

ASSIGNMENTS

1. Choose a fairly sophisticated technical article from a professional journal in your field of study or in a field that interests you. Using the substance of the article, write an article of your own for one of the audiences listed below. To be sure that your article will be appropriate for the new audience, fill out the Document Analysis Worksheet (see Figure 3.6) *before* you start writing.

   a. You have been asked by a high school counselor to write an article on a subject related to your field of study. The purpose of the article is to acquaint high school seniors with the subject so that they might begin to think about possible majors in college.

   b. *Science Digest, Time,* or *Newsweek* (choose one) has asked for an article from you on a subject of interest and importance to the general readership.

   c. Your boss (middle management) has asked you for an article on a subject that is important to a current or future company project. Your boss has little technical background in the subject, but needs to appear knowledgeable at the next meeting of the board of directors.

2. Case Study

The Situation

You are a member of the Personnel Relations Committee of Omni International, a highly diversified firm with interests in many areas. The committee is charged with reviewing personnel problems within the firm and making recommendations to James Peterson, Vice President of Operations. The chair of the committee, Joseph Doakes, has presented you with this problem: his boss, Peter Mason, a regional sales director for the Consumer Products Division, has been showing signs of wear. His last two quarterly reports were late, sales in his region were down 5 percent for the last quarter, he missed two important meetings with sales representatives in the last 2 months, he has been absent 7 days in the last month, and he sometimes doesn't make it back to his office from lunch.

Mason is sixty-two, has worked for Omni for 25 years, is eligible to retire, but doesn't want to until he's sixty-five. Doakes points out that Mason has done an excellent job until recently, and has been very good to those who work for him, especially to Doakes himself, whom Mason has been grooming to take over his job when he retires.

The Task

A. Doakes wants the committee to recommend a course of action to Peterson, but because of the sensitive nature of his relationship to Mason, wants to withdraw from the deliberations. He claims that he will go along with anything you recommend to Peterson, who is a no-nonsense person and who is well respected for his efficiency and fairness.

B. In this case, you have two audiences to analyze and write for. Your primary audience will be Peterson, because he wants your recommendations and will, in

Figure 3.6
Document analysis worksheet

DOCUMENT ANALYSIS WORKSHEET
(Adapted from work done by John Harris and Donald Cunningham)

Name of the document or situation
that requires that it be written: _____

Primary Purposes for Writing

1. Record Keeping/ Formal Documentation?

2. Supplying Information?

3. Changing Opinion (Persuading)?

4. Moving to Action (Persuading to enable decision making)

Secondary Purposes for Writing

1. Creating, maintaining, or improving professional image?

2. Maintaining or improving interpersonal relations, either internally or externally, or both?

3. Creating, maintaining, or improving a sense of trust or reliability?

Audience(s) Intended for this Document

1. Who are they? (Primary? Secondary?) What are their backgrounds, levels of education, and technical expertise?

Primary:

Secondary:

Figure 3.6
(*Continued*)

2. What positions, biases, attitudes are they likely to have on or toward the subject?

3. What purpose do they have for reading this document

4. What should they know (or become) after reading this document?

5. What should they be able to do after reading this document?

Preliminary Plan for the Document

1. What sources are available and should be used to gather data?
   Primary (collected first-hand, not published)?
   Secondary (collected second-hand, already published)?

2. What limitations need to be set for gathering data? (i.e., what is the scope of the proposed document?)

3. How might the information of the document be organized, and why?
   Inductively? Deductively? Chronologically? Climactically?
   Reverse climactically?

4. What graphics are necessary, and why?

part, base a decision on them. But you have a secondary audience in Doakes, who is both the chair of the committee and your colleague, and who has entrusted you with recommending a solution.

C. Specifically, you are to do two things:
   1. Analyze your audiences and the situation according to the considerations and methods discussed in this chapter.
   2. Write a memo to Peterson recommending a plan of action to deal with Mason. Remember that Doakes will review the memo before he sends it along.

Some Tips

Although your ultimate recommendations should be your own (and you will have to invent some of the details to round them out), here are some possibilities to start you thinking:

A. Force Mason to retire in December. This, of course, would reduce his pension, but it will save the company money and would probably elevate Doakes to Mason's position.

B. Force Mason to retire in December, but pay him his pension as if he had retired at age sixty-five.

C. Reorganize the regional pecking order so that Doakes takes over many of Mason's responsibilities until he retires at age sixty-five. Raise Doakes's salary; keep Mason's as it is.

D. Make Mason a consultant to the company at a reduced salary, but pay him his normal pension when he reaches age sixty-five. Elevate Doakes to Mason's position.

Note: Firing Mason outright is not an option.

TERM PROJECT OPTION

Assuming you have chosen a problem from your field to work on, researched it, and written an annotated bibliography, you are now ready to interview an expert to help you put your research into perspective and to clarify any questions you might have about your project.

First, conduct your interview, having prepared good, interesting questions, not basic questions you should be able to answer yourself from the research. Then write up the essence of your interview for your instructor. This is a basic rhetorical problem, because your instructor was not at the interview and will have to rely totally on your report for a sense of what was said and why it is important. Your report on the interview should cover the following topics:

1. Context of the interview

2. Introduction to the interviewee (who the person is, his or her position and qualifications as an expert)

3. Interview goal

4. Conclusion about the effectiveness of the interview

5. Summary of the three most important questions asked and their answers

6. Attitude of the interviewee

7. Plans for using the interview material

You should end up with about a page and a half of typed or word processed material. This material can then constitute another source for your proposal and your final written project.

SOLVING PROBLEMS

THROUGH PROPOSALS

Preview of the Chapter

Fundamentals of a Proposal
  Purpose and Rationale
  Kinds of Proposals

Analyzing the Process of Proposal Writing
  Statement of the Problem
  Analysis of the Audiences
  Statement of the Objectives of the Work Proposed
  Review of the Literature and Previous Work
  Methods for Doing the Work
  Facilities
  Personnel
  Budget and Schedule
  Expected Results and Evaluation Plan

Format of a Proposal
  Basic Format
  Expanded Format

Conclusions

February 1, 1990
7:30 A.M.
Patricia Wynjenek's office
College Hall, 367
Department of Anthropology
Hastings University
Las Palmas, New Mexico

Patricia Wynjenek got to her office early. She was anxious to get going on writing a proposal for more fieldwork. Although she had been to Indigo, Texas, before to do some fieldwork in linguistics, she was anxious to return to study the city and its poverty-level population more thoroughly, especially as to how they survive economically and still keep their families intact.

Indigo, Patricia believed, is unique among cities in the southwest. Situated on the border between Mexico and the United States, it has a population of 100,000, the political and commercial infrastructure is predominantly Mexican-American, it has the lowest per capita income of any city of its size in the United States, and yet its family structure has not disintegrated as have so many in other American urban areas with similar problems of poverty. Patricia wanted to know how and why Indigo is different, and how Indigo might be used as a model for different kinds of social programs that would serve the needs of its people.

Patricia would need some money, of course, to do the necessary fieldwork, and she'd need some time off from Hastings; and the only way she could get time off from Hastings would be to get some external funding. She thought of the sources that might fund her. Two came immediately to mind: the National Science Foundation (NSF), which had funded her Ph.D. dissertation fieldwork, and Las Almas Buenas Foundation, which was privately endowed and which funded projects particularly concerned with the economic survival of Mexican Americans. Las Almas Buenas had a special emphasis on health care, and how that is taken advantage of and afforded by Mexican Americans—not only in the southwest, but also in other areas where migration has taken them.

Patricia knew she would have to write separate proposals for the two groups, with different emphases. But they both could be informed by the information she already had about Mexican Americans in the southwest, particularly those of Indigo, and more information that she could use from reviewing the work of others. She would have to talk specifically about poverty in Indigo—how it comes about, what forms it takes, and how people deal with it. For Las Almas Buenas, she would have to direct her attention to health care—what access people have to established, modern medical facilities; how they use traditional methods: remedies, cures, and people who bring them about, apart from the establishment.

It would be a little tricky, but Patricia knew that if she defined carefully the problem and objectives of her work; the background of the problem as she knew it and what others had done to research it, or problems like it; how she would go about performing the work, and how long it would take; and how much it would cost, she could appeal to all parties: NSF, Las Almas Buenas Foundation, and Hastings University.

She certainly had some work to do, but she was buoyed by her conviction that her work was worthy of support, and that in the end she would get funding for the work she believed she had to do.

FUNDAMENTALS OF A PROPOSAL

Hardly anything gets started or changed in the professional world without proposals. They may be written or oral, informal or formal, solicited or unsolicited, but whatever form they take, they become the basis for initiating practically any kind of work.

Purpose and Rationale

Proposal writing happens in all areas of the professional world. People in business, for example, may propose changes in the way something is made, entirely new products, new markets, and new ways of appealing to those markets. Successful proposals may alter office procedures; they may bring about changes in personnel or corporate moves to new locations. They are often written to improve financial arrangements or to change investment strategies. In fact, all areas of business and industry, if they are going to remain active and productive, at some time will require proposals for change. The opportunities for preparing proposals are almost limitless.

There are similar opportunities for writing proposals in other areas. Scientists regularly propose to research new avenues for cures for cancer and heart disease. Engineers propose new systems and modifications to equipment. Lawyers propose methods of handling their clients' legal problems. Teachers propose new courses of study, changes in administrative practice, ways of expanding educational opportunities to neglected groups of the population. Government workers propose changes in bureaucratic functions, ways to make government services more efficient, appeals to foreign governments on future relations in trade, and cultural exchanges. And the list goes on. Every profession is involved at some time in writing proposals, because it's a professional responsibility to take the initiative.

Regardless of the subject, all proposals have the same basic purpose: persuading someone in a position of influence that something feasible needs to be done for a reasonable cost within a reasonable time.

This is why proposals offer a perfect example of the problem-solving activities of all professionals. Those who prepare proposals assume at the outset that some kind of problem exists—a procedure is inefficient, a market is untapped, the course of a disease is not fully understood. They further assume that solutions to these problems are necessary—that with changes in procedure, or cultivation of new sources of revenue, or discovery of a turn in the way a disease develops, both the quality of professional work and the quality of life in its broadest sense will improve. Finally, they reason that they can do the work and come up with the appropriate solutions.

Kinds of Proposals

As we mentioned earlier, there are many kinds of proposals. Some are informal and mentioned only in passing, maybe over a cup of coffee. Most, however, are more formal than that, and require close attention to style, form, and content. The process of writing proposals takes up a large part of the time professionals spend communicating—telling someone what needs to be done, how it can be done in the best way, and what the rewards are going to be for having done it. Proposals are categorized according to whether they are solicited or unsolicited and whether they are research or practical (see Figure 4.1).

Solicited Proposals

Proposals are *solicited* when they are requested by those who want certain work done or a certain problem solved. The impetus for solicited proposals comes, therefore, from the potential sponsors of the work rather than from the proposal writers themselves. The *felt need*, something we have mentioned several times before, lies with the potential sponsors, and the proposal writers, if they want the work, must respond to the specifications of the requested work as they are laid out in what is called a request for proposal (RFP), a request for quote (RFQ), or a request for bid (RFB). RFPs generally come from public and private foundations and government agencies that usually, but not necessarily exclusively, are interested in having research done. RFQs or RFBs, on the other hand, generally come from business and industry sources that are looking for more specific or tangible work to be done.

Various professional areas request proposals. For example, government agencies like the National Science Foundation, the National Endowment for the Humanities, NASA, or private foundations like the Rockefeller Foundation all have programs that need to be carried on to fulfill their missions. To do this, they send out RFPs—extensive documents that outline the particulars of the agencies' programs and the areas in which they want work to be done. These RFPs are sent to research institutions, both public and private. Researchers then respond with proposals in their areas of expertise and are judged competitively on how well they understand the agencies' needs, how they propose to meet those needs—with what facilities and personnel, within what time span, and at what cost.

The same kind of interaction happens in the private sector. Visionometrics, Inc., in San Jose, California, for example, wants a new automated inventory control system to keep up with its growing business. The company sends out to private computer engineering firms, like Hewlett Packard, RFQs or RFBs that

Figure 4.1
Kinds of proposals

Kinds of Proposals

Type of Proposal	Solicited	Unsolicited
Research	•	•
Practical	•	•

outline the extent and kind of inventory it has and is likely to have in 5 to 10 years, and the kinds of problems that the present system has already caused or is likely to cause. Firms interested in getting the business then respond with proposals to solve the problems by means that lie within their capabilities. Contracts to do the work are awarded on a competitive basis to the proposers who, in Visionometrics' judgment, are best able to do the work at a reasonable cost and within a reasonable time.

Unsolicited Proposals

Unlike the solicited proposal, the impetus for *unsolicited proposals* comes from proposal writers, not from potential sponsors. In this case, the proposers, not the sponsors, perceive a problem or a felt need; they must convince potential sponsors that the problem exists, and that they are capable of solving it, if they are to get the work. In this case, too, preparing proposals runs the gamut of the professional world, but the competitive edge, which we already know exists in responding to solicited proposals, is even keener. Government agencies like the National Institute of Education (NIE), for example, have a portion of their budgets set aside for work in which they have interest and for which they have set up broad guidelines, but for which they have issued no specific RFP. It is up to proposers, in competition with others, to convince NIE that a problem actually exists, that they have possible solutions to it, and that they can solve it at a reasonable cost and within a reasonable time.

The same is true in the private sector. Proposers have to convince potential sponsors, clients, or customers that problems or needs exist within their operations. Thus Visionometrics may be using an inventory control system that a proposer sees could be brought up to date and made more efficient, but that Visionometrics itself has not yet thought to change. These situations, therefore, call for even keener persuasive techniques—again convincing sponsors that something is wrong or, if not wrong exactly, could be made better, when that need has not yet been seen or fully understood by the potential sponsors themselves.

Unsolicited proposals can be generated from both inside and outside an organization. They require that someone define a problem and devise a reasonable way of addressing or solving it—the basics of a proposal. Then the real work of writing a proposal, which will convince someone to support the work, begins.

Research Proposals

Research proposals address problems to which there is yet no tried or proven solution. This does not mean that what they proposed is in some way unreasonable. It means, rather, that although the problem has been defined, the actual results of addressing the problem, or attempting to solve it, remain in an area of speculation. Researchers working on the AIDS epidemic, for instance, may take several different directions, not knowing exactly what they will find, in an attempt to find a cure for the disease.

87

Many of the projects sponsored by government agencies are generated from research proposals, and virtually all of them are solicited. Sponsoring agencies know that problems exist; in fact, these agencies have been established and mandated by Congress to solve them, and they know that they must contract the best researchers possible to find the solutions. No one expects that a cure for cancer will be found tomorrow; nor is it known how a nuclear repository will ultimately affect an ecosystem, but everyone expects a careful search for cures and answers. Thus the National Science Foundation or the Environmental Protection Agency solicits research and later supports it, when, according to the best of its knowledge, that research is reasonable and promises progress toward cures and answers. In this way, research proposals address broad and prevailing concerns of our modern society: how to cure and prevent disease, how to educate significantly a large and heterogeneous population, how to sustain and improve the quality of life.

Practical Proposals

For our purposes, those proposals not based on the kind of research described above are called *practical proposals*. This is not to imply that research cannot be practical, or have practical results, because in fact most of it is intended for ultimate practical application. But the focus of research proposals is on the study of what is not yet known or proven, whereas the focus of practical proposals is on a product or service within the known capabilities of the proposal writers. A computer engineering firm's proposal to Visionometrics to revamp its inventory control system, therefore, qualifies as a practical proposal. The proposers know what has to be done, know how to do it, and most often have already done it for other clients. Indeed, most of the work of business and industry is generated by practical proposals. They are also, in contrast to research proposals, generally shorter, less scholarly, and less fully documented, because the process that generates them operates within the private sector and is not subject to public, bureaucratic scrutiny.

ANALYZING THE PROCESS OF PROPOSAL WRITING

The process of writing proposals can be analyzed by asking several basic questions. The answers to them can translate into the various parts of a proposal. (See Figure 4.2.) These questions, considered as thoroughly as possible, not only will define the basic purpose for writing a proposal, but also will provide an outline of the necessary content. We now need to consider the context of a proposal in detail.

Statement of the Problem

As we indicated in Chapter 1, the question that needs to start any problem-solving process is, What is the problem? Proposers need to define the problem clearly and

Figure 4.2
*Questions to ask
and answer to
define the
contents of a
proposal*

QUESTIONS THAT PROPOSALS ANSWER

Statement of the Problem
- What problem or problems will the proposed project address or attempt to solve?
- In other words, what is the felt need?

Analysis of the Audiences
- Who will benefit from the proposed work?
- Who will review the proposal and either accept or reject it?
- Are the groups who will benefit from the proposed work and who will accept or reject the proposal the same?
- If the groups are different, what relationship do they have to each other?

Statement of the Objectives
- What are the objectives of the work proposed?
- What are the goals?
- What specifically will result if the work is done in the way it is proposed?

Review of the Literature and Previous Work
- What previous work has been done in the area of the problem?
- How does the problem fit into the larger context of work done in the area?

Methods for Doing the Work
- How will the work be done?
- What methods will be used to solve or address the problem and to achieve the objectives as defined?

Facilities
- What resources exist for getting the work done?
- Specifically, what facilities are available to bring about the objectives?

Personnel
- Who will do the work?
- How are they qualified to do the work?

Budget and Schedule
- How much will the work cost?
- How long will it take?

Expected Results and Evaluation Plan
- What results can be expected?
- How will the results be evaluated?

precisely, because the definition establishes the basic reason for proposing. Without a problem and an idea of who feels the need to have it solved, there is no need to propose.

Defining the Problem for a Solicited Proposal

Defining is easier in the case of solicited proposals, whether research or practical. The RFPs or RFQs are by their very nature defining documents. They set out the problem as it is perceived by the potential sponsors, and by virtue of the request also establish how it should be perceived by proposers. Proposers must then respond and show how their understanding of the problem coincides with the sponsors'. So, if Visionometrics sees that it has an inventory control problem and calls for proposals to solve it, proposers must attempt to see the problem in the company's terms. If the proposers find that they need to redefine the terms of the problem, they should do so as long as they keep in mind Visionomentrics' basic understanding of the problem. To do otherwise would be insulting. Organizations don't send out RFQs or RFPs on vaguely felt, ill-defined needs.

The same is true of a government agency like the National Endowment for the Humanities (NEH). Within its broad Congressional mandate, NEH has defined several areas of concern for furthering the study, knowledge, and appreciation of the humanities. One such area is secondary education and the need for high school teachers to maintain a high level of awareness of and education in the humanities. This, the Endowment thinks, can be done through collaborative efforts between colleges and universities and secondary school systems. So NEH calls for proposals on how such collaborative efforts could bring about a rejuvenated awareness and teaching of the humanities in the public schools. Universities and school districts, if they are willing and able to collaborate, would submit proposals that must demonstrate why they think collaboration would be beneficial, and how it would be possible.

Defining the problem, or understanding the felt need, in the case of solicited proposals is not difficult as long as the areas of concern and expertise of both sponsors and proposers are evenly aligned. If proposers work actively in the areas in which sponsors want work done, and if proposer and sponsor perceptions within those areas are similar, then this first step in the analysis of the problem of writing the proposal should be fairly easy to accomplish.

Defining the Problem for an Unsolicited Proposal

Defining the problem is harder when writing an unsolicited proposal, when a potential sponsor does not necessarily perceive a problem and must be convinced that one exists. In this case, the burden of proof lies completely with the proposers. They must have not only up-to-date knowledge of their own areas of expertise, but also a full understanding of the areas of expertise of their potential sponsors. Let us return to our example of Visionometrics, Inc. A computer engineering firm that specializes in designing inventory control systems knows through contacts in the industry that Visionometrics uses a system that is outdated or inadequate, given the nature and growth of its business. The task for the computer firm, then, becomes one of convincing Visionometrics that the problem exists and that the proposers can solve it. The firm will have to show in its statement of the problem that it understands the peculiar needs Visionometrics has for inventory control, how its present system, though at one time adequate, is no longer so, and that the firm has designed and installed systems that would better meet Visionometrics' needs. Although the basic job of any proposal is to persuade, for the unsolicited proposal, persuasion becomes even more important. Proposers have to realize that ideas of what needs to be done may not be shared initially by potential sponsors. They must, therefore, be sure that those ideas are clearly, thoroughly, and accurately delineated.

Analysis of the Audiences

Direct Beneficiaries of the Work to Be Done

Although the answer to the question of who will benefit from the proposed work may seem obvious if the problem has been defined clearly, it is still important to know who will be the *direct beneficiaries* of a solution or address to a problem, and whether they are the same people who will review the proposal. In the case of Visionometrics, the groups are the same: Visionometrics will benefit from a new inventory control system, and it will also review the proposal for one. This makes the proposers' job somewhat easier, since there is only one audience that needs to be analyzed.

In the case of research proposals, however, especially those sponsored by public agencies, those who will benefit from the work to be done and those who review the proposal are most often separate audiences. If we talk about AIDS research, for instance, the direct beneficiaries are those who have the disease and those who are at risk of contracting it. The reviewing audience (in this case, perhaps a group from the National Institutes of Health) is made up of agency personnel and experts in medical research of various kinds, such as genetics, virology, and immunology. They will look at the proposal objectively and judge it on its general scientific, technical, and otherwise professional merit. The reviewers usually hold themselves apart from the direct beneficiaries of the research. It should be noted here, however, that a cure for AIDS will in the end benefit all of us, and to that extent, the beneficiary and reviewing audiences are the same. But for purposes of this discussion, it is useful to talk about the direct beneficiary and review groups as being separate audiences.

Analyzing carefully the needs of the group who will benefit directly from the work is important, then, for several reasons. It helps proposers reflect on the problem and the felt need, to see that they are clearly defined. It also helps define specific objectives of the work to be done. And it may also suggest certain methods that need to be used to fulfill the objectives.

Reviewing Audiences

If the beneficiary and reviewing audiences are not the same, a close analysis of the reviewing audience of a proposal is fundamentally important. These reviewers will ultimately decide whether to offer a contract to do the work. Although defining the problem or felt need is the first step in writing a proposal, to do so without analyzing the reviewing audience carefully is akin to choosing the right vegetable to plant in the spring, given a particular climate and growing season, without preparing the soil. The choice of what will grow may be just right, but without a thorough preparation of the growing medium, the crop will yield only poorly or not at all. Good analysis of the reviewing audience is good preparation of the soil.

Besides the usual questions about audience we have already considered in Chapter 2—What does an audience already know? What does it want to know? What does it need to know?—particular attention should be paid to understanding the reviewing audience's background. Proposers should know as thoroughly as possible the nature of potential sponsors' operations, what projects they are presently involved in, and what kinds of projects they are likely to support in the future.

To the fullest extent possible, proposers should understand what philosophical biases sponsors are likely to have and how those might influence their review of proposals. Both public and private sponsors of research on viruses, for example, want to know how viruses operate so that vaccines may be produced, but may not want to support research that requires genetic engineering of some kind. Although information on biases may be hard to pin down, much can be learned from reading annual reports of an organization's activities or the policy statements produced in some form by all organizations, both public and private. Also, in the case of government agencies, reviewing past years' RFPs will be helpful in learning the history of interests and directions agencies have taken. Personal contact with representatives of potential sponsors, if at all possible, will yield even more meaningful audience information.

The Review Process

Finally, and again to the greatest extent possible, proposal writers should determine how potential sponsors review proposals and award contracts. We do not claim that all proposals, written for either the public or private sectors, would be reviewed in exactly the same way. Although individual differences exist, the following discussion outlines general procedures and areas for consideration.

Public Organizations   Government agencies supported by public funds make the review process publicly known, and it usually happens on three tiers. After an initial screening process to see whether the proposals fit within the agency's general view and RFPs, they are sent to privately contracted reviewers, experts in the general field the proposals address. These reviewers read the proposals according to guidelines supplied by the agency and supported by their own expertise, and then make recommendations about whether to pursue the proposals further.

Proposals are then reviewed by a middle-level committee of agency staff that first considers the reviewers' recommendations and then, depending on the agency's mission, makes recommendations of its own. Finally, the decision to support the proposed projects is made at an executive level.

We take the time to mention this procedure because it so clearly illustrates the need for close audience analysis. In these cases there are three audiences reading proposals. All have similar interests and backgrounds, but each will use the information of the proposal differently. The outside reviewers are experts in the field in question and so will read the proposals with much greater concern for technical accuracy, the need for the proposed work, and its feasibility.

The middle-level staff committee, once satisfied from outside reviewers' comments that proposed projects meet certain technical criteria, will be concerned more with how the projects fit into the general mission of the agency. One way to do this is to see how closely proposers have responded to the letter of the RFP. It is at this level that all proposals live, die, or are given a second chance.

If the outside reviews are universally negative, however, there is virtually no chance a project will be supported. If the comments are universally positive, a project will be recommended for support, perhaps with slight alterations in procedure, budget, or timing. But if the evaluations are mixed, and if the project otherwise fits into the agency's mission, the committee may turn down the proposal initially, but ask the proposer to revise and resubmit it for reconsideration.

A good percentage of revised proposals are funded, mainly because proposers get copies of the outside reviewers' comments (they are submitted anonymously) and can see where they have gone wrong. Numerous proposals may be rejected initially, but are eventually funded because the projects had merit, and the proposal writers were able to revise in areas that had caused problems.

But this is no invitation to sloppy preparation—a bad proposal, one that reflects no care in the consideration of its audience, will be flatly rejected. Those that show promise, however, and otherwise good quality are often reconsidered after changes have been made.

The last level of review—the executive committee—deals only with proposals that have been recommended for support at the first two stages of review. This committee, like its middle-level counterpart, is also concerned with the general mission and goals of the agency, and with the ideas of the outside reviewers, but ultimately it is concerned with costs. Although the executive committee is unlikely to turn down a proposal if it has reached them, it is more than likely to negotiate the budget—scrutinizing every item and its justification—that the proposer has supplied. It is rare indeed that a project is funded entirely, without question, but the extent of the negotiations will be determined (and eased) in large part by how well and how reasonably proposers have presented their requests for money.

Private Organizations   We have talked a good deal about how government agencies deal with proposals, but have not considered how private firms and industry evaluate them. There is good reason for this. As we mentioned earlier, government agencies, by virtue of their dependence on public funds, generally have to make their actions much more public. The same is not true of the private sector, where proposals (either solicited or unsolicited) are reviewed on an individual basis, according to the firm's particular needs and wants.

Proposals may be evaluated by committees set up to evaluate a proposed project, or by selected individuals. The main difference is that proposals in the private sector work through an internal procedure, with the company relying on its own technical and policy-making personnel to make recommendations and decisions.

Writers of solicited proposals must anticipate concerns of these audiences by paying close attention to the RFPs. RFPs are usually very specific, outlining in detail the work needed, within limits of cost and time. Proposers must address every specification within their capabilities and facilities to have even a chance at securing a contract. In the case of unsolicited proposals, however, the situations are less well defined and less formal. The chances of securing a contract are, therefore, more dependent on how well proposers have researched the operations, have analyzed the needs of potential sponsors, and have established personal contacts with them.

It is clear that review procedures for both public and private sectors are complex and thorough, the audiences multiple and demanding. Each audience wants a strong, global impression of the proposed project, but each also has special interests, determined by its purposes for reading, its background, and its biases. For proposal writers, there is no task more demanding than audience analysis. The audience must be kept in mind always; knowing the audience must thoroughly inform the entire proposal-writing process.

Statement of the Objectives of the Work Proposed

It is important for proposers to realize that defining a problem and defining what is to result from the proposed work are different. It is one thing to know and understand clearly what is wrong, lacking, or unknown; it is quite a different thing to know what realistic objectives, goals, and results can be achieved from doing the work proposed. These are separate issues and they should be thought of separately.

Take the case of the Seattle-based educational consulting firm responding to an RFP from the U.S. Department of Education for drug education programs in public schools. The firm understands clearly the problem of drugs among America's youth. It knows the demographic and cultural backgrounds of those children who use drugs; it understands the effects drug use has had on the conduct of family and public life. It has data on the effects drug use has on children physically and psychologically. Armed with this body of information, the firm can write an impressively clear, thorough, and precise statement of the problem, and it will rely on this background to imply its objective: a generalized drug educational program.

The Department of Education wants to see, however, a specific list of realizable objectives. These might include workshops for parents to bring them up to date on the drug problem as it affects their children; in-service training for teachers for similar purposes, but stressing the physical, psychological, and sociological effects drugs have on their students; and an integrated, graduated curriculum for grades K through 12 that would involve team teaching specific units on various aspects of drug use in health, physical education, and social studies classes.

Proposers should remember a couple of points here. First, most proposed projects have a set of objectives that may make up one large objective. Reviewers want to know what that set of objectives is, or how the larger objective is constituted, to see that proposers fully understand the problem and the task at hand. Thus in the example above, proposers have at least three subobjectives to meet before the larger objective—a generalized drug education program—can be achieved.

The second point to remember is that the objectives section of a proposal is reserved for telling reviewers *what* is to be done, not *how* it is to be done. Proposers often confuse these and try to answer both questions at this point in the proposal, whereas the answer to how something is to be done is reserved for the later section on methods. Again the drug education example is helpful. In thinking of the larger objective, proposers might mistake the three subobjectives as methods of achieving the larger objective and include information about how the workshops for parents would be taught, what the in-service training for teachers would require, how the team teaching of the integrated curriculum would work. Although this information is necessary, it is not needed or expected at this stage of the proposal. Reviewers want and need a simple logical progression: What is the problem (definition)? What is to be done about it (objectives)? How that is to be done (methods) comes later.

Review of the Literature and Previous Work

The answers to the questions of what has been done in the area of the problem and of how the problem fits into the larger context of work done in the area suggest some important elements in the proposal-writing process: the proposers' experience, their awareness of what is going on in the field, and their notion of how the particular problem in question fits into a larger scheme of problems. The differences between research and practical proposals show up fairly clearly here and help illustrate how the answers to these questions add depth and credibility to the proposal.

Proposers of a research project want to show that they know what other work has been done in the area and how it helps define or influence the problem as they have proposed it. They, therefore, refer to and discuss in some detail the studies of other researchers—what they did, how they did it, and what their ultimate findings and analyses were. They also refer to their own past work, how it compares with or contrasts to the work of others, and how it has informed or influenced their present work. This discussion in research proposals is usually referred to as the review of literature, because indeed that is what happens: proposers review and analyze the published findings of their own and of others' research in order to present the problem in a larger context, and to demonstrate to reviewers that they understand that context. This is an important activity. It shows reviewers, depending on the literature reviewed, that the proposers are up to date on work in the field and that they perhaps subscribe to a particular school of thought. It helps reviewers place the proposal in the appropriate context, and therefore helps them decide whether to recommend it or turn it down.

A review of literature is not simply a list of sources or an annotated bibliography; it is a conclusive, evaluative discussion that must show the relationship of the proposed work to other work being done in the field. As such, it should follow all the conventions of documentation (citation) of secondary sources used in the field.

There is a similar task in writing the practical proposal. Proposers want to refer to previous work, but not in the way called for in a review of literature. They want to point specifically to projects they have completed successfully for other clients or customers, projects that had similar problems as their central focus, similar objectives, and similar solutions. They, of course, want to point to the success with which the problem was solved and the project completed. None of this requires reference to published materials, though sometimes proposers will include brief testimonies to the success of a project from former clients or customers.

The previous work section talks only of the *proposers'* previous work, or of their understanding of work that needs to be done based upon their experience. It does not usually discuss work that others have done; or if it does, it does so only obliquely, without specific references for obvious competitive reasons.

And thus in the case of the proposal to design and implement a drug education program for Seattle public schools, the group would speak of other special educational programs it had established. It would want to refer perhaps to the work it had done in sex education, another integrated and graduated program involving students, teachers, and parents at all levels, K through 12. It would point perhaps to the work it has done with school dropouts: identifying who they are and the kinds of families they come from, and the efforts made to get dropouts to return to school or to study for general education diplomas.

Proposers to Visionometrics, Inc. would want to demonstrate how they had set up new inventory control procedures for firms that were of a similar size, with similar growing pains.

A review of the proposers' experience is necessary in the practical proposal. The same idea applies as in the review of literature of a research proposal: to demonstrate that proposers are thoroughly up to date and have done the work necessary to solve the kinds of problems identified in the proposal at hand. The review, however, is rendered in a different way; instead of academic references, the review points to results the proposers have already successfully realized, those well removed from theoretical speculation.

Methods for Doing the Work

Potential sponsors want to know not only how proposers conceptualize problems, but also how they plan to solve them. The two processes clearly complement each other: a thorough definition and analysis of a problem will point to what should be done to address it; a clear and feasible plan to address a problem will demonstrate how well proposers have analyzed it. Proposers should be very careful, once again with audience in mind, to state *how* they want to achieve the objectives they have already set out. We are reminded at this point of the difference between the *what's* and the *how's* of a project: *what* needs to be done is the objective(s); *how* to achieve the objective(s) is the method.

As with all other sections of a proposal, the methods section should be written to persuade. Clear plans, with explanations and justifications for what methods will be used, need to be laid out. Reviewers will be aware of the best techniques for getting jobs done, and they will want to know whether proposers will use those techniques and how they will apply them. Even more specifically, they will perhaps evaluate the merits of one procedure over another, given the problem to be addressed or solved.

An example of this activity is the case of Patricia Wynjenek (which opened this chapter and which was discussed in Chapter 2). Patricia wanted to study the economic survival strategies of low-income Mexican Americans living in Indigo, Texas. In her proposal to the National Science Foundation, she had to lay out specifically her methods of primary research, the ways she would collect her data in the field. First, she would become a participant observer, taking up residence in one of the poorer neighborhoods of the town, establishing contacts with key individuals in the neighborhood, and generally taking part in the life of the community.

But beyond participant observation, a time-honored method of anthropological research, she would have to collect specific information on how people, who were underemployed or unemployed and who had limited access to social economic programs, survived economically. To do this, she proposed to choose at random 102 households from the neighborhood in which she lived, to hire four residents from the neighborhood as interviewers, and then to have them interview the members of those households. Interviewers were to ask from a preestablished set of forty-five questions about such areas as employment (family income), education, medical care, and family life. The 45-minute interviews would be tape-recorded, and both interviewers and those interviewed would be paid $5 per interview. (The number of interviews would be more or less evenly divided among the four interviewers, thus allowing each to make about $125.)

The tape-recorded interviews would then be transcribed and analyzed to see what similarities, differences, patterns, or trends might exist among the answers. From this analysis, conclusions would be drawn about how this particular group of low-income families survives economically, and what might be done to plan social programs for them and people like them in the future.

This example demonstrates the need for detail in statements of method. Reviewers have to be persuaded that proposers know how to address a problem and that the method for getting the necessary information will in fact do that. In Patricia's case, for instance, reviewers would want to read and evaluate the forty-five questions planned for the interviews, in addition to the details already provided; they would then be able to tell more about her ability to analyze the problem in general, and also about her ability to match the approach to that analysis.

We have spoken here mostly about research proposals, but the same generally holds true for practical proposals. Those who want to take on new approaches to problems, like that of Visionometrics, Inc., the firm that needs to update its inventory control system, have to know how proposers would bring about such a change. They need also a detailed statement of method: what new software will be necessary, why it will be necessary, to what degree it will replace or interface with existing software, what changes in hardware need to be made, and how the changes in either or both areas will be coordinated while day-to-day business is still being conducted.

The approach needed to appeal to the audience in the methods section of a proposal is perhaps less theoretical than practical, but it is no less important, since practice always reflects theory. A forthright, detailed and logical statement of how to get the proposed work done is an essential part of the process of writing proposals.

Facilities

All work, of course, needs physical support; whether the proposal is based in research, practice, or both, proposers need to demonstrate that they have sufficient facilities to do the work they propose. Even in those proposals written to procure advanced equipment, proposers need to talk about existing facilities, if for no other reason than to show that they are no longer adequate and thus to justify a proposal for new equipment.

Whatever the case, all physical facilities needed to perform or support the work of the proposed project need to be described. These would include libraries, their holdings and services; laboratories, including the essential equipment necessary for the project; and computing facilities, including the systems available to the proposed project.

Again, as with any section of a proposal, the intent here is to be persuasive. Proposers want to convince reviewers that the physical support is adequate—maybe even more than adequate—to perform the proposed work. If all preceding parts of the proposal, but especially the section on methods, are convincing and compelling, the use of facilities that may require slightly higher costs than those of competing proposers may be justified.

Some idea of how the facilities will favorably affect the duration of the project is also important to include here. Potential sponsors are especially keen to inefficiencies of time caused by use of outdated equipment or facilities with lesser capacities for doing prescribed work. But they are also keen to demands put upon contemporary, up-to-date operations. Normally workers on any individual project are not going to have unlimited access to an organization's facilities; therefore, a realistic projection of access and how that influences duration should be reflected.

Personnel

Just as the physical resources that will support the work need to be described, so do the human resources. Even though earlier questions about previous work point to experience proposers have had, reviewers have come to expect a full statement of the qualifications of those who will be doing the work.

Proposers should write biographical sketches that highlight the experience of each of the principals and the kind of work they will be doing for the proposed project. These sketches are then expanded into full résumés of all principals that may be included in the personnel section or in an appendix at the end of the proposal.

Sponsors especially want to know about the personnel's experience in the field of the proposal: what previous research has been done; what has been published and where; what other recognition has been gained professionally. The personnel résumés should emphasize such experience.

The same is not so true of the practical proposal, especially as prepared by large, well-established companies. Prospective clients or customers in business or industry will rely more on the reputation of the proposing organization than it will on those of the individuals actually doing the work. While executive résumés are often called for, general employees' résumés are omitted. A section on personnel might even be replaced by a section on the history of the firm and its work in the field.

For smaller, younger companies, however, which depend heavily on personalized service to clients and customers, the personnel section remains centered on individuals. Résumés act as documentation of the qualifications of those who will be doing the work.

Budget and Schedule

Cost and time are obvious and very important considerations of any proposal. Although budget and schedule presentations are usually separate parts of a proposal, questions about each surface simultaneously, and with good reason. Potential sponsors want to know not only how much something will cost, but also how long their money will be tied up paying for the proposed project.

The test of cost and time is reasonability. If proposal writers are realistic about what a project will cost and how long it will take, the chances for getting a contract, all other things being equal, are much greater. This means that proposers must take care to list and justify each major expenditure and the time needed to complete each phase of the project.

Since it is the job of reviewers to know what things cost and how long they will take to accomplish, the proposal with the reasonable budget and schedule, given the problem and the methods of approach to it, will be more likely supported, even if it is not the least expensive. Reviewers are often suspicious of markedly low budgets or short time lines, because they can indicate several possibilities: the proposers are desperate for the work and are willing to cut corners; or they think they will be able to plead for additional funds and time after the contract is granted; or they have been simply naive or sloppy in making estimates. Whatever the case, it is very important that proposers not appear to be budgeting insufficiently, in terms of either money or time.

Having said this, it should be noted that as a practical matter, very few research proposals are supported at the full level requested, and most budgets are negotiated downward before contracts are granted. Practical proposals, however, may well be awarded to the lowest bidder, as long as the bid is reasonable, and in fact some public, governmental agencies are required to take the lowest bid, as long as the bidders meet the minimum requirements for doing business.

Expected Results and Evaluation Plan

All sponsors, no matter what the circumstances, want to know what the results of a project will be, but those organizations that solicit work, especially in the private sector, already have firmly in mind what they want to have at the end of a project. They expect to read a statement that summarizes the expected results, and more importantly, one that specifies how the results will be evaluated. These statements should lay out the means by which work will be evaluated and specify that the results will be presented in what are known as performance reports.

The same is true of the public sector, especially in the case of research proposals. Even when the work is solicited, potential sponsors expect a separate statement in which proposers detail what they expect to find, and more important, how they propose to disseminate that information to a larger community of researchers and scholars. Dissemination of information acts as a means of evaluation, since the community of researchers and scholars closely analyzes the proposed research and often will try to replicate it as it is done (or is proposed to be done) by those who are proposing the research. The process, whether done in the private or public sectors, should be evaluated.

Sponsors of publicly supported projects, both in research and practical areas, may expect a plan for third-party evaluation, whereby a team of outside evaluators gives impartial interpretations of the quality and impact of the work done. An evaluation plan needs to outline in detail how the evaluation will be made, how long it will take, and the credentials of the evaluators.

Although this kind of plan would not be required of practical proposals in the private sector, potential sponsors will want to know how well a project is progressing, and then once it is established, how well it works. Proposers must include, then, a plan for a series of periodic reports and performance reports. These plans would indicate how many reports would be written, at what intervals, and by whom. Though it is possible that outsiders would evaluate the work, most likely internal technical personnel would evaluate the project.

FORMAT OF A PROPOSAL

The preceding discussion of essential questions establishes the basic ingredients of most every kind of proposal—solicited or unsolicited, research or practical. But we should point out that not all proposals will answer each question in equal detail or necessarily in the order we have suggested. In fact, the formats will vary according to emphases the proposers want or need to make, and according to conventions of proposal writing within their fields of interest.

Figure 4.3
Elements included in the basic proposal format

Basic Proposal Format

- Statement of the Problem
- Statement of the Objectives
- Methods for Doing the Work
- Budget and Schedule
- Expected Results and Evaluation Plan

Basic Format

The elements included in the basic format (see Figure 4.3) are typical of most proposals. They may be arranged differently, however, to emphasize a particular element. With this basic format, most potential sponsors have what is necessary to make an informed and intelligent decision.

Expanded Format

In the case of more formal, solicited proposals, potential sponsors want additional information, usually specified in a section on format in the RFP, RFQ, or RFB. In the case of solicited practical proposals, where the RFQ or RFB may not specify any format, potential sponsors nevertheless expect certain information beyond the basics to be included. Figure 4.4 lists the elements of this expanded format. Most of these elements have already been discussed; the following sections provide information on the additional elements included in the expanded format.

Figure 4.4
Elements included in the expanded proposal format

Expanded Format

- Letter of Transmittal ———————————— separate from the document

- Cover Page
- Abstract or Executive Summary
- Table of Contents
- Statement of the Problem
- Statement of the Objectives
- Review of the Literature and Previous Work — complete document
- Methods
- Facilities
- Personnel
- Budget and Schedule
- Expected Results and Evaluation Plan
- References Cited

Letter of Transmittal

As its name indicates, the function of the letter of transmittal is to transmit, or send, the final proposal to the potential sponsor (reviewing audience). The essential ingredients of the letter should state that the proposer is sending a proposal (it needs a title), that the proposal addresses a certain problem and suggests what should be done about it (a summary of the problem and objectives), that the proposed work will take a certain time (total time commitment), and that it will cost a certain amount (total budget figure).

The opening of the letter should state the auspices under which the proposer is submitting the proposal. If the proposal is in response to an RFP, the proposer should say so, and specify the date of the request. If the proposal is unsolicited (no request for proposal), the proposer should say something to the effect that he or she is submitting the proposal on a problem the reviewers would have interest in having solved. The closing of the letter should state (politely) the proposer's hopes for a favorable review. The sample letter shown in Figure 4.5 indicates the general format to follow.

Cover Page

Also called the title page, the cover page formally identifies the proposal. Usually in equal quarters of the page, it states the proposal's title; the name, position, and address of the recipient; the name, position, and address of the proposer; and the date. Figure 4.6 presents a sample cover page.

Abstract or Executive Summary

The abstract or executive summary is the first substantive statement, beyond the transmittal letter and the cover sheet, that reviewers read in an expanded proposal. It should always be conclusive, not merely descriptive. Since potential sponsors usually have numerous proposals to review at a given time, they want to know immediately, and in summary, all the substantive highlights of the project, from problem to objectives to cost to time. They are not interested in descriptive statements that set out only the general topics the proposal will cover. These are not appropriate or useful, since preliminary decisions about continuing a review of a proposal are often made on the strength of the abstract or executive summary alone. Therefore, proposers need to speak of the best qualities of their proposed projects in a condensed form. Many RFPs call for limits of 150 to 300 words or will provide forms with designated spaces (not to be exceeded) that will not allow for more than 150 to 300 words. Thus, the abstract or summary must be truly conclusive and condensed.

Although the abstract or summary is among the first items of the proposal to be read, it is one of the last to be written. Proposal writers are usually not able to write abstracts or summaries until everything else in the proposal has been written. It is among the last of the problems to be solved in writing proposals, but it is often, because of the initial impression it makes, one of the most demanding.

THE AVERY MICROCOMPUTER LAB
Avery Hall   Department of English   Howell State University   Howell, Delaware 06164-5020

June 6, 1991

Donald L. Johnson, Vice Provost for Instruction
Driscoll Administration Building
Howell State University
Howell, Delaware 06164-5020

Dear Dr. Johnson:

Opening, stating what the proposal is and under what auspices it is being submitted—block paragraph

Summary of problem and objectives—block paragraph

Summary of time and costs—block paragraph

Closing, asking politely for a favorable review—block paragraph

Sincerely,

John P. McKenzie
Associate Professor

Encl.

Figure 4.6
Sample cover page
for a proposal

A Proposal to Research the Effects of Institutionalized
Computer-Assisted Instruction on the Writing
Program, Department of English,
Howell State University

Submitted to

Donald L. Johnson
Vice Provost for Instruction
Howell State University
Howell, Delaware 01164-4040

Submitted by

John P. McKenzie
Department of English
Howell State University
Howell, Delaware 01164-5020

June 6, 1991

Table of Contents

For long proposals, a table of contents should be included. It shows the contents and organization of the proposal, allowing the reader to turn immediately to specific pages to read different parts of the proposal at will. It is sometimes written to the second level of specificity, section headers and major headers within sections, but often includes only the main sections of the proposal.

The table of contents includes lists of appendixes and may include lists of figures or illustrations, but sometimes lists of figures and the like appear immediately after the table of contents. The table of contents does not list material preceding it, such as the title page.

The table of contents is paginated as other front matter with lowercase Roman numerals. Like the executive summary, it is one of the last parts of the report to be written. Authors should wait until all changes have been made in the proposal before adding page numbers; otherwise they may simply have to do it again.

Graphic Depictions of Schedule

Depending on the RFP requirements, proposers may find they can organize material best by presenting schedule details graphically. For complicated schedules or schedules containing several subdeadlines, a graphic schedule is the only sort that will make much sense. Although schedule formats may be adapted for any audience, reviewers in industry are probably most accustomed to reading the three forms discussed here.

The first form is called a GANTT chart. The strength of the GANTT chart is that it can show the times of several simultaneous activities, such as those required to move a whole office full of people to another building (see Figure 4.7). The GANTT chart delineates time across the x axis and task down the y axis, and can

Figure 4.7
Example of a GANTT chart showing change of location

	MONTHS FROM START					
TASKS	1 July	2 Aug	3 Sept	4 Oct	5 Nov	6 Dec
Administration						
Arrange Lease	——C					
Arrange Phones, etc.	———			——C		
Arrange Design Bid	————	——C				
Design: Contracted						
Create/Submit Office Design		—————	——C			
Deliver Equiptment					——	
Engineering						
Dismantle Conference Room					————	
Inspect Electrical System		————	——C			
Assemble New Conference Room					————	——C

indicate critical path activities with a *C*. The *C*s mark activities that cannot be allowed to slip without jeopardizing the schedule.

A PERT chart is more appropriate for depicting sequential activities than simultaneous activities. It looks like a flow chart and is most useful when the process by which the schedule will proceed is complicated. For example, a schedule that depends on a number of approvals and validations would be effectively rendered by a PERT chart (see Figure 4.8). In order for this schedule to work, all involved will have to meet or beat their deadlines. While they can try to alert people to impending action, they can't really carry out these actions simultaneously.

The third form is the milestone chart (see Figure 4.9). This chart is suitable for a long-range schedule comprised of several phases. The milestone symbols indicate subcategories of actions (which may overlap) that feed into completion of the overall project. We can see from the chart in Figure 4.9 that these proposers have already gotten their work started, indicated by the filled-in milestone triangles. It doesn't make sense to use a milestone chart to indicate purely sequential actions; a PERT chart would be better for that kind of schedule.

References Cited

For proposals that require a formal review of literature or that cite other sources in other sections of the proposal, a list of references cited within the text should appear at the end of the proposal. Such a list provides reviewers with all the pertinent information about the sources at a glance. Since there are several bibliographical formats in use, proposers should use the one considered standard in their field. These formats can be found easily in standard reference books or in the lists of references cited at the end of articles published in professional journals. There are also now computer programs that properly format such lists.

Figure 4.8
Example of a PERT chart showing steps of a design procedure

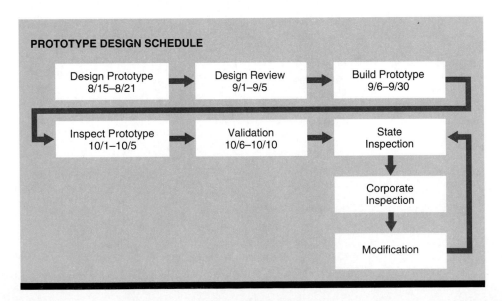

Figure 4.9
*Milestone chart
showing the
establishment of a
new drug program*

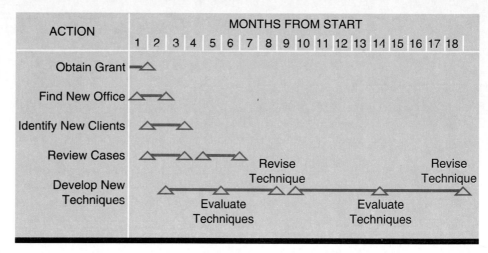

A list of references cited differs from the annotated bibliography discussed in Chapter 2 in that it is just a list, without annotations, of only the sources actually used and cited in the text of the proposal. Most lists of references cited are made up of only printed or published sources, but for those who have used interviews with experts to write their proposals, the names of the persons interviewed, their positions, addresses, and dates of the interviews should also be listed.

CONCLUSIONS

The process of writing proposals is varied and complex, and since virtually all the professional world's work is initiated or changed by proposals, there is really no way to avoid writing them. There may be some consolation, however, in knowing that proposals are often written with others, or collaboratively. We see evidence of this in the profiles of professionals in Chapter 1, and we will take up the topic of collaborative writing in detail in Chapter 10.

But as demanding as the work is, writing a successful proposal—convincing a potential sponsor that the proposer can recognize a problem and suggest reasonable, effective ways of addressing or solving it—can be one of the more rewarding tasks of professional life.

EXERCISES

1. Case Study

The Situation

You work for Educational Consultants, Inc., a Portland-based firm that runs special programs for, among others, the Portland Public School District. You are approaching the end of a 2-year program, funded by the Mary Wilkins MacKenzie

Foundation, on drug education in the Portland public schools, grades 7 to 12. You want to get a continuance grant that will pay for another 2-year program, but at increased expense.

The Task

You and your team need to persuade the MacKenzie Foundation that your program is worthy of additional funding. Therefore, you will have to demonstrate need for continuing the program as well as at least some degree of successful performance in the existing program.

To start planning your proposal, you had support staff collect some data on what has taken place in your program over the last 2 years and what has happened in other programs during the same time. They have listed the data below. You will need to evaluate the data for accuracy and usefulness and then decide where certain pieces of information would go in the format of your proposal. Although you will have to keep all sections of the proposal in mind, you may find that some sections are not covered by the data. You will then have to instruct the support staff to collect that information.

The Data

A. John C. Babes in *Drugs and Youth Today* (New York: Harper & Row, 1982) says that alcohol abuse among teenagers is more serious than other drug abuse. There has been a 35 percent increase in the number of adolescents who drink to excess in the last 3 years. (Our program has put little or no emphasis on drinking as a problem.)

B. Government findings (1988) show that marijuana use is on the decline. Our program has found the same: from a high of 45 percent of schoolchildren, ages 13 to 17, using marijuana once a week in 1987, the percentage has decreased to 27 percent by June 1989. (Use of marijuana has been one of our focal points.)

C. Although use of cocaine has decreased among Portland students, use of crack has increased. Three years ago, crack was hardly known among school-aged children, but since then it has grown dramatically in popularity. (We need to realign our emphases in the cocaine area.)

D. Our use of team teaching involving teachers of biology, social topics, history, and physical education has worked well for special workshop presentations: students' attention is centered on the drug problem at least four times a semester. But reports from Bay Area and Los Angeles school districts indicate they are having success integrating drug topics directly into the curricula of the various subject areas.

E. Tricia C. Blount reports in her article "Drugs Are Here to Stay" (*Newsweek*, October 30, 1988) that most education programs still have to fight the notion adolescents have that drugs are a way of life—either because they themselves take them or because their friends do.

F. Surveys of parents of children in grades 7 to 12 need to be continued to determine attitudes towards drugs, knowledge about drugs, and first-hand experience with children using drugs. This information is valuable for continued updating of our program.

G. Our "Celebrities Talk about Drugs" feature has been quite successful, with majorities of students reporting that they were most impressed with that part of the program. But preliminary investigation indicates that speakers' fees will rise about 15 percent in the coming year.

H. The Department of Health and Human Services reports that amphetamines are being used by 15 percent of schoolchildren in grades 7 to 12. This represents an increase of 3 percentage points over 2 years. A combination of amphetamines and barbiturates is being used by 12 percent of the same age group, up from 10 percent over the same period. (Our records indicate that Portland students rank with the national average, even though our program has placed good emphasis on this area of the problem.)

I. In-service training for teachers needs to be continued. They need to be updated on all aspects of the drug problem, how well our program has been received, and how well it has worked.

J. The overall program will see an average increase in costs of 15 percent over the next 2 years. This is compared to an average increase of 11.5 percent for other programs like it in the northwest.

K. Since the program began, those whose grades had dropped five or more percentage points since they began using drugs now report that their grades have returned to former levels, but have gone no higher. They also report that they still use drugs at least once a week.

L. Drug rehabilitation centers in the northwest report that they have seen an increase in enrollment of 22.5 percent among schoolchildren ages 15 to 17 over the past 2 years.

The Final Product

At the end of the exercise, you and your team will have produced a proposal outline, specifying which data belong in which sections of the proposal, as they have been outlined and discussed in this chapter, and which additional data need to be collected. You may also decide that some data are useless, and some are potentially useful—if they were to be developed further. Specify both cases and your reasons for the determination, and instruct your staff accordingly.

A. As we have pointed out earlier, proposals can be written individually or in groups, collaboratively. Choose a problem, either one you want to work on and have already defined, perhaps in your work in Chapter 2, or one that you and others want to work on. Plan and write a rough draft of the four main parts of a proposal: statement of the problem, objectives, review of literature or previous work, and methods. Each individual or group will submit the draft to a review team for evaluation. Use the peer review worksheet provided in Figure 4.10 to organize comments on the drafts.

Figure 4.10
*Peer review
worksheet for
proposals*

PEER REVIEW WORKSHEET FOR PROPOSALS

Reviewer's Name: _____

Author's Name: _____

Answer the following questions as thoroughly as possible.

1. Statement of the Problem
   a. Does the statement of the problem actually define a problem? Can you identify that something is wrong, lacking, or unknown? In a sentence or two, restate what you think the problem is.

   b. Does the author provide sufficient background to the problem? Do you know how the problem developed, when, where, to what extent? Suggest improvements, if necessary.

   c. Is it clear who will benefit from a solution to the problem? Specify who will benefit and how.

2. Statement of the Objectives
   a. Do the objectives actually state what will be done through the research? Or does the author somehow confuse what will be done with how it will be done (method)? Explain.

   b. Do the objectives follow logically from the statement of the problem? Do they seem reasonable goals to achieve? Explain.

   c. If the objectives are listed or bulleted, are the entries in parallel construction? If the objectives are written in narrative, or paragraph form, is it still clear what will be done? Suggest improvements where necessary.

Figure 4.10
(*Cont.*)

3. Review of the Literature and Previous Work

   a. Is the review a discussion, that is, is it integrated, and does it cohere, or come together, as one piece?

   b. Does the review expand on the statement of the problem, that is, does it show clear connections to the problem? If not, suggest improvements.

   c. In general, does the review discuss the pertinent highlights of the problem the author is pursuing? If so, summarize those highlights here. If not suggest those that need to be addressed.

   d. Is the review conclusive or purely descriptive? If it is only descriptive, suggest ways of making it conclusive.

4. Methods for Doing the Work

   a. Do the methods grow naturally and logically out of the objectives of the author's project? That is, would the objectives be met if the methods were performed.

   b. Are the methods presented in logical order? That is, is there a sense that once certain tasks are done, others should follow? Explain.

   c. Given the reviewing audience for the proposal, are the methods fully explained and detailed? Is there any doubt about how something will be done? Explain.

ASSIGNMENTS

1. Following this "Assignments" section are examples of proposals written by students (see Figures 4.11, 4.12, and 4.13). They are not perfect examples and shouldn't be used as models to be copied, but they are representative of what some students can do when assigned to write their first formal proposal. Consider them carefully and decide how closely they adhere to the principles discussed in this chapter. What are their strengths and weaknesses? Please use the Peer Review Worksheet provided in this chapter to evaluate the proposals.

TERM PROJECT OPTION

Write a proposal on the research problem you have decided to work on this semester. Depending on time allotted by your instructor and the purpose of the proposal, you may follow the basic or expanded format provided and discussed in this chapter. According to your instructor's wishes, you may write the proposal to your instructor (who may not be an expert in the field in which you are proposing the work) or to another audience, one that would likely be in a position to support the proposal work if you were writing the proposal in the world of work.

Figure 4.11
Student
proposal 1

Proposal to Investigate the Effect of AIDS Knowledge and
Concern on the Sexual Behavior of ISU Students.

Sheryl Soderstrom

English 307
Spring 1991
Dr. Tracy Montgomery

40 Oakwood Dr. #114
Pocatello, ID 83204
233-5854

Figure 4.11
(Cont.)

Abstract

AIDS is a growing threat to the heterosexual young adults of Idaho due to a feeling of immunity and continuing risky sexual behaviors. Studies and documentation are needed to establish that risky behaviors are engaged in here and that students at Idaho State University are susceptible to contracting the HIV virus in spite of a high level of knowledge of transmission and protection. In addition, information is needed to isolate what discourages people from engaging in safe sex, what affects changes in sexual behavior, and how to best proceed with education efforts. It is expected that future education must center on self-esteem, decision-making skills, negotiation skills, and behavior modification to be effective in preventing the further spread of HIV.

This proposal requests $1,486.00 to undertake a survey that addresses the issues of AIDS knowledge, perception, concern, opinion, and behavior at ISU. A journal article will be prepared from the survey results and will be submitted to the instructor on April 22, 1991. This article will subsequently be submitted to Sociology and Social Research. Results will also be released to the ISU Bengal and the ISU AIDS Education Committee.

Figure 4.11
(*Cont.*)

PROPOSAL TO INVESTIGATE THE EFFECT OF AIDS KNOWLEDGE AND CONCERN ON THE SEXUAL BEHAVIOR OF ISU STUDENTS.

1.0 Statement of the Problem

1.1 Today, having unprotected sex is like playing Russian roulette because of a small, fragile, but deadly virus known as HIV. (See 1.2 Glossary.) The HIV virus causes a breakdown of the human immune system. When this happens, opportunistic diseases and infections invade the body. The presence of these specific diseases and infections leads to a diagnosis of AIDS. AIDS is a terminal condition. There is no cure.

The cause of AIDS is a virus, not a lifestyle or a particular activity. But HIV can be transmitted by the body fluids exchanged in unprotected sexual activities (semen, vaginal fluid, blood) (9.22, 9.9). Since information about how to protect oneself has been available since 1983 (9.3, 9.9), there is no reason for anyone to contract HIV (and subsequently receive a death sentence) through sexual activities.

The presence of HIV in our society and its fatal consequences should cause responsible people to change their sexual practices to protect themselves and others. However, articles in Mademoiselle (9.14), U.S. News & World Report (9.2), and Newsweek (9.20) indicate that AIDS is spreading into the heterosexual population, and misinformation about AIDS is rampant. Results of a Centers for Disease Control (CDC) study of student blood samples from universities across the country show that 1 in 300 students are HIV positive (9.3). It appears that the threat of AIDS has done little to curb sexual activity among heterosexuals and especially among college students (9.26).

In conservative southeastern Idaho, one might question the validity of these observations. We've somehow gotten the idea that AIDS only happens somewhere else, to certain other groups of people. We think we are immune because of the heavy religious emphasis in this area, our conservative nature, our isolation from urban areas known to harbor ''at risk'' populations, and because ''we don't engage in any risky behaviors.''

However, a 1989 survey of ISU students indicated that risky sexual behaviors are prevalent (9.27). Additionally, there have been 81 people diagnosed with AIDS and there are 280+ HIV infected people (that we know of) in Idaho (9.9). We are also aware that there are HIV+ people and PWA's going to school at ISU (9.3, 9.9). In fact, if we extrapolate from the CDC study (9.3, 9.2, 9.20) and another blood sample study (9.12), ISU with a student enrollment in excess of 10,000, probably has 20-30 HIV infected students. The scary side of this is that most of those people don't know they are infected and are probably continuing to engage in risky sexual behaviors.

As long as people in Idaho and people at ISU continue to believe they are not at risk of contracting HIV, and that they as a whole don't engage in

Figure 4.11
(*Cont.*)

any risky behaviors, they will continue to take the information they are given about AIDS and toss it away as not applying to them. Until it is brought home to individuals that it can happen to them—we will not see a change in behavior and AIDS will spread exponentially in Idaho as it has in other states.

As someone who has friends who are HIV+ and who have AIDS, and as someone who has lost friends to AIDS, I am concerned that no more people be sentenced to an early death because of sex. An investigation is needed to study the effect of the threat of AIDS on populations of sexually active, mobile, young adults who still naively believe it will never happen to them (9.23, 9.26:52, 9.17). A local study will (hopefully) be taken more seriously by Idahoans and may convince them that they are at risk, just like anyone else in the U.S. engaging in the same risky activities. Information gathered in this survey may better equip us to deal with AIDS in Idaho, will tell us what people think about it and are doing to protect themselves, and how we as educators can best reach Idahoans and get them to protect themselves.

While the HIV virus is transmitted in ways other than just sex (blood, shared needles, mother's milk), the proposed survey only looks at sexual transmission. This survey is intended to show ISU students that they are not so different from students elsewhere. It is intended to serve as a baseline to determine how successful AIDS education has been, how concerned people are, and whether their sexual behavior has changed as a result of the threat of AIDS. It also looks at people's opinions on a couple of AIDS-related issues and PWA's.

The final product, an article reporting survey results from ISU, may alert not only ISU, but other schools/students in isolated areas to the relevancy and need for AIDS education that concentrates not only on providing information about transmission, but also speaks to behavior modification.

1.2 Glossary

　1.2.1 AIDS—Acquired Immune Deficiency Syndrome. A condition characterized by a compromised immune system (caused by HIV) and the presence of specific opportunistic diseases/infections, including, but not limited to, Kaposi's sarcoma and Pneumocystis carinii pneumonia (PCP).

　1.2.2 HIV—Human Immunodeficiency Virus. The virus identified as the cause of AIDS.

　1.2.3 PWA—Person With AIDS.

　1.2.4 PLWA—Person Living With AIDS.

　1.2.5 Knowledge—For this survey, knowledge refers to answers to items testing knowledge of protection, transmission, and outcome.

　1.2.6 Perception—For this survey, perception refers to answers to items testing level of concern about personally contracting AIDS/HIV, level of concern about children contracting AIDS/HIV,

Figure 4.11
(*Cont.*)

and perception of AIDS as a health problem both nationally and in Idaho.

1.2.7 Behavior—For this survey, behavior refers to answers to items testing willingness to discuss the problem and solution with one's children, willingness to participate in identified safer sex practices, and avoidance of risky behaviors.

1.2.8 Opinion—For this survey, opinion refers to answers to items testing personal view of three controversial issues: condom machines on campus, HIV infected children in public schools, and AIDS as a punishment from God.

2.0 Objectives

2.1 To write an article for Sociology and Social Research.

2.2 To report the results of my survey to the students, faculty, and staff of ISU, via the ISU Bengal, and to the ISU AIDS Education Committee.

2.3 To determine if increased knowledge about AIDS is correlated to changes in sexual behavior.

2.4 To determine if increased concern about AIDS is correlated to changes in sexual behavior.

2.5 To discover how ISU compares to other universities regarding knowledge, concern/perception, opinions, and sexual behavior.

2.6 To establish a baseline of proof (if any) for the need for continued education about AIDS.

2.7 To determine the direction future AIDS education at ISU should take.

2.8 To determine if students at ISU do engage in risky sexual behaviors and are therefore susceptible to contracting HIV.

2.9 Expected results:

2.9.1 Basic knowledge will be high.

2.9.2 Personal concern will be low.

2.9.3 Level of knowledge will have no effect on behavior.

2.9.4 Level of concern will have some effect on behavior.

2.9.5 People will support condom machines on campus and HIV infected children in schools.

3.0 Review of Literature

My research for this project centered on four categories of material, which provided me with background information and comparison figures focusing on AIDS and the college student.

The first category, and by far the most extensive, is previous surveys. Most of the surveys I found were done at other universities in the U.S. (9.1, 9.7, 9.8, 9.11, 9.17, 9.18, 9.25, 9.27, 9.28, 9.29, 9.31). Of these, two surveys were specifically aimed at measuring knowledge (9.1,

Figure 4.11
(*Cont.*)

9.31), and two dealt with sexual behavior (9.7, 9.18, 9.29). One paper reviewed a number of surveys (9.11) some of which I have included in my research, one looked at peer pressure and homophobia (9.17), and one article reported on two ISU surveys concerning condom machines on campus (9.25). The final source in this section is a paper on a small survey (n=84) done at ISU that looked at perception, concern, and some safer sex practices (9.27). A few surveys were done at universities outside the U.S. (9.13, 9.15, 9.24), and some were done with specific populations (other than college students) (9.4, 9.6, 9.21). In general, these surveys report that basic knowledge is good, but concern is low, and sexual behaviors are not changing.

The second category is information about AIDS. This includes the need for education (9.16, 9.23), reports on misconceptions, precautions, fears, hysteria, prejudices, and risks (9.10, 9.14, 9.30), facts about AIDS (9.22, 9.9), and activities on some campuses to fight AIDS (9.5).

The third category features statistics about AIDS. Two articles report on the Centers for Disease Control (CDC) study of the incidence of HIV on campuses in the U.S. (9.2, 9.20), and another reported on a different blood sample survey also documenting incidence of HIV infection in college student populations (9.12). One source is my interviewee, Dr. Larry Farrell, who provided incidence statistics both nationally and locally (9.9). I also include as a source in this category a local epidemiologist, Jack Bennett, who contributed Idaho AIDS/HIV Statistics (9.3).

The final category focuses on sex and the college student and includes just two resources. The first reports on sexuality and sexual behaviors of college students in 1980, before anyone knew about AIDS (9.19). The other article reports on the spread of AIDS among heterosexuals, especially on campus (9.26). It was published in 1987 and shows relatively little change (if any) in sexual behavior since the threat of AIDS.

4.0 Method

4.1 Research previous surveys done at ISU, other universities, and the general public.

4.2 Research information on AIDS, sexual behavior of college students.

4.3 Test a preliminary survey for understandability, needed changes, etc.

4.4 Design and administer survey dealing with knowledge, perception, opinion, and behavior.*
*See copy of survey attached at end of section 4.0.

4.5 Analyze returned surveys for frequency.

4.6 Cross-tabulate data.

4.7 Analyze cross-tabulated data.

4.8 Interview Dr. Larry Farrell, microbiologist and AIDS lecturer.

Figure 4.11
(Cont.)

4.9 Write up findings for journal article.
4.10 Report findings to ISU Bengal, ISU AIDS Education Committee.
4.11 Submit journal article to Dr. Tracy Montgomery for evaluation.
4.12 Present oral report of survey/article to class.
4.13 Submit article to Sociology and Social Research.

5.0 Facilities/Equipment

Facilities:
        Eli M. Oboler Library,
        Idaho State University
Equipment:
        ABsurv—survey analysis program
        First Choice—word processing program
        Computer
        Printer
        Paper
        Reference Books
        Copy Machine

Figure 4.11
(*Cont.*)

CONFIDENTIAL AIDS SURVEY

1) Did you attend a lecture by Richard Carper during the week of October 22-26, 1990?
   __YES → When?
   __NO → Go to #9.
     __Wed. night public lecture
     __In a class
     __Friday luncheon

3) Did you learn anything new?
   __YES __NO
   __About AIDS
   __About risky behavior
   __About how to prevent AIDS
   __About how it feels to have AIDS
   __Other _____
   _____

5) Do you think Richard Carper was effective in his presentation of the subject?
   __YES __NO __SOMEWHAT

6) Has your opinion of people with AIDS changed since hearing Richard Carper?
   __YES __NO __SOMEWHAT

7) Have you made any changes in your lifestyle because of Richard Carper's presentation?
   __YES __NO __SOMEWHAT

2) Why did you attend?
   __extra credit
   __information about AIDS
   __interested in subject
   __curiosity
   __normal class period
   __other _____

4) Prior to the lecture by Richard Carper how did you feel about people with AIDS? _____
   _____
   _____
   _____

8) Additional comments about Richard Carper and/or his presentation(s): _____
   _____
   _____
   _____
   _____
   _____
   _____
   _____

9) The only safe sex is_____.

10) The next safest sex is ____.

11) AIDS is transmitted by:
   __coughing   __giving blood
   __kissing   __sharing needles
   __tears   (drugs)
   __mother's milk   __hugging
   __semen   __vaginal
   __breathing   secretions
   __blood   __blood
   __sharing eating   transfusions
     utensils   __toilet seats

13) Do you personally know anyone who is HIV+ or who has AIDS?

12) How have you learned about AIDS?
   __class   __magazine
   __TV   articles
   __friends   __parents
   __children   __special
   __books   lectures
   __other _____

__YES __NO

Figure 4.11
(*Cont.*)

CONFIDENTIAL AIDS SURVEY (*Cont.*)

14) There is a cure for AIDS. ___YES ___NO ___UNDECIDED

15) AIDS is something most people should be
    concerned about. ___YES ___NO ___UNDECIDED

16) People can catch the AIDS virus from
    public toilet seats. ___YES ___NO ___UNDECIDED

17) AIDS can be transmitted from females as
    well as from males. ___YES ___NO ___UNDECIDED

18) Most people who become infected with the
    AIDS virus will not get fully developed,
    fatal AIDS. ___YES ___NO ___UNDECIDED

19) Would you stop being friends with a
    person if you discovered that he or she
    had AIDS? ___YES ___NO ___UNDECIDED

	STRONGLY AGREE	AGREE	DISAGREE	STRONGLY DISAGREE	NOT APPLICABLE
20) AIDS is the most urgent health problem facing the U.S.	SA	A	D	SD	NA
21) AIDS is the most urgent health problem facing Idaho.	SA	A	D	SD	NA
22) AIDS affects only limited, specific groups of people.	SA	A	D	SD	NA
23) I am personally concerned about contracting AIDS.	SA	A	D	SD	NA
24) I am concerned about my teenage children getting AIDS.	SA	A	D	SD	NA
25) I have or will discuss AIDS with my children.	SA	A	D	SD	NA
26) I have or will discuss safer sex practices with my children.	SA	A	D	SD	NA

Figure 4.11
(Cont.)

CONFIDENTIAL AIDS SURVEY (*Cont.*)

	STRONGLY AGREE	AGREE	DISAGREE	STRONGLY DISAGREE	NOT APPLICABLE
27) Because of AIDS I have increased the length of time I date someone before engaging in sexual intercourse.	SA	A	D	SD	NA
28) Because of AIDS I am more likely to ask a potential sex partner about his/ her sexual history.	SA	A	D	SD	NA
29) Because of AIDS I have made the decision to remain celibate prior to marriage.	SA	A	D	SD	NA
30) Because of AIDS I am more likely to use condoms when having intercourse.	SA	A	D	SD	NA
31) Because of AIDS I am less likely to engage in oral sex.	SA	A	D	SD	NA
32) Because of AIDS I am less likely to engage in anal sex.	SA	A	D	SD	NA
33) Condoms should be available in the bathrooms on campus including in the dorms.	SA	A	D	SD	NA
34) HIV infected children have a right to go to public school.	SA	A	D	SD	NA
35) There is little that can be done to prevent the spread of AIDS.	SA	A	D	SD	NA

Figure 4.11
(Cont.)

CONFIDENTIAL AIDS SURVEY *(Cont.)*

	STRONGLY AGREE	AGREE	DISAGREE	STRONGLY DISAGREE	NOT APPLICABLE
36) AIDS is a punishment sent by God because of people's immoral behavior.	SA	A	D	SD	NA

37) AGE: _____

38) SEX: ___ MALE   ___ FEMALE

39) MAJOR: _____

40) HOME STATE: _____

41) CLASS: ___FRESHMAN ___SOPHOMORE ___JUNIOR ___SENIOR ___GRAD
                                                                      STUDENT

42) MARITAL STATUS: ___MARRIED→ HOW LONG? ___YEARS. ___DIVORCED
    ___SEPARATED ___SINGLE ___WIDOWED
    ___LIVING WITH SOMEONE (SEXUAL RELATIONSHIP)→ HOW LONG? _____

43) SEXUALLY ACTIVE? ___YES→ # OF PARTNERS IN LAST YEAR _____.   ___NO

44) RELIGION: _____ ___ACTIVE
                         ___INACTIVE

45) To what extent have your religious beliefs affected your sexual
    behavior?
           ___NOT AT ALL   ___SOMEWHAT   ___VERY MUCH

Figure 4.11
(*Cont.*)

6.0 Personnel

6.1 Sheryl Soderstrom, Principal Investigator

    I began this investigation out of my own curiosity about whether the AIDS education we have access to has affected people's behaviors, perceptions, concerns, knowledge, and opinions. My active membership in both the ISU AIDS Education Committee and The Southeast Idaho AIDS Coalition further spurred my desire to obtain some measurement of where students on our campus were at on these issues. I have had classes in Social Research, Social Statistics, and AIDS, and I have participated in a team research project involving a small survey on behavior changes because of AIDS here at ISU. I have also completed successful independent research projects. I am qualified to handle this project and my resume will support my suitability.

    6.1.1 My resume is attached.

6.2 Dr. Larry Farrell, Interviewee.

    Dr. Farrell is a professor with the Department of Biological Sciences at ISU, specializing in microbiology. He teaches a class on AIDS at ISU and has been hired by the State Board of Education to do in-services on AIDS for teachers in the public school system. Dr. Farrell has also done a number of community presentations on AIDS. He has been at ISU since 1972 and so is familiar with the school and the community. He is an active member of the ISU AIDS Education Committee, the Southeast Idaho AIDS Coalition, the Idaho AIDS Foundation, and the State Board of Education's Drug, Alcohol, and AIDS on Campus Committee. He is generally considered one of the area's leading authorities on AIDS. Dr. Farrell's background and involvement clearly establish his expertise in the field of AIDS and his value and authority in speaking about ISU students.

    6.2.1 Dr. Farrell's Curriculum Vitae is attached.

Figure 4.11
(*Cont.*)

SHERYL SODERSTROM
40 Oakwood Dr. #114
Pocatello, ID 83204
(208) 233-5854

EDUCATION   Current Status: Senior   4.0 GPA

Idaho State University—Pocatello, ID   1989-Present
    Bachelor of University Studies; Major—Thanatology, Sociology;
    Minor—Psychology, Philosophy. Dean's List every semester. Trained as
    AIDS/Safer Sex Peer Educator.
        > ASISU Scholarship—Fall 1990
        > Independent Research (not for class):
          Confidential AIDS Survey (n=245)
Hospice Volunteer Training—Pocatello, ID   1991
University of Alaska—Fairbanks, AK   1987-1989
    Major-Psychology; Dean's List every semester.
Life, Death & Transitions Workshop—Wasilla, AK   1988
    Elizabeth Kubler-Ross 5-day Retreat and Training Session
Headquarters Beauty Academy—Fairbanks, AK   1981-1982
    Licensed in State of Alaska 1983-1986.
Galileo-Adams Community College—S.F., CA   1980-1981
    Took courses in Licensed Vocational Nursing,
    Certified as Nurse's Assistant 1981.
Flathead High School—Kalispell, MT
    Graduated with Honors 1974; State Speech Champion 1974.

EXPERIENCE—VOLUNTEER

Muscular Dystrophy Association Telethon
    Phone Supervisor—Idaho Falls, ID   1990
        Recruited, trained, scheduled, and managed over
        80 volunteers. Coordinated with local radio and
        TV personalities, various businesses, and
        organizations. Assisted Telethon Coordinator.
        Worked independently.
    Mail Room Supervisor—Fairbanks, AK   1984-85, 87-88
        Located, trained, and managed 5-10 volunteers.
        Handled and readied pledges for mail out. Worked
        independently.
    Phone Volunteer, Mail Room Volunteer   1980, 1983
The Compassionate Friends
    Co-leader—Pocatello, ID   1989-Present
        Organize, plan and present the monthly topic.
        Facilitate and conduct support group meetings.
        Assist with public relations and presentations.
            > Wrote Dedication speech for the Children's
              Memorial Garden at BRMC—1990.
            > Designed birth-death announcements.
            > Met with the Mayor and other city officials
              about cemetery conditions/maintenance.
    Member—Fairbanks, AK; Pocatello, ID   1985-1989

Figure 4.11
(*Cont.*)

EXPERIENCE—PROFESSIONAL

<u>LDS Church</u>: Full-Time Missionary, PA   July 1986-July 1987
    Enhanced public relations. Wrote weekly reports.
    Wrote, updated and conducted surveys. Designed
    pamphlets. Kept records. Team taught a series of six
    presentations.

<u>The Prime Cut</u>, Fbks, AK: Hairdresser   Nov. 1985-July 1986
    Scheduled appointments, sold products, did end-of-day
    bookkeeping. Helped plan advertisements, specials, and
    promotions.

<u>Happy Faces Day Care</u>, Fbks, AK.   Aug. 1985-Nov. 1985
    Licensed Operator. Self-employed. Cared for 5 children
    daily. Kept the books. Wrote the policy statement and
    parent contract. Kept required state records. Wrote
    reports.

<u>Gooden Services</u>, Fbks, AK: Bus Aide   Jan. 1985-July 1985
    Assisted driver in providing safe transportation to and
    from school for mentally and physically handicapped
    people, ages 5-20.

<u>Wedgewood Hairstyling Salon</u> and <u>The Split End</u>,
Fbks, AK: Aug. 1982-Jan. 1985
    Hairdresser

PAPERS & PRESENTATIONS

"Death and Dying" Guest Lecture.   1991
    Dr. Larry Farrell's AIDS class—ISU, Pocatello, ID.
"Belief in Life After Death as a Measure of Death Attitudes
as Established through Epitaphs" Original Research.   1990
    > First Place—2nd Annual Idaho Conference for Students
      in the Social Sciences and Public Affairs—Boise
      State University, Boise, ID.
    > Honorable Mention—The National Undergraduate Social
      Science Conference—Weber State College, Ogden, UT.
    > 17th Annual Western Anthropology/Sociology
      Undergraduate Research Conference—Santa Clara
      University, Santa Clara, CA.

MEMBERSHIPS

<u>Southeast Idaho AIDS Coalition</u>
    Served on Mission Statement/Goals Committee. Designed
    and marketed "Condomgrams."
<u>ISU AIDS Education Committee</u>
    Student Representative to the State Board of Education's
    Committee on Drugs, Alcohol, and AIDS on Campus—1991.
    AIDS/Safer Sex presentations.
<u>Foundation of Thanatology</u>
<u>Association for Death Education and Counseling</u>
<u>Elizabeth Kubler-Ross Center</u>

<u>REFERENCES</u>   Furnished upon Request.

Figure 4.11
(*Cont.*)

LARRY DON FARRELL

CURRICULUM VITAE

Personal
> Born—November 5, 1942. Woodward, Oklahoma.
> Married—August 8, 1965. Two Children.
> Present address: Residence—843 North 10th
> Pocatello, Idaho 83201
> Telephone: (208) 234-0334

> Business—Dept. of Biological Sciences
> Idaho State University
> Pocatello, Idaho 83209
> Telephone: (208) 236-3171

Education
> B.S.   May, 1964, University of Oklahoma, Microbiology.
> M.S.   August, 1966, University of Oklahoma, Microbiology.
> Major Professors, Drs. John Lancaster, Donald Cox, Robert Collier.
> Research topic, Phage replication and sporulation in Bacillus subtilis.
> Ph.D.   August, 1970, University of California at Los Angeles, Bacteriology.
> Major Professors: Drs. Frederic A. Eiserling and William R. Romig.
> Research Topic, Development of the genetic system of Bacillus subtilis bacteriophage SP02.

Academic Experience

1989-present	Professor, Dept. of Biological Sciences, Idaho State University, Pocatello, Idaho 83209.
1988-present	Assistant Chairman, Dept. of Biological Sciences, Idaho State University, Pocatello, Idaho 83209.
1984-1988	Associate Professor, Dept. of Biological Sciences, Idaho State University, Pocatello, Idaho 83209.
1978-1984	Associate Professor, Dept. of Microbiology and Biochemistry, Idaho State University, Pocatello, Idaho 83209.
1977-1984	Department Chairman, Dept. of Microbiology and Biochemistry, Idaho State University, Pocatello, Idaho, 83209.
1972-1978	Assistant Professor, Dept. of Microbiology and Biochemistry, Idaho State University, Pocatello, Idaho 83209.
1970-1972	Instructor, Dept. of Microbiology, University of Illinois, College of Medicine, Chicago, IL 60680.
1966-1967	Teaching Assistant, Dept. of Bacteriology, University of California, Los Angeles, California 90024.
1964-1966	Teaching Assistant, Dept. of Botany and Microbiology, University of Oklahoma, Norman, Oklahoma 73019.

Figure 4.11
(*Cont.*)

Courses Taught:

Introductory Microbiology
Acquired Immune Deficiency Syndrome (AIDS)
General Virology
Bacterial Virology Laboratory
Survey of Electron Microscopy
Microbial Genetics
Medical Microbiology
Advanced Bacterial Virology
Practical Electron Microscopy
Principles of Molecular Biology

Research Experience

1967-1970   Graduate Student, Dept. of Bacteriology, University of
California, Los Angeles, California 90024.
1970-1972   Postdoctoral Fellow, Dept. of Microbiology, University
of Illinois College of Medicine, Chicago, IL 60680.
Mentor, Dr. Harvard Reiter.

Since 1972, I have directed my own laboratory at Idaho State
University. A total of eleven students have completed M.S. degrees
under my direction, seven have gone on to Ph.D. programs and one to a
D.O. program. I have been awarded a total of five research grants by the
Faculty Research Committee of Idaho State University and one grant by
the Academic Dean's Council of Idaho State University.

My primary research interests are in the area of microbial
genetics, as specifically applied to bacterial viruses. I am currently
working on the viruses of Sphaerotilus natans, a bacterium of
commercial importance because of the problems it causes in sewage
treatment plants.

Professional Organizations

International Society for AIDS Education
Society of the Sigma Xi
American Society for Microbiology (both national and Intermountain
Branch)
American Association for the Advancement of Science

Involvement in Professional Organizations:
Member—Volunteers Committee for 78th annual meeting of the
American Society for Microbiology, Las Vegas, NV, 1978.
Papers presented at several meetings, Intermountain Branch, ASM.
President, Intermountain Branch, ASM, 1980-81.
Chairman—Volunteers Committee for 85th annual meeting of the
American Society for Microbiology, Las Vegas, NV, March, 1985.

Professional Activities

Organizer and Liaison for the Idaho Committee of Correspondence,
National Center for Science Education.
Idaho AIDS Foundation, Member of the Executive Board, Co-Director
of Education Task Force.

Figure 4.11
(*Cont.*)

Pocatello AIDS Task Force, Interim Director (1988)
Invited reviewer for chapter on Microbiology in Campbell's
Biology, Second Edition, Benjamin/Cummings Publishers.

Special Recognition

Listed in 14th edition of "American Men and Women of Science"
Listed in 22nd edition of "Who's Who in the West"
Listed in 6th edition of "Who's Who in Technology Today"
Listed in 1st edition of "Who's Who in Pocatello"
Listed in 2nd edition of "Who's Who of Emerging Leaders In America"
Listed in 2nd edition of "Five Thousand Personalities of the World"

Publications

"Observations of single phage-infected cells of Bacillus subtilis"
Journal of Ultrastructure Research 25:501-506 (1968).

"Phleomycin-stimulated degradation of deoxyribonucleic acid in
Escherichia coli" (With H. Reiter) Antimicrobial Agents and
Chemotherapy 4:320-326 (1973).

"Phleomycin-stimulated degradation of deoxyribonucleic acid in
Escherichia coli. II. Inhibition of solubilization by bacteriophage
T4" (With H. Reiter) Canadian Journal of Microbiology 22:645-53
(1976).

"The effects of bleomycin on Ehrlich ascites carcinoma in suspension
culture" (With J. T. Eells and L. J. Fontenelle) Proceedings of the
Western Pharmacological Society 20:199-203 (1977).

"Handwashing: Ring Wearing and Number of Microorganisms" (with G.
Jacobson, J. Thiele and J. McCune) Nursing Research 34:186-188 (1985).

"Use of Serological Techniques for the Detection of Bacteriophages in
Dairy Products" (With M. Oswald) J. Idaho Academy of Science 22:15,
1986. ABSTRACT.

"Electron Microscopic Studies of Phage-Infected Sphaerotilus
natans" (with R. Pithawalla) J. Idaho Academy of Science 22:16, 1986.
ABSTRACT.

"Isolation and Characterization of Bacteriophages for Different
Strains of Sphaerotilus natans" (With D. Roberts) J. Idaho Academy of
Science 24:10, 1988. ABSTRACT.

"AIDS Education—An Opportunity for Interdisciplinary Education"
(With J. Girvan) Accepted for publication in Education.

"Developing an Effective Half-Day Secondary School Inservice on
Acquired Immune Deficiency Syndrome (AIDS)" (With J. Girvan) The
Clearing House 62:381-383 (1989).

Non-Refereed Publications

"AIDS Update" (With J. Girvan). A series of articles appearing in the
Idaho State Journal during 1987-88.

"AIDS in Idaho: The Facts, the Fears, and the Information Resources"
Idaho Librarian 40:32-34, 1988.

Figure 4.11
(*Cont.*)

7.0 Budget

7.1 Personnel
    7.1.1 I am the only investigator working on this project. My research and analysis fee is $15.00/hour. I foresee a total of 80 hours of labor to complete the project.

80 hours $15.00/hour =	$1200.00

    7.1.2 Dr. Larry Farrell, consultation fee:

1 hour X $50.00/hour =	$ 50.00
	$1250.00

7.2 Supplies and Equipment

ABsurv program =	$ 160.00
Survey copies (275 copies of 2 page survey)	
550 pages X $0.05 per page =	$ 27.50
Printer ribbon (1) =	$ 10.45
Computer paper	
600 sheets X $0.0125 =	$ 7.50
3-hole punch (1) =	$ 12.95
Hiliter (1) =	$ 1.00
Pens, pencil =	$ 2.50
Binder (1) =	$ 5.35
Columnar pad (1) =	$ 2.50
	$ 229.75

7.3 Research Material

Copies of articles	
125 pages X $0.05 =	$ 6.25
7.4 Total Budget =	$1486.00

8.0 Schedule

10/90-11/90, 2/91-3/91 Library Research, reading articles
10/27/90 Preliminary survey
11/1/90-11/15/90 Administer Survey
12/15/90-1/15/91 Analyze for frequency
2/1/91-3/25/91 Analyze cross-tabulated data
3/8/91 Interview—Dr. Larry Farrell
3/14/91 Proposal due
3/15/91 Personal Conference—defend proposal
3/25/91 (week of) Interview report due
4/15/91 (week of) Progress report due
4/22/91 Major project due
4/29/91 (week of) Oral presentation due

Figure 4.11
(*Cont.*)

9.0 References

9.1 AIDS Survey, 1990, AIDS Task Force. Lewis-Clark State College, Lewiston, Idaho.

9.2 A Scary Little Survey of AIDS on Campus. 1988. U.S. News & World Report. 14 November: 12.

9.3 Bennett, Jack. 1991. Lecture notes. Guest speaker in Dr. Larry Farrell's Biology 469 Microtopics: AIDS class. Idaho State University. Pocatello, ID. 29 January.

9.4 Bezilla, Robert, ed. 1988. The Gallup Study on America's Youth 1977-1988. The Gallup Organization, Inc. Princeton, NJ.

9.5 Bruno, Mary, et al. 1985. Campus Sex: New Fears—AIDS is the latest STD to hit the nation's colleges. Newsweek. 28 October: 81-82.

9.6 Bryan, Clifford. 1989. Study sponsored by NAACP and CDC and Idaho Department of Health and Welfare. Reported in the Idaho State Journal. Found on Sociology Department bulletin board, Idaho State University. Fall.

9.7 Carroll, Leo. 1988. Concern with AIDS and the sexual behavior of college students. Journal of Marriage and the Family. 50:405-411.

9.8 College Students only 'Paying Lip Service' to Safe Sex Message. 1990. Pediatric News. Orlando, Florida. May.

9.9 Farrell, Larry D. 1991. Personal Interview. Idaho State University, Pocatello, ID, 8 March.

9.10 Fear of AIDS virus spreads to colleges nationally, 1985. CPS, carried in The ISU Bengal. 1 November.

9.11 Fennell, Reginald. 1990. Knowledge, Attitudes and Beliefs of Students regarding AIDS: A review. Health Education. July/Aug. 21:20-25.

9.12 Gayle, Helene D., et al. 1990. Prevalence of the human immunodeficiency virus among university students. New England Journal of Medicine. 29 November. 323:1538-41.

9.13 Greatorex, Ian Frederick & John Michael Valentine Packer. 1989. Sexual Behavior in University Students: Report of a Postal Survey. Public Health. 103:199-203.

9.14 Hacinli, Cynthia. 1988. AIDS, straight: A Heterosexual-risk update. Mademoiselle. August:138.

9.15 Hanna, Jack. 1989. Sexual Abandon: The Condom is unpopular on the campus. Maclean's. 25 September:48.

9.16 Hepworth, Jeri and Michael Shernoff. 1989. Strategies for AIDS Education and Prevention. Marriage & Family Review. 13:39-80.

9.17 Hirschorn, Michael W. 1987. AIDS is Not Seen as a Major Threat by Many Heterosexuals on Campus. The Chronicle Of Higher Education. 29 April. 33:1, 32-34.

9.18 Ishii-Kuntz, Masako. 1988. Acquired Immune Deficiency Syndrome and Sexual Behavior Changes in a College Student Sample. Sociology and Social Research. October. 73:13-18.

Figure 4.11
(*Cont.*)

9.19 Katz, Joseph and Denise M. Cronin. 1980. Sexuality and College Life.
     Change. F / M:44-49.

9.20 Leslie, Connie, et al. 1988. Amid the Ivy, Cases of AIDS-College
     campuses offer students no sanctuary. Newsweek. 14 November:65.

9.21 Masters, William H., Virginia E. Johnson & Robert C. Kolodny. 1988.
     Crisis: Heterosexual Behavior in the Age of AIDS. New York: Grove
     Press.

9.22 McGinnis, Lee. 1987. AIDS panel voices concern. The ISU Bengal.
     13 November. 11:9.

9.23 Newman, Frank. 1988. AIDS, Youth, and the University—An interview
     with Admiral James D. Watkins, the chairman of the AIDS
     Commission. Change. September / October:39-44.

9.24 Nutbeam, Don, et al. 1989. Public Knowledge and Attitudes to AIDS.
     Public Health. 103:205-211.

9.25 Ragan, Kelly. 1988. Bowen gives 'Thumbs down' to condom machine
     proposal. The ISU Bengal. 22 January. 14:1.

9.26 Smilgis, Martha. 1987. The Big Chill: Fear of AIDS—How heterosexuals
     are coping with a disease that can make sex deadly. Time.
     16 February:50-53.

9.27 Soderstrom. Sheryl, et al. 1989. Has the threat of AIDS influenced
     sexual attitudes and practices on the ISU campus? Unpublished team
     project for Sociology 206—Social Research. Idaho State
     University. Pocatello, ID. Fall.

9.28 Threat of AIDS having little impact on sex habits of college
     students. 1990. (AP) Idaho State Journal.

9.29 Ward, Sally K. and Susan Ault. 1990. Fraternity and Sorority
     Membership, AIDS Knowledge and Safe-sex practices. Sociology and
     Social Research. April. 74:158-161.

9.30 Webster, Keeley, 1988. Condoms are to sex as seatbelts are to
     driving. The ISU Bengal. 11 November, 15:10.

9.31 Winslow, Robert W. 1988. Student knowledge of AIDS transmission.
     Sociology and Social Research. 72:110-113.

Figure 4.12
*Student
proposal 2*

1100 N.E. Myrtle St.
Pullman, Wa. 99163
February 23, 1989

Mrs. Martha Messersmith
Washington State League of Women Voters
1312 Rainier St. Suite 101
Seattle, Wa. 98166

Dear Mrs. Messersmith:

The attached document is a proposal to conduct a study on the effect the
television networks' early release of election predictions and results
has on issues within Washington State. The proposed study will survey
registered voters throughout Washington State who chose not to vote in the
1988 election. The results of the survey will determine if the networks
influenced the voters' choice not to vote, and if so, how the voters would
have voted on Initiative 518, Initiative 97 and 97b, and House Joint
Resolution 4222. From this information, the study will determine if these
lost votes could have swayed the outcome of these Washington State issues.

We hope that your organization will recognize the need for addressing this
problem. We are confident the results of this study will be of benefit to
political organizations and voters throughout the state, and hope that you
will decide to fund our research project.

Sincerely,

Susan Otis

Susan Otis

Kay Andreini

Kay Andreini

Eric Wheeler

Eric Wheeler

Figure 4.12
(*Cont.*)

Proposal to study the effect the networks' early
release of national election results has on issues
within Washington State.

Submitted to Washington State's League of Women Voters.

Submitted by Eric Wheeler, Kay Andreini, and Susan Otis on
February 23, 1989.

Figure 4.12
(*Cont.*)

Abstract

This proposal will address the problem of network election projections on election night. This practice of projecting the outcome of presidential races has been linked to decline of voters on the West Coast in several studies. Unfortunately, these studies have been flawed in various ways, and the networks have avoided changing this practice.

We are concerned that this decrease in voters could be sufficient to skew the outcome of state elections and state issues being voted on at the same time. We propose to conduct a survey of registered voters who did not vote in the 1988 election. We will ask why they did not vote, and how they would have voted. In this way, we can discover if network projections affected voting habits, and if it affected voting sufficiently to change outcome.

The proposed study will last eight and a half months, and will cost approximately $91,640.

Figure 4.12
(*Cont.*)

Statement of the Problem

During the last few elections, the American public has complained about the television networks' policy of broadcasting presidential election predictions based on East Coast returns before West Coast polls have closed. In an early victory, the networks will even announce a presidential winner to West Coast voters before they have had a chance to vote. When these voters receive this information, studies have shown that many people who intended to vote on the presidential race decide not to vote at all. The result is a decline in voter participation on the West Coast.

The networks' policy is harming America's democratic system, because only through optimum participation by voters can fair representation of the public's interest be insured. Even though the presidential election may have been decided and the loss in votes will not affect this race, many important issues at the state and local levels will need to be decided. A study done by Michael X. Delli Carpini ("Scooping the Voters?: The Consequences of the Networks' Early Call of the 1980 Presidential Race." *Journal of Politics* 46: 866-85, Aug. 1984, p. 866), concluded that in 1980 as many as fourteen congressional level races were decided by margins small enough to have been affected by the impact that the networks' early release policy may have had on voter turnout. These state and local issues are not of secondary importance to the presidential race. They are important to people's everyday lives, and the networks' election coverage policy is adversely affecting the number of votes these issues are receiving. As a result, the final vote on these important issues may be unrepresentative of the entire public's best interest.

Objectives

We propose to conduct a study which will determine the effect early network election releases and predictions have on Washington State voter turnout. The study will also analyze the effect a decrease in voter turnout has on the Washington State issues of Initiative 518 on increasing the minimum wage, Initiatives 97 and 97b on hazardous waste cleanup, and House Joint Resolution 4222 on increasing the personal property tax exemption for heads of households within Washington State. After these two topics have been analyzed, we will draw conclusions on the extent of the problem, and make recommendations for its resolution.

Review of Literature

The debate over early election predictions is nothing new. In 1964, Johnson was projected to beat Goldwater well before polls closed on the

Figure 4.12
(*Cont.*)

West Coast, and in 1972, Nixon was projected to beat McGovern more than two hours before West Coast polls closed (*Television Coverage of the 1980 Presidential Campaign* edited by William C. Adams, Ablex Publishing Company, 1983). In all cases, Congress investigated the effects of these early projections. In 1972, the Senate passed a bill that called for twelve hours of nationwide voting, with all polls to close at 11 pm EST. In 1974, the Senate passed a bill prohibiting disclosure of results before midnight, EST. Neither bill was picked up by the House.

While there had been concern over the networks' early projections before 1980, it was nothing compared to the surprise and upset over NBC's sudden predictions in 1980, which unfortunately set a precedent for election night coverage.

To backtrack, there are two methods of counting votes. One is the system used to count all votes in the United States. This is used by the News Election Service, and the networks use it only when the race is very close and unpredictable. The other is used to project a winner quickly, and each network designs its own. These have traditionally been a combination of exit polling and target precinct results. But in 1980, NBC changed that.

What NBC did was to rely solely on exit polling. In this way, NBC could project an outcome in a state even before a state's polls closed, and air the projection immediately. For instance, NBC predicted that Reagan would win in Ohio forty seconds after its polls closed. (While NBC aired predictions minutes or seconds after a state's polls closed, it never breached protocol by projecting a state before it finished voting.)

NBC also got a jump on the other networks by airing election projections during its nightly news program. Traditionally, networks did not begin election coverage until 7:30 EST, after the news program was over. NBC started its news broadcast by announcing that Reagan seemed to be headed for a landslide victory. NBC's exit polling allowed them to call twenty-five states first, and correctly call the presidency at 8:15 EST, two hours and forty-five minutes before West Coast polls closed, and about forty-five minutes before Carter conceded the victory.

The reason this broadcast caused such a reaction, and why critics say turnout was so affected on the West Coast, is that Reagan won by a landslide when no one expected a landslide. Social scientists believe that a voter's participation depends on how important the person believes his vote is. If the predictions follow expectations, i.e. projecting a close race when people believe there will be a close race, or projecting a landslide when people expect one, there is little effect on voters. But if voters expect a close race and then hear that one candidate is winning by a huge margin, they believe that the race is over already. They believe that their vote will make no difference on the outcome, and thus do not vote.

The networks deny any connection with their projections and voter behavior. They point to the fact that some Mountain and Pacific time zone states had higher voter turnout than in the previous election. But critics

Figure 4.12
(*Cont.*)

say that voting was badly affected during the three-hour period between the beginning of election coverage and the poll close. People were seen leaving poll lines, and many calls were made to election officials complaining of the coverage.

Two studies seem to support this theory.

In one study conducted by Los Angeles County Supervisor Edmund Edelman, L.A. County voting declined by 3.23% after 6 pm PST from the 1976 election. Voting declined another 4.12% between 7 and 8 pm PST. The main weakness in this study is that it cannot conclusively connect nonvoting directly to the early projections. Networks point to Carter's early concession.

The Center for Political Studies, University of Michigan, conducted the most extensive study, with funds from ABC News and the Markle Foundation. They examined the National Election Study, 1980, using the data from post-election re-interviews. They found that among those who had not voted by the time election coverage started and still had time to vote, the estimated proportion of voting dropped by 20 to 25%. In the entire sample, there was a 6 to 11% drop off ''as a result of nonvoting among those who had not voted when they heard news of election outcome.'' They also concluded that election projections and Carter's concession speech had an equal effect.

Many proposals have been made so far, but all of them either violate the First Amendment, are impractical due to expense or technological difficulties, or underestimate the networks' incentives to be first with the story.

Several studies have been undertaken in recent years to determine the effect of early election predictions on the nation's voters. Conclusions vary. John Jackson (1983) employed a 1980 National Election Study and a telephone survey to conclude that early network predictions resulted in a 6 percent to 12 percent decline in voter participation (''Election Reporting and Voter Turnout.'' *American Journal of Political Science* 27:615-35).

Philip L. Dubois (1983) analyzed the effect of early predictions on the 1980 presidential election and found ''considerable evidence of a decline in western voter turnout in 1980 that is attributable to the network television broadcasts'' (''Election Night Projections and Voter Turnout in the West.'' *American Politics Quarterly* 11:349-64).

Tannenbaum and Kostrich (1983) were unable to find conclusive evidence on the effect of network predictions on voters, stating, ''The evidence is mixed and the jury, ourselves among them, has still to issue a verdict'' (*Turned-on TV; Turned-off Voters*. Beverly Hills: American Enterprise Institute, 1983, p. 83).

Epstein and Strom added to the controversy by finding no effect at all on voters. They concluded, ''The decision to vote—on the West Coast or anywhere else—is the result of a complicated combination of factors, none of which is related to information received on election day'' (''Election

Figure 4.12
(Cont.)

Night Projections and West Coast Turnout.'' *American Politics Quarterly* 9:470-92, p. 486).

Finally, Michael X. Delli Carpini (1984) adjusted for what he termed the ''weaknesses'' of previous studies and found the network predictions to have a ''small but measurable impact'' on voter turnout. Carpini concluded, ''While the overall impact was too small to have affected the outcome of the presidential race, at the congressional level as many as fourteen races were won by margins smaller than the estimated impact of the early call in those districts'' (''Scooping the Voters?: The Consequences of the Networks' Early Call of the 1980 Presidential Race.'' *Journal of Politics* 46: 866-85, Aug, 1984, p. 866).

Our proposed study will further delineate the problem by ascertaining to what degree Washington State voters in particular are affected by early network predictions. Because no study has specifically addressed the problem in Washington State via a voter survey, the proposed work will be a valuable addition to the general foundation of materials already available.

Method

This study will gather most of its data from a voter survey to be designed by Andreini, Otis, and Wheeler and conducted by an independent polling service. The survey will be employed in door-to-door and mail-in applications. Washington Poll Service of Yakima, Washington, will conduct a door-to-door survey in the following nine cities:

	Population*
Seattle-Everett	1,607,469
Tacoma	485,643
Spokane	341,835
Portland (Clark Co. portion)	192,227
Yakima	172,508
Bremerton	147,152
Tri-Cities	144,469
Olympia	124,264
Bellingham	106,701

*Bureau of Census 1980 figures

In each city, only registered voters of Washington state who did *not* vote in the 1988 presidential election will be polled. This limitation eliminates the variance that would occur from counting voters who would not have voted regardless of early network predictions because they were not registered.

Of the 550,000 registered voters who did not vote in 1988, a total of 40,500 will be polled. This sample size is sufficient to accurately

Figure 4.12
(*Cont.*)

reflect the views of the universe of nonvoting registered voters (Council for Advancement and Support of Education, *Attitude and Opinion Research: Why You Need It/How To Do It*, 3rd edition. Washington, D.C.: CASE, 1983, p. 34).

In each city, 500 voters will be polled for a total of 4,500 door-to-door surveys. An additional 36,000 surveys will be mailed to voters in rural areas in order to more accurately canvass the cross-section of Washington voters. The higher number of mail-in surveys is required because response is generally only 10 percent, while door-to-door surveys carry an 80 percent response rate (Parten, *Surveys, Polls, and Samples*, 1950, pp. 95, 73). Although the mail-in surveys are much less expensive than door-to-door interviews (see budget), experts prefer the personal interview for its higher degree of accuracy in survey results (Webb and Hatry, *Obtaining Citizen Feedback: The Application of Citizen Surveys to Local Governments*, Washington, D.C.: Urban Institute, 1973, pp. 48-49).

The survey will be designed to determine why registered voters chose not to vote in either of the last two presidential elections and to what degree television networks' early predictions influenced their decision. Questions will be carefully phrased to assure an objective representation of voter attitudes.

In-house research will be conducted by Andreini, Otis, and Wheeler to determine the effect of early predictions on the outcome of local issues within the state. Evaluation of data will produce conclusions and recommendations to the League.

Facilities

We plan to utilize various Washington State University facilities throughout the completion of our study. To conduct the necessary research for our report, we will use W.S.U.'s extensive and versatile library system. This system consists of five major libraries and over three million items including books, journals, magazines, newspapers, government documents, microforms, manuscripts and other material. In addition, it offers a night search program, a computer bibliographical database called Coug-a-log, an interlibrary loan service, and a knowledgeable and helpful staff. Another Washington State University facility we plan to use is the Avery Microcomputer Lab. This campus resource provides Macintosh Computers equipped with Microsoft Word, Cricketgraph and Superpaint programs. A laser printer is also available for the printing of both the graphics and the text of our report. Finally, to compile the data collected from our survey, we plan to employ Washington State University's Computer Science Department.

Time Line

The survey of Washington State voters' attitudes toward the early election projections will be scheduled as follows.

Figure 4.12
(Cont.)

Design of survey	3 weeks
Survey send out and return	24 weeks (6 months)
Compilation of results	3 weeks
Examination and interpretation of results	4 weeks

The project will begin June 1st and continue to mid February.

MONTH	June	July	Aug.	Sept.	Oct.	Nov.	Dec.	Jan.	Feb.
Week	1 2 3 4	1 2 3 4	1 2 3 4	1 2 3 4	1 2 3 4	1 2 3 4	1 2 3 4	1 2 3 4	1 2 3 4
1. Design									
2. Send & Return									
3. Compile									
4. Examine & Interpret									

━━ Length of Activity   △ Activity completed

In addition to these Washington State University facilities, we will contact county court houses within the nine cities and rural areas of our study to obtain information on the number of votes received and the margin of victory in the three Washington State issues included in our report. We will also obtain lists of voters who were registered to vote but chose not to. The last facility we plan to utilize for our report is the Washington Poll Service of Yakima, Washington. This reputable survey company will be employed to distribute our survey by mail and door-to-door to the list of registered voters who chose not to vote in 1988.

Personnel Report

Kay Andreini: Majored in Political Science at Washington State University in 1987. Wrote Masters thesis on the effects of media in the election process. Worked for the Washington State Republican Convention as a poller in 1984.

Eric Wheeler: Majored in Sociology at Washington State University. Graduates in May, 1989. Emphasis on scientific methods of survey and statistical analysis.

Figure 4.12
(*Cont.*)

<u>Susan Otis</u>: Majored in Political Science at Washington State University. Graduates in May, 1989. Volunteered as surveyer/interviewer of Snohomish County Parks and Recreation Committee in 1983.

Budget

Salaries
  Study Team—design, research and evaluation of survey

Kay Andreini	10 weeks, 40 hours/week, $15/hour	$ 6,000
Susan Otis	10 weeks, 40 hours/week, $15/hour	6,000
Eric Wheeler	10 weeks, 40 hours/week, $15/hour	6,000
		$18,000

Survey contract—to Washington Poll Service, Yakima, WA

4,500 door-to-door surveys in metropolitan areas @ $15 ea.*	$67,500
36,000 mail-in surveys in rural areas @ 20 cents ea.*	5,400
	$72,900

Computer Access	$ 500
Supplies	150
Preparation of Final Report (including labor and computer fee)	90
	$ 740

TOTAL	$91,640

*Webb, Kenneth and Harry P. Hatry. *Obtaining Citizen Feedback: The Application of Citizen Surveys to Local Governments*. Washington, D.C.: Urban Institute, 1973, pp. 45, 54.

Expenditures

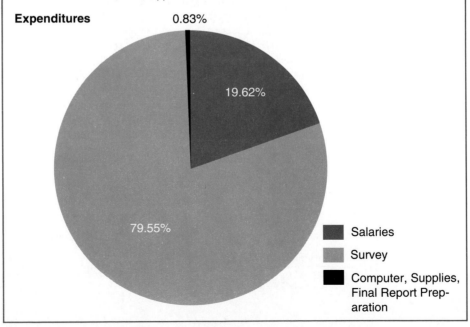

Figure 4.12
(*Cont.*)

Expected Results

Several studies have been undertaken on a national level in recent years to determine the effect the early release of election results and predictions have on voters. Conclusions from these studies vary, but the more extensive studies have determined a significant effect on voter turnout. We expect the results of our survey to be consistent with these earlier national studies, and verify the existence of this problem within the state of Washington. We also expect the results of our report to show that because of the drop in voter turnout, the outcomes of one or more of the state issues we are focusing on have been altered due to network interference.

Figure 4.13
*Student
proposal 3*

Diane Maree Desselle
421 Campus Vista
Pullman, WA 99166

Dr. P. R. Gavin
Department Head
Department of Veterinary
Clinical Medicine and Surgery
College of Veterinary Medicine
Washington State University
Pullman, WA 99164-7012

August 1, 1991

Dear Dr. Gavin:

The attached document is a proposal to conduct a study on
alternatives to live animals in student surgery laboratory. The
study will consist of interviews with professionals and other
concerned parties and research into various types of alternative
models. The results of the study will determine the best alternative
methods available, depending upon usefulness and price.

I hope you will realize the need for this problem to be
addressed. I feel confident that this study will prove beneficial to
the veterinary community.

Sincerely,

Diane Desselle

Diane Desselle

Figure 4.13
(*Cont.*)

PROPOSAL TO STUDY THE METHODS AND EFFECTS OF ALTERNATIVE
TRAINING IN VETERINARY SURGICAL LABORATORY

Submitted to the Washington State University
College of Veterinary Medicine

Submitted by Diane Desselle on August 1, 1991

Figure 4.13
(*Cont.*)

Table of Contents

Abstract 2

Statement of the Problem 3

Objectives 4

Review of Literature 4

Methods 6

Facilities 7

Personnel Report 8

Budget 8

    Salary 8

    Overhead costs 8

    Total cost 9

Time Line 9

Expected Results 9

Evaluation 10

Figure 4.13
(*Cont.*)

Abstract

This proposal will address the need for finding the best alternative models for live animal use in student surgery laboratory. The demand for decreasing the use of live animals for training purposes is steadily growing, and the best training possible is necessary to produce quality veterinarians.

Several alternative models are in use today, but this study proposes to find the best model both in quality and in cost. I propose to conduct interviews with various people in the field including veterinarians, veterinary students and veterinary professors. I will ask students and veterinarians how they feel about alternative methods, why they feel that way, and whether to continue in this manner. I will ask professors what kind of effects those methods have on the quality of education.

The proposed study will last 13 weeks and will cost approximately $1,560.

Figure 4.13
(*Cont.*)

Statement of the Problem

In veterinary schools around the country there is a growing concern among students that doing live animal surgical practice for the sake of learning does not mesh with the ideals of medicine. As students of veterinary medicine their goal is to promote and maintain the good health of the animal, not to cause pain.

Performing surgery on live animals which don't require the surgical procedures at best makes some students uncomfortable and at worst makes some students abandon veterinary medicine.

In order to remedy the situation a number of substitutes to live animals for surgical training have been introduced, in practice and in theory, ranging from the use of cadavers to highly technical holographic techniques. Substitutions using these techniques can be costly and/or time consuming, both to the veterinary school and to the students.

These substitutions could also have the effect of not adequately preparing the veterinary students for actual surgery once outside of the academic world. Surgery in actual practice has to be accurate, yet quick, because mistakes and/or wasted time could mean the death of the animal. However, in a surgery in which no live animals are used the surgeon may have the tendency to relax and make more mistakes.

Finding the best substitution for live animal surgery available will prove useful to veterinary schools as a way to better the quality of the education available. It will also prove useful for veterinary students who will be able to learn surgical techniques without having to harm live animals. The veterinary community as a whole will benefit because students who learn surgery using these techniques will most likely become better veterinarians. Animal deaths because of training will be lessened and animal rights groups may be placated.

Good training is important to the well-being of the animals and to the livelihood of the veterinarian. This good training can only be achieved if the best methods available are utilized.

Objectives

One of the major objectives of this research would be to determine which alternative training method or methods would be the best academically and financially. This determination would be based upon information obtained on each type of method currently used or proposed. There would be a cost analysis, and a summary of the pros and cons of each method. Also, interviews with those in the field would provide a background of which method they feel is the best among those they use.

A second objective of this research is to determine the effects of alternative training on the performance of the veterinary student both pre-graduation and post-graduate. If the effects are negative, different alternative approaches need to be found.

Figure 4.13
(*Cont.*)

The final product would be an article proposing the best alternative technique and would give the veterinary colleges the chance to compare their own surgery laboratory practices with those proposed in the article.

Review of Literature

The ideas for using surgical substitutes gained recognition in the mid 1980s. Veterinarians, veterinary colleges and the non-veterinary community all have opinions on live animal use. There is a common theme among all: veterinary surgical training needs to decrease the use of live animals through alternative methods, but complete eradication of live animal use is not an option.

Dr. P. B. Jennings, Jr. (1986) listed several alternatives to the use of live animals in student surgery laboratory. These techniques ranged from the use of cadavers and synthetic models to the training of veterinary students in the same way medical students are trained, with lots of internship and residency which is most costly and time consuming. ("Alternative to the Use of Living Animals in the Student Surgery Laboratory." *Journal of Veterinary Medical Education* 13: 14-15.)

Dr. Eberhard Rosin (1986) finds that although using live animals in surgery laboratory raises ethical questions, alternatives fail to teach the necessary skills required of professional veterinarians, and should not be the only training available. He feels strongly that live animal use is necessary in order for the skills to be taught adequately. ("The Importance of Using Living Animals in the Small Animal Student Surgery Laboratory." *Journal of Veterinary Medical Education* 13: 11-13.)

DeYoung and Richardson (1987) find that the use of bone models for orthopedic teaching is superior as a *primary* teaching device for students. They claim that the students' self-confidence is bolstered and control and comprehension are superior to those who do not use models. ("Teaching the Principles of Internal Fixation of Fractures with Plastic Bone Models." *Journal of Veterinary Medical Education* 14: 30-31)

Dr. Franklin M. Loew (1989) found that Tufts University has implemented a program in which live animals are not used for unnecessary medical practices. This was an action requested by students. To make up for not using live animals the students who take the course will be required to spend extra time in surgical and clinical rotation. ("Tufts Develops Alternative Program for Teaching Surgery." *Journal of the Veterinary Medical Association* 195: 155)

Bernard Z. Rollin (1990) advocates the rights of the students who find live animal surgery morally wrong. He feels that the veterinary profession will benefit from these students because they show the kind of concern necessary for a caring practice. ("Changing Social Ethics on Animals and Veterinary Medical Education." *Journal of Veterinary Medical Education* 17: 2-5)

Figure 4.13
(Cont.)

Dr. James Lincoln, in an interview (1991), discussed various techniques used at Washington State University for surgery laboratory. He stressed that live animal use should not be completely taken out of the program because they are necessary in some cases. He believes that the quality of education when using alternative methods is dependent on the students' attitudes.

Finally, Nils Soren Peterson, a computer programmer and representative, (1991) discusses the use of computers in the place of live animals. He points out that the computer is far superior in such exercises as the study of Mendelian genetics. He also states that many new innovations are just prototypes but advances are being made rapidly in order to improve education while reducing animal use. (''Education, Computer Software and Animal Welfare.'' *Animal Welfare Information Newsletter* 2: 3+)

Methods

This study will gather most of its data from interviews with veterinary professors, veterinary students and veterinarians in the community. The interviews will be one on one. The questions will be designed to discover how the interviewee feels about live animal surgery laboratory and whether he/she feels that substitute methods give accurate training. In addition, professors will be asked what kinds of alternative methods are used and which ones they feel are most useful.

Answers will be evaluated by myself based on a compilation of all interviews. These interviews will provide useful information not only about how the general veterinary community feels about alternatives to live animals, but also what alternatives professors feel are the most useful.

The rest of the data will be gathered at the Washington State University College of Veterinary Medicine's library or at the Owen Science and Engineering Library as secondary information.

Facilities

The various facilities of Washington State University will be utilized. Research will be conducted primarily in the Veterinary Medical/Pharmacy Library and in the Owen Science and Engineering Library, with the other three library facilities employed as needed. These libraries allow access to books, journals, magazines, newspapers, government documents and other materials, and have over three million items on hand. The various computer services that the libraries give access to, such as Coug-a-log and the night search, will also be utilized. The Veterinary Medical/Pharmacy Library has many useful journals and monographs on hand that may be

Figure 4.13
(*Cont.*)

employed to conduct research. Washington State's Computer Science
Department will also be used to complete the finished article. The CMS
system will be employed to format the text and it will be printed using the
laser printers available for student use.

In addition, interviews will take place in the Washington State
University College of Veterinary medicine and at various veterinary
clinics around Pullman. Dr. James D. Lincoln, an associate professor in
clinical medicine and surgery at the College of Veterinary Medicine will
be one of the interviewees. Dr. Lincoln has been with Washington State
University since 1977. He has been on the faculty of the College of
Veterinary Medicine since 1980 and teaches small animal surgery
laboratory with an emphasis on orthopedics. Dr. Lincoln's laboratories
use alternatives to live animals for most surgery laboratory periods.
Other professors and students will be interviewed. An interview may also
take place at the Washington State University College of Engineering and
Architecture.

Personnel Report

Diane Desselle: Investigator. Zoology major at Washington State
University. Bachelor of Science anticipated in May, 1993. Applied for
admission to the College of Veterinary Medicine, October, 1991. Worked in
a veterinary clinic as an assistant from 1988 to 1991. Will do research,
evaluation, compilation and final draft of report.

Budget

Salary

My fee for design, research and evaluation of the information is $12/hour.
I foresee 130 hours of work for a total of $1,560.

Overhead Costs

Overhead costs include computer use at $250 and the preparation of the
final report (including labor and printing fee) at $70.

Total Cost

The total cost of the project is $1,830.

Time Line

The schedule for this article will be as follows:

Figure 4.13
(*Cont.*)

- Research of previous work .... 2 weeks
- Interviews .... 4 weeks
- Compilation of results .... 3 weeks
- Examination and interpretation of results .... 4 weeks

    The project will begin in early September and will end in mid December. Some parts of the schedule, such as the research and the interviews may run concurrently.

Expected Results

Several methods have come forth in previous years as alternatives to using live animals in surgery labs. It is important to do a thorough review of these methods to find the best alternative available and how alternative surgical training affects student performance. The importance of proper training cannot be understated. I expect the results of my work to highlight the most workable alternative method available in order to increase training productivity.

Evaluation

Once a new program based on the results of this article is implemented, it will be necessary to evaluate its usefulness in an actual situation. The most important evaluation would be student performance. Student performance could be evaluated during the forth year of classes. During this year, students actually work on clinical cases, where their performance is already evaluated. The performance of students trained on the alternative method described in the article could be compared with the performance of students trained in other alternative methods.

    Another method of evaluating student performance is through employers after graduation. Employers are only going to hire the veterinarians they feel are most qualified to work for them. If employers are more pleased with the veterinarians trained using the new alternative methods than those trained on methods already in use, then the new program is useful. Employer responses could be gained through surveys over a three year period, comparing the performances of new graduates trained on the alternative method described here to those trained in other ways.

Figure 4.13
(Cont.)

Curriculum vita
DIANE M. DESSELLE

Campus Address
SW 421 Campus Vista
Pullman, WA 99163
(509) 332-2301

Home Address
3011 Boundary St.
Olympia, WA 98501
(206) 943-6312

Education
1991-   Washington State University
              Bachelor of Science in Zoology
              Expected in May 1993

1988-1991   Centralia Community College
              Associate of Science in Pre-veterinary medicine
              Received in June 1991
              G.P.A. 3.04

Experience
1988-1991   Veterinary assistant, Kitty Klinic
              Lacey, WA 98503

              Assisted in reception area, examinations, and
              surgery. Filled prescriptions. Did laboratory
              work. Cleaned cages.

1990-1991   Stall cleaner, James Gang Ranch
              Lacey, WA 98503

              Cleaned horse stalls. Assisted in training.
              Assisted in veterinary work. Fed, watered and
              blanketed horses.

Activities
1991-   Partnership for Equine Therapy and Training.

1991-   Organization for Future Veterinarians.

1991-   People-pet partnership.

SOLVING PROBLEMS THROUGH PROGRESS (PERIODIC) REPORTS AND COMPLETION REPORTS

Preview of the Chapter

Fundamentals of a Periodic Report
  Purpose and Rationale

Questions That Periodic Reports Answer
  What Project or Work Is Being Reviewed in the Report?
  What Period of Time Does the Work Cover?
  In Summary, What Has Happened during This Period?
  What Work Has Been Accomplished?
  What Problems Arose While Doing the Work?
  Is the Work on Schedule and within Budget?
  What Work Has to Be Done in the Future?

Format and Substance of a Periodic Report

Sample Professional Periodic Report

Fundamentals of a Completion Report
  Purpose and Rationale

Questions That Completion Reports Answer
  What is the Problem? Why Does It Warrant Special Attention?
  What Work Was Done? How Was It Done? What in General Were the Results?
  What Conclusions Can Be Drawn from the Work That Was Done? How Can the Data Be Interpreted? What Decisions, if Any Are Necessary, Can Be Made Given What Is Now Known?

Format and Substance of a Completion Report
  Elements of the Format for a Nonacademic Audience
  Elements of the Format for an Academic, Research-Oriented Audience

Sample Professional Completion Report

March 1, 1991
11:00 A.M.

Leah Feldstein's Office
EDUCARE, Inc.
1200 Stone Way, Suite 500
Seattle, Washington

Leah Feldstein was nearing the end of the third quarter of the second year on a $300,000 grant from the John T. Elliston Foundation, a grant she had had a big part in writing the proposal for. Although she had already written six quarterly reports on EDUCARE's Program Drugfree, *she was particularly concerned about this one, because Elliston was embarking on a close review of all funded projects, with an eye to possible cuts. She knew that if she weren't persuasive about the progress EDUCARE had made in drug rehabilitation, the firm could lose part or all of its funding on the renewal grant that had to be proposed next quarter.*

She also knew that EDUCARE had what Elliston saw as problems with Program Drugfree. *Her readers in Washington would certainly have a keen interest in what EDUCARE had done to solve the problems and what the future looked like for continued improvement.*

Leah quickly reviewed the problems. First there was the relatively static client population. In the almost 2 years since this funding period began, the number of clients had stayed right around 150, even though she had hired three new counselors for a total of eight. The ratio of eighteen to twenty clients per counselor she believed was favorable—counselors could spend more time with each client—but unfortunately the people in Washington were often more concerned with funding formulas and wanted to see higher ratios; more clients per counselor meant to them greater impact for total expenditures.

This reality led directly to the second problem. Leah did not believe in aggressive recruitment. She thought that enlisting clients should be done by existing means: referrals by teachers, parents, and other social service workers in the Seattle area. There was also, of course, the occasional self-referral. Through these means the program had enlisted a total of 198 new clients, replacing those who had passed out of the program, either successfully or unsuccessfully, over six quarters. Although she knew Elliston would like to see higher enlistment rates, she wanted her staff to spend their energies working with existing clients, not on beating the bushes looking for new ones. Leah thought that good work done with the existing pool was more important than expanding the pool, and thus perhaps risking a dilution of their primary effort: good and effective counseling, which meant getting clients off drugs for good.

This problem of recruitment was related, as was the first, to the last problem, which in many ways was the most difficult to confront. Leah wondered whether she was going to be able to convince Elliston that Program Drugfree *indeed was effective in getting clients off drugs and in keeping them off. The amount of time clients spent in counseling both in and out of school, the number who had gotten off drugs, and the number who had stayed off drugs were all comparable to figures of other programs she knew about. In some cases EDUCARE's success rate was even better. But she was not sure, given the problems of counselor-client ratios and recruitment, that the results would be viewed as favorably by her readers. That, she concluded, she would have to keep foremost in mind while she wrote her report.*

There was a lot riding on this report, but having defined the problems at least, Leah decided she was ready to start writing.

FUNDAMENTALS OF A PERIODIC REPORT

Purpose and Rationale

Periodic reports are sometimes referred to as *progress reports*. This is a misleading term because many people think of a progress report in only one way: a document reporting positive change in the condition of ongoing work over time. The difficulty hinges here on the notion of "positive change." Not all progress reports can document positive change over time. Sometimes they must report negative change. So instead of being able to report on how well a new marketing strategy has worked for a new product, for example, some manufacturers may have to admit that the product had less appeal than they originally thought it would, or that the strategy to market it was poorly conceived or timed. But those who are responsible for documenting the progress of the marketing campaign (progress thought of here in the most general of terms—how the campaign is getting along over time) must still write reports.

These reports may be written weekly, bimonthly, quarterly, or on any other schedule that seems to fit the needs of the situation. That is why many have come to call progress reports *periodic reports*, a more useful term. This term describes the fact that they are written at distinct intervals, and it removes the idea that they must report only positive changes.

Periodic reports, then, are written to document changes in conditions, either positive or negative, of any ongoing work of an organization that is crucial to its operation. They are not usually written to document what might be called the everyday work of an organization—work that does not essentially change over time or does not affect major policy decisions.

Another important element of periodic reports is that they are written to those in managerial positions so that these people can make decisions; therefore, the reports must be informative and persuasive in a way that makes options for action clear. Management relies on these reports to decide whether a project is on the intended track, whether stated goals are being met, whether the budget is sufficient, and finally, whether the project or plan of action is on schedule.

One additional and important factor having to do with purposes for writing and reading periodic reports needs to be considered, especially in Leah Feldstein's case. Most writers of periodic reports write only for the managerial audience of the organization they work for, who for Leah was John Fiske, Director of EDUCARE. But because EDUCARE is funded by external means, it is obliged, often by contract, to report periodically on the progress of projects to agencies that fund it. This was Leah's situation. John Fiske always expected Leah to write the periodic reports to Elliston, even though he was the signatory of the report. So Leah had to write for not only John Fiske but also the program officers at Elliston.

She found, however, that she could take good advantage of necessity. John Fiske became, in a significant way, a reviewer and editor of her periodic reports to Elliston. He could consider not only problems that were strictly internal, such as those having to do with scheduling and personnel, but also those problems that

Elliston would be concerned about, like client-counselor ratios, recruitment, and the overall success rate. Leah found that writing for John Fiske, which she had to do anyway, was a good built-in editing device that made for better reports for Elliston.

In general, periodic reports, whether they are written strictly for internal audiences or also for external audiences, play an integral part in decision making. They become, therefore, one of the more important kinds of writing professionals are required to do.

QUESTIONS THAT PERIODIC REPORTS ANSWER

Different audiences will require different formats, but essentially, periodic reports should cover the following topics:

1. *Orienting information*: project addressed, time reported on, background, changes in report format
2. *Evaluative overview of progress for current reporting period*: the report's thesis and a conclusive statement of what happened
3. *Current status*: a review of the major actions and their significance in moving the project along, problems encountered, and recommendations
4. *Conclusions*: a summary of the significance of what has happened, including a preview of future work and objectives

The answers to several questions will help specify the purposes for writing and reading periodic reports, and therefore help determine the basics of their contents (see Figure 5.1).

What Project or Work Is Being Reviewed in the Report?

Most organizations have multiple projects going on at the same time, so it is necessary to identify the one the report discusses. This can be done simply by using a familiar title or name, sometimes in combination with a code number. In

Figure 5.1
Questions to ask and answer to define the contents of a periodic report

QUESTIONS THAT PERIODIC REPORTS ANSWER

- What project or work is being reviewed in the report?
- What period of time does the report cover?
- In summary, what has happened during this period?
- What work has been accomplished?
- What problems arose while doing the work?
- Is the work on schedule and within budget?
- What work has to be done in the future?

writing for Elliston, Leah has to identify not only EDUCARE, the group responsible for the work, but also the project, Drug Rehabilitation (as distinguished from Drug Education, which is a different project), and the contract number Elliston has assigned to it. Since Elliston has hundreds of contracts with many organizations, it would have trouble finding the documentation in its database without the contract number.

Leah usually identifies her reports in this way:

```
EDUCARE, Inc., Seattle, WA, Drug Rehab, Ell DRA x15-023
```

What Period of Time Does the Report Cover?

Since periodic reports are written after distinct periods of time, it is important to identify the particular reporting period in order to keep the report separate from previous and future reports. Leah is about to report on the activities of the third period, but it is the third period of the fiscal year that begins in July, the customary working calendar of government and many industries. She will write then, very simply:

```
                  Period Covered
        Third Quarter, January-March, 1991
```

In Summary, What Has Happened during This Period?

Readers of all reports need to read a general summary of the activities and work of a project and an evaluation of their results. As in the case of proposals, discussed in Chapter 4, an abstract or executive summary lays out the conclusive results—what actually happened and what it means—for readers. Readers, but especially upper management, can, after reading the summary, decide what part they have in continuing the work or furthering the goals of the project; they can evaluate better who should know about the activities and what kinds of questions about completing the project successfully need to be asked and answered and by whom.

Some readers, depending on their positions, will make decisions about what has to happen immediately, based on what they learn from the summary. Others will pass the report along to others for them to make decisions. In either case, the evaluative summary is important at initial stages in considering what has to happen and who is responsible for making it happen.

In this section Leah has to cover the whole gamut of concerns: the specific activities of her staff, the changes she and her staff have proposed in completing those activities, the results of their activities to date, and the likely results of future activities, both as they have been carried out in the past and as they may change, based on new activities proposed.

What Work Has Been Accomplished?

Clearly, readers of periodic reports need to know what has happened during the reporting period. They look to see whether the activities projected for the period actually conform to what was done and whether anything was done differently. But most important, readers want to know whether overall goals of the project are being met by the work of the period. Therefore, writers must not only describe clearly and thoroughly what has happened, but also explain how that has furthered the purposes and objectives of the project.

In her report Leah has to review the usual activities of her counseling staff and show how they have been promoting the goals of drug rehabilitation as defined by both EDUCARE and Elliston. But for this report in particular, since so much is riding on it, she has to stress also the initiatives she and her staff have taken to move clients successfully out of the program. Her report, then, has to include discussion of the changes in group counseling: the formation of smaller groups (no more than seven per group, rather than the usual ten to twelve) that met more frequently (on the average of twice a week, rather than once a week). Although she cannot point to a significant increase in the number of clients moving successfully out of the program, reports from her staff on the progress of their individual counseling activities indicate that their clients enjoy their new group sessions, because they are more intimate. They are also glad to meet twice a week, because they think the sessions are becoming more helpful. Her staff predicts that with these generally more positive attitudes, the success rate will be higher during the next quarter.

What Problems Arose While Doing the Work?

In many ways the problems section of a periodic report is more important than the section on work accomplished, because problems, if they exist, require management to make immediate decisions about how to solve them and get the project back on track, and then, perhaps, to make decisions about how to avoid similar problems on similar projects in the future.

The problems section requires analysis and decision making not only from the readers, but also from the writers. In fact, it is the job of the writers to help their readers make decisions about trouble spots in the projects they are reporting on; so they must be analytical and make decisions about what to include in this section. If a relatively minor problem has cropped up, say some procedural snare in the routing of information that was solved quickly and without implications for the future, writers should know not to include discussion of it. But if a procedure that has been followed for some time has become increasingly more burdensome as more work is accomplished or has become more complex—for example, the ways payments are made to vendors or consultants—then writers should analyze and describe the problem in detail: what has gone wrong, what is the source of the problem, and how has progress specifically and generally been affected?

But the analysis should not stop here. Good reporters of problems will also analyze and suggest possible solutions. This is very important for two reasons: it shows that the writers are doing their jobs responsibly and not expecting upper management to do their thinking for them, and it helps readers decide on a solution or on a plan of action more efficiently. Even if the ultimate solution is not one that writers suggest, readers at least have some options, so that they can better decide that something else needs to be done.

When planning what she would include in the problems section of her report to Elliston, Leah had a slightly different situation to analyze from the one she had in writing for EDUCARE's internal review. Since she did not see the static population or lack of aggressive recruitment of clients as real problems, even though she thought her readers would, she decided she could not reasonably discuss them as problems. If she did, she would have to suggest some solutions, like changes in methods of observation and referral, that she didn't believe in. The only legitimate problem, in her view, was the rate at which clients successfully left the program. She knew that rate could be higher, even though EDUCARE's success rate was comparable to several other programs of the same size. And further, she believed that the initiatives she and her staff had taken in group counseling would soon show more positive results.

She decided, then, to discuss the success rate as the main problem of this reporting period, and then to refer to the initiatives she had discussed in the work accomplished section as a solution already being tested. She could also project an increase in the success rate for the next quarter based on reports from her staff. In this way she would demonstrate that she had assessed the problem intelligently and was doing something reasonable about solving it. This would also leave room for the program officers at Elliston to suggest some fine-tuning of the initiatives, if they saw fit.

In summary, there are four things to remember about writing the problems section of a periodic report:

1. If a problem has already been solved, and it is not likely to become a problem again, it shouldn't be mentioned. Doing so just wastes time for both writer and reader.
2. If a problem exists that can be solved easily without other managerial intervention, it shouldn't be mentioned either. To do so would also waste the reader's time, and worse, would show lack of initiative on the writer's part.
3. If legitimate problems exist that impede the crucial work of the organization, they should be analyzed and described in detail: what needs to be done, how it should be done, who needs to do it, and when. If the solutions will cost additional money or take more time, a general statement outlining the additional costs and time should also be included.
4. If no problems exist, they shouldn't be created.

Is the Work on Schedule and within Budget?

If the work is on schedule and within budget, then a simple statement to the effect is all that is necessary for this section. But if work has fallen behind schedule or is likely to in the near future, or if costs are exceeding projections or are likely to in the near future, these realities should be part of the discussion of problems. Management appreciates as much honest troubleshooting as possible about cost and time so that disastrous consequences can be averted.

This section, then, should be reserved for how far the work has fallen behind or will likely fall behind, or for how much the budget has been exceeded or will likely be exceeded. Writers need to supply detailed statements, including time lines or budgets that compare the original projections for time and costs with those that are now in place or soon to occur. Refer to Chapter 4, pages 105 to 107, for a discussion of schedule graphics.

Although suggestions on how to minimize time and cost overruns should be part of the discussion of solutions in the problems section, amplifying them here in detail is a good idea. It not only will reinforce the discussion of problems, but also will allow readers who are most interested in time and costs to skim the problems section and get to the details of the overruns in this section.

Leah's situation with regard to costs and time is slightly different from others'. Since EDUCARE is wholly dependent on external funding to carry out its programs, it is also bound by negotiated contracts that stipulate exactly how much will be spent and in what areas, and how long the project will last. If Elliston agrees to pay $300,000 over a 2-year period, that is all it will spend in that time. Although it may agree to a new contract, that will have to be negotiated, and once it is agreed to, it allows for little or no flexibility.

Leah, then, does not have to worry much about this section of the periodic report, but writers in the private sector, who generate their own funds and can alter spending and schedules to meet contingencies they hadn't planned for, often find this section very important. They want to suggest reasonable alternatives to the original plan, to get the project back on track with as little disruption as possible. Thoughtful, careful analysis and appropriately addressing readers' concerns can do that.

What Work Has to Be Done in the Future?

Not only does management need to know what has gone on in the recent past, and what is going on in the present, it also wants projections about what will likely happen in the future. Since planning is of crucial importance to all organizations, the need to know about future activities and how they fit in with what has already happened is compelling. Writers should talk about the specifics of what will happen—what work has to be completed, who will do it, how it will be done—all with the general objectives of the entire project in mind.

For Leah, the task is fairly simple. She will talk again about the initiatives taken in group counseling, and suggest, based on further information she gets from her counselors and from clients, how the success rate can be improved. This discussion will include plans for changes in individual counseling sessions and staff development.

In these ways Leah thought she could bolster the success rate of her clients in the future. Her plan certainly makes good sense philosophically, and is probably practically sensible, but it will have to be tried, something that is within her abilities and resources, and something that she needs to lay out for both John Fiske's and Elliston's considerations in this section.

FORMAT AND SUBSTANCE OF A PERIODIC REPORT

Leah wrote her report in a format she and Elliston had agreed to in the past, but certainly it is not the only format that can be used. Often periodic reports are less formal than Leah's, especially to in-house recipients. In roughing out the draft, Leah was grateful that she didn't have to deal with the endless forms that government agencies, like Health and Human Services, required of their funded programs. There is generally no informal agreement on format when it comes to reporting for the government: format is described in minute detail, not allowing for the kind of narrative discussion that Leah felt more comfortable with.

SAMPLE PROFESSIONAL PERIODIC REPORT

Figure 5.2 is the rough draft of Leah Feldstein's periodic report to the Elliston Foundation on the activities of EDUCARE's drug rehabilitation program for the third quarter of 1991. Leah will send the report with a letter of transmittal (for more specific information on letters of transmittal, see Chapter 8) signed by John Fiske, even though Leah is the author of the report. She has also identified the report as a draft and has dated it. This will allow Fiske time to make changes before the report is due at Elliston, and more practically, it will help ensure that the report will not somehow be sent out in its present form, that is, without editorial review.

EXERCISES

1. You are a counselor on Leah Feldstein's staff at EDUCARE. She has asked you to help her plan the final quarterly report to Harper St. John at Elliston on the activities of EDUCARE's drug rehabilitation program. You are at the end of the second month of the quarter, so you are certainly able to comment on your own activities for the period and for the year, but you need to talk to your colleagues about their activities. You decide to get together with two or three others to discuss what the report should contain.

Given your knowledge of what was said in the last quarterly report, decide, with others, what the final report should discuss. Be sure to think about the basic elements of a periodic report: work accomplished, problems encountered, and the future, given what you think the future might hold. An outline of the contents of the report should be the result of your discussions.

2. Put yourself in Harper St. John's position at the Elliston Foundation. You receive periodic reports from many programs reporting on their activities and have to evaluate and make judgments on them all. You want to do the best job as easily

Figure 5.2
*Leah Feldstein's
periodic report*

*This first material is
the orienting informa-
tion. Because John
Fiske, the Executive Di-
rector, is the signer of
the report, Leah shows
his office as the report's
origin. Other informa-
tion designates the
period of reporting, the
recipient, and the pro-
ject name and contract
number. All of the iden-
tifying information
shown is necessary, be-
cause organizations like
Elliston fund numerous
projects and need to be
able to draw up infor-
mation from their files
quickly and accurately.*

*The summary of project
activities lays out all
the significant activities
of the period. As is true
of all conclusive sum-
maries, this one will
allow readers to make
decisions about how the
project should proceed,
whether new directions
need to be taken,
whether existing direc-
tions need to be
bolstered, whether ev-
erything should remain
basically as it is estab-
lished. In solving the
rhetorical problem of
writing any report, but
perhaps especially of a
periodic report, a con-
clusive summary anti-
cipates questions read-
ers will have and al-
lows them to decide
whether the project is
meeting the goals as set
out in a proposal or
through other less
formal means.*

EDUCARE, INC.

1200 STONE WAY, SUITE 500   SEATTLE, WA 98706   206-457-7789   FAX: 206-345-9900

OFFICE OF THE EXECUTIVE DIRECTOR

DRAFT—MARCH 15, 1991
THIRD QUARTERLY REPORT—JANUARY-MARCH, 1991—TO
THE JOHN T. ELLISTON FOUNDATION ON
PROGRAM DRUGFREE, EDUCARE, INC.

Project

EDUCARE, Inc., Seattle, WA, Drug Rehab, E11 DRA x15-023

Period Covered

Third Quarter, January-March, 1991

Summary of Project Activities for the Period

Program Drugfree is making the kind of progress projected for this
quarter. And in an attempt to boost our success rate, we have begun two
changes that affect both clients and staff. Group size has been reduced
and frequency of meetings has increased. Since we retain the same number
of counselors, we have rearranged their coverage so that each counselor
now meets on the average two groups, twice a week, for an hour each
session. Counselors have found these smaller group meetings to be
positive. In general, the sessions are more client-directed than
counselor-directed.

The cumulative success rate has remained at 27% for the third quarter,
but the positive responses to the new initiatives in group counseling
encourage us to think that the rate will increase to 38% next quarter.

The staff is considering two other modifications to the program:
additional client-directed individual counseling sessions and increased
staff development. An additional individual session per month would be
directed mainly by clients and would focus on role playing. In staff
development, the staff plans to meet weekly instead of every 2 weeks,
devoting the additional time to reviewing new findings in the field and
reporting on professional meetings. We hope in this way to improve our
service to EDUCARE's clientele.

Figure 5.2
(Cont.)

The first paragraph reviews the highlights of the period, establishing (or reestablishing) some of the basics of their work: how many clients they see, how often, where, and for how long. She also is sure to reiterate that the primary areas of concern in their individual counseling approach remain the same. Thus, she continues to orient the readers to a context that might be difficult to remember otherwise.

The remaining paragraphs of this section lay out the new approach to group counseling. Keeping her audience in mind, and the problem they may see with client-counselor ratios, Leah is quick to point out that the new arrangement requires about twice the time of each counselor for group counseling.

In paragraph three Leah details the configuration of the new groups, which on the surface might seem unnecessary. Since this is a new arrangement, she wants to show that the configuration was based on good theory; familiarity and friendship are effective means of getting people to open up, to say what they have to say without embarrassment or intimidation.

Leah talks in paragraphs four and five about how meeting more often and in smaller groups has encouraged more open responses from clients, making

Work Accomplished

Individual and Group Counseling

The drug rehabilitation counseling staff of EDUCARE, Inc., has continued to meet regularly in both individual and group sessions with 152 registered clients. The individual sessions have been conducted, as usual, both in the schools and in the four outreach centers in Seattle and larger King County. They continue to stress the four primary areas of concern: family relations, relations with friends, relations with persons of authority, and self-esteem building. Clients still meet counselors individually at least four times a month for an hour each time.

The conduct of group sessions has changed, however. Instead of meeting once a week in groups of 10-12, the groups have been reduced in size to no more than seven clients, and they meet usually twice a week. This means that we have had to rearrange counselor coverage so that each counselor now meets, on the average, two groups, twice a week, for an hour each session. Accounting for preparation and debriefing time, counselors are now spending an average of 7 hours a week on group counseling, roughly twice what they were spending under the old plan.

In devising the new plan for group counseling, we took special care not to break up the old groups arbitrarily. We took into account friendships or good relations that seemed to have been formed among clients, and no individual has been reassigned to a smaller group made up totally of relative strangers. We have also tried to keep the same counselors for the new groups: in every case at least half the group has worked with the same counselor in the past. These measures reassure us that clients' useful contributions to group discussions will not be unduly restrained.

In general, we have retained the format and content of group sessions. Each session is based on a theme derived from one of the four counseling areas mentioned above. But the additional meeting per week allows for more immediate reinforcement or continuation of discussion that may have been artificially abbreviated under the old plan.

Counselors have found that clients are in general more forthcoming in the smaller groups. They tend to talk more, more specifically, and to the point. The greatest, most positive change, all counselors agree, is that clients are directing their comments more often to each other, and not strictly to the counselor. Discussions have become friendlier, more expansive, and more spontaneous; the general atmosphere has become more client-directed, and less counselor-directed. Instead of saying what they think the counselor wants to hear, clients are now saying what they want to hear from themselves and from others, and are comparing and contrasting their experiences, failures, and successes. One counselor reported recently that in a discussion of relations with parents, her clients seemed to have forgotten her, and that there was so much talk back and

Figure 5.2
(*Cont.*)

their experiences more client-directed than counselor-directed: a distinct and sound goal of the program, in both EDUCARE's and Elliston's eyes.

Her concluding paragraph for this section does what all good conclusions do. It looks ahead, inviting the readers to think of possibilities that lie beyond the scope of the report.

The success rate is important for Leah to discuss. It is something the project must look out for and something the readers of her report at Elliston will want to know about.

She talks about the "slips" in clients' performance outside the program, specifying what happened to them and their decisions to return to the program. She even tries to inject a little humor (although understated and dry), recounting one client's substitution of marijuana for crack and the results: he reported that "he was feeling better," but he "was also invited to return to the program."

Leah sums up the current client enrollment and the success rate in percentages for at least 90 days. She also mentions, however, and this is important, that she sees the new initiatives as promising improvements in the success rate. She wants to put the best face forward on the

forth among the members of the group that she could barely get a word in edgewise. She said, "I felt left out, rather useless, but I was thrilled. My clients got more said, and in more particular and articulate ways, than they had said in all sessions in the last 2 months."

Counselors have also reported from individual sessions that clients like the intimacy of the new group sessions, that they feel less shy and more willing to take part, and that they actually look forward to meeting twice a week with their groups. Though many admit that their individual battles with drug abuse have not yet been won, the same number agree that they are more able and willing to discuss their battles, and that in itself has given them greater confidence that they will eventually win.

Success Rate

We have moved clients out of the program successfully at about the same rate as last quarter. In the first third of the quarter, twenty-eight clients left the program with staff consent and approval. Follow-up interviews, conducted 1 month and 2 months later with clients, teachers, parents, and other social service workers indicated that twenty-three clients had remained free of drugs. Five had slipped "once or twice," but showed no recurring habitual pattern. And three who had slipped often and were returning to habitual patterns were invited to come back to the program. Two have returned within the last 10 days.

In the second third of the quarter, twelve clients left the program with staff consent and approval. Follow-up interviews with all concerned indicated that nine have remained drug-free; two have slipped once or twice, and one reported that he had substituted marijuana for crack and was feeling much better. He was also invited to return to the program.

The percentage who have left the program unsuccessfully, that is, without staff consent and approval, and who, again with information from follow-up interviews, we believe to remain on drugs, stays at about 9%.

With returnees and new clients, current enrollment is 152, and the success rate remains, as it had for the second quarter, at about 27% for those who have been in the program for at least 90 days. But we believe that with the initiatives we have taken in group counseling, the success rate will increase. The change in attitudes toward counseling in general has been oustanding. Clients are particularly pleased that they are able to feed back information from their group sessions to their individual sessions, not only because they feel a new comraderie and openness with their fellows in the groups, but because they are also usually dealing with the same counselors; they don't have to start from the beginning—most of what they think about and understand about their problems with drugs has already been brought up and discussed in some way.

On the basis of this, counselors now predict an increase in our success rate. They have identified nineteen clients beyond those who would normally leave successfully who will be ready to leave the program successfully in the next quarter. That, with the cumulative 21-month

Figure 5.2
(*Cont.*)

work of the period and show that there is promise for the future.

In the problems section Leah identifies the problem she is willing to admit is a problem. She does not mention client-counselor ratios or recruitment, issues Elliston may want to consider problems, but she does not. She is specific about dates and figures, but she is quick to predict how the problem may be solved with the new group counseling procedures. She suggests that the predicted success rate of 38 percent is one that Elliston would be pleased with.

In the second paragraph she begins to discuss other measures she thinks will help improve the success rate.

The other measure responds to another problem, counselor stagnation, certainly related to the success rate, but perhaps more indirectly. The staff's decision to meet more often and to devote the additional time to discussing developments in the field is both a good idea for the obvious benefits that can accrue, but also as a demonstration of the staff's commitment to the program. This change in priorities Leah hopes will positively impress her readers and perhaps effectively reduce criticism of client-counselor ratios and unaggressive recruitment.

success rate factored in, would raise our success rate to almost 38%, an 11% increase in the rate we have been achieving, and substantially more than the rate for other programs of our size.

Problems Encountered

Our modest success rate remains our biggest problem. Though the rate has increased from 21% in the first quarter of 1990 to 27% in the first quarter of 1991, it has remained at 27% for the last two quarters. But as we have indicated, new group counseling procedures have already had a positive impact, based to date on observation and anecdotal evidence. We look forward with confidence to the next quarter when we think we can expect the rate to increase to as much as 38%. Though 38% is still not ideal, it is a respectable and encouraging figure, and if it can be gradually improved, the program will have met the long-term objectives that were set at the beginning of the funding period, and will have exceeded the quarterly objectives by 2%.

The staff is currently considering two other modifications to procedures that are likely to have a positive effect on the success rate. The first has to do with individual counseling sessions. We are thinking of adding one session per month, either at the beginning or at the end of the month, depending on scheduling needs, that will be almost entirely client-directed. Clients will choose from the previous month's discussions a topic that they want to pursue further. The topic can have anything to do with the four major areas of concern: family, friends, authority figures, or self-esteem, but clients are supposed to ask of counselors the same kinds of questions normally asked of them. Counselors will respond in ways that their clients would: sometimes reticently or incompletely, sometimes volubly or expansively. The point is to allow clients to ask their own questions and to receive the kinds of responses that they themselves are likely to give.

This kind of exchange has been suggested as a way for clients to investigate areas of insecurity or indecision in their own thinking and to see how adults, who have no familial or other extra-therapeutic ties to them, respond to problems they feel and have confronted in their own lives. It is also a means by which clients are able to exercise some measure of control, something, we have always known, clients lack and sorely feel the need of.

The other change has to do with staff development. Though we conduct staff meetings weekly, the time is usually spent discussing administrative and procedural matters: revising schedules, reporting on meetings with school officials or other social service agencies, and documenting clients' progress. Little time is spent discussing the theoretical or practical approaches to drug counseling, or the results of professional meetings staff members have attended. The result is a certain stagnation and lethargy in our thinking.

Figure 5.2
(Cont.)

The schedule and budget information speaks for itself, and the plans for the future are itemized, specific, and clearly connected to what has already been discussed. There can be no questions about what is supposed to happen, including EDUCARE's intentions to seek additional funding, clearly something Leah and EDUCARE want Elliston to look upon favorably.

> To correct this situation, we have decided to devote at least one meeting a month to seminar discussions, reviewing new findings and happenings in the field and suggesting how they might be applied to EDUCARE's clientele. This will add no additional hours to already full schedules, and the staff has agreed that the active exchange of ideas, in an arranged setting, will be beneficial.
>
> ### Schedule and Budget
>
> The project remains within the contractually set limits of schedule and budget.
>
> ### Plans for the Next Quarter
>
> While plans for the next quarter have been detailed in other sections of this report, the following summary lists them.
>
> 1. We will continue the initiatives taken in group counseling to boost our success rate to 38%.
> 2. We will begin additional individual counseling sessions that will be more client-directed than counselor-directed.
> 3. We will increase the number of staff meetings from twice a month to four times a month, with at least one of the meetings devoted strictly to reviewing findings and developments in drug counseling.
> 4. In addition to a discussion of how these program changes have worked, we will produce a final report on the activities of EDUCARE's drug rehabilitation program (HHS DRA x15-0023) for the funding period, 1990-91.
> 5. We will propose a renewal of the grant for the funding period 1992-93.

and efficiently as possible in the best interests not only of Elliston but also of the programs. You therefore look for and admire thorough but efficient reporting, because it makes your job easier and your work more effective.

Given what you know of the activities in drug rehabilitation that EDUCARE has taken on in the past, especially in the last quarter, what would you expect to read in the last report of the funding period? What would you expect to be able to do, given what you have read? An outline of the expectations should be the result of your thinking.

ASSIGNMENTS

1.   Your discussion group at EDUCARE has decided to write a memo to Leah Feldstein on its thoughts about what should be included in the final periodic report to Harper St. John at the Elliston Foundation. You want to make sure that you have represented your activities well, but that you also have taken into account the difficulties that normally arise in the course of your work. You also want to make some intelligent suggestions for the future. Write the memo to Leah, and send a copy to John Fiske, Executive Director of EDUCARE.

2.   As Chapter 8 discusses, people often write memos for purposes of documentation only; they are called memos "to file." Among other purposes, they serve as reminders of what has been done about a particular problem, how successful the action has been, what problems have arisen (and how they might be solved), and what needs to be done in the future.

Since EDUCARE is on the questionable list for renewed funding, Harper St. John wants particularly to document his reactions to what EDUCARE has been doing to keep to the goals that both EDUCARE and Elliston have agreed to for *Program Drugfree*. That way St. John can call up the information on EDUCARE quickly, and determine more efficiently whether continued funding is in order.

Assuming Harper St. John's position, write his memo to file.

TERM PROJECT OPTION

Write a periodic report on the project you are currently working on. It should be directed to the same audience who received your proposal. Remember to make your report conclusive and appropriately explanatory about the significance of the actions you have taken. After you have drafted the report, edit it once for passives and nominals, which tend to abound in periodic reports. Refer to the Appendix on selected problems of usage and style if you aren't clear about these constructions.

January 13, 1991
7:30 A.M.

Patricia Wynjenek's Office
Department of Anthropology
Hastings University
Las Palmas, New Mexico

Patricia Wynjenek felt good. She had recently returned from a highly successful sabbatical leave to the Mexican-American border, specifically to Indigo, Texas, where she had studied economic survival strategies of low-income Mexican Americans. She had chosen Indigo because it is unique among border cities of its size (100,000) or larger. It is 93 percent Mexican-American, is in general politically and commercially run by Mexican Americans (not Anglos, as is the case with most other border cities), and has the lowest per capita income of any city in the United States. Yet the problems of crime, drug abuse, and family disintegration that plague most other urban areas are greatly diminished in Indigo. It is an area that needed to be studied, both to determine the factors that make it unique, and to suggest social policies and programs that the state and federal governments might adopt to serve more effectively their poorest citizens.

As is typical of many anthropologists (and many other academicians), Patricia's sabbatical was partially funded by outside sources—government agencies and private foundations, who have interests in the kind of work she does. One such group, Las Almas Buenas Foundation, which is particularly concerned with medical problems and access to medical facilities among Mexican Americans, had funded 25 percent of her expenses while she was in the field. She needed now to report finally on her findings of how low-income Indigoans use and pay for medical facilities to treat ailments and stay healthy.

Patricia felt pretty confident that she could report intelligently. She had collected a lot of good information on health care practices in Indigo, had analyzed it, and thought she was able to draw some meaningful conclusions. She actually felt not only confident, but also pleased about the report she would write. Her contact at Las Almas Buenas, Dolores Sanchez, had written her to suggest the form her completion report might take. Even though Dolores had received periodic reports from Patricia on her work in Indigo, she wanted a final report that would appeal to the Board of Directors of Las Almas Buenas, a report that would lay out specific information in terms that they could understand. That meant she would have to repeat information that Dolores and other readers of her periodic reports had already read. But in so doing, Patricia could write the report for a broader, professional journal-reading audience, who would need the background information.

Patricia saw the possibility of meeting the needs of two situations with one report, an efficiency she was rarely able to practice, but one that she was eager to try. She sat down at her computer to start writing the report with more enthusiasm than she could remember having for such jobs in a long time.

FUNDAMENTALS OF A COMPLETION REPORT

Purpose and Rationale

There are basically two kinds of completion reports: those written for an audience in the private sector (sometimes called final reports) and those written for a more academic, research-oriented audience (sometimes called research reports). They both fulfill the same purposes:

- To define and/or address professional problems
- To explain what work was done to solve or address the problems
- To conclude what the work ultimately means
- To make recommendations for future work, if necessary

Although completion reports can take different forms, the rhetorical basis for them is the same. Someone who has been principally responsible for work on a specific project needs to report on what has gone on, why it has gone on, what the results were, and what the results mean; and someone closely interested in the work, usually a managerial audience, needs to know the same. Just as they do with periodic reports, the rhetorical concerns on both sides of completion reports—writer and reader—readily coincide.

The important difference to remember between completion reports and periodic reports is that the work for better or for worse has come to an end by the time a completion report is written. The goals of the project may or may not have been met, and there may be more that can be done in the future, but the immediate need is to report on the end, or completion, of the project. Both writers and readers need to tie things up to see the end of something and perhaps to see the beginning of something new. The process allows for a certain orderliness in the conduct of anyone's business.

This difference thus implies the final rhetorical element in the need for completion reports. Completion reports are written to document the activity of special projects; they are not written to document the course of everyday business. If a software manufacturer regularly designs, upgrades, and markets software programs for the computer industry, the conduct of its business is documented in other ways: periodic reports on sales and relations with customers, performance reports on the technical workings of programs and packages, and annual reports both to upper management and to stockholders. Only when particular work is thought of as contained by time, as finite, and when certain special expectations are established and work has been performed to fulfill them is there need for a completion report. Thus, completion reports are appropriate for projects supported by grants, special assignments, temporary assignments, and replacement service, to name a few of the situations that apply.

171

QUESTIONS THAT COMPLETION REPORTS ANSWER

As in the case of a periodic report, the questions to ask when planning to write a completion report are simple and direct. The answers again will help determine the basics of the content. (See Figure 5.3.)

What Is the Problem? Why Does It Warrant Special Attention?

All organizations, both public and private, take on new initiatives, new programs, or new projects from time to time. They do so to keep current and/or competitive, and they understand that taking on something new is ultimately beneficial and productive, that without such moves, the business of the organization can stagnate.

Thus they have to consider new problems, define them, and build a case that defends the need to solve them. Any of the cases we have been looking at can serve as examples. When OUTERWARE, Inc., designed ENCONTRO (see Chapter 3), for instance, it had in mind a new, comprehensive system that would control ambient temperatures at any site from a central location. In a large and complicated physical setup like the capitol building in Hartford, controls like these are necessary, and they are within OUTERWARE's and the capitol building's capabilities. But as with all new design projects, close definitions of the need and the means (including methods, time, and costs) of problem solving have to be laid out carefully not only in proposals, but also later in completion reports. The element that needs to be added in completion reports is the results of the work: what actually happened, what it means, and how it coincides with the goals of the project. Only then can a system or program be replicated and marketed, sold, and installed for other customers on a continuing basis, the work no longer requiring documentation through completion reports, but perhaps through periodic or performance reports.

Figure 5.3
Questions to ask and answer to define the contents of a completion report

QUESTIONS THAT COMPLETION REPORTS ANSWER

- What is the problem?
  Why does it warrant special attention?

- What work was done?
  How was it done?
  What in general were the results?

- What conclusions can be drawn from the work that was done?
  How can the data be interpreted?
  What decisions, if any are necessary, can be made given what is now known?

But the problems that are the proper subject of completion reports are not limited to those involving design and marketing of a new product or service. They may also have to do with theoretical issues of research that when subjected to various laboratory or fieldwork experimentation and study suggest answers to problems that are yet to be fully tested. The anthropologist, Patricia Wynjenek, who has identified the severe economic problems of U.S. urban populations living along the border of Mexico and the United States, thinks it necessary to determine how those populations get along. She wants to study survival strategies—the means by which impoverished urban populations use the infrastructure of the community, both public and private, to overcome severe economic handicaps.

Patricia may be funded by some group like the National Science Foundation (NSF) for the general research she does or by private groups like Las Almas Buenas Foundation (LAB) for the practical implications her work would have. Supported by funds provided, she lives among the people she is studying, participates in and observes the life of the community, and with the help of local people, conducts surveys of area residents about the ways they survive economically.

Her ultimate analysis of the problem and her suggestions for better social programs become the necessary substance of a completion report directed to those who have funded her. The problem is identifiable, the time for its solution is finite, and NSF or LAB wants to know the results and whether its money has been spent wisely. After the completion report she might also prepare a report, with a different format but essentially the same substance, to be published in a professional journal, so that she can reach a larger, academic audience with her findings.

What Work Was Done? How Was It Done? What in General Were the Results?

Readers of completion reports want to know specifically what kind of work was done and how it helped solve or address the problem defined by the project. Also, and especially true of completion reports that later will also serve as academic reports on research, readers want to know how the work was done—specifically, the methods, materials, and conditions under which the work was performed. This permits readers to analyze and evaluate the results in light of how they were achieved, thus allowing a closer scrutiny of the reporter's interpretation of them.

In the case of OUTERWARE's installation of ENCONTRO for the capitol building in Hartford (discussed in Chapter 3), upper management wants to know how the design of the program was adapted to fit the capitol building's needs—what assessments of present systems for environmental control and physical inspections took place and how existing computer facilities were adapted to accommodate the new system. It wants to know what training and orientation were necessary for the capitol building personnel to get the new system up and running. Finally, it wants to know what problems arose in doing the work, whether and how they were solved, and what predictions for the success of future work of a similar kind can be made.

The case of Patricia Wynjenek is similar. She needs to report on the ways she determined that segments of populations in urban border cities would be observed and surveyed, how the samples of population would be made up, who would do the surveying and why, what the protocol for surveying would be, and what results were expected. These goals require explanations of the various parameters: the kinds and frequency of participant observation (meetings, social gatherings, informal contacts), the number of respondents to the survey (including how they were chosen—at random or by stratification as to age, gender, and other demographic characteristics), the same kind of demographic description of the surveyors, the questions that were included in the survey, and the raw data by numbers and percentages that resulted from the answers to the survey questions.

For both cases, the answers to these questions map out the work that was done and show how it was done, so that readers can begin to determine whether the conclusions of the report seem reasonable, given the methods of collecting the data. The ultimate validity of interpretation is a separate issue.

What Conclusions Can Be Drawn from the Work That Was Done? How Can the Data Be Interpreted? What Decisions, if Any Are Necessary, Can Be Made Given What Is Now Known?

The answers to these questions form the third element of the rhetorical basis for the completion report. It is the most important because it explains the significance of the work. Without an educated evaluation of what the work accomplished means, organizations can't know whether directions they are taking make sense, whether they are effective, or whether they can be made effective. Upper management makes important decisions based on information provided in this area—decisions that affect not only the conduct of business, but also the future of research. These decisions need to be made, if solving problems through good analysis is going to continue to be effective.

OUTERWARE, therefore, uses Mary Anne Cox's interpretation of how ENCONTRO has worked at the capitol building in Hartford to make decisions about similar projects. Understanding what went on, what problems arose, how they were solved—many of the same problems periodic reports discuss—and finally, what the whole project means for the present and future helps question and perhaps affirm basic directions of the company. Such activity also helps establish initiatives and new directions for the future.

The same is true of Patricia Wynjenek's work. Her understanding and discussion of the dynamics of economic survival along the Mexican-American border is important in two ways: it helps fill out the knowledge of Mexican-American culture, the fastest-growing minority group in the United States today, especially as it exists in border areas; and it suggests ways that social programs might be made more responsive to the needs of those they are supposed to serve.

FORMAT AND SUBSTANCE
OF A COMPLETION REPORT

As we have indicated, completion reports are written for special purposes, purposes that go beyond the conduct of everyday business, and they therefore require some special treatment. The quality of the production is dependent on several factors: time, costs, and of course purposes for which the reports are written. They are often specially printed, complete with four-color graphics and illustrations, and bound. The binding can range from three-hole ring binding to sewn book binding; again the method of binding is dependent on resources and on the purpose of the report.

Although the four points in rhetorical problem solving—purpose, audience, context, and ethical stance—are the most important elements to consider in any technical and professional writing, different formats are helpful to define and organize those rhetorical elements. We suggest two generic formats for completion reports; these elements can be used in the absence of formats supplied or required by those who have called for the reports. The first format would be appropriate for a report written for private agencies, government, or industry—a nonacademic audience; the second, for an academic, research-oriented audience. (See Figure 5.4.)

Elements of the Format for a Nonacademic Audience

Letter of Transmittal

The letter of transmittal records the production and delivery of the entire finished report. (For a full discussion of letters of transmittal, refer to Chapter 8.) If the

Figure 5.4
Elements included in a completion report for a nonacademic audience

Format of a Completion Report for a Nonacademic Audience

- Letter of Transmittal ——————————————— separate from the document

- Cover
- Title Page
- Acknowledgments
- Executive Summary
- Table of Contents
- Introduction   complete document
- Analysis and Discussion
- Conclusions
- Recommendations
- Works Cited
- Appendixes

report is intended for an internal audience, one within the organization the author works for, the letter may be written as a memo, but if the report is being sent to an external source (in Patricia Wynjenek's case, for instance, Las Almas Buenas Foundation) it is written in conventional business letter format. The letter formally identifies the report, reiterates why the report was written (including reference to any contractual obligations), and often summarizes the highlights of the work that was done and the main conclusions that were drawn. If the report's organization or structure departs from what would normally be expected, the letter identifies the departures. It also identifies any discrepancies between work proposed and what was actually produced.

Writers usually close letters of transmittal with an invitation to the reader to comment on the report and some indication that they look forward to continued interaction and service in the future.

As we have also indicated in Chapter 8, the letter of transmittal includes a list of those to whom copies of the report have been sent. The list may be short—only those who have a vital interest in the report—or it may be long, including those who have vital interest and those, who by virtue of their position or as courtesy dictates, should get a copy. The author of the report has to decide, in keeping with the purpose of the report and with protocol, who will receive copies.

One structural element in the production of the report is good to remember. As noted above, completion reports are often specially printed and bound. Annual reports to stockholders are a good example, because they go out to a wide variety of readers. The letter of transmittal is not normally bound with the rest of the report; it is attached to (or covers) the report; thus another term for a letter of transmittal is the *cover letter*.

Cover

The cover of the report, no matter the range of appropriate production styles available, must contain some basic information: the title of the report, sufficiently descriptive of the contents; the name and corporate address of the author or the group that produced the report; and the date. Sometimes the name of the primary recipient of the report is also included. Cover graphics, if appropriate, should also suggest the basic purpose of the report and reflect the desired corporate image of those who have produced it.

Title Page

The first page of the report is the title page. It contains the title of the report (exactly as it appears on the cover), the name and address of the recipient, the author's or originating organization's name and corporate address, and the date. No graphics are expected or necessary, but convention nevertheless calls for a title page. It reflects the formality of the report and helps identify what the report is, if for some reason parts of it get separated.

The title page shows no pagination, but it is often counted as the first of the total number of pages of front matter, that is, material that precedes the main substance of the report.

Acknowledgments

If writers of completion reports have received extraordinary help from others to write the report, they should acknowledge that help formally. But it is important to understand what extraordinary help is. If people go out of their way to supply information or are consulted on matters that lie within their knowledge and expertise, but go beyond their usual structural and professional responsibility to supply that information, they should be acknowledged.

Most completion reports written in the corporate sphere involve the help of those who are expected to supply it. It is a part of their professional responsibilities, and they supply information routinely. They need not be acknowledged formally; in fact, to do so would look silly. Acknowledgments should be reserved for those special cases of extraordinary help.

Under these circumstances, readers expect to know in what areas the help came. Therefore, it is customary to specify not only the person(s) who supplied the help, but what kind of help it was: "For her help in suggesting appropriate investment strategies for the coming year, I must thank Jane Drussel of Smithson and Company, Toledo, OH."

If an acknowledgment page is included, it is counted in the total number of pages of front matter and paginated with a lowercase Roman numeral either (i) or (ii), depending on whether the title page is also counted in the total number of pages of front matter. The numeral is placed either in the bottom center of the page or in the upper right-hand corner.

Executive Summary

The executive summary is an abridged version of the whole report. Because decisions, even if they are preliminary, are often made on the basis of summaries, they need to be conclusive rather than simply descriptive. Conclusive summaries tell the whole story in brief: what was the problem, how it was approached or solved, what conclusions were drawn, and what recommendations were made. Relative to the length of the whole discussion, it is fairly short, usually running no more than 500 words (about two double-spaced pages), but it can run as long as 10 percent of the original.

Since the executive summary is a condensation of the entire report, it should be one of the last parts written. It is also considered front matter, and is paginated in lowercase Roman numerals.

Table of Contents

For longer reports a table of contents is absolutely necessary. It shows the contents and organization of the report, allowing the reader to turn immediately to specific pages to read different parts of the report at will. It is usually written to the second level of specificity: section headers and major headers within sections.

The table of contents includes lists of appendixes and sometimes lists of figures or illustrations. If the lists of figures and tables don't appear in the table of contents, they should appear separately with their own headers. Lists of figures

177

and the like appear immediately after the table of contents. The table of contents does not list material preceding it, such as the title page.

The table of contents is paginated as other front matter with lowercase Roman numerals. Like the executive summary, it is one of the last parts of the report to be written. Authors should wait until all changes have been made in the report before adding page numbers; otherwise they may simply have to do it again.

Introduction

The introduction educates and prepares readers for what is to come in the report. It outlines the purpose and scope of the report and provides background material so that readers can read the discussion intelligently.

The introduction is clearly very important. Beyond the executive summary, it is the first substantive piece in the report, and as such, it needs to lay out the reasons for the report, how it should be used, and any particular information necessary to place the subject and purpose of the report into a larger context.

The section can be headed "INTRODUCTION," in all-capital letters and centered as a major heading, or may be called something else, as long as the heading clearly identifies the material that follows as introductory. The heading, whatever it is, should follow the title of the report (this is the third time, if covers are used, that the title appears).

Pagination of the main body of the report, as separate from the front matter, begins with the first page of the introduction, but it is customary not to show a numeral on the first page. Therefore, Arabic numerals begin to appear in the upper right-hand corner of the second page: 2. Pagination continues throughout the body of the report, through any appendixes and the index (if one is necessary).

Analysis and Discussion

The analysis and discussion form the main narrative of the report and provide all the data, evidence, and interpretation needed to show the following:

- What the authors were trying to do
- Why they were trying to do it
- What they actually did
- What they found out
- What it all means
- What, if anything, the work implies for the future

The section is normally broken down into smaller units or topics for discussion, each given a descriptive header (or topical heading) to identify it. It is important that the breakdown be logical and consistent, showing a hierarchy of development. Since not all topics require equal billing or are themselves thought of as distinct subtopics of other larger topics, a series of major and minor headers should be established and then consistently used.

The choice of entering major headers in uppercase letters, as in

GENERAL USE OF MEDICAL FACILITIES ALONG THE BORDER

and of justifying (aligning) minor headers to the left-hand margin in upper- and lowercase letters, as in

Use of Conventional Facilities

is really up to the author. You will notice that the documents in this book use different systems of heading levels. Whatever system an author decides on should be clear to readers, and it must be used consistently throughout the report. To do so is rhetorically persuasive. It helps organize reading and thinking, and it allows, as is so important in technical and professional writing, retrieval of information in a nonlinear way.

Conclusions

Once again, in order to provide easy access to important parts of the report, conclusions, even though they may have been implied in the preceding analysis and discussion section, should be summarized in a separate section. Many the busy reader will read the executive summary, skim the introduction, and then turn directly to the conclusions to see what the authors have decided about the problem discussed in the report. Readers can then decide whether they need to fill themselves in on how the conclusions came about and read parts of the analysis and discussion at will.

Separating the conclusions from the analysis and discussion is a good idea not only for readers but also for authors. Authors, in summarizing conclusions in a separate section, are forced to look at the report as a whole and decide whether what they have implied as conclusions is reasonable. Writing a section on conclusions helps authors specify their thinking about the problem and its implications.

Recommendations

If the analysis and discussion and conclusions suggest that specific actions need to be taken, they should be presented separately as recommendations. They can be listed and enumerated or bulleted, but they need to be fairly specific as to how they would be carried out.

Vague notions of what should be done are of no use to most readers; they want and need the particulars, so that they can make decisions more easily. The finer details of a plan can be worked out later, but the basic outline of what needs to be done and why should be stated concisely.

Works Cited

Most completion reports require secondary sources of some kind. The material can be obtained from printed sources or from the personal commentary of people considered experts in the area the writer is investigating. In either case, courtesy and professional integrity require acknowledgment (or as it is often called, *citation*) of those sources. (A similar section, called "References Cited," is discussed in Chapter 4, page 106.)

The acknowledgment of printed sources is more formally prescribed. Not only must borrowed material (either quoted or paraphrased) be cited parenthetically in the text, but in addition, full information on the source of the material must be included in this section in a list, usually headed "Works Cited." The basics required are the bibliographic information: author's name (listed alphabetically by last name), title of the work, and publishing information (place of publication, publisher, and date). In the case of articles published in professional journals or in edited collections, inclusive page numbers in which the article appears are also provided. Citation styles vary from field to field and are often published in individual style sheets; writers should use the conventional citation style of the field in which they are reporting.

Citing information gleaned from personal interviews is less formally prescribed, but no less necessary. Writers often name the source in the text and parenthetically cite the place and date of the interview. Then, in this section, sometimes in a list separate from the printed sources, they include the name, position, and professional affiliation of the source; sometimes they repeat the date and place of the interview. This separate list is often headed "Other Sources."

Appendixes

An appendix (singular form) or appendixes or appendices (plural forms) are added-on pieces of information that enhance the presentation of the report but that are not absolutely necessary to readers' understanding it. They come at the end of the report and take the form of charts, tables, photographs, specifications, test results, or computer program printouts, sometimes with explanatory narratives. They are not included in the text because they are not immediately pertinent and would be disruptive to the arrangement and flow of the discussion.

Appendixes are meant to bolster the main discussion of the report and should not be thought of as a dumping ground for irrelevant data, impressive only as padding. If there is more than one appendix, each is individually lettered A, B, C, and so on, and titled:

APPENDIX A: CENSUS DATA ON USE OF MEDICAL FACILITIES
FOR AMERICAN-MEXICAN BORDER MUNICIPALITIES, 1990

or

APPENDIX B: CORRELATIONS BETWEEN NUMBER OF YEARS
OF FORMAL EDUCATION AND USE OF MEDICAL FACILITIES
AMONG AMERICAN-MEXICAN BORDER POPULATIONS

If there is only one appendix, it is simply labeled as such, with no A or B designations:

APPENDIX: CENSUS DATA ON USE OF MEDICAL FACILITIES
FOR AMERICAN-MEXICAN BORDER MUNICIPALITIES, 1990

Appendixes are paginated only if they are longer than one page. If, as in some cases, they are to be paginated separately from the rest of the text, the visible pagination begins with the second page and continues for the length of the appendix. The upper right-hand corner of the second page would show Appendix A-2, the third page, Appendix A-3, and so on.

Thus the basic format is complete; it organizes and explains the whole process of problem solving for any particular project from beginning to end. Although some organizations may design and require authors to use their own formats for writing completion reports, the format we have discussed above serves all the rhetorical needs of completion reports and may be used in the absence of company formats.

Elements of the Format for an Academic, Research-Oriented Audience

As suggested at the beginning of this discussion, completion reports are also often written for more academic, research-oriented audiences. Although the rhetorical needs are essentially the same, reports on research place more emphasis on two areas: the theoretical underpinnings and environment of the work and the methods and means used to carry out the work. Readers need this additional emphasis so that they can more completely assess and evaluate the reporter's interpretation and claims of significance for the work completed. (See Figure 5.5.)

The following format, similar to that of the completion report already discussed, is useful for reporting on primary research in a final, formal way. With

Figure 5.5
Elements included in a completion report for an academic, research-oriented audience

Format of a Completion Report for an Academic, Research-Oriented Audience

- Letter of Transmittal ——————————————— separate from the document

- Cover
- Title Page
- Acknowledgments
- Abstract
- Table of Contents
- Introduction
- Review of Literature
- Methods and Materials   complete document
- Results
- Discussion
- Summary and Conclusion
- Works Cited
- Appendixes

some modifications it may also be used for articles intended for publication in professional journals. We have noted, when appropriate, the differences between this format and that of the completion report outlined and explained above.

Letter of Transmittal, Cover, Title Page, Acknowledgments

In general, the front matter for a research report is handled the same way it is in the nonacademic completion report. But if the report is being submitted to a journal as an article for possible publication, the cover and title page would be eliminated, and the letter of transmittal would be altered to reflect the difference in the author's purpose for submitting the report.

Abstract

The rhetorical purpose of abstracts is slightly different from that of executive summaries in that readers do not normally make decisions for subsequent action (except whether they might bother to read the report in the first place) based on the contents of the abstracts. Abstracts, however, still perform a summarizing function, and in that regard they should still be conclusive, stating the major conclusions of the work and their significance.

If a report is intended for publication in professional journals, authors may also be asked to list in their abstracts key words or phrases that will clue readers in to the kind of material covered in the report. These key words also help libraries index the report in automated databases. Abstracts are often published separately to help researchers narrow down a search for secondary material that will be helpful and pertinent to their own research. In Patricia Wynjenek's case, if she were submitting her report for publication, she might list the following key words or phrases: *poverty among Mexican Americans along the border; health care among Mexican Americans; economic survival strategies among Mexican Americans*. Researchers in any or all of these areas would then know that her article discusses in some way areas they are interested in.

Abstracts, like executive summaries, are supposed to be short—some say no more than 5 percent, others no more than 10 percent, of the length of the entire report—but many journals, particularly in the sciences and applied sciences, set arbitrary limits of from 150 to 200 words.

Table of Contents

The table of contents, including lists of figures and appendixes, is presented in the same way as it is for nonacademic completion reports. But the table of contents is not included if the report is being submitted as an article to a journal.

Introduction

The introduction serves the same purpose as it does for the nonacademic completion report. It discusses the purpose and objectives of the research, some background, and the scope or limitations of the report. If the plan of development and the arrangement of the report are unconventional, the introduction explains them.

Review of Literature

The review of literature is the first additional section required of research reports; generally, it is not required of nonacademic completion reports. As is true of the review of literature written for proposals (see Chapter 4, pages 95 to 96, for a detailed discussion of the review of literature), the purpose of the review is to place the writer's work in a larger theoretical context of work already done, or being done, in the field. Readers want to know how the writer's work has been influenced by, or will influence, other similar work done in the field in order to understand more completely the writer's interpretations of and conclusions about his or her own work.

In reviewing others' work, however, writers shouldn't avoid differences in theoretical approach, methods, findings, interpretations, and conclusions. In fact, they are often the meat of meaningful discussion, but writers need to state specifically why other research may differ from their own. In this way, they can prepare readers even more thoroughly than they can in the introduction for what is to come later in the report.

Reviews of literature should also be thought of as expansions of the statement of the problem, the essential element of the introduction. It is important for writers of research reports to demonstrate that problems they address are not formed in a vacuum, that they are a part of a larger set of problems that people are trying to solve. The review of literature demonstrates this larger context.

Finally, writers should keep in mind (something also emphasized in Chapter 4) that the review is not merely an annotated bibliography. It is a *discussion* that must adhere to all the elements of development, coherence, and interpretation expected of any discussion. It shows ultimately that researchers have done their homework, and that they are aware of what is going in the field and how their own work fits into it. Research is now so specialized that writers must provide this context of previous research for their readers. Without the review of literature, it would be difficult for other specialists to appreciate what the writer has done.

Methods and Materials

The second additional section typical of a research report, but not of the non-academic completion report, is a discussion of methods and materials. This section allows readers to match methods and materials, or how the research was performed, with interpretations and conclusions to see whether they are reasonable. In some cases readers may want to replicate the methods and materials to see whether they come up with the same interpretations and conclusions.

To satisfy this need, writers must describe the conditions under which data were collected: the kind, setup, and operation of the equipment; the way results were recorded and analyzed; and the peculiar constraints of the method and operation of the research. This kind of description must thoroughly cover deviations from the conventional, explaining what they were and more important, why they were used.

Results

The results section in reports on primary research is very clear-cut. It lays out the recorded data, often in tabular form, of the investigation in question, accompanied by all necessary written explanations: prefaces, labels, and footnotes. When anomalies or peculiarities occur, those, too, are noted, but they are not usually explained in any detail, since it is still common practice to reserve interpretation for the next section.

Discussion

One of the most important sections of the primary research report, the discussion reviews, analyzes, and draws conclusions about the data presented in the results section. In essence, the discussion explains what the research has meant, given the context of which it is a part: it suggests, through the researcher's interpretation, what is now known that wasn't known before the research was done and assesses the significance of the new knowledge.

The discussion also explains any questions that the results may pose. Are there anomalies, irregularities, or blanks in the data? Were there recognized flaws in measuring and recording the data? If so, how do these problems affect the conclusions that have been drawn? It is important for the researcher to discuss these problems openly, rather than have a reviewer call them out, as if the researcher didn't know about them. Professionals understand that problem solving often yields unanticipated new problems, so there is no need to try to hide research problems.

Summary and Conclusion

Often, but not always, a separate section is reserved at the end of the report for writers to assess the significance and worth of their research. It is important here, as with any good conclusion, that there be some speculation about what the research implies for the future. Is more work of the same kind necessary? What more can be learned from additional research? Or should research in the same area take a different path? If so, why, and how would the path be defined?

Answers to questions like these help summarize and justify the work that was undertaken and suggest directions for related work.

Works Cited and Appendixes

Treatment of works cited and appendixes is virtually the same here as it is in the discussion of completion reports above. The only inhibiting factor has to do with space if the report is being submitted to a journal for publication. Often journals set strict word or page limits, and appended material would be the first to go in order to meet them.

SAMPLE PROFESSIONAL COMPLETION REPORT

Figure 5.6 is the rough draft of Patricia Wynjenek's completion report to Las Almas Buenas Foundation on the activities of her work in Indigo on economics and health care. She wrote it in the basic format of the second completion report discussed above, but one that could also serve for an article for possible publication in a professional anthropology journal.

Because precedent did not call for it in Las Almas Buenas's case, Patricia did not have the report specially printed and bound. After the letter of transmittal, the report begins with the title page and ends with conclusions and works cited. The report does not contain appendixes.

EXERCISES

1. Patricia Wynjenek's report to Las Almas Buenas is a combination of the two formats for completion reports outlined in this chapter. It does not take the exact form of the nonacademic completion report for government, corporate, or industrial groups; neither does it take the exact form of the report of primary research for academic groups. And yet the commentary has claimed the formatting and reporting successful. Do you agree?

Given Wynjenek's obligations to Las Almas Buenas and to another, later academic (and professional) audience, analyze specifically how the report is set up and whether it is successful in meeting the needs of both audiences and of Wynjenek herself. You will have to define what those needs are in each case.

Do this as a class or in small groups, and be specific in your analysis.

2. The kinds of completion reports discussed in this chapter are by no means the only ways of presenting the results of research. Several others, such as manuals, brochures, and pamphlets, can be the appropriate products of legitimate research; it all depends on the purpose of the research and the audience who will benefit from reading about it.

If your research calls for a different kind of final presentation, you should plan its formatting before the work is actually completed. To aid in this, go to the library and find at least two samples of final presentations that would be appropriate for the kind of research you are doing. Analyze them for how well they meet the needs of both audiences and writers. Consider not only what has been written but also how it has been presented, and then decide how the presentations may be adapted to fit your needs.

You may do this with others who are working on similar kinds of projects.

Figure 5.6
Patricia
Wynjenek's
completion report

The front matter of
Wynjenek's completion
report is conventional.
The letter of transmittal
identifies the report
(including the contract
number in the reference
line) and sends it to the
appropriate person at
Las Almas Buenas. It
summarizes briefly
Wynjenek's main con-
clusions, preparing the
reader for the executive
summary.

Patricia N. Wynjenek
Department of Anthropology
Hastings University
Las Palmas, NM 70812

January 16, 1991

Dolores Sanchez, Associate Director
Las Almas Buenas Foundation
1752 Alamo Drive
San Antonio, TX 68201
Re: LAB 990-30-01-15-90

Dear Ms. Sanchez:

Enclosed is my final report on health care practices among low-income
residents of Indigo, Texas. I have called it POVERTY, TRADITION, AND
HEALTH CARE: THE EXAMPLE OF A TEXAS BORDER CITY. It is the last of three
reports I have written for LAB, and it represents my final ideas and
conclusions on part of the work I did in Indigo from January to December,
1990.

I have found generally that the case of Indigo, in contrast to reports of
other Mexican-American communities, does much to reaffirm the diversity
of the Mexican-American population as a whole. Family size has decreased
dramatically in the last 20 years; modern or "scientific" medical care is
sought when available, but access to it is still restricted by economic,
bureaucratic, and professional barriers; and traditional healing
practices are well integrated with scientific ones. Decisions about
health care are based on perceived acuteness of condition, expense, and
failure of previously employed therapies.

I hope you find the report helpful and informative, and that perhaps I can
be of further service to LAB in the future. Please let me know if you have
any questions.

Sincerely,

Patricia N. Wynjenek

Patricia N. Wynjenek
Associate Professor

Encl.

cc: Gunther T. Eliot, Chair, Department of Anthropology
    Lois M. Charing, Dean, College of Arts and Sciences
    David J. Price, Provost

Figure 5.6
(Cont.)

The title page includes necessary identifying information: title, author, contract number, recipient, and date.

POVERTY, TRADITION, AND HEALTH CARE:
THE EXAMPLE OF A TEXAS BORDER CITY

Submitted to

Las Almas Buenas Foundation
1752 Alamo Drive
San Antonio, Texas

Submitted by

Patricia N. Wynjenek
Department of Anthropology
Hastings University
Las Palmas, NM 70812
(LAB 990-30-01-15-90)

January 16, 1991

Figure 5.6
(*Cont.*)

The acknowledgments section mentions the people who were of special help to Wynjenek in her work, and she makes sure to include those who supported her financially.

ACKNOWLEDGMENTS

For their enduring patience and good will, I thank first of all the people of La Fabrica. They put up with my intrusive presence and questions, because they are generous people and they thought that some good might come of my interruption of their lives. I sincerely hope it does.

I also have to thank personally Jose Vela and his family for their help, care, and friendship. Without them, I could not have survived, and without people like them, anthropologists like me could never complete the work they believe they are supposed to do. Along with Jose Vela and his family, I also need to thank, for their personal help, Maria Cortez, Magdelena Moreno, and Eduardo de Playa.

For their professional help, and also good friendship, I want to thank my colleagues at Hastings University, James Bowdle and Alan Littleton.

Finally, for their financial support and their intelligent professional assessment of my work, I thank Las Almas Buenas Foundation, the National Anthropological Society, and the Arts and Sciences Research Committee of Hastings University.

ii

188

Figure 5.6
(Cont.)

The executive summary is conclusive, not descriptive. Wynjenek mentions the four areas about which she was able to draw significant conclusions, but more important, she is sure to mention, or allude to, the reasons they are significant. This clues readers to the fact that Wynjenek's work has turned up new or different information about Mexican-American culture, and suggests those areas of the report readers may want to turn to for a full discussion.

Executive Summary

An investigation of the family planning and other health care practices of the residents of an impoverished barrio in the border city of Indigo, Texas, carried out via traditional ethnographic methods and the administration of a standardized, open-ended interview, yielded the following results:

1. Family size has decreased dramatically in the last 20 years. Despite unaltered adherence to the Catholic Church, women of childbearing age cite economic considerations for their choice to limit the size of their families.
2. The increased availability of modern, "scientific" medical care has greatly reduced reliance on *parteras*, or lay midwives, with generally, though not universally, beneficial results, and increased the frequency and timeliness of medical care generally. Access to medical care is still restricted by poverty and by governmental and professional bureaucracies.
3. Traditional healing practices continue to be employed in definable circumstances. They are well integrated with the resort to scientific medicine, and both traditional and scientific concepts of illness appear to be held without conflict. Decisions about health care are based on perceived acuteness of condition, expense, and failure of previously employed therapies.
4. These findings for Indigo, in their variation from the findings reported for other Mexican-American communities, reaffirm the diversity of the Mexican-American population as a whole.

iii

Figure 5.6
(Cont.)

The table of contents lists major and minor headings, so that readers can turn quickly to particular areas they may have interest in knowing more about. In fact, the main purpose of all front matter (with the possible exception of the acknowledgments) is to identify, summarize, and generally make it easier for busy readers to select parts of the report they consider of greatest interest and importance. This is one of the primary purposes of the kind of formatting we find in technical and professional writing: it allows efficient consideration of a document without requiring a complete linear reading from beginning to end.

CONTENTS

Acknowledgments ii

Executive Summary iii

Introduction

    Early Ethnographic Studies and Their Successors 1

    More Recent Studies 1

    Background of This Study 2

Availability of Health Care

    Indigo's Medical Establishment 3

    Mexican Alternatives to the Medical Establishment 5

Family Size

    Birth Rate 6

    Reasons for Limiting Family Size 7

Childbirth

    Access to Prenatal Care 9

    Traditional Midwives 10

Traditional Healing

    Home Remedies 12

    Traditional Healers 12

    Ambivalence and Integration 13

Conclusions 15

Works Cited 17

iv

Figure 5.6
(Cont.)

Wynjenek's introduction does what a good introduction should do. It provides the necessary background of what has been done in the area of study, who has done it, when, and what it means for the basis and purpose of her study. It essentially sets the scene and prepares the reader for an intelligent reading of the rest of the report.

Since Wynjenek does not include a separate review of literature (specified as appropriate for research reports in the second format discussed above), her specific references to older and more recent studies others have done help supply the kind of information a review of literature normally supplies.

POVERTY, TRADITION, AND HEALTH CARE:
THE EXAMPLE OF A TEXAS BORDER CITY

Introduction

Early Ethnographic Studies and Their Successors

Studies of health and health care among Mexican-American populations in the United States generally fall into two categories. The first, and by far the older, focuses on the culturally distinctive features of Mexican-American life, particularly the practice of *curanderismo* and other aspects of traditional healing. These studies include not only influential ethnographic works of the sixties and seventies, such as those of Madsen (1964, revised 1973), Rubel (1966), Warner (1977), and Achor (1978), but also more recent writings, some of them with an applied focus, that derive from the same tradition. Thus, Maduro (1983) in his discussion of *curanderismo* stresses the significance of "folk illness" in Latino cultures and the beliefs held by Latinos about the causes and treatments. McKenna (1989), in an analysis of the health care needs of elderly Mexican Americans that relies on studies dating from as early as 1951, refers to the "passivity," "passivistic-collectivistic value orientation" and "fondness for traditionalism" of the group under study. And in *Transcultural Concepts in Nursing Care* (1987), a textbook designed to introduce nurses and nursing students to the medical implications of cultural variation, Boyle and Andrews urge nurses to respect the culture-specific needs of many Mexican-American patients who seek "spiritual treatment" from *curanderos* and *espiritualistas*.

More Recent Studies

In contrast to the focus of the traditional and traditionally based studies cited above, new foci in studies of Mexican-American health and health care have emerged in the last decade. Scheper-Hughes and Stewart manifest at least two of these in their 1983 article, "Curanderismo in Taos County, New Mexico—A Possible Case of Anthropological Romanticism." Drawing on their own work among Spanish-Americans in rural New Mexico first studied by Saunders in 1954, Scheper-Hughes and Stewart found that in the 30 years since Saunders's report, health care practices of at least this population have changed greatly. In contrast to Saunders's finding of pervasive reliance on traditional concepts of health and illness and on traditional healers, Scheper-Hughes and Stewart conclude that "*most* Spanish-Americans of Taos County rely primarily on the same explanatory model as Anglos with regard to the definition of health and illness," and that "*curanderismo* in northern New Mexico today has moved from being a primary and important source of medical care to an alternative and very occasional source" (Scheper-Hughes and Stewart 1983:80).

Figure 5.6
(*Cont.*)

In addition to these specific findings, Scheper-Hughes and Stewart stress the need to acknowledge and explore the great diversity that exists within the Mexican-American population, rather than to lump together the rural, the urban, the economically secure, the poor, the minority and the majority populations. Indeed, calls for the recognition of Mexican-American diversity have become increasingly common and urgent in a variety of academic disciplines (see Winkler 1990).

An important trend in recent students of Mexican-American health and health care is the move away from a focus on distinctive subcultural variation to a more general demographic and epidemiological focus. Such studies do not aim at ignoring cultural variation where it has a demonstrable effect on the perception of illness or on health care decisions, but they point out that the health of Mexican Americans increasingly presents a profile that is not dramatically culturally distinctive. Rather, it is typical of the social class to which they belong. However, "since a large proportion of the Mexican origin population is poor, health problems which are associated with poverty are particularly important in the study of the health of this group" (Angel 1985:413).

A final topic, less frequently addressed, is what Foster (1987), in his examination of international health agencies, refers to as the "bureaucratic" issue. That is, to what extent are the perceptions of health care and the decisions relating to it the result, not only of subculture, social class, biology, and epidemiological risk factors, but also of the governmental and professional bureaucracies that deliver medical care?

Background of This Study

The following discussion explores these issues as they affect the low-income Mexican-American population of the border city of Indigo, Texas. Data are derived from ethnographic fieldwork (supported by Las Almas Buenas Foundation, the National Anthropological Society, and the Arts and Sciences Committee of Hastings University) conducted from May through December, 1990. Ethnographic fieldwork involved both traditional participant observation in a neighborhood in which I had lived and worked off and on over a period of 14 years, as well as the tape-recorded administration of an open-ended interview schedule by four local residents, who acted as research assistants. One hundred household heads, most of them women, were interviewed in Spanish. Addresses were chosen at random from a list of the slightly more than 300 houses in the neighborhood, which is referred to by the pseudonym of *La Fabrica*.

Indigo is an interesting choice for the exploration of factors involved in Mexican-American family size and other medical choices because of its extreme cultural conservatism. A city of roughly 100,000, Indigo is 93% Mexican-American, with an almost unbroken history of 250

She also mentions under the heading of the background of her study the basic methods she used: participant observation and interviewing. She says that the interview schedule (survey) was open-ended (questions not limited to a choice of possible answers) and specifies the way the interview was administered, including how many interviewers there were, how many people were interviewed, and how those people were chosen. She does not mention, perhaps because her audience would assume it, that not only the interviewers but also the interviewees were paid. Her introduction thus satisfies the

Figure 5.6
(*Cont.*)

need for information on methods and materials, suggested above as appropriate for reports on primary research.

The discussion is not headed "Discussion," but rather is divided from the beginning into four major areas of investigation with appropriate headings: "Availability of Health Care," "Family Size," "Childbirth," and "Traditional Healing." Each major area is then subdivided into smaller areas of interest and given a minor heading: "Indigo's Medical Establishment," "Mexican Alternatives to the Medical Establishment," and so on. In this way, Wynjenek has organized her discussion to present the overall problem as one that is naturally made up of distinct parts—parts that need to be analyzed and commented upon as they contribute to an understanding of the whole.

Using the first major area of discussion, "Availability of Health Care," as an example, we can see the three basic ways Wynjenek has researched and analyzed the problem. We see these ways repeated, more or less consistently, throughout the report.

1. She uses purely secondary material, often in the form of Census reports, to establish some of the basic facts of the problem: how many doctors and dentists practice in this city of 100,000, where and

years of economic solidarity and self-direction. Though the city has the lowest per capita income of any city in the United States, it also has an old, entrenched Mexican-American political, commercial, and professional elite. Except for its much larger sister city, Pollo Blanco, Naranjas, Mexico, directly across the international bridges over the Rio Grande, Indigo is isolated from any other settlement of more than a few hundred by 150 miles of scrub desert in every direction, and by the Texas system of independent county governments.

Availability of Health Care

Indigo's Medical Establishment

For a border community in Texas, Indigo enjoys good medical services. Though the city has only ten dentists for 100,000 inhabitants, it has sixty-five doctors, for a rate of 64.5 per 100,000 persons, a respectable showing in Texas. Indeed, Indigo has something of a local reputation as a medical center, and patients from rural towns as far as 80 miles away, as well as from Pollo Blanco and other, smaller Mexican settlements, often go to Indigo for medical care. The city has two hospitals, one of them a proprietary hospital in the new, wealthy suburb of Del Mar, which is never patronized by Indigo's poor. Faith Hospital, located in a central, impoverished barrio, is by far the larger of the two hospitals, and accepts medically indigent patients for emergency and urgent care.

In addition to private physicians, dentists, and hospitals, residents of Indigo have access to several neighborhood clinics. La Fabrica, the barrio in which I conducted the interviews cited in this paper, has its own modern clinic within easy walking distance of all houses in this awkwardly situated barrio, isolated from other parts of the city by a large web of railway tracks. The clinic offers routine well baby care, including immunizations; family planning services; and a drop-in clinic for general health care and referrals. It does not handle prenatal care, but it does offer some dental services. The residents of La Fabrica agitated for such a clinic for many years, and its realization, in Mexican colonial-style stucco, has been a source of pride and gratification to the whole barrio.

Aside from the official medical outlets described above, people in La Fabrica can patronize several other sources of health care. There are doctors, dentists, and pharmacies in Pollo Blanco; *parteras*, or lay midwives, in Indigo; and *curanderas*, or traditional healers, on both sides of the river.

Only 18 of the 100 barrio residents surveyed said that anyone in their households had ever visited a dentist in Indigo, and most of them noted that these dental visits had taken place at the clinic. Dental care has an extremely low priority in La Fabrica. Throughout the city it is common to see middle-aged and older people with missing or visibly decayed teeth.

193

Figure 5.6
(Cont.)

how they have been educated and trained, and how these compare with other figures.

Thus readers find out that the number of doctors, a rate of 64.5 percent per 100,000 persons, is "respectable" for Texas as a whole.

2. She uses primary information gleaned from interviews about the following topics: how many people (usually in raw numbers and percentages) use established medical facilities—doctors, dentists, hospitals, and neighborhood clinics; how often they use the facilities; how those who use them pay for them—(Medicare, Medicaid, private insurance, unassisted means). Wynjenek implies that those who must use unassisted means to pay for medical care rarely do, simply because they don't have the means.

3. She uses participant observation, reported anecdotally, to determine how various residents respond to the medical care available to them.

Thus readers are told that the private medical establishment, particularly, holds itself aloof from most of its patients; that patients have to wait long periods of time to see doctors; and that they often leave doctors' offices angry and frustrated, knowing very little more about what is wrong with them, or how they should go about making themselves better, than

Sixty-three respondents reported that someone in the household had visited a private doctor in Indigo. This group included all those respondents with Medicare (19%), Medicaid (12%), or medical insurance (11%), since these programs pay for office visits that many barrio residents cannot otherwise afford. Unless they have a longstanding relationship with a doctor, most barrior residents believe that they will be turned away if they cannot pay at once for physicians' office visits. While this is certainly true in some cases, it may not be true in others. It is, however, a pervasive view throughout South Texas, and is often responsible for the delaying of medical care.

Most of Indigo's physicians are Mexican-American and have been trained in Mexican medical schools. Many preserve a reserved, sometimes distant manner with their patients, speaking little to them and explaining less. Patients are often held to be too ignorant to understand details of their conditions and treatments and too irresponsible to arrive at the office at a specific time. Thus most doctors make no appointments, and patients often wait 2 or 3 hours or longer to see a doctor. After such long waits patients are angry and frustrated, feelings that are often intensified after they leave the office with diagnoses and advice they often fail to understand completely but are too intimidated to ask about. Rich or poor, Indigoans almost universally respect modern medicine, but many barrio residents are antagonistic toward Indigo's physicians. Thus even people whose economic resources are limited often seek medical care in San Antonio or Corpus Christi, each 150 miles away. Both cities have large Mexican-American populations, although the cities themselves are much more oriented to Anglo-American culture than Indigo. Still, many Indigoans believe that doctors outside Indigo, whether Anglo-American or Mexican-American, are likely to treat them with greater consideration and respect. One resident of La Fabrica, a middle-aged woman whose eye injury was misdiagnosed in Indigo as permanently incapacitating, now seeks all medical care in Corpus Christi. This not only represents a substantial investment in time and money, but also puts the woman, a dynamic and articulate force for barrio improvement, in a difficult and demeaning position. Since she cannot drive, speak any English, or read or write more than her name, any visit to the doctor now requires the services of her husband or daughter as a driver and translator. Her story, which is only one of many I have heard in Indigo, is powerful testimony of the enormous effort to which some barrio residents will go to avoid having to deal with the Indigo medical establishment.

Most people in La Fabrica, of course, cannot travel 150 miles outside the city for medical care, and must make do with the services Indigo has to offer. This exacerbates rather than tempers their general dislike and mistrust of Indigo's doctors. The most commonly voiced complaint was that "they make you wait and wait, and then it's $30." But despite its 100,000 people, Indigo seems in many respects a much smaller place, and the reputations of individual physicians, as well as stories of their

Figure 5.6
(*Cont.*)

*they did before their
visits.*

*Specific anecodotal
evidence, like the case of
the woman with the eye
injury, illustrates and
particularizes the expe-
riences of the people in
their dealings with the
medical establishment.*

rudeness, favoritism, and maltreatment of patients, are well known
throughout the city. Whether or not the stories are apocryphal, the
dislike is real.

Because doctors are expensive and time-consuming, and because they
are considered arrogant and unsympathetic, few residents of La Fabrica
have a regular doctor (the "family physician" of American folklore).
Instead they, like many other impoverished Americans, often turn to the
emergency room at Faith Hospital. Sixty-seven percent of those interviewed said they or someone in their family had used the emergency room at
least once. Often these visits are occasioned by children's illnesses that
have worsened during the night, when the clinic is closed, or by acute
conditions in adults for which the clinic does not provide services and
for which families cannot afford a visit to a private physician, who may
turn them away.

More and more people in Indigo are making use of neighborhood clinics:
73% of those surveyed in La Fabrica said they or their families used the
neighborhood clinic regularly. The proximity of the clinic and the fact
that its services are available free or at very low cost have undoubtedly
improved health care for those in the barrio, especially children. One
barrio resident who worked tirelessly to bring the clinic to La Fabrica
(the woman with the eye injury mentioned earlier) said that her greatest
sense of achievement came from the realization that "now people don't
wait when their children are sick until they are almost dead" to seek
medical care for them.

Mexican Alternatives to the Medical Establishment

Sixteen residents of La Fabrica told interviewers that they patronized
doctors or dentists in Pollo Blanco, and sixteen (an overlapping but not
identical group) said they bought medicines in Pollo Blanco's pharmacies.
The decision to seek medical or dental care across the river is usually
based on cost: most office visits and procedures are less than half as
expensive as they are in Indigo. In addition, some people find Pollo
Blanco's physicians more sympathetic and less distant. This is difficult
to understand, since most of Indigo's doctors (and virtually all those
patronized by barrio residents) are Mexican-American, some are Mexican-
born, and many are graduates of Mexican medical schools. One would expect
that their demeanor would be similar to that of their counterparts across
the river. Finally, Mexican pharmacies offer not only several kinds of
patent medicines believed by many Indigoans to be extremely effective, but
also some kinds of drugs that can be bought over the counter in Mexico but
only by prescription or not at all in the United States.

The use of Mexican health care facilities correlates neither with low
income nor with advanced age nor with briefness of residence in the United
States. It seems to be an unpredictable, idiosyncratic choice. Some
respondents said brusquely, "*No, nada de eso*" (No none of that), when

Figure 5.6
(*Cont.*)

asked if they went across the river for health care. Others responded, "Yes, sometimes, for reasons of economy" (*por economia*). My landlady provides a good example of the mixture of elements involved in choosing where to seek medical care. She is a strong, almost passionate, believer in American medicine; she has a good income by barrio standards, as well as medical insurance, thanks to her husband's rare union job; she is an American citizen, having lived 40 years in Indigo, although she was born in rural Naranjas. She would not consider going to a doctor in Pollo Blanco, but all her dental work is done there, at fees that are roughly a third of U.S. dental fees for comparable work. And she is very partial to some Mexican patent medicines, which she considers superior to anything available in the United States.

As mentioned earlier, we see this pattern of analysis and reporting repeated. Under the major heading of "Family Size," Wynjenek provides Census data on the birth rate in Indigo and how it has decreased dramatically; primary data from respondents on how and why they limit family size; and finally, interpretive notions, based on participant observation of limited family size (for one male respondent the births of only two children in 13 years of marriage) that have to do with how people think they are responding to culturally approved norms, and how they actually appear to be responding to them.

Family Size

Birth Rate

In 1968 the birth rate in Johnson County, Texas, of which Indigo is the county seat and only city, was 43.8 per thousand. Twenty years later the birth rate had declined to 26.6 per thousand, nearly 40% lower. It is interesting to note that, although Johnson County has the second highest concentration of Mexican Americans of any county in the United States, its rank in birth rate is only seventieth. It should also be remembered that figures for Johnson County are inflated by the large numbers of residents of Mexico who give birth in Indigo so that their children may claim U.S. citizenship. Indeed, the first thirty-seven places in the birth rate sweepstakes go, not to counties with high Hispanic populations, but primarily to counties in Kansas, South Dakota, North Dakota, and Utah, with high Hutterite, Mennonite, and Mormon populations.

A look at Indigo's 5-year age cohorts in the 1980 Census report gives graphic evidence of the city's declining birth rate:

      under 5 years: 10,350
         5-9 years: 10,755
       10-14 years: 11,154
       15-19 years: 11,165

These figures are all the more remarkable because of the constant emigration of Indigoans who cannot find work in the city (whose official unemployment rate has recently ranged from 12 percent to 36 percent) and the constant immigration of Mexican nationals, who may be even more culturally conservative than lifetime or longtime residents of Indigo.

Reasons for Limiting Family Size

Johnson County's birth rate is nearly twice as high as that of the state of Texas as a whole, which is 19.2 per thousand. Its dramatic decline over the last two decades, however, seems to indicate that Mexican-American birth

Figure 5.6
(Cont.)

rates, even in such a traditional and isolated enclave as Indigo, are not mere cultural epiphenomena, but that they respond to the same kinds of conditions as do the birth rates of other populations. Shrinking opportunities for migrant farmworkers, the need for longer schooling, the increased acceptability of women's working outside the household, and necessity for women to do so have all had an effect on family size. These phenomena are consistent with the patterns that not only prevail in developed, industrial countries, but that have emerged in the developing world as well. They are also, and at least equally significantly, specifically expressed in the words of Indigo residents as well.

Feelings about family planning in the barrios of Indigo are both interesting and fairly clear-cut, and they provide insight into the human realities of family planning that is not available from Census statistics. In the survey of households in La Fabrica, answers to questions about family size fell into three categories. Just over half of those questioned favored birth control outright. Nearly another quarter believed that birth control was essential in contemporary life, but they regretted its necessity. Only a quarter said they believed in having "all the children God sends."

People with an apparently unalloyed preference for family planning included men and women of all ages, and their reasons were always economic. "You have to think, how many can I support, feed, educate, protect, and defend against everything," said one young woman with energy, while an eighty-three year-old mother of five sons responded urgently, "I tell my grandchildren that they must limit their children to one or two—or three." The different options for rich and poor informed many responses. "If you make good money you can have a hundred children, but if you're poor, you have to plan," one man stated firmly.

A common response of barrio residents was that family planning had not always been necessary, as it now was. One great-grandmother represented this view in her response: "You used to be able to have all the children God sent; everyone had five. But in these times, no. Now you can have only one." A middle-aged woman offered a similar opinion: "Before, you could have twelve, fifteen, twenty children. Now everything is so expensive you can't maintain them." People who mentioned an earlier era nearly always regretted the necessity of birth control, as, indeed, did those who compared the rich to the poor in this respect. The desire for numerous children is still present for many people in Indigo's impoverished barrios, although most have decided that they cannot afford to indulge this desire.

The makeup of the group of barrio residents who said that they favored having all the children God sent is extremely interesting. It includes primarily men, older women who had never been married, and women over forty, some of whom had had as many as ten or fifteen children. Some of the responses in this category were religious in form. One of the never-

Figure 5.6
(*Cont.*)

married women gave the most doctrinaire response: "According to my religion, marriage is for having a family, and to limit one's family would be a sin." But a seventy-year-old mother of four answered similarly: "I think you should have all the children God sends you. To limit them would be a mortal sin." Most of the reasons married women gave for preferring not to limit their families, however, were references to their own children. "No, I don't like family planning," said one woman, "because I had fifteen, myself." None of the men gave any reason for not liking birth control, nor did any of the interviewers, all of whom were women, press them. An interesting feature of their responses, however, was that their professed desire for "all the children God sends" seldom seemed to accord with the number of children they actually had. In 13 years of marriage one of these men had had two children, who were eleven and twelve years old. Another had had two in 7 years, and a third had had three in 17 years. It seems clear that either these men were responding according to a culturally approved model while acting according to economic self-interest, or they believed they were acting according to cultural rules while their wives were acting according to economic self-interest.

While there is still a strongly voiced minority sentiment in Indigo's barrios that opposes limiting family size, it is not the sentiment of women of childbearing age. All but five female respondents aged forty or under said they favored birth control, as, of course, did many men and older women. Whatever the motivation of the men opposed to birth control, the size of their families seems to be determined not by their stated views, but by those of their wives.

Only one of the household heads interviewed in Indigo identified herself as anything but Catholic, and she was a former Catholic, now converted to the Jehovah's Witnesses. Though there is a great range of piety and degree of formal religious observance, virtually all Indigoans consider themselves Catholic, and all adults are well aware of the prohibition of the Catholic church on artificial methods of birth control. For a small minority, like the two women quoted earlier, this prohibition was given as the reason for which they did not approve of birth control. It should be noted, however, that several of those interviewed who disapproved of birth control on religious grounds were women who had never married (and who had no children). Those persons who favored birth control and who also mentioned the position of the Church were divided as to their feelings about not complying with Church teachings. One mother of two in her early twenties said, "If a person knows that he is poor, he can't have too many children, if you accept what God sends, he could send a bunch [*un bonche!*]." Though this woman is remarkably cheerful and self-reliant, and apparently unmoved by Church teachings on birth control, some of her neighbors were less insouciant. "They say, 'Have faith,'" one older woman remarked bitterly, "but it's too many." And the father of ten children under sixteen, a man who now favors birth control, responded similarly: "They say it's a sin, but I say you can't support them."

Figure 5.6
(*Cont.*)

The same happens with "Childbirth" and "Traditional Healing," although purely secondary material, like Census data, is noticeably lacking, mainly because respondents are even more reluctant to report such information to Census takers than they are to people like Wynjenek and her research assistants. Thus information about access to and use of prenatal care, traditional midwives (parteras), and curanderas, *can be obtained only through primary means (answers to interviewers' questions).*

Primary evidence seems to take over in these sections of the report. Readers learn about how many women take advantage of prenatal care, how many use parteras, *how many go to professional physicians to find out about complications of their pregnancies, and how much they have to pay for such services. Anecdotally, readers also learn about how midwives work, how often their services are used, and what they charge.*

Childbirth

Access to Prenatal Care

The fundamentally economic basis for birth control in Indigo is mirrored in the way other medically related decisions are made. One of these concerns childbirth, which, because of Indigo's location on the U.S.-Mexican border, is marked by some unusual features. Not only do Mexican nationals living in Pollo Blanco come across the river, sometimes while in labor, to give birth in Indigo and thus assure their children of U.S. citizenship, but both residents of Pollo Blanco and Indigoans themselves make use of the services of *parteras*, or lay midwives.

Pregnant women who do not plan to give birth in a hospital often spend the last week or so of their pregnancies at the house of a *partera* in one of Indigo's barrios. Here the woman's vital signs are monitored, and if obvious problems arise, the *partera* can usually send her patient to Faith Hospital for care and delivery. *Parteras* are usually shrewd, cautious, and experienced women, who much prefer to lose a patient to the hospital than to death, should complications arise.

A woman in labor, with acute preeclampsia or toxemia, or with severe postpartum complications will not be refused admission to Faith Hospital, whatever her economic situation, residence, or nationality. In this, Indigo is very different from many other settlements along the border or elsewhere in South Texas, where there are no medical facilities at all, or only privately funded hospitals without a federally mandated obligation to accept indigent patients. Although the hospital provides inpatient maternity care to virtually anyone who requires it, it does not provide prenatal care, nor does any clinic or physician provide this service at low or no cost. The only alternatives available to pregnant women are a private physician (most of whom require a fee of roughly $700, payable in cash by the fourth or fifth month of pregnancy), a *partera* (whose fee, usually $200 to $300, must also be paid in advance), or no prenatal care at all, culminating in arrival at Faith Hospital in labor. Because of the high unemployment and underemployment in Indigo, common unreported employment (involving payment "off the books" or "under the table," to benefit the employer), as well as thousands of long-term jobs that simply offer no employee benefits, only eleven of the households surveyed reported any coverage by employment-related insurance. Twelve households reported coverage for some family members by Medicaid, and nineteen elderly householders reported that they or their spouses received Medicare, a program that is of little assistance in defraying the costs of childbirth.

Traditional Midwives

In the households I surveyed, 37% of the female household heads had given birth with the assistance of a *partera*, 50% had been attended by a doctor,

Figure 5.6
(*Cont.*)

and 2% had employed both during the course of their reproductive lives. The rest had had only the assistance of their families. Of those who had employed *parteras*, only two said they preferred them to doctors. All the others cited a lack of money to pay a doctor, or, in the case of two elderly women who had lived on remote ranches, the unavailability of doctors. Those who had been delivered by doctors were almost universal in citing the greater security or safety of physician-attended births. Five women added that they had been forced to turn to doctors because of complications surrounding their pregnancies or deliveries: hemorrhaging, preeclampsia, or the need for a caesarean delivery. Another three women volunteered that they had been afraid to go to a partera. Formal interviews in La Fabrica did not request information about the complications of pregnancy or delivery, although some women volunteered them. Among my friends in other barrios in Indigo I have heard, however, several stories of problems accompanying delivery by *partera*. One involved the death, shortly after delivery, of a young woman who lived in Pollo Blanco and worked in Indigo (a "commuter"). The woman had been staying at the house of an Indigo midwife awaiting delivery. The baby was born healthy, and the mother appeared healthy as well. Shortly after delivery, however, complications arose in the mother, who was immediately sent to Faith Hospital. She died shortly after admission. Without more information it is impossible to know whether delivery in a hospital would have saved the mother's life, but it seems likely. Another story, more typical, involves complications that, while less tragic, would certainly never have occurred in a hospital delivery. The midwife in this case performed an episiotomy on her patient, and the baby was born healthy. The episiotomy, however, was never sutured. It healed slowly and painfully, with infection and the development of awkward scar tissue that necessitated caesarean delivery for the next pregnancy.

One of the interviewers, a former migrant farmworker, all of whose children had been born in hospitals, some of them in northern states, occasionally asked respondents who had had doctor-assisted births whether they had done so because they had been "afraid." Though I have no further evidence than this, it seems as though there is some vestigial virtue that can be attached to the courage involved in foregoing a doctor. Whether or not this is true, few Indigo residents are choosing delivery by *partera* these days. No respondent in her twenties had employed a *partera*, and only five in their thirties at the time of the interview had done so. This is in great measure the result of Faith Hospital's relatively recent policy of accepting all patients for delivery and emergency inpatient prenatal and postnatal care. It cannot necessarily be seen, however, as unalloyed progress, since many women who would once have had some prenatal oversight from a *partera* now have none at all, their only goal being hospital delivery.

The story of Maria Esmeralda Diaz (a pseudonym) illustrates the

Figure 5.6
(*Cont.*)

difficult position of impoverished pregnant women in Indigo, as well as the style of the city's medical community. Maria was born 25 years ago in Chicago to parents who came from Indigo. She lived in Chicago off and on until she was married, at 23. She then returned to Indigo with her Puerto Rican husband so that she could be near her parents, who lived in La Fabrica. She wanted to be near her family when her first child was born, and she wanted to escape Chicago's crime. But her husband had trouble finding a job in Indigo's crisis economy, and the couple had little money. Meanwhile, Maria's pregnancy was advancing, but since she could not put together either $200 for a midwife or $700 for a doctor, she relied on her mother's care and advice and put off medical assistance. When it began to seem as though Maria's pregnancy was continuing too long, she made an appointment with a prominent Indigo general practitioner. This woman refused to accept Maria as a patient because she had come to her only in the ninth month of pregnancy. Now more concerned than ever, Maria immediately took a bus to Chicago, where her aunt still lived. The morning after she arrived, she went straight to a hospital, where (despite her indigence) she was examined, the fetus was examined via ultrasound, and for reasons of which Maria was not entirely sure, doctors decided to induce labor immediately. It is chilling to consider what would have happened if Maria had lacked such energy, experience, and family connections.

The growing conviction that modern medicine, however and whenever acquired, is superior to traditional care has created new difficulties for impoverished pregnant women in Indigo. In addition, time spent in the maternity ward of Faith Hospital is for many women a rare chance for respite from their strenuous household duties. One informant, who had developed preeclampsia during her last two pregnancies and had spent several weeks in the hospital before each birth, told her interviewer with enthusiasm, "*Me encanta el hospital* (I adore the hospital)." It is thus clear that in Indigo, as Scheper-Hughes and Stewart report for Taos, the use of *parteras* does not represent reactionary adherence to a dangerously maladaptive cultural practice, but rather a locally available optional strategy employed primarily for economic reasons and eagerly discarded as soon as possible from economic and/or medical motivations, even when it might prove beneficial.

Traditional Healing

Home Remedies

It remains to consider the issue of traditional medicine, including both household remedies (*remedios caseros*) and traditional healers (*curanderas*). Two-thirds of the household heads interviewed in La Fabrica said they resorted to home remedies first when family members were ill. These remedies are usually herb teas of various leaves, flowers, or barks,

Figure 5.6
(*Cont.*)

Further, readers learn about midwives, home remedies, traditional healers, and the ailments they treat. Wynjenek is sure to point out that although there is a certain embarrassment (she more significantly calls it "opprobrium") attached to traditional healing methods, the people of La Fabrica take part in them. The evidence Wynjenek presents in these sections is more clearly and dramatically anecdotal, even more convincing because it comes from individual sources, who have decided for any number of reasons to be forthcoming in their responses. One involves the death of a young woman who lived in Pollo Blanco, who had come to a partera *in Indigo for the delivery of her child; another tells about a woman who traveled back to Chicago, where she had an aunt living who could help her in the last hours of her pregnancy, because she could not get the help she needed in Indigo; and one deals with the problem of one of Wynjenek's informants and friends who had been suffering from a stomach ailment, who*

many of which can be bought in small cellophane bags at the grocery store. Indeed, Indigo is the home of La India, a company whose packaged medicinal and culinary herbs can be found in stores serving Mexican-American customers all over the western and southwestern United States. For other, more recherché ingredients, some barrio residents go to special herb shops in Indigo or Pollo Blanco. In addition to teas to bring down fevers, settle queasy stomachs, or relieve insomnia, some women can make poultices for cuts, burns, pains, and fevers, and soothing syrups for coughs. Among those interviewed who said they could do this were both old and young women, including two nurse's aides.

Traditional Healers

Besides the ability to cure everyday discomforts with home remedies, some women can cure such disorders as *mal de ojo* (usually translated as "evil eye," though this distorts the nature of the illness), *empacho* (intestinal blockage), and *susto* (fright). Though social scientists usually treat these disorders as a separate category of "folk" or supernaturally caused illnesses, they do not seem to be regarded universally as a distinct category by Indigoans. One woman, for example, said she takes her young son to the neighborhood clinic when she suspects him of having *susto*, while at least one respondent seemed to distinguish *mal de ojo*, as supernaturally caused, from *susto* and *empacho*, which had natural causes (and the latter of which was curable by Pepto Bismol). Similarly, respondents do not use the term "*curandera*" to designate all women who can cure *ojo*, *susto*, or *empacho*. I did not hear of a single man who engaged in traditional curing, although there are some in the region, including some who are extremely well known. Some women can cure these ailments in their own children, while others have sisters or friends who are particularly good at it. Only when an adult is suspected of having *empacho* (usually only children or adolescents are afflicted with *ojo* or *susto*) and home remedies and patent medicines have failed, would most families consider looking for an official *curandera* whom they do not know personally.

Ambivalence and Integration

An extremely unfortunate flaw in the interview schedule resulted in unreliable responses to questions about *curanderas*. Naively, I had constructed the questions using the term "*curandera*." In response to all questions using this term, every informant responded that she never consulted such persons. One interviewer, however, an extremely bright and insightful young woman, simply rephrased questions involving traditional healers. Instead of asking whether the informant ever consulted *curanderas*, she asked, "When someone in your family is ill with *susto* or *empacho* or something like that, do you know how to cure him, or do you know someone who does?" To such a question, virtually everyone responded

Figure 5.6
(Cont.)

had first used established medical means to diagnose and treat the ailment, then when none of that seemed to work, had gone to a curandera *in Pollo Blanco, and finally, when that had not worked, had gone back to established medical care in Indigo. His review of the steps he took to get better indicates that although the established means of his cure eventually worked, he couldn't rule out the traditional means, mainly because he perhaps hadn't believed strongly enough in them.*

affirmatively, and then proceeded to discuss such techniques as rolling an egg across the forehead of a child to remove a fever, or rubbing the body with holy oil to cure *empacho*.

Clearly, even in Indigo's impoverished barrios, people are well aware of the opprobrium attached to *curanderismo*, especially when it is clearly identified with the traditional lexical label. They are embarrassed to admit that they resort to it when asked directly, but readily describe their use of the system when the interviewer both assumes that they use it and refrains from labeling it. I have had a number of discussions with Indigo's barrio residents about traditional concepts of health, traditional healing, and supernatural power generally, and only one person, my monolingual, nonliterate, but very modern landlady, resolutely maintained disbelief. Indeed, her dislike for or discomfort with such topics was so great that it took days of pleading to discover why an old woman and her great-grandchild came regularly to gather leaves that had fallen from a particular tree in the neighborhood. It was a *pirul* tree, the leaves of which are used in many traditional curing rituals, but having finally told me that, my landlady burst out, "You will think we are savages. You will think we are crazy. It's nothing but witchcraft" (*Pura brujeria*)."

It is safe to say that most impoverished Indigo residents continue to believe in traditional concepts of medicine together with modern western concepts. Many accounts of Mexican-American *curanderismo* stress its conflict with the practice of contemporary western medicine. The results of my experience and surveys in Indigo, however, paint a picture of traditional and scientific medicine as an integrated system, in which there is little conflict for most barrio residents. Home remedies, simple homeopathic and sympathetic curing practices, and patent medicines, such as aspirin and Pepto Bismol, are the first choice for curing sick or injured family members. They are cheap and easy to procure, and they disrupt the family very little. If these attempts fail, and the illness or injury does not improve, the patient is usually taken to the clinic, the emergency room, or a private doctor. Only if these latter measures fail after some time is a patient likely to look for outside help in traditional curing. Most barrio residents seem to consider the majority of maladies susceptible of cure by either traditional or scientific medicine, depending on circumstance, severity, and the individual. Certainly no Indigoan of my acquaintance would hesitate to consult a doctor for an obvious acute condition, whether he or she thought it was *susto* or heart trouble.

A medical anecdote from the life of a friend of mine of twenty years' standing, a man I will call Jose Vela, illustrates the ways in which traditional and scientific medicine may be combined in Indigo's barrios. In the spring Jose's stomach, which had been troublesome for some time, began to give him genuine pain. Jose, the thirty-eight-year-old son of uneducated Mexican migrant farmworkers, who himself had earned a B.A., had

Figure 5.6
(Cont.)

been a medical corpsman in the Air Force, and the pattern of his discomfort seemed to him to indicate an ulcer. Since over-the-counter remedies and his mother's teas had no effect, Jose made an appointment with a general practitioner. The doctor examined him, ordered several tests, and ultimately concluded that Jose did not have an ulcer. Seeing that Jose's job was very demanding, he decided that the stomach pains were caused by "tension," and prescribed a mild tranquilizer. When, after several weeks, Jose's stomach had not improved, his mother, who does not like or trust doctors in Indigo, persuaded him to consult a physician in Pollo Blanco. This doctor agreed that Jose did not have an ulcer, and prescribed something to "calm the nerves," presumably another tranquilizer.

A month later, when Jose felt no better, his mother and wife conferred and came to the conclusion that Jose must have *empacho*. Since he was by now miserable and living on Rolaids, Jose allowed his mother to take him to a *curandera* in Indigo's central barrio of La Virgen (a pseudonym). The *curandera* was a pregnant middle-aged woman, whose unemployed husband was often at home doing chores around the house, a situation that made Jose extremely uncomfortable. What made him more uncomfortable was having to take his clothes off, not only in front of the *curandera*, but in front of his mother as well!

The treatment, repeated several times a week apart, consisted of a vigorous massage, preceded by prayerful invocations and succeeded by downward brushing with leaves of the *pirul* tree, also accompanied by prayer. In between treatments Jose was to drink a bottle (about half a pint) of Pompeiian olive oil a day. The *curandera* asked for no payment; her skills were a gift from God. But if her patient was cured through her efforts, he was expected to give her a monetary gift.

Jose gave the *curandera* a gift, but he was not cured. In desperation he made an appointment with an Indigo internist, who diagnosed and treated him for diverticulitis. Within a week Jose's pain had subsided.

When I asked Jose, a thoughtful, insightful, educated, and intelligent man, what he had thought about the *curandera*, he replied that although he had disliked the treatments, he knew of many cases in which *curanderas* had effected cures for people who believed in the process. "I guess I didn't believe strongly enough," he said.

Conclusions

Most of Indigo's population is extremely poor, and nearly all of it participates in the most conservative Mexican-American culture anywhere in the United States, with the possible exception of the culturally distinctive area of highland New Mexico. Indigo's cultural system offers its participants traditional medicinal and healing options not open to most other Americans who participate more fully in the majority culture. And the city's location on the Mexican border offers scientific western medicine in a slightly different setting and at a much lower cost. But it

Wynjenek's conclusions, although implied throughout the report, are separately laid out for readers to consider immediately if they want to. They expand upon and develop the conclusions she has offered in both the letter of transmittal and the executive summary, and again they suggest the significance the study has had,

204

Figure 5.6
(Cont.)

not only for the time in which it was done, but also for the future.

Readers can decide from her conclusions whether what she has done and what she thinks it means is significant enough to ask her for specific recommendations about what should be done in the future, or whether projects like hers should be supported in similar ways in the future.

Patricia Wynjenek has written a typical completion report. With a few modifications, it is also in good shape to submit to a professional journal for possible publication.

would be a mistake to believe either that (1) Indigoans do not themselves participate to a great extent in Anglo-American culture, or that (2) they make decisions informed primarily by considerations shaped by their own distinctive subculture. In most matters that directly affect their health, well-being, and family size, Indigo's barrio residents appear to make choices based on the same values as any other Americans: they want to maximize their well-being and minimize the cost wherever possible—cost being of great importance in Indigo. Thus, as child and infant mortality declines, and as the raising of children becomes more and more expensive, considering urban life, prolonged schooling, and the cessation of income derived from child labor, people in Indigo, like people everywhere for whom this is true, simply have fewer children. They are aware of the teachings of the Church, but with more or less pain they, like most other Catholics, and certainly like most other American Catholics, have decided that they must ignore those teachings.

In the cases of prenatal care and delivery, Indigoans, like most other Americans, are convinced of the superiority of doctors and hospitals over *parteras*. When they could not afford doctors or hospitals, or could not reach them, Indigoans have turned to *parteras* simply *"por economia,"* as most respondents stated, with evident amazement that anyone would wonder why they had done so. They have not feared or mistrusted modern medicine; they have not been moved by modesty; they have not been put off by Anglo-American medical personnel (most doctors and virtually all nurses in Indigo are Mexican-American, in any case). They have simply not had any other economic option.

As for *remedios caseros* and *curanderismo*, these again represent primarily a low-cost alternative to very expensive scientific medical care. As Anglo Americans turn to Tylenol, Indigoans turn to *yerbas* (as well as to Tylenol) as a first line of attack. And as Anglo Americans turn to psychiatry, chiropractic, and various alternative strategies when mainstream modern medicine fails, Indigoans turn to *curanderismo*. It is not a substitute for scientific medicine, but an adjunct to it. And if impoverished Mexican Americans rely more heavily on *yerbas* and *curanderas* than Anglo Americans do on their alternative strategies (and I am not sure that this is the case), this is far less because they are Mexican-American than because they are impoverished. In the end, Indigoans' decisions about health care are based on essentially the same considerations addressed by other Americans: perceived acuteness of condition, expense, and failure of previously employed therapies.

Figure 5.6
(*Cont.*)

Works Cited

Achor, Shirley
  1978 Mexican Americans in a Dallas Barrio. Tucson: University of Arizona
      Press.

Angel, Ronald
  1958 The Health of the Mexican Origin Population. *In* The Mexican-
      American Experience. Rodolfo O. de la Garza et al., eds. Austin:
      University of Texas Press.

Boyle, Joyceen S. and Margaret M. Andrews
  1989 Transcultural Concepts in Nursing Care. Glenview, Illinois: Scott
      Foresman.

Clark, Mark
  1970 Health in the Mexican Culture. Berkeley: University of California
      Press.

Foster, George M.
  1987 Bureaucratic Aspects of International Health Agencies. Social
      Sciences and Medicine 25 (9):1039-1048.

Madsen, William
  1964, revised 1973 Mexican-Americans of South Texas. New York: Holt,
      Rinehart and Winston.

Maduro, Renaldo
  1983 *Curanderismo* and Latino Views of Disease and Curing. The Western
      Journal of Medicine 139:868-874.

McKenna, Margaret
  1989 Twice in Need of Care: A Transcultural Nursing Analysis of Elderly
      Mexican Americans. Journal of Transcultural Nursing I (1):46-52.

Rubel, Arthur J.
  1966 Across the Tracks: Mexican-Americans in a Texas City. Austin:
      University of Texas Press.

Saunders, Lyle
  1954 Cultural Differences and Medical Care: The Case of the Spanish
      Speaking People. New York: Russel Sage.

Scheper-Hughes, Nancy and David Stewart
  1983 *Curanderismo* in Taos County, New Mexico—A Possible Case of
      Anthropological Romanticism? Western Journal of Medicine
      139:875-884.

Winkler, Karen J.
  1990 Scholars Say Issues of Diversity Have "Revolutionized" Field of
      Chicano Studies. Chronicle of Higher Education, 26 September,
      1990:A4-A8.

ASSIGNMENTS

1. Following the "Assignments" section is a completion report written by a student in a technical and professional writing class (see Figure 5.7). The student proposed her own project in her major, set up the audience she wanted to address, and decided on the form she thought would best address her readers. The report gives you an idea of what students can accomplish in their majors, as they put together their first formal completion report. We don't intend it as a model you should copy, but as a demonstration of work done by a fellow traveler.

Evaluate the student report. Your comments should address not only audience considerations, but also such issues as consistency with the proposal work and the extent to which the report adheres to the principles discussed in this chapter. What is admirable about the report? What is weak?

TERM PROJECT OPTION

Write a completion report [or whatever final product is appropriate (see Exercise 2, page 185)] for the work you formally proposed in Chapter 4. Besides adhering to the principles discussed in this chapter and elsewhere in the text, you should edit your project for the problems of usage discussed in the appendix and for problems of basic grammar and sentence structure.

Whatever form your final project takes, write an executive summary that serves two functions. First, it should do the conclusive summarizing required of an executive summary. Second, it should explain to your instructor exactly what decisions you made about audience and form and how you adapted your choice of words, level of abstraction, and the like, based on those decisions. You'll also want to discuss the purpose, context, and ethical considerations you saw for this project.

Figure 5.7
*Student
completion
report*

40 Oakwood Dr. #114
Pocatello, ID 83204

April 23, 1991

Dr. Tracy Montgomery
LA #212
Idaho State University
Pocatello, ID 83209

Dear Dr. Montgomery:

I am submitting my major project, an article for the journal Sociology and
Social Research. I have also attached my graded proposal per your request.
This article is primarily based upon an original survey administered to
ISU students in the Fall of 1990.

I have made several changes since submitting my proposal. First, I changed
the title to "AIDS Education and Variables Affecting Safer Sex Behavior
in a Conservative State University." This reflects a slight change in
emphasis to how AIDS education should proceed and also the addition of two
variables in my examination of what affects behavior. My interview with
Dr. Farrell and my further review of previous studies influenced my
decision to incorporate these additional two variables. My five variables
now include behavior, knowledge, concern, attitude, and contact with a
person living with AIDS (PLWA). All five of these variables were tested on
the original survey instrument.

Second, although many of the schools where previous studies have been done
are of similar size to ISU, most are probably not as conservative. My
article (and the title) reflect this difference in emphasis. Third, I
chose to include only works cited as my references because of the length of
the list. I have used three works that I had not reviewed at the time of my
proposal and I have dropped several sources which did not fit in my
article. Fourth, in my proposal I said that I would turn in this project on
April 22, 1991. However, I have extended this self-imposed deadline by one
day to finalize my project.

This survey found that ISU students are sexually active and do put
themselves at risk of contracting HIV. Further, no one variable is
effective in promoting all the safer sex behaviors measured in this
survey. Recommendations call for a comprehensive education plan
incorporating all of these variables because they all have some influence
in changing some behaviors.

Sincerely,

Sheryl Soderstrom

Sheryl Soderstrom

Figure 5.7
(Cont.)

AIDS Education and Variables Affecting Safer Sex Behavior
in a Conservative State University

Sheryl Soderstrom

Submitted to
Dr. Tracy Montgomery
Instructor
Professional Writing
Idaho State University

April 23, 1991

Figure 5.7
(*Cont.*)

AIDS EDUCATION AND VARIABLES AFFECTING SAFER SEX BEHAVIORS
IN A CONSERVATIVE STATE UNIVERSITY

Executive Summary

This paper reports the results of a survey of ISU students (n = 245) during the fall semester 1990. The survey tested five variables: behavior, knowledge, concern, attitude, and contact with a person living with AIDS (PLWA). Results indicate that students are sexually active (68%) and are placing themselves at risk of contracting AIDS because of sexual behavior. Other findings include the following: 90% gave accurate answers to knowledge questions, 76% expressed a high level of concern, 92% indicated a positive attitude about AIDS, 34% have had contact with a PLWA, and 78% claim that they are practicing safer sex because of AIDS. Basic transmittal knowledge was high (95%), personal concern was low (47%), 92% supported condoms on campus, and 95% supported the right of an HIV+ child to go to public school.

Respondents were more willing to discuss AIDS/safer sex with their children (98%/97%) than to take positive action in their own sexual behavior. Remaining celibate until marriage (only 44% Strongly Agree/Agree), and giving up oral sex (only 49% SA/A) were the least popular of the safer sex behaviors on the survey. This was followed by dating longer before having sex (only 76% SA/A). None of the variables can be correlated to changes in all eight behaviors tested, but accurate knowledge, high concern, and positive attitude do affect some behaviors. Contact with a PLWA had no effect on behavior, but did have an effect on concern which in turn affects some behaviors. Recommendations include a comprehensive format that enhances all these variables for the individual (especially personal concern) to facilitate behavior changes, and modules on self-esteem, decision-making skills, negotiation skills, and condom use skills. Education at ISU needs to reach males, LDS students, and freshmen in particular. AIDS education for everyone must move from the general and basic to the specific and detailed, and it must move from the statistical "other" to personal concern and the realization that no one is immune.

The audience for this article are the readers of Sociology and Social Research. These are the professionals in the field of Sociology (and perhaps other social sciences) as well as Professors and students in this field. They should be familiar with the research format and the use of tables, cross-tabulations, and surveys and will thus understand my methods and results as presented. They should also be familiar with AIDS and the various studies conducted in the past to the extent of their personal interest in this area.

To appeal to this audience I followed the typical social research format. I reviewed past research in this area and tried to do something different that would pique their interest. For instance, I looked at five

Figure 5.7
(Cont.)

variables instead of just two or three, and I did my survey at a
conservative school. I used language and style appropriate to this
particular journal and comparable to other articles already published in
this journal. I used a modified "Scientific Articles" format which
includes Abstract, Introduction (not identified as such), Literature
Review (not identified as such and basically incorporated into the
Introduction), Methods, Results, Discussion, and Works Cited. These
modifications reflect the pattern typically seen in articles published in
this journal. I attached four tables of information (which are discussed
in the text) at the back of the article to meet with the convention of this
journal.

Within the section on Methods, I divided my report into two sections:
Sample and Survey Instrument. The section on sample describes the
demographic information on my respondents. The section on Survey
Instrument defines the variables in terms of the survey items measuring
them and gives a brief recounting of how the data was gathered and
analyzed. In the Results section, I chose to begin with information about
students' sexual activity, followed by the overall percentages for each
variable. Next, I reported on the variables broken down by demographic
information. Then I went into some detail about each of the variables, and
finally I addressed the influence each of the variables wields on safer
sex behavior. All discussion of results is confined to the section labeled
Discussion and is limited to the major points. Also in this section, I
address limitations of the study and recommendations for future AIDS
education.

Figure 5.7
(*Cont.*)

AIDS EDUCATION AND VARIABLES AFFECTING SAFER SEX BEHAVIOR
IN A CONSERVATIVE STATE UNIVERSITY

Abstract

Past research has focused on four variables relating to AIDS: behavior, knowledge, concern, and attitude. However, most previous studies did not look at all four of these variables. This study of students at Idaho State University (n = 245) examined all four of the variables listed above as well as contact with a person living with AIDS. Results indicate that students at this conservative school are at risk of contracting HIV sexually and that no one of the variables examined is sufficient to cause a change in all the safer sex behaviors examined. Different behaviors were affected by different variables, leading to the conclusion that AIDS education must be comprehensive to include all these variables and to cause a change in sexual behaviors.

Figure 5.7
(*Cont.*)

AIDS Education and Variables Affecting Safer Sex Behavior in a Conservative State University

Today, having unprotected sex is like playing Russian Roulette because of a small, fragile, but deadly virus known as Human Immunodeficiency Virus (HIV). While HIV is transmitted in ways other than just semen and vaginal fluid (blood, shared needles, mother's milk), this study only looks at sexual transmission—perhaps the primary route of transmission on college campuses. This study of 245 students at Idaho State University found that students are indeed sexually active (68%) and are putting themselves at risk of contracting HIV. General knowledge of AIDS was high, but personal concern was low. Further, it was determined that a comprehensive system of education that addresses myths and brings concern down to a personal level will be the most effective in bringing about safer behavior.

For years, college campuses have had a reputation of sexual freedom and experimentation, and coupled with the relatively high density of single people, one would expect this population to be particularly vulnerable. However, one might question the validity of this observation in a small public university set in an extremely conservative community and state. But if the observation and reputation hold true at the small school, then they can be expected to be true (and perhaps multiplied) at larger, more liberal universities. One would also expect a university population to be better educated, and better informed on a variety of current events and issues than the general public. Given these factors, it would, therefore, be an appropriate place to measure HIV/AIDS awareness and concerns in relation to sexual behavior.

The presence of HIV in our society and its fatal consequences should cause responsible people to change their sexual practices to protect themselves and others. However, articles in Mademoiselle (Hacinli, 1988), U.S. News & World Report (—1988), and Newsweek (Leslie, et al., 1988) indicate that AIDS is spreading into the heterosexual population, and misinformation about AIDS still exists. Results of a Centers for Disease Control (CDC) study of student blood samples from universities across the country show that 1 in 300 students are HIV positive (Bennett, 1991). Most researchers believe that the threat of AIDS has done little to curb sexual activity among heterosexuals and especially among college students (Smilgis, 1987; Hirschorn, 1987; Gayle, 1990; Greatorex, 1989; Masters, et al., 1988).

In a quest to prevent unnecessary deaths, AIDS educators are searching for "the key" to producing sexual behavior changes in people. Many previous studies have looked at three factors—knowledge, concern, and attitude. While knowledge about HIV/AIDS—its transmission and its prevention—has increased (Winslow, 1988; —1990a; Ward & Ault, 1990), it has not been sufficient to produce behavior changes (Ward & Ault, 1990; Ishii-Kuntz, 1988; Fennell, 1990; —1988; —1990c). Most agree that knowledge alone is not the answer in behavior modification (Fennell,

Figure 5.7
(*Cont.*)

1990). Researchers note that concern about HIV/AIDS has led to some reported changes in sexual behavior on some campuses (Carroll, 1988; Ishii-Kuntz, 1988; Bruno, 1985), but on others the effect was nil (Ward & Ault, 1990; Ahia, 1991; —1990c; Hirschorn, 1987; Smilgis, 1987). And Carroll noticed some discrepancy between reported and actual behavior changes (1988). Fennell reported that attitudes improved over a 30-hour AIDS class that included critical thinking skills, ethical discussions, and group activities, but did not investigate the relationship between attitude and behavior (1991). A study done with high school students found that 61% overall had positive attitudes toward HIV/AIDS and PLWAs, but again did not check for the effect attitudes had on behavior (Jones, et al., 1991). Others found a change in attitude, but not behavior(—1990b; Hirschorn, 1987; Smilgis, 1987).

Overall, most agree that sexual behavior has not changed over the last 15 years. Young people are still as sexually active as always, and they continue to engage in risky behavior (Newman, 1988; Hanna, 1989; —1990b; —1990c; —1988; Hirschorn, 1987; Katz & Cronin, 1980; Smilgis, 1987). The current study looks at the variables "knowledge," "concern," "attitude," and "contact with a PLWA," and their effect on reported sexual behavior.

Methods

Sample. The 49-item survey was administered to a non-random sample of undergraduate students in Sociology and Social Work classes at Idaho State University (ISU) during Fall semester 1990 (n = 245). These lower division classes provided a cross-section of ISU's students, although not in the same proportion as the school's actual population. Most of the survey respondents were female (62%) (See Table 1, p. 15). More than 10 majors were identified with the largest field, social sciences, accounting for 27% of the total. Freshmen represented the largest class (35%) and almost half (44%) of the respondents were LDS (Mormons). Respondents ranged in age from 18 to 50 years old. For ease of handling, they were grouped into five age categories. Almost half (46%) were single, while a little more than a third (37%) were married. Married respondents reported marriages ranging from 1-35 years long, while respondents living with a significant other in a sexual relationship reported that those relationships had been ongoing for up to 5 years. Sixty-eight percent of the respondents reported being sexually active.

Survey Instrument. This survey measured five variables: behavior, knowledge, concern, attitude, and contact. Questions measuring behavior ranged from discussing AIDS/safer sex with children to six behavior questions borrowed directly from the Ishii-Kuntz study (1988). These six items began with the phrase "Because of AIDS" to isolate that the threat of AIDS was the motivation behind these reported behaviors. Responses were

Figure 5.7
(*Cont.*)

analyzed and cross-tabulated with the four other concepts, and then grouped to indicate safer sex and not safe behaviors. Six items testing awareness of transmission methods, prevention, and outcome of an AIDS diagnosis determined level of knowledge. Responses were then analyzed and grouped as accurate or inaccurate knowledge. Concern was measured by five items testing the individual's perception of the magnitude of the AIDS problem both in the U.S. and in the State of Idaho, and the extent of the individual's concern: everyone should be concerned, I am personally concerned, I am concerned about my teenagers. Responses were grouped to reflect high and low concern. Attitude reflects opinion of AIDS and persons living with AIDS (PLWAs), as well as two important social issues: condom dispensers on campus including in the dorms, and the right of HIV infected children to attend public schools. Responses to the five attitude items were grouped as either positive or negative. Two items measured contact: attendance at one (or more) of a PLWA's (Richard Carper) lectures two weeks prior to taking the survey, and "Do you personally know anyone who is HIV+ or who has AIDS?"

Most survey questions were offered on a Likert scale—strongly agree (SA), agree (A), disagree (D), strongly disagree (SD), and not applicable (NA). Some items gave the choice of yes, no, or undecided, some were mark-all-that-apply, and some were fill-in-the-blank. Collected data was analyzed for frequency and then cross-tabulated with the ABsurv survey analysis program. Percentages for each item testing a particular variable were grouped, adjusted to remove those who thought the particular item did not apply to them, and a mean was obtained. Answers to individual questions were also adjusted, polarized by variable, and then a mean was obtained for the polarized ends of that variable.

Results

Forty-five percent of the singles reported they are sexually active, while 52% of the divorced respondents, and 75% of the separated respondents also reported that they were sexually active. To compound their risk factor, of those reporting the number of partners they've had in the last year, 7% of the married reported 2-3 partners; 75% of divorced reported 2-5 partners; 50% of separated reported 2-3 partners; 61% of singles reported 2-20 partners; and 21% of those living with someone reported 2-5 partners.

Overall, 92% of respondents indicated they had a positive attitude about AIDS, 34% have had contact with a PLWA, 76.4% expressed a high level of concern, 90.3% gave accurate answers to knowledge questions, and 78% claim that they are practicing safer sex because of AIDS (See Table 2, p. 16).

More females have accurate knowledge (91%) than males (86%), and more females also have a positive attitude (91%) compared to 81% of males (See Table 3, p. 17). There is little difference between males and females on

Figure 5.7
(*Cont.*)

concern or behavior. Fewer people with no religion had accurate knowledge (82%) than either Catholics (91%), Protestants (91%), or LDS (90%). More Catholics expressed high concern, positive attitudes, and safer behavior than the other religion groups. Fewer LDS people expressed a positive attitude (82%), although that is still a majority, and less than half (46%) reported safer sex behavior because of AIDS. There is a negative relationship between class level and reported safer sex behavior. However, more seniors expressed accurate knowledge (94%), high concern (72%), and a positive attitude (94%), than did their lower class mates.

A high percentage of respondents, (See Table 2, p. 16), gave accurate answers on the questions testing knowledge of AIDS (90%), but 39 people still believe AIDS is transmitted by giving blood. More respondents were unsure of the correct answer to a question about whether AIDS is fatal or not than other knowledge questions, but still more than half (62%) gave the correct answer. Seventy-eight percent of respondents reported that they have, will, or are more likely to engage in safer sex behaviors. This ranged from a high of 98% reporting that they have or will discuss AIDS with their children, to a low of 44% who SA/A they have decided to remain celibate prior to marriage. Also unpopular was giving up oral sex—only 49% SA/A they are less likely to engage in oral sex. Regarding the variable "concern," the more general the concern statement, the more people SA/A. For example, 97% SA/A that AIDS is something everyone should be concerned about, but only 47% admitted that they were personally concerned about contracting AIDS. In spite of an overall positive attitude reported by the majority, 16% indicated they SA/A with the statement "AIDS is a punishment sent by God because of people's immoral behavior."

Accurate knowledge appears to heavily influence the decision to remain celibate prior to marriage (See Table 4, p. 18). Forty-five percent of those with accurate knowledge SA/A, while only 23% of those with inaccurate knowledge SA/A to remain celibate. All other differences between accurate and inaccurate knowledge, regarding any of the behaviors, was small, but it is interesting to note that the safer behaviors of using condoms, and not engaging in oral or anal sex were more popular among those with inaccurate knowledge. Regardless of knowledge, a high percentage (> 70%) say they are engaging in safer sex, with the exception of being celibate and giving up oral sex. A positive attitude seems to have an important effect on six of the eight behaviors. However, 56% of those with a negative attitude SA/A to remain celibate until marriage because of AIDS as opposed to only 42% of those with a positive attitude. The biggest difference between positive and negative attitudes in relation to behavior is on using condoms: 88% of those with a positive attitude SA/A, while only 67% of those with a negative attitude SA/A. High concern seems particularly effective in getting people to date longer before sex, and to not engage in oral sex. It is only moderately effective in getting people to ask for a potential partner's sexual history, to use condoms, and to not engage in anal sex. Having had contact with a PLWA had

Figure 5.7
(Cont.)

no major effect on any behavior; however, it does have a positive effect on concern, which in turn has an effect on behavior.

Discussion

It appears that at least at ISU, conservative morals have little effect on college students. If the behavior indicated on the survey is true, ISU students are indeed similar to their cohorts across the country. They are sexually active and they are engaging in risky sexual behavior. And if people in this morally conservative area are sexually active to the point of putting themselves at risk, it seems reasonable to assume that people in more liberal areas are doing the same.

This risky behavior cannot be attributed to ignorance, lack of concern, or a poor attitude because the majority of respondents expressed accurate knowledge, high concern, and a positive attitude. While no one variable was effective in influencing safer behavior across the board, knowledge, concern, and attitude all had a major effect on at least one behavior. In particular, increasing personal concern seems to be effective in getting people to practice safer sex. One way to increase personal concern is to increase contact with PLWAs. Dr. Larry Farrell explained that, "the most effective thing I've seen so far is for people who are diagnosed or infected to make themselves known. . . . That establishes some real immediacy. . . . It's no longer an abstract idea. It's no longer an invisible statistical entity. It's a person" (1991). Personal stories can open some people's eyes to the reality and risk of their own actions. All these variables, then, must be encouraged and nurtured in the individual to increase safer sex behavior.

Consistently throughout the various cross-tabulations and in spite of one's position with regard to any variable, people were not agreeable to remaining celibate or to giving up oral sex. The other behavior viewed with less favor was dating longer before having sex. This should send a clear message to the school, the community, and the state that people are sexually active in spite of AIDS, in spite of religious influences, in spite of moral conservatism, and in spite of "knowing better." Although we know that the only safe sex is no sex, those groups who insist that that is all that should be taught are fooling themselves.

This small study is subject to the same limitations that any survey research is subject to, i.e., are respondents telling the truth or are they marking answers to meet assumed expectations? Additionally, the following limitations are noted: first, this survey did not ask which safer sex behaviors people actually did or how often they did them, but instead focused on what they were likely to do. Second, this survey tied all safer sex behavior to the motivation or threat of AIDS; however, at this school people may be agreeing with these statements for other reasons. Parallel statements without the "Because of AIDS" qualifier may have made this distinction clearer.

Figure 5.7
(*Cont.*)

AIDS education to date has been effective in providing basic knowledge about AIDS and the transmission of HIV. But as Fennell reminds us, "Changes in knowledge without subsequent changes in behavior are not sufficient when dealing with HIV because of its potentially fatal consequences." The next step is to bring that knowledge down to a personal level. We must remove the notion that AIDS can be handled in a coldly statistical manner, and we must change people's perception that AIDS only happens to other people so different, so far removed from themselves that they are not at risk.

Future education should incorporate more detailed knowledge of AIDS to deal with the myths and misconceptions. It should also incorporate modules on self-esteem, decision-making skills, negotiation skills, and familiarity with condoms (Fennell, 1990; Farrell, 1991). Education at ISU should be particularly aimed at males, LDS students, and freshmen. As educators we need to boost the personal concern level of the individual, and we need to rid people of the negative attitudes associated with AIDS because negative attitudes act as a barrier to hearing the message and thus protecting oneself.

This study finds that none of the variables examined is, by itself, sufficient to cause a change in sexual behavior. However, different variables seem to be related to different safer sex behaviors. Therefore, a comprehensive education plan incorporating all these variables in a format that requires the student to think, to role play, to participate in activities, and to interact with PLWAs and HIV+ people may be our best hope to accomplish sexual behavior changes in this population which considers itself "not at risk."

Figure 5.7
(*Cont.*)

Works Cited

———1988. A Scary Little Survey of AIDS on Campus. U.S. News & World Report. 14 November: 12.

———1990a. AIDS Survey. AIDS Task Force. Lewis-Clark State College, Lewiston, Idaho.

———1990b. College Students only 'Paying Lip Service' to Safe Sex Message. Pediatric News. Orlando, Florida. May.

———1990c. Threat of AIDS having little impact on sex habits of college students. (AP) Idaho State Journal.

Ahia, Ruth N. 1991. Compliance with Safer-Sex Guidelines Among Adolescent Males: Application of the Health Belief Model and Protection Motivation Theory. Journal of Health Education. Jan./Feb. 22: 49-52.

Bennett, Jack. 1991. Lecture notes. Guest speaker in Dr. Larry Farrell's Biology 469 Microtopics: AIDS class. Idaho State University. Pocatello, ID. 29 January.

Bruno, Mary, et al. 1985. Campus Sex: New Fears—AIDS is the latest STD to hit the nation's colleges. Newsweek. 28 October: 81-82.

Carroll, Leo. 1988. Concern with AIDS and the sexual behavior of college students. Journal of Marriage and the Family. 50:405-411.

Farrell, Larry D. 1991. Personal Interview. Idaho State University. Pocatello, ID. 8 March.

Fennell, Reginald. 1990. Knowledge, Attitudes and Beliefs of Students regarding AIDS: A Review. Health Education. July/Aug. 21:20-25.

———1991. Evaluating the Effectiveness of a Credit Semester Course on AIDS Among College Students. Journal of Health Education. Jan./Feb. 22:35-41.

Gayle, Helene D., et al. 1990. Prevalence of the human immunodeficiency virus among university students. New England Journal of Medicine. 29 November. 323:1538-41.

Greatorex, Ian Frederick & John Michael Valentine Packer. 1989. Sexual Behaviour in University Students: Report of a Postal Survey. Public Health. 103:199-203.

Hacinli, Cynthia. 1988. AIDS, straight: A Heterosexual-risk update. Mademoiselle. August:138.

Hanna, Jack. 1989. Sexual Abandon: The Condom is unpopular on the campus. Maclean's. 25 September:48.

Hirschorn, Michael W. 1987. AIDS is Not Seen as a Major Threat by Many Heterosexuals on Campus. The Chronicle of Higher Education. 29 April. 33:1, 32-34.

Ishii-Kuntz, Masako. 1988. Acquired Immune Deficiency Syndrome and Sexual Behavior Changes in a College Student Sample. Sociology and Social Research. October. 73:13-18.

Figure 5.7
(*Cont.*)

Jones, Herb, et al. 1991. HIV Related Beliefs, Knowledge and Behaviors
of Ninth and Eleventh Grade Public School Students. Journal of Health
Education. Jan./Feb. 22:12-18.

Katz, Joseph and Denise M. Cronin. 1980. Sexuality and College Life.
Change. F / M:44-49.

Leslie, Connie, et al. 1988. Amid the Ivy, Cases of AIDS—College
campuses offer students no sanctuary. Newsweek. 14 November:65.

Newman, Frank. 1988. AIDS, Youth, and the University—An interview with
Admiral James D. Watkins, the Chairman of the AIDS Commission. Change.
September / October:39-44.

Smilgis, Martha. 1987. The Big Chill: Fear of AIDS—How heterosexuals
are coping with a disease that can make sex deadly. Time. 16
February:50-53.

Ward, Sally K. and Susan Ault. 1990. Fraternity and Sorority
Membership, AIDS Knowledge and Safe-sex practices. Sociology and
Social Research. April. 74: 158-161.

Winslow, Robert W. 1988. Student knowledge of AIDS transmission.
Sociology and Social Research. 72:110-113.

Figure 5.7
(*Cont.*)

TABLE 1   DEMOGRAPHICS

	#	%
SEX		
MALE	93	38
FEMALE	151	62
AGE		
18-20	84	35
21-25	60	25
26-30	32	13
31-35	26	11
36-50	39	16
RELIGION		
CATHOLIC	25	11
PROTESTANT	63	29
LDS	97	44
NONE	34	16
CLASS		
FRESHMEN	86	35
SOPHOMORE	60	25
JUNIOR	64	26
SENIOR	33	14
MARITAL STATUS		
MARRIED	88	37
DIVORCED	23	10
SEPARATED	4	2
SINGLE	110	46
LIVING WITH	15	6
SEXUALLY ACTIVE		
YES	159	68
NO	74	32
MAJOR		
SOC. SCIENCES	65	27
BUSINESS	40	17
HEALTH RELATED	34	14
EDUCATION	37	15
COUNSELING	16	7
SCIENCES/MATH	8	3
ENGL/PHIL/MC	6	3
MISC	35	15
PARTNERS		
1	90	66
2-3	32	24
4-5	9	7
6-10	3	2
11-15	1	1
16-20	1	1

Figure 5.7
(*Cont.*)

TABLE 2 POLARIZED VARIABLES BY SURVEY QUESTIONS

	ACCURATE	INACCURATE
KNOWLEDGE		
AIDS is transmitted by: (All-that-apply)	95%	5%
There is a cure for AIDS.	93%	7%
People can catch the AIDS virus from public toilet seats.	96%	4%
AIDS can be transmitted from females as well as from males.	99%	1%
Most people who become infected with the AIDS virus will not get fully developed, fatal AIDS.	62%	38%
There is little that can be done to prevent the spread of AIDS.	97%	3%
MEAN	90.3%	9.6%

	SAFER	NOT SAFE
BEHAVIOR		
I have or will discuss AIDS with my children.	98%	2%
I have or will discuss safer sex practices with my children.	97%	3%
Because of AIDS I have increased the length of time I date someone before engaging in sexual intercourse.	76%	24%
Because of AIDS I am now likely to ask a potential sex partner about his/her sexual history.	87%	13%
Because of AIDS I have made the decision to remain celibate prior to marriage.	44%	56%
Because of AIDS I am more likely to use condoms when having intercourse.	86%	14%
Because of AIDS I am less likely to engage in oral sex.	49%	51%
Because of AIDS I am less likely to engage in anal sex.	83%	17%
MEAN	78%	22%

	HIGH	LOW
CONCERN		
AIDS is something most people should be concerned about.	97%	3%
AIDS is the most urgent health problem facing the U.S.	89%	11%

Figure 5.7
(*Cont.*)

TABLE 2   (*Cont.*)

	HIGH	LOW
AIDS is the most urgent health problem facing Idaho.	67%	33%
I am personally concerned about contracting AIDS.	47%	53%
I am concerned about my teenage children getting AIDS.	82%	18%
MEAN	76.4%	23.6%

	POSITIVE	NEGATIVE
ATTITUDE		
Would you stop being friends with a person if you discovered that he or she had AIDS?	96%	4%
AIDS affects only limited, specific groups of people.	95%	5%
Condoms should be available in the bathrooms on campus including in the dorms.	92%	8%
HIV infected children have a right to go to public school.	95%	5%
AIDS is a punishment sent by God because of people's immoral behavior.	84%	16%
MEAN	92%	8%

	YES	NO
CONTACT		
Did you attend a lecture by Richard Carper during the week of Oct. 22-26, 1990?	54%	46%
Do you personally know anyone who is HIV+ or who has AIDS?	14%	86%
MEAN	34%	66%

TABLE 3 VARIABLES BY DEMOGRAPHICS (MEANS)

	Knowledge Accurate	Knowledge Inaccurate	Concern High	Concern Low	Attitude Positive	Attitude Negative	Contact Yes	Contact No	Behavior Safer	Behavior Not Safer
Male	86%	14%	64%	36%	81%	19%	29%	71%	49%	51%
Female	91%	9%	66%	34%	91%	9%	38%	62%	51%	49%
18-20	87%	13%	63%	37%	85%	15%	25%	75%	57%	43%
21-25	87%	13%	61%	39%	85%	15%	30%	70%	45%	55%
26-30	93%	7%	66%	34%	91%	9%	42%	58%	47%	53%
31-35	92%	8%	72%	28%	93%	7%	33%	67%	57%	43%
36-50	91%	9%	70%	30%	89%	11%	53%	47%	47%	53%
Cath	91%	9%	75%	25%	97%	3%	46%	54%	57%	43%
Prot	91%	9%	63%	37%	90%	10%	34%	66%	54%	46%
Lds	90%	10%	63%	37%	82%	18%	28%	72%	46%	54%
None	82%	18%	64%	36%	88%	12%	35%	65%	47%	53%
Fresh	88%	12%	63%	37%	82%	18%	20%	80%	55%	45%
Soph	89%	11%	63%	37%	87%	13%	33%	67%	51%	49%
Jun	88%	12%	65%	35%	92%	8%	44%	56%	47%	53%
Sen	94%	6%	72%	28%	94%	6%	53%	47%	48%	52%
Married	93%	7%	67%	33%	88%	12%	42%	58%	40%	60%
Divorced	91%	9%	73%	27%	97%	3%	37%	63%	61%	39%
Separat.	75%	25%	50%	50%	80%	20%	50%	50%	41%	59%
Single	87%	13%	64%	36%	86%	14%	27%	73%	58%	42%
Liv. with	85%	15%	64%	36%	88%	12%	37%	63%	48%	52%
Sex. Act.	89%	11%	67%	33%	90%	10%	36%	64%	50%	50%
Not Sex. Act.	89%	11%	60%	40%	82%	18%	27%	73%	53%	47%
1 Partner	98%	2%	58%	42%	91%	9%	37%	63%	47%	53%
2-3 Part.	91%	9%	63%	37%	95%	5%	30%	70%	59%	41%
4-5 Part.	89%	11%	69%	31%	95%	5%	45%	55%	55%	45%
6-20 Part.	100%	0%	75%	25%	100%	0%	50%	50%	68%	32%
Not At All	95%	5%	62%	38%	93%	7%	35%	65%	52%	48%
Somewhat	96%	4%	57%	43%	92%	8%	31%	69%	57%	43%
Very Much	98%	2%	53%	47%	80%	20%	35%	65%	43%	57%

Figure 5.7
(*Cont.*)

TABLE 4 VARIABLES X SAFER SEX BEHAVIOR (SA/A)

	Discuss AIDS	Discuss Safer Sex	Date Longer	Sexual History	Remain Celibate	More Likely To Use Condoms	Less Likely Oral Sex	Less Likely Anal Sex	Mean
Knowledge									
Accurate	98%	97%	76%	88%	45%	86%	49%	82%	78%
Inaccurate	88%	93%	71%	73%	23%	90%	56%	88%	73%
Concern									
High	99%	98%	80%	89%	44%	89%	52%	85%	80%
Low	95%	92%	45%	76%	56%	74%	29%	78%	68%
Contact									
Yes	99%	98%	65%	83%	47%	82%	52%	77%	75%
No	98%	98%	80%	88%	43%	88%	48%	84%	78%
Attitude									
Positive	99%	98%	78%	87%	42%	88%	48%	83%	78%
Negative	87%	90%	58%	75%	56%	67%	41%	84%	70%

6

SOLVING PROBLEMS THROUGH TRIP REPORTS, FEASIBILITY STUDIES, AND LAB REPORTS

Preview of the Chapter

Fundamentals of a Trip Report
  Purpose and Rationale

Analyzing the Process of Writing a Trip Report
  Introduction
  Overall Assessment of the Work Done
  Problems and Solutions
  Conclusions and Recommendations

Format and Substance of a Trip Report

Sample Professional Trip Report

Fundamentals of a Feasibility Study
  Purpose and Rationale

Analyzing the Process of Writing a Feasibility Study

Sample Outline for a Feasibility Study

Sample Engineering Feasibility Study

Fundamentals of Scientific Writing
  Evolution of Scientific Writing
  The Professional Writing Continuum

Format and Substance of a Scientific Report

Sample Student-Authored Scientific Article

April 2, 1991
8:30 A.M.
Bruce Kennewick's Office
The Brighton House
1530 Shore Boulevard
Ozark Lake, Missouri

Bruce Kennewick had just gotten back from his task force assignment in Mexico. Brighton Hotels' head office had sent him to Puerto Vallarta to straighten out the Catering Department at its new hotel, Brighton Playa–Puerto Vallarta, that had opened at the beginning of November, the start of the winter tourist season. Although all the departments of the hotel had gone through the usual task force treatment before a new hotel opens, which involves a team of experts in various areas of a hotel's business coming to the new property to establish procedures and train personnel, the Catering Department had met with unusual reverses. Fifty percent of the personnel hired had quit or been fired and the Director of Catering, a Mexican national, had quit suddenly to take a better job in Guadalajara with a competing hotel chain.

Brighton Playa–Puerto Vallarta was certainly in business, but needed some help—especially in the Catering Department. That's where Bruce Kennewick came in. After some 12 years with Brighton Hotels, in various capacities of providing food, beverage, banquet, and meeting and convention services, Bruce was a good person to send to Brighton Playa. He could assess the problems quickly and begin to solve them, or at least suggest how they might be solved. And so on November 22 he got his assignment to be in Puerto Vallarta on December 3 to run another mini-task force, specifically for the Catering Department.

Bruce accepted the assignment willingly. He knew a lot about running a Catering Department, he was willing to take an interim assignment if the company wanted him to, and he had never been to Mexico. What could be better?

Although it seemed ideal, the job turned out to be sometimes troublesome and frustrating. He had trouble with language and cultural differences that made for some tensions and misunderstandings between him and the people he worked with. He also had been away from home and his family for a prolonged period—4 months—and that had created other problems. In fact, Bruce Kennewick was bone tired. He thought, in the end, that he had done well on his special task force assignment, but there it was, sitting on his desk, the form for reporting company activities off of home site. He would have to fill it out, but it would mean at this point a major effort, one that he would have to put a good deal of thought into, and one that could not reflect how tired he was.

Despite his fatigue, he decided he would have to put the best face on it. His task force effort in fact had worked pretty well. He left Brighton Playa–Puerto Vallarta with a better staff, one that could work well with the new management, one that showed promise in developing new business along the Brighton lines. Bruce had done basically what he was supposed to do, but he knew also that there were still some problems he would have to discuss, problems he felt sure that he had addressed, and in some cases had solved, but ones that Brighton needed to know about so that it could plan for the future.

Pushing aside for now the other paperwork demands on his desk, Bruce turned his attention to this important trip report he had to write.

FUNDAMENTALS OF A TRIP REPORT

Purpose and Rationale

Trip reports have a very specific purpose. They are written to record the activities of someone away from the usual work site. Organizations send their employees on trips for any number of reasons: to drum up new business, to check the progress of business already underway, and to assess and solve problems that have cropped up with business already underway. Management needs to know what has gone on, what is going on, or what needs to be done, so that it can plan for the future. In this way, trip reports are very much like periodic reports, because they answer the same kinds of questions.

Bruce Kennewick's case is typical of organizations like Brighton Hotels. They regularly send out people to start up new hotels, a process called task forcing—an effort by veteran employees to establish local standard operating procedures (LSOPs) at a new site consistent with the general standard operating procedures (GSOPs) throughout the chain. The work involves analyzing the needs and setup of the new site, defining the operations and procedures of the chain in light of the situation at the new site, training new employees, and working through the usual functions of the hotel to anticipate and forestall problems.

Bruce had been a member of numerous task forces, which usually worked for a month or so away from their own home assignments. But he had never been on a follow-up or troubleshooting task force. He had also never gone to an international property, where there were differences in language, culture, and delivery of services that had to be coped with. This assignment was special in those ways, requiring him to report more thoroughly and thoughtfully on the outcome of his trip.

All trip reports, whether special or routine, can be organized under the following five general topics:

1. Introduction
2. Overall assessment of the work done
3. Problems
4. Solutions
5. Conclusions and, perhaps, recommendations

ANALYZING THE PROCESS OF WRITING A TRIP REPORT

Again the answers to several questions help define the purposes for writing and reading trip reports, and therefore help determine their basic contents (see Figure 6.1).

Figure 6.1
*Questions to ask
and answer to
define the
contents of a trip
report*

Questions That Trip Reports Answer

Introduction
- Where was the work done?
- With whom?
- When?
- For how long?
- Why?

Overall Assessment of the Work Done
- What work was done?
- How did it meet the goals of the assignment?

Problems and Solutions
- What problems were encountered?
- Were they solved?
- How?
- If they were not solved, how might they be solved?
- By whom?
- When?

Conclusions and Recommendations
- What work has to be done in the future?
- When should it happen?
- Who should do it?

Introduction

As is true of periodic reports, trip reports must establish the basics to orient the reader. The audience—again middle to upper management—needs to sort out one project from another and make decisions based on the answers to several other questions. So at the outset readers need to know where the writer went, whether singly or as part of a team, when the trip happened, who authorized it, how long the trip lasted, and finally, why the trip was taken—what purpose it was to serve.

To this, Bruce was able to respond fairly easily because Brighton Hotels, typical of many organizations, had provided a format to fill in. The first page of Bruce's trip report shows this format (see Figure 6.2, p. 233).

Overall Assessment of the Work Done

As we have already suggested, management calls for trips to be taken for a number of reasons. A new sales territory may need to be established, which could call for market testing or contacts with potential customers to be made; or perhaps a new product needs to be introduced in an already established market, in which case specific local marketing strategies need to be devised. Also, as in the case of Brighton Hotels, management needs to know whether operations are being conducted according to plan, whether expectations are being met, including how and to what extent. It wants to know whether its short- and long-term goals are being served, and if not, why not. If an organization spends money sending someone to another place to find out what is going on there, then clearly a full report of what happened on the trip needs to be written.

Although these needs can often be met on any individual site by those who work there, sometimes it takes a fresh and practiced eye, someone not connected to the day-to-day business, to assess accurately the situation. That's where Bruce Kennewick comes in for the Brighton Hotels. His years of experience in the food and beverage areas of the hotel business, but particularly in catering for Brighton, have enabled him to analyze and evaluate a property's operations and to make certain changes that will further the effective and smooth running of the business. Thus the work he had to do in Puerto Vallarta—general reorganizing of the Catering Department, soliciting business, and training personnel—becomes the necessary substance of this section of his trip report.

Problems and Solutions

This part of the trip report mirrors the same section of the periodic report. If problems exist that have implications for the future, they need to be analyzed in this section of the report. Readers want to know the nature of the problems, how they were solved, and how and when they may happen again. If the problems cannot be solved within the trip period, writers need to explain why and suggest how they might be solved in the future and by whom.

Besides the usual problems of finding reliable personnel, Bruce Kennewick had the additional problems of working in a foreign culture and speaking a different language. Although he knew some Spanish, it was limited pretty much to a basic "getting around" vocabulary, not a facility for carrying on business easily. And even though the hotel had hired some bilingual employees, they were often in key positions and had their own work to do. At the beginning of his assignment, therefore, he found he had to spend a good deal of time learning the language and finding people who could translate and interpret for him.

But the bigger problem was the cultural differences, especially in the way of conducting business. Bruce's task force experience had been limited to properties in the United States, where he could usually rely on a large pool of skilled labor that delivered services quickly and efficiently. And even though Puerto Vallarta is a resort town, geared in many ways to the service and hospitality industry, its pool of skilled labor is nevertheless small and in great demand. Therefore, services cannot be rendered in the same way as they might be in the United States. The need for electricians, carpenters, and people versed in audiovisual and computer technology is great and is met sometimes haltingly.

Problems like these have significant impact over the long term. They need to be addressed so that management can plan for the future, so that future task force operations can be made more efficient, and so that follow-up task force assignments, like the one Bruce was on, could be reduced in frequency, or eliminated entirely.

Conclusions and Recommendations

Once again, this section is very similar to the section that answers the same questions in the periodic report. The difference is that in the periodic report, writers and readers are reporting on the general, ongoing activity of a project over time, whereas in the trip report, the interest lies in an activity that is specified at a particular time. Concern about the future in the periodic report is normal as a project evolves; concern about the future in the trip report is more specifically directed toward follow-up activities or toward predictions about what may happen.

Thus Bruce Kennewick will reserve this section to suggest how follow-up task force actions may be made less frequent or eliminated entirely. Making sure, for instance, that the initial task force has at least one bilingual member and someone who is familiar with the cultural differences of the country in question would make initial training and contacts with service personnel more efficient.

The future work section of a trip report, then, requires specific recommendations to management, rather than a review of work already projected.

FORMAT AND SUBSTANCE OF A TRIP REPORT

Bruce Kennewick wrote his report on a form that was provided by Brighton Hotels. When no company form exists, however, the basic format of his report can be followed.

SAMPLE PROFESSIONAL TRIP REPORT

Figure 6.2 presents the rough draft of Bruce's trip report to T. P. Simpson on the activities of his follow-up task force assignment.

Figure 6.2
*Bruce
Kennewick's trip
report*

BRIGHTON HOTELS, INC.

3200 LAKESIDE DRIVE, SALT LAKE CITY, UTAH 70121   801-326-9800   FAX: 801-243-1864

OFF-PROPERTY REPORT

Primary Reporter: Bruce Kennewick, Director of Catering, 044-34-4739

Home Property of Primary Reporter: The Brighton House, Ozark Beach, MO, 1530

Authorization: T. P. Simpson, Vice President, International Division, Salt Lake City, Utah, November 10, 1990

Reporting Property: Brighton Playa, Puerto Vallarta, Mexico, 1720

Other Members of the Reporting Team: None

Dates of Assignment: December 1, 1990-April 1, 1991

Purpose of the Assignment: Reestablish and refine GSOPs, Catering Department, in light of difficulties with personnel changes. Specifically, train new Assistant Catering Director to take over as Catering Director.

Figure 6.2
(*Cont.*)

The first paragraph summarizes briefly the work done on site during the time spent there. It identifies the four areas of concern and concludes what Kennewick did to solve the problems of each, the problems he encountered in solving them, and what has to be done to solve those not yet solved. As in a periodic report, this introductory section serves as an executive summary, which lays out the substance of the report so that busy readers can find out immediately what happened and then return to the report to study any details.

Work Accomplished

Summary

General Activities

This assignment fell within the usual guidelines and expectations of a follow-up task force. I identified four general areas of concern: personnel, administration, sales, and support services. The problems with the four areas were either solved or substantially diminished to the point that productivity has increased steadily over the last 2 months. I spent the first 10 days assessing the local operations to see where strengths and weaknesses lay and then started to decide which areas needed the most improvement, in line with GSOPs, and how that improvement could be brought about quickly and be sustained over a longer period of time.

Following are the significant accomplishments in each area:

Personnel:

1. Trained the Assistant Catering Director to take over as Director of Catering, with ultimate recommendation that he be promoted
2. Hired and trained a new banquet manager and coordinated his efforts with the Assistant Director of Catering's, according to GSOPs
3. Hired and trained four new waiters

Administration:
Set up the following on the property's computer system:

1. A reorganization of the Catering Department's central filing system
2. A separate trace and file system on local groups and businesses
3. A new database of menu information

Sales:
With the help of the Director of Sales and the Food and Beverage Director:

1. Developed yacht sales (sales to private yachts docked at Puerto Vallarta)
2. Planned weekly theme parties

Support Services:
Finding skilled, reliable vendors of support services proved to be something of a problem, but we established at least the beginnings of a vendor network.

Figure 6.2
(*Cont.*)

The "Personnel" section identifies the work that Kennewick had to do with regard to personnel: hiring and training new waiters and a banquet manager, and continued training of the assistant catering director. He is specific about who the principal parties are and where they come from, but does not waste time going into detail about their qualifications, since that kind of information is available more completely and efficiently through the personnel office.

Kennewick speaks of the specifics of his work with Moreno and Vasquez, keeping in mind the purposes of the assignment—to reestablish and refine GSOPs and specifically to train the new Assistant Catering Director to take over as Catering Director. And he specifies the activities he and his trainees took part in to show how he was meeting those purposes. He comments briefly on how the training for the two went generally.

In the fourth paragraph Kennewick writes specifically about his training of Moreno in sales procedures, a crucial element in the operations of the Catering Department. He shows how he involved the Banquet Manager and refers the readers to a later part of the report for greater detail.

Problems

Differences in language and culture initially slowed down the reorganization effort, but by the end of the period both problems had been significantly diminished.

Recommendations

1. Provide at least one bilingual member who is also versed in the mores of the host culture on task force teams to international properties.
2. Establish a pool of reliable, competent off-property service personnel as soon as possible at international sites.
3. Hire an audiovisual manager at Brighton Playa.

Details of the Report

Personnel

On the property when I arrived were an assistant catering director, Sr. Jose Moreno, who had been hired only 3 weeks before; a banquet manager; a catering manager; and eight waiters, three full-time, five half-time. Within 3 weeks the banquet manager and four of the waiters, one full-time, three half-time, had quit. We advertised the positions in the local press and through local contacts, and at the end of the first 2 weeks, we were able to hire four new waiters and a new banquet manager, Sr. Pedro Vasquez.

The most important work of the period was to prepare Sr. Moreno to take over as Director of Catering and to train the new banquet manager, Sr. Vasquez. The two men have combined experience of 7 years with Hilton and Stratton in Mexico City and Guadalajara, but both are new to Puerto Vallarta. Their complete résumés are available through Central Personnel.

It was essential to coordinate the efforts of these two people to meet the standards of Brighton's GSOPs. I therefore reviewed with them, over a 3-week period, the paperwork involved in ordering, preparation, and presentation, and was able to take advantage of a short lull to supervise a dry-run rehearsal for a large convention at the end of the month. The two men worked well with me and soon began to understand their relationship in planning and coordinating clearly. They also worked well with waiters, bringing them up to standard performance in about 3 weeks.

During this time I also gave special attention to Sr. Moreno's training in sales procedures, pointing out and clarifying his responsibilities for coordinating local bookings with those of our own booking centers in the United States. We also worked together on plans for increasing local sales (discussed in greater detail below). We involved Srs. Vasquez and Castorena (Catering Manager) in several of our meetings so that they could better understand the relationship of sales to their parts of the operation.

In general, work with personnel went smoothly, though a bit slowly, and I felt confident at the end of the period that the Catering Department was working well as a team.

Figure 6.2
(Cont.)

In the three paragraphs under "Administration," Kennewick refers to three administrative chores he accomplished: reorganizing the central filing system, establishing a trace and file system, and setting up a database of menu information. Since the latter two have a direct influence on sales, he is sure to point that out, given the primary importance of sales to any operation of this kind. He is also specific as to the effects the changes will most likely have.

Administration

A number of important administrative chores had to be completed before the department could run smoothly. The existing filing system for such things as sales orders, purchase orders, and disbursements had to be reorganized to conform to Brighton's central system. A good deal of miscommunication had resulted from using the ad hoc, local system the original Director of Catering had established, and that apparently only he understood.

I also established a separate trace and file system for soliciting sales from local groups. As a subset of the main filing system, the new database now provides quick and easy access to information on local groups and businesses in order to solicit new business and to encourage repeat business. Although 4 months was not enough time to test the system fully, we were able to book four new meetings and two repeat meetings for the 1991 Christmas season, an encouraging indication of the new file's future utility.

The last administrative chore was to establish a database of menu information based on several considerations: time of year (accounting for seasonal differences, especially in fish, fruits, and vegetables), local service availability, kind of meeting, size of meeting, and costs (including customer's budget). Having this information, and being able to update it according to changes in production and the economy, will make our sales efforts both more efficient and convincing.

The "Sales" portion of the report is the longest, again because of the central importance sales have to the Catering Department. Kennewick explains in some detail the two local initiatives he was able to put into place: yacht sales and theme parties. He explains how the initiatives will work and offers in paragraphs three and five the underlying business rationale, besides increasing profits, for the moves.

Sales

With the help of the Director of Sales and the Food and Beverage Director, the Catering Department was able to suggest two local initiatives for local sales. The first is yacht food sales, something new to our business, but that Hilton has tried already with some success. The procedure is fairly simple. A "grocery list" of foods and meals available is delivered by uniformed personnel to private yachts docked in the port, and the customers are invited to decide what they might want delivered to them, ranging from uncooked foods to complete dinners, including full service.

Customers may order uncooked foods to be prepared on ship by their own staffs or a complete banquet delivered and served by Brighton personnel. There are of course variations of service available between the two extremes.

The initiative capitalizes on the leisurely resort atmosphere of Puerto Vallarta. And even though this initiative may require some additional outlay, such as more delivery equipment and additional servers, the move could also prove very profitable. People with the means to take private cruises are also willing to pay for courteous, efficient, and tasteful service.

The modest beginnings of yacht sales when I left—ten or so orders, mostly of small dinners of six to seven people—were profitable. We were able to use existing hotel equipment and personnel, without hindering

Figure 6.2
(*Cont.*)

Finally, Kennewick is quick to mention the help he received from the Director of Sales and the Food and Beverage Director. This is important because it demonstrates the interconnectedness of the operation, but also because it shows he is willing to draw on other in-house resources, a central part of the notion of team playing that Brighton Hotels strongly fosters.

Kennewick ends the "Work Accomplished" section with talk of support services. Although he found the work in this area problematic, Kennewick is able to point to some success with the physical therapists' meeting and to suggest a reasonable way of solving the problems he came across.

Kennewick speaks of two basic problems typical of any international

operations, and the rewards, both in revenue and customer satisfaction, were substantial. A more detailed report on this initiative will follow from the Director of Sales.

The other local initiative, which will prove beneficial for extra-local sales, is the theme party. Based on successful specials, happy hours, and seasonal parties at hotels in the United States, the Catering Department, with help from the Food and Beverage Director, has decided on weekly theme parties that will be held in the Aztec Room (a Grade B banquet room) on each Wednesday. The themes will vary from the mystery of the sea to the culture and mythology of the Aztecs, but we plan an Aztecan theme at least twice a month. The kind of food and beverages will attempt to reflect the theme, although choices from the bar and menu will also include standard, nontheme items; waiters will wear appropriate costumes in keeping with the theme. Service will be mostly buffet style, but waiters will serve cocktails, coffee, and dessert, as requested. Music will also be provided, mostly by recording, but sometimes live. Theme parties will start at 7:00 P.M. and food service will conclude at 11:00 P.M. Bar service, including hors d'oeuvres and music, will continue until 2:00 A.M.

Support Services

Support services were in some ways the most troublesome of all the work for the period. Although Food and Beverages has trouble with timely delivery of some of its commodities, Catering is able nevertheless to piggy-back on its orders for most of our functions. But Catering requires other support services that F and B doesn't require, such as stage construction and audiovisual services, and finding vendors for these services was a problem (to be discussed in some greater detail below).

We were able, however, to find some local plumbers, carpenters, and electricians who could serve our needs in a fairly reasonable time. For the first meeting of the American Association of Physical Therapists at Brighton Playa, we were able to section off areas by collapsible partition and in some cases construct performing stages for various demonstrations of new techniques in physical therapy. We also provided minimum services for audiovisual requirements, such as overhead and slide projectors. The meeting was successful, although we got some complaints about the immediate availability of these services. Given some time, and an established network, these services can be as easily rendered as any other. But it will take time and practice. More of this later under "Problems."

Problems Encountered

Differences in language and culture were the biggest problems I had to confront for most of the time on the property. Although I spoke some Spanish when I arrived, I soon realized that I did not speak enough to get

237

Figure 6.2
(*Cont.*)

property: differences in language and culture. He is specific about how language was a problem, especially in training personnel, since he is not bilingual, and those who are were not always available. This made for some misunderstanding and confusion and in general tended to slow down the operation. But he also points out that time and practice in Spanish made him at least functionally fluent toward the end of his stay.

along easily. The GM and all other department heads are bilingual, but the manager's level has only a few who are bilingual, and Srs. Moreno and Vasquez are not among them. Although they speak better English than I do Spanish, their facility in English is halting at times, which at the beginning of the training period caused some difficulties. They seemed to understand the basic concepts of the GSOPs, for instance, but when I attempted to alter them for specific local needs, they frequently misunderstood what I was trying to explain.

The problem was even greater in the training of waiters and setup personnel. At that level everyone speaks only Spanish. And the same is true for off-property service personnel: carpenters, electricians, and the like. Even though Srs. Moreno and Vasquez took a willing hand in training waiters, there were times when they were either unavailable or themselves had trouble understanding and explaining the kinds of procedures I wanted waiters to follow. At the times I had to deal with service personnel, Moreno and Vasquez would have to do almost continuous translation, and if they were not around, I would have to find someone else to translate for me.

Over the course of 4 months I was able to learn much more Spanish and became at least functionally fluent in the needs of day-to-day business. Nevertheless, much of the slowness at the beginning of the reorganization efforts I must attribute to problems with language.

The other problem, cultural differences, is more delicate and difficult to solve. But Kennewick does a good job of defining the differences as they affected him and his operation, without making qualitative judgments. Referring to the differences as a "clash of expectations," he is careful not to diminish the mores of the host culture, and in speaking of "compromise," he gives credit to both sides for their willingness to take part in that activity.

The other main problem has to do with cultural differences, especially in the general area of punctuality. North Americans in business usually operate on the notion that time is money, that meeting a fairly rigid schedule of operations will in the end be profitable. Mexican nationals in business, at least at the mid to lower levels, however, tend to operate on more flexible schedules, those that allow for more relaxed interactions between people, interactions they believe in the end will also be profitable. The result of the two is a clash of expectations: North Americans expecting a more rigid conformity to schedules, Mexicans expecting a more flexible schedule. The two notions can eventually come together or be compromised at some point, but I found that it takes time, and neither group is immediately comfortable with the other's expectations.

I tended to complain about lateness to meetings and missed appointments by both hotel and off-property personnel; they tended to show confusion about why I was complaining. It took us both a while until such difficulties could be compromised, which meant essentially changes in planning and schedules on both of our parts; but eventually a much smoother working relationship was worked out.

Recommendations for the Future

The recommendations for the future are brief and straightforward

Several recommendations for the future grow immediately out of the problems I encountered, although others might simply move business along more expeditiously and profitably.

Figure 6.2
(Cont.)

and grow directly out of problems Kennewick came across. When possible, as in the case of item #2, some idea of how the recommendation could be carried out is included.

1. Initial Task Forces on international properties should have at least one member who is fluent in the native language and who has clear ideas of cultural differences that will affect the conduct of business. The two usually go together, but not always. This will make conduct of business much easier and more efficient.

2. A pool of reliable, competent off-property service personnel should be established as soon as possible. This involves some research: finding vendors who have worked well on other properties in the area and determining their availability or perhaps getting recommendations for vendors from the local Chamber of Commerce.

3. At Brighton Playa in particular the Catering Director needs to hire someone to manage audiovisual services.

EXERCISES

1.   Taking a trip on a company's business obviously costs something, both in time and money. Trips, therefore, have to be planned in advance so that time and money are spent wisely. Bruce Kennewick, for example, spent several hours of several days planning what he would do when he got to Puerto Vallarta, and anticipating as well as he could the problems he might confront. This made his work more efficient when he got on site.

Using a problem that you and your instructor have agreed is worthy of attention and that would require a trip to help address, plan what you would do, how you would do it, and why.

An example might be the decision of the city in which your college or university is located to establish a comprehensive solid waste recycling program in response to new state mandates for such programs in all municipalities of 10,000 people or more. The city council has turned to the college or university for help in planning and implementing the program.

The problem would require a review and assessment of existing recycling efforts and facilities. When planning this work, you might consider a visit to the mayor, or city manager, or city planner to ask questions about the city's current recycling efforts and how they might be changed to meet the new state mandates. You would also want to visit the current recycling facilities to see how they operate.

Imagine yourself a member of an assessment team, and decide what it is you need to find out from the visits suggested above. In addition to deciding on the kinds of questions you would ask and the kinds of operations you should observe, anticipate any problems you might have that would interfere with your plans.

Remember that you will eventually have to report on your visits to someone. Define that audience carefully, and keep it in mind as you make your plans.

A specific outline of your plans for the audience intended should be the result of this exercise.

2.   Plan a trip to gather data for any other problem that may exist on your campus or in the community: access to facilities for handicapped students and visitors, the extent of and access to computer facilities for students, a safety program for women traveling alone on campus, programs for reeducation and reemployment of workers who have been laid off at a local or regional manufacturing facility.

ASSIGNMENT

TERM PROJECT OPTION

Based on the principles discussed in this chapter and elsewhere in the text, write a report on a trip you have taken to collect data on the research problem you are attempting to address or to solve.

June 13, 1988
11:45 A.M.
Somewhere on the Llano Estacado in New Mexico
Temperature 115° F

Al Robinson took another swig from his canteen. He and his crew had been running pilot holes into the desert for 4 months now to find a spot that could support the project his company was interested in: burying nuclear waste. This exploratory work had turned up some interesting things; the pilot holes had first of all looked like diagonals instead of verticals because of the unexpected resistance they had encountered from various soils. A number of methodological changes were then instituted. Another problem, expected but not in its current frequency, was the volume of brine infiltration the crews encountered.

After consulting with the hydrologists and mining engineers, Al made some significant adjustments to the pilot hole rationale. After those changes the crew started getting some reliable numbers for depth, time, and costs. Unfortunately, these numbers were not exactly what Al's management seemed to be looking for, from what Al could perceive. As a result of the memos and preliminary reports he had seen, Al had the impression that management was interested in a simple project, not one that would require greater depths and, therefore, greater costs than a standard potash mine would require.

Al felt like he was in a dilemma. Was he obligated to report all the work they had done to conduct the feasibility study? Should he try to do his managers' thinking for them by leading them to what he thought was a reasonable answer, or should he just lay down the facts and let them form their own opinions? He didn't think it was his job to place undue influence on his higher-ups. Exactly what should he do to write up this feasibility study?

As a last resort Al called Tammy, the technical writer he had worked with on procedures. She was not knowledgeable in the technical aspects, but she still understood how to write up technical subjects. She had some good advice for him. She was a cool breeze in the middle of the desert.

FUNDAMENTALS OF A FEASIBILITY STUDY

Purpose and Rationale

A feasibility study reports exploratory work performed to assess whether a larger project is advisable. The advisability can be based on any parameters the authors want considered, like cost, physical feasibility, or schedule. This kind of report used to be called a recommendation report, because that is the essence of the report's importance.

More important than the description of work done to try to determine feasibility is the logic of the conclusion the authors draw. A feasibility study is not complete without the recommendation; yet, the recommendation cannot be evaluated without the data on which it was based. So a feasibility study will usually contain two distinct sections, a descriptive section and an evaluative section. The descriptive section, like that of a lab report, will review in appropriate detail the tests performed to try to determine feasibility. The evaluative section will pull all the discrete conclusions together into an overall recommendation.

While feasibility studies are not difficult to write, they may be more difficult to make readable than other types of reports because they have so much descriptive work to do. The temptation for the writer is to get bogged down in descriptive details instead of subordinating these details to the readers' concerns. Different audiences will read feasibility studies for different reasons, but whenever possible the writer should structure one report for ease of reading by a number of audiences, rather than write different versions of the same report.

Although feasibility studies may take various forms and may be addressed to varying audiences, the following ground rules always apply:

1. Make the report conclusive.
2. Review reasonable alternatives.
3. Provide sufficient detail and analysis to support conclusions and recommendations.
4. Include specific recommendations.

ANALYZING THE PROCESS OF WRITING A FEASIBILITY STUDY

The essential questions that feasibility studies answer are summarized in Figure 6.3.

A good feasibility study will state its conclusions up front, either in the report's introduction, in an abstract, or in an executive summary. This sort of recommendation report is very tempting to structure like a detective novel instead of like a professional report because one of the purposes of the report is to give a definitive answer to a specific question: Should we take on this project or not? Will this project be worth financing? Is this project doable? The writer gets caught up in the suspense of the enterprise. But the readers want answers immediately; the suspense wastes their time. So the author must be forthcoming with the conclusions. Responsible audiences will read on. With the suspense gotten out of the way, the reader can immediately read for coherence between test data and conclusions.

Reviewing reasonable alternatives means that the writer will consider choices to originally projected actions in a responsible way. For example, if an author were estimating the feasibility of burying nuclear waste in bedded salt in a specific site, the author would have to review alternatives in good faith, not skipping any which, for personal reasons, did not appeal. Thus, the writer would have to admit that a site with an extant but defunct potash mine shaft might work, despite the fact that the company would rather test out all kinds of innovative shaft-sinking technology

Questions That Feasibility Studies Answer

- What is the problem being studied?
- Briefly, what alternatives are being considered?
- What is the recommendation?
- What evidence supports this recommendation?
- What financial and schedule consequences result from this recommendation?
- What further work needs to be done?

and would, therefore, prefer virgin territory. It is tempting to "load" alternatives into a feasibility study, but it is better to try to cover only the reasonable ones, since lack of coverage of those might be apparent to reviewers and provide them with reason to dismiss the report.

To establish credibility, the feasibility study must show clear logical connections between the descriptive data it provides and the conclusions and recommendations it reaches. Thus, it is not enough to expect the facts to speak for themselves. Instead, the facts must be analyzed for the reader, the logic spelled out in clear, simple prose. So, an analysis section is at the heart of a feasibility study. It serves as the connection between the raw data and the conclusions the data support.

It is important for those writing the feasibility study, and who, therefore, have the most detailed and current understanding of the possibilities in a situation, to write specific recommendations based on their findings. These findings, although perhaps rejected in their specific language, may provide the model of acceptable choices. They essentially instruct the reader in how to think about the project's implications. If a feasibility study dodges this responsibility, then the report may lose all credibility.

SAMPLE OUTLINE FOR A FEASIBILITY STUDY

Having reviewed these particulars with Tammy, Al had a much better idea of what to include in his report. He decided that some brief mention should be made of their early drilling problems, just to honor the accuracy of the descriptive information section, but he wouldn't need to dwell on these problems. He also decided that the use of defunct potash mine shafts should be clearly explained as an alternative, despite the fact that he didn't think his own management was very interested in that alternative. He would also walk his readers through the process of elimination that he had gone through to come up with what he saw as the most feasible alternative: keep looking. His report thus became a very straightforward job, with the following organization:

I. Abstract

This section of the report contains Al's conclusion that the project is not feasible in any of the sites so far. He also notes here his recommendation to keep looking, but to shift the search to the southwest by 50 miles.

II. Description of the problem and summary of testing

This is where Al summarizes the problem of finding new sites and presents a chronological summary-level review of the 4 months of testing.

III. Discussion

Briefly, Al summarizes the alternatives being considered.

IV. Conclusions and recommendation

Al lists these for his readers.

V. Analysis

Al walks his readers through the evaluation and process of elimination by which he reached his conclusions and recommendation. This discussion serves as the rationale for his recommendation and includes financial and schedule consequences that would result from his recommendation.

VI. Future needs

Al lays out what work has to be done from this point on.

Note that short reports could combine sections III and IV, as long as they emphasize analysis.

SAMPLE ENGINEERING FEASIBILITY STUDY

We have included a copy of an engineering feasibility study from a professional source (see Figure 6.4). You'll note that this feasibility study follows the same organization as Al's, but does not use organizational headers as much as topic headers. It also adds a section on the history of such projects.

This study is a fine model of explicitness. Note that the abstract is conclusive; we know what the upshot of this feasibility study is without having to search through the report to find it. The report is also well marked with descriptive headers, topic sentences, and an explicit conclusions section.

Perhaps the most overwhelming aspect of this report is its reliance on graphics. They are most effectively used for two reasons. First, the tables organize several elements needing comparison. Note that the authors discuss the tables in the text. They don't just expect the tables to speak for themselves. The drawings, of course, visualize for the reader the sort of technology these authors have in mind. Since feasibility analyses concern areas of speculation, drawings help a great deal to make the speculations seem rational and well grounded in reality.

We think this report is a fine example of professional and technical writing. You may also note that the authors write in first person plural (*we*), which allows them to avoid many passive constructions (refer to the Appendix for an explanation of passives). They also express several opinions in this study. Thus the persuasive purpose of so much technical and professional writing is acknowledged and taken up in this study.

Figure 6.4
Sample professional engineering feasibility study

ENGINEERING FEASIBILITY OF A 150-kW IRRIGATION PUMPING PLANT USING SHALLOW SOLAR PONDS

E. A. Platt
R. L. Wood

April 3, 1978

Work performed under the auspices of the U.S. Department of Energy by the UCLLL under contract number W-7405-ENG-48.

LAWRENCE
LIVERMORE
LABORATORY
University of California/Livermore

Figure 6.4
(Cont.)

Printed in the United States of America
Available from
National Technical Information Service
U.S. Department of Commerce
5285 Port Royal Road
Springfield, VA 22161
Price: Printed Copy $; Microfiche $3.00

Page Range	Domestic Price	Page Range	Domestic Price
001 - 025	$ 4.00	326–350	$12.00
026–050	4.50	351–375	12.50
051–075	5.25	376–400	13.00
076–100	6.00	401–425	13.25
101–125	6.50	426–450	14.00
126–150	7.25	451–475	14.50
151–175	8.00	476–500	15.00
176–200	9.00	501–525	15.25
201–225	9.25	526–550	15.50
226–250	9.50	551–575	16.25
251–275	10.75	576–600	16.50 [1]
276–300	11.00	601–up	
301–325	11.75		

[1] Add $2.50 for each additional 100 page increment from 601 pages up.

Figure 6.4
(*Cont.*)

LAWRENCE LIVERMORE LABORATORY
University of California / Livermore, California / 94550

UCRL-52397

ENGINEERING FEASIBILITY OF A
150-kW IRRIGATION PUMPING PLANT
USING SHALLOW SOLAR PONDS

E. A. Platt
R. L. Wood

MS. date: April 3, 1978

Figure 6.4
(*Cont.*)

CONTENTS

Abstract 1
Introduction 1
    Comparison with Alternative System 3
    Comparison with Other Solar Systems 5
    Projected Costs 6
Historical Background 7
Current Activity in Solar Pumping Stations 9
The LLL Study 10
    General 10
    Ponds 11
    Storage Reservoir 13
    Pond Flow Controls 14
    Heat Engine Subsystem 17
Conclusion 22
Acknowledgments 23
References 23

iii

Figure 6.4
(*Cont.*)

ENGINEERING FEASIBILITY OF A
150-kW IRRIGATION PUMPING PLANT
USING SHALLOW SOLAR PONDS

ABSTRACT

We have analyzed the economics of a field of shallow solar ponds that presumably supplies the heat for a Rankine cycle engine using refrigerant R-113 for the working fluid. When operating, the engine supplies 150 kW of shaft power, 125 kW of that is available for deep-well irrigation pumping. The system components have been chosen to produce the maximum net energy — April through October — per dollar of installation cost. Weather data are from Inyokern, California, 1962 records for most calculations.

We estimate that, for a private investor, the real internal rate of return for this installation would be positive only if in the forseeable future the cost of conventional energy were to inflate 8% faster than the cost of the commodities needed by the solar system. A 17% differential inflation rate would produce a 10% rate of return. Reduction in cost of the shallow solar ponds potentially could reduce the system installation cost by about 20%.

INTRODUCTION

Collector array costs are by far the major expense of solar thermal power systems. Specific costs vary by collector type but, generally speaking, those designed to operate at higher temperatures — such as concentrating collectors — cost substantially more than those designed to operate at lower temperatures. High-temperatures are obviously desirable for power production. But question has arisen as to whether one could economically use lower-cost, low-temperature arrays for solar-powered irrigation. The suggested principle is that the savings in array costs might more than offset the lower conversion efficiency from sunlight to mechanical work, thus yielding a lower overall cost per kilowatt-hour.

To test this concept's feasibility and compare the economics against those of alternative power sources, we have studied and projected costs for a solar irrigation system that uses relatively low-temperature heat from shallow solar ponds to run a Freon engine of the waste-heat-recovery type. We chose 150 kW as the nominal capacity of the engine so as to compare our results directly with studies of other systems that specify concentrating collectors. Our work has been mostly calculational although the engine data are from engineering studies and the assumed weather data — for Inyokern, California,

April through October 1962 — are from actual meterological records.

Figure 1 shows the physical plant, the principle elements of which are a field of shallow solar ponds, a water storage pool, circulation pumps and piping, a standby diesel electric generator, and a powerhouse containing the heat exchangers, the turbine, and a motor generator. A local water well supplies the condenser cooling water. The pump for this well connects directly to the output shaft of the engine. A generator also connects to the shaft to provide power for other wells at a distance.

What size farm this system could irrigate depends on the crops, the annual rainfall to be supplemented, and the water table level. A farm in the southwestern U.S., for example, might need 0.5-m coverage from a 100-m total head system.[1] For an overall pumping efficiency of 55% and average 115-kW input, 1.97 million cubic meters of water could be delivered. This would be enough for a typical irrigated farm of about 400 hectares (~1000 acres). Land dedicated to the solar pond system would take up about 0.5% of the farm. We use these data in the projections that follow.

Figure 2 shows the cumulative cash flow needed to build and maintain this station during its lifetime. Also shown are data for comparable irrigation

1

Figure 6.4
(Cont.)

Fig. 1. Shallow solar pond irrigation pumping station. The fifty 5- × 60-m ponds are on 6 acres. When operating, the shaft output is 150 kW. The net useful power averaged from April to October (Inyokern, California, 1962) is 115 kW.

Fig. 2. Costs for a shallow solar pond irrigation system compared with a diesel-electric-generator powered system and with purchased electric power. All systems supply 115 kW average during a growing season of 6 months.

systems using either purchased electric power or a diesel engine — generator set. These costs, summed without regard for the time value of money, are presented as a schedule of disbursements in constant dollars.

We used a computer simulation of the solar pumping system and the Inyokern weather data to arrive at the base cost of the solar system. We scaled costs to the most appropriate parameters and calculated from hourly data the net mechanical energy produced from April through October, which is the normal growing season. Critical system parameters were varied until we identified the irrigation system with the lowest cost per average kilowatt over the growing season. For this "optimum" system, the April-October average useful power was 115 kW. The power supplied to the pumps during system operation was 125 kW, and the online time was 89%.

2

Figure 6.4
(*Cont.*)

Table 1 gives unit costs of the system, Table 2 provides size parameters of the most cost-effective system, Table 3 gives performance data for the optimum system, and Table 4 is a cost breakdown.

Comparison with Alternative System

For the alternative irrigation system using purchased electric power, the cost of the power was based on current Pacific Gas and Electric Company rates for a farmer with an annual contract. It was assumed that he would not pay for new transmission line. Normalized to the average output of the solar system and the 6-month operation cycle, electrical costs were $180/kW. For the diesel engine – generator system, the cost was calculated by relating the cost of the engine-generator unit together with a 10,000-gallon fuel tank to the output of the solar system. We assumed diesel fuel would cost

Table 1. Shallow solar pond power system unit costs.

Item	Unit	Cost ($/unit)	Life (years)	Operation and maintenance ($/year)
Site preparation	m^2	1.40	–	100
Pond bed leveling	m^2	0.76	15	
Fencing	m	4.59	30	25
Ponds				
Water bags	m^2	7.00	7.5	
Top glazing	m^2	3.81	15	
Lower glazing	m^2	0.20	7.5	
Moisture barrier	m^2	0.20	15	
Insulation	m^2	4.04	30	
Curbing	m, pond edge	13.74	–	
Glazing end clamps	m, pond length	1.75	–	
Weather seal	m, pond length	0.66	7.5	
Bow assembly	m, pond length	9.80	–	
Panel clamp	m, pond length	1.15	–	
Misc. hardware	m, pond length	4.08	–	
Installation	m, pond length	15.02	7.5	
Manifolding	ea. pond	223	15	
Flow controls	ea. inlet	400	15	150
Installation	ea. inlet	385	15	
Piping	m^2, wetted area	191	30	100
Pumps	kW	350	15	20
Accumulator	$kg^{2/3}$	35	30	
Storage pool				
Excavation	m^3	2.75	–	
Concrete	m^3	192	–	
Diffuser and plumbing	ea	2500	15	
Cover	m^2	5	7.5	
Building	$kW^{1/3}$	1200	30	
Conversion machinery				
Turbine and gearbox	$kW^{1/3}$	3200	–	75
Generator and switchgear	kW	60	–	20
Instruments and controls	$kW^{1/2}$	1200	–	50
Regenerator	kW/C	1000	20	
Other heat exchangers	kW/C	100	20	
Installation	kW	200		
Stand-by diesel	kW	7800/kW + 80	20	150
Operator				10,000

3

Figure 6.4
(*Cont.*)

Table 2. Size of shallow solar pond power system.

Item	Value
Area of site, m^2	25000
acres	6.0
Collector (pond) area, m^2	15000
acres	3.7
Perimeter fence, m	640
	(185 × 135)
Number of ponds	50 (5 × 60 m)
Number of inlets	25
Total length of pond, m	3000
Total length of curbing, m	6500
Wetted area of piping, m^2	132
Circulating pump capacity, kW	18
Accumulator capacity, kg	2200
Parasitic power, kW	25
Storage pool:	
Volume of excavation, m^3	1760
Volume of concrete, m^3	270
Area of cover, m^2	200
Conversion machinery:	
Shaft power, kW	150
Regenerator UA, kW/C	20
Preheater, vaporizer, and condenser UA, kW	825

Table 3. Performance data for the optimum shallow solar pond power system (Inyokern, April - October, 1962).

Parameter	Value
Total irradiation, MJ/m^2	5460
Total energy collected, kWh	5.29×10^6
Total pond flow, kg	4.08×10^8
Net shaft output, kWh	5.04×10^5
Average shaft output, kW (W/m^2)	115 (7.60)
Average collector efficiency, %	23.3
Average cycle efficiency, %	9.52
Average overall efficiency, %	2.21
Specific cost, $/kW	7060

36.5¢/gal and the engine fuel consumption would be 0.095 gal/kWh. The slope of the shallow solar pond line in Fig. 2 represents salaries and routine maintenance charges of $100/kW-yr. The step costs are for periodic replacement of major components as indicated in Table 1. The major replacement charges we anticipate are for new water bags on a 7.5-year schedule and new heat exchangers on a 20-year schedule. We have only limited information about the useful life of plastics in this hot and wet

Table 4. Shallow solar pond power system cost breakdown.

Item	Cost ($)	Production/first unit
Ponds		425,000/475,000 (52.3%/43.2%)
Water bags	105,000	
Curbing	89,000	
Glazing	63,000	
Insulation	61,000	
Other	106,500	
Conversion system		215,000/375,000 (26.5%/34.0%)
150-kW Rankine engine (See Tables 11 and 12)	171,570/329,000	
Building and installation	33,600	
Stand-by diesel	9,800	
Storage pool		60,000/80,000 (7.4%/7.3%)
Concrete	52,000	
Excavation	4,800	
Diffuser and plumbing	2,500	
Cover	1,000	
Site preparation		47,000/60,000 (5.8%/5.5%)
Pumps and plumbing		45,000/60,000 (5.5%/5.5%)
Instruments and controls		20,000/50,000 (2.5%/4.5%)
		812,000/1,100,000

4

Figure 6.4
(Cont.)

environment and to be conservative have specified short lives and expensive materials; however, less expensive alternatives may be practical.

At the present time, natural gas is available in many farming areas in the Southwest, and in these locations it is the least expensive power source. However, since natural gas shortages are apt to occur relatively soon, we have not considered its cost in the following discussion. Also, where transmission lines exist or can be extended without cost to the farmer, the purchased power and local power generation using a diesel engine cost nearly the same. Therefore, for the purpose of economic comparison, we have only considered the shallow solar pond and the purchased electric power irrigation systems.

Figure 3 shows an annual cost comparison of these two systems. In our evaluation, we have used the methods of Ref. 2, with the following constants:

- 25-year study period (system life).
- 10% investment tax credit.
- 51% income tax.
- Straight-line depreciation.
- Zero salvage value.
- Equity financing.

Fig. 3. Annual cost of a shallow solar pond irrigation system compared with the cost of purchased electric power to provide the same service versus the cost of money. Lifetime of the system is 25 years.

In Fig. 3 we have calculated the after-tax annualized costs of the two systems as functions of the interest rate, or the effective return on the money involved. Only those costs which are not shared are included, and, in addition, we have neglected the cost of not farming the six acres needed for the solar system. The solid lines depict the annual cost per average kilowatt for the solar system for various write-off times. The dashed lines are the annualized costs of electric power, together with operation and maintenance. Relative to the solar system, no first cost and no depreciation is involved. We have shown 5%, 10%, and 15% differential inflation rates for electric power: that is, the inflation of power rates in excess of the inflation of solar system maintenance and replacement costs. It appears that the solar pond system can show an economic advantage only if energy costs increase rapidly. If the cost of power inflates less than 8% faster than the commodities needed to maintain the solar system, the solar system would not be economically feasible and would be a losing investment for the farmer.

If debt financing rather than equity financing is used, as would often be the case, the after-tax cost of money will change the picture presented by Fig. 3. At the tax rate we have presumed, the actual cost of borrowed money is only half the interest rate. This circumstance favors the more capital-intensive solar irrigation system.

If the farmer is already using purchased electrical energy for irrigation, the shallow solar pond system may be viewed as a possible cost-reduction investment. In this case, an important question is the internal rate of return on the investment. The rate of return is numerically equal to the interest rate which makes the annual costs equivalent as shown in Fig. 3, at the points where the curves intersect.

Figure 4 is a plot of the real internal rate of return for the solar system as a function of the future differential inflation rate for electrical energy. We have again assumed a 25-year life and a 10-year write-off period. If, for example, the farmer can expect a minimum 10% return on his capital, the solar system becomes economically attractive only if he anticipates a 17% differential inflation rate for purchased electrical energy. If and when such extreme conditions occur, they may be associated with economic and social problems that would complicate the rate-of-return analysis.

Comparison with Other Solar Systems

It is not within the scope of this report to compare the cost of power from shallow solar ponds with that from other solar collectors in detail. We

5

Figure 6.4
(*Cont.*)

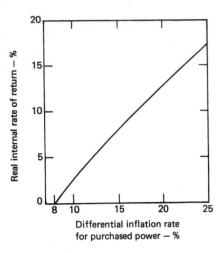

Fig. 4. Real internal rate of return for equity investment in the shallow solar pond irrigation station versus the differential inflation rate for purchased electrical power in excess of the inflation rate affecting solar system maintenance costs. System life, 25 years; write-off period, 10 years.

Table 5. Shallow solar pond power system performance using Albuquerque, NM weather data, January-December, 1962.

Parameter	Value
Total irradiation, MJ/m^2	7920
Total energy collected, kWh	5.25×10^6
Total pond flow, kg	7.00×10^8
Net shaft output, kWh	4.70×10^5
Average shaft output, kW (W/m^2)	53.6 (3.57)
Average collector efficiency, %	15.9
Average cycle efficiency, %	8.95
Average overall efficiency, %	1.42
Specific cost, $/kW	14,700

Table 6. Shallow solar pond power system performance using 1-year Inyokern weather data, January-December, 1962.

Parameter	Value
Total irradiation, MJ/m^2	8380
Total energy collected, kWh	6.10×10^6
Total pond flow, kg	7.43×10^8
Net shaft output, kWh	5.64×10^5
Average shaft output, kW (W/m^2)	64.4 (4.30)
Average collector efficiency, %	17.5
Average cycle efficiency, %	9.25
Average overall efficiency, %	1.62
Specific cost, $/kW	12,200

believe, however, that the cost of the first shallow solar pond plant would be less than that currently being spent on a demonstration irrigation pumping system using parabolic-trough concentrating collectors to produce about the same net output. The system using concentrating collectors is calculated to average 63.2 kW over the year on the basis of Albuquerque, New Mexico, 1962 weather data. For comparison, we applied Albuquerque weather data to the shallow solar pond plant. The results are shown in Table 5. Over the year the average power is 53.6 kW. Table 6 shows the all-year performance for Inyokern, California, where the somewhat more favorable weather gives an average power of 64.4 kW.

Projected Costs

If the shallow solar pond system we have studied were built, the first units would cost appreciably more than the production units, as we have shown in Table 4. The ponds themselves are not much affected by this cost escalation since they are low-technology, on-site conventional construction.

However, the cost of the rest of the system could possibly double because of initial design time, testing, and rework. In this event, the cost of the first system could rise to $1.1 million and the specific power cost based on the 6-month operation time would rise to about $10,000/kW.

Solar system power output is sometimes averaged over various lengths of time for the purpose of reporting performance. It is common to report "peak performance": that is, short-time average power at noon in summer. This figure of merit is undoubtedly useful for comparing systems that are similar otherwise, but it is not generally useful for economic evaluation since energy rather than power is the commodity of value. We have used a 6-month average for most calculations of the output of the shallow solar pond system to correspond with the heaviest irrigation load. Other time periods, such as the full year, would change the specific costs of both

6

Figure 6.4
(Cont.)

the solar and the electric alternatives, but the rate-of-return evaluation should remain about the same. If one designs for peak performance, the results can be misleading. The cost of the peak energy may be deceptively low because components operate at their highest efficiency, and no energy storage is required. If, for example, the shallow solar pond plant were designed for lowest cost peak performance, the installation cost might be less than $400,000, and relative to the 150-kW peak output, the specific cost might be as low as $2500/kW. However, the total work done during the growing season would be only ¼ to ⅓ as much as would be done with our system using a 6-month average.

There are valid prospects for cost reduction in the pond construction and for improvement in its high-temperature performance. We have specified chlorosulfonated polyethylene,* at $7/m^2, for the

water bag material because of the considerable experience with this material in water reservoirs, and because wrinkle-free bags can be made with it. It is believed, however, that the high-temperature polyolefin resin polybutylene,† at about $0.50/m^2, would be adequate. It is presently available in blown tubes of sufficient diameter for the pond width. This 12% decrease in the first cost of the installation and the large reduction in replacement costs would be reflected in a comparable reduction in the annual costs. In addition, it is expected that the transmission-reflection performance of the pond glazing can be improved by using an inner glazing of greater transmission and lower refractive index. Such an improvement would apply directly to the total energy collected. The total reduction in specific costs could approach 20% from these modifications.

*Dupont, Hypalon.

†Witco Chemical Corporation, Witron.

HISTORICAL BACKGROUND

Man's rapid use of petroleum and the coming problem of doing without it suggest the situation of a person who, having been left a legacy of money and using it for current expenses, forsees the time when his supplementary funds will be gone. With perhaps a twinge of panic he begins to consider ways and means of supporting the standard of living to which he has become accustomed. Unhappily, no solution to his problem presents itself immediately. In both the imagined and the real situation, it may be that no satisfactory solution to the problem necessarily exists. Our living standard may indeed decline when petroleum becomes scarce, no matter how diligently we investigate other sources of energy. Nevertheless, it is prudent for us to find the most effective alternate energy source available to us. At best, the loss of petroleum will cause economic difficulties and changes. Our failure to plan and prepare adequately for the difficulties could lead to uncontrollable social and political upheaval.

For the most part we are going over old ground in solar energy research. Work on solar systems, with the exception of photovoltaics, predates the recent heavy reliance on petroleum. [3,4] The engineer John Ericsson constructed seven solar engines between 1868 and 1875. [5] His engines used arrays of mirrors on a curved framework to concentrate sunlight onto either a steam boiler or an air chamber. He reported

that with the steam boiler he obtained 1 hp/100 ft^2 (80 W/m^2) of reflecting surface. Ericsson was at first exceedingly enthusiastic about solar engines powered by concentrating collectors. Finally, however, he was disillusioned, and he wrote: "The scheme is impracticable on account of the great cost of the needed apparatus. The fact is that although the heat is obtained for nothing, so extensive, costly, and complex is the concentration apparatus that solar steam is many times more costly than steam produced by burning coal." Ericsson's conclusion notwithstanding, in 1898 a similar engine of 1000-ft^2 aperture was put into operation to pump water for a Pasadena, California, ostrich farm. The 6 hp (48 W/m^2), this machine could develop was obtained with an inverted umbrella collector configuration having the boiler in the handle. The cost was estimated at $5/ft^2.

Flat-plate collectors also have a long history, Tellier used the glazed heat box type for raising water as early as 1885. [6,7] In 1907, Frank Shuman of Philadelphia constructed a water pumping engine equipped with a flat-plate collector which vaporized and subsequently expanded ether in a reciprocating engine. [8] On the basis of the pumping power of this system, Shuman calculated that one would need 160 ft^2 of collector per horsepower (50 W/m^2), and he concluded that a practical power plant of this kind must necessarily be based upon an inexpensive

7

Figure 6.4
(*Cont.*)

collector design. He proposed the plant illustrated in Fig. 5 which is reproduced from the May 13, 1909, Engineering News. For an output of 750 kW, he proposed 20 closely spaced shallow solar ponds, covering 4 acres, with an asphalt foundation and a glass cover. Hot water from the ponds would be stored temporarily in a tank and eventually run through the turbine. The turbine was described as being of the total-flow type, working at a low pressure so that part of the hot water would flash into steam and accelerate the remaining water. The condenser cooling water would be from a well. After passing through the condenser, the cooling water could be used for irrigation.

Shuman's proposal seems remarkably farsighted, although we can point out some details we believe would have caused trouble if the scheme had been reduced to practice.

1. The loss of heat to the sky and the surroundings at night would be particularly heavy, and some additional insulation between the water and the ground would likely have been cost-effective.

2. The size and cost of the low-pressure turbine and condenser would be an important consideration, and Shuman would almost certainly have been disappointed in the performance of the total-flow turbine because the liquid as droplets would not rebound from the turbine blades properly and behave as the homogeneous mixture he predicted.

3. The cooling water requirements of more than 1000 gpm might also have been a special problem.

An actual irrigation water pumping station using shallow solar ponds for the heat source had been built and operated near Needles, California by Willsie and Boyle as early as 1905.[9] Figure 6, also from Engineering News, is a photograph of this plant in its final form. The solar ponds were insulated on all sides by dead air spaces, and were separated into a first section with a single glazing and a second section with double glazing. It was found that a thin layer of water and relatively rapid circulation worked best. The hot water was stored in a tank and used as needed as the heat source for a sulphur dioxide Rankine cycle engine. Both the

Fig. 5. Shuman's shallow solar pond proposal (1909).

8

256

Figure 6.4
(*Cont.*)

Fig. 6. Willsie's shallow solar pond pumping plant, Needles, California (1905).

evaporator and the condenser were of the drip type which had the water flowing downward over vertical arrays of pipes containing the sulphur dioxide. The condenser was in a thatched-roof shed, open on the sides. The cooling water, which was part of the pumped irrigation water, was supplied to the condenser in limited amounts so that a considerable part of the cooling came from evaporation of the water in contact with the condenser tubes. The two heater sections made up about 1000 ft^2 of collector. Willsie reported the outlet temperature as 180°F with variations according to weather conditions. He thought that the reciprocating sulphur dioxide engine produced as much as 15 hp, but he estimated the collector requirements for continuous running as 400 ft^2/hp (20 W/m^2). The collector cost was about 25¢/ft^2.

In the early 1970's, the Lawrence Livermore Laboratory studied again the use of shallow solar ponds as a way of producing large-scale electric power from solar energy.[10] The overriding consideration was the same as Shuman's, that since collector costs dominate solar energy systems, minimizing collector costs would probably be of first importance. Willsie's plan was not changed in principle, although modern plastics were now used in pond construction and the Rankine cycle engine made use of Freon for the working fluid. A provision was made for draining the ponds at night to conserve heat, and the heat rejection capacity was supplied by cooling towers or evaporative ponds. In this study, year-long average power output was considered rather than peak performance. The collector area needed per kW was 133 m^2 (7.5 W/m^2). The estimated collector cost (including piping) was $16/m^2 ($1.49/ft^2). Relative to the estimates of 25¢/ft^2 made by both Shuman and Willsie in 1909, the modern estimate must be considered inexpensive since an inflation factor of only 2.74%/year implies equal real cost. Subsequent experience in shallow solar pond construction indicates that the actual collector cost is roughly double this estimated figure.

CURRENT ACTIVITY IN SOLAR PUMPING STATIONS

Two solar-powered irrigation stations in the 25- to 50-hp range have recently been put into service. Both systems use about 6000 ft^2 of sun-tracking, parabolic trough collectors. The 50-hp no-energy-storage system at Gila Bend, Arizona is a cooperative venture of Northwestern Mutual Life Insurance Company and Battelle Memorial Institute. The 25-hp hot-oil-storage system near Williard, New Mexico is a joint effort of the Department of Energy and the State of New Mexico.

Three recent studies of 150-kW deep well pumping stations have been completed for the Department of Energy. Energy Resources Center, Honeywell, Inc., has studied the parabolic dish with central receiver — presumably the Pasadena solar engine design. Black and Veatch Consulting Engineers have studied the central receiver in a field of sun-tracking mirrors. Acurex Corporation, Aerotherm Division, has studied the parabolic trough system in the larger 150-kW size. The Acurex Corporation design has been chosen for demonstration, and is scheduled to be constructed by early 1979. Based on the Albuquerque 1962 weather data, it is said to average 63.2 kW.

9

Figure 6.4
(*Cont.*)

THE LLL STUDY

General

The performances of both solar collectors and Rankine cycle engines are well understood and can be characterized by a few parameters, given uncomplicated input variables. Unfortunately, when collectors and engines are coupled and the input depends on weather conditions, it becomes difficult to generalize about system performance. The system responds in complicated ways to a number of parameters, some of which can be controlled by the designer and some of which cannot. Chief among the factors which cannot be controlled are:

● Weather, including foreseeable seasonal insolation variations and unforeseeable short-term variations of cloudiness, haze, and air temperature.

● Temperature of the available heat sink.

Some of the important factors which the designer must manipulate are:

● Balance between engine capacity and collector area.

● Hot water storage capacity in relation to the collector area.

● Relationship between collector temperature and enthalpy extraction rate.

● Heat exchanger capacities and flow rates to match power demands and hot water availability.

● Working fluid selection.

● Collector thermal design and material selection.

● Pond water thickness profile.

The present study has relied on a computer simulation of the total system based on hourly weather information. The weather information came from the insolation climatology data base for the southwestern United States, prepared for the National Science Foundation by Aerospace Corporation, El Segundo, California. For most of the calculations, the data for Inyokern, California, for 1962 were used. Some comparative studies were made for Albuquerque, New Mexico, 1962. The data used were the total horizontal insolation, the normal incidence radiation, the percent of possible radiation, the dry-bulb temperature, and the solar azimuth and elevation.

Figure 7 is a general flow diagram for the irrigation power system. Only one of the water wells that might be connected is shown. The local well supplies the condenser cooling water which is then available for irrigation. That part of the pumping power for this well lost in the condenser is considered parasitic. In addition to the condenser flow, three fluid circuits in the system can be distinguished. The pond flow is drawn from the bottom of the thermal storage pool by the main system pump. When the system is active, the pump charges the accumulator with 2 m^3 of water at a head of about 8 m. This arrangement is calculated to give the lowest cost compromise between accumulator size and pump on-time. The ponds are operated in pairs, being deepest at the inlet and gradually shallowing to 2 cm at the outlet. The outlet temperature is regulated according to a plan to be described below by on-off control of the inlet valve. In hot weather some steaming at the outlet is to be expected, and the vapor is vented at this high point. The overflow hot water from the outlet returns by gravity flow to the top diffuser of the thermal storage pool. The ponds are drained at night to conserve heat by reversing the direction of flow in the ponds. The accumulator is isolated from the ponds, and the by-pass piping to the storage pool is opened. The pond water flows by this return path to the bottom diffuser of the storage pool.

When the engine is running, the hottest available water is drawn from the storage pool and pumped through the vaporizer and the preheater, returning either to the storage pool or the ponds. The system is characterized by four separate relatively large and expensive heat exchangers. The gaseous R-113 leaves the turbine with valuable superheat remaining, and it is cost-effective to remove some of this superheat in a regenerator. Condensation occurs in the condenser at a low pressure. The liquid R-113 out of the condenser is pressurized by the condensate pump, reheated in the regenerator by the turbine exhaust, raised to boiling temperature in the preheater, and boiled in the vaporizer. The temperature and pressure of the R-113 vapor depend on the temperature of the hot water supply and the fact that the turbine flow is controlled for 150-kW output.

The gearbox which reduces the turbine output to a convenient rotational speed is connected by an overrunning clutch to the generator which can also serve as a motor. At startup or when hot water is unavailable, the system can be energized from a standby diesel electric unit, not shown.

The amount of energy available from the conversion machinery is relatively sensitive to the temperature of the water available for the condenser. In our calculations, 18°C has been assumed for the baseline system. Figure 8 shows the relation of the installation cost to well-water temperature. If the well temperature were as high as 25°C (77°F), the cost per useful kilowatt would increase by 30%.

10

Figure 6.4
(Cont.)

Fig. 7. Shallow solar pond power system flow diagram.

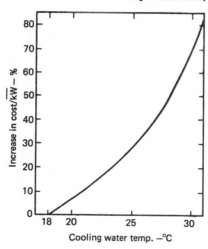

Fig. 8. Percentage increase in system cost per average kilowatt produced during the growing season in Inyokern, California in 1962 versus cooling water temperature. All system component sizes fixed.

Ponds

The general construction details of shallow solar ponds for heating water to between 25 and 60°C have been reported elsewhere.[11] In this temperature range, we have found a single dead air space (single glazing) to be most effective. For power production, high engine efficiency depends on obtaining the highest feasible source temperature, and for this service we have added an inner glazing to form two dead air spaces. The result of this modification is to reduce both the rates of heat absorption and heat loss so that higher temperature performance is enhanced at the expense of lower. Because of the higher temperature operation, we have specified chlorosulfonated polyethylene rather than polyvinyl chloride for the water tube material. It is expected that vinyl lifetimes would be shortened by the loss of plasticizer at temperatures higher than 60°C. There are virtually no strength requirements for the intermediate glazing which can be stretched over a light wire lacing between the pond curbs. The material of choice for this glazing is thin polycarbonate film. Figure 9 illustrates the construction of these ponds.

11

259

Figure 6.4
(*Cont.*)

Fig. 9. High-temperature shallow solar pond.

For lower temperature operation, it is convenient to heat water in the ponds in daily batches so that the pond depth may be as much as 10 cm. For power production the shallowest possible depth appears to be best, as Willsie [9] had observed. As the heating-time constant of the collector is reduced more flexible control plans are possible, and the system can react to take advantage of favorable weather changes or minimize the consequences of an unfavorable change. The limit with respect to making the pond shallower depends on pond bed leveling techniques and the stability of the underlying material. Dry spots in the pond during periods of bright sunlight may reach a temperature of 190°C and eventually result in holes in the absorbing layers. Obviously, the shallow solar pond system cannot be allowed to remain dry on sunny days, and high spots in the bed will cause trouble. In our calculations we have used 2 cm for the water depth at the pond outlet under the assumption that we can expect soil stability within about 1 cm over the 60-m bed. The optimization program indicates that the pond bed should be sloped up toward the outlet so that the water depth at the inlet of the first of the coupled ponds is about 5 cm. The tapered depth makes it possible to control the outlet temperature more smoothly, and has the added advantage of promoting faster draining at the end of the day.

For batch operation or when the heat units collected have roughly the same value at all temperatures, it is possible to analyze pond perfor-

mance from time-averaged insolation data and the temperature-dependent collection efficiency of the pond, based upon noon conditions. For the thin flowing pond with a premium value on high temperature, it is not clear how long-term averages can be used to predict performance. We have used in our calculations a differential model of the pond heat balance in which hourly average direct and diffuse insolation, the hourly average air temperature, and the associated sun angles are the input data from weather records and the pond local temperatures and heat-up rates are the output. The pond performance parameters involved are: the heat-loss coefficient, the radiation absorption coefficient, and the dependence of the latter on the sun's elevation. These parameters can be described respectively as the heat loss from the water per degree of temperature excess over the ambient, the fraction of overhead sunlight that could reach the water, and the degree to which large angles of incidence reduce this fraction. To determine best values for these parameters, an instrumented pond was modified by adding an intermediate glazing, and water and air temperatures as well as insolation intensity were recorded for a number of variations of water depth and starting temperature. These data were tried in three variations of the mathematical model of the heat balance described above, and the performance parameter values which the operational data indicated were identified. We observed some scatter in the data, but we feel the

12

Figure 6.4
(Cont.)

averages of a large number of points are reliable enough for our purpose. We found the heat loss coefficient to be 4.36 $W/m^2/°C$, the radiation absorption coefficient to be 63%, and the sun angle effect to be best described by a function of the solar zenith angle, α, of the form

$$\cos\left[\frac{\pi}{2}\left(\frac{2\alpha}{\pi}\right)^{1.24}\right]$$

to be applied to the direct component of the sunlight only.

We used a fairly complex computer subroutine to model the performance of each pond unit. (In the proposed system, two ponds in series make up one pond unit.) The complexity was necessary because of the relatively long length of the unit (long residence time) and because of the relatively high thermal capacitance of a full unit (long lag times). The unit was broken down into several smaller elements along its length so that the effects of having a relatively cold pond near the inlet (high efficiency) and a relatively hot pond near the outlet (lower efficiency) could be accounted for.

Each element is a thermodynamic control volume on which a mass and energy balance is performed for each time step during the simulation. All the water within an element is at a single uniform temperature, the bulk temperature of the element. For ease of calculation, the mass and enthalpy flow is done in a separate step from the external heat transfer.

The pond inlet flow rate and the overall length of the time step are specified when the subroutine is called. The subroutine may take the time step in a number of smaller steps, depending on the flow rate and on how full the unit is. The total input flow is put into the first pond element and mixed with the water already there before any is allowed to flow into the next element. Any water in excess of the amount that should be in that element, as determined by the flow rate, the weir height, and the slope of the bed, is then put into the next element and mixed with the water already there. This wave of water goes through each element in turn, and the overflow from the last element is put into the return pipe.

After the flowing part of the time step has been completed, the thermal time constant for each element is calculated. The effecitve collector stagnation temperature,

$$\overline{T}_{stag} = T_{ambient} + \frac{\overline{\tau\alpha}}{U}\,I_0$$

is calculated based on the weather data input file and the pond optical and thermal parameters. Each element is then allowed to approach $\overline{T}_{stag}$ according to an exponential decay function for the duration of the time step.

A negative flow rate causes the pond to drain with a 0.5-hour time constant.

Storage Reservoir

The thermal storage pool, Fig. 10, is of conventional construction with a diameter-to-depth ratio of 2 when it is full. Filling the ponds reduces the water level in the reservoir by about 2.5 m so that in operation the daytime depth is 5 m and the nighttime depth is 7.5 m. The volume of the thermal storage pool relative to the area of the collector is selected to minimize the cost of energy from the system. Figure 11 shows the way in which the cost of the 150-kW plant increases with respect to the base case as either pool capacity or pond area is changed, and illustrates the kinds of parameter studies that were made to select the baseline system. The thermal storage pool has inlet and outlet diffusers to prevent jetting and unwanted mixing of hot and cold water; however, long-term stratification of the thermal layers is not expected to be a

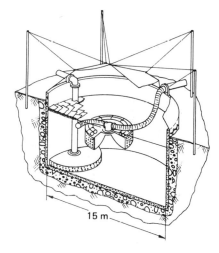

15 m

Fig. 10. Thermal storage pool.

13

261

Figure 6.4
(Cont.)

Fig. 11. Increase in cost per average kilowatt versus collector area and tank capacity. Costs per average kilowatt produced the growing season in Inyokern, California in 1962 expressed as percentage above the minimum for various collector field sizes and tank sizes varied around the base case. All other components fixed.

problem since the flow rate to the heat exchangers can be equivalent to more than four changes of the pool water a day.

Thermal losses from conduction and convection are apt to be small compared to the heat flux. We can prevent losses from the surface of the water by floating a cover of "bubble pack" material made of polybutylene on the surface. The thermal inertia of the ground should minimize losses from the sides and bottom. After the initial warming period, the rate of heat exchange between the water and the surrounding ground of the underground reservoir tends to be proportional to the square of a characteristic dimension of that reservoir while the total heat content of the reservoir is proportional to that dimension cubed. These trends make the problem of heat loss and the question of additional insulation for large thermal storage reservoirs of minor importance relative to small reservoirs. For an uninsulated pool of the size required here, calculations suggest that the daily heat loss would be a few tenths of a percent of the useful heat stored.[12] Much more rapid heat loss would occur during the month after cold start-up, but the overall heat loss problem seems small enough so that a simple conductivity model of the pool thermal response should be sufficient.

14

Three subroutines model the thermal storage subsystem in the simulation code. One subroutine removes water from either the top or the bottom of the thermal storage tank, and also reports the bulk temperature of water removed. Water is put into the tank by the second subroutine. The amount of water and the temperature distribution in the tank are recorded with a pigeonhole, or bin, system. One hundred bins are set up, each corresponding to an integer number on the Celsius temperature scale from 1 to 100. If an amount of water at 81.62°C is to be put into storage, the second subroutine adds 62% of it to the 82nd bin and the other 38% into the 81st bin.

The third subroutine takes the bin distribution and calculates a new distribution some time Δt later, based on internal and external heat transfer. A coarse finite element heat transfer model is set up with 100 nodes equally spaced from the top to the bottom of the tank. Each node is charged with the thermal capacitance of 1/100th of the total mass of water in storage, and the appropriate initial node temperatures are calculated through consideration of the bin data. Intratank conductances are calculated by assuming the water is a solid. Wherever an upper layer of water is cooler than the layer below, the conductance value involved is multiplied by 60 to account for the natural convection that would occur. The third subroutine uses a forward difference integration method in a series of steps to accomplish the desired relaxation.

Pond Flow Controls

The sizes of the supply and drain piping for the ponds have been selected for a field gradient of 2%. The pipes of the drain manifold are large enough so that gravity flow can accommodate all of the ponds flowing simultaneously. Two-inch pipes are required at the pond outlets, and the drain manifold ends in a 6-in. flexible pipe connecting to the floating diffuser in the thermal storage pool. The circulating pump draws water from the bottom diffuser in the pool and delivers it to the 25 control valves at the inlets of the pond pairs. For the purpose of sizing supply piping, we have allowed a friction gradient of 5% in addition to the lift required by the field terracing. The pumping head required is 8 m and the main supply line is 5 in., reducing in steps to 2-in. control valves. The supply manifold becomes a drain manifold when the ponds are to be emptied. Most of the pond water can be returned to storage in 30 minutes, after which flow will taper off for several hours.

Figure 6.4
(*Cont.*)

Appropriate control of the solar pond temperatures through flow rate control is critical in maximizing the total work produced by the Rankine cycle engine over the season. Collection efficiency goes down with increasing temperature. To maximize the amount of thermal energy gain, collectors are operated at the lowest possible temperature the load can utilize. On the other hand, the conversion efficiency of a heat engine goes up with increasing supply temperature. It is not obvious at first glance what the best control method is for a collector/engine combination.

The following analysis of an idealized collector/engine system will illustrate the approach finally taken. Flat-plate solar collectors are often described by the classical "straight line" efficiency relationship,

$$\eta_{collector} = \overline{\tau\alpha} - U\left[\frac{T_{collector} - T_{ambient}}{I_0}\right], \quad (1)$$

or

$$\dot{Q}_{collected} = I_0\,\eta_{collector}$$

$$= \overline{\tau\alpha}\,I_0 - U\left[T_{collector} - T_{ambient}\right]$$

$$= U\left[\overline{T}_{stag} - T_{collector}\right], \quad (2)$$

where

$$\overline{T}_{stag}\left(= \frac{\overline{\tau\alpha}}{U}\bigg|_{T_{collector}} I_0 + T_{ambient}\right) \quad (3)$$

is the *effective* collector stagnation (asymptotic) temperature. For some collectors, $\overline{\tau\alpha}$ and U are functions of collector temperature. If allowed to stagnate, the collector temperature will approach

$$T_{stag} = \frac{\overline{\tau\alpha}}{U}\bigg|_{T_{stag}} I_0 + T_{ambient}\,.$$

In Eq. (2), T_{stag} is the only environmentally dependent variable.

For many fluids, the conversion efficiency of a low-temperature Rankine cycle engine tends to be a constant fraction, ψ, of the theoretical maximum (Carnot) efficiency as defined by the actual boiling and condensing temperatures, T_B and T_C respectively. (Temperatures in absolute scale.)

$$\eta_{cycle} \equiv \frac{\dot{W}_{out}}{\dot{Q}_{in}} = \psi\,\frac{T_B - T_C}{T_B}\,. \quad (4)$$

If a flat-plate solar collector is used as a Rankine cycle boiler, the implied mechanical output power is

$$\dot{W}_{out} = \psi\,\frac{T_B - T_C}{T_B} \cdot U\left[\overline{T}_{stag} - T_B\right]. \quad (5)$$

The maximum power possible for the given T_{stag} and T_C is

$$\dot{W}_{max} = \psi\,UT_C \cdot \left(\sqrt{\frac{\overline{T}_{stag}}{T_C}} - 1\right)^2$$

and is obtained only if

$$T_B/T_C = \sqrt{\frac{\overline{T}_{stag}}{T_C}}\,.$$

It can be shown empirically that in a similar system in which a flat-plate collector is used to heat a fluid (liquid-vapor) from temperature T_C to T_{max} in a supercritical Rankine cycle engine, the optimum collector outlet temperature for maximum power output is given approximately by

$$\frac{T_{max}}{T_C} = \left(\frac{\overline{T}_{stag}}{T_C}\right)^{0.72}$$

In both these examples, a few critical assumptions were made. We assumed no temperature drop between the collector and the boiling Rankine cycle fluid, which is not true if an interceding heat exchanger is used. Also, a solar collector with a finite flow rate and no boiling does not operate at a single temperature, but rather it operates over a continuous range of temperatures along its length from inlet to outlet. This is a considerable effect in a collector as long as a shallow solar pond. Finally, we assumed steady-state weather and flow conditions. The effect of thermal storage and system thermal capacitance on the performance is not clear. If the goal is to maximize the total work output over some period of time, it is possible that a control logic which defers maximum performance during marginal periods to enhance performance during better periods (or *vice-versa*) may be best.

Finding and verifying the truly optimal pond control logic could be a very difficult task, and is

15

263

Figure 6.4
(Cont.)

beyond the scope of this study. Instead, we tried a few simple control strategies, including one that will be referred to as theta control in which the pond outlet temperature was controlled such that

$$\frac{T_{outlet}}{T_{ambient}} = \left(\frac{\bar{T}_{stag}}{T_{ambient}}\right)^x .$$

We simulated the pond/engine system for each strategy and for several values of x between 0.35 and 0.80. Each strategy also included an over-temperature mode meant to minimize pond boiling and a provision for draining the ponds if the incoming water were warmer than the stagnation temperature (nighttime). Theta control was superior to all the other control strategies tried. The best value for x was between 0.45 and 0.60; the exact value is not critical in that range. Again theoretical evidence supports $x = 0.50$.

The desired outlet temperature under given conditions is then

$$T_{desired} = T_A \left(\bar{T}_{stag/T_A}\right)^{0.5}$$

$$= \left(T_A \cdot \bar{T}_{stag}\right)^{0.5} .$$

Let $\delta = \bar{T}_{stag} - T_C$, so that

$$T_{desired} = \left[\left(T_A + \frac{\delta}{2}\right)^2 - \frac{\delta^2}{4}\right]^{1/2} .$$

If $\delta^2/4$ is small compared to T_C^2 (in absolute scale), then

$$T_{desired} \approx \left[\left(T_A + \frac{\delta}{2}\right)^2\right]^{0.5} = \frac{T_A + \bar{T}_{stag}}{2} .$$

The system shown schematically in Fig. 12 accomplishes this control. The logic circuit that performs the theta control operation is very similar to a standard differential temperature thermostat (DTT). A possible circuit minus various auxilliaries is shown schematically in Fig. 13 for illustration only. Other types of circuitry may be less costly or more reliable.

X: if $T_1 > T_2$, close B then open A
    if $T_2 > T_1$, close A then open B

Y: if $T_3 > \dfrac{T_4 + T_5}{2}$ open C

    if $T_3 < \dfrac{T_4 + T_5}{2}$ close C

Fig. 12. Pond flow control schematic.

16

Figure 6.4
(Cont.)

τ_3, τ_4, τ_5 — thermistors

$\tau_4 + \tau_5$ identical
$\tau_3 = 2$ of same in series

Function:

if $T_3 > \dfrac{T_4 + T_5}{2}$ open C

if $T_3 < \dfrac{T_4 + T_5}{2}$ close C

Fig. 13. Possible pond control circuitry.

Heat Engine Subsystem

An organic-fluid Rankine cycle (R/C) engine converts heat energy to mechanical power. The engine sits atop an irrigation water well and directly drives the well pump to produce 2×10^5 kg/h (900 gpm). An on-shaft motor/generator converts additional output mechanical power to electrical power. The solar collector system uses a portion of the electrical power produced, and the balance can be used to drive other local irrigation pumps or other farm machinery. The Barber-Nichols* concept of this unit is pictured in Figs. 14 and 15.

Heat from the solar collection network preheats and vaporizes Refrigerant 113 (R-113) which flows

*Barber-Nichols Engineering Company, Arvada, Colorado, designed the engine hardware.

through a nozzle bank feeding the turbine. Vapor exiting the turbine contains a significant amount of superheat, a thermodynamic characteristic of R-113 and many other refrigerant vapors. As a result, the turbine exhaust vapor possesses energy that can be recovered and used in the cycle, increasing its efficiency. This superheat is recovered by introducing a regenerative heat exchanger which extracts a portion of the superheat in the turbine exhaust vapor and transfers it to liquid refrigerant leaving the feed pump on its way to the preheater and vaporizer. After the vapor loses this superheat, it enters the condenser. Here, irrigation water pumped from the well absorbs the latent heat of vaporization, converting R-113 vapor to liquid. A pump pressurizes the liquid R-113 and feeds it through the liquid side of the regenerator to the preheater and vaporizer heat exchangers, completing the loop. By passing

17

265

Figure 6.4
(*Cont.*)

In
out
Solar H$_2$O
Preheater
150-kW motor generator
Well head
Regenerator
Gearbox
Turbine
Condenser
Vaporizer
Feed pump
Out
In
Cooling irrigation water
Control box
L
24 ft
H
6 ft 6 in.
W
6 ft 6 in.
Overall package dimensions
18

Fig. 14. Solar irrigation system conversion machinery.

Figure 6.4
(*Cont.*)

Fig. 15. Conversion equipment fluid circuits.

through the regenerator, R-113 liquid gains thermal energy from turbine exhaust vapor, thus increasing Rankine cycle efficiency by decreasing the amount of heat necessary from the external heat source (i.e. collector network).

Initially, we considered several working fluids (see Table 7). Where a constant supply of hot water is available, we thought that a supercritical or near critical Rankine cycle might have some advantages over a subcritical cycle like the R-113 cycle. The hot water which "fires" a supercritical cycle is cooled to a relatively low temperature. The large temperature drop is accompanied by a low hot water flow rate and a high solar collector efficiency to offset the low engine efficiency. (Where the conversion efficiency is so necessarily low, the power required just to circulate the hot water is considerable.) Almost all of the heat input to a subcritical cycle goes to boiling the working fluid at a constant temperature. In passing through the boiler, the hot water is cooled to near the working fluid's boiling temperature

Table 7. Candidate fluids.

Fluid (by Ref. No.)	Critical temp. (°F)	Critical pressure (psia)
R-12	233	597
R-13 B1	153	575
R-22	205	722
R-32	176	454
R-113	420	503
R-115	176	451
R-142b	279	598
R-152a	236	652
R-290 (propane)	206	617
R-C318	239	401
R-500	222	642
R-502	180	591
R-504	154	696
R-600a (isobutane)	274	529
R-717 (ammonia)	271	1657
R-1270 (propylene)	197	670

19

Figure 6.4
(*Cont.*)

which must be as high as possible to keep the conversion efficiency high. To get the same thermal power, the hot water flow rate must be high. Only a small part of the thermal energy available in the hot water stream is syphoned off in passing through the boiler. If the discharged water is discarded at this point, the thermal energy source would be poorly utilized.

The thermal storage tank makes an important contribution to selecting the subcritical R-113 cycle. The hot water in storage circulates through the boiler several times during the night, each time taking a drop in temperature. The working fluid boiling temperature slowly decreases overnight with the associated drop in conversion efficiency. By morning the tank has been depleted, and the coldest water is sent to the collectors. As far as the collector is concerned, it makes no difference whether the water is cooled all in one step (as with the critical cycle), or in several smaller steps (as with the subcritical cycle); the cold water brings the same high collector efficiency and low collector flow rate. With that possible advantage eliminated, the supercritical cycles could not compete with the higher conversion efficiency, more manageable pressures, and higher operational flexibility of the subcritical R-113 cycle. Comparisons by computer system simulation showed the R-113 to be a better performer in this application. Had there been no storage, it is not clear which fluid would have won.

Over 24-hour periods and seasonally, the hot water temperatures supplied to the boiler will vary considerably. We wish to maximize the net amount of mechanical work produced over a season. In a system of fixed physical size (heat exchangers, turbine, etc.), only the flow rates and pressures can be varied (perhaps not independently). We assume that they will vary as functions of the hot water supply temperature and the condenser cooling water temperature.

Finding an optimal control system was beyond the scope of this project. Instead, we selected a relatively simple control scheme which made the system simulation calculations least complicated. For purposes of calculation, hot water and cooling water flow rates are fixed and (in effect) the refrigerant flow rate, pressures, and turbine admission angle are controlled to keep the gross turbine mechanical output fixed at 150 kW. If the supply temperature is too low to enable the engine to produce 150 kW at the prescribed water flow rate at an efficiency no less than 4%, the engine shuts down completely. At the shut-off point, the refrigerant flow rate is at maximum and the turbine is at full admission. With higher supply temperatures, the

boiler pressure (and temperature) is raised, increasing the conversion efficiency. To keep the gross power at 150 kW, the fluid flow rate and turbine admission angle are reduced. It is not clear whether another control mode (modulating boiler water flow, for instance) might have produced more power. We think that perhaps a 10%-20% improvement in the cost per average kilowatt could be achieved over the reported value through optimization of the system controls.

A Fortran subroutine was written to calculate Rankine cycle engine performance. This subroutine covers information about the working fluid properties, hot and cold water flow rates, supply temperatures, and the heat exchanger capacities. An iterative method is used to determine the water return temperatures and the boiling and condensing temperatures. Guesses are made for the boiling and condensing temperatures. Based on these guesses, we can calculate the cycle efficiency. The requirement of producing 150 kW and the calculated efficiency defines the heat rates in the boiler and condenser. A check is made to see if the heat exchangers are large enough to achieve these heat rates at the guessed temperatures. If not, the exchanger temperature difference is increased by lowering the assumed boiling temperature or raising the condensing temperature (and *vice versa*). The pinch-point temperatures are checked. Again, if the supplied temperatures are inadequate to produce the 150kW efficiently, the engine is shut down.

Computer simulations of the pond/power system were performed to select appropriate sizes for the heat exchangers and turbine, and flow rates as well as other operating data. Table 8 summarizes the approximate engine specifications which were selected through iterative attempts to minimize the capital cost per total kilowatt-hour produced in the growing season.

With this specification as a starting point we examined the engine components in more detail.[*] The four heat exchangers, preheater vaporizer, condenser, and regenerator were sized using the effectiveness — number of heat-transfer units (ϵ-NTU) approach. We estimated costs of production units based on current cost data from heat exchanger manufacturers. Table 9 shows selected heat exchanger data.

An axial flow turbine is proposed. Design parameters for a possible turbine configuration are

---

[*]Analyses of organic fluid cycle efficiencies were done by Barber-Nichols Engineering Company.[3]

Figure 6.4
(Cont.)

Table 8. Approximate Rankine engine specifications resulting from iterative system simulations.

Parameter	Value
Boiler and preheater capacity, kW/C	400
Condenser capacity, kW/C	375
Hot water flow rate, kg/h	2×10^5
Cold water flow rate, kg/h	2×10^5
Cold water temperature, °C(°F)	18 (64)
Hot water temperature maximum, °C(°F)	100 (212)
minimum (shut-off), °C(°F)	68.9 (156)

Other system temperatures at shut-off:	Temp., °C(°F)
Refrigerant boiling temperature	57.9 (136)
Refrigerant condensing temperature	30.02 (86)
Solar water into vaporizer	68.9 (156)
Solar water out of preheater	58.7 (138)
Cooling irrigation water into condenser	18 (64)
Cooling irrigation water out of condenser	27.6 (82)

given in Table 10. The turbine design point should be based on the most probable delivered pond temperatures. This involves examination of a time and temperature weighted turbine work cycle to maximize the overall turbine efficiency integrated over the entire growing season. This was considered to be beyond the scope of the present analysis. The turbine, in this case was sized, as were the heat exchangers, at the shut-off point. Multiple turbine staging and reheat are other refinements of the turbine design, the details of which are beyond the scope of this study. While these complications would increase the cost of the conversion machinery, the increased efficiency would be directly reflected in reduced collector field size, and the additional heat exchangers might be cost-effective overall.

The computer simulation of the system assumed that the pumping power load could be made to match the power available at all times. In a real operation the load might occasionally drop below system capability. Flow control of the working fluid is therefore based upon turbine speed, as indicated by the generator output frequency.

An electro-mechanical valve controls flow to the turbine by allowing flow through various numbers of nozzles, thereby changing the arc of admission. A frequency signal from the motor-generator controls this valve. The turbine is designed to run at full admission and design speed at the shut-off point (68.9°C supply temperature). As the water temperature increases above shut-off temperature, the turbine and thus the motor-generator speed up. The resulting increased frequency of the generator output is sensed, causing the flow through one nozzle to be stopped. The turbine slows down, resulting in lower generator output frequency. The opposite response is elicited by a decrease in pond temperature (i.e., the arc of admission increases). Thus the generator output frequency can be controlled within fixed limits.

Rankine cycle engine cost estimates were made for the first unit and for quantity production units. These are summarized in Tables 11 and 12.

Table 9. Heat exchanger design data.

Parameter	Preheater	Vaporizer	Condenser	Regenerator
Effectiveness	0.910	0.808	0.792	0.687
UA, kW/C	37.9	399	388	19.9
Overall coefficient (U), kW/m²·°C	0.567	0.567	0.567	0.034
Surface area (A), m²	66.7	703	684	584
Cost function, $/UA	99.5	110	94.8	997
Cost, $	3,770	44,200	36,800	19,800

21

Figure 6.4
(*Cont.*)

Table 10. Turbine design parameters.

Parameter	Value	
	At 68.9°C(156°F) Pond temp. (shut-off)	At 95°C(203°F) Pond temp.
Hardware		
Rotational speed, rpm	3600	3600
Pitch diameter, in.	15.37	
Blade height, in.	3.27	
Blade chord, in.	0.75	
Blade number	80	
Nozzle number	25 (full adm.)	6 (partial adm.)
Nozzle angle, deg	16	
Nozzle area ratio	1.097	
Efficiency	0.808	0.700
Fluid conditions		
Inlet temperature, °F	136	193
Inlet pressure, psia	20.4	49.1
Exit pressure, psia	8.0	8.0
Specific speed (cfs units)	78.0	35.0
Isentropic Mach number	1.33	1.83

Table 11. Production costs for 150-kW Rankine engine.

Item	Cost ($)
Heat exchangers	
Preheater	3,770
Boiler	44,200
Regenerator	19,800
Condenser-desuperheater	36,800
Turbine-gearbox	17,000
Generator-switch gear	10,000
Miscellaneous (insulation, pumps, etc.)	40,000
Total	**171,570**

Table 12. Cost for first 150-kW Rankine cycle engine.

Item	Cost ($)
Analysis and design	35,000
Hardware	230,000
Assembly	29,000
Test	25,000
Heat source (boiler) rental	10,000
Total	**329,000**

CONCLUSION

It is our belief that shallow solar ponds make possible the lowest cost solar thermal power system that has been proposed to the present time. Nevertheless, it does not seem likely that a farmer would invest in such an installation in the foreseeable future on the basis of its economic merits. It is, of course, possible for solar power to be intoduced into farming by government stimulation through subsidies and changes in tax laws. Such an artifice would likely increase rather than decrease the cost of the solar power but would distribute the cost more widely.

22

Figure 6.4
(*Cont.*)

ACKNOWLEDGMENTS

The authors wish to express their appreciation for the assistance of W. C. Dickinson and A. F. Clark, and for the participation of Richard Parsons and Alan Casamajor in developing the data we have used.

Thanks also go to Robert E. Barber and Daryl Pigmore of Barber-Nichols Engineering Company for their contributions to this project.

REFERENCES

1. D. L. Larson et. al., "Feasibility of Using Solar Energy to Drive Irrigation Pumps," Paper No. 76-2531, American Society of Agricultural Engineers, St. Joseph, Michigan, 1976.
2. W. C. Dickinson and H. J. Freeman, *An Economic Methodology for Solar-assisted Industrial Process Heat Systems: The Effect of Government Incentives,* Lawrence Livermore Laboratory, Rept. UCRL-52254, (1977).
3. A. S. E. Acherman, "The Utilization of Solar Energy," *J. Royal Soc. Arts,* 538 (April 30, 1915).
4. H. W. Newkirk, *Solar Technology Applications: A Literature Review of Solar Thermal Powered Irrigation Systems,* Lawrence Livermore Laboratory, Rept. UCID-17510 (1977).
5. J. Ericsson, "Sun Motor," *Harper's Weekly,* **31**, (January 10, 1887).
6. C. Tellier, "Equipment for the Activity of a Pump Apparatus for Solar Heat," German Patent No. 34749 (August 15, 1885).
7. "The Utilization of Solar Heat for the Elevation of Water," *Scientific American,* 214 (October 3, 1885).
8. "Power from the Sun's Heat," *Engineering News,* **61** [19], 509 (May 13, 1909).
9. H. E. Willsie, "Experiments in the Development of Power from the Sun's Heat," *Engineering News,* **61** [19], 511 (May 13, 1909).
10. A. F. Clark, J. A. Day, W. C. Dickinson, and L. F. Wouters, *The Shallow Solar Pond Energy Conversion System: An Analysis of a Conceptual 10-MWe Plant,* Lawrence Livermore Laboratory, Rept. UCRL-51533 (1974).
11. A. B. Casamajor and R. E. Parsons, *Design Guide for Shallow Solar Ponds,* Lawrence Livermore Laboratory, Rept. UCRL-52385 (1978).
12. J. Shelton, "Underground Storage of Heat in Solar Heating Systems," *Solar Energy,* **17**, (2), 137 (May 1975).
13. D. Prigmore, *A 150 kW Rankine Cycle for Use with Shallow Solar Ponds,* Barber-Nichols Engineering Company, Arvada, Colorado (December 1977).

VRS/gw

23

EXERCISES

1.   Investigate the possibility of adding a special interest class to the curriculum in your field. First, you'll need to obtain the necessary data on the requirements to add a new course in your department. Then, you'll need to do some exploratory work on the interest other students might have in such a course. You might write up a brief questionnaire to assess interest. Finally, putting the procedure and interest assessment together, write a brief report to your English instructor on the feasibility of your idea. Consider your English instructor a first-level reviewer; if you get the go-ahead from her or him, you might then submit your report to your department chair.

2.   Investigate the possibility of establishing a new student service or facility or enhancing an existing one: an after-dark transit or escort service for women, a counseling service for minorities, an up-to-date computer lab. As in exercise 1, you'll have to obtain the necessary data on the need for such a service or facility and whether existing resources can accommodate or be expanded to accommodate the change you think is necessary. Your investigation can be preliminary, but it should be specific about what needs to be done and how it should be done, although the work may have to happen in the future. Keeping these things in mind, prepare a short report to an appropriate audience of students (perhaps members of the student government) or administrators.

FUNDAMENTALS OF SCIENTIFIC WRITING

Scientific reports, including lab reports, fall into the category of professional writing we call science writing or scientific writing. There are many fine texts devoted solely to science writing, for example Michael Alley's *The Craft of Scientific Writing*. While the rhetorical choices the author has to make are the same as those in other types of professional writing, the conventions are very different. Scientific reports are dictated virtually entirely by convention. Beyond any obvious advice for writing lab reports, such as to use precise information and provide all the data requested, there is not much general advice we can give. To explain the format-driven nature of lab reports, we will consider the evolution of science writing and the place of science writing in the field of professional writing.

Evolution of Scientific Writing

In the early days of scientific writing, the scientists told each other about their work through stories, little narratives that described the experiment chronologically. In the early volumes of *The Philosophical Transactions of the Royal Society* Sir Isaac Newton tells the story of his research on Optiks. He says, in effect, "I took me a prism and set it up in such and such a place to get such and such an angle of light. . . ."

By the nineteenth century, scientific discourse looked very different. Especially in the discourse of scientists addressing other scientists, the form became rigidly conventional. No longer could experimental work be reviewed in the leisurely form of a story because there was so much more work than there had been 200 years before. Instead, scientists used standard categories to describe their work. These categories, which predominate in science writing today, include method, conclusions, previous work, and so on. The use of a conventional format allows other scientists to skim work quickly so that they can stay current in their field.

Contemporary scientific writing is even more rigid than its nineteenth-century counterpart. One factor is the great increase in scientific research today. Another factor is the fierce competition for funds and reputation, which has made reproducibility, so important to Newton, secondary to other concerns, such as the review of literature and speculation about other necessary work. Such changes mean that science writers must familiarize themselves with the conventions that dominate both their field of expertise and the particular journal they want to publish in.

The effect of such rigid convention in science writing is not altogether constructive. A great deal of the writing is mindlessly passive. And more and more, illustrations, photographs, and other graphics are expected to carry the weight of meaning. There is little attempt in some scientific publications to incorporate into the text the significant aspects of the graphics. Instead, the text seems to exist to orient the reader to the graphics. While not all science journals have gone this way, others certainly have.

The Professional Writing Continuum

A look at the continuum of types of professional writing (see Table 6.1) shows the place of scientific writing. Some interesting things about professional writing as a whole are reflected in this continuum. First, as one moves from scientific writing to administrative writing, the audience becomes more varied and less expert. The audience for administrative writing is even more generalized than that for technical and professional writing. While many different users must interpret most

TABLE 6.1 *Continuum of Professional Writing*

	Scientific writing	*Technical and professional writing*	*Administrative writing*
Document types	journal articles lab reports	technical reports procedures manuals feasibility studies proposals	letters memoranda brochures
Style	conventionalized	varying styles	varying styles
Tone	"objective"	somewhat objective	subjective

technical and professional reports, they are generally "insiders," whereas correspondence, the primary type of administrative writing, can also go to "outsiders," people who have nothing at all to do with the authoring organization.

Where style and format are concerned, science writing is by far the most conventional. One can find technical and professional reports of many arrangements and formats, but such variety cannot be found in scientific writing, for the reasons discussed above. If any change is to occur in science writing to challenge established conventions, it will probably come only from those scientists who can write, who will then understand the advantage of some flexibility for rhetorical reasons. In technical and professional writing, there is some flexibility of arrangement and style, while in administrative writing the only standards are the purely arbitrary standards of setting up letters and memos.

The level of objectivity also changes across the continuum. On the scientific writing end, objectivity is at a premium, the notion being that the investigator will draw conclusions from objective data instead of from personal opinion or prejudice. Thus, there is much passive construction in science writing; the scientist is trying to emphasize the objective nature of the work, performed by accepted protocols. Yet all scientists acknowledge the importance of the observer, who reads measuring instruments, sees reality from an individual orientation, and interprets, no matter how objectively, as a human being.

The continuum shows that objectivity is partly in evidence in technical and professional writing but is not at all the goal of administrative writing. In other words, as one moves across the continuum, the writing becomes no longer a matter of presenting objective facts to an audience, such as one might find through experimentation; instead, the writer is trying to persuade the reader to accept the view of reality presented in the particular report. Proposals are at the more obviously persuasive end of technical and professional documents, and cover letters and brochures are obviously persuasive. In fact, at the administrative end of the continuum, subjectivity, a focus on the person behind the message, is a real strength, something to be sought for in the writing. Thus, a job application letter that paints a vivid picture of the writer is admirable, not unprofessional.

Technical and professional writing as a whole used to be defined as we, in this text, define science writing. Generally, people thought that all the documents produced in the workplace were somehow about the serious, objective work of engineers, businesspeople, bankers, all the standard professions associated with the work professionals do. This work was all about numbers and costs and schedules and other objective parameters, that is, measurable parameters. The current notion is more sophisticated. Professionals understand that the objective data do not speak for themselves. They must be framed in a context, within a purpose, and for an audience with expectations and logical requirements. In other words, these data must be conveyed effectively; to accomplish this, the writers use rhetorical techniques to persuade the audience that certain "facts" make sense and certain conclusions are more or less reasonable. One can see, then, that it is a mistake to equate technical and professional writing with total objectivity or with rigid format conventions. As a matter of fact, the writing that best fits into this old-fashioned notion of technical and professional writing is scientific writing, a small part of the whole professional writing field.

FORMAT AND SUBSTANCE OF A SCIENTIFIC REPORT

For the scientific report, then, our discussion is descriptive instead of prescriptive. One type of scientific report is the lab report, usually an in-house document that reports interim findings informally, before they are written up as a formal scientific report. Thus, an engineer will record in a lab report the preliminary data from an experiment in progress. But this report makes few demands on the writer, since it usually is a sort of fill-in-the-blanks report that requires the writer to transfer essential information from personal notes.

The scientific report is simply a more thorough, formal documentation of findings arising from a number of related lab reports. The scientific report adds the review of literature section, to situate the work in significant other work in the field; an abstract (since it would be addressed to outsiders, other scientists at other facilities); formal citations; and suggestions for further investigation. One pitfall of the scientific report's abstract is that it may simply be a tease, telling the reader what the article is supposed to be about, instead of reporting very concisely what conclusion the researchers came to. So, again, the concern is to be conclusive, to know how to write the main report clearly, knowing that the point is not to string the reader along, but to respect the harried reader's limited time and attention span where professional reading is concerned.

The best general advice we can give to science writers is to follow the rhetorical principles in this book, while writing within the conventions that dominate the field, understanding that these conventions are not written in stone; many of them are relatively new rules, but subscribed to as if they were the only way one could write well about science. In the range of professional documentation, science documentation is the most rigidly prescribed, partly because the audience wants certain essential information from the writing and partly because the most appropriate language for relaying scientific information is not discursive but symbolic. Mathematicians and musicians are not expected to convert all their symbols into prose any more than scientists are expected to convert their symbols into prose. Such symbolism is appropriate only for an expert audience, and most scientists understand this.

SAMPLE STUDENT-AUTHORED SCIENTIFIC ARTICLE

Authored by a chemistry student in a technical and professional writing class, the following sample (Figure 6.5, page 277) is an award-winner that translates the student's field notes into a professional-level article that was submitted to a competition for chemistry undergraduates. This student had published before in his field and so was accustomed to writing to professional conventions.

In his executive summary you will note his attention to details of paragraph structure, for example, which he adjusted appropriately for his audience. You will also note that he understands the loss of coherence he risks by adhering to the convention of not using topic sentences for paragraphs in the experimental section. The other sections of his article are very well signaled by topic sentences, and his abstract is conclusive. As a student, he is in no position to challenge the conventions of publishing in chemistry; the important thing is that he understands the place of conventions in his field and he has the flexibility to write both for chemistry professionals and his English professor, to whom he addressed his executive summary.

Finally, this sample clarifies our earlier point about the need for scientists to use symbolic language. At certain points, this student had to start writing in formulas because they expressed most clearly and accurately what he had to say. He simply adhered to the conventions of including formulas in a text; note his spacing and standard discussion of the elements in the formulas. This symbolic writing is absolutely appropriate to his audience, specialists in chemistry. It would be a big mistake, however, for him to speak in formulas to a group of lay listeners.

EXERCISES

1. Analyze the sample article for its effectiveness. You don't have to be a chemistry major to do some basic rhetorical analysis. You can compare the author's stated purpose and audience as described in the executive summary to the level of language, thoroughness of coverage, and degree of explicitness in the article.

2. Analyze the difference in publishing conventions among *Scientific American, Science,* and the *Journal of the American Medical Association* (JAMA). How would you describe their audiences, their purposes, their structures, and their formatting conventions?

Figure 6.5
Student scientific article

Jon Sutter
2534 S. Fairway
Pocatello, Id. 83201
April 24, 1991

Professor Montgomery
Department of English
Idaho State University
Pocatello, Id. 83207

Dear Professor Montgomery:

Enclosed is a copy of my final project for the Spring semester of English 307. As you may recall, the title of my project is "Convergence of Generalized Simulated Annealing with a Variable Step Size for Function Optimization." The paper was written for a group of PhDs in Chemistry (namely the Kent State Undergraduate Research Symposium reviewers). The paper will discuss two major topics. These topics are generalized simulated annealing (GSA) and generalized simulated annealing with a variable step size (GSAVS).

It is necessary to discuss GSA since GSAVS is a modification of this well known optimization technique. Dr. Kalivas and I created GSAVS and it is my intention to show that GSAVS is able to converge to exact global conditions, whereas GSA is not. A comparison will be drawn between GSA and GSAVS to show that this is true. Also, GSAVS will be used to perform a chemical analysis (predict concentrations of an unknown sample) to present some of the possible uses.

The data used in this paper were all taken from experiments performed by me last summer. I also did a great deal of research on this topic to support claims that were not achieved through my research. I consulted Dr. John Kalivas, an expert in the field of chemometrics, to explain the importance of this research and the long term goals of GSAVS. A combination of all three are represented in this paper.

Sincerely,

John Sutter

Jon Sutter

Enclosure
JS/js

Figure 6.5
(*Cont.*)

Executive Summary:

The need to optimize chemical processes is often a must in the field of chemistry. Over the years many approaches have been investigated, some with limiting features that render them impractical. After much research generalized simulated annealing (GSA) was found to be the best in that it is able to find the area of the best conditions, therefore generalized simulated annealing with a variable step size was created to find the best conditions, which is the discovery through research presented in the paper.

GSA is a computer program that requires user assistance. First, the user must pick a set of parameters s (the initial conditions such as time, temperature and concentration of reactants of a chemical reaction). GSA uses the parameters to calculate the cost function (the numerical answer of a mathematical equation that represents the situation being optimized, using the parameters as the variables). GSA then randomly selects a new set of parameters in the neighborhood of the previous parameters, calculates a new cost function, and compares the two cost functions. If the new cost function is better than the old cost function, GSA accepts this new step and continues by selecting new parameters. If the new cost function is worse than the old, GSA may accept the step based on a probability number P. GSA is able to find the near global (best) conditions due to the fact that it accepts some detrimental (bad) steps. The equation of the probability of accepting a detrimental step is based on Boltzmann's distribution and is represented as:

$$P = \exp(-\beta \Delta C(rs)/C(s) - C(o))$$

This equation is based on the differences in the last two cost functions and also the difference between the new cost function and the best cost function (predicted by the user). Beta is a constant adjusted by the user to keep P in a range of values that will allow GSA to work for different experiments (p must be between 0.5 and 0.9 at first). If P is greater than a random number from 0 to 1 then the detrimental step is accepted. Theoretically, the P values should go to zero when GSA is close to the best conditions since the difference between the current cost function and the predicted best cost function will be small. This will cause detrimental steps to be rejected and GSA to converge to global conditions. Unfortunately, the step size is often too large and GSA steps over the exact global. It is at this point that GSAVS will automatically shrink the step size and converge to the exact global conditions. GSAVS adjusts step sizes based on a number resulting from the number of steps accepted divided by the total number of steps in a certain block of steps. Since this number is small when the P values are at zero, GSAVS shrinks the steps.

Three major things had to be determined in order to make GSAVS work. First, through trial and error, a block of 20 steps was used to calculate

Figure 6.5
(*Cont.*)

the acceptance ratio. Second, beta was adjusted until the *P* values were between 0.2 and 0.7 so that a forced increase of the step size was not induced. Third, beta was adjusted after every step size change to keep the *P* values consistent. The adjustment is based on a ratio of the old beta and the corresponding difference in cost functions and the current difference in the cost functions.

GSAVS was used to optimize two situations, a mathematical equation and a chemical analysis. First, GSA and GSAVS were both used on a mathematical equation starting from points that should give no difficulties for either technique. Here it was evident that GSAVS was able to converge to exact conditions where GSA was not. A figure of the response surface was supplied to show the readers the difficult starting conditions (close to global conditions and a local optimum). GSAVS was started at these difficult areas and was still able to converge to global conditions. Second, GSAVS was used to perform a chemical analysis. A figure of the curves are presented in a figure. The assumption here was that the reader would know that spectral overlap would cause difficult selection of concentrations by any technique. This is not an unreasonable assumption since the readers are all chemistry PhDs (Kent State Undergraduate Research Symposium reviewers). Despite the spectral overlap, GSAVS was able to find the concentrations of the unknowns. Noise was then added to this spectra and GSAVS was compared to a well known technique of predicting concentrations (the K-matrix approach). Here it was shown that GSAVS did a better job at predicting concentrations in areas of spectral overlap than the K-matrix approach.

In conclusion, when global conditions are absolutely needed, GSAVS is a technique that can find them.

This paper was written under the assumption that the readers were well versed in chemical procedures, but not in the field of chemometrics. Therefore, a great deal of emphasis was placed on the description of how the optimization techniques worked. The paper was written in accordance to the stipulations created by the reviewers of the Kent State Undergraduate Symposium and also technical papers written in the field of chemistry.

Each entry had to include a short abstract, an introduction section, an experimental section, a results and discussion section, and a works cited section which had to be presented in order of appearance in the paper. Since the reviewers were interested in the student's contribution to the project, I wanted to make this come through clearly in the paper. Therefore, I tried to use simple language that would make the paper clear.

Also, in regards to the experimental section, the paragraphs don't contain topic sentences since this is not standard procedure of the papers written in chemistry. The experimental sections are usually short sentences that simply state what kinds of instruments were used and other technical details that would help to recreate data. Tables and figures were included so that the reviewers could more easily visualize details of GSAVS. I tried not to use passive tense, but it was difficult not to in some areas without using first person.

Figure 6.5
(*Cont.*)

Jon Sutter
Dr. Montgomery
Technical Writing

**CONVERGENCE OF GENERALIZED SIMULATED ANNEALING WITH A VARIABLE
STEP SIZE FOR FUNCTION OPTIMIZATION**

Figure 6.5
(*Cont.*)

Convergence of Generalized Simulated Annealing with Variable Step Size for Function Optimization. Jon Sutter, Department of Chemistry, Idaho State University, Pocatello, Idaho 83207.

Over the years, numerous diverse methodologies for optimization have been developed. However, many of these optimization techniques are impractical due to the amount of time needed or due to their tendency to converge to local optima rather than the global optimum. Generalized simulated annealing (GSA), unlike other optimization techniques, has the ability to converge to global or near-global conditions. GSA uses a fixed step-size. By making slight modifications to GSA, generalized simulated annealing with a variable step size (GSAVS) was developed. GSAVS has the ability to converge to the exact global optimum by means of automatic reductions or increases in the step size. GSA and GSAVS will be discussed in detail and a comparison will be made of the two.

Figure 6.5
(*Cont.*)

Introduction

The need to optimize chemical processes is often a must in the field of chemistry. Over the years many different optimization techniques have been developed. Unfortunately, research has shown that many of them have limited uses (1-4). The limiting factor can be the amount of time required to perform the optimization or simply that the technique converges to a local optimum rather than the global optimum. Whatever the reason, often the optimization technique is considered useless for certain situations.

After much research in the area of Chemometrics, an optimization technique called generalized simulated annealing (GSA) has been found to be the best (4-8). GSA does not require much time to perform an optimization, and it is almost guaranteed to find the area of the global optimum.

This paper is concerned with a modification of GSA that will allow convergence to the exact global optimum rather than the area of the global optimum. The modification is the addition of a variable step size. Thus the technique will be referred to as generalized simulated annealing with a variable step size (GSAVS). Since the paper is concerned with GSAVS, only a brief description of GSA will be offered. For a more detailed description of GSA refer to reference 5. For a comparison of GSA and another optimization technique (simplex) refer to reference 4.

For the sake of clarity, it is necessary to give a qualitative description of how GSA works and how it differs from other optimization techniques before describing the quantitative features of GSA. GSA has been suitably called a semi-random walk, because it is able to walk off of local optima and onto the global optimum due to the fact that, unlike other optimization techniques, it will accept some detrimental steps. To begin GSA the user must pick a set of parameters s; GSA then computes a cost function $C(s)$ using these parameters, takes a random step from s and obtains the set of parameters r, computes a cost function $C(r)$ based on the set r, and finally compares the two cost functions $C(s)$ and $C(r)$. In the case of a minimization, GSA accepts $C(r)$ if it is less than $C(s)$, and it accepts $C(r)$ if it is greater than $C(s)$ based on a calculated probability P. This procedure is repeated until the area of the global optimum is discovered. Whenever cost functions are compared it will be referred to as a step or iteration in this paper. A more detailed description of GSA will now be given.

Quantitative Description of GSA

Through research, GSA was developed by Bohachevsky (5). It is a variation of simulated annealing which is related to the annealing process of a solid. The reason this technique is able to walk off of a local optimum and locate the area of the global optimum stems from a statistical

Figure 6.5
(Cont.)

equation that is derived from the Boltzmann's distribution. This equation is:

$$P = \exp(-\beta\Delta C(rs)/C(s) - C(o))$$

where β is a constant adjusted by the user, $\Delta C(rs) = C(r) - C(s)$, $C(r)$ is a randomly selected cost function, $C(s)$ is the last computed cost function, and $C(o)$ is the predicted optimal cost function selected by the user.

This equation is used to determine whether a detrimental step will be accepted or not. In the case of a minimization, when $C(r)$ (the selection of the set r will be discussed later) is greater than $C(s)$, GSA has taken a detrimental step. Most optimization techniques would not accept this step, which will allow them to converge to a local optimum in certain situations. GSA, however, will accept this step if P is greater than a random number that is taken from a uniform distribution from zero to one. This makes GSA a semi-random optimization technique and thus allows it to walk off of local minima and into the global area.

This process of accepting the good steps and accepting detrimental steps based on the P value is continued until GSA finds the global area. When GSA finds the global area the P values will go to zero because $C(s)$ will be close to $C(o)$, and the detrimental steps will be rejected. This allows GSA to find and converge on the global area.

In order to find $C(r)$ it is necessary to find a random set of parameters r. These random parameters are found by the equation:

$$r = s + \Delta r \times y$$

where s is the set of the previous parameters used to compute the cost function $C(s)$, Δr is a step size chosen by the user, and y is an array of normalized random numbers selected from a normal distribution with mean zero and standard deviation one.

The step size is the main discussion of this paper. The problem is that if the step size is too large, GSA will often miss the global optimum by simply jumping over it. Many times it is necessary to perform GSA over and over, reducing the step size each time in order to find the global optimum. This procedure may be too time consuming for all practical purposes. GSA with a variable step size should solve this problem.

This paper is based on a variable step size that is calculated by use of an acceptance ratio. If more than 90% of the steps in a block of GSA steps are accepted it means that GSA is far from the global and therefore the step size should be increased. If less than 20% of the steps in a block of GSA steps are accepted it means that GSA is close to the global and therefore the step size should be decreased. The incorporation of variable step size with GSA will be discussed in detail later.

Figure 6.5
(*Cont.*)

Experimental

All computer programs were written in Fortran 77. The computers used were all 100% IBM compatible.

Simulated data was constructed by Gaussian curves with a range of 1-100. The peaks have bandwidths of 5 and amplitudes of either 10 or 5.

The responses of real data were taken from a UV-Vis spectrophotometer.

For GSA coupled with the variable step size, β was chosen by doing 100 iterations and adjusting β until the average of the P values was approximately 0.4. If the optimal cost function was not known an estimate was used. If GSAVS found a cost function below the estimated cost function a lower value was inserted. There is no need to re-adjust β after the new minimum is selected, since β is automatically adjusted after each step size change (this will be discussed further in the results and discussion section of this paper.)

Results and Discussion

In order to use the acceptance ratio variable step size with GSA, three major changes had to be made to GSA. They are general changes that work for every case tried in this paper. They were used in every analysis, unless otherwise specified.

First, the acceptance ratio was calculated at the right amount of steps in order to make GSAVS work. The calculation had to involve enough GSA iterations, so that the changes needed to be made to the step size could be determined. The calculation also had to be made after a small enough number of GSA iterations so that the procedure would not take an unnecessary amount of time. After much trial and error, it was discovered that the block of GSA iterations before an acceptance ratio calculation should be 20. An iteration block of 20 seemed to give enough information so that GSAVS could make an acceptable adjustment of the step size by use of the calculation of the acceptance ratio without wasting time with unnecessary iterations.

Second, the initial β had to be adjusted so that GSAVS would work. If the suggested β of GSA (such that P was between 0.5 and 0.9) (5) was used, the step size would always increase after the first acceptance ratio calculation. The reason for this was that β was adjusted so that the P values were between 0.5 and 0.9, which caused about 80% of the first set of detrimental steps to be accepted. This would almost guarantee that the acceptance ratio would be greater than 90% and therefore increase the step size. Since an increase in the step size is not always necessary on the first acceptance ratio, something had to be done with the β value. It was discovered that the best thing to do was to adjust β so that the P values were between 0.2 and 0.7. This would reduce the chance of a forced increase in step size, while still allowing GSAVS to walk off of a local optimum.

Figure 6.5
(*Cont.*)

The third and final change that was made to GSA was an automatic adjustment of β. This change was necessary because when the step size changed it would sometimes considerably change the difference between $C(r)$ and $C(s)$. This difference is a major factor in the calculation of the P value. Since the P value plays a very important role in the GSA technique, something needed to be done to preserve the consistency of the P value. Because the inconsistency in the P value was caused by the difference of $C(r)$ and $C(s)$ the following equation was derived:

$$New\beta = FDIF/DIF \times Old\beta$$

where $FDIF$ is the average of the difference in $C(r)$ and $C(s)$ in the first three iterations, DIF is the current difference in $C(r)$ and $C(s)$, $Old\beta$ is the first β value that is given by the user (this is the β that is first used so that the first P values are between 0.2 and 0.7), and $New\beta$ is the β used after the step size change. $New\beta$ is calculated each time the step size is changed.

First, GSAVS was used to optimize a simple math equation. This optimization was compared with an optimization using GSA. The math equation optimized was:

$$R = X^2 + 2Y^2 - 0.3\cos(3\Pi X) - 0.4\cos(4\Pi Y) + 0.7$$

where X and Y are the parameters and R is the cost function. In this case R is minimized and the global optimum is $R = 0.0$ and $(X, Y) = (0,0)$. The results are presented in Table 1.

TABLE 1. GSA and GSAVS Optimization of a Mathematical Function

Optimization Technique	Initial Step Size	Initial X, Y	Final X, Y	Final R	Number of Steps
GSAVS	0.15	0.85 0.85	0.000 0.000	0.00	2204
GSA	0.15	0.85 0.85	0.058 0.033	0.08	105

For this minimization, β was adjusted so that the P values were between 0.5 and 0.9 for the case of GSA alone and 0.2 and 0.7 for GSAVS. Notice that the exact global was found using GSAVS and only the global area was found with GSA alone.

Figure 1 is a 3-D plot of the response surface of this math function. Notice that at the starting points 0.85 and 0.85 the response is not on a local minimum. The optimization was started on a local minimum and also in the global area to see if GSAVS would converge to the global. The results are presented in Table 2.

Figure 6.5
(*Cont.*)

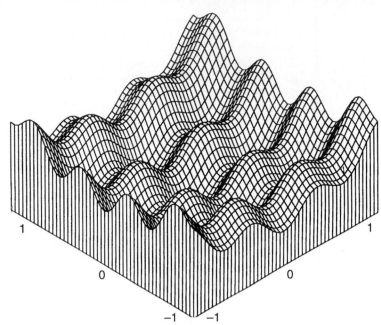

FIGURE 1.

TABLE 2. GSAVS Optimization of a Math Function Starting on a Local Minimum

Optimization Technique	Initial Step Size	Initial X, Y	Final X, Y	Final R	Number of Steps
GSAVS	0.15	−0.5 −0.5	9.3E-7 4.7E-7	1.3E-12	2857
GSAVS	0.15	0.003 0.003	3.7E-8 4.0E-7	3.2E-13	4757

Table 2 shows that GSAVS is able to converge to the global from a local minimum and from the global area.

The final step size in these optimizations was decreased to the precision of the machine. During the last few iterations of GSAVS $C(s) = C(r)$, which means that the step size is so small that it doesn't move anywhere when finding the random set of parameters.

Finally, GSAVS was used to perform a chemical analysis. The cost function was calculated by t   ollowing equation:

$$|r_s - cK|$$

where r_s is the vector of instrumental response for the unknown sample, c is the vector of the unknown concentrations (the parameters of the

Figure 6.5 (*Cont.*)

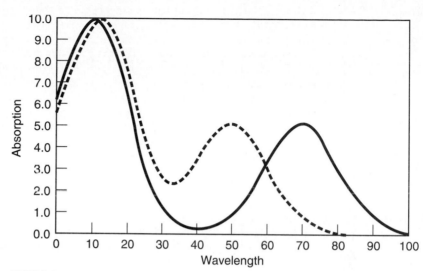

FIGURE 2.

optimization), and *K* is the *K*-matrix derived from Beer's law. *K* is calculated by dividing the concentrations of the pure component spectra into their corresponding instrumental responses. The bars around the equation indicate that the vector norm is taken.

First an optimization was performed using simulated UV-VIS data. The Gaussian curves of a simulated two component system are represented in Figure 2. The analysis was performed using select wavelengths and all wavelengths. The results are presented in Table 3.

TABLE 3. GSAVS Optimization of Simulated Chemical Predictions without Noise

λ's	Initial Conc.	Final Conc.	Relative Errors*
ALL	0.001	0.5	0.0%
	0.001	0.5	0.0%
10,70	0.001	0.5	0.0%
	0.001	0.5	0.0%
1-30	0.01	0.5	0.0%
	0.01	0.5	0.0%
35-100	0.01	0.5	0.0%
	0.01	0.5	0.0%

* Relative errors were calculated by dividing the difference of the predicted concentration and the true concentration by the true concentration.

Figure 6.5
(Cont.)

Notice that it does not make a difference if there is spectral overlap or not. GSAVS is able to find the global optimum. Because of this, the chemical analyses from this point on were performed using all wavelengths.

Noise was added to these data and the optimization of the chemical analysis was performed. Three and five percent relative noise was used because it should illustrate the worst case scenario. The results were compared to the classical least-squares approach (also known as the K-matrix approach. These results are presented in Table 4.

Note that the GSAVS gives better estimates at higher degrees of noise. The two components have different degrees of errors in all cases. One component consistently has a higher relative error than the other component due to spectral overlap. Note that GSAVS is not affected by the spectral overlap as much as the K-matrix approach seems to be (1.5% vs. 4.1% relative error). This suggests that GSAVS can be an effective tool for many different situations.

This study seems useless from a practical point of view because GSAVS obviously takes more time than the K-matrix approach. It seems pointless to do this analysis using GSAVS because of this. Actually, this is a precursor to other research ideas, such as analyzing for a single component in a mixture without knowledge of what the other components are. Obviously, the K-matrix approach could not solve this problem. The study presented in Table 4 was performed in order to test the validity of GSAVS for such problems as chemical analysis. It was assumed that if GSAVS did not work on this problem, it wouldn't be able to solve more complicated problems such as the one component analysis.

TABLE 4.   Optimization and CLS Results for Simulated Chemical Predictions with 3% and 5% Relative Noise

Analysis	RSD	Estimated Conc.	Rel. Error
GSAVS	0.03	0.0997	0.3%
		0.5011	0.22%
GSAVS	0.05	0.0985	1.5%
		0.5013	0.26%
K-matrix	0.03	0.1010	1.0%
		0.4989	0.22%
K-matrix	0.05	0.1041	4.1%
		0.4965	0.7%

Figure 6.5
(Cont.)

In summary, GSA is an effective tool to use for global optimizations. Unfortunately, GSA does not always find the exact global optimum. Using the acceptance ratio to adjust step sizes accordingly allows GSAVS to converge to the exact global optimum. According to certain experts in the field of Chemometrics (namely Dr. Kalivas), global conditions are not always necessary or feasible; but it is good to know that if global conditions are needed, GSAVS exists to find them.

Figure 6.5
(*Cont.*)

References:

(1) Edgar, T.F.; Himmelblau, D.M. **Optimization of Chemical Processes**; McGraw-Hill: New York, 1988.

(2) Bayne, Charles K.; Rubin, Ira B. **Practical Experimental Designs and Optimization Methods for Chemists**; VCH: Deerfield Beach, FL, 1986.

(3) Box, George, E.P.; Draper, Norman R. **Emperical Model-Building and Response Surfaces**; Wiley: New York, 1987.

(4) Kalivas, John H.; Roberts, Nancy; Sutter, Jon M. **Anal. Chem. 1989**, *61*, 2024.

(5) Bohachevsky, Ihor O.; Johnson, Mark E.; Stein, Myron L. **Technometrics 1986**, *28*, 209.

(6) van Laarhoven, P.J.M.; Aarts, E.H.L. **Simulated Annealing: Theory and Applications**; D. Reidel Publishing: Dordrecht, 1988.

(7) Vanderbilt, David; Louie, Steven G. J. **Comput. Phys. 1984**, *36*, 259.

(8) Johnson, Mark E., Ed. **Am. J. Math. Manag. Sci. 1988**, *8* (3 & 4).

SOLVING PROBLEMS THROUGH POLICY STATEMENTS, MANUALS, AND PROCEDURES

Preview of the Chapter

Distinguishing among Policy Statements, Manuals, and
   Procedures
   Policy Statements
   Manuals
   Procedures

Rhetorical Problem Solving for Policy Statements, Manuals,
   and Procedures

Guidelines for Writing an Enforceable Policy Statement

Sample Policy Statement

Guidelines for Producing a Functional Manual
   Formatting
   Readability
   Organization
   Appendixes and Attachments

Sample Outline for a Manual

Guidelines for Writing a Logical Procedure
   Essential Characteristics of Procedures
   Model for Procedure Writing

Sample Administrative Procedure

Sample Operations Procedure

Analyzing an Administrative Procedure

Conclusions

Postscript

February 15, 1989
10:50 A.M.
Ruth Warner's Office
Public School District 16
Administration Headquarters
Elko, Nevada

Ruth Warner began to realize just how big this problem of the new reader was going to be for the sixteenth district. Recently the Elko School Board had approved a new reader for sixth-graders on civics, or embryonic political science. Our Global Family was the latest book for sixth-graders and had the virtue of incorporating the apparent end of the cold war in its last chapter. As the elementary curriculum coordinator, Ruth had been especially pleased with this text choice.

Not everyone in Elko shared Ruth's enthusiasm, however. To her horror she found church groups and civic organizations rising up in indignant protest over the text choice. They expressed their dissatisfaction in various ways, almost all of them uncivilly. Ruth received reports of their activities every day. One group sent a mass mailing to a sixth-grade teacher who was using the book. Another group went directly to the district superintendent, bypassing classroom teacher, department head, principal, and several layers of administration in between. Some individuals transferred their children to other schools. Others directed petitions to neighbors and students.

Ruth knew that the superintendent could be swayed by such protests, despite their lack of reason-ableness and their mob-rule tactics. Ruth herself was outraged by these displays. She decided to meet with Jack Kelsey, the superintendent, to remind him of state-level support for the procedures the school board followed. Then she affirmed this support at the state level. With such clear-cut support from important sources, Ruth decided to seize the advantage. She would write a policy statement on what the school administration regarded as appropriate channels of protest. Ruth was determined to cut off the chaos of ad hoc protests. The protesters' energy, if channeled well, could be constructive; as it was currently being acted out, she saw it as destructive and irresponsible, as well as a very poor example to all children in the school district.

While it would be difficult to obtain agreement on a policy statement, because bureaucrats are loathe to take clear stands on policy, Ruth would do what she could. These protesters who were giving her such a headache were actually doing her a favor as well; they were giving her the opportunity to point out the need for a clear policy. She doubted she'd get much argument on that point.

July 29, 1990
9:00 A.M.
Bob Hanley's Office
St. Luke's Hospital
Denver, Colorado

Bob Hanley knew that the fierce Rocky Mountain heat was actually a plague visited on him by a punitive desert god. He loosened his tie in his boxy office, kept barely cool by its few vents from the central air-conditioning system. Someone had played with the thermostat again, and the temperature was 80 degrees. If you turned the thermostat down too abruptly, or directly, or harshly—Bob didn't know exactly what the crime was, but he knew the punishment well—the gods put the system on vacation. Trying to work in an 80-degree office in a building with windows that wouldn't open was all but impossible. Twenty years ago, when St. Luke's was a university instead of a hospital, the students who had been protesting the war from his office wouldn't have let something like hermetically sealed windows stop them from cooling off the place.

Despite these less than ideal atmospheric and theological conditions, he had to summon up the patience he didn't have to train his new administrative assistant. Bob usually enjoyed his job as a hospital administrator in charge of personnel, but he didn't have a moment to spare. Training a new assistant consumed much of his time and often his finally trained assistants then took better positions elsewhere. This almost constant process meant that he had to absorb the time crunch, taking home briefcases full of paperwork each night for several weeks.

Bob decided to talk to Doris Lippincot, his counterpart at Denver General, a woman with 25 years of experience in the business. She was one of the old school, as her name suggested. Doris had proved an invaluable ally, since she knew many of the people Bob worked with. But she also enjoyed watching this college graduate flounder in his new position. Bob had earned a degree in hospital administration when it was still a fairly new degree. He then spent 3 years learning the ropes, as if from scratch, when he worked with her at Denver General. "I would think you might have solved your training problem by now, Bob," Doris brayed. "You've only been through this about once a year for the past 5 years." Doris was really enjoying his misery.

It was hard, though, for Doris to dangle Bob along too much in such miserable heat. Instead, she took pity on him. "Why don't you commission a manual for your administrative assistant position," she suggested. The suggestion was so simple and so reasonable that Bob could have jumped out the window for not thinking of it himself. He would contact the technical writing group several floors beneath him, beneath the whole hospital for that matter, and see whether they could bail him out in time for the latest in his long string of assistants.

August 31, 1970
11:15 A.M.

Professor Allen's American History Class
Room 1595
St. Luke's University
Denver, Colorado

The semester had no sooner begun than Rick Allen wished he had stayed at his cabin in the Uintas. His upper-division students were getting more enraged by the minute because he didn't seem to be giving them the answers they wanted about U.S. involvement in Vietnam. He wasn't sure how much longer he could control the situation. He was getting sick of being shouted down in his own classroom. Today some of the quieter students left in the middle of the class, apparently intimidated by the dramatics and perhaps disgusted by the lack of order in the ivy-covered halls of St. Luke's.

What worried him most were the students who seemed in control through a sort of self-possession that Rick had never had and really couldn't imagine having, since he wasn't inclined to any absolutist positions about anything. He thought he had organized his life to function in a similarly nonabsolutist environment, a university, but was now wishing he had at least a little strong advice about how to handle the difficult situation in his American history class.

Rick felt that if he or the university mishandled the students, then he and the university might be liable. The St. Luke's faculty was considered in loco parentis, *and so could not comfortably take an adversarial position with the rebelling students. Rick felt he personally could not take such a position because it violated his sense of the humanistic education. But he also realized that someone might get hurt if he didn't cool down the situation.*

After checking with the administration, Rick found that a certain document did exist to respond to his dilemma—"Policies and Procedures in Case of Classroom Disruption." When Rick read the document, he had to laugh. The procedure was a mishmash of badly ordered information, few firm directions, and plenty of waffling language, qualifications that made it almost impossible to understand exactly what was expected of professors who found themselves confronted with disrupted classes.

In order to clarify the procedure for himself and to press administrators to take a firm stance on the issue, Rick decided to critique and rewrite the procedure, with the hope that exposing the vagueness and waffling would force the original authors to take a clearer stand. Rick had his work cut out for him, as we can see from reading the following document:

POLICIES AND PROCEDURES IN CASE OF CLASSROOM DISRUPTION

The following provides the faculty member or teaching assistant facing willful classroom disruption with guidelines which he may wish to follow in attempting to control the situation. These guidelines have been formulated to provide the instructor, the peacable [sic] students in the class, and the institution maximum protection under the university *Code of Conduct* and the legal structure of the courts.

If followed, they would also permit a relatively uniform across-campus response to disruptive situations, with consequent obvious advantages.

The suggested procedure in case of intentional class disruption, whether by students enrolled in the class or by others, is as follows:

1. The instructor should attempt to persuade the disrupters to desist and leave the classroom. At this point, threats of criminal, civil, or disciplinary sanctions are not appropriate.
2. If these efforts are unsuccessful, the instructor may wish to dismiss the class. If he does not and the situation escalates at any time to where life or property is endangered, the instructor should then dismiss the class without delay.
3. If the class remains and the disruption continues, the instructor, or a messenger, if feasible, should telephone the university security office and describe the difficulty. The security office will immediately contact the Dean of Students or his representative, who will proceed to the classroom at once. At the same time, a security officer, ordinarily in plain dress, will be dispatched to assist. While awaiting aid, the instructor should continue attempting the de-escalation of the situation. On arrival of professional assistance, the instructor should relinquish authority to these persons.
4. If the instructor is unable to follow the procedure in item 3 and wishes to retain his class and continue his effort to restore order, he should inform those interfering with the class that further disruptive conduct will subject them to university disciplinary proceedings and criminal or civil charges. If he is unsuccessful, the class should be dismissed.

Whenever disruption occurs, the instructor should:

1. Attempt to describe and identify the disrupters
2. Secure detailed written statements from as many students as possible, describing the disruption and the role of the participants
3. Prepare a report for the Vice President of Academic Affairs, embodying the data in items 1 and 2 above

Only with clear statements of witnesses identifying the offenders and describing their wrongful conduct can the university investigate the disruptive event and support disciplinary action and civil charges.

Rick was confused; what was he obligated to do and what did he really have a choice to do? This procedure gave him so many options that he finally couldn't use it as written. It would have to be revised.

DISTINGUISHING AMONG POLICY STATEMENTS, MANUALS, AND PROCEDURES

There are real distinctions among policy statements, manuals, and procedures as document types. These distinctions, however, are inconsistently applied within the professional world. For example, the document that Rick Allen found, "Policies and Procedures in Case of Classroom Disruption," shows a confusing mix of policy and procedural statements. Such a mix is unfortunate, because the statements vary in their level of generalization and in their intent. The following discussions point out the distinctions among the three types of documents, considering them in a hierarchy by level of detail, beginning with the most general, the policy statement.

Policy Statements

Policy statements are extremely general rules. As rules, they have very general application. "Work shall be done safely" and "Decisions shall not be affected by race, creed, national origin, or gender" are examples of such general rules. Policy statements do not account for their own implications; if a policy is not well implemented, one cannot find the way to implement it within the language of the policy itself. The Ten Commandments provide a good example of some clear policy statements, but what happens to those who break them is a matter of speculation. And exactly how we are to honor our parents is not prescribed, as it would be in a procedure on the subject.

Manuals

Manuals are descriptive documents. They present more specific information than policy statements do about narrower topics. Thus, manuals describing the duties of a certain position are common. Manuals may also describe the function of a group as a whole or of a piece of equipment. For example, the manual that comes with a personal computer describes how to put the equipment together and how to maintain it. Since initial start-up is a one-time activity, we don't consider this set of instructions in the manual to be procedural.

An important function of a manual is to document, that is, to record officially the status quo of the topic in question. Such documents as federal government facility descriptions and site plans fall within this category. These documents officially record information of a specific, descriptive sort, for example, a detailed description of all the buildings on a particular government site. Such a document will be used by planners and assessors.

The important point about manuals is that the descriptive material they contain does not provide the necessary level of detail to affect employee actions in specific situations. For example, a manual will contain a general description of the duties of an administrative assistant, but not a daily prescription of those duties.

How to carry out these duties will depend on various circumstances that a manual doesn't intend to account for. So there is a great deal of flexibility in the use of manual descriptions. Unfortunately, most people think of procedures and manuals interchangeably.

Procedures

Procedures provide step-by-step instructions for performing a specific activity repeatedly. If written well, a procedure will ensure that the activity proceeds uniformly no matter who performs it. Thus, banks have set up procedures for using their cash machines. If people try to reverse the order of the procedures, they will not get any money. The procedure is absolute; and it must be, because it has serious financial implications.

Besides ensuring uniformity, procedures should be regarded as a logical test of the activity concerned. Generally, however, the format of procedures tends to dominate their logical basis. People are so intimidated by procedures, knowing how seriously professionals take them, that they are tempted to regard them as above criticism, above analysis. This awe, though, is finally harmful and encourages the perpetuation of mindless activity.

Because procedures are so serious, sometimes with life-or-death consequences, they should be written sparingly. If readers are to focus intensely on procedures, writers need to ensure that the topic of the procedure deserves such attention. Thus, a procedure for miners to contact each other underground certainly seems necessary. But a procedure for miners to shower after their shifts is unnecessary, unless there is a safety consideration to such showering, for example, the need for miners in uranium mines to rinse off radioactive particles. Procedures on trivial subjects seem like opportunities for those with a bit of power to assert themselves to the many.

A good question to ask to decide whether a procedure is called for is this: Does this topic have any safety, financial, or quality (especially, ethical) ramifications? If not, then the topic does not need to be turned into a procedure. If so, then it should definitely be written up as a procedure. And every procedure reader should be a troubleshooter, the role Rick chose for himself after reading the classroom disruption procedure.

Table 7.1 summarizes the distinctions among policy statements, manuals, and procedures.

TABLE 7.1 *Distinguishing among Policy Statements, Manuals, and Procedures*

	Policy statements	*Manuals*	*Procedures*
Level of generality	High	Moderate	Low
Common forms	Rules Principles	Information Description	Directions
Purpose	Assert image	Provide guidelines	Specify actions
Function	Identity	Reference	Performance

RHETORICAL PROBLEM SOLVING FOR POLICY STATEMENTS, MANUALS, AND PROCEDURES

While policy statements, manuals, and procedures require the same rhetorical problem-solving process as reports do, their major concerns are different. Because the discourse of these documents is essentially directive, persuading the audience is not often a major part of the rhetorical problem, as it is in discursive reports. The writer does not have to present persuasive reasons for the reader to follow medical protocols, for example, or justify the logic of the company organization chart in the new employees manual. Thus, rhetorical problem solving for these documents takes on a different cast.

Instead of worrying about persuasion, the writer must be concerned with usability, verification, and logically sound reasoning. The clarity and accessibility of the documents are crucial. In fact, manuals and procedures are the documents that most clearly adhere to the old-fashioned notion of hard-core technical writing. They seem to dwell in the land of objective truth, objective data, and unambiguous writing, where a word means one thing and one thing only.

This old-school impression of technical writing, that it deals only in the facts, ma'am, is basically true of manuals and procedures, but with one qualification. The level of detail in manuals and procedures will determine the level of truth the document communicates. If, for example, Linda Rogers, a building supervisor, is writing a procedure on conducting fire hazard inspections, she will have a choice of the level of detail to go into. She might make the procedure essentially administrative, focusing on the paperwork to be completed, the reports to be filed, and the areas to be inspected, on the assumption that she need not mandate to a trained fire inspector how to look for hazards. If she takes this high road, though, which is built on the weak foundation of assumption, she is letting herself in for all sorts of liability. If the procedure she writes is too vague and general, it will contain logical gaps that require the reader to improvise, thus rendering the fire inspection almost ad hoc instead of standardized. If, on the other hand, she is very detailed about the steps in the procedure, she will find that she is back to the more impressionistic world of human disagreement over the proper method, the proper goal, and the proper responsible party. Manuals and procedures assign responsibility; they are therefore often very difficult to write well and approve.

Yet, despite the vagaries of their composition, manuals and procedures are extremely important documents with very serious ramifications. Badly written procedures can slow down response in places like nuclear power plants. Poorly written manuals can sit on the shelf, forever unused, when, if written well, they would be reliable descriptions of the way business is done in an organization. If a large corporation has a poorly written comptroller's manual, for example, then it will receive numerous variations on the annual report to headquarters. The professional world takes manuals and procedures very seriously; they are far more complex than the notion of a procedure as a "recipe."

Policy statements are far more obviously persuasive than manuals and procedures because they are rules. But they are absolutes, not arguments. They are more abstract, more general, and are intended to reach a more varied audience than are manuals and procedures. They may be intended for internal audiences, external audiences, or both. They may also be drafted differently for different audiences, which can certainly lead to an ethical problem.

The challenge of writing good policy statements is to turn them into meaningful prose; they tend to be written as motherhood statements, which assert uncontestable and extremely general values. For example, this policy statement appears in one form or another in several American industries: "Workers will work in accordance with safe work practices." As a policy, this statement is hardly trendsetting or even very meaningful. It means that safety is a concern of the employer and that federal agencies that oversee workplace safety, such as the Occupational Safety and Health Administration (OSHA), have a presence of some sort at the facility. OSHA might conduct regular inspections; the Personnel office might be contacted for quarterly accident reports. What this policy statement really means is that the company that posts it obeys federal laws about occupational safety. Need any company post a policy that says, in effect, we respect federal law?

Ruth Warner's challenge will be to draft a policy statement that the district's administrators will approve and that will still have teeth in it to deal with the book opponents. Policy statements are difficult to write because they are a company's internal laws, yet won't necessarily have any legal teeth to them. Implementing a policy often requires extensive legal review.

For the purposes of this chapter, the policy statement is a helpful concept because it makes the function and intent of manuals and procedures clearer. The point to remember is that policy statements are general rules, not concrete directions for people to follow to accomplish specific activities. Therefore, Rick Allen needs a procedure, not a policy statement, to direct him in his time of chaos. The policy statement is the document to think about, to meditate on, to recollect in tranquility; the procedure should specify appropriate actions in specific circumstances.

 ## GUIDELINES FOR WRITING AN ENFORCEABLE POLICY STATEMENT

It is not easy to write an enforceable policy statement, because so many legalistic decisions go into it and because so many people must take a stand on its content. It's very difficult to get people to agree about such statements, either their content or tone. Generally, though, the following guidelines can help:

1. State the policy as simply as possible. Too many qualifications will both obscure the content and water down the force of the policy statement.
2. State only policies that can be enforced. It damages an organization's credibility to state a policy that it has no power or will to enforce.
3. Maintain the identity of the policy statement by keeping general descriptions and procedural detail out of it.

The enforceability of a policy statement is a vital consideration. "We suggest that students attend 80 percent of their classes" is unenforceable, whereas "five or more absences result in an automatic F for the class" is specific and clear enough to be enforceable, as long as it is also legally possible. A more moderate statement of the absence policy might be "five or more absences constitute grounds for failing the course." Thus, the instructor would have some flexibility to judge individual circumstances. Most instructors would want to make a distinction between students who had missed class because of illness and those who had missed class because of a bowling date.

The difficulty in writing a policy statement, then, is not so much in drafting the statement, except for the three rules above, as it is in getting agreement on the statement.

SAMPLE POLICY STATEMENT

Ruth Warner needs a policy statement to bring some order to the chaos of the Elko textbook rebellion. She needs a policy that will establish a channel for communicating discontent with School Board and District decisions, so that individuals involved, as well as innocent bystanders or innocent students, won't get their time taken up with ad hoc attacks and complaints. Fortunately for Ruth, she has the autonomy to draft the policy herself and then get it approved by the School Board and the District Superintendent, only four people.

After analyzing the problem, Ruth knows what teeth she's going to put in the policy before she even knows what policy to advocate. The teeth will be that any route for complaints other than the one described by School Board and District policy will lead nowhere: the School Board will hear only those complaints that come via the approved route. Thus, the consequence of ignoring the policy will be that one's complaint will not get official consideration. Although most people don't like to encounter this sort of bureaucratic response, large organizations must have orderly channels of communication.

Since Ruth intends to be so strict about this policy and since she knows she has an enforceable consequence, she decides to make the policy statement itself as simple as possible. She could certainly write her policy to stymie any protest at all, but she doesn't really want to stifle protest; she wants to organize it. She decides on this simple wording: "Objections to School Board policy must be submitted in writing to the District Superintendent."

While he has no objection to being the conduit for complaints about School Board policy, the Superintendent does comment that Ruth will be lucky if her audience—the people of Elko—will know what kind of issue the School Board would rule on. He suggests that she somehow explain what topics would be covered by her policy statement. To solve this problem, Ruth decides to add a description of the scope of School Board decisions: "Such issues as scheduling, discipline, text selection, administrative hiring, and standardized testing come under School Board purview." "What are the citizens of Elko, Nevada, going to know from 'purview?'" asks the Superintendent; so Ruth makes a change in the policy wording: "The School Board rules on scheduling, discipline, text selection, administrative hiring (as opposed to teacher and staff hiring), and standardized testing." This revision allowed Ruth to sharpen her own thinking and exclude the waffling language in her first draft of the explanation: "such issues as," "under . . . purview." The fact is, those are the issues the School Board addresses; why imply that they are some of the many others, when there are no others?

Having addressed audience issues and clarity, Ruth then knows it's time to draft the consequence section of the policy statement. Again, she wants to write it clearly, but not necessarily in tones that would threaten an outsider audience. She needs a fine line between firmness and intimidation. She tries and rejects the colloquial—"If you don't submit your complaint in writing, we won't read it"—because it sounds too threatening, because it sets up an antagonistic we-you relationship with the audience, and because she's afraid all those negatives might confuse the readers. Instead, she chooses a more neutral version: "Only those complaints submitted in writing to the Superintendent will be addressed."

The new policy statement, then, is clear, specific, and understandable by an outsider audience:

> Objections to School Board policy must be submitted in writing to the District Superintendent. The School Board rules on scheduling, discipline, text selection, administrative hiring (as opposed to teacher and staff hiring), and standardized testing. Only those complaints submitted in writing to the Superintendent will be addressed.

This is an enforceable policy, written in explanatory tones; it should encourage cooperation, not discourage participation.

GUIDELINES FOR PRODUCING A FUNCTIONAL MANUAL

Besides adhering to the principle that the content of manuals should be descriptive, not procedural or policy-oriented, the biggest job in putting together a manual is document design. There are many aspects to document design, but they all converge in a single purpose: to make the manual functional. Document design is an issue with all types of professional documents, and we devote Chapter 11 to it, but we introduce it here in connection with manuals because the task of making a manual readable is an extremely difficult one.

Formatting

One important aspect of document design that is usually considered important for the wrong reasons is formatting. Formatting is important because it sets up a consistent structure for the manual, a structure readers can predict. Formatting is not so important simply for aesthetics or image. A system of headers, footers, and other internal identifiers must be consistent, not primarily to please the eye, but to signal the reader appropriately. Manuals contain the largest accumulations of prose in a work environment, yet must somehow make their information accessible.

Formatting consistently makes this access possible, because it sets up expectations in the reader. When these expectations are fulfilled, the reading goes faster, with greater comprehension. This business of predictability is very important to encourage in readers, since study after study has correlated the ability to predict text with a high level of comprehension.

Readability

Besides having consistent formatting, the manual should be readable. The writer's style certainly affects readability, and some style concerns are covered in the Appendix. But readability is also a matter of form. Here we refer to *form* as distinct from *formatting*, which is primarily a concern of word processors. Form concerns paragraph length, sentence type, and all other matters of arranging the words on the page. Generally, the more successful manuals do not rely on large, unbroken chunks of written material. To encourage the harried and bored reader, the successful manuals provide breaks, such as bulleted lists, tables, charts, figures, and all the variety of technical illustration available. Since manual material is essentially descriptive, the illustrations and graphics are appropriate for carrying the message to the reader.

Organization

Although this may seem so obvious that it need not be said, a manual must also be organized logically. Given sufficient time, most departments would put together organized manuals. But manuals are so often delivered in a rush to satisfy some internal demand for documentation that their disorganization is often shocking. The usual logical organizing schemes are functional, covering tasks in order of their importance, or chronological, describing activities from the beginning to the end of the working day. The bare minimum of organizing schemes would be alphabetizing topics by chapter. Another important organizer for manuals is the index. People need some way to get to the information they need quickly.

Professional and technical manuals are often revised, since all aspects of the workplace are constantly changing. To accommodate almost constant revision, the manual author needs some provision for indicating which revision is reflected in the manual, perhaps by indicating this information on each page. The author should also consider numbering each chapter separately. Thus, each chapter would have an alphanumeric starter that renders the chapter independent of the rest of the manual. For example, the pages of Chapter 3 would be numbered 3-1, 3-2, and so on. With separate chapter numbering, when a section or an entire chapter is revised, only the chapter involved will have to be renumbered. With continuous pagination, however, any revision of sections or chapters would require renumbering of the entire manual.

Appendixes and Attachments

Appendixes are sometimes called attachments, but the two are distinct. Appendixes are usually substantial self-contained sections of text; attachments are usually short supplements, like copies of forms and other paperwork. Appendixes and attachments are similar, however, in that both are supplementary to the main text; both present pertinent but secondary information that would be intrusive if put into the main text of the manual.

SAMPLE OUTLINE FOR A MANUAL

Bob Hanley's manual for his administrative assistant will succeed if he follows the principles of consistent formatting, attention to readability, and clear organization. While we don't need to include the text of a whole manual here, we can certainly outline topics for it (see Figure 7.1). Even in this outline we can see attention to signaling the reader through repetition of key words and phrases, such as "applicants" "overview," and "current," and good summary-level chapter titles.

Bob has a good plan for his manual. His arrangement of topics is logical, his chapter headings are descriptive and logically organized (according to the job search process), and he includes an index.

The four appendixes in Bob's manual contain information important enough to go in the manual, but not important enough to go in the main text. Appendixes 1 and 2, current organization charts for the whole hospital and for the personnel department, would require constant updating, so it would be foolish for Bob to include these in the body of the manual. Appendixes 3 and 4, legal and illegal interview questions and pertinent Colorado legislation, contain related information, some of which elaborates on points made in the manual, but which is of secondary importance to the text. St. Luke's is more concerned to get federal legislation straight than it is to get Colorado legislation straight, because the federal rulings are more complex than are the state-level rulings.

Bob's manual as planned is thorough, logically organized, and informative. It should be enough to teach his new administrative assistants the essence of their job.

GUIDELINES FOR WRITING A LOGICAL PROCEDURE

The three main guidelines for writing procedures are the following:

1. Include only procedural discourse in the procedure; eliminate policy and manual material.
2. Organize the procedure by process instead of by participant.
3. Review all procedures for their logical soundness.

Figure 7.1
*Sample outline for
a manual*

A HANDBOOK FOR THE ADMINISTRATIVE ASSISTANT
IN THE PERSONNEL DEPARTMENT

Chapter 1: An Overview of St. Luke's Hospital

Chapter 2: General Description of the Personnel Office

Chapter 3: Overview of Administrative Assistant Duties

Chapter 4: Writing Advertisements

Chapter 5: Screening Applicants

Chapter 6: Acknowledging Applicants

Chapter 7: Setting Up Interviews

Chapter 8: Interview Duties

Chapter 9: Coordinating with Hiring Departments

Chapter 10: Handling Unsolicited Applications

Chapter 11: Orienting New Employees

Chapter 12: Handling Terminated Employees

Chapter 13: Reporting Commitments

Chapter 14: Monitoring Employment Legislation

Appendix 1: Current Organization Chart: St. Luke's Hospital

Appendix 2: Current Organization Chart: Personnel Department

Appendix 3: Legal and Illegal Interview Questions

Appendix 4: Pertinent Colorado Legislation Index

Index

One of the most important functions of a procedure is to get the procedural information, the steps for performing the activity, separated from policy statements and manual descriptions. A procedure should be a very pragmatically written document. It is not the place for philosophizing and speculating. Neither is it the place for justifying (the job of policy statements) or describing (the job of manuals). If a procedure mixes the three levels of information, then the procedure operator may have difficulty distinguishing the essential actions required by the procedure. Even if the user can distinguish the actions from the policy, the time required to do so is still costly.

Procedures are often organized according to who is performing the action. If the procedure is performed by only one person, this organization is not a problem. But if more than one person has a part to play in the procedure, then instruction based on a participant's role is a big mistake. It is like trying to write a procedure for a *pas de deux* by first describing all the prima's steps and then describing all her partner's steps. Such a procedure would give no sense of the *pas de deux* as a whole; it wouldn't integrate the activities of the two people who together make a whole out of a series of steps.

The justification for writing procedures by performer is that people need to know what their part is in a procedure. While it is true that people need to know their responsibility in a procedure, they also need to know how their part coordinates with other people's parts; that way, they can act more cooperatively and thus enhance the procedure's successful completion. While the procedure performer doesn't need to know everything that everybody else does, the sequence of activities must be clear.

The sequence of steps within an activity must be logically sound and should be the main emphasis of a procedure. Even if people, because of human nature, do tend to be interested only in their own part, procedure writers should not pander to this narcissism. One of the most notable characteristics of a professional is a general concern for quality instead of a myopic obsession with one's personal duties. Professionals are not expected to complain, "That's not my job," if they receive a request. Instead, they must see to it that the person who does do the job gets the message.

Essential Characteristics of Procedures

Procedure writers must keep in mind the following five essential characteristics of procedures:

1. Accuracy
2. Feasibility
3. Specificity
4. Honesty
5. Thoroughness

Testers can walk through draft procedures to determine their accuracy, but feasibility is often a matter of logical analysis, because sometimes feasibility of "solutions" in procedures can't be tested under normal conditions. For example, the procedure can state that classroom instructors should get a message to the security office if their class is disrupted, but can make no guarantee in advance that such an action will be feasible for the instructor. What if the disrupters are blocking the door or holding the instructor hostage? To provide a feasible way for the instructor to reach security, the procedure writer might have to propose another solution, which would require the approval of all those responsible for the procedure and which might even prompt new policy decisions.

The specificity of procedures is a matter of constant evaluation. Whatever level of specificity an author chooses, one rule of thumb is constant: a procedure step should limit itself to one action only. One noteworthy aspect of the procedure on classroom disruption is that several steps are embedded within each numbered step in the procedure. For example, step 3 contains at least five individual steps, depending on what decisions the administration would make about policy vagueness (see page 295). As Rick rewrites this procedure, he'll need to separate individual steps. Discrete steps not only enhance procedure readability, but also allow author and reviewer to get a clear sense of the procedure's logic.

The honesty with which a procedure is written is an ethical consideration that has serious ramifications. If, for example, Jason Wells, a midlevel executive, must write procedures, which are to be reviewed by outside reviewers, to document how his group does business, then he must be sure to report how business is actually done. If he tries to create more appealing procedures than the ones actually used, he will be lying, of course, and will also probably get caught by the Quality Control group in his own organization, which will audit his group by the extent to which his activities are procedurally correct. If his own organization doesn't catch him, then the outside reviewers will, which would be all the more humiliating as far as his organization is concerned. Many the job search group has had its work come to nothing when the affirmative action auditor notes that decisions were not made in accordance with affirmative action procedures. It does no good, then, to write procedures that bear little resemblance to the reality of the work environment, but authors are often tempted to do so when external auditors are reviewing them.

Thoroughness is contingent on a procedure's specificity. Thus, a badly written procedure might contain three badly written steps that amount to something like this: (1) Begin project in accordance with rules learned in training; (2) Complete project by deadline; and (3) Draft a report for the General Manager on the success of the project. While easy to write, this procedure is absurdly general and therefore very difficult to perform thoroughly.

The link between level of specificity and thoroughness, then, is clear.

There is another aspect of thoroughness that is often overlooked in procedure writing: alternative action in decision areas. In the two schools of procedure-writing theory one school says that those who carry out procedures are thinking human beings, and the other school says that they are "knuckle-draggers." Those who believe the former will leave the decision making to the user. That's what Rick's university administrators did. Those who believe the latter will try to write procedures that allow no decision making by the users. There is a middle ground, however, between these optimistic and cynical schools: the prudent school. This school advocates the idea that users and operators are capable of judgment, but should not be left without guidance. Thus, the users should not have to invent their own alternatives to decision areas because the author will write down which actions are appropriate based on possible outcomes.

Model for Procedure Writing

The work Dr. Daniel Plung and associates did with procedures at the Waste Isolation Pilot Plant Project in Carlsbad, New Mexico, provides a fine model of prudently written procedures, both operations procedures and administrative procedures. The procedures are prudently written because they give sufficient guidance to people making decisions, without oversimplifying the procedure to eliminate all decision areas. Dr. Plung seems to assume that people who carry out procedural work are neither knuckle-draggers nor free spirits.

He bases his graphic procedure format on the flowcharts in computer science. Plung's system uses different symbols to indicate different logical operations required of the user—acting, warning, deciding, cross-referencing, and qualifying. The rectangle, circle, and diamond constitute the main action line in a procedure, which runs down the middle of a page.

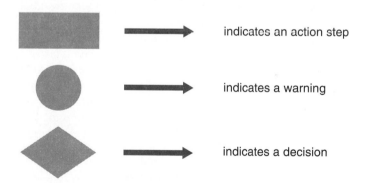

The triangle and oval appear to the side of the main action line, connected to a rectangle or diamond by an unbroken line. They appear to the side because they concern extra information, not crucial to performing the basics of the procedure.

Flowchart Components

Sample Action Step

Note that the person performing the action is identified at the beginning. Note, too, that only one action is contained in the step.

Technician tests
the water sample.

Sample Warning

A warning will sit right on top of an action step, so the person who should heed the warning need not be identified in the warning itself. The warning is worded so that the most important information appears first in the statement. Many warnings in other forms obscure the crucial information in qualifications and prepositional phrases.

Wear
asbestos
gloves to
remove the
cap.

Sample Decision Step

Note that the decision step is written as a question, because more than one outcome is possible. People tend to assume that decision areas in administrative procedures are pro forma, but for the procedure to be well written, all reasonable consequences should be accounted for. Just because a general manager tends to sign off on any report that crosses his desk does not mean that his replacement will rubber-stamp work so routinely. The principles of the procedure must override the personalities of employees who currently hold the positions referred to.

In this example the decision step presents only two possibilities, yes and no. The procedure author draws these consequences out in alternate sections of the procedure, immediately following the diamond. Other lines and arrows indicate where the particular path of consequences rejoins the main action line of the procedure.

No   Does General   Yes
      Manager approve
      the report?

Sample Cross-Reference

Cross-references serve a couple of important functions in a procedure. First, as in the one above, the cross-reference will set up a loop of actions, where a loop is needed. For example, until a certain approval is obtained, the user may need to be in a cycle of reviews; until the appropriate signature has been obtained, there should be no progress in the procedure. Another function of the cross-reference is to direct the user to related procedures and appended information at the back of the current procedure. Cross-references help the user make major moves through a complex procedure that has many alternative paths to account for.

Return
to
step 5.

Sample Note

The main principle governing the use of notes is that they concern only secondary information. Notes don't affect the activities on the main action line; they contain only adjunct information and qualifications. Procedure writers need to keep notes at a minimum because they can distract from the procedure's essential actions. If the writer finds that a procedure seems to require a greater number of notes, chances are that the author needs to write some of the descriptive information in a manual or to cross-reference the information in an appendix at the back of the procedure.

Other copies should go to
the General Manager and Vice
General Manager if the
loss exceeds 5K.

SAMPLE ADMINISTRATIVE PROCEDURE

Put together, these graphics form a clear path of actions that follows the logic of process. Figure 7.2 shows a sample administrative procedure presented in a flowchart per Dr. Plung's model. In addition to the flow chart there are four categories on the first page of the procedure that orient the reader to the procedure's limits (scope statement), any peculiar definitions, references, and general statements that pertain to the procedure as a whole. The general statements are usually some kind of rules pertinent specifically to the procedure; they are not rules general enough to qualify as policy statements.

For people accustomed to standard procedures, this procedural format can appear daunting, at first. Since each step truly is only one step and since each decision area is called out as a real decision instead of a rubber-stamp area, the procedure appears quite lengthy. The fact is, though, that it is the explicitness of the procedure that makes it seem longer than the standard procedure. Rick Allen will find that when he rewrites his procedure for classroom disruption, he will have many more steps than the four currently making up the procedure.

Note, though, that this explicit format makes some realities much clearer than they would be in the old embedded style. First, we can see exactly how bureaucratically rigid this process of getting an administrative leave is. One misstep and a person's request would be nullified. And since the process takes so long, it would be difficult to summon the stamina to start the application all over again.

Another truth that becomes apparent is that this procedure puts a great deal of power in the hands of the department chair. While this may or may not be good news for the applicant, it is a fact that any procedure reviewers should consider. Administrators might question how much they want department chairs in charge of

Figure 7.2
Sample administrative procedure

A scope statement at the beginning of the procedure does not concern essential action, but explains to whom the procedure applies, what circumstances it covers, and who falls outside its provenance.

Any term that might be ambiguous or that needs to be understood in a very narrow sense or that is too technical for the procedure audience should be defined before the procedural steps themselves are described.

In this section, list all references used to write the procedure.

PROCEDURE 15: APPLYING FOR ADMINISTRATIVE LEAVE

I. Scope: This procedure describes the process for obtaining administrative leave. It applies to professors and administrators. Others wishing administrative leave, particularly hourly workers, should follow procedure 25.

II. Definitions:
   Administrative leave: a leave of absence taken to accommodate consulting work or off-campus research.
   Administrator: all employees from category A-6 on.
   Professional leave: a leave of absence taken to accommodate a sabbatical.
   Professor: permanent faculty on 9-month appointment, tenured or untenured.

III. References:
   St. Luke's University Handbook, 1976

IV. General:
   A. Leave proposals are considered twice a year, in December and in April.
   B. The decision process takes at least three months, under the best of circumstances. It is therefore wise to begin it early.
   C. Any applicants who do not follow this procedure will automatically be dropped from consideration.

V. Procedure:

Figure 7.2
(*Cont.*)

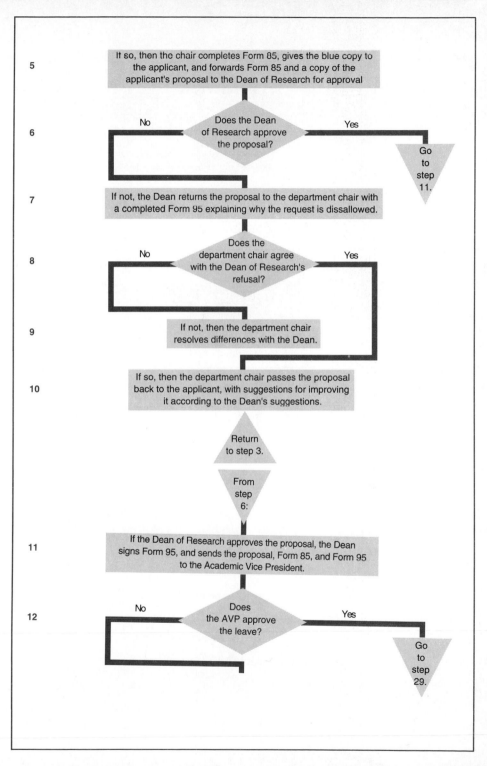

5 — It so, then the chair completes Form 85, gives the blue copy to the applicant, and forwards Form 85 and a copy of the applicant's proposal to the Dean of Research for approval

6 — Does the Dean of Research approve the proposal? No / Yes — Go to step 11.

7 — If not, the Dean returns the proposal to the department chair with a completed Form 95 explaining why the request is dissallowed.

8 — Does the department chair agree with the Dean of Research's refusal? No / Yes

9 — If not, then the department chair resolves differences with the Dean.

10 — If so, then the department chair passes the proposal back to the applicant, with suggestions for improving it according to the Dean's suggestions.

Return to step 3.

From step 6:

11 — If the Dean of Research approves the proposal, the Dean signs Form 95, and sends the proposal, Form 85, and Form 95 to the Academic Vice President.

12 — Does the AVP approve the leave? No / Yes — Go to step 29.

Figure 7.2
(*Cont.*)

Figure 7.2
(Cont.)

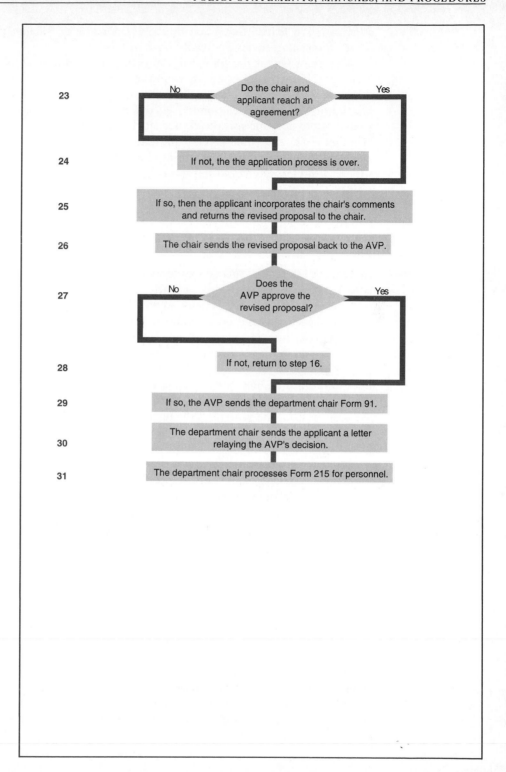

administrative leave. Does that option open the way for any possible abuses? That's a question reviewers would have to face.

The point is that the format of the procedure makes such biases clear for all reviewers. If any of the alternatives in the decision areas had not been specified, this error would appear graphically as an arm that attached to nothing else in the procedure, a path that dead-ended. As this procedure stands, it is not perfect, but it does try to account specifically for all the consequences of the decision areas. Whether reviewers would agree with these consequences or not is a question they would have to ask themselves during the procedure review process. But at least with this format they could tell what the consequences were.

SAMPLE OPERATIONS PROCEDURE

In general, operations procedures tend to have fewer decision areas than administrative procedures do. This is partly because the procedures will not be so specific that they provide lessons in standard technical operations for the user. They will focus instead on a sequence of actions that constitutes an operational whole. Thus, for example, a technician would not find a procedure on how to change the oil in the company car, because this is a standard activity that has little degree of specialization attached to it. On the other hand, the technician would find procedures on how to work a specialized piece of equipment, like a one-of-a-kind nuclear waste forklift, or procedures on how to respond to a nuclear spill on the premises. All the principles the technician had learned about cleaning up spills would be qualified by site-specific rules and parameters. The procedure in Figure 7.3 is a simple operations procedure that conveys the flavor of such procedures.

While it may seem that this procedure has been written for knuckle-draggers, there are two good reasons for its specificity. First, there is a concern for quality control. The Loadem Company wants to be able to guarantee professional loading for its customers, who might decide to find another shipping company if they get poor results. The second reason is that Loadem's policy to penalize packers for damaged goods could result in constant disputes about who was responsible for the damage. To ensure that the packer is not responsible, Loadem requires a signed inspection at the end of the process. This inspection protects the packer and furnishes Loadem with the documentation necessary to recover any damage fee from the truckers.

It is inspection step 16, however, that provides a loophole for the packer. The implicit decision required by an inspector has been flattened out in this procedure, as if the inspector will always find that the pallet has been properly packed. In order to make it clear that this inspection is not a rubber stamp, the procedure should be revised to make step 16 a decision instead of an action.

While other operations procedures may be far more technical, in that they contain more technical information, their structure will be an elaboration of this sample operations procedure.

Figure 7.3
Sample operations procedure

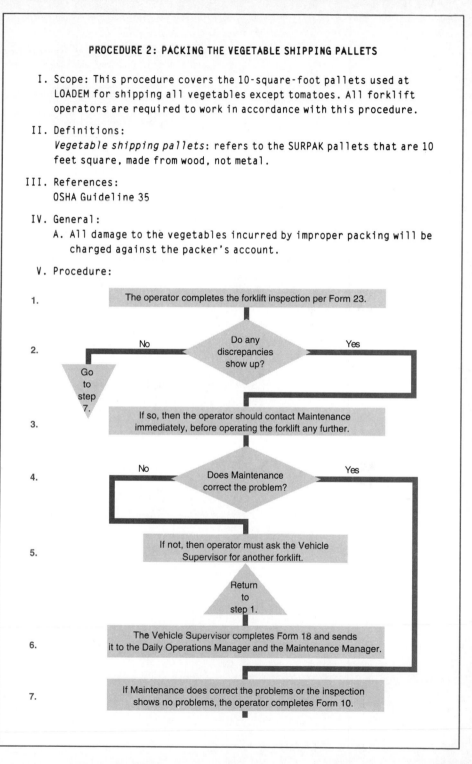

PROCEDURE 2: PACKING THE VEGETABLE SHIPPING PALLETS

I. Scope: This procedure covers the 10-square-foot pallets used at LOADEM for shipping all vegetables except tomatoes. All forklift operators are required to work in accordance with this procedure.

II. Definitions:
Vegetable shipping pallets: refers to the SURPAK pallets that are 10 feet square, made from wood, not metal.

III. References:
OSHA Guideline 35

IV. General:
A. All damage to the vegetables incurred by improper packing will be charged against the packer's account.

V. Procedure:

1. The operator completes the forklift inspection per Form 23.

2. Do any discrepancies show up? No / Yes
Go to step 7.

3. If so, then the operator should contact Maintenance immediately, before operating the forklift any further.

4. Does Maintenance correct the problem? No / Yes

5. If not, then operator must ask the Vehicle Supervisor for another forklift.
Return to step 1.

6. The Vehicle Supervisor completes Form 18 and sends it to the Daily Operations Manager and the Maintenance Manager.

7. If Maintenance does correct the problems or the inspection shows no problems, the operator completes Form 10.

Figure 7.3
(Cont.)

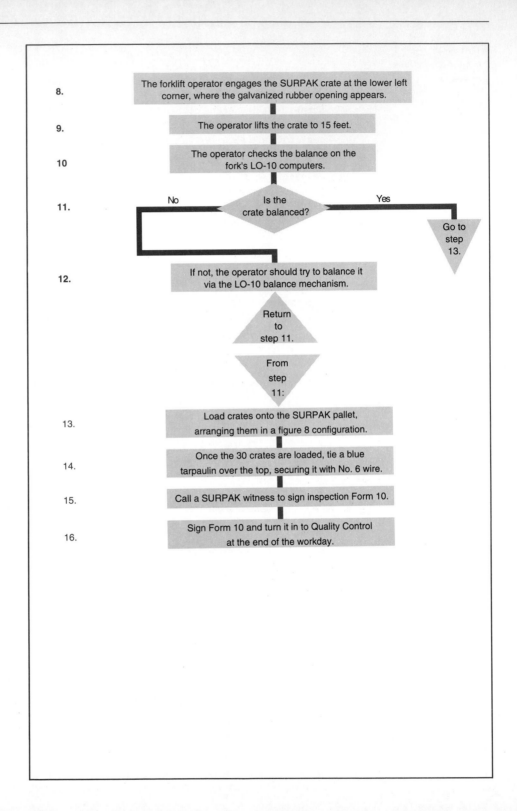

8. The forklift operator engages the SURPAK crate at the lower left corner, where the galvanized rubber opening appears.

9. The operator lifts the crate to 15 feet.

10 The operator checks the balance on the fork's LO-10 computers.

11. No ← Is the crate balanced? → Yes

Go to step 13.

12. If not, the operator should try to balance it via the LO-10 balance mechanism.

Return to step 11.

From step 11:

13. Load crates onto the SURPAK pallet, arranging them in a figure 8 configuration.

14. Once the 30 crates are loaded, tie a blue tarpaulin over the top, securing it with No. 6 wire.

15. Call a SURPAK witness to sign inspection Form 10.

16. Sign Form 10 and turn it in to Quality Control at the end of the workday.

ANALYZING AN ADMINISTRATIVE PROCEDURE

Professor Allen is so disgusted with the administration's poor attempt to commit itself to a procedure that he decides to try to motivate a revision. It is a task worth doing: not only are he and the university facing liability from several directions—parents, involved students, bystander students, staff, professors—but also as a matter of principle the university should have a coherent policy in place on such a potentially dangerous issue. Rick knows that it will take a long time to get agreement on a procedure about such a controversial issue, but a good place to start would be to make explicit all the embedded decision areas in the existing procedure. Figure 7.4 presents Rick's revision and analysis of the classroom disruption procedure.

When flowcharted, the procedure looks as unwieldy and uninstructive as Rick suspected it was. In fact, the flowchart shows how weak the procedure really is. If a professor's simple logical analysis could get at the weaknesses in the procedure, a skilled trial lawyer could have a wonderful time with it. Even assuming that the procedure were on the right track, we can see that there are holes in it at steps 16 and 20; that is, the procedure reaches a dead end, with absolutely no guidance for the instructor who has come to that pass.

One of the most amazing points about Rick's analysis is seeing how many steps actually were embedded in a procedure that listed only four procedural steps, with another three added on the end as an afterthought. Rick's twenty-two-step analysis is as lean as he can make it without violating any of the decision areas embedded in the procedure's logic. On the other hand, the three steps added on the end of the procedure actually constitute only one step in Rick's analysis of the procedure.

Converting a procedure into a flowchart is an invaluable tool for detecting logical problems both in procedures one is writing and in procedures one has been assigned to review. You may recall that the professional profiles in Chapter 1 listed procedure review as a major part of a professional's job. Using flowcharts gives the reviewer a method and a very graphic representation of both procedural chaos and procedural quality.

CONCLUSIONS

This chapter distinguishes among three different types of directive discourse: policy statements, manuals, and procedures. Policy statements are very general rules; the primary concern is to write them so that they say something meaningful. Manuals provide descriptive and basic information; they are not as general as policies or as specific as procedures. They present guidelines but not to the point of describing a single process step by step, the way a procedure does. The major concern with writing manuals is designing them appropriately for their audience and organizing them logically. Procedures present step-by-step directions for performing a certain activity in a uniform manner. This uniformity is necessary for any activity that has important quality, financial, or safety implications. Procedures are essential when a process must be performed with no deviation.

Figure 7.4
*Rick Allen's
analysis of the
classroom
disruption
procedure*

PROCEDURE FOR HANDLING CLASSROOM DISRUPTION

Note to Administrators: I have converted our current procedure on classroom disruption into a flowchart to point out some problems with it. You will see below how many of the decisions are thrown in the lap of the instructor, with few guidelines for the instructor's protection. My comments appear throughout the procedure in brackets.

I. Scope: This procedure applies to the entire teaching staff at St. Luke's University, tenured and nontenured, full- and part-time. It applies to any disruption in a classroom that could endanger students or property [and/or faculty?]. Disruption that is not physically [or psychically?] threatening, i.e., uncooperative attitudes, disagreement with the professor and long debate about the disagreement, does not fall under this procedure. Such benign disruption is covered under Procedure TBD (to be determined)[I assume there must be another such procedure].

II. Definitions:
Disruption: behavior that is physically threatening to students or property. [We don't want to forget faculty here either or psychic disturbances.] It impedes an instructor's ability to conduct class.

III. References:
St. Luke's University Code of Conduct

IV. General: (None)

V. Procedure:

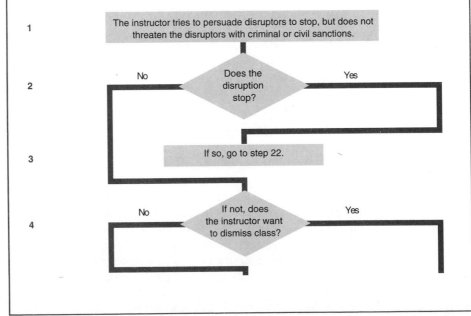

1   The instructor tries to persuade disruptors to stop, but does not threaten the disruptors with criminal or civil sanctions.

2   Does the disruption stop?   No   Yes

3   If so, go to step 22.

4   If not, does the instructor want to dismiss class?   No   Yes

Figure 7.4
(*Cont.*)

Figure 7.4
(Cont.)

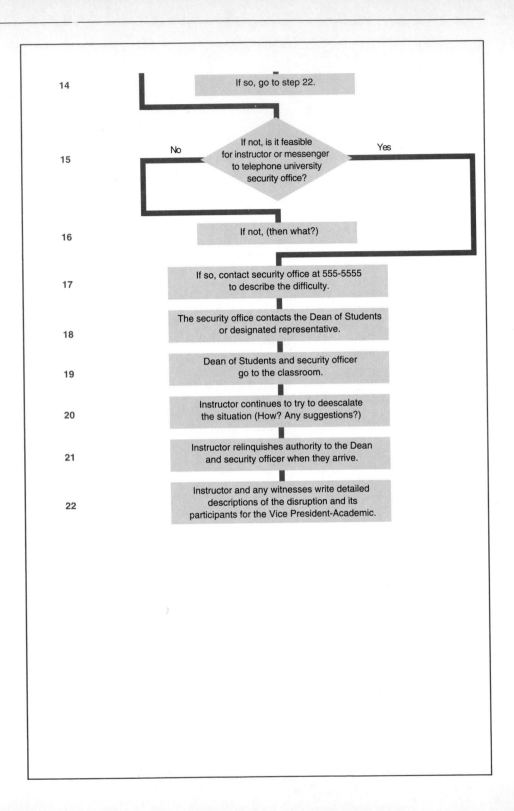

14   If so, go to step 22.

15   No   If not, is it feasible for instructor or messenger to telephone university security office?   Yes

16   If not, (then what?)

17   If so, contact security office at 555-5555 to describe the difficulty.

18   The security office contacts the Dean of Students or designated representative.

19   Dean of Students and security officer go to the classroom.

20   Instructor continues to try to deescalate the situation (How? Any suggestions?)

21   Instructor relinquishes authority to the Dean and security officer when they arrive.

22   Instructor and any witnesses write detailed descriptions of the disruption and its participants for the Vice President-Academic.

POSTSCRIPT

Ruth Warner's policy statement was partially successful. Those who bothered to read it tended to abide by it, but the textbook issue was so hot that Ruth and the others in the school district's administration found they had to initiate some meetings and public forums to put themselves at the center of the dispute, all the better to put it into some kind of controlled deliberation.

Bob Hanley's manual was a great success. His new administrative assistant, Joe, spent a day with it while he was still training, and then used it as a reference until he was skilled in all aspects of the job. Joe realized, in fact, that he should update the manual to add another duty to the job description there: maintain the Administrative Assistant's Handbook. He did maintain it faithfully; and when he decided to leave to become a law student, Bob turned the training over to him. The switch from Joe to Jeannine was the smoothest staff transition Bob ever had.

Rick's procedure efforts were a qualified success. He certainly made it clear to St. Luke's University administration that the current procedure on classroom disruption was inadequate. But because the higher-ups could never agree on policies that would clarify actions in the procedure, the old procedure remained on the books. Rick got another teaching job, because his insistence about having a reasonable procedure in place got on some administrative nerves. The next year one student was hurt in a disrupted class at St. Luke's and successfully sued the university. Part of the suit's success derived from the fact that the university had no coherent procedure in place to deal with classroom disruption. Very soon thereafter St. Luke's University became St. Luke's Hospital.

EXERCISES

1. Using Rick's procedure analysis as a base, revise the classroom disruption procedure. Write a flowcharted procedure that will resolve the open issues in the first draft and streamline the procedure as a whole. Exchange revised procedures and critique a partner's revision.

2. Obtain a procedure sample from a business or organization in your community. Critique that procedure orally for your class according to the principles discussed in this chapter.

3. Analyze some of the policies you may find in your school's bulletin. Do they fulfill this text's criteria for policies?

ASSIGNMENT

1. Convert the following sample into a logical flowcharted procedure that adheres to the principles discussed in this chapter. You should note that this draft procedure is not organized by the logic of its actions, but by another criterion: responsible person.

REPORT AND INVESTIGATION OF OCCUPATIONAL INJURY OR ILLNESS

I. POLICY

It is the policy of this contractor to provide medical treatment to
employees injured while working at a corporate facility, to take all
necessary actions which will eliminate work-related hazards, and to
develop methods to achieve these goals.

II. SCOPE

This procedure specifies the appropriate actions to be taken following an
occupational injury or illness to a contractor employee.

III. DEFINITIONS

Occupational injury or illness: Any injury or illness that occurs or is
alleged to have occurred in the course or as a direct result of an
employee's work assignment

Investigation report: A study and subsequent report of pertinent
information necessary to determine the accident cause and corrective
actions necessary to prevent a recurrence

Serious injury: Any occupational injury that precludes the injured from
returning to his or her regular work assignment and/or identified as a
reportable injury for inclusion on OSHA Form No. 200

Recordable injury: Any occupational injury resulting in one or more of the
following:
1. A full shift's absence from work
2. Any amputation
3. Any fracture
4. Any medical procedure exceeding first aid measures, e.g., suturing.
5. Any loss of consciousness

Travel on company business: Any authorized travel or temporary assignment
outside the main headquarters

IV. GENERAL

The procedure describes actions needed to provide adequate medical
treatment for injuries received by employees while in the course of their
regular work assignment; establishes investigation and reporting systems
necessary to compile information for use in the prevention of accidents

and to supply information to appropriate state and federal agencies as required; and establishes a recording system of all job-related injuries.

V. RESPONSIBILITIES

1. Injured Employee
   A. If physically possible, inform supervisor immediately of a job-related injury or illness.
   B. Provide supervisor with pertinent information regarding accident.
   C. If traveling on company business, advise cognizant manager of accident or injury as soon as it is practical.
   D. Work according to safe working practices established in training.

2. Other Employees
   A. If injured employee is physically unable to report accident, advise cognizant manager of injury immediately.
   B. If able, provide assistance to injured employee.
   C. If a witness to the accident, provide supervisor with pertinent information regarding same.

3. Cognizant Manager of Injured Employee
   A. Advise Project Manager, Manager of Safety, and Manager of Personnel of accident or injury immediately.
   B. Assist Personnel Department in securing medical attention if required.
   C. Complete Record of Occupational Injury or Illness form and forward copies of same to Manager of Personnel and Manager of Safety.
   D. Conduct investigation of accident within 24 hours, forwarding copies of investigation report to Manager of Personnel, Manager of Safety, and Project Manager.
   E. Identify and implement corrective actions required to prevent recurrence of accident.

3. PERSONNEL MANAGER
   A. Maintain emergency medical procedure for Project office.
   B. Maintain pertinent emergency notification and health information for all project participants.
   C. Secure emergency medical care for job injuries as required.
   D. Distribute pertinent accident or injury information to appropriate company organizations.

4. MANAGER OF SAFETY
   A. Assist in accident investigation.
   B. Review and approve corrective action required to prevent recurrence of accident.
   C. Inspect area to ensure corrective actions identified have been implemented.
   D. Maintain OSHA Form No. 200 and make appropriate entries to same.

SOLVING PROBLEMS THROUGH LETTERS AND MEMORANDA

Preview of the Chapter

Memos and Letters as Problem Solvers
> *Documenting with Memos and Letters*
> *Distinguishing between Memos and Letters*

Format of a Letter and a Memo
> *Standard Letter Format*
> *Standard Memo Format*

Conventions of Administrative Writing
> *Structure and Content*
> *Length*

Reading and Writing Professionally at Two Levels
> *The Literal Level*
> *The Implicit Level*

Analyzing the Administrative Writing Process
> *Isolating the Main Problem*
> *Identifying Underlying Problems*
> *Applying the Principles of Rhetorical Problem Solving*

Sample Professional Memo Written to Solve a Problem

Postscript

Transmittal Letters as Problem Solvers
> *Functions of a Transmittal Letter*
> *Copy Notation for a Transmittal Letter*

Sample Professional Transmittal Letters

Writing for Someone Else's Signature
> *Considering the Audience*
> *Analyzing the Rest of the Rhetorical Situation*
> *Proofing the Document*

Conclusions

January 27, 1991
Super Bowl Sunday
3:20 P.M.
Jay Dalton's Cubicle
The Write Solution, Inc.
Santa Fe, New Mexico

The technical writers at The Write Solution, Inc. (WS) were really disgusted this time. They often had to work on weekends to finish last-minute jobs, but this weekend was pushing the abuse too far. A major client, Texas Oilcats, annually contracted its stockholders' report with WS. The job was a big one: about 150 pages of text and as many photographs. It essentially paid WS's January expenses and brought a small bonus if produced correctly the first time, without revisions. But, as welcome as this client was to WS, Texas Oilcats was always difficult to work with. The salt was rubbed in the old wounds this time, because the staff was working on Super Bowl Sunday.

The staff—writers, graphic artists, and word processors—were well trained and conscientious, but they were salaried, and so worked overtime without compensation. It's difficult to consider the perks of salaried work when a person is missing the Super Bowl and in danger of missing it every year because the client is late. This abuse of staff was causing morale problems, and WS couldn't afford to lose anyone.

Besides not adhering to WS's schedule, the Oilcats had also argued about the bonus. For example, the Oilcats often didn't make a distinction between a second time through production to correct WS errors and a second time through because someone at the Oilcats changed a passage, reordered the table of contents, or withdrew a section from the galleys. Thus, WS often found itself losing bonus money because changes were needed to correct its "errors."

As Jay Dalton saw it, the fault was not in the stars but in WS. While he wouldn't deny that Texas Oilcats was a difficult client, he felt it was up to WS to protect itself from financial liability and its staff from abuse. It was clear to Jay that the Oilcats depended on WS; after 5 years of producing the report, WS could produce it more efficiently than any other technical writing contractor. Texas Oilcats was consistently happy with the final product, and it took much less of the Oilcats' time to produce because WS was so experienced. That experience gave WS some leverage, in Jay's opinion.

How to start wielding that leverage? Jay had some ideas about this problem. He had thought about it every January for the past 4 years, as soon as it was evident that the Oilcats would be difficult to control. He also had hopes that a successful resolution of the Oilcats problems would demonstrate his own executive ability; that's how people got promoted to management at WS. In such a small company—only thirty employees—there weren't many managerial slots. Jay would do his best to get one. He would start by writing a few memos.

MEMOS AND LETTERS AS PROBLEM SOLVERS

As noted in Chapter 6, professional writing is classified into three categories: scientific, technical and professional, and administrative. The focus in this chapter is on the administrative category, which may be the most prevalent form of professional writing, but which is most easily treated simplistically or even dismissed as essentially formulaic. While the structural conventions of this kind of documentation are quite rigid and thus somewhat formulaic, careful writers must otherwise be as thoroughly critical of their administrative writing as they are of their technical and scientific writing. Good administrative writing is the grease that makes day-to-day business in the working world go smoothly.

Memos and letters, the primary examples of administrative writing, are two of the most frequently used means of solving problems in the professional world. While a banker may never write a feasibility study and an engineer may never write a lab report, they will both write letters and memos. These documents cut across all disciplinary boundaries.

Documenting with Memos and Letters

We start our discussion of administrative writing with the question "Why not simply pick up the phone?" This is the fundamental question and one that all professionals should remember to ask as they do their day-to-day business. The fact is that much business does get conducted by phone. But even those telephone contacts will often be followed up with a piece of paper, a memo or letter, that puts in writing the upshot of the discussion. Why would people double their labor like that? The primary reason is the need to document, to keep a record of the way events transpire. This record may never be pulled out of the file, but if it is needed later to solve a dispute over the contents of the oral agreement, it is, indeed, precious and utterly essential.

Professionals learn with experience what should be documented and what should not. Here are some guidelines to recognize the situations requiring documentation:

1. Oral agreements, especially with people outside your organization
2. All personnel issues, whether you are the manager or the managed, including time and money disputes, all travel expenses, health-related issues, injustices, potentially troubling situations
3. Significant work accomplishments, which you should keep in a file for your use in revising your résumé and for support in your annual employment review
4. All internal work agreements, especially with people who tend to be unreliable and with people from other departments, especially important when interdepartmental projects have absolute deadlines
5. All important requests you make

This sampling gives some idea of the occasions in working life that require documentation. While some of these, like significant accomplishments, could be listed informally at the back of a calendar, they are all invaluable for tracking the work professionals do and the working realities they experience.

Distinguishing between Memos and Letters

Professionals use both memos and letters to solve problems and to document information. The primary difference between these two types of administrative writing is the audience each addresses. Memos are written to people inside one's organization; letters are written to people outside the organization. This difference in audience is the basis for other distinctions between memos and letters.

Memos, because they are sent to insiders, are considered less formal than letters. The style, format, and tone of a memo are less formal than is the case for a letter. However, the informal style is less important than the fact that a memo, like a letter, documents; that is, it records an opinion, an action, a plan, or a train of events for legal purposes. Professionals often record information for themselves in memos addressed to their own file simply to keep track of important issues.

Letters solve problems with outsiders—customers, clients, contractors, and so on. Because letters address an external audience, they are more formal in their presentation, format, and, in particular, word choice than are memos. Chances are that an external audience will not share the same insider language appropriate within an organization. Since the external audience is, in a sense, uninitiated, more focus is required on background and introductory information in a letter than in a memo. The letter writer is responsible for keeping the reader oriented to time, purpose, and history. Additionally, the tone in a letter will be more restrained, less open than in a memo, although the same level of sincerity is certainly possible and desirable.

In certain situations letters rather than memos are sent to people inside an organization. Examples of in-house letters include congratulatory letters (also known as "attaboy" letters), recommendation letters, and disciplinary letters.

FORMAT OF A LETTER AND A MEMO

This chapter briefly reviews standard letter and memo format, but it is more important to understand the problem-solving function of memos and letters. There are two reasons for not dwelling on format. First, once at work in the professional world, writers will either turn the formatting job over to a secretary or look up company recommendations on letter formatting. Often companies set their own conventions for correspondence to achieve some uniformity, some company look. They virtually always set memo formats, ordering stationery with that format imprinted on it. Second, the best-formatted letter in the world cannot overcome the structural and rhetorical gaffes that come from inadequate problem solving.

No one is going to ignore a well-written letter if the date appears on the left side instead of on the right. The truth is that professionals often don't notice such offenses, whereas English teachers are notorious for noticing them. The workaday professional is most interested in the technical and rhetorical sophistication of the documentation: How well does it solve its technical problem? How well does it communicate its purpose to its audience, within a certain context and the writer's ethical constraints?

Standard Letter Format

In lieu of company formatting guidelines, the standard block letter format (see Figure 8.1) is useful. The essence of this format is that everything begins at the left margin.

Standard Memo Format

The standard memo format (see Figure 8.2) works well for communication between student and instructor, for example. Students might write a memo to their professional and technical writing instructor—to ask for assignment extensions or to explain absences, and for whatever administrative purposes the instructor expects written communication. The writer centers the whole memo on a full-length page. Note that the memo dispenses with the salutation, addresses, complimentary close, and signature. The subject line needs a descriptive phrase; this line orients the reader to the memo's purpose.

These standard formats should provide consistent-looking letters and memos for the student, job seeker, and private citizen. Employees of professional organization may find these formats superseded. What will not be superseded, however, is the rhetorical discussion that follows in the rest of this chapter.

CONVENTIONS OF ADMINISTRATIVE WRITING

Because professionals must read so many memos and letters from so many sources—some estimates indicate as many as 140 pages a day by the year 2000—they have devised conventions to ensure the most efficient reading possible. *Efficiency* is the key word here because no one reads these letters and memos for fun; professionals read and write these documents to do their work. The strength of administrative writing conventions is that they address the reader's concerns, not the writer's concerns. Thus, these conventions make a text very reader-friendly.

Figure 8.3 presents a structural and rhetorical analysis of the memo. In other words, the memo is described as a professional would read it, with the questions the professional would be reading for called out in italics. The same analysis applies to letters. For the most efficient, effective administrative writing, the writer must honor these conventional expectations of the reader. In the same way, scientists honor the conventional expectations of their readers when they structure their scientific articles by a standard order of standard topics.

Figure 8.1
*Standard block
letter format*

Date	April 15, 1992
(Skip 3 lines)	
Sender's return address	2840 Andrews Center Littlefield, TN 44365
(Skip 1 line)	
Recipient *Recipient's title,* *company, and* *address*	Ms. Ramona Weathers Director of Marketing ALY, Inc. 12 Century Square Moscow, GA 30303
(Skip 1 line) *Salutation, starting* *with* Dear *and ending* *with colon*	Dear Ms. Weathers:
(Skip 1 line)	I want to thank you for the interview you so graciously participated in last week. Your answers were most helpful and should go a long way to dispel some of the myths the public has about marketing.
(Skip 1 line)	Regarding your question about the number of marketing graduates coming from Moscow University each year, I did some research and found that the totals have been coming down about 10 percent each year. In 1989, MU graduated 512 majors; in 1990, 460; and in 1991, 416.
(Skip 1 line)	If you need anything further, please let me know. I'll send you a transcript of our interview next week and a copy of the draft article in about six weeks.
(Skip 1 line)	
Complimentary close	Sincerely,
(Skip 4 lines *to printed name)* *Sender's signature*	*Ryan Abernathy*
Sender's name, printed	Ryan Abernathy

Figure 8.2
Standard memo format

Initial your memo here

(Skip 2 or more lines, depending on the length of the memo)

(Skip 1 line)

TO: Professor Albertson
FROM: Junior Van Dyke *JVD*
DATE: March 18, 1990
SUBJECT: Annotated Bibliography Deadline

Because several items from my annotated bibliography can be obtained only through interlibrary loan, I will need an extension. All sources should be here by March 25, so I could get the bibliography in to you on April 7.

Please sign at the bottom of this memo if you approve the extension. If not, I would appreciate a conference with you as soon as possible.

Figure 8.3
Structural and rhetorical analysis of administrative writing in a memo format

---

MEMORANDUM (with accompanying memohead)

TO: Direct addressee
FROM: Signator (Remember, this is not necessarily the author of the
           document.)
DATE: As close to the date signed as possible
SUBJECT: Key words to describe the problem to be solved

The first paragraph provides an *introduction*, consisting of the following
elements:
  1. A *purpose statement*, which tells why the author is writing the memo,
     for example, to request help, to provide information, to request a
     meeting.
  2. *Background information*, as needed, which should be kept brief.
  3. If the memo is intended to provide an *answer* to some question, the
     answer should be summarized here. Memos are not detective stories to
     be read for pleasure; the sooner the author can make the main point,
     the better. It is stylistically and practically offensive to play coy
     in a memo.
  4. If this memo is in response to another, provide *reference to other
     correspondence*. The references usually take the form of letter
     numbers or correspondence dates.

The middle paragraph or paragraphs form the *body* of the memo. Here the
author will develop *pertinent details, explanations,* or *arguments*
required to expand on the point of the memo. The author may also provide
alternatives for solutions to problems on which the recipient must make a
decision. The author should not rely on the recipient to devise solutions
for which he or she has done no thinking, especially if the recipient is a
higher-ranking person on the organizational chart.

The final paragraph provides the *conclusion*. Here the author may request
specifically any desired action, including the dates by which the action
should be completed. The author should comment in closing on his or her
willingness to cooperate. This should be done with a formal statement such
as "If I can help with resources, please let me know."

gg/EC/MO   [Typist's initials, author's initials, and ghost writer's
             initials, if necessary]

Enclosures   [Number and titles of any enclosures are listed here.]

             [Memo number may be noted below the enclosures or, if there
             are none, below the initials.]

Structure and Content

For both letters and memos, the basic structure is absolute: an introduction, a body, and a conclusion. Writers must always incorporate this structure into their administrative writing. Now this doesn't mean that every memo and letter will have three paragraphs in it, one devoted to each part of the structure. Sometimes the whole structure will be taken care of in one paragraph, sometimes within a multipage document.

The fundamental administrative writing structure is elaborated in Figure 8.3. In this case, a memo illustrates the structure's parts, but a letter would work out exactly the same, except for the different letterhead formatting (see Figures 8.1 and 8.2). Note how well this structure addresses the rhetorical issues of purpose, audience, and context. The fourth issue, ethical stance, calls for the writer's full attention. There is nothing in this structure that automatically incorporates attention to ethical stance.

A few points about the model memo are worthy of attention. First, note that requests for action are pulled out of the body of the memo and put in the conclusion. Doing this isolates the action so that the reader does not skip over requests that are embedded in the details of the problem, in the body. The main question on any reader's mind upon receiving administrative writing is, What do I have to do? And if *what* is the first concern of the reader, *when* is the second concern, so the author must always specify the date by which an action is to be accomplished.

It's also worth repeating that any answer the administrative writing has to deliver should appear immediately in the introduction. The explanations and rationale can appear in the body, but the reader should know as soon as possible what the answer is. So, for example, if a manager asks for three worthy candidates from the fifty who applied for a position, the search committee should list the three names in the first paragraph of the memo that makes the recommendations. Writers may resist delivering bad news so directly, but if it is embedded in the body of the writing, the reader may miss it. If it's personal bad news, the reader will only resent being strung along before the boom is lowered.

Length

Sometimes technical and professional writing students are given rather arbitrary length specifications. They are told not to write long sentences, long paragraphs, or long pages. Although such limitations may be necessary when writing newspaper articles, they are not necessary in administrative writing. Conventions of length, such as limiting memos and letters to one page, are simply superstition, put forth as if there were some quantitative formula for strong professional and technical writing. The fact is that clear, explicit prose is so easy to read that it doesn't matter whether a memo runs over a page, or a job application runs over a page, or a résumé runs over a page. The professional reader will not be counting pages, but will be looking for substance; and if the writer writes substantively and clearly, then deviations from so-called standard length will not arouse hostility. To assume that readers will be offended by a so-called nonstandard length sells the professional readers short. They are not mindless cogs in a wheel, but thoughtful people trying to do their work well. In fact, they are apt to get a bit hostile if a one-page formula letter is so badly written that it conveys nothing and thus requires the reader to waste time using other means to clarify the message.

READING AND WRITING PROFESSIONALLY AT TWO LEVELS

Whenever professionals read memos and letters, they read them on more than one level. The literal level, what the document actually says, certainly needs to be clear to the recipient; but the implicit level, what is not said very directly, must also be clear. Seasoned professionals read on both levels after picking up the company way of doing business. Entry-level professionals can certainly put these principles to good use as well.

The Literal Level

The reader must be able to understand the literal level of a letter or memo. As obvious as this injunction sounds, it is often easier said than done. For example, a quick reading of the following memo (Figure 8.4) leaves the reader with the impression that the memo has no purpose; the memo simply appears to record a lot of information that is apparently useless.

Keeping in mind the conventions described in Figure 8.3, we can surmise how Wilcox will read this memo. He will glance at the subject line for orientation, skip to the last paragraph for his action and the date by which he needs to complete that action, go back to read the first paragraph, all the while skimming the body as needed. After reading this memo, James Wilcox has just one question: Why is Russ Walton telling me this? Because there is no clear statement of purpose in the memo, Wilcox has no way of understanding the writer's intention. And if the purpose of the memo isn't clear, the reader will have problems puzzling out the literal level of meaning.

If the writer violates the conventions or isn't sure of the purpose of the memo and so is unable to make purpose and action clear, then the reader will become frustrated and either file the memo in the trash or telephone the author to clarify the message. A phone call takes time that need not be spent if the memo is written correctly in the first place. And the fact that Walton has even written a memo about his trouble with Mixum tips off Wilcox that he will, indeed, have to call to straighten out the Walton request. The issue must be important; otherwise Wilcox would never have put his request in writing.

An in-depth look at the memo reveals its weaknesses. First, the subject line is very vague. All Wilcox knows is that the memo is about some annual report, but whose report this is and what year the report was produced are mysteries. The

Figure 8.4
*Memo with no
apparent purpose*

JetStream, Inc.

Memorandum

TO: James Wilcox, Legal Counsel
FROM: Russ Walton, Accounting
DATE: January 15, 1990
SUBJECT: Annual Report

Our client for the past several years has been Mixum Paint and Supply. We often do several jobs for Mixum with the understanding that this work is to be paid on a commission basis.

Last year Mixum had Accounting prepare a report to summarize its actions with various subsidiaries. This report was a rush job and as such did not partake of the same status as the usual contingency jobs would.

In our billing for the special report we have received determinations that our basis for payment will not be met as we had thought it would. Subsequent talks with Mixum confirmed that there had been an error that Accounting must avoid in the future.

I wanted to hear from you about this.

cc: Joanna Belmont

subject line of a memo should accurately describe the content of the memo by key words. The best way to think of this function of the subject line is to imagine having to code a document in an index; in this example, the code "Annual Report" gets the reader only to genre, or type of document, referred to. It does not indicate what Wilcox should focus his attention on. The *to, from, date,* and *subject* lines are not pro forma parts of a memo. They have a specific function and form a substantive part of the document.

The memo's first paragraph is puzzling. It is in the first paragraph that the reader expects to see a purpose statement, one that would clearly elaborate on the information in the subject line. This memo, however, contains no clear purpose statement. What has the writer accomplished in the first paragraph? From what Wilcox knows about the subject, he can tell that the writer is providing some background information. While it is true that background information does go in the introduction, this information is secondary to a purpose statement. The conventions of memo writing require that all secondary information be kept to a minimum. The aim is to provide as much essential information as necessary in as concise a form as possible.

The subsequent paragraphs focus on a particular problem the Accounting Department has had with Mixum. The reader sees that there has been a misunderstanding and that Mixum seems to be holding out on some kind of payment that Accounting feels is its due. This whole scenario has a kind of shady feel to it, however, because, for one thing, the language is so abstract; "as such did not partake of the same status as the usual contingency jobs would" is a good example of this vagueness. Is a contingency job the same thing as a commission job? Using substitute terms for the same idea can be very confusing to a careful reader. The first part of the phrase is simply wordy and badly written; the author apparently is incapable of writing something directly and concretely.

"We have received determinations that our basis for payment will not be met as we had thought it would" provides another example of the problematic diction in this memo. Here Wilcox wonders who made the "determinations," whether Accounting will be paid at all or whether the client intends to dribble out payments, and whether any direct meeting has occurred about this issue between Accounting and its client. The vague diction lets in all kinds of possibilities that the reader cannot interpret for lack of information.

The final paragraph, where the reader expects to see future actions spelled out, is as vague as the rest of the memo. In the first place, the past-tense construction "wanted" suggests that Walton had wanted Wilcox's help at one time, but now has given up, and so just wanted to pass along this note of disappointment. Even if Wilcox overlooks the tense problem in this sentence, however, he is still left with the fact that Walton requests no specific action. If the memo is simply informational, then it should say so, in language like this: "I wanted you to know the background of this situation before Mixum's lawyers call you next week." Then Walton might have closed with an offer of help. A thorough reading of the memo brings the reader no closer to any certainty about what the writer is talking about than a careless reading does. The reason why this memo is so dysfunctional is not only because its author seems to be dysfunctional, but also because it breaks all the conventions of memo writing.

Analysis of the Revised Memo

If Wilcox were to "translate" Walton's memo, he would find that Walton has made a very simple request in a very complicated way. His request is simply bogged down in ambiguity and vagueness. Essentially, Walton wants Wilcox to review the payment problem to see whether Accounting has any legal leverage with Mixum. Figure 8.5 presents Walton's message within the conventions of memo writing.

The memo that follows the conventions of administrative writing is a few paragraphs longer than the incomprehensible memo. Yet the added length does not affect the quality of the revised memo because the memo does all the work it is intended to do. Therefore no follow-up action is required of the reader. Wilcox has no need to make phone calls or visits to Walton to clarify the translated version of the memo. So, even though the second memo is a bit longer, it is far more efficient than the first.

The revised memo follows the conventions of memo writing so well that Wilcox can read efficiently the way professionals do, from subject line to last paragraph, and back up to the first paragraph. The second paragraph concisely describes a situation about which Wilcox has no information at all, so the description occupies two paragraphs, one to describe the problem and one to describe Walton's attempted solution.

In addition to fulfilling all the conventions, Walton's revised memo also addresses the reader well, anticipating accurately what Wilcox may and may not know about the situation. For all Walton knows, Wilcox may think that Mixum is one of JetStream's own subsidiaries instead of a client. So it is appropriate for Walton to identify Mixum, even though the information may seem obvious. This sort of thoroughness saves extra time later on. It allows the reader to get the literal message as efficiently as possible.

The most important virtue of Walton's revised memo is that it is conclusive. He thought through what he wanted to say; in fact, he drafted what he wanted to say before sending off his ideas. Walton's first memo looks like a rough draft because it is so inconclusive, uncertain, unorganized, and vague. That's the way draft writing looks. As long as the writer doesn't actually send the draft version, it doesn't matter what it looks like. It may well take a draft for the author to figure out what needs to be said and to discover what the memo's purpose really is. Especially when a person wants to write a memo in response to a touchy problem, it is useful to draft the memo first so that it can be transformed into readable text for its audience.

Remember, the strength of administrative writing conventions is that they address the reader's concerns, not the writer's concerns. Clarity is absolutely necessary for the reader to understand the literal level of the message.

Common Errors in Administrative Writing at the Literal Level

While Walton's original memo is certainly badly written, it is not unusual. It instructively embodies the four most common errors committed by administrative writers:

1. Neglecting purpose statements
2. Burying the main point in the body

Figure 8.5
*Revision of the
purposeless memo*

JetStream, Inc.

Memorandum

TO: James Wilcox, Legal Counsel
FROM: Russ Walton, Accounting
DATE: January 15, 1991
SUBJECT: Request for Legal Review

I need your help on a matter with one of our clients, Mixum Paint and
Supply. The Mixum file needs a legal review because of a mix-up Accounting
had with the company last month.

Briefly, we did some extra work for Mixum on the assumption that this work
would be paid for in the same manner as the other commission (or per piece)
work. Mixum, however, claims that this extra work is covered by the
regular fee schedule, some 25 percent less than the commission schedule.

I've talked to Mixum's administrative manager, Dot Taylor, but she sees no
way for the work to be paid for as I think it should. She referred me to
Mixum's attorney, Ralph Wainright, if I have any further questions.

Will you look at this file by January 25th to see whether we have any legal
leverage to claim the work as commission work? I need to know your opinion
so that I can institute a suit, if necessary.

If you need further information, please let me know.

fm/enclosures: Mixum file
                December file

3. Including background information not pertinent to the reader's purposes (a result of poor audience analysis)
4. Writing vague calls for action

The Implicit Level

We mentioned earlier that professionals read on two levels at once, the literal level and the implicit level. This section takes up the implications of administrative writing, which tend to be political implications. Everyone in an organization, from the mailroom attendant up, reads administrative writing at the implicit level. Authors should be able to read their own writing at this level, to avoid inadvertently putting themselves at a disadvantage.

There is a lot to read in a memo on a literal level, and the conventions of memo writing help standardize the process. But the implicit level—which is largely political—may yield far more related information than the reader could ever get from the literal level.

Elements to Consider at the Implicit Level

There are several elements that contribute to one's understanding at the implicit level.

Writer's Tone   The most obvious element contributing to implications in memo writing, tone conveys the importance of a subject for the writer. The tone tells whether an assignment seems urgent *to the writer*. This information is important, not because the reader must also believe the situation is urgent, but because the reader can be alerted to others' likely responses. The emotions associated with the topic and the value attached to the topic constitute the tone of a document.

Identity of the Author and Indication of a Ghostwriter   The *from* line gives the signator of the memo. But the person who signs the memo is not necessarily the author. A highly placed executive, in fact, will rarely be the author of a memo or letter, choosing to delegate such work to administrative assistants, deputy managers, or secretaries.

Therefore, if the document lists a highly placed executive as the author, the canny reader immediately looks for clues as to the true author of the memo. One place to find that information is at the bottom of the memo, where the typist, who is not necessarily the author's secretary, lists typist's initials, signator's initials, and ghostwriter's (or actual author's) initials. This information is important because it tells the reader whose policy, or problem, or position is currently in favor with the signator. Furthermore, such information tells the reader who needs to be persuaded or dissuaded about any issue that might be causing trouble.

For example, Mark Thibadeaux receives a memo from Assistant Comptroller Sharon Weist telling him that the company is changing its policy on copy machine use. At the bottom of the memo Mark sees this: jm/SW/JH. This tells him that

Janet Monroe typed the memo, which is reasonable since she is Sharon's secretary. It also tells him that JH, Jeff Holz, is the true author of the memo, which implies that he is the one responsible for this policy change. Because Mark doesn't agree with the change, he can start trying to reverse it by speaking to Jeff. Sharon will be more likely to reverse her decision if Jeff encourages her to do so.

Recipients of Copies   The copy notation will appear in different places in a letter or memo depending on a company's habit, but will usually appear directly below the heading or at the bottom of the document, as it does in the first version of Walton's memo.

The people listed in this section indicate who is also involved in the situation under discussion. In effect, the copy notation provides further context about the topic. Some of this context is simply organizational, as when an author will send a copy to a subordinate who is in charge of a project under discussion but who has no actual administrative authority in the matter.

More than organizational information, though, the copy notation provides political information, answering such questions as the following: Who are the "players" in this situation? Who are the major powers behind this policy? Who is being groomed by the author? Who is being subordinated or snubbed in the situation, by virtue of being excluded from the copy notation? Who are the insiders and who are the outsiders?

The copy notation also can be a persuasive device in a letter or memo. If, for example, the author feels that the reader will be hesitant or reluctant or un-enthusiastic about taking a requested action, the author may send a copy to the reader's supervisor or the author's own supervisor to apply some extra pressure. For example, if Olivia Draper wants a refund for some defective perfume she bought, she will probably get the refund quicker if she sends a copy of her letter to the salesperson's manager. Intelligent use of copies eliminates the need for any desperate threats because several readers are in on the problem that needs to be solved. The rationale is that concerted attention will take care of problems more efficiently than sequential contacts, one letter or memo at a time.

Another prudent use of sending copies is to alert higher-ups to actions the author is taking to resolve certain potentially messy problems. If, for example, Ed James has discovered a design flaw in the plans for a nuclear waste forklift, he will want to address this problem in written communication because it has potentially damaging consequences. Because of safety concerns and legal liability questions, Ed will write a memo to the head of the design group, thus documenting the problem, and will send copies to his own boss and other higher-ups (like the Manager of Safety) who should be aware of the problem, that is, *cognizant* of the problem, to use the workplace language. The copy notation should eliminate any hesitation in the design group about correcting the problem. While overuse of copies can be annoying, especially if used mainly for self-promotion, their reasonable and prudent use can promote better business practices.

While reading for implications may seem Machiavellian in an academic dissection, it is a necessity for sophisticated action in the corporate world. All experienced employees read for what is implied as well as what is directly stated. Professionals need to incorporate sophisticated reading strategies into their everyday lives to be more effective in their work.

ANALYZING THE ADMINISTRATIVE WRITING PROCESS

Jay Dalton wasn't an experienced technical writer for nothing; he knew how to solve problems with memos and letters. The process he went through can be outlined as follows:

1. Isolate and articulate the specific problems that need to be solved.
2. If more than one problem needs to be solved and the problems are not related, then prioritize the problems and take them on in separate letters or memos.
3. If the audience is internal, write a memo.
4. If the audience is external, write a letter.
5. If the problem is a personnel problem within an organization, write a letter. A letter carries more official weight than the informal memo does.
6. Follow the conventions of administrative writing (see Figure 8.3) for structuring the documentation.
7. Clarify the literal purpose by writing a draft of the documentation. Writing through a draft may bring up the principle behind the specific problem; in other words, drafting is actually part of the thinking process in writing and is not an indicator that the author is inefficient or inexperienced. Especially if the issue is one the author feels strongly about, the documentation should be drafted and revised. If the author writes a memo or letter about something that really makes him or her angry, writing a draft will allow the author to vent emotions that, if sent along in the final document, might alienate the reader. There's nothing wrong with indicating one's displeasure, but drafting allows the writer to decide how much to tone down the language, not necessarily to save the reader's feelings, but to protect the writer.
8. Once the literal purpose is clear, state it in the first paragraph of the document. Be sure to make the document conclusive. So, for example, if the document is intended to relay an opinion, state it up front. Don't lead up to it dramatically in the final paragraph.
9. Review the draft for its implications. Check through all the elements that contribute to an implied reading of the document.
10. If the memo is intended to propose a solution to a certain problem, then present the reader with alternatives to choose from.
11. If the memo is intended to transmit a policy or solution to subordinates, then present a rationale as well. Remember that subordinates, even if they don't hold professional titles, deserve the courtesy of basic explanations.
12. Proof the document after it is typed or word processed. Remember that the signator is responsible for any errors in the document, whether or not the signator typed it.

Isolating the Main Problem

As number 1 states, writers should isolate and articulate, at least to themselves, the specific problems that need to be solved. There may be a way to solve more than one problem at a time as long as their overall presentation is uncomplicated. In fact, it may be most efficient to solve related problems at the same time. But the writer needs to be sure that the relationships are real and that the presentation is clear. For example, Jay had to decide here whether the problem with Texas Oilcats was an isolated problem or whether it was the most disturbing manifestation of an underlying problem.

Identifying Underlying Problems

The distinction between an isolated problem and one that underlies other problems is an important one to consider. If a problem is mislabeled "isolated" and treated as such, yet is actually only a manifestation of a deeper problem, then any solution for that isolated problem will be, ultimately, inadequate. The following example demonstrates this issue:

John Smith is disturbed about the difficult attitude that he has noticed recently in his subordinate, Kathy Marsh. Whereas Kathy used to be supportive and cooperative, she is now sarcastic and truculent. She seems to be sniping at him instead of communicating with him, and frankly, this bad attitude of hers makes him want to avoid her. As he sits down with his problem, he brainstorms a few options for dealing with it:

OPTION 1:   He can ignore the problem, do nothing, and wait for Kathy to change back to her old supportive self.

OPTION 2:   He can call her into his office to discuss this problem and to get more information.

OPTION 3:   He can write a letter to her file, citing her difficult behavior as cause for a lower-than-average raise.

OPTION 4:   He can write a memo to all employees about the importance of professional behavior in the workplace.

His most reasonable option of the four is number 2. If he takes this option, he will discover that Kathy is in the middle of a divorce and suffering from that upheaval in her life. John will also realize that he has no reason to take this sniping personally; Kathy is just running on a short fuse because of the stress of her divorce. Assuming they have a satisfactory conference, there will probably be no need to document this problem at all, so no memo or letter will be necessary.

If John takes the first option, to wait, he may also get a satisfactory result. After several months, as Kathy gets adjusted, she will calm down and things will return to normal. But avoiding discussion of the problem will increase the time necessary for its solution and build up a wall that will be difficult to overcome once Kathy regains her good temper; in the meantime, John will have suffered, and he may find it difficult to be open with Kathy once she decides to cooperate again. Kathy needs to know that John is feeling some flack from her difficulties.

The third option would be disproportionate, given the long good relationship John and Kathy have had before this sniping began. If John writes a letter to her file, he will be relieved a bit because he has taken some action, but he will have to understand that this documentation could hurt Kathy in the long run. If John leaves the letter in her file even after she recovers from her difficulties, she will have a permanent blot on her record even though her difficulties were transient. In that light, John's documentation would seem a bit harsh and unforgiving. He could avoid any kind of permanent damage by removing the document from her file as soon as he felt better. But, if he intends to make the letter a permanent part of her file, no matter what, then he is ethically bound to let her read the letter and respond to it. If company policy does not require such fairness and John does not initiate it, then he should ask himself some questions about whether he would want his manager to treat him so punitively if the situation were recast with him in the role of sniper.

While the fourth option may seem ludicrous, it is popular with those who want to avoid confronting a single subordinate. It is a sort of "scattershot" approach to send out a general lecture in response to a specific problem that concerns a specific employee. It is also an approach that managers use all too often in business. The problem with taking this approach is that it can cause more instead of less trouble. The intended subordinate may overlook the connection, and the other subordinates may get offended by such a general lecture that they can see no cause for.

Jay wants to take the most efficient approach possible to the Oilcats problem. After thinking about it for some time, he realizes that this problem is, indeed, an isolated incident. For no other account do he and the other employees have to do such unreasonable deadline work. He will address the problem as a single problem, then, instead of pulling in other "related" problems as long as he's going to be proposing solutions. It's important to take problems on one at a time unless the specific problem is actually a symptom of a larger one.

Applying the Principles of Rhetorical Problem Solving

Having decided the nature of the problem, Jay considers it in light of the rhetorical problem-solving process that has always been useful for him. This process is presented in detail in Chapter 3.

Jay determines his audience first. He decides to address more than one audience at a time in this memo, because several of the people he reports to are concerned in the problem. His immediate manager, Jim Rothschild, fields all the work with the Oilcats, but the main contact between WS and Texas Oilcats is actually Jim's manager, Tom Fields. Jay decides that he wants Tom to be aware that the Oilcats is a problem account and that he has a workable solution to the problem, but he respects the organizational channels in WS and doesn't want to jump over his own manager's head with all his bright ideas. Therefore, he decides to make Jim his main addressee, but will send a copy of his memo to Tom so that he can be aware of the situation.

Jay's notion of the purpose of his memo is already clear. He wants to propose that a chronic problem be solved. Since that is his purpose, he will organize his memo accordingly. An intelligent strategy for a problem-and-solution memo is to describe the problem concisely, but focus mainly on the solution to the problem, providing alternative solutions as the audience might require them.

The context for this memo is fairly complicated. Recall that context concerns the political and emotional aspects. So, for example, a touchy issue, one that the recipient doesn't want to hear about, would require a different strategy from that of an issue that seems to be a simple matter of fact. Personnel problems are particularly touchy issues and should be approached with great sensitivity. A new operations policy, on the other hand, rarely evokes a strong emotional reaction. In the Texas Oilcats case, the problem is the struggle between the employees' interests and the company's interest, which often coincide, but not always. To satisfy the company's best interest—to please a difficult and demanding client—the employees must work unreasonable hours for a few weeks during the year. Jay decides he must be careful to show he understands the company's interest in this problem, but that it is also in the company's interest to treat staff respectfully.

Finally, the ethical considerations in this problem are fairly substantial. Jay must first determine what his ethical stance is in this situation and then what his actions will be in response to that stance. His position is that in a small company like this one management should treat employees as partners. The management, in fact, does treat WS employees that way in a number of policies; for example, all WS employees may choose profit-sharing programs and protected savings programs. Nevertheless, Jay decides that since the employee abuse over Texas Oilcats has been going on so long, he is obligated to voice his concern. He also believes there are several alternatives to consider, that the situation is not a simple black-and-white matter. He will be able to live with himself better knowing he has defended his principles and tried to be constructive in this situation.

SAMPLE PROFESSIONAL MEMO WRITTEN TO SOLVE A PROBLEM

After putting his problem through the rhetorical problem-solving process, Jay is much clearer about the direction he will take in his memo. All this prewriting analysis will save him several drafts of the final copy. Figure 8.6 presents the final copy of Jay's memo.

A few things about Jay's memo deserve comment. First, WS's memo heading style is different from the heading style that JetStream uses. The point of this is simply that different companies use different memo styles. It is unnecessary therefore to memorize heading formats as long as the style contains all the essential parts—*date*, *subject*, *to* and *from* lines, and copy notation. The advantage

Figure 8.6
Jay Dalton's memo

Memorandum

January 31, 1991

Subject: Proposed Solution to the Texas Oilcats Deadline Crunches
From: Jay Dalton
Telephone: 509-236-2198

To: Jim Rothschild
cc: Tom Fields

We seem to have done such a good job accommodating Texas Oilcats that the
company has no need to change its pattern of doing all its business with us
at the last minute. This pattern has caused a lot of trouble within our own
ranks. I think the solution is to contract help for these crunches, making
sure that the Oilcats bear the cost.

Since the Oilcats are such an important client, we are in a difficult
position. All our other clients who tried to ignore our deadlines were
either educated or refused. We learned that turning away a few difficult
clients was worth it, both for financial and morale reasons. But the
Oilcats account pays our January bills and then some. If we turn this
account down, we will take a major loss; we have tried education, with no
success. If we try education again in some kind of formal, serious way, we
might well be wasting our time and we might also come across as if we are
asking the Oilcats to solve our own problems. At this point, the Oilcats
have no problem—we should remember this.

On the other hand, if we solve this problem on our own, we will not have to
engage the Oilcats in a time-consuming and unguaranteed education
process, yet we will still respect our own people. My idea is that we fill
in the labor gap with contract editors and printers.

My estimates show that the cost of contract labor for the overtime hours we
normally work for the Oilcats would be about 10 percent of the usual cost.
We should tack this 10 percent onto the usual fee; the Oilcats will gladly
bear the extra cost because the quality not only will remain consistent
but also will probably be enhanced. Our own people, who will not be burned
out on the job, will be sharper during the process, thus eliminating some

Figure 8.6
(*Cont.*)

of the costly alterations (and further chance for error) that the process usually demands.

The gain in morale from this move will make the step worthwhile. We have made a point of hiring reliable, consistent people. We have treated them respectfully—except for this job. If we don't take some action on this problem, we risk losing our people to places that pay overtime. When employees work overtime, they want to get paid for it. Our system makes no provision for overtime pay for salaried employees.

What we need, simply put, are more hands on the job. If we add a few hands, we will have no further problem with the Oilcats; we will retain our own people, who know the Oilcats account inside and out; and we will have upheld our own policy of putting our own people ahead of any unreasonable demands of our clients.

Please let me hear what you think of this proposal by February 15. I have to meet with the Oilcats then to set up next year's schedule and budget.

of WS's style is that the reader sees the *to* line and copy notation together, all the better to analyze audience and purpose of the memo. Neither this style nor any other, however, will account for any blind copies, which are copies sent to people not listed on the memo itself. Jay's memo is a straightforward proposal and problem analysis; his sending a copy to Jim's manager, Tom, is a message to Jim that he wants serious consideration of this proposal. It is also a message to Tom that he is a constructive problem solver with administrative capacity.

One thing that bothers Jay about his memo is that it exceeds one page. However, Jay has done the reasonable thing: said what he had to say as concisely as possible. If a memo must exceed one page, it should be clear and well-written so that the reader will not feel put out. Jay's memo adheres to these guidelines.

One of Jay's more successful accomplishments in this memo is making it extremely explicit, which can be seen in three places: his subject line, thesis, and topic sentences. The subject line tells the reader that Jay is proposing a solution to the Oilcats problem. It doesn't state exactly what that solution is, but it cues the reader, eliminating the need for a lot of identification in the first paragraph. Jay knows that his audience knows as much (Jim) or almost as much (Tom) about the Oilcats account as he does, so he is relieved of the need to provide a lot of background or introductory information. In essence, the introduction to Jay's memo appears in the subject line.

Despite the fact that the memo exceeds a page, it is not an onerous job to read it because the reader knows immediately where Jay intends to go in the memo. The last sentence of the first paragraph contains his thesis, his main point, his conclusion, his reason for writing, his results—all these terms are a way of naming the most important information that the writer has to relay. This placement does the reader the courtesy of getting to the point. Once the reader knows the point, he can switch gears to examine the logic of Jay's argument.

This order—a signaled solution, followed by arguments in favor of it—is the opposite of the order seen in the hard sell. This other rhetoric often reviews logical support before presenting the solution or alternative that is being argued for. For example, television advertising often begins like this: "Do you want to feel like a king? Do you want to get rid of the drudgery in your life? Do you want to have the nicest yard in your neighborhood? Then you'll love Edge-O-Matic!" The "reasons" are presented before the solution, all to build suspense, excitement, and interest in the product. In professional writing all such suspense-building should appear in the public relations and public affairs writing departments, the most frankly persuasive arms in any organization. The workaday departments rely on a much more explicit, straightforward presentation. Jay's audience is already interested in his solutions; it is Jim's job to be interested in Jay's solutions, and just to ensure that added bit of attention, Jay sent a copy of his memo to Tom. Jay's thesis statement clearly states his conclusion and, as a bonus, explains who is going to pay for it, always a major concern when someone proposes to bring in more people to help with a project.

The rest of his memo reads so smoothly because of his excellent topic sentences. The test for topic sentences is simple: read only the first sentence in every paragraph to discern any order and sense in the memo. Following is a paragraph consisting of only the topic sentences of Jay's memo:

> We seem to have done such a good job accommodating Texas Oilcats that the company has no need to change its pattern of doing all its business with us at the last minute. Since the Oilcats are such an important client, we are in a difficult position. On the other hand, if we solve this problem on our own, we will not have to engage the Oilcats in a time-consuming and unguaranteed education process, yet we will still respect our own people. My estimates show that the cost of contract labor for the overtime hours we normally work for the Oilcats is about 10 percent of the usual cost. The gain in morale from this move will make the step worthwhile. What we need, simply put, are more hands on the job. Please let me hear what you think of this proposal by February 15.

These topic sentences give a very accurate precis of the whole memo. All the major topics—cost, benefits, problem analysis—are clearly signaled. And each paragraph devotes itself to the function determined in the topic sentence—introductory, developmental, concluding. Jay's memo will require significantly less follow-up time for his reader than would be the case with Mr. Walton's original memo. Jim Rothschild will not have to spend time trying to decipher the memo and will not have to make follow-up calls or visits.

The principles of solving problems in memos and letters are constant, although their application is myriad, given the infinite variety we find in human nature.

POSTSCRIPT

Jim liked Jay's suggestions very much. The Oilcats grumbled about the extra cost, but didn't want to lose the "experts" on its report, so it agreed to the change and then rushed its efforts even less. The extra help eased employee tensions considerably. The quality of the document was enhanced. The WS employees put away their résumés for a while. Jay's good efforts brought him a raise and a promotion to line manager. Jay slept very well for a few months, until the next crisis presented itself.

TRANSMITTAL LETTERS AS PROBLEM SOLVERS

Of the many types of letters companies write, one tends to be overlooked—the transmittal letter. Customer-oriented letters tend to get handled by the public affairs or public relations branches in companies, but the other professionals, including scientists, engineers, and technicians, will have to write transmittal letters. The transmittal letter is a sort of preface to the document it sends. It may summarize the document's organization and structure; it may explain, in the case of a completion report, what expectations found in the proposal did not work out in the actual research. These discrepancies should be explained at a summary level. It is worth considering the problems transmittal letters address.

Functions of a Transmittal Letter

The three major functions of the transmittal letter are the following:

1. To reach a wide audience for a regularly produced document
2. To record production and delivery of an important document
3. To orient the main addressees to any changes in purpose, format, or audience that may have been decided on from issue to issue

In fact, any change that might be seen as a discrepancy from previous conventions and expectations needs to be signaled in the transmittal letter. Even if the recipients initiated the changes, it is important to remind them in the transmittal letter so that they can adjust their expectations for the way they should read the document.

People are so accustomed to reading standard reports a certain way that it throws them if the report doesn't look familiar in a particular issue. And, given professionals' huge reading requirements, familiarity is essential. That's why the transmittal letter must clue them in to the fact that something about the familiar document has changed. Readers would be shocked, for example, if *The Wall Street Journal* began to publish in a *National Enquirer* format. So, too, are professional and technical report readers shocked by any violation of their reading expectations.

Transmittal Letters as Documentation

A very important function of the transmittal letter is to record the fact that a report was produced and distributed on time, per previous agreements with the recipients. When companies are doing contract work, for example, reports are often contractually required and constitute a major source of income. Much of the work done for the federal government is this sort of contract work, most commonly associated with the Department of Energy and the Department of Defense. The contractors to these agencies may be paid on a fee system that requires delivery of status reports that document that certain contracted work was completed. It's very important that these reports are truthful, since they become the basis for paying the contractor. It's also important for the transmittal letter to be signed only after the sender is satisfied that the report is truthful, because the transmittal letter is a sort of certification for whatever it transmits. The signator should be able to stand by the information enclosed.

Copy Notation for a Transmittal Letter

It is not uncommon for transmittal letters of major quarterly reports, for example, to contain numerous names in the copy notation. Besides the main addressees, which might number ten, one might find a copy notation with thirty-five names in it. In such cases it is unreasonable to consider all these entries as audience problems when drafting the report. Such a list is only functional, serving as a distribution list. It may have some political significance in its honorific additions or punitive subtractions, but intensive attention to the list as an audience issue is not necessary. Many people included in the copy notation shelve their copy of the report, keeping it only for reference. In fact, certain libraries and reading rooms often appear in copy notations for major reports.

The major concern for the author is to update the list of recipients. While a secretary keeps the typed list current, the author is ultimately responsible for providing the names of recipients.

SAMPLE PROFESSIONAL TRANSMITTAL LETTERS

Two sample transmittal letters on the following pages indicate some of the functions discussed. The first letter (Figure 8.7) is from The Write Solution to the Texas Oilcats. It is the transmittal letter WS has been sending the Oilcats for the past 5 years, with updated names on the distribution list, which is lengthy since it lists the recipients of an annual report. Many people would have an interest in such a report.

The second letter (Figure 8.8) is from WS to another client, who requested some changes to the format of the report that WS prepared. That change is summarized for the client, so that she won't be stymied by a new format.

WRITING FOR SOMEONE ELSE'S SIGNATURE

As we noted in Chapter 3, one way problems get solved in the professional world is for subordinates to write memos and letters for their managers to sign, so that the subordinates become ghostwriters, in effect. This responsibility can demonstrate how well suited a subordinate may be to make the move from salaried professional to manager. Such a demonstration would require that the professional show evidence not only of writing competence but also of problem-solving competence.

Considering the Audience

The difficulty about ghostwriting a memo or letter is that even though there may be only one addressee—no copies, blind or noted—the writer must always address at least two readers, the addressee and the signator. This is a matter of addressing audience correctly, and professionals will find this job easier to do the better they know the signator.

Analyzing the Rest of the Rhetorical Situation

The second thing to remember about writing for someone else's signature is that it is crucial to analyze the rhetorical aspects of the job, sometimes referred to as

Figure 8.7
*Transmittal letter
from the Write
Solution to Texas
Oilcats*

THE WRITE SOLUTION

2355 La Tertulia Dr.   Santa Fe, NM 88000

January 31, 1990

Mr. Cecil Simons, Manager
Public Affairs
Texas Oilcats
1499 Live Oak Boulevard
Dallas, TX 54666

Dear Mr. Simons:

We are pleased to deliver *Oilcats Internationale* for your review and
approval. It seems the Oilcats have had another good year. We hope the
coming year holds the same success for you.

Please contact me if you have any comments or suggestions about the
report.

Sincerely,

Tom Fields

Tom Fields, Manager
Production

sr/TF/JW

cc:
M. Cummings, WS
J. Cushing, WS
A. Campbell, WS
W. Jenkins, WS
B. Williston, WS
E. Gonzales
R. Winchell
M. Aguirre
S. Schatz
A. Montfort
R. Hitchcock

Figure 8.8
*Sample
professional
transmittal letter*

THE WRITE SOLUTION

2355 La Tertulia Dr.   Santa Fe, NM 88000

January 31, 1991

Ms. Rachel Ramon, President
Southwest Technologies
P.O. Box 199
Albuquerque, NM 88102

Dear Ms. Ramon:

We are pleased to deliver the hydrology report for the second quarter, 1990. As usual, the production process was very smooth. The report's revised format seems to be a real improvement for the reader.

I would remind you of the four changes in this issue that we agreed on in our meeting last July 25th:

1. We changed the photography from black and white to full color.
2. We published in the new cover format worked out with your public affairs people last November.
3. We reordered the report to eliminate two small sections—fire safety and laser applications—and to combine three other sections under the heading "Education." This new order appears below.
4. Finally, we revised the back cover logo per instructions from Southwest's public affairs department.

The new order of chapters is as follows:

  I. Highlights of the Second Quarter
 II. Laser Research
III. Defense Work
 IV. Automotive
  V. Education

This new order should enhance coherence in the report. If you have any questions or comments, please call me.

Sincerely,

Tom Fields

Tom Fields, Manager
Production

sr/TF/JW

cc: J. Dalton

"scoping out the job," before anything gets written. This means that the writer must know exactly who is to be addressed and for what purpose, what the context is (political and otherwise), and what the signator's ethical stance is on the subject. In other words, authors must be sure to put the writing task through the rhetorical problem-solving process the same way they would if they had initiated the task themselves.

Proofing the Document

The third important point about ghostwriting is that signators may well insist upon a standard of perfection from the ghostwriter that they would never expect of themselves. This added responsibility can be weighty because the writer cannot count on the signator finding all the errors that need correcting at the draft stage. That would leave errors in the final stage and add numerous revisions for minute offenses.

When any signator or manager demands perfection of a document, the writer has no choice except to work with a partner to proof the document. Remember that computer programs that check spelling will find obvious typographical errors, but not the homonyms that constitute improper usage or the errors that form real, but inappropriate, words: *pubic* for *public*, for example. The writer and a partner will have to undertake the painstaking process of going through the document page by page. It is intense work but will often reveal errors that the writer just can't find anymore after having read several versions of the same page.

CONCLUSIONS

This chapter emphasizes the rigorous analysis that administrative writing requires. It is conventional in that professionals have expectations that the structure needs to fulfill. But it is a matter of individual problem solving as well, since each occasion for a memo or a letter requires the writer to ask, first of all, whether any documentation is really necessary, and second, the questions involved in the rhetorical problem-solving process. Length is less important than clarity and logic; format is less important than essential structure. Problem solving through memos and letters is the most common and potentially effective means any professional has to work more efficiently.

EXERCISES

1. Interview a professional or graduate student in your field to determine what kind of situations require documentation.

2. Case Study

The Situation

You have just been promoted to management. To celebrate, you are taking a vacation before you start your new position, Manager of Daily Operations. You stop by your new office to check your mail before you drive to the airport. You are already in your bermudas; you cannot stay longer than 1 hour in your office, or you will miss your plane. When you get to your desk, you see that you have three problematic situations already waiting for you.

The Task

Write the documentation you feel is appropriate for the situations listed below. First, you must determine what about the situation requires documentation. Then, you need to analyze the rhetorical situation. Finally, you should remember to use copies effectively.

After you've written the documentation you think appropriate for these situations, write a memo to your instructor providing a rationale for all your important decisions, both your business decisions and your compositional decisions, such as whom to address, whom to send copies to, and the like.

The Problematic Situations

A. In a move calculated to impress you, Sam Young, your administrative assistant, authorized two secretaries to track the comings and goings of all sixty-five employees in your building. The employees are now very angry to have received memos, signed by Sam with a copy to you, totaling lost work time from late arrivals and early departures. The sixty-five then authored a memo to you complaining that the company no longer trusts them and they don't appreciate being nickled and dimed to death.

B. The engineering group that reports to Daily Operations designed a special forklift for moving nuclear wastes. The prototype is ready and sales are lined up. As you look over the design, however, you discover that the forklift has inherent instability that will make it lurch on the slightest grade (the prototype was tested in a flat area).

C. You read in the weekly accomplishments report that the scientific group reporting to Daily Operations is very close to perfecting the no-run nylons that the world has been waiting for. Yet, you know, but the scientific group does not, that the no-run nylon project is about the scrapped. The scientific group never made the importance of the project or its nearly completed status clear to the budget people. The project will be dropped in a week if you do not step in. You are certainly not anxious to lose either the project or the cooperative stance that the scientific group has the reputation for.

ASSIGNMENTS

1. With an eye to the organization chart provided below, and bearing in mind the process of analyzing the rhetorical situation, write the summary memo that will

most clearly and honestly describe the following problem. Feel free to define Project X as you wish.

Project X is behind schedule. The project is scheduled to be completed in 1 month, but because of various problems you are effectively 3 months behind schedule. As the lead on the project, you feel you must write an overview of the situation for your manager's signature. The general manager must know what is going on so that he can authorize steps to help you meet the deadline. In business, the bad news must be revealed quickly so that the consequences can be mitigated if at all possible. People don't simply let deadlines slide by without taking some kind of action, at the least informing responsible managers in enough time for them to try to change the outcome. Your overview should be addressed to the general manager, who has a long-standing professional relationship with the supplier (his cousin).

Contributers to the Problem

A. The supplier, C Corp, has consistently missed delivery dates, once delivering material 3 weeks after the contracted date.
B. The technician from the engineering group has been out of the office five times in the last month. This technician is the sole expert on the computer graphics necessary for your project.
C. Your own scientific group's work has been hampered by miscalculations on the part of Mr. Hamilton, who will retire in a year after 35 years of service to the company.

Complicating Factors

A. Your manager wants to push Hamilton into early retirement.
B. Hamilton taught you everything you know about the company.
C. Your company will lose 50 percent of its fee if the deadline is not met.

Organization Chart

General Manager
(Les Michaels)
Addressee

Engineering
Group Manager
(Karen Wolcott)

Computer Technician
(Sam Cruikshank)
Contributor

Scientific Group Manager
(Rudy Larsen)
Signator

Project Lead
(You)
Writer

(Mr. Hamilton)
Contributor

The Rhetorical Situation

A. You are working for a promotion to management. You have a problem, though, because as the lead you are responsible for the success of the project but you have no true administrative power.
B. Les Michaels is always interested in the bottom line.
C. According to the organization chart, you are on the same level as this un-cooperative computer technician.
D. Your own manager, Rudy Larsen, will be loathe to inform Les there is a problem unless he has also thought of a solution.

After you have written the overview you think is appropriate given the constraints of this situation, exchange with a classmate, who, acting as your manager, Rudy Larsen, will decide whether to sign the memo as written, or whether to send the memo back for changes.

TERM PROJECT OPTION

Write a transmittal letter to your instructor to introduce your major project. Not only will you want the letter to appear in some recognizable format, but you will also want to adhere to the demands of the transmittal letter outlined in this chapter. Be sure to document any changes from your proposal that your instructor might be surprised by. For example, if you have decided to address your project to a different audience from the one you designated in your proposal, you'll need to account for that change.

SOLVING PROBLEMS

IN THE PROFESSIONAL

JOB SEARCH

Fundamentals of the Job Search
> *Appealing to Employers*
> *Common Job Application Errors*

The Job Search Process
> *Reactivate Placement File*
> *Approach Recommenders*
> *Research Possible Employers and Find Position Descriptions*
> *Update Résumé*
> *Sample College Résumé*
> *Sample Professional Résumé*
> *Write Cover Letters*
> *Sample Position Description*
> *Sample Cover Letter for an Advertised Position*
> *Submitting an Unsolicited Application*
> *Sample Cover Letter for an Unsolicited Application*

Postscript

Shaping up a Student Résumé
> *First Draft of the Résumé*

Revised Student Résumé

Fundamentals of the Interview Process
> *The Interviewer*
> *Interview Guidelines*

Conclusions

April 15, 1990
6:15 P.M.

Interstate 285
Atlanta, Georgia

John Loomis sat up straight in the driver's seat on his commute home as he felt the indecision of the past few months resolve into a cold certainty: he must begin another job search. This decision was the one he dreaded because it meant taking on a very time-consuming, painstaking "second job" to find a new one. His current job as staff geologist at GEOLAB more than filled his workweek. But he and GEOLAB had not worked out.

For the third time in as many years John was passed over for promotion to management. More serious was his doubt about the direction GEOLAB had taken, especially the contract work with industries responsible for pollution, work that he found more difficult to excuse. His unflattering findings about these industries' activities may well have been responsible for his static position. He was more than competent, but this competence had proved to be rather inconvenient for GEOLAB's management. This latest deferment on his promotion sent him a clear message: be a team player or be ignored. While John was willing to cooperate with a company's often contradictory missions, he was unwilling to bury the results of his work. He knew that other companies would appreciate his scruples; he need not accept that his work and his values had nothing to do with each other.

His decision made, John began to realize that his new job search would be a far cry from his first. As a graduating geologist, John had put together a rather traditional cover letter and résumé for the university placement office, which put them on file for the recruiters to read. He then interviewed with six different companies, three of whom made him an offer. He chose GEOLAB because its offer was the most generous. The whole procedure that time was simple. He had only to follow the placement office's suggested résumé format and attach a rather perfunctory cover letter that said, in effect, "you'll see the basics of my education and experience on the enclosed résumé and I'll be looking forward to talking to you about an entry-level position." He made the ten copies of these documents the placement office required and then waited for the messages to materialize on his answering machine.

Now there were no recruiters lined up to interview him. His 5 years out of school seemed like a lifetime. It was hard to recall the brief points on the placement office handout, but John had an ace up his sleeve: he had experience with the hiring end of the job search. This thought encouraged him, so he turned up the air-conditioning and began to think through the job search process.

FUNDAMENTALS OF THE JOB SEARCH

John Loomis's job search contains some more sophisticated twists and turns than an entry-level search will simply because he has some professional experience and has been out of school for 5 years. Yet, John is not so very advanced. For example, he does not yet have a graduate degree; many of this book's readers, on the other hand, will be going on to graduate or professional school before taking on a very serious job search. Also, as a traditional student, John may be younger than some readers who are nontraditional students. He may be less experienced than our readers are as well.

John's story is important because it depicts the deeper rhetorical considerations that we all must accommodate when engaged in a serious job search. His story provides a feel for the decisions professionals make as they conduct their search. Those contemplating getting their first job out of college may not care much about the finer points of the search; they just want to do anything to get that first job, and may assume that their college credentials will do the trick for them. Yet, unless the economy begins to boom very soon, very few job seekers will be able to rely only on college credentials. Most will have to distinguish themselves from the pack of other job seekers, all with similar college credentials.

Appealing to Employers

The most important point we have to make in this chapter is that job seekers must persuade potential employers that they are the best candidates for the job; they cannot rely on their college credentials or their job experience to speak for them. So, as they look for a job, they must take an actively persuasive role in their job application materials: the cover letter and the résumé. If they do not take on this persuasive job, they will have a longer, more discouraging search. A persuasive cover letter and résumé, on the other hand, will give them the edge to proceed to the interview. Persuasive letters and résumés will gain the writer leverage, because more people will be interested, and, thus, enhanced options.

In Chapter 3 we made the point that the quality of technical problem solving is only as good as the ability to convey it effectively. In Chapter 11 we say that document design can make a good document better, but it cannot make a bad document good. The same principle holds true for the job search: the applicant's credentials and experience are only as good as the presentation of them. While an attractive-looking résumé can make good credentials look better, it cannot make bad credentials look good. In fact, an expensive résumé that says virtually nothing always looks absurd. On the other hand, the writer's ability to select and highlight those details that will appeal to a prospective employer will enhance a mediocre-looking background. Rhetorical skill will separate the job seeker from the mass.

So applying for jobs is not simply a matter of formatting a cover letter and résumé according to some formula and then waiting for the employers to choose according to the objective criteria advertised. First, the writer is not the passive

359

applicant in this process, but has some control over how the materials will be received: rhetorical control. Careful writers can present their case more effectively than other applicants do. Second, the application process is not strictly objective. People, not machines, are being considered. And the application reviewers know all too well that hiring mistakes are very difficult to overcome and can make many people's lives miserable in the process. Think how much of their waking time people spend at work.

We will explore the rhetoric of the job application process, getting at the essential principles that transform a standard-looking résumé and cover letter into outstanding ones. John's case extends beyond simple formulas and into the harder questions people need to be asking as they look for a job. We will also look at a student résumé, with an eye to making the best of the student's lack of experience and education.

Remember that John won't be doing anything that an entry-level applicant won't be doing, unless the applicant plans to work only through recruiters on campus. Even those who fall into this category should take John's search seriously because, like him, they may one day decide they want a new job.

Common Job Application Errors

John understood the sort of work he had cut out for him, because at GEOLAB he had served on three reviewing committees for new hydrology managers. In the course of this review work he must have read through 500 application packages that included cover letters, résumés, recommendations, and GEOLAB application forms. Being on the other side of the application package, as evaluator instead of applicant, had been a shocking experience. John remembered some of the rejects:

- The "canned" letters
- The perfunctory letters
- The illiterate letters
- The uninformative résumés
- The résumés with suspicious gaps in time
- The inflated résumés

John was taken aback by the overall arrogance—or was it naivete?—of those applicants who seemed to assume that their fervent desire to work at GEOLAB warranted special consideration. These applicants didn't understand that their desire was shared by all the other applicants, that the reviewers had duties other than reviewing applications, and that most applicants fulfilled the basic objective requirements for entering first-line management and, therefore, had to make a persuasive case for themselves in order to stand out. Figure 9.1 presents one of those rejected letters.

The rejected applications bore an uncanny resemblance to John's own first cover letter and résumé. Perhaps his father's years of service at GEOLAB *had* played a part in his getting that entry-level position. Nor did many of the applicants John screened receive much help from their recommenders, many of

Figure 9.1
*Rejected
application letter*

Dear Sir:

    As I am ready to graduate this semester, I am eager to speak with you about suitable job openings.

    I have known about the advantages of engineers and have prepared since high school for working in a big company like yours.

    My résumé lists all my qualifications for employment.

    I look forward to a call from you to set up an interview at your earliest convenience.

                    Sincerely,

                    Tom Jones

                    Tom Jones

whom responded either as if they hardly knew the applicant or as if this applicant were a trusty collie, loyal to the end.

It had been grim work to sort through those packages, some obviously put together at great expense. Many of those applicants might as well have spent their money on another wok; the reviewing committee eliminated half the applicants after a 10-second reading of the application materials. The rest were pared down almost as quickly, when a second reading revealed gaps in time or unanswered questions about such things as the number of job switches in an applicant's résumé.

The short-listed applications were more carefully considered and then ranked, after some debate among committee members, for substantive accomplishments and recommendations. The quality of the application package itself mattered even more at this point. Professionals must write well; their judgments must be well supported, their style succinct, and their attention to detail meticulous. These characteristics would be evidenced in their cover letters by their ability to anticipate and counter any arguments against their "pitches." In fact, the cover letter itself was more of a pitch than John had ever realized when as a student with a sought-after major, he could pitch randomly. Those applicants at the top of the short list were called for interviews that would begin an evaluation cycle of a much more intense nature.

John well understood, after so many hours with other people's application packages, that his package, if thoughtful, distinctive, and substantive, would get his foot in the interviewer's door. He had no intention of being rejected because of his own poorly written documents. He already had a wok he didn't use.

THE JOB SEARCH PROCESS

John's new job search wouldn't be taking place under the rosy auspices that had surrounded his job search as a graduating senior in geology. He and his friends in engineering, hotel administration, and business had been fortunate then that the economics in their fields produced interviewers bidding for the best of their graduation class. His friends in the social sciences and humanities, on the other hand, had not been so warmly greeted for 20 years, and so had to tackle the more complicated job search immediately out of college. Now John would have to concentrate as his friends with English and history majors had done from their first search.

John felt fortunate he still had an income to pay the bills while trying to square his values with his job description. As an older and wiser searcher, he knew this process would take time. His friend Cheryl, an accountant, searched on her own for a year before finding a job in her home state that allowed her to make the jump into management. Although she had sent out seventy-five impeccable letters and résumés, her search was prolonged by applying to companies that had not advertised positions. John knew he could expect a shorter search time since there was still some movement in his own discipline.

His decision made to take on another job search, John ate a hearty dinner for the first time in weeks, then settled down to work. He first drew up a list, breaking down the tasks ahead of him as follows:

1. Reactivate placement file.
2. Approach recommenders.
3. Research possible employers and find position descriptions.
4. Update résumé.
5. Write cover letters.

John knew that the planning and detail work he put into the front part of his job search would shorten appreciably his overall search time. He cheered at the thought of the graceful resignation memo he would write GEOLAB. There would be no need to burn bridges; he might find himself working for a former GEOLAB employee one day. The professional world, he found, can be a rather close-knit community. Professionals switch companies as easily as mercenaries switch armies. The days of the one-company career are over.

Reactivate Placement File

John knew this service was well worth the nominal fee of $25 at his alma mater. Not only could he use the service to house his recommendations, but he also could expect the office to forward any listings appropriate for his position and field to him. The confidential recommendations he had solicited were more appropriately handled through such a professional intermediary than by John himself. The résumés he had reviewed that listed references separately at the bottom of the page appeared amateurish and of dubious confidentiality. And while he didn't expect to find many leads appropriate to his experience, he felt it worthwhile to review the listings available.

To update his file, John wrote to the placement office requesting a revision of his dossier—now 6 years old—and included a check for the fee. He then updated the placement file's summary-level forms on positions held and classes taken. He had taken postgraduate courses in Atlanta and requested transcripts of those classes be sent to the placement office in Gainesville.

John carefully revised his objectives statement. Now that he had clarified his objectives, he could improve on the standard entry-level objective he had written 6 years ago: "To find an entry-level geologist's position in industry or research." He changed this to "Manage a research and development group investigating pollution in aquatic environments." I may as well shoot for the job I really want, he reasoned.

His objective updated, John then perused the list of recommenders he had written on his college form. Of the seven he had listed originally, only two could comment on his recent work with any authority. One was his major undergraduate geology professor, whom he saw at the national geology conferences. Another was one of his Atlanta-based graduate professors. The other five he had lost touch with. John decided to replace those five with three current recommendations from among those who knew his work at GEOLAB. He would tell the placement office to destroy the old recommendations from his fraternity president and his supervisor at Ed's Eats, where he had worked summers.

John could cross step 1 off his list. This step had required three letters—two to the placement office and one to his Atlanta school—and 2 hours. It was April 22, a week after his decision to begin his search.

Approach Recommenders

While this second step on his list would not be time-consuming for him, John knew it could be tricky. He needed to find people who knew him well, who were enthusiastic supporters, who were reliable, and who could write well. These apparently obvious descriptions were not so easy to find combined in single individuals. His immediate manager, Sue Jackson, was definitely enthusiastic. She had supported him for promotion the three times he had bid. She also knew him well, having been his manager for 3-1/2 years. She wrote well. But her performance in the reliability category gave him pause. While Sue, no doubt, would maintain confidentiality at GEOLAB, she might take a very long time to get this correspondence written. It had once taken her 2 months to write a recommendation for John's co-worker, Alice, whose job search was thereby prolonged. John decided to ask Sue after approaching some more efficient candidates; he was in a hurry.

Toby Graham and John had worked together on a big project in 1989. They had respected one another, worked well together, and collaborated on the project's final report. As a bonus, Toby had come to GEOLAB from SeaScience, which had been sorry to lose him and which was high on John's list of possible new employers. Toby gladly took on the task of recommending John.

Nathalie Schuster and Marv Roebling were similarly suitable and willing. Nathalie was Sue's boss, but had been John's immediate supervisor before Sue was hired. Marv was the company's comptroller and had consulted often with John about his section's budget and schedule priorities. Marv's recommendation would lend evidence in support of John's bid to come into his new company as one not only technically proficient, but fiscally proficient as well.

Now that he had enlisted three extremely reliable recommenders, John decided to ask Sue. She was delighted to oblige and, predictably, responded within 9 weeks of the placement office's request. Because his other recommenders had been prompt, John's search was never stalled by Sue's busy schedule. Neither was Sue put in the position of hearing from Nathalie—her boss—that John was looking around. Most important, John had a current recommendation from his immediate manager, and, although slow in coming, it would be useful for the next 2 years.

As of April 25, then, John was ready to start his job search in earnest.

Research Possible Employers and Find Position Descriptions

John knew what he valued about his work: rigorous science, important projects, ecological commitment. Now he had to find the company that also valued those things. While he had built up several impressions of other companies from his fellow geologists, he decided to formally research the ones he was most interested in, SeaScience and Aquatics, Inc. He was interested mainly in the types of projects these companies took on and in their clients.

To do this research, John obtained copies of the companies' annual reports. These gave general descriptions of past and current projects, as well as partial client lists. From this information, John could see that SeaScience was probably the company he should aim for; it had performed several analyses for the state of Alaska after the oil spill in the Prince William Sound. Aquatics, Inc., was contracted with several of the same companies he already had done work for, so John decided to eliminate that company.

But John didn't want to limit his search to one company, so he continued his research. He scanned the professional journals for employment listings. He also contacted the employment centers of the professional societies he knew and respected. From these sources he obtained another dozen listings, although none for SeaScience. He then did the basic annual report work on the dozen listed companies, from which he could pare his list to eight. With nine contacts to be made, John was ready to get his résumé updated and his cover letters written.

Since John did this research while he arranged for recommenders, he was still only 2 weeks into his job search.

Update Résumé

With a shudder John stared at his old résumé. He had updated it only cursorily in the past few years, usually to send to chairs of panels on which he had presented a few papers, to provide them with background information for their introductions.

This old résumé was embarrassingly uninformative and a sure candidate for the rejects pile. In his anxiety to keep it to a page, which is what his placement office had advised him to do, he had what looked like merely an outline for a complete résumé.

Basics of a Strong Résumé

Having been on the other side of the hiring process, reviewing others' applications rather than submitting his own, John understood the basics of a strong résumé.

Purpose   Its purpose is to give a concise picture of the applicant through well-selected and well-explained details. People read résumés for dates, so dates are crucial. The dates should present a clear picture of the applicant's activities for the past several years. The applicant who hasn't been working for a few years should explain that on the résumé.

Audience   Because the applicant doesn't know who will be reading the résumé and cannot count on that person's familiarity with local detail, concise explanations of the local and regional details are required. For example, the reader won't necessarily know what Job's Daughters is. Remember to orient the reader. Remember, too, to highlight through boldface type or italic type or capitalization those details readers must notice.

Arrangement   There are several ways to organize résumés—for example, by dates (chronological résumé) and by categories of work performed (functional résumé). The chronological résumé (listing education, experience, and so on) is the most common type. The point is to choose one organizational pattern and stick with it consistently. That pattern sets up reader expectations that will be violated if the writer is inconsistent.

Sample College Résumé

While reading through John's old college résumé (see Figure 9.2), examine how well he seems to have considered purpose, audience, and arrangement. This résumé is not an impressive document. Of course, in 1984 John had no professional experience in geology, but he had made very little of the experience he did have. Following are some of the mistakes John made:

- He failed to annotate his senior thesis; a brief summary statement would have sufficed.
- He forgot to mention that he financed his undergraduate education by himself through grants, loans, and scholarships, impressive information about an undergraduate that any prospective employer would appreciate knowing.
- He undercut his one award by omitting the fact that this first-place time was a national record, officiated in an NCAA competition.
- His grade-point average (GPA) was missing, but was provided on the placement office forms which the recruiters, at least some of them, had read. His was impressive, a 3.9, which undoubtedly accounted for the six interviews he did get. So, for that entry-level position, he had been fortunate to have two backups, the placement office forms and his father's association with GEOLAB.

Plan for Updating the College Résumé

For his current purposes his résumé needed a massive overhaul.

Revising Content   John's first task was to revise content. He needed to add information pertaining to the past 6 years, provide information that was missing, and delete items that no longer were necessary or appropriate.

Figure 9.2
*John Loomis's
college résumé*

RÉSUMÉ

JOHN LOOMIS
P.O. Box 3857
Gainesville, FL 32601
Answering Machine: 904-372-0055

Objective: To find an entry-level geologist's position in industry or research

PERSONAL: Single   Weight - 180 lbs.
Height - 6'2"

EDUCATION: 1984 - B.S. in Geology, University of Florida,
Gainesville, FL
Senior Thesis: ''Effects of the Glencoe Slide''
Major Professor: Dr. Fred Thompson

1980 - High School Diploma, Glencoe High School, Orlando, FL

EXPERIENCE: 1983 - Summer; Ed's Eats, Orlando, FL, waiter
1982-1983 - Sigma Delta Alpha Fraternity House, University
of Florida, Gainesville, FL, cook

1980-1982 - Fair Oaks Country Club, Gainesville, FL, caddy

AWARDS: 1983 - First place, 300-m Freestyle, University of Florida
Swim Team

REFERENCES: Please contact

The Placement Center
Student Pavilion, Box 94
University of Florida
Gainesville, FL 32706

OBJECTIVE STATEMENT   He would omit the objective statement. For one thing, he would make his objective clear and more convincing in his cover letter. This letter would establish a strong connection between his management objective and his qualifications. In other words, he could demonstrate that his objective was warranted. Objectives are just pipe dreams if you can't make a case supporting them.

For another thing, he rarely ever saw an objective statement on any résumé except an entry-level one, where it was usually so vague (as his was) that it said very little. He certainly didn't want his résumé to look amateurish.

Finally, he didn't want to limit the way he was categorized by his reviewers. Chances were that an objective statement specific enough to be substantive might give a reviewer grounds for dismissing him from consideration for a position he might not have foreseen as a possibility. He wanted to keep his options open and would never reject out of hand a combined professional and managerial position, should someone want to consider him for it.

PERSONAL INFORMATION   In the personal information category he would omit his height and weight information, a frivolous vanity he had indulged in the first time around; while his height was the same, his weight was not. Since he was not applying to be a Chippendale dancer, this information was irrelevant.

EDUCATION   In the education category he would add his postgraduate courses and more fully describe his senior thesis. He would also add the name of his graduate professor, a major figure in geology.

EXPERIENCE   In the experience category John needed a full description of his work over the past 6 years. He would add descriptive information to give an overall view of his duties and a significant accomplishments category to highlight the substantive projects he performed alone and participated in with others. This way he could reasonably believe that this experience would stand out from the experiences of those who had listed only their experience, without explanation.

Because he was interested in a managerial position, he would also be sure to call out his current administrative experience, despite not yet having attained a formal designation as manager.

PUBLICATIONS AND PAPERS   John could now add a new category, related in substance to the experience category: publications and papers. He had one article in a respectable journal and two conference papers. This work helped establish his professionalism as a geologist, contributing to the academic work in his discipline in addition to the applied work he did for a living.

AWARDS   In the awards category besides better describing his swimming prize, he could add his GEOLAB award for best professional, another testament to the consistent high quality of his everyday work. Of course, he would put this award first to adhere to the reverse chronological order he used throughout the résumé. That way, his readers would catch the most current information in each category with the least amount of reading.

REFERENCES   In the references section John might list the names and addresses of his recommenders. Application reviewers sometimes prefer to know from whom to expect letters of recommendation.

Attending to Readability   As for overall readability of the résumé, John knew he should consider certain principles.

LENGTH   Since he was no longer a fresh college graduate with little to report, John found that it would be very difficult to keep his résumé to the one-page limit he had formerly adhered to. Now he had really substantive professional accomplishments to his credit. He also had a bit of persuading to do about his managerial preparedness, and he intended to do this explicitly, but succinctly. He would throw caution to the wind and extend to a second page.

While he was uneasy at first about this decision, he remembered that all the top candidates he had reviewed as a selection team member had two-page résumés. This extension to a second page was required because of the detail, summaries, and persuasive tasks their résumés had to accomplish.

WHITE SPACE   The interesting thing was that the two-page résumés John had read actually were easier to read than most of the one-page résumés his selection committee had received because of this: they used white space attractively and pragmatically, so that the whole résumé appeared balanced and proportioned. The white space also helped emphasize and subordinate information unobtrusively. He wouldn't have to rely solely on typography to accomplish these rhetorical tasks.

TYPOGRAPHY   John would enjoy changing font and point size on his Macintosh PC. Palatino was particularly readable, with an edge of grace that might set his résumé apart from the turgid standard fonts. He flirted with the idea of a humorous font, like Western script, but resisted, realizing he was beginning to enjoy this job search far more than he should. At least he wasn't considering a small portrait of himself in the upper righthand corner of the résumé, like the one the selection committee had all enjoyed laughing at. It had broken the tedium of their search but was quickly discarded as unprofessional. Nor did it help the author's case that he was not particularly attractive. And, as one selection committee member had pointed out, such a portrait was a rather sly way of appealing to stereotypical considerations the law had gone a long way to putting out of bounds.

He would also highlight and subordinate information with boldface type, italic type, and underlining. He would set up a consistent system that his reader could rely on to signal first-, second-, and third-level categories.

Sample Professional Résumé

After working for two evenings John was satisfied with the results of his work. Combining all the considerations of rhetoric—his purposes and audience—with format considerations to promote readability, John produced the résumé shown in Figure 9.3, putting it together carefully, as if he were solving a puzzle.

RÉSUMÉ   as of 5/1/90

JOHN LOOMIS
52 Tuxedo Park
Atlanta, GA 30300

EXPERIENCE   Home Telephone: 404-563-0987   Spouse: Cynthia
                 Office Telephone: 404-371-2112   Child: Gregory

EDUCATION   1989 TO PRESENT   15 hours (5 classes) toward an MS in
                     Geology; Georgia State University, Atlanta, GA

                 Current Research: "Mapping the Piedmont River Fault"
                 Major Professor: Dr. Susan Richardson

                 1984   B.S. in Geology; University of Florida,
                     Gainesville, FL 32706

                     GPA Overall—3.9
                         in major—4.0

                 Senior Thesis: "Effects of the Glencoe Slide"
                     Research demonstrating the demise of Glencoe River beaver
                     populations north of Orlando, as a result of the '79 slide
                 Major Professor: Dr. Fred Thompson

EXPERIENCE   1984 TO PRESENT   Senior Staff Geologist

                             GEOLAB
                             30 Peachtree Drive
                             Atlanta, GA 30300

                 Description:
                             Administer field studies for five of the ten
                                 largest clients, including NASA, DOE,
                                 and DOT

                             Administer budget for geology and hydrology
                                 groups, approximately 50 employees in all

                             Conduct all training for geology and hydrology
                                 field-workers

Figure 9.3
(Cont.)

John Loomis/Résumé
Page Two

Significant Accomplishments:
Achieved consistent EXCELLENT rating from DOE
and DOT, which earned GEOLAB $5 million in
bonuses over 1985-1989

Reduced geology budget 30% and hydrology
budget 40% by eliminating duplication of labor
from several procedures

Discovered role of gophers in undermining
Chattahoochee River levees

PUBLICATIONS AND PAPERS

"Effects of the Glencoe Slide." 35,
Geology Journal, 1986, 18-35.
"Further Observations on Glencoe."
Paper delivered at the 35th Professional
Geologists Association Conference.
Pasadena, CA. October 1988.
"Fault Mapping in Aquasystems," Paper
delivered at the 12th Geology in
America Conference. University of
Minnesota, Minneapolis, MN. 1986.

AWARDS

1989—Best Professional; selected by GEOLAB
International

1983—NCAA Gold Medal; 300-m Freestyle Champion;
National record set (still unbroken) at the
75th NCAA competition, University of
Alabama, Birmingham, AL

REFERENCES

Available upon request from

The Placement Office
Student Pavilion, Box 94
University of Florida
Gainesville, FL 32706

For this job search John wanted a *person* to be apparent in his résumé, not just a functionary. He had a family he was proud of and so gave them some lines. This also sent the message that he was not an unformed slot filler, but a responsible man who had achieved some integrity between his life and his work. He was surprised by the difference 6 years had made in his résumé. The new résumé made the contrast rather dramatic.

John's résumé took a good week to fix up. He was now 3 weeks into his job search, staring at May 5 on his calendar.

Write Cover Letters

Now came the most difficult part of John's problem-solving task: writing cover letters that effectively correlated the categories of his résumé and the demands of the positions he wanted to apply for. His updated résumé would give prospective employers a condensed picture of what he had done; the cover letter would explain how his past was a useful basis on which to build a future together.

Again, from his selection committee experience, John knew that his cover letter should embody certain principles:

1. Adapt, where legitimate, for audience needs.
2. Inform through summary.
3. Persuade through evidence.
4. Synthesize as necessary to correlate experience and requirements of the position.

Adapt, Where Legitimate, for Audience Needs

This first point is qualified by the phrase *where legitimate* for both ethical and pragmatic reasons. The pragmatic reason is that it does no good to present oneself falsely in a cover letter because this falseness will eventually be discovered and will have wasted the time of both the prospective employer and the job candidate. The interview, in fact, is designed to detect such falseness. So, for example, if John is not a real team player, then he should not try to project himself as such.

The ethical problem with "overadapting" for an audience is apparent, but worth stating, since many sources in society instruct people to do just that—overadapt. This advice parallels that which mothers used to give to their pubescent daughters: pretend to be interested in everything he says. It is important to find a job, to be financially secure, to build a solid professional history. But there is no need to see this as the only important thing in life.

Society is not so unreasonable yet that every other facet of life must be subordinated to career. And if you proceed in the belief that all comes second to career, you will be in real danger of losing your integrity. You should be aware of your boundaries. Ask yourself: How far can I go to present myself as suitable for the position I want to apply for? If you have any sense of yourself, there will be clear limits to any answer to that question.

Inform through Summary

This second principle clarifies the difference between the cover letter and the résumé. While the cover letter should preview the important points in the résumé as they apply to the position description, it should not simply rehash all the details contained within the résumé. The résumé serves an outline function, arranging all the details necessary to document activity; the cover letter, however, deals in relationships between these documented activities and the positions applied for. These relationships have to be articulated and supported (the topic of principle 3) in a reasonable way. One of the worst things an applicant can do is to claim relationships where, in fact, none exist. Often such an application will be thrown out because of the hostility of the reader to the applicant's trying to "pull something" in the cover letter.

Persuade through Evidence

The third point is also an important one. John had read too many cover letters (and had even written one himself) that were essentially transmittal letters, referring the reader to the résumé. This strategy puts the onus on the reader to pull the applicant's case together. John remembered being simply too rushed and too tired to make a case for those who had not made their own. It had cut his work considerably when applicants had been professional enough to show him, very explicitly and directly, how their experience matched, exceeded, and approximated the position requirements.

Synthesize as Necessary to Correlate Experience and Requirements of the Position

Where holes were left that constituted gaps between the applicants' experience and the position description, the responsible applicants had addressed them, instead of trying to hide them. It was not uncommon for conscientious applicants to realize that they fulfilled all but a few of the requirements very well. The few mismatches were no reason not to apply for a job they wanted. Instead, the applicants suggested alternatives to the holes, strategies for overcoming them. Even when such arguments had to be discounted because the gaps were simply too big or the alternatives inadequate, John felt some respect for the honesty of these straightforward applicants.

He knew that not all his colleagues agreed with him, seeing a hole as a hole and perhaps admiring those who tried to cover up their inadequacies. But John was keeping the larger issue in mind: he might one day be working for one of these applicants. He preferred to think of working for one who would try to solve problems that existed to one who would try to cover them up.

Problems could probably be solved adequately once they were acknowledged. Refusal to acknowledge them never helped any company, he had learned. NASA's problems with the Hubble Space Telescope, designed for use in orbit around the earth, had demonstrated that principle clearly enough. John had read that the lens makers had ignored unfavorable test results because of their belief that a certain lens was superior. As a result, the space center's mission had failed to produce the photographs it had sought to capture. Moreover, this problem could not be corrected from Earth. So the faulty equipment languished, awaiting a repair vehicle that would not reach it for some years to come.

Sample Position Description

John kept these principles in mind as he analyzed the position descriptions he had collected, including one from *Oceanique, Lmtd.* (Figure 9.4). The lack of such a description for SeaScience was a separate problem he would address later. His analysis of position descriptions was mainly to clarify for himself exactly what requirements he would need to address in his letter. Sometimes these requirements were specified; sometimes they were implied.

While this position description was a bit daunting, since it emphasized an experienced manager, John was not put off. He had real administrative experience from three important projects, even though he didn't have a managerial title with GEOLAB. He would make this point in his cover letter.

From the sequence of professionals listed on the description, he suspected that this company might prefer an oceanographer; oceanographers might be in the majority in this group. But he could play a strong second as a geologist. In addition, he had done DOT contract work before, with smooth progress. His research background was strong although more terrestrial than aquatic, but he was serious about shifting emphases, and so would try to make that argument part of his case. With his proven administrative record, yet no previous managerial title, OCEANIQUE might see that his salary requirements could be less onerous than those of a Woods Hole manager, for example.

Sample Cover Letter for an Advertised Position

In response to this description John wrote the letter shown in Figure 9.5, which highlights his attempts to synthesize his qualifications for his reader; that is, in several places John will spell out exactly how he is a good match for the position description.

Throughout this letter John tries to summarize and to persuade his reader. These communication skills take far more effort than simply referring the reader to the résumé, good as his revised résumé may be.

Because the difficult part of John's argument is to persuade his reader that he is qualified for a managerial position, despite the fact that he has never held one before, he devotes the bulk of the letter to that argument. His research background is solid and well detailed in his résumé, so he mentions it as further proof, but does not detail it in the letter because he wants to keep the letter concise. Only in very complicated situations would one want to write a cover letter that is longer than a page. Yet, it is important that the cover letter be complete enough to serve as a good introduction to the résumé.

Figure 9.4
Sample position description

OCEANIQUE, LMTD.

4580 Falmouth Dr., Suite 925 Boston, MA 02200

POSITION TITLE

The Boston branch of OCEANIQUE, LMTD., requires a manager for its research division. Applicants should send current résumé and cover letter to Ms. Angela Rowan, Personnel Manager, Box 2155, Boston, MA 02200. Material should be postmarked by 6/1/90.

DUTIES

Supervise a 16-member team of oceanographers, geologists, hydrologists, and computer specialists. Administer multimillion-dollar budget for a US DOT project investigating the shipping routes in the North Atlantic for degradation.

REQUIREMENTS

An experienced manager with a strong research background. B.S. at minimum. Salary negotiable.

Figure 9.5
*John Loomis's
cover letter in
response to an
advertised
position
description*

April 30, 1990

52 Tuxedo Park
Atlanta, GA 30300

Ms. Angela Rowan, Personnel Manager
OCEANIQUE, LMTD.
Box 2155
Boston, MA 02200

Dear Ms. Rowan:

I am most interested in the Manager of Research position I saw advertised in March's issue of *Geology Today*. My previous experience administering projects for US DOT and my background in geology, hydrology, and aquatics are particularly suited to the requirements you specify in the position description.

I have been the lead on several important projects at GEOLAB, where I am now employed. I am experienced in fulfilling contractor expectations. For example, I have been the lead for the past three years on a US DOT project investigating the breakdown of Chattahoochee River levees. DOT appreciated the efficiency of my team's work, awarding us an EXCELLENT rating for all three years. My other contractor experience includes work for DOE on the stability of mine shafts in New Mexico and work for NASA, analyzing samples taken from the moon. Both of those projects received EXCELLENT ratings, as well.

My budget experience comes from lead positions on major projects. While I have yet to administer a multimillion-dollar budget, I have administered those in the $500k range. I assume your budget requires CPAF documentation, which I am practiced in. At GEOLAB, I have compiled and administered budgets on both the CPAF system and a standard corporate system.

It is the nature of the work you've advertised that attracts my attention—investigating possible environmental degradation in the North Atlantic shipping routes. I am looking for another position, not only to take on a management title, but also to take on the interesting work of environmental investigation. The GEOLAB projects don't have the same ecological emphasis as the one you've identified in the advertisement. My research background is hardly challenged by standard contract work. I am eager to put my postgraduate experience to work, especially in aquatic research. My previous work on aquatics has been well received.

My résumé, which I have enclosed for your review, lists my work and home phone numbers. I look forward to discussing this position in more detail, at your convenience.

Sincerely,

John Loomis

John Loomis

/encl

John wrote seven other cover letters adapted to the position descriptions he had found in his research. These letters followed the principles he had followed when writing to OCEANIQUE because they were all in response to specific position descriptions. John's letter to SeaScience would have to be a bit different, though, since he was not responding to a written description.

Submitting an Unsolicited Application

With the SeaScience application John was trying to break into a closed system that, in fact, might not have any openings. He had to rely on his own knowledge about the company and on his research; that is, using his knowledge and research about the company, he had to argue that a mutually beneficial relationship could be established. John's first decision was that he would address his letter to Rick Stewart, Vice President in Charge of Research. John did this with some confidence because he had met Stewart at a conference and had discussed research interests with him. Stewart had seemed receptive and impressed by John's panel. While normally he would not address a cover letter to an executive, John thought it was worth a try in this case because he had some previous dealings with this executive. For formal reasons, though, John would copy the letter to the manager of personnel at SeaScience. He didn't want Stewart to think that John expected him to do all the legwork for this contact with SeaScience; John could contact Stewart and still do his own legwork.

Since he was so interested in the company, John thought it would be worthwhile to mention his colleague, Toby Graham, who was formerly employed by SeaScience. That can be a risky strategy simply because the mutual acquaintance might not be well regarded by the reader. But everything John knew about Toby Graham, that he was generally respected in his field, persuaded him that it would only help him to mention his name.

For this letter John followed these principles:

- Make the previous relationship with the addressee clear from the beginning of the letter.
- Mention a mutual acquaintance only if there is reason to believe the person is well regarded, and only if the person is truly a mutual acquaintance. It is legitimate to use an "in" as long as that person truly can provide a means of access to whoever will be considering the applicant's request.
- Make a strong case for the mutually beneficial relationship that might be worked out, but make the case formally and respectfully, using the principles of persuasion and evidence one would use to respond to a position description.

When applying this final principle, John must remember to balance his previous knowledge of the reader with his own status as an outsider. John may know Rick, but not as a co-worker would, so he wouldn't want to overdo any informality.

Sample Cover Letter for an Unsolicited Application

John's letter to SeaScience appears in Figure 9.6. Two points are worth mentioning about this letter. First, John violated his own page-limit rule with a cover letter that ran one-and-a-half pages. This was a risky strategy because he had no guarantee that Stewart would want to take the time to read such a long letter. All John could be sure of was that if he was going to send such a long letter, it would have to be well written.

The problem is not that people adhere to fixed page limits for any quantitative reason; the problem is that since so many people write poor letters, the chances that a letter will be poorly written, and thus defeat the author's purpose, increase with each paragraph. Thus, the poorer writers generally benefit from shorter letters. On the other hand, a good writer, who considers audience, who has a pleasant style, and who makes substantive points throughout the letter, can write a longer letter *when necessary*. In this case a longer letter is justified by the fact that John is writing an unsolicited cover letter, so he has to do a bit more explaining than he would in a solicited letter. This letter length is also justified because John writes well. Even though he exceeds one page, he writes very efficiently, considering all his letter must accomplish.

Another interesting point about this letter is that John ends it with the statement that he will call Stewart at a certain time. This is also a risky strategy and not one to be used in standard letters. For example, if John were to use this tactic with OCEANIQUE, he might come off as pushy, trying to rush the search forward for his own convenience, as if he were the only applicant. He knows he is not the only applicant since he is responding to a nationally advertised search. But John is the only applicant for the SeaScience job, as far as he knows, since no search has been advertised.

Furthermore, John's call not only will inquire about the status of his own application, but also will touch base with a colleague. He will inquire whether such a position is available, and he will also follow up on any possible procedural difficulties with the way he has approached the company.

So in this case the follow-up call is justified. It will accomplish reasonable business and follow up on a contact John already has.

With this letter to Stewart, John reached the end of his cover letter stage. Since he wrote each letter individually, sometimes adopting paragraphs from other letters, but always approaching each letter as a fresh rhetorical problem, this stage was quite time-consuming. By the time he was finished, it was the end of May, not surprising since John was still working full-time and living a life with his family.

POSTSCRIPT

On May 17 John called Rick Stewart at SeaScience. Since Stewart was out of town until May 25, John had no choice but to wait on his contact. He preferred to talk to Stewart before he talked to the personnel manager, who might toss his application

Figure 9.6
*John Loomis's
cover letter to
inquire about a
possible position*

May /, 1990

52 Tuxedo Park
Atlanta, GA 30300

Dr. R. D. Stewart, Vice President
SeaScience
P.O. Box 85
St. Augustine, FL 30333

Dear Dr. Stewart:

I'm not sure that you will remember me without some explanation. I met you last year at the Geology in America conference in Fort Worth. You had attended the session I chaired on aquatic fault lines in the Atlantic, and we exchanged data a few weeks later. Toby Graham, formerly employed by SeaScience and now senior hydrologist at GEOLAB, told me he had quite a good experience at SeaScience and encouraged me to write you. Apparently he worked with you quite extensively in 1985 on the Cousteau project.

I am particularly interested in your company because of the environmental work you do. I very much admired SeaScience's study of the ozone hole over Antarctica and would like to devote my energies to such work. My experiences in administration and research might be attractive to SeaScience, since I am accustomed to working on tight budgets and producing consistently verifiable research.

That said, I wanted to let you know that I am currently looking for another position and am most interested in anything that might be suitable at SeaScience. While the bulk of my experience has been as lead of research projects, I am interested in taking on a formal managerial role in research.

My experience as the lead on several important projects at GEOLAB, where I am now employed, has taught me how to fulfill contractor expectations. For example, I have been the lead for the past three years on a US DOT project investigating the breakdown of Chattahoochee River levees. DOT appreciated the efficiency of my team's work, awarding us an EXCELLENT rating for all three years. My other contractor experience includes work for DOE on the stability of mine shafts in New Mexico and work for NASA, analyzing samples taken from the moon. Both of those projects received EXCELLENT ratings, as well.

My budget experience comes from lead positions on major projects. I have administered several in the $500k range. In Fort Worth you mentioned that

Figure 9.6
(*Cont.*)

R. D. Stewart
Page 2

your budget requires CPAF documentation, which I am practiced in. At
GEOLAB, I compiled and administered budgets on both the CPAF system
and a standard corporate system, so I can adjust to whatever budget
documentation requirements SeaScience must meet.

I am sending a copy of this letter and résumé to Mr. Arnold in SeaScience
Personnel, just so that he can put the copy on file. But since you are the
administrator of the SeaScience Research Section, I wanted you to know
about my job search. While I am applying for other positions advertised
in the journals, I am particularly interested in coming to work for
SeaScience, where I think we all would find a good match between mission
and ability. I hope to call you the week of May 15 to discuss any offerings
that might come up. In the meantime, I look forward to discussing my search
further at your convenience.

Sincerely,

John Loomis

John Loomis

/encl

because he did not go through the orthodox channels. In the meantime John heard from OCEANIQUE on May 20, where he was short-listed for the managerial position. Replies to his other seven letters were polite, but unencouraging.

On May 25 John did talk to Stewart, but because Stewart called him. Stewart was pleased to get John's letter, enthusiastic about John's interest in the company, and encouraging about actually establishing a position for John. Since this position would be an additional one, John would have to be willing to wait for several weeks for the bureaucracy to go into gear. John was willing; he began his wait.

On June 10 OCEANIQUE called John for an interview. He went to Boston on June 15, returned to Atlanta on the 17th, wrote a formal thank-you letter for the interview on the 18th, and was offered a position on the 30th. While John was terribly pleased to have an offer so efficiently in hand, only 10 weeks from the beginning of his search, he hesitated because of his desire to work at SeaScience. He called Stewart to apprise him of the situation and Stewart asked him to hang on a little longer; the extra position was only halfway through the SeaScience system.

By July 15 OCEANIQUE began to press for an answer. John negotiated for some time, until August 1, and called Stewart again. This time Stewart had bad news. The extra position could not be approved until the next fiscal year, which began October 1. Stewart felt John's chances would be excellent then, but could not make any guarantees. John was stuck. He decided to push from another end.

On July 25 John informed his immediate supervisor, Sue, that he had received another offer. Sue was sorry to hear that he would be leaving, but didn't seem to feel moved to make a counteroffer. John suspected that Nathalie Schuster, Sue's superior and his former supervisor, might be willing to counteroffer, so he wrote a memorandum explaining his offer, and copied the memo to Nathalie. As he predicted, Nathalie was indeed interested in a counteroffer, so she asked him for a week to consult with her superiors to determine how much and what position she could offer him. Within 3 days she returned with an offer for a 12 percent raise, but no change in position. John rejected this counteroffer since his position at OCEANIQUE would include a managerial position title and perks. In 2 more days Nathalie came back with the 12 percent and a managerial title. She obviously wanted John to stay.

John then had to think about the reasons he had for wanting to leave GEOLAB in the first place. Besides his frustration over being passed over for management, he felt unfulfilled in his work, that his results were pushed under the rug because they were unflattering to the government contractors who had commissioned the studies. Was he willing to continue doing work for these contractors, knowing they were hostile to his results, after being stroked a bit by a salary increase and a managerial title?

At this point John realized he would have to talk to Nathalie again to clarify this problem. Nathalie encouraged John to persist in his research, despite unflattering findings, and pledged to support his conclusions as much as she could. But she could not guarantee that he would receive the full support of upper management; in fact, he could expect to have to fight for his principles.

John appreciated Nathalie's honesty and began to perceive that perhaps he never would be able to have the kinds of guarantees he craved from his employer.

His choices, then, were to stay where he knew the problems but had wrested some respect, to go to an unknown but receptive environment (at least it seemed receptive), to continue his search, or to wait for SeaScience. His decision would not be an easy one; on the other hand, it was a decision he relished and a far cry from the sort of decision he was making 3 months ago in the rush-hour traffic on I-285.

In the end John decided to stay with GEOLAB, to try on this new hat in the company. He gracefully declined OCEANIQUE's offer by phone call and letter. He contacted Stewart with his decision, who was pleased that John had not counted out SeaScience. October was close; now that John had a managerial position at GEOLAB, it would be much easier to justify the new managerial slot for him. The job search, if it did nothing else, opened a number of new opportunities for John, making him realize how much he had to offer a company.

In the future John would not see the search as a signal of the end of his career satisfaction, but as a chance to assert himself in his profession. While he couldn't imagine that he would skip from company to company—he was not that ambitious—he could imagine taking on another job search when his values and his work became too unrelated.

SHAPING UP A STUDENT RÉSUMÉ

In this section we will work with an entry-level application by a student applying for an engineering job. In fact, the student is Joe Brown, whose professional profile appears in Chapter 1. From this profile we know that Joe made it eventually into his engineering field. How much did his student résumé contribute to his success?

First Draft of the Résumé

The first draft of Joe's résumé (see Figure 9.7) doesn't look particularly promising. While reviewing it, note the points that could be strengthened to appeal to an engineering recruiter.

Purpose

Joe wants to convince prospective employers that he is well suited to an entry-level position. Because an entry-level position in engineering isn't a specialized calling, Joe needs to focus on the strengths in his academic preparation and in his work experience. While the latter may not exactly relate to engineering, it will show a bit about his character as an employee.

Has Joe achieved his purpose with this résumé? He has made a good start, but needs to do a better job of highlighting his strengths: significant work experience and academic diversity, branching off from engineering into computers and math.

Figure 9.7
*Sample first draft
of a résumé*

JOE BROWN
1015 Smithfield
Twin Falls, ID 83897
(208) 534-9786

OBJECTIVE   Entry level position with opportunities for research and
                   development, advancement, and further education.

EDUCATION   Senior enrolled at Mountain State University, Twin
                   Falls, Idaho.Graduation expected in May 1992 with a
                   Bachelor or Science in Engineering and a Minor in Math.

EMPHASIS   Currently taking the Thermal Fluids and Measurement and
OF STUDY   Control Systems sequences.Known computer languages
                   include Cobal, Fortran, and Basic.

CAREER-RELATED   Tutored Engineering, Math, and Physics
EXPERIENCE   independently 1988 to present. Instructed 1 to 3
                   students per semester through junior level
                   courses.

WORK EXPERIENCE   Mechanic House of Fords, Twin Falls, Idaho
                   1982-1990.Achieved ASE certifications in Brakes,
                   Engine Repair, and Heavy Trucks. Job required
                   dealing with customers on a regular basis.

REFERENCES   Upon request

Audience

Joe has appealed somewhat to his audience, which is recruiters for engineering firms. In other ways, he has missed them.

He has been successful in that his résumé is very focused on the essentials pertinent to the position he's looking for. In fact, his objective statement is one of the more substantive ones seen on a student résumé. Since he has been asked to submit only a résumé, his objective statement is useful here. He has not added a lot of superfluous material. His writing is concise.

But he has missed his audience through a few errors. First, he has not proofed his work carefully; we see spelling errors and spacing problems. It is also a bit difficult to read this résumé for dates, although it looks like he was out of high school for several years and then decided to go on to college. Finally, the reader doesn't get much of a feel for the person behind this résumé. This is a problem since Joe is submitting only his résumé, with no cover letter, per recruiter requests. He could probably come up with some impressive personal information if he thought about it.

Arrangement

Joe has written a chronological résumé, organized into the standard categories of objective, education, experience, and references. He has added emphasis of study as a separate category, instead of making it a subcategory of education; it's not clear why this should be a separate category. He has also made a distinction between career-related experience and work experience. This may well be a meaningful distinction, since students often do work to get themselves through school that has nothing to do with their intended career. Joe may also be trying to distance himself from the mechanical aspects of his experience, since he is educating himself in engineering and math.

It would seem reasonable for Joe to keep the work experience distinctions, but to subordinate emphasis of study to education. He should not give short shrift to his mechanical experience, though, especially since he worked at House of Fords for 8 years. This is significant work experience for a student to have.

An aspect of arrangement is typography, how the words are word processed or typed on the page. There are few typographical distinctions in Joe's résumé. In fact, the only ones he makes are between all-capital category names and upper- and lower-case descriptive material. He could use others to highlight his résumé: boldface type, underlinings, and italic type are quite common. Another mistake he has made is to use paragraphs instead of lists to outline his qualifications. Paragraphs are more difficult to sort out in résumés than are lists, since most information on a résumé is at the same level of generalization; that is, each sentence in a paragraph is just as important as the others.

REVISED STUDENT RÉSUMÉ

Joe's revised résumé is shown in Figure 9.8. His revised résumé is a real improvement over his first one. Through attention to purpose, audience, and arrange-

Figure 9.8
Revision of the sample résumé

JOE BROWN
1015 Smithfield
Twin Falls, ID 83897
(208) 534-9786

OBJECTIVE   Entry-level position with opportunities for research and development, advancement, and further education.

EDUCATION   1988 to present; Mountain State University, Twin Falls, ID, 83897. Expect to graduate in May 1992 with a B.S. in Engineering and a math minor.

Area of concentration: Thermal Fluids and Measurement and Control Systems.

Computer Languages: COBAL, FORTRAN, and BASIC

Accomplishments:
—self-financed college education
—maintained a 3.5 GPA
—worked full-time during college
—received Bart Jones scholarship, 1989-90

CAREER-
RELATED   1988 to present; tutor engineering, math, and physics students through junior-level courses; instruct 1 to 3
EXPERIENCE students per semester

OTHER WORK 1982-1990. House of Fords, Twin Falls, ID, 83897; Mechanic.
EXPERIENCE Dealt with customers on a regular basis.

Accomplishments:
—Earned ASE certifications in brakes, engine repair, and heavy trucks.

REFERENCES Available on request from

Placement Office
Mountain State University
Twin Falls, ID 83897

ment, he has highlighted his strengths and made the résumé easier to read, despite the fact that the second one is actually longer than the first.

FUNDAMENTALS OF THE INTERVIEW PROCESS

Interviewing is, of course, a very important part of the job search process. The documentation gets the candidate to the interview step, but by no means guarantees a successful interview. On the other hand, many have learned the hard way that a successful interview does not guarantee a good future employee. Some people interview very well but prove very difficult to work with. Others do not interview dramatically well but prove to be solid choices for a position. So, to round out the interview scenario, we can say with assurance that everyone involved in the interview is trying to feel his or her way through it as best as possible. There is no scientific process to guarantee the best choice for all involved.

The Interviewer

It is worthwhile to consider the interviewer's position in this stressful situation. It is taken for granted that the candidate will feel nervous and on the spot, but the interviewer's state of mind complicates the situation. One important thing to remember about those who are doing the interviewing is that this task is just one of many they have to get through that day. While the candidate has only the interview to focus on, the interviewers have many other things to focus on—the everyday tasks that constitute a day on the job—and may regard the interview as an interruption; interviews are certainly time-consuming for those in charge of them.

So, much as the writer of correspondence must keep in mind the image of the harried reader who must plow through many letters and memos, the candidate facing an interview needs to keep in mind an image of the harried interviewer. Such an image should help the candidate remember to be as businesslike as possible in the interview. And given the fact that the interviewer may well be interviewing several candidates for a position, it obviously is important for the candidate to make some kind of distinctive impression, to come across as a real person, instead of as an actor who takes no risks but just wants to play the part of the perfect interviewee. The fact is that interviewers are interested not only in a candidate who seems to fit all of their criteria, but also in the person who might be coming to work for them.

Interview Guidelines

Beyond the obvious etiquette of interviewing, it is helpful to understand the rhetoric of the situation. A candidate is brought to an interview, often at considerable company expense, because the hiring organization has reason to believe that the candidate has some good things to offer the company. The purpose of the interview is to get a feel for the candidate's personality. The interviewers will be as variable as people can be.

It is difficult to advise candidates about the interview because so much depends on the characters of unknown people. Interviewing is a very subjective business, and it is a fact that a good interview impression may be overlooked for reasons over which the candidate has no control: another candidate may have made an equally good impression or someone conducting the interview may have been threatened by a candidate's accomplishments.

Because there are factors over which the candidate has no control, it makes sense for the candidate to concentrate on those factors over which she or he does have some control: responsiveness, preparedness, finesse with trick and hostile questions, and honesty.

Responsiveness

The candidate should be forthcoming and cooperative with the interviewers. This means that candidates should answer questions fully, developing reasonable answers but not rambling. Nothing is more painful for interviewers than extracting answers from a candidate who may be too nervous or too immature to volunteer any more than the most cursory answers. On the other hand, it is almost equally painful to listen to a candidate ramble in a series of broken-off sentences that never come to an end. Although the interviewer may realize that this stream-of-consciousness answer is a result of the candidate's nervousness, he or she will not overlook this type of response.

Candidates should think about their answers for a minute, clarify the question if necessary, and generally try to be as concise as possible. After getting through any kind of detailed answer, the candidate might ask a simple question like "Are you with me?" to give the interviewer a chance to ask any minor questions the answer might have raised.

Another aspect of responsiveness is for the candidate to listen well. Sometimes candidates are so nervous that they simply don't hear introductions, explanations, and the like. The candidate who is too nervous to listen can miss a great deal, at the least, and present an unattractive picture, at worst, so as to be eliminated from consideration. No one wants to work with someone who doesn't listen.

Preparedness

Interviewees are often cautioned to be prepared, but this advice usually refers to researching the company. Since a candidate will have already done the research necessary to apply for a position, we are using *preparedness* in a different sense. This means that if a candidate is to give a presentation during the interview, for example, then a formal presentation should be completely ready to go. It makes a very bad impression, implying a real lack of interest in the job, to stumble through an unprepared talk when expected to present a formal one.

387

This may well mean that the candidate will have to do some scrambling to pull a prepared talk together, but this is all part of the extra job one takes on to look for another one. Being prepared also means that the candidate should be able to speak specifically to those areas of expertise that are advertised in the job position. Thus, a potential personnel director should have some specific things to say about running the interviewer's personnel department.

Finesse with Trick and Hostile Questions

Interviewing is a stressful business, but every interviewee should understand that there are interviewers who enjoy making it even more stressful, to see what kind of reaction the candidate will have to such stress. Trick questions and hostile questions fall into this category of interviewing games. If the candidate can accept that these strategies are typical of interviews, then the questions won't seem so powerful and the candidate shouldn't be thrown by them.

Trick questions are those speculative questions that one has no way of answering too well. "Where do you see yourself in 5 years?" or "When do you think you would want to get into management?" or "What are your weaknesses?" are all questions to beware of. If nothing else, they are a good test of the candidate's ability to give a no-answer answer in a very charming way. It is never a good idea to answer the questions about weaknesses too sincerely, since the question is designed to put the candidate in an unfavorable light. Generally, good interviewers will not ask these questions.

Hostile questions are not necessarily the mark of bad interviewers because the questions themselves can be genuine. The charged-up feeling behind the questions may or may not be genuine; nevertheless, the situation puts the candidate's character to the test. What kind of grace under pressure can the candidate muster? The candidate may be confronted with remarks like these: "Surely you're not implying that . . ." or "If what you say is true, then how do you account for . . . ?" or "This sounds to me like the latest version of snake oil."

When confronted with this apparent hostility, the candidate must not take it too seriously. Chances are good that the remark is not serious, that the remarker is just showing off, that the remarker is the group curmudgeon, or that the remarker is trying to earn some kind of points with the local authority figures. The candidate's best strategy is patience, good humor, and objectivity, on the assumption that not everyone is going to like everything the candidate has to say. Above all, it is important not to retaliate out of defensiveness. It may well be that the questioner is too hostile to be overlooked or distracted with a joke, and so the candidate will feel that some firmly held stance is appropriate; but it's best to avoid insults and viciousness, the same way one would try to avoid such behavior to a host.

The important point in this section is that the candidate should not do anything that would compromise integrity. We do not believe that a candidate should do just anything to get a position; the qualification is always understood that the candidate will do what is reasonable and ethical to get a position. But the competitiveness of the interview can evoke extreme responses from candidates.

Honesty

Because the candidate is on the spot, yet wants to make a good impression, it is easy for him or her to fall into habits that are less than honest. First under this category are all attempts to be agreeable to the interviewer when those attempts do not at all reflect the truth. Candidates may find themselves saying things that are very difficult to live up to later: "I don't mind driving 45 minutes into the desert in the morning to get to work"; "I don't need a window in my office"; "Straight commission work is fine with me." If candidates agree to things that are too difficult to live up to, then, when they try to renegotiate those points, they seem to be backing out on implied promises.

Another type of honesty error is the inability of many candidates to admit they don't know something they think they are supposed to know. While there are many dodges, the interviewer usually spots them quickly and the candidate loses credibility. It is better to admit lack of knowledge than to bluff. One form of bluff is to move the conversation back to an area the candidate does know something about; another is to answer a different question. For example, the interviewer may ask, "Why would a teacher want to work in a mining outfit?" The candidate, unsure of the reasons, replies: "It is very gratifying to work with others, to know that one can enhance a child's future. I'm looking forward to the same type of opportunity with you." This answer still does not tell the interviewer why the teacher wants to move into mining. The candidate should understand that interviewers are looking for just such dodges as these.

In the long run everyone is best served by honesty. It will win the candidate little to be hired based on false expectations set up in the interview. And it will benefit the hiring organization little to take on someone who evokes real doubts in the interview. It is very difficult to fire most professionals. A case must be carefully built up during a probationary period, supported by documentation, and accompanied by plenty of counseling. It is not easy to undo mistakes made in the interview. A genuine interviewing style goes a long way to eliminating bad matches before they happen.

CONCLUSIONS

This chapter emphasizes the persuasive job that applicants take on when preparing their cover letters and résumés. Therefore, the rhetorical considerations of purpose, audience, and arrangement are paramount. In addition, applicants must take political considerations into account at several points in the job search process. Finally, applicants should not be afraid to stand by their ethical constraints. The job search is not a product-processing enterprise, but a rather unpredictable encounter among human beings. The process is both objective and subjective, and candidates should do their best to evoke the person behind the qualifications.

EXERCISES

1. Write a cover letter and résumé to apply for the position described in Figure 9.9. You should not make up any facts for these application materials; instead, you should work with your real experience, highlighting your strengths and correlating them with the terms of the job description.

2. Your class should form evaluation groups to review the applications for the liaison position. Then you should all make enough copies of your cover letter and résumé to distribute to the evaluation groups.

These groups will then review the candidates for the position based on how well their cover letters and résumés reflect the principles discussed in this chapter. The position description is multidisciplinary, so no one student has any better qualifications than any other. Your instructor will be interested mainly in how well you correlate your own qualifications with the demands of the position.

Each group should choose three top candidates. Then the group should write a memo to the instructor explaining why group members chose the three. Make a recommendation that they be brought in for an interview.

ASSIGNMENTS

1. Contact the placement office at your school for brochures and pamphlets or any other pertinent advice available on the job search. Do you see any discrepancies between the principles in this chapter and the advice your placement office has for you? What rationale lies behind the discrepancy? Discuss this in your class.

TERM PROJECT OPTION

Prepare a résumé that appeals particularly to your proposal audience. This résumé will document your suitability to act as principal investigator for your major project. Your résumé should show evidence of being directed toward this audience. For example, you should highlight any experience you have that is consistent with your proposed research project.

Figure 9.9
*Position
description*

POSITION DESCRIPTION

The Westwood Corporation requires a liaison to the eastern Idaho region. This is a part-time position. Duties include the following:

1. Report directly to the manager, Rocky Mountain Division, on such issues as demographics, potential markets, technical and scientific research in the area, and university relations

2. Sit on a committee for personnel relations

3. Write reports, summaries, and procedures

4. Speak to corporate and community groups on topics of interest

Qualifications include familiarity with eastern Idaho, good communication skills, ability to work with a team of professionals from a variety of fields, and a strong academic record. Students are encouraged to apply. Applicants should indicate how many hours a week they could devote to the work described above.

Westwood offers benefits for part-time employees, such as medical insurance and paid holidays. Salary open.

Please send cover letter and résumé to

Jane Doe, Personnel Manager
Rocky Mountain Division
Westwood Corporation
Salt Lake City, UT 83303

SOLVING PROBLEMS THROUGH COLLABORATION AND EDITING

Preview of the Chapter

An Overview of Professional Collaboration
   The Role of the Lead

The Collaboration Process
   Initial Planning and Organization and Assignment of Tasks
   Establishment of a Tracking System
   Drafting
   Review and Comment
   Final Revision and Production Preparation
   Distribution and Document Control

Postscript

Conclusions

August 15, 1990
2:45 P.M.

Alfred Gutierrez's Office
Cash Valley Bank
Mumford, Missouri

Alfred read his memo from Vice President Ralph Edwards and cheered. After years of needling, demanding, and threatening, Alfred had finally convinced Ralph that Cash Valley banks needed a more unified image to present to the world. Ralph gave Alfred the people and dollars to produce a style guide that would apply to all Cash Valley banks.

As the administrator in charge of customer service, Alfred had found that with the increasing sophistication and complexity of the bank's operation, its documentation demands increased. Alfred's group of twenty customer relations specialists had become more harried every day trying to sort out the different demands of the different audiences within the bank's operation. Alfred had expected to adjust for external audiences, but internal audiences need not have such varied requirements. Another concern was that the bank branches be able to present some sort of united face to their customers, instead of producing a patchwork of unrelated-looking documents as different from each other as a McDonald's menu from a church bulletin.

Eager to capitalize on this concession of Ralph's, Alfred made a quick list of the steps he would take to bring this project to completion. First he would call a meeting of representatives from each branch to explain the overall project, divide writing tasks, and agree on purpose and general audience statements to keep some consistency in the document. He would also devise a schedule based on input from the branch representatives. He would try to accommodate individual participant's schedules yet keep the momentum going on this project. This first meeting would be crucial to getting this project successfully defined and launched.

After the initial meeting the next step would be the writing. The difficulty here would be keeping the writers on task. Their usual duties would be a constant distraction, from Alfred's perspective. People didn't like to take extra time to produce once-in-a-lifetime documents. These documents did come up often, though, and as professionals, the participants were accustomed to writing them. One person from each branch would most likely be assigned to the task, probably a new hire who wasn't quite so bogged down yet with daily responsibilities. In fact, Alfred hoped for new hires, because they would work hard and would be fairly eager to please. No matter who the writers were, however, at this stage it would be important for him to keep the project on track. Alfred intended to devise some documentation to help ensure timely submissions.

The review and comment stage could be extremely long and drawn out, and Alfred was determined not to let his project founder there. This stage required all parties concerned to read and comment on the draft document. Three possible snags could occur. First, and most common, many reviewers would simply not meet the due date for comments to be in. They would be busy with other projects. Second, and less common but more difficult, some reviewers would object to substantive issues and require negotiation with the others involved. Alfred certainly didn't mind conflict resolution, but he wanted to accomplish it efficiently. A third category of reviewers would claim they didn't like the document but would be unable to produce any substantive comments to illustrate their dissatisfaction. Such complainers usually had only editorial objections, not substantive ones. Alfred had learned that the way to handle them was simply to incorporate the editorial changes they wanted—if those changes made any sense and were grammatically correct—and ignore any extraneous and insulting remarks.

After the review and comment stage, Alfred's staff could go to work on the document. Alfred had no worries about this stage, because at this point his group would be in control of the document again. His group would produce final copy, arrange graphics and printing, and take care of any document control and records matters that needed to be attended to.

The process would be a long one, particularly because so many groups had to review the draft style guide. But Alfred knew that if he structured the process well, the style guide would be completed as efficiently as possible.

AN OVERVIEW OF PROFESSIONAL COLLABORATION

Collaboration in professional and technical writing is not the same experience it is in college English classes intended to prepare students to write academic prose. Professionals in the workplace do not normally gather round a table to discuss a document. Document reviews usually occur simultaneously among several individuals in the privacy of their own offices. Nor do professionals gather round a table to compose a document together, although a company going after a big job will pull together a proposal team of employees from across the country. These people will all contribute their pieces of the proposal, often consisting of the boilerplate common in pro forma documents. The result of such a collaboration can be a massive document, hundreds or even thousands of pages long.

Yet many of the documents produced in a professional setting are collaborative, in that more than one person writes and edits them. The significance of collaboration for this textbook is in its logical dimension. Since collaboration is a fact of life in the workplace, there is no need to advocate it. What we argue for is that documents flow logically through an organization. This logical flow will ensure efficiency, thoroughness, and some logical coherence in the document.

The Role of the Lead

One quickly learns in collaborative situations that the original writers will protect their own schedules by adjusting deadlines for rhetorical effect. Project leads must learn to do the same thing; they must insist on deadlines that give them some slack to handle uncooperative participants. Otherwise, the people in final production will find themselves pulling very late hours to accommodate the casual performances of people who were to have cooperated with some original schedule, which now is in shreds.

Uncooperative collaborators, perhaps an oxymoron but nevertheless a fact of life, are difficult to handle, often because of political consequences that no one wants to cope with. Following are a few suggestions for handling uncooperative participants:

- Work through the chain of command (the organizational hierarchy) to reach managers who can do something about the uncooperative employee.
- Send memos and letters, as appropriate, to document the problem and provoke some action (see Chapter 8, "Documenting with Memos and Letters," p. 327).
- Break down large jobs into sequential steps, each with a firm deadline. This tactic makes procrastination more difficult than it would be if only one date is given for the completion of the entire task.
- Assign tasks meaningfully, so that people do work appropriate to their skills and interests.

All professionals are vulnerable to finding themselves in the uncomfortable role of the lead on a major project. The lead is a professional with administrative accountability and responsibility for keeping other participants on track, but without administrative authority. We know that Alfred is the lead on the style guide project; he will be coordinating the efforts of people from all branches, people who all have their own bosses, who will not regard the lead as a boss, and who will feel only compulsory obligation to cooperate with the lead. After all, these people are compelled to work on a project that will not necessarily benefit their own branch, except abstractly; it is the lead's branch that will receive the glory for the project. So participants' loyalties can be divided. The lead must motivate, cajole, and otherwise guide all participants through the collaborative process.

The benefit of being in the lead is that it indicates one may be management-bound. Successful leads often find themselves up for promotions because they have demonstrated they can complete projects and inspire a group of people to cooperate. So, while the lead position is not necessarily enviable, it is certainly one way to give oneself a professional boost, as long as one succeeds.

THE COLLABORATION PROCESS

We can distinguish seven stages in the sort of large-scale collaboration Alfred's scenario is concerned with:

1. Initial planning (or more rhetorical analysis)
2. Organization and assignment of tasks
3. Establishment of a tracking system
4. Drafting
5. Review and comment

6. Final revision and production preparation
7. Distribution and document control

Initial Planning and Organization and Assignment of Tasks

Responsibilities of the Lead

As lead on the project Alfred was responsible for these two stages. He first thought through the whole process of producing the style guide, before he ever met with all the people who would contribute to the project. It was too inefficient for him to pull the participants together so that they could brainstorm methods to accomplish the job.

The workaday world is production-oriented, although much of the work is, by its very nature, collaborative. In contrast, while certainly productive, much academic work is solitary. Professors have to really concentrate on doing work collaboratively, and so might be very amenable to a kickoff meeting that debates methods for getting a job done. For them, collaborative work is the exception, not the rule. Since it is the rule for many other professionals, the kickoff meeting must be less exploratory and more introductory.

So Alfred prepared several materials for the upcoming kickoff meeting. He drafted a schedule that he truly believed he could live with. He found that a GANTT chart was most appropriate (see Chapter 4). And, since he already had a list of participants, which his secretary had gathered, he assigned individuals to take on the various actions depicted on his schedule. This gave him an action item list that became the backbone of the collaborative project. This list provided a schedule of activities with deadlines and, most important, the names of those responsible for each activity. Alfred himself would oversee the production process.

Responsibilities of the Participants

While individuals sequestered in their offices perform the actual writing and reviewing of collaborative documents, a general meeting of writers and editors at the beginning of the job can ensure that everyone will be more or less on the right track during the writing process. It is well worthwhile for people to spend time working out the document's general purpose; for example, it is essential to do so when the originators of the document don't seem to be clear about it. Those participating in a collaborative project must never assume that the originator of the document is clear about its purpose. Often various groups receive assignments to produce documents and, without thinking them through, start looking for others in the organization who should be helping out with this onerous task. It is impossible to take requests for help at face value.

This initial skepticism we are advocating is necessary to the "scoping out" process that everyone must do when first presented with the request for a writing job. As reviewed in Chapter 3, this initial overview of a writing task considers purpose, audience, context, and ethical implications of a job. A collaborative writing task demands no less an assessment by its participants. In fact, it is even more crucial to ask these questions of collaborative tasks since, in the face of group momentum, it can be almost impossible to rework assumptions that everyone has already agreed to. For example, one can imagine people from varied groups within an organization gathered to write parts of a general employee manual. If the lead proceeds from the assumption that new employees are suspect until proven trustworthy, then the whole tone and level of detail of the manual will be affected. It will be very difficult to argue for a different philosophy of the new employee's nature once everyone is halfway finished with the project. Therefore, the time and place to articulate any doubts about a project is in an initial kickoff meeting.

Establishment of a Tracking System

As lead, Alfred also was responsible for tracking the group's progress. To do this most effectively, he set interim milestones that left plenty of room for delay. He organized a "tickle file" to remind participants of approaching deadlines. Finally, he asked that all extension requests come in by a certain date, so that they could be negotiated with those concerned.

Drafting

Drafting took place individually. Because the tasks were clear-cut and effectively thought out, Alfred believed that this stage would proceed smoothly. While drafting was underway, Alfred organized infrequent meetings to troubleshoot the drafting and to check progress. He knew that people usually will get themselves organized if they must give some formal accounting of the work they've done to date.

Review and Comment

One way to get the unwieldy review and comment process under control is to require reviewers to record their comments on separate sheets, usually forms designed for the purpose. Figure 10.1 presents a sample form for review and comment. The use of such a form is a great advantage for the comment incorporators, who usually are the original authors of a particular section, because the form will summarize comments for the author, saving the need to page through the whole document looking for comments and corrections. A separate form also discourages the noting of minute editorial comments, which are not the concern of this stage.

While typos may be noted at the review stage, it is enough for a reviewer to ask for a general editorial review for typos and mechanics rather than to spend time as a copy editor. For one thing, this minute level of editing is best undertaken when the copy is in final draft form. Editorial errors will disappear as sections get rewritten, so there is no need to point them out until the final preparation stage.

Figure 10.1
*Sample review
and comment
sheet*

SAMPLE REVIEW AND COMMENT SHEET

Reviewer: _____   Author: _____

Department: _____   Department: _____

Please review by: _____

Document Title and Number: _____

Manager's Signature: _____

_____ Acceptable as written; no changes necessary

_____ Acceptable after changes indicated are incorporated

_____ Revision necessary; will not sign until new version is reviewed

Page	Original Text	Suggested Revision	Commenter's Initials

Note that the review and comment sheet requires the reviewer's signature, so that even if the review job gets delegated to an underling, the original reviewer must pay some attention to the comments that are made. There is plenty of space for reviewers to cite suspect passages and an area for corrected versions to be submitted for the author's consideration.

Especially in those organizations with networked word processing systems, it is imperative that the review process be organized so that only the author of a text has access to the text to make any changes. One can easily imagine the chaos that would result if reviewers were allowed access to a text. Comments that normally need to be negotiated among reviewers and authors would simply compete for the same space, with reviewers canceling out each other's efforts.

It is also important for reviewers to keep the bigger issues in mind as they review a document. Reviewers themselves can be distracted by petty errors and fine points, while overlooking the larger issues, like the essential truth of a passage, its feasibility, its impact on one's own organization, its implications for budget and schedule. Such issues are much more easily resolved at the draft stage than at a formal revision stage, which would occur after a version has already been published. Once a document has been published, it is normally revised only on a periodic schedule, perhaps once a year for frequently used procedures, and far less often for manuals and larger documents. In such a case, those who want changes must often wait far longer than they believe they should to get their changes incorporated.

The review and comment stage can be managed so that the author and reviewer are not in a constant cycle of argument over any sticking points. Assuming the parties involved are all trustworthy, the reviewer will trust that the author has incorporated important criticisms in the spirit in which they were meant. The review and comment sheet is a great help to the reviewer at this stage because it serves as irrefutable documentation of the sorts of changes the reviewer wants the author to make. Since the reviewer has detailed the changes on the standard form, and signed the form, the reviewer has a record. An uncooperative author violates the spirit of the whole process, and of professionalism, by ignoring reviewer comments.

In the long run it does no good to push through a document whose reviewers and co-authors are not satisfied. They will tend to subvert the document. A reviewer faced with an uncooperative author, one who has refused to incorporate significant comments, can then take the review and comment sheet over the author's head to try to get satisfaction. Upper management would be appropriately involved at this stage, possibly resulting in real damage to the original author's credibility.

If an author behaves professionally, then the comment resolution stage can be less intimidating, but perhaps equally complicated. The best bet for resolving large sticky issues in the text would be to call a meeting and get all the large issues resolved at once, instead of laboriously sending paper back and forth across an organization. It is important for any professional to know when it is advisable to use paper to solve a problem and when it is not. Meetings and telephone calls can often be more effective. Everything does not have to be committed to paper; on the other hand, any issue requiring a credible record demands some paper, at least a form. To that end, it is important to remember to make documentation solve the problems that occur when managing collaborative projects.

Final Revision and Production Preparation

After the reviewers' comments have been resolved, after the copy editing has taken place, and after the final version of the text has been approved, the final production begins. Although the production of a collaborative document is fairly standard and easy, it often is complicated by pressing deadlines that hardly leave sufficient time for a decent job. It is axiomatic in professional workplaces that the final production people will have to make up everyone else's schedule. For all the slips in schedule allowed to the writers and reviewers, the final production staff will have to pay. It is, therefore, Albert's responsibility, as the lead, who serves as liaison between the various writers and the editors, artists, and printers, to protect final production time by whatever means work.

Distribution and Document Control

This facet of collaborative document production required Alfred to ensure that all essential personnel received the style guide. He set up another tracking system to do this. He assigned a number to all recipients. Then he sent out the style guide with a letter that the recipient must return, stating that the document was received at a certain time. This letter then was filed with all the others for the style guide.

There are many methods of document control. The point is that often collaborative projects result in the need for documentable distribution. This last step may or may not be pertinent to a particular project.

POSTSCRIPT

Eighteen months from receipt of his memo from Ralph, Alfred inspected his new style guide, fresh from the printing office. He was impressed that the document was delayed by only 6 months from his original aggressive 1-year schedule. While overall cooperation had been good, the style guide itself was not a high-priority document for the bank, so the schedule had to be adjusted several times to accommodate more pressing matters.

His colleagues also found themselves daunted at first by the review and comment sheets Alfred insisted they use. They complained that the sheets took too much time to complete and that it was easier just to make their marks on the original draft as they saw errors occurring. Alfred did find, however, that since the review and comment sheets did not allow reviewers to bury themselves in minutiae, their comments generally seemed more substantive and more sophisticated. This helped produce a higher-quality document than Alfred had hoped for.

CONCLUSIONS

Collaboration is a process that must be managed successfully to be effective. It is helpful to think of it as a seven-stage process, the final stage of which may or may not be necessary, depending on the sort of document produced. Besides effective managers, collaborative projects need critical participants. They cannot assume that the schedule and tasks the lead organizes will necessarily make any logical sense. The time to troubleshoot the process is early on, in the kickoff meeting. The review and comment stage must be carefully managed and documented so that disputes between authors and reviewers are settled professionally.

EXERCISES

1.   After choosing a local organization that interests you, interview the publications manager, document specialist, or administrative manager about the logical flow of collaborative documents through the organization. Do you think the organization's system is efficient, thorough, and professional?

2.   As the representative of a group with a vested interest in the document, review and comment on a document produced by a group in your class. This document might come from a procedure assignment or a proposal assignment, for example.

   Make your comments on a review and comment sheet, and negotiate with the authors until you reach a compromise on the concerns you all have.

3.   Author a document for review by your classmates that attempts a compromise position on an issue with serious implications for the rest of the class. For example, you might negotiate for some change in a class deadline or for suggestions on how the class should be taught next time.

ASSIGNMENTS

1.   Divide yourselves into groups to produce a document completely within your class. Your instructor will assign the document to you. You will need these groups: organizers, authors, reviewers, and final production people.

   When the project is completed, each group should author a memo to the instructor assessing the group's effectiveness and its success in collaborating with the other groups. If the project misses its deadline, the memos should try to assign responsibility for that failure.

2.   Using an agreed-on draft document, edit the document for fine points that need not have been attended to during the draft stage. Use proofreaders' marks assigned by your instructor. Know that any points you miss will come out of your paycheck at the rate of $1 per error. Will you take home any money that week?

SOLVING PROBLEMS

THROUGH

DOCUMENT DESIGN

Preview of the Chapter

The Importance of Presentation

Elements of Document Design
   White Space
   Text
   Graphics

Sample Professional Document Design

Creativity versus Convention in Document Design

Conclusions

September 23, 1991
7:30 A.M.
Kevin Ersting's Office
Office of International Education
Westminster College
Little Rock, Arkansas

Kevin Ersting arrived at his office in Tollan Hall just after 7:30 A.M. It was a little earlier than he usually got to the office, but today he was excited and a little nervous about proposing his idea for a newsletter for the overseas programs section of the Office of International Education (OIE) in this morning's staff meeting. The OIE was having a successful year, thanks in part to the new director, Feona Dalton, and her efforts to consolidate the office and its many tasks into a self-sufficient, cost-effective unit. This transition proved to be very timely; recent budget cuts had drastically reduced funding for several other similar offices on campus that relied almost entirely on the administration hierarchy for both leadership and funding. However, with most of the decisions on programs and finances being made in-house, new ideas and projects had to be carefully proposed and considered for both their cost effectiveness and practical use of people's time. Kevin, the Foreign Study Advisor for Overseas Programs, one of three major divisions of the office, knew that the newsletter's budget was going to come primarily from his section and he was very eager to use what limited funds existed carefully and productively.

The idea of a newsletter came as a result of last week's staff meeting, after the group began discussing various recruitment ideas that would possibly increase the numbers of students interested in overseas programs and increase the awareness and knowledge of the office throughout the campus. Kevin had posed the idea of a newsletter, but it was met with divided interest. Several of the staff members, specifically those from the International Students and Faculty section, felt that a newsletter would not be of much benefit and would have little effect on recruitment. Others, including Feona and Kristina Elwood, Kevin's assistant, felt that it was an idea worth looking into. So Kevin decided to do that.

Monday he began by considering what the audience would be interested in reading and what the OIE would want to emphasize in order to meet the predetermined goals of the production. Kevin found that the needs of the audience and the needs of the office were quite close. The audience, if interested in the happenings of the Office of International Education, would want to know about some of the various opportunities for students, faculty, and staff overseas and news on what many of the international students and visiting faculty were currently doing on the Westminster campus. In addition, information about the office itself—its various tasks, personnel, and subdivisions—would be of interest. As for the needs of the office, as Kevin had learned in last week's staff meeting, Feona wanted some projects that would aid in the campuswide advertisement of the office and its functions. For this purpose, a newsletter would be ideal.

However, as good as the idea was, Kevin knew that one of the first things people would ask was how much the newsletter would cost. As it was, the office was running on a tight budget and was not expecting any budget increases within the next two quarters. As a result, Kevin had to consider his expenses. How would he be able to produce an informative and appealing newsletter within a very limited budget? The answer to this came to him quickly—produce the newsletter in-house on the office computer system.

This answer, however, would pose other questions about the office's capability to produce such a document. It was here that Kevin hoped his experience in technical writing and especially in designing documents, would help convince Feona and others that they could produce a professional-looking, informative newsletter economically and efficiently in-house.

Kevin knew from courses and his experience in technical and professional writing that audience consideration and carefully written text were not all that a writer was able to do to accommodate and influence an audience effectively. He also knew the importance of page design and how a well-designed document can have positive rhetorical effects on its readers. Therefore, he collected some of the best examples of documents he had written and designed, or that he had helped others produce, and wrote short rhetorical analyses to show the staff how the documents appealed to their audiences and that they could be produced with existing facilities and limited funds.

After a week's preparation Kevin felt pretty confident that his office would soon be producing its first newsletter.

THE IMPORTANCE OF PRESENTATION

Presentation is a key element in many areas of the professional arena. In situations in which competition is very strong, the way a product is presented may determine its eventual success or failure. Presentation helps persuade consumers that the product does what it is supposed to do, and does it well. In the restaurant business, for example, taste is not the only consideration for a successful meal. A high priority is placed on how the meal looks on the plate. The same is true for the clothing and automobile industries, or any other industry that depends to a large degree on aesthetics to sell its products.

However, the power of presentation is not simply in the attempt to beautify an item for the sell alone. In Kevin's case, for instance, the design of his newsletter—how information is presented on the page—would also affect how well it informs its readers. Kevin's experience both as writer and reader showed him that he learned much more, and learned it more easily, from documents that had been carefully designed and laid out than from those that were simply dense blocks of words.

Many think, though, that designing pages of a document, considering how and where to lay out text and graphics, is a task best saved for the professional printer, designer, or graphic artist. This is true in part—graphic artists, designers, and printers make their livings by laying out, designing, and producing documents for clients or customers. Writers, however, also can use many of the same techniques that printers, designers, and graphic artists use, especially with the sophisticated capabilities of many personal computers. But even if those facilities are not available, writers still must keep in mind the visual impact of what they are writing—and must plan for it—if they are going to write effectively and per-suasively.

The documents professionals write can be designed in many different ways. Just by looking at all the written communication generated daily, especially that which comes from the professional sector, we find that those pieces that are the most effective are also the best designed. Visual enhancement and displays ranging from stunning, multicolored pamphlets and manuals with varieties of font styles and sizes and with graphics within the text, to simple and clean, well-planned typewritten pages of an in-house report give a positive impression of the organization and its professionalism.

A piece of technical or professional writing when first presented to the intended reader is very much like a new tool being introduced to the market. When presenting it to prospective buyers, the producers will present a well-polished product and will display it in a manner that best depicts its abilities and usefulness. In other words, the tool will be presented in as visually informative a setting as possible. The professional and technical document must do the same.

This need for a piece of writing that is as informative visually as it is textually may seem difficult, for there seem to be as many variations in design as there are documents to write. However, all designs, if they are successful, accomplish three basic tasks:

1. A successful design *creates an immediate positive impression* for the reader. A well-designed document demonstrates a writer's ability, and perhaps more important, a writer's commitment to producing a professional piece of writing.
2. A successful design *highlights the major topics* of the document. Effective and consistent use of headings, bullets, and other textual formatting, such as underlining and use of boldface or italic type, gives the reader a sense of order, hierarchy, and logic. In addition, well-designed highlighting facilitates both close, detailed reading and skimming for topical information.
3. A successful design *helps the reader read effectively*. A clear and effective document design helps readers follow a surer path from one element to another, making their reading faster and more efficient.

Thumbnail sketches allow the designer to compare a number of possible layouts side by side and experiment with such things as location of graphics, organization of text, and use of columns and margins. The designer will look for the layout that best suits the purpose intended by the document for the given audience. Consider the thumbnail sketches of documents in Figure 11.1. The designer has laid out two possibilities for presenting the content of the piece. The design of document A, with its use of subtitles, graphics, and tables, is perhaps more appropriate for a formal, technical report, whereas the design of document B, with its use of double columns and boxes highlighting portions of the text, may appear more appropriate for an article in a periodical. The point is that even without a hint of the actual content of the piece, the design of visual elements creates initial reactions and expectations in readers that designers should consider.

At this point it is important to remember that page design and graphic layout alone are not enough to sell a piece of writing. Written communication must say

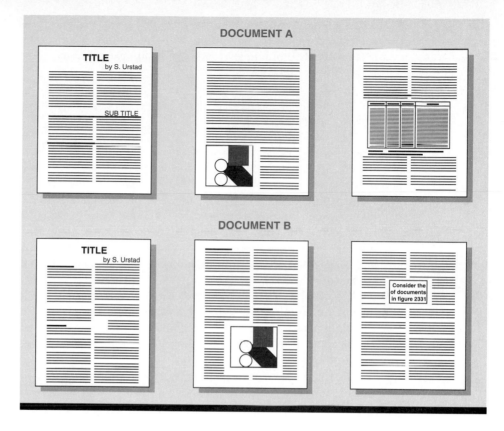

Figure 11.1
Thumbnail
sketches for a
report

what is intended clearly, concisely, and effectively, following considerations of tone, audience, and purpose discussed in earlier chapters. Only after these elements of the written message have been considered can designing the document begin. Font variations, multiple columns, and flashy graphics will be of little or no use if the text proper is weak and unconvincing. An effective design will make a well-written document better—but it won't make a poorly written document good. With this in mind we will now consider how the physical design of a document can enhance already effectively written communication.

ELEMENTS OF DOCUMENT DESIGN

Writers, when designing documents, look at individual pages differently from the way most readers look at them. They actively consider aspects of the text, margins, and graphics that most readers see only passively. To writers and designers, the page has three key elements:

1. White space—the portion of the page not written or drawn on
2. Text—written portion of the document, consisting of readings and bulk text
3. Graphics—all items that stand outside the text proper, such as graphs, illustrations, tables, and the like

These elements are the building blocks of a well-designed page, and they can be considered in order, beginning with the white space of the blank page and systematically building a structure of headings and titles, and finally filling in the rest with text and graphics.

White Space

The white space of the page seems at first thought to be of little concern to writers, since many see their job as filling up the space with words. However, this space, often referred to as the *negative space*, is the frame in which all other elements are placed. The pages of this book provide a good example of the use of white space. To begin, each page is framed with margins, balanced borders of white, on either side of the page. Margins are something often taken for granted, but with effective use of margins, a document can be more readable. Chapter titles and page numbers add information but still keep the overall frame intact and balanced.

Figure 11.2 illustrates differences that variations in margins can make in a document. From left to right, the pages come from an engineering textbook, a copyright contract, and a glossary of medical terms. In each case the margin format has become conventional for the particular form of writing, because it meets certain rhetorical needs.

Textbooks (format A) commonly use single-column text with standard margin widths. This format allows for a good deal of text to be printed per page, but without overcrowding. Thus the primary purposes of textbooks—to inform and to persuade—can be accomplished in a fairly confined space, still permitting other visual and organizational enhancements, such as headings and graphics, to be included. Most documents in technical and professional writing—reports, position papers, proposals—use similar margin formats.

Format B, that of the contract, also responds to rhetorical purposes. Contracts, the basis for legal commitment, are one of the most meticulously analyzed forms of documentation written and as such are often designed with wide left and right margins that condense the text into shorter lines. Often the lines are numbered in the margin, which allows specific portions of the contract to be identified easily by line number. The wide margins provide space for notes to be written.

Format C is typical of a glossary or dictionary, primarily a reference source, which provides definitions of various terms used in a particular field. Through the use of double columns and small margins, writers can provide maximum information in a minimum of space. Since readers use glossaries to gain specific information at specific times, and do not read them to understand and evaluate unifying expositions or arguments, glossaries are designed with maximum efficiency in mind. White space is kept to an absolute minimum.

In each of these cases writers have tried to accommodate the purpose and use of the document in the design. They have decided to use formats that have become conventional, because their use over time has proven effective. But it is necessary to remember that while conventions often dictate the common path to

Figure 11.2
Margin variations in document design

follow, they should be considered first for their rhetorical effectiveness, and only second for how widely they are used.

If we look again to the use of white space in this textbook, we see more complex uses: to set off headings, to indicate paragraph indents and spacing, to highlight lists, and to separate major sections of text. These separations are very important, for they help readers categorize each section, visualizing the closing of one section and the preparation for a new one. The space around a list of bulleted or numbered items allows the list to be highlighted outside the text without distracting the reader, or worse, breaking the continuity of the written text.

Text

As mentioned earlier, bulk text and headings, the written portions of a document, form the second design element. For the goals and purposes of this discussion, the text should be considered in its visual form, not for its content. Textual formatting, manipulating the look of the text and headings, will affect how the reader views the document. Through variations in typeface and choice of column format and line justification, both text and headings can establish positive impressions for the reader. First we will discuss the role of headings as indicators of the organization and hierarchy of topics. Then we will discuss the elements that affect how the headings and text look—typeface, columns, and justification.

Headings

Writers of longer documents with more than one component should use headings. Headings provide clear organization of major sections, subtopics, and common elements, and a quick view of the overall content of the document. They aid the reader in making transitions by signaling the end of one section and the start of another. Without the order established by headings, the reader may become confused or lost.

Good headings complete two tasks in a piece of writing. First, they encourage a close, precise reading of the text by providing tags or markers of various topics, both major and minor. Second, and in contrast to the first, headings allow a document to be skimmed. Often readers want to glance through an entire piece to see what information has been provided before beginning a closer reading, or they may want to concentrate on or return to a section, after having read the document, and don't want to have to reread the entire piece. Without headings that tag various sections, topics, and subtopics, a lengthy piece of writing has to be read almost in its entirety each time—a time-consuming, inefficient process for busy people.

Headings also act as a form of outlining for the text proper. Many writers use outlines when organizing thoughts for a piece of writing and creating a hierarchy for the subject and purpose of the document. Two of the common forms of outlining are illustrated in Figure 11.3. These two systems, an alphanumeric system (a combination of letters and numbers) and a decimal system, are identical in their purpose: to organize topics and thoughts in a logical hierarchy.

When the outline is expanded with addition of text, for short or long documents, the various divisions of the outline become headings, and each heading represents the sequential and subordinating order of the outline. In texts of ten pages or fewer the alphanumeric system is easy to follow, but for longer documents, writers often prefer the decimal system, because it keeps track of major and minor divisions. Finally, as is the case with this text, the alphanumeric or decimal notations are eliminated, and divisions are made clear with variations in type style and size to establish a consistent hierarchy of topics. Figure 11.4 shows two styles of headings. Style A uses varying styles and sizes of type to show the

Figure 11.3
Two systems of outlining

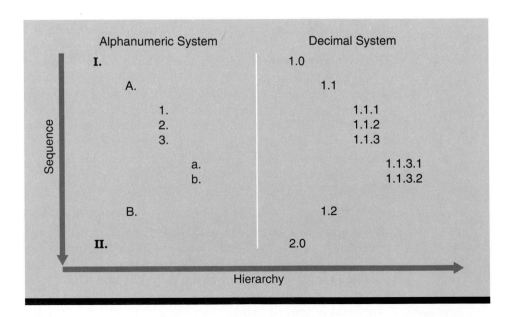

Figure 11.4
Sample heading systems

Heading Style A   Heading Style B

hierarchy of major and minor headings. Style B uses the decimal notation to accomplish the same purpose.

Because the primary purpose of a heading system is rhetorical, to help readers be informed, understand, and be able to make decisions, it is important that writers be consistent in their use of headings throughout the document. With consistent headings, writers control and manipulate the presentation of the text, which in turn sets up expectations in readers' minds. For example, if minor headings are *italicized* in the first section of the document, readers will expect that they be *italicized* in all following sections. Transitions from major headings (which may be **boldfaced**) to minor headings (which may be *italicized*) should remain the same from section to section. Once established, heading styles should be consistent throughout each portion of the document. Otherwise the effect will be to confuse readers, not to aid them.

With this thought, let us now move to the discussion of typefaces used for text and headings, column formats, and justification of text and headings.

Typefaces

The term *typeface* refers to *all* type of a single style; the term *font* refers to a set of type all of one style and *one size*. Many computer software programs offer the writer a wide selection of typefaces. Here, for example, are four different styles of type:

Typeface	Example
Chicago	The rain in Spain falls mainly in the plains.
Helvetica	The rain in Spain falls mainly in the plains.
Times	The rain in Spain falls mainly in the plains.
Serifa	The rain in Spain falls mainly in the plains.

Different typefaces affect readers differently. The Chicago typeface, for instance, seems bold and progressive, stating the message with strength and conviction. But

Helvetica is softer, quieter, more elegant perhaps. Writers using word processing software programs should choose typefaces that help present the message and an image in keeping with the purpose of the document they are writing. But a word of caution: changing fonts frequently or using too many of them can be distracting; readers begin to pay more attention to the variety and changes in the text than they do to the content. Font styles should be used to enhance the purpose and tone of the document; they should not become items of interest in themselves.

All typefaces can be categorized into two types: *serif* and *sans serif*. Serif typefaces are those with small hook strokes, called *serifs*, extending off from the character, as illustrated in Figure 11.5.

Many typesetting manuals will recommend serif typefaces for block text, because they supposedly are more readable and pleasing to the eye. Serifs link characters together well, allowing the eye to proceed easily word by word on a line of print. Thus, large portions of bulk text are more readable in serif typefaces.

However, sans serif typefaces can also be used effectively. They may be used for headings and figure legends to help highlight these portions through their contrast with the text proper. Sans serif typefaces are also commonly used for résumés and manual graphics because of their clean design and ability to distinguish white space so effectively.

Columns

Bulk text can be laid out on the page in several formats: single-column, multi-column, and note-marginal (see Figure 11.6). Single-column format, also referred to as *block text* layout, is the common layout for most memos, reports, textbooks, and proposals; multicolumn formats are often the norm for pamphlets, brochures, and articles intended for general audiences. Like different typefaces, different column formats serve specific rhetorical strategies. Single-column text usually appeals to a specific reader or group of readers who generally share a common knowledge of the topic being discussed. And quite often, the level of discussion and technicality is high and complex. The readers of such a document, be it a memorandum written to a supervisor documenting a problem with employee relations or a report on a new method of gene splicing being prepared for a technical oversight committee, will be better able to read sentences of greater length and complexity in a single-column format than they would if the same were presented in a multicolumn format.

Figure 11.5
Serif versus sans serif typefaces

Figure 11.6
*Typical column
formats*

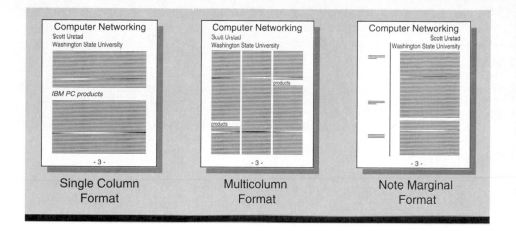

Single Column Format

Multicolumn Format

Note Marginal Format

For example, a report on the video surveillance system for a nuclear facility is written specifically for the engineers and technicians who will be using the system. Given the equally high technical level of the audience, the writer will discuss the system's installation and application in an appropriately high technical level, and would most likely format the text in single columns. Should, however, this same report be rewritten to appear as an article in *Scientific American*, which caters to a knowledgeable but more diverse audience, the tone of the article would need to be changed and the technicality reduced to address adequately this new group of readers. As a result, this text may be placed in a multicolumn format, as *Scientific American* features, using shorter paragraphs with simplified information, to appeal to a more general level of readership. In each of these writing situations, the format reflects primary rhetorical considerations: what is the purpose of this document and who will be reading it?

The third format, note-marginal, is a combination of both single- and multi-column formats. The document is laid out in a disproportional two-column format with the smaller of the two columns placed either to the right or left of the larger column. The smaller column is for writers' or readers' editorial commentary or notes on the text, or for extending graphics beyond the text. Manuals, handbooks, and textbooks are often produced in this way. In fact, Chapter 2 of this text demonstrates the use of a note-marginal format in the presentation of Mary Ann Cox's memos.

Justification

Designers of a document should also consider justification of the text. *Justification* refers to the alignment of text along one or both margins (see Figure 11.7). Generally, block text is justified to the left, with a ragged alignment on the right margin, or to the right and left (sometimes referred to as *full justification*) with both left and right margins evenly aligned. The choice is mostly aesthetic, but some writers believe that full justification produces cleaner, more professional-looking documents.

Figure 11.7
*Text alignment
formats*

But a note of caution: Documents that are professionally printed, or that are produced on advanced word processing systems, use a pictal-proportional system that equally divides the spaces between all words and all letters in the line being justified to avoid large gaps in the text. Less advanced word processing programs often divide the spaces proportionally between the words alone, creating noticeable gaps in the text:

```
Although the technology existed,  microprocessing was   often
ignored as a viable method of development.  However, with the
introduction of digital circuitry, microprocessing  has become
```

The inconsistent spacing between words is distracting and makes the lines difficult to read, which obviously detracts from the most important element of the document—its content.

Just a word on right justification: Although block text usually is not justified to the right, often headings are, to highlight and to vary the format of the text. But as is true of all formatting techniques, right justification should be used consistently, according to the hierarchy the writer wants and needs to establish.

Graphics

Graphics are used to enhance the explanation of data for readers. In technical and professional writing, graphics seldom, if ever, are used purely for the purposes of embellishment or aesthetic appeal. They are needed to simplify complex design descriptions, to highlight and clarify trends and relationships found in numerical data, and to clarify complicated procedures or processes. Graphics play an important role in the success of technical and professional writing and must be used carefully if they are to be effective.

Knowing what a graphic is and knowing why it should be used are not necessarily the same thing; deciding when and where to use graphics within a document depends on a number of considerations. Keep in mind the following rules of thumb for the use of graphics:

- Place graphics immediately after (or as close as possible to) their textual reference.
- Consider the technical level of your audience carefully.
- Choose the best type of graphic for the situation.

When large graphics or numerous graphics are being used in a particular document, placement is not always an easy task. Smaller graphics may be incorporated directly into or following the paragraph in which they are referenced. Larger graphics, of a half or full page, should appear on the facing or following page. In any case, it is important to preface the graphic with text to prepare readers for its appearance and to establish its purpose. If readers turn the page of a document to find a full-page graphic diagram of the electrical wiring of a cooling system, before the text has begun discussing it, they will certainly not be prepared and more than likely will be confused.

Just as the text must meet the needs and expectations of an audience, so must the graphics. Highly technical diagrams and charts that a group of engineers may understand very clearly will have little success with a more general lay reader. This is not to say that graphics are good only for one particular audience. Almost all audiences can benefit from graphics as long as the designer chooses a type appropriate for the audience in question. Technicians or specialists may be very interested in the specifics of a particular system and perhaps would expect a table of values in the report. A group of managers, on the other hand, may expect and understand better more vivid representations of essentially the same data in the form of a graph or a pie chart. In either case, the use of graphics needs to be considered carefully to meet the needs and expectations of the intended audience.

It is not by coincidence that so many different kinds of graphics are used. Tables, bar graphs, illustrations, photographs, and the like all serve tasks specific to their forms and all have strengths and weaknesses. Writers, when choosing a graphic to depict and explain data, must decide which type will be most effective for their purpose and most appropriate for the intended audience. The seven most commonly used forms are discussed below. Any other types are most often variations or spin-offs of these basic seven.

Displaced Text

Displaced text often is not thought of as a graphic, but when considering the rhetorical task of any graphic—to enhance or make clearer the information expressed through the text—displaced text becomes very much a graphic element of a piece of writing. Displaced text can be any text that is related to, but not directly incorporated into, the main text. Such forms as highlighting bullets, standout quotes or marginalia, and writers' editorial notes all act as graphics and must be considered carefully for use. Figure 11.8 shows a common way of displacing text.

Displaced text can highlight specific points that the author wants to emphasize. Bullets or numbers emphasize points made within the discussion by removing them from the density of the main text. Throughout this text, for example, we have used bullets and numbers to set off certain pieces of information we want readers to remember or pay special attention to. In addition, displaced text works much like headings by working with the hierarchy to allow the reader to skim a section for the major points. *Stand-out quotes* are found often in journals, magazines and newsletters to highlight specific statements. Unlike bullets and numbers, they

Figure 11.8
Displaced text

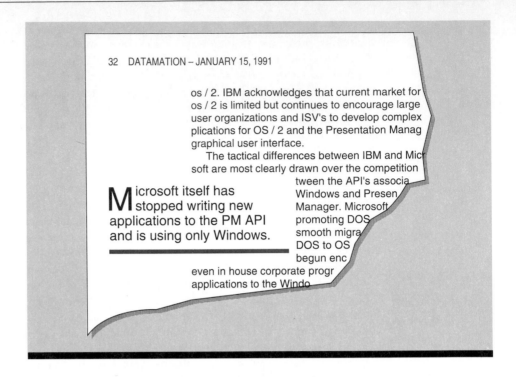

act as a sort of advertisement for what is contained in the piece as a whole. Like all graphics, stand-outs should appear after they are used in the text proper.

A final note to remember: too much displaced text throughout a piece of writing will distract the reader from the general text. Choose what to displace and where it should go carefully, for the reader will quickly know when text is being highlighted for purely aesthetic reasons, rather than for specific rhetorical and informative purposes.

Tables

Tables are used to list values of at least two variables (perhaps amount of money [variable 1] spent over fixed intervals of time [variable 2]) in rows and columns (or on x and y axes), organized with headings. A table requires at least two variables to be considered a table; otherwise it is a list. Figure 11.9 shows the table Leah Feldstein used to quantify information on EDUCARE's clientele for her oral presentation.

Writers use tables as organizing devices to display and compare statistical data and to make the discussion of the data easier to follow. If writers were to attempt to lay out and discuss the values corresponding to multiple variables in a block of text, their readers could get irretrievably lost. But by organizing the variables and values in a confined, tabular form, writers are then free to discuss only the highlights of the data in the text, permitting readers to concentrate on those

Figure 11.9
Sample table

	Mean Age	Sex		% Return	% Complete
EDUCARE CLIENT PROFILES		% M	% F		
1987 – 88	15.4	79%	21%	n.a.	11%
1988 – 89	14.8	61%	39%	57%	21%
1989 – 90	12.1	74%	26%	36%	34%
Average	14.1	71.3%	28.7%	46.5%	22%

highlights, and then to consider the rest of the data as presented in the table in their own time, and as they see fit.

Tables are effective for displaying absolute values and precise comparisons of discrete items, but are less useful if the purpose is to show relationships proportionally or in trends.

One final note: tables are always called *tables*, and if there are several, they are labeled sequentially, Table 1., Table 2., Table 3., and so forth. All other graphics are called *figures*, no matter what type they are, and are also labeled sequentially.

Pie Charts

Pie charts (or pie diagrams) are most commonly used to show proportional comparisons of the parts of a whole population or field by percentage, as is illustrated in Figure 11.10.

If writers want to highlight visually two or three main elements as they relate proportionally to the whole, such as time spent on sick leave or annual leaves or educational workshops, pie charts work well. However, they do not display absolute values effectively unless the value is added as a label to its respective piece of the pie. Also, if writers want to point out differences between two relatively similar percentages (say the difference between 7 percent and 9 percent), pie charts, because they are not precise enough, do not show these differences well. Finally, a pie chart will not work well if the pie is divided into two many "slices," making it hard for the reader to see the relationships between a specific part and the whole or other parts.

Bar Graphs

Like pie charts, bar graphs present data often found in tables in a more accessible and vivid way. But as Figure 11.11 illustrates, bar graphs, unlike pie charts, can

Figure 11.10
Sample pie chart

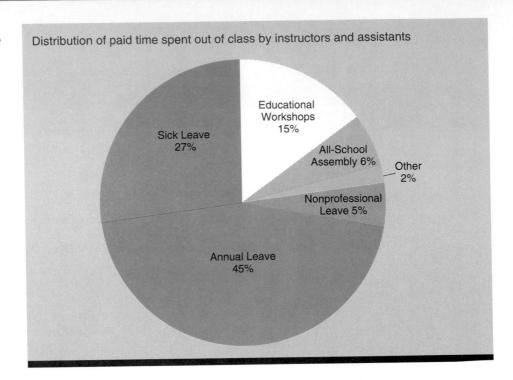

Distribution of paid time spent out of class by instructors and assistants

display more graphically both discrete quantities (frequency of signal) and trends (general increases) over time.

In addition, bar graphs can depict other elements or variables. Figure 11.11, for example, is actually a *stack graph*, which also shows proportional relationships of parts to the whole, as pie charts do. Differences in signal frequency are compared

Figure 11.11
Sample bar graph

Figure 11.12
Sample line graph

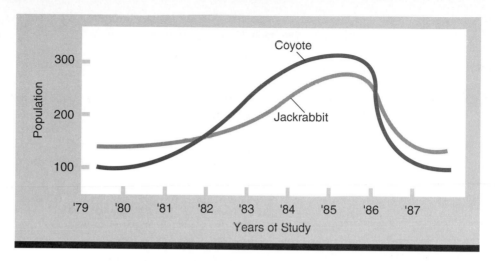

over time, but the graph also illustrates (or *stacks*) the proportional differences between signal A and signal B at each measured point in time.

Line Graphs

Line graphs are excellent for showing trends, and two or three elements can be compared effectively. The line graph in Figure 11.12 compares population histories of coyotes and jackrabbits more immediately and effectively than separate tables of the same figures would. But in situations where more than two or three elements are being compared, bar graphs or multiple graphs may be better.

The primary weakness in line graphs is the inability to depict proportions or percentages of a whole. However, by using an *area format*, illustrated in Figure 11.13, proportions are captured graphically. Readers can see both the total number

Figure 11.13
Sample line graph using an area format

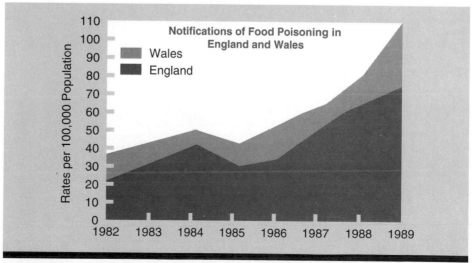

of notifications of food poisoning in England and Wales and how the numbers of notifications in each place compare to the whole over time.

Photographs

Photographs, such as the one in Figure 11.14, can be used when accuracy is important or when drawings or illustrations cannot capture the fine detail the writer is discussing. However, using photographs effectively can be difficult. Unlike drawings or illustrations, photographs cannot be embellished easily without specific placement of the camera, special lighting, or arrangement of the object or scene.

Nonetheless, if all these factors can be attended to, photographs lend a very impressive and often dramatic quality to a document. As with any other graphic, it is important to consider the audience. Before using a photograph, decide whether the audience is truly in need of such specific representation.

Illustrations and Drawings

In many technical areas, drawings and illustrations are the most commonly used form of visual description of parts, processes, and systems. Unlike photographs, drawings allow the writer more freedom to highlight specific aspects of the item in

Figure 11.14
Sample photograph

Figure 11.15
Sample drawing

question. Drawings are best for describing parts of a piece of equipment or showing mechanisms or processes inside a unit that a photograph would not be able to capture, as shown in Figure 11.15. It was not the writer's intention to sketch a perfect still life of a mass spectrometer, but to illustrate the process of decomposition taking place within the apparatus and to label the parts that a reader needs to know to understand the process.

Graphics, when used with careful consideration, play an important rhetorical role in technical and professional writing. Carefully considering the right graphic helps present technical or complex data, processes, systems, and descriptions clearly and descriptively. The right graphic will save the writer explanation, will prevent confusion, and will leave a favorable impression on the reader.

SAMPLE PROFESSIONAL DOCUMENT DESIGN

After a rather heated debate over the usefulness of a newsletter for the Office of International Education, Kevin had successfully convinced the staff of the benefits such a publication could have. From that point the meeting became quite productive. Jessica Haysmith, Assistant Director for International Students and Faculty, recommended something that Kevin hadn't considered. In addition to reporting the general happenings of the office, each of the three sections—Overseas Programs, International Students and Faculty, and the Intensive English Language Center—should provide an article addressing a current issue or concern in the respective areas. She also suggested that the newsletter be distributed bimonthly to save on production costs.

Kevin thought that these were good additions to his initial proposal. It could be excellent publicity for his Overseas Programs section, while allowing each member of the staff to participate in writing and producing the newsletter. In addition, Kristina Elwood, Kevin's assistant, reminded him that if the newsletter proved successful, they could consider applying for grant money to distribute it to alumni supporters and other international education programs nationally.

On Saturday afternoon Kevin found himself in the position he wanted to be in, but was much aware of the large task before him. He had finished writing the article for the Overseas Programs section, a profile of the newly established Russian programs and agreements that Westminster and the OIE had worked very hard to establish, and he had received the articles from the other two sections of the office as well. With the exception of the article that Feona would write as Acting Director, Kevin was ready to begin designing the newsletter.

Kevin's first step was to draw up a set of thumbnail sketches of various design ideas for the newsletter. Several of the figures in this chapter, such as Figures 11.1, 11.2, and 11.6, are thumbnail sketches. By drawing several thumbnails of the first page, Kevin would be able to find a general format that he would like to see the entire newsletter follow. Figure 11.16 shows Kevin's sketches.

Having produced thumbnails for six possible front pages, Kevin began to consider the image that the staff, during Thursday's meeting, had wanted to project. They wanted a professional-looking document that both faculty and students could read easily. Kevin pondered his choices before choosing the last sketch in the first row—a four-column layout with a large graphic in the center of the page. This was a practical design that would allow readers to browse through a number of article titles and subtitles to find topics of specific interest. More important, since the primary audience would be readers who were interested in international education, but who had diverse levels of knowledge and expertise, the tone and style of the articles he and his peers had written were appropriate for a general, educated audience and were perfect for a multicolumn format.

Kevin also knew that the purpose and image of the newsletter would be enhanced by choosing the front-page article carefully. The title of that article, coupled with the masthead and a strong graphic, should give readers an immediate understanding of the kind of document this was intended to be.

From here, Kevin thought, the task would be a little easier. He decided to make all remaining pages of the document follow a similar format. In choosing the headings, Kevin wanted to create a hierarchy both within each of the feature articles and between the articles and other special interest sections. He wanted to have a graphic on each of the inside pages, but he knew not to force graphics into text when they were not needed. There was time enough for including graphics sensibly. The topics for future articles that he and other members had presented in Thursday's staff meeting were all interesting and relevant, several of which he

Figure 11.16
Thumbnail sketches of OIE newsletter

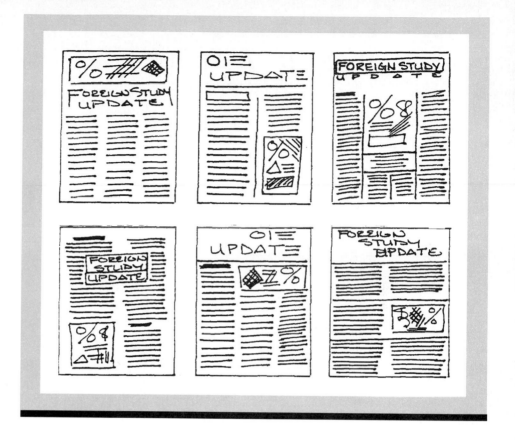

knew immediately would be complex and require a graphic of some kind to help explain the ideas to readers.

Kevin chose to open the newsletter with his article about the new Russian programs. He knew he would get a ribbing from the others for choosing his article to appear on the front page, but the news was exciting and fit in well with current affairs. In addition, a photograph of Moscow on the front page would be eye-catching and appropriate for a newsletter coming from the Office of International Education.

With his general page layout complete, Kevin began developing the heading sequence for the newsletter by choosing the typefaces and deciding on the locations for the headings. Remembering what he had learned from past reports he had written, and the successes and failures that resulted, he decided to lay out a heading sequence on a separate page to see whether it worked well. For a newsletter, like many reports, he liked using typeface variations rather than an alpha numeric outline to organize the hierarchy of the piece. Large sans serif fonts would make for clear and readable titles and major headings. The text itself would be written in a serif font because it is easier to read. By lining up his choices in vertical order, Kevin could see how well they were separated from others.

423

Newsletter title

Foreign Study
U P D A T E

Major article heading — **OIE Takes Part in Glasnost**

Minor article heading — ***From the Director's Desk***

Subheadings — Program Deadlines
Language Requirements

Once Kevin was happy with his choice for headings, it was time to build a template (a standard design or layout that can be reproduced whenever necessary) on his computer from the thumbnail he chose and incorporate the other articles into it. The office was producing the document on the office computer system, and the other writers had all written their pieces on the same system, so Kevin had only to insert the documents into his template and begin proofing to be sure all textual references preceded the respective graphics, and that the layout of each article was consistent with the previous one. Kevin was nearly finished.

Kevin's template (see Figure 11.17) shows how he wanted the title and organization to be displayed and where his graphic was to be placed both to make the text easier to understand and to encourage the reader to continue. In addition, the four-column design allows the reader to preview the title and subheadings before beginning a close reading.

CREATIVITY VERSUS CONVENTION IN DOCUMENT DESIGN

A balance between creativity and convention is important to discuss at this point. Technical and professional documents must compete with others for the attention of their readers. As a result, writers may be tempted to embellish their writing visually for purely competitive reasons. But by so doing, they may go beyond the bounds of convention and forget that the primary purposes of technical and professional writing are to inform, perhaps to persuade, but above all to be useful to readers. New and creative document designs can be productive pieces of written communication as long as they continue to serve the rhetorical needs the documents require.

Figure 11.17
Kevin Ersting's template for OIE newsletter

CONCLUSIONS

With thoughtful visual design, writers can positively influence their readers' acceptance and use of any document. But writers don't have to have a computer on their desks to get this done. All they need is a clear idea of what makes writing easier and more enjoyable to read; they need ultimately to make the writing useful. Intelligent notions of formatting and the use of graphics can accomplish that goal.

When two documents present information of equal quality and usefulness, the one with the more professional appearance and effective use of design will often be viewed as the better of the two. However, writers must remember that although a good design can make a good document better, it cannot make a bad document good.

EXERCISE

With the help of your instructor, form small groups according to major fields of study. As a committee, find three different documents written for readers in your field of study: perhaps a newsletter for alumni, an announcement of a change in your major's curriculum, and an article from a professional journal reporting on research. Analyze the physical design of the documents based on the principles and techniques of document design discussed in this chapter. Decide how well the designs work depending on the purposes for which the documents were written. Write a short committee report for your classmates that lays out your analysis.

ASSIGNMENT

TERM PROJECT OPTION

Following an outline you have written of the contents of the results (product) of your term research, write a plan for the physical design of your project. Be specific about how the design will appeal to your intended readers and will serve the purposes for which you are writing the document.

SOLVING PROBLEMS

THROUGH ORAL

PRESENTATIONS

Preview of the Chapter

The Naturalness of Oral Communication
  Practical Limitations Resulting from the Setting

Rhetorical Analysis of an Oral Presentation
  Purpose
  Audience
  Context
  Ethical Stance

Essential Elements in the Preparation of an Oral Presentation
  Knowing the Material
  Knowing What Is Important to Discuss
  Planning the Physical Aspects of the Presentation
  Practicing

Planning the Text for an Oral Presentation
  The Introduction (or the Appetizer)
  The Body (or the Main Course)
  The Conclusion (or the Dessert)

The Mechanics of Effective Public Speaking
  Relax
  Speak Loudly Enough to Be Heard
  Maintain Eye Contact with the Audience
  Keep the Body Poised and Vibrant
  Talk—Don't Read
  Don't Take the "Sleepers" Personally

Tips for Giving Oral Presentations to Specific Groups
  Committees
  Civic or Special Interest Groups
  Boards of Directors

Conclusions

October 12, 1990
9:30 A.M.
EDUCARE, Inc.
1200 Stone Way, Suite 500
Seattle, Washington

Leah Feldstein returned to her office at a markedly slow pace. She had just come out of a meeting with EDUCARE's director, John Fiske, who had let her in on some very unsettling news. He confirmed the rumors that had been flying around that the U.S. Department of Education was planning to cut its funding to drug education and rehabilitation programs, and that an assessment team was on its way to the West Coast to determine which programs in the major cities should be cut or saved. If EDUCARE were cut, that could mean a loss of up to 25 percent of its funding. That, coupled with other likely cuts from the U.S. Department of Health and Human Services and the state of Washington, would effectively wipe out EDUCARE's funding. All that would be left would be money from private foundations and private donations, which currently accounted for only 23 percent of the budget.

The long-term future looked pretty bleak but was still unknown. The immediate future, on the other hand, was very clearly known, and its bleakness was beside the point. EDUCARE would have to wage an all-out effort to convince the government that it was a program that needed to be saved. And Leah's part in that effort, she found out today, would start with an oral presentation to the assessment team coming out from Washington. As Director of Client Relations, Leah had responsibility for the general direction of the drug education program in the public schools, outreach work to identify adolescents who are using drugs and who would benefit from specific education and rehabilitation, and supervision of other social workers who act as counselors of adolescents inside and outside the public schools. John Fiske wanted her to present to the team, due to arrive for their initial assessment on October 25, the strongest achievements the program had made in client relations, especially with regard to education. The rehabilitation element of the program would have to wait for now, since the threat of cuts came immediately from the Department of Education. In addition, Fiske wanted Leah to lay out her plans for her presentation in a meeting on Wednesday, October 17, with Fiske and the budget director, who also had to present his story to the assessment team.

Leah was no stranger to oral presentations. In the 3 years she had worked for EDUCARE, she had given eight or ten presentations to PTAs, to teachers for in-service training, and to the boards of directors of private foundations and of the United Way. But she had never talked formally to members of the government's bureaucracy, and furthermore, she had never had to talk in a way that could determine whether EDUCARE and she, as its Director of Client Relations, would survive.

Leah's problem was clearly defined, but the specifics of how she would appeal to the assessment team were yet to be determined. She knew, as she sat thinking at her desk, that she probably couldn't take a real lunch break today, or maybe for some days to come.

THE NATURALNESS OF ORAL COMMUNICATION

Every time Leah was asked to give an oral presentation, she was reminded of her college days and of a technical writing teacher who started off his course with a short lecture on the unnaturalness of writing. He pointed out that, historically, human activity relied on a much older oral tradition, and that written communication is a relatively recent phenomenon, arising independently in different civilizations only about 6,000 years ago. He would point to the oral art of poets like Homer, whose *Iliad* and *Odyssey* were strictly oral accounts of the glories and tragedies of the Greeks, written in the forms known today only after centuries of oral presentation passed on regularly from one generation to another. He would talk also of the great Greek and Roman orators, who through oral language attempted to sway their fellow citizens to adopt some course of action for the betterment and preservation of the state.

He would also point to what is known of human development to make his case. Children master oral language long before they master (and *master* is the key word here) written language. By the age of five, children have learned and essentially mastered the intricacies of their grammars, and can communicate most of what needs to be communicated to get along. But it's not until years later that they master writing. And some, he was quick to note, never learn anything but the basics of writing their names. He would cap it off by reminding his students that most of the world's peoples are still nonliterate, and that the activities of their lives are carried on only through oral means.

Leah smiled in remembering that her teacher's purpose in mentioning all of this was to establish that writing wasn't a "natural" act and that they shouldn't feel bad about not being able to master it right away. Further, he wanted to suggest that since oral communication is more natural, the presentations his students would have to give at the end of the semester would be easier to produce than any of the corresponding tasks in writing. That an oral presentation would be easier than a written one she knew, even at the time, couldn't be true on the face of it, but it wasn't until later that she would fully understand how much that was stretching the truth.

Practical Limitations Resulting from the Setting

Leah knew from her experience in college when she gave her first oral presentation and from her experience in speaking before groups since then that oral communication may be more natural in the general scheme of things, but it's not much easier to produce in formal settings than writing is. She still had to run through the steps of technical problem solving (definition, research, analysis, resolution and synthesis, and implementation) and of rhetorical problem solving (evaluating purpose, audience, context, and ethical stance). Leah had realized, with the help of her teacher, the practical ways in which oral communication is limited as a natural act:

- *As the number of listeners increases, the self-consciousness of the speaker increases.* These kinds of questions, for instance, come to mind: How do I look and sound? Am I making sense and covering the points that need to be covered? Do I have enough time to say what I need to say? Or, perhaps, am I taking up too much time? Some self-consciousness on the speaker's part is good, even necessary, if the speaker is to speak effectively. But too much self-consciousness translates into visible nervousness, which if not controlled, becomes distracting for both speaker and audience.

- *As the size of the audience increases, the sense of intimacy between speaker and audience can decrease.* This situation can create psychological distance between speaker and audience, which in turn can cause awkwardness on both parts. But a loss of intimacy is not inevitable. In fact, the successful, effective speaker creates intimacy even in large groups. Thus after a good campaign speech a politician can say, "I really had that crowd with me."

- *The physical surroundings can cause problems.* The room may be too big or too small, too hot or too cold, too light or too dark. The acoustics of the room or the quality and condition of the audio equipment may make it difficult for a speaker be heard easily. All these factors can create interference (what communication specialists call *noise*) between speaker and audience. And as the noise increases, the clarity and understanding of the message the speaker wants to send decrease.

As Leah reviewed all the things she had learned about oral presentations, she kept coming back to this notion of noise, which for her was a good metaphor for the things that were apt to disrupt her efforts at conveying information effectively. All kinds of factors contributed to noise. They could be the physical or psychological elements, but in her experience they mostly had to do with her preparation and all that that implies. Leah remembered that the times she had done well in speaking before a group, she also had prepared well. Likewise, she remembered the times with little preparation, and how unsuccessful, sometimes bordering on the miserable, they were. As is true of most of us, Leah remembered the bad times more vividly than she remembered the good.

On this occasion Leah could not afford a bad presentation. Too much was riding on it—the future of the agency and her own job were clearly at stake—and she would simply have to do the very best job she could. So she began the usual process of preparing her presentation, making sure that every step was as thoroughly thought through and as accomplished as possible.

 ## RHETORICAL ANALYSIS OF AN ORAL PRESENTATION

As with everything she wrote, Leah knew that beyond defining the problem, which she and John Fiske already had been able to do fairly clearly, she would have to analyze the rhetorical aspects of the situation for her oral presentation. That meant deciding four things (all of which have been discussed in Chapter 3 and elsewhere): purpose, audience, context, and ethical stance.

Purpose

In her analysis of purpose Leah first asked herself, What purpose does my audience have for listening to me and what purpose do I have for giving the presentation? Since Leah knew the purpose of the audience's visit, she also knew that its purpose for listening and hers for presenting must coincide in some way. But she needed to sketch out the purposes consciously to make sure that she emphasized in her presentation those elements that needed emphasis.

Leah knew that the main purpose of the visit was for the team to assess the effectiveness of EDUCARE's education program in light of its costs. So like it or not, Leah knew the team would be looking keenly for weaknesses, anything it could recommend for cutting. Like any other program, EDUCARE's had its weaknesses. The most troubling had to do with the outreach part of the program. In outreach, social workers acted as counselors to adolescents whom they had identified as drug users, and who would benefit from specific education and rehabilitation outside of school. The idea was that students generally would be more willing to meet counselors outside of school, rather than in school where they would be singled out for special attention, no doubt an embarrassing situation for many.

The trouble lay in the numbers. Although Leah didn't have the figures immediately at hand, she knew that the ratio of counselors to clients was a bit too favorable from the government's point of view. Although she and her staff knew that keeping the ratio low was good, that better work could be done when counselors had fewer clients, she also knew that the Department of Education would want to see how widely EDUCARE had been able to broadcast its efforts. This was in an area, Leah further knew, where the two interests would never completely coincide, the one more concerned with the quality of the work being done, the other with costs. For Leah, the ideal was to hire more counselors so that more clients could be served, and served well. The government's ideal was to serve the most clients possible at the least cost. For better or for worse, Leah knew that those working for the government, no matter what they personally thought the ideal was, would be looking for inefficiencies in EDUCARE's counselor-client ratio.

As she prepared her presentation, Leah would have to research the figures and analyze them, and then try to make the best impression possible—put the best face on it—within the limits of time. Her specific goal would be to show that what the team might perceive as weaknesses were really strengths in some ways, and that increasing numbers could be served without significant budget increases.

Her general goal would be to show that the program as a whole was working both within and outside the schools, that it had the potential to keep working, perhaps even more effectively, and that it should be fully funded for these reasons.

The next question Leah asked herself was, What should my audience do after listening to my presentation? Closely related to the question of basic purpose, this question looks forward to what will happen as a result of the presentation. This is something speakers (and of course writers) need to think about, since the purposes for speaking (and writing) should prepare an audience in ways that it had not been prepared before. This is true even if immediate decisions or actions are not expected from the audience, even if initially the only purpose for the presentation is simply to inform.

Leah had quite specific ideas about what her audience should do. She wanted the team to decide that EDUCARE's program was working well, that it was working as efficiently as any program of its kind could work, and that it should be maintained at full funding levels. (Actually, she wanted the team to decide that the program should get increased funding, but she knew that that wasn't going to happen, given the specific purpose the team had for visiting.) In many cases, the answer to the questions of basic purpose and the question of what the audience should do are closely related. However, it is still a good idea to address the second question. Doing so helps add that little bit of clarity and persuasive emphasis to the speaker's presentation, which may make the difference between ultimate success or failure of the presentation.

Audience

For Leah, answering the next question was an easy task. Who will be listening to me and evaluating my presentation? In this particular case Leah could find out specifically who the people on the team would be: their names, positions and areas of responsibility, length of employment, and so forth. From other records she could find out their educational backgrounds, where they had gone to school, for how long, and what degrees they had received. All this information would help Leah determine their likely prejudices, their leanings, their ways of thinking, and the ways that she might appeal to them.

As she had predicted, she was able to come up with some interesting particulars. She found out that there were to be three on the assessment team coming out from Washington—two men and a woman. They all were program officers at the national level, which meant they were responsible for reviewing the drug education programs that had been approved and funded by the Department of Education for at least the past year. She learned also that all had been hired under the Reagan administration and had been retained by the Bush administration without interruption, so they all had had reasonably long experience and would know the ins and outs of funded programs such as EDUCARE's.

Leah was pleased to discover that she had met one of the team—Mary Stamper—at a meeting in Washington of urban program directors she attended with John Fiske over a year ago in September. She and Mary had gotten along well, both having similar educational backgrounds and professional interests. Mary struck her as bright, reasonable, and committed to similar goals as hers—furthering innovative and effective drug education programs at local levels through grass roots efforts.

The assessment team from Washington would be joined in Seattle by the regional director of the Department of Education and his assistant, a woman, who were in charge of following the progress of funded programs regionally. Unfortunately, although Leah knew their names and had met them on several occasions, she did not know them well. They worked out of the regional office in San Francisco, and the problems and programs in California seemed to demand most of their attention. They got to Seattle only occasionally, and then only for brief stays.

Leah's check on the educational backgrounds of the five turned up some common ground. The team from Washington all had gone to medium to large state universities, two in the east, one in the midwest. The two regional people had gone to schools—also state institutions—in the west. All held master's degrees in education, social work, or sociology. Four had been secondary school teachers in public schools for up to 5 years before working for the government. Everyone was between the ages of thirty-one and forty-five.

Given this information Leah could sketch out a fairly close and useful profile of the members of her audience. They were young to middle aged, educated, experienced both in teaching and in government work, and likely to be conservative, but not reactionary, given whom they were presently working for and the kind of work they did.

In all, Leah could say with some confidence that they wouldn't be a hostile audience. But since they were coming to Seattle for a very specific purpose—to determine whether EDUCARE should continue to get government funding—she knew, too, that they wouldn't be too easy to convince. Her audience most likely would be courteous and attentive, but also thoughtful, careful, and undoubtedly probing. The one idea she thought would unite them was the need for drug education programs, but ones that could continue to operate effectively in times of budgetary restraint.

Although Leah was able to draw a rather detailed audience profile in this case, she knew that specifics like these are not always possible to collect. In the past she had had to go on much more general analyses for some of her oral presentations. The audiences were larger, came from more diverse backgrounds, and although apparently drawn together on common ground, often based their decisions on distinctly different thinking.

She remembered, in fact, the talks she used to give at the beginning of EDUCARE's work in the schools to large groups made up of school board members, administrators, teachers, and parents. Although everyone was there ostensibly to learn about what might be done to educate schoolchildren about drug use and abuse, many came with different ideas of how that might be done effectively, and some came with a well-developed skepticism that it could be done at all. In some cases the range of ideas and attitudes went from conservative approaches to education that viewed innovations in the classroom suspiciously to distinctly liberal positions that embraced, often uncritically, almost any innovation in education. Then there were those who held the position that problems with drugs, like problems with early sexual activity, are not rightfully the business of schools, that they are moral problems that only the home and the church should deal with.

Audiences like these are difficult, although not impossible, to analyze. Leah had had to do it in the past, and she knew there would be times in the future when she would have to do it again. She was simply glad that this wasn't one of those times.

Finally Leah wanted to be realistic about the whole subject of audience. While this presentation would be the highlight of her day, she was fairly sure it would not be the highlight of her audience's day. Chances were good that her audience would listen as carefully as possible, but would not bring a high level of intensity to that task. Leah could remember being on the listening end of a presentation when she attended professional conferences. She could calmly and coolly focus on the presentation's content while the presenter worked. It was helpful to recall this lack of intensity the audience feels, which is in contrast to the intensity and self-consciousness felt by the speaker. Speakers perhaps can feel less nervous if they remember they are not the center of the audience's universe. All eyes may be focused on the speaker, but the minds behind the eyes are sometimes thinking about other things, like the room temperature, the person sitting in the next chair, the dessert served at the luncheon, the lines at the restroom. Audiences often have short attention spans; this fact is both a blessing and a curse for the speaker.

Context

Leah's analysis of the context of her presentation focused on the considerations of place rather than those of time. The issue is not time, because the team controls the timetable for decision making. Leah need only be ready when she is scheduled. But the considerations of place, specifically the political constraints, must be a vital part of Leah's analysis. She knew that the context of this presentation ushered in all the political problems of a federal bureaucracy. As government employees, the team must adjust its policy to political decisions made at a higher level. Thus, it would be useless and destructive for Leah to argue that it was unfair to make cuts; the team has already received its mandate to do so. The fact is that the team's political survival depends on its ability to make cuts.

It's important for Leah to maintain her professionalism for this kind of audience. If she were too defensive or attributed personal vendettas to the team, she would hurt her organization. Instead, she must rely on clear, rational appeals, using EDUCARE's good history with the Department of Education to overcome the political difficulties of this situation.

Ethical Stance

The question of ethical considerations was the final aspect of Leah's rhetorical analysis. Having decided to take a clear stand and fight for EDUCARE's programs, Leah decided she had no ethical difficulties with this upcoming speaking task. She might have had real problems if she had been told to offer up some part of EDUCARE's work for the team to cut. But saved from such a fate, Leah decided she would stand her ground, refusing to sacrifice quality for cost efficiency.

ESSENTIAL ELEMENTS IN THE PREPARATION OF AN ORAL PRESENTATION

Knowing the Material

Nothing can make a speaker more confident than knowing the material. Leah had learned this from past oral presentations: the times she felt most confident were those when she had known the material most thoroughly and when she had anticipated carefully the questions her audience was likely to have. The former requires some research, even of a topic that the speaker knows well; the latter requires fitting the research to the audience analysis.

Leah realized that in this presentation she would have to answer some very specific questions, questions that she was anticipating and that would require some more specific research. Again, she would have to concentrate on the weak areas of the program, or at least areas that the assessment team would consider weak, such as the counselor-client ratio in the outreach portion of the program.

The figures that Leah was able to dig up showed that in 1987, when the program got started, EDUCARE hired twelve outreach counselors. In the first year of the program they identified and counseled 1,000 adolescents in both group and individual sessions. That meant that each counselor had contact with about eighty-three clients in either individual or group sessions, or both, within a week. In the second year of the program EDUCARE hired ten more counselors—five full-time, five part-time—and increased the client pool to 1,700. That meant that full-time counselors had contact with about seventy-seven clients in both kinds of settings within a week, and part-time counselors saw about thirty-three clients.

In the third year of the program the ratio stayed the same for 5 months and then decreased slightly. The program lost 250 clients, but retained all counselors. Full-time counselors saw seventy-three clients in both settings; part-time counselors saw about thirty.

It was this loss of clients, Leah thought, that would trigger criticism from the assessment team. Ironically, any decrease in the counselor-client ratio, which from EDUCARE's point of view was something positive, would be seen by the government as a problem, an indication, perhaps, that the program had served its purpose and its effectiveness was beginning to wane. Leah would have to counter this with information on how well counseling was working. She would have to be specific about how many clients had made progress in cutting down or giving up drug use, and how that progress was connected to counselors' efforts. She would have to draw from the monthly reports counselors were required to write and from the results of interviews and questionnaires that were held or administered regularly in the outreach program.

Leah was convinced that counselors were doing a good job, but she would have to translate her conviction into specific figures and percentages, so that the assessment team would also be convinced. There is no substitute for a thorough knowledge of the material one has to talk about, and Leah knew this. She decided that for this presentation she would have to show a particularly close, thorough knowledge of the working and effects of the outreach program; after all, the future

435

of EDUCARE and her own job was riding on how well she could tell her audience about the program's success.

Knowing What Is Important to Discuss

Leah also remembered that in the past she had had to discriminate among pieces of information, to decide which elements of the problem she was speaking about needed to be included, which could be left out.

Whereas writing contains limitations of space, speaking contains limitations of time. A speaker may feel the need to talk about all the elements of a problem, but time limitations make such coverage impossible. Leah thought that she would like to talk about all EDUCARE's dealings with clients, but she knew, given her audience's purpose for listening, that she would have to limit her talk strictly to EDUCARE's efforts in education. Any information on EDUCARE's rehabilitation efforts would have to wait for another time and another audience. (Actually, Leah was pretty sure she wouldn't have to wait long, since it was likely that the Department of Health and Human Services would be conducting a similar assessment of EDUCARE's work in rehabilitation.)

Leah then decided to sketch out the topics that would be of interest to her audience (see Figure 12.1). Leah knew that she would not be able to cover all the topics with equal thoroughness, nor would she even be expected to. The information on in-service training and the curriculum, for instance, would be pretty well known to her audience, so she could cut down on detail there. But the outreach counseling, which she had already identified as a potential problem, would require more time and greater detail, since the philosophies and practices of outreach counseling can differ markedly from program to program. She knew that she would have to take a chance that the audience's philosophy would not differ too much from hers. She also knew, as she thought about this, that it is impossible to anticipate every detail in preparing any presentation—either written or oral—and that she would just have to go with the best preparation she could muster.

Figure 12.1
Leah Feldstein's topics of interest for her audience

EDUCARE Presentation Topics of Interest

Topic 1. In-service training for teachers at both elementary and secondary levels

Topic 2. Drug education curriculum taught in health units and in physical education and social studies classes

Topic 3. Special seminars and presentations to update present information on the problems of drug use

Topic 4. In-school counseling done by EDUCARE's personnel

Topic 5. Presentations for PTA and community groups to explain what drug education has come to mean and how it is conducted

Topic 6. Public information presentations through various media – newspapers, radio, and television – aimed at the general public

Topic 7. Outreach counseling done by EDUCARE's personnel

Planning the Physical Aspects of the Presentation

It is obvious that Leah had already begun to plan. Her rhetorical analysis and coverage notes clearly are forms of planning. But good preparation involves other, more specific kinds of planning. John Fiske had told her that she should talk for a half hour, which meant that she would have to allocate bits of time to the various topics she had to cover. She would also have to plan the kinds of support, such as visual aids, she would need. Would they be charts and graphs in the form of handouts, or would transparencies or slides that she could project onto a screen be better? Or maybe she should combine the two. An outline of the outreach counseling practices would be easier to follow from an overhead projection or from a large poster. Then she could duplicate the outline on a handout that she would give her audience at the end of her talk, one they could have for future reference.

Leah knew from her experience that she would have to plan the physical details of her talk carefully. On several occasions in the past she found the overhead projector distracting: it was noisy, and unless she positioned herself correctly, the projection couldn't be seen by everyone. She also knew, however, that using a chalkboard could be awkward, since when she was writing on it, she would have to have her back to the audience. Leah liked to see her audience face-to-face at all times, and use of the overhead projector allowed her to do that.

She had used handouts in the past but found out that unless she passed them out just at the right time—when she was going to refer to them—they, too, could be distracting. If she passed them out too early, people tended to read them or fiddle with them and stopped paying attention to what she was saying.

Posters could also be trouble, especially with large audiences. If they weren't drawn in large figures and dominant colors, they couldn't be seen by people in the back of the room. At these times only half the audience benefited from the graphic illustration.

Leah then had to think of the room. For this talk she would use the conference room, in which there was a large table surrounded by comfortable chairs. There wasn't much space between the head of the table, where there was a chalkboard and a screen for projection, and the table itself. People sitting closer to the front might have to strain to pay attention to the projection, whereas people sitting at some distance would probably be comfortable. The same might be true, however, if she used the chalkboard, but if she used the chalkboard at least there wouldn't be the distraction of the bulk and noise of the overhead projector. In any case, these were considerations that she had to take into account. Elements such as these, which could make the difference between a successful and an unsuccessful presentation, reinforced the need for careful planning.

Finally, there were the amenities. She would want to check on the temperature of the room. There had been times when it was too hot or too cold. Coffee and tea and perhaps some pastries would have to be supplied. Since the meeting was planned for 10:00 A.M., and John had told her it had to be over by 12:00, allowing for his general introduction and conclusion and for the budget director's presentation, she was somewhat relieved. At least she wouldn't be speaking to people who had just had a big lunch. She always had to account for sleepiness in afternoon presentations, something she found difficult to deal with.

Leah found her planning to be easier for this presentation than for others. The audience would be small and she knew the territory, her capabilities, and those of the facilities she would be using. All in all, this was a fairly easy presentation to plan.

Practicing

Even though the presentation was fairly easy to plan, Leah didn't want to push her confidence too far. She remembered from her school experience and previous presentations that she was always better off when she practiced, going through the actual steps of her presentation in a kind of dry run. That meant checking to see whether the equipment was working properly; making sure that there were extra bulbs for the overhead projector (if she should decide to use it); going over slides (if she decided to use any) to see that they were in the right order and were appropriate; testing the slide projector to be sure that the remote control advance mechanism was working. (She remembered one time in a talk for a high school PTA when the remote control mechanism didn't work and she had to advance the slides by hand. The talk wasn't a disaster, but it was certainly inhibited by her not being able to move around freely.)

Leah knew that these were all steps she could take under the best of circumstances—in places that she knew and had free access to, like the conference room in EDUCARE's office. There were other places, however, to which she had less access, but that she could get to without too much trouble before a presentation. Simpson High School auditorium, where the school board met monthly, was one. She knew the facilities there pretty well, since she had spoken there several times before. She always went there at least a day before a presentation to make sure that the equipment she needed was in place and working.

But there were several times when she couldn't do any advance practice in person, like for the talk she gave at the offices of the Superintendent of Public Instruction in Olympia last year. In that case, and in others like it, she had to prepare the premises by telephone—talking to people to make sure that whatever she needed would be provided. In these situations Leah usually had a backup plan that she could use if her telephone arrangements had not worked out. Instead of an overhead projector, for instance, she could use a chalkboard or easier-to-read topical handouts. In the end she knew that the physical circumstances shouldn't daunt her and that alternatives she had thought about carefully would probably serve as well.

Most important for Leah was pacing herself, actually delivering the talk and timing how long it took. One of the hardest things for her was knowing, fairly surely, how long a presentation would take. She could plan all she wanted—2 minutes for the introduction, 8 for the background, 17 for major findings, and 3 for a conclusion—but if she didn't actually give the talk to somebody, even to herself, she wasn't sure she could keep within her time limits.

Before she was married, Leah used to deliver her talks to her roommate, and then after that, to her husband. They were pretty agreeable to her requests and would even suggest changes she might make, since they would play the role of whatever audience she had in mind. But what she really wanted to know was whether what she had to say would fit into the time allotted her. That she knew was very important. If she ran out of time, she wouldn't be able to conclude strongly. If she saw that she was running out of time, she might hurry over points that needed more development, thus ill-preparing her audience for her conclusion. If she raced through her talk, nervous about time, she might gloss over major points, and worse yet, leave an awkward time after the talk to be filled in by poorly informed questions from her audience (because she had rushed over essential material) or by polite applause and then complete silence—the absolute dread of any speaker.

Timing is of the utmost importance. Every speaker has to worry about it. And even if one has advanced beyond the stage of dragging others into listening to a talk, there's no excuse for the speaker's not having timed it in some way. Leah knew this, and although in recent times she had let her husband off the hook, she still delivered her talks in the privacy of her own office at work or in her study at home. Often she would use a tape recorder and a mirror, so that she could both hear (later) what she was talking about and see (immediately) how she was talking about it.

After enough experience in giving oral presentations, Leah thought she knew the ropes. She could anticipate most problems and most questions from her audience. But she never gave up a little practice before actually delivering her talks. Very few whose jobs require oral presentations can do that. Leah held onto the notions of preparation, planning, and practice very closely.

PLANNING THE TEXT FOR AN ORAL PRESENTATION

Speakers can prepare, do research, discriminate among pieces of information for proper emphasis, and practice the talk, but if the text of the presentation is not well organized and does not highlight the important points, the talk will not be effective. Leah's college instructor thought of a well-organized text in terms of a basic three-course meal: the appetizer, the main course, and finally, the dessert (see Figure 12.2). The appetizer is supposed to whet the pallet, get the juices flowing, interest the diner in what's to come. The main course is supposed to put things together—tastes and textures and colors—so that the substance of the meal is interesting and satisfying, and the dessert caps it all off—a complement to what has come before, a suggestion, perhaps, of what is to come in the future. Leah agreed that the formula for a good meal was the same as one for a good presentation.

The Introduction (or the Appetizer)

Suggestions for good introductions in speaking follow similar suggestions for good introductions in writing. Good introductions are supposed to grab the listeners, get

Figure 12.2
Comparison of menu topics and presentation topics

MENU	PRESENTATION
Appetizer	Introduction
Main Course	Body
Dessert	Conclusion

their attention, prepare them for an intelligent appreciation and understanding of what is to come. Bad introductions do the opposite: they confuse listeners, lead them away from the substance of the presentation, or simply bore them from the very outset.

Leah knew this from her experience in college, when she was criticized for starting her first presentation with, "The subject of my talk is . . ." and then going on to state it in the blandest of terms. Even then she knew there was no interest in that kind of beginning, but she felt scared and shy and thought she should get on with the substance of her talk. She didn't realize until later that she had had to work doubly hard to get her audience interested and to keep them with her through the rest of her presentation.

Beginnings are often troublesome. When people begin anything, unless they are veterans, they feel awkward or shy or silly, sometimes stupid. And many speakers and writers, who are otherwise fully versed in what they have to say, often sit for what seems like hours agonizing over how to begin the presentation. To alleviate the problem, some speakers begin their planning with the body of the talk: they know what they want to say, and map it out, step by step, including, in some cases, the conclusion. Then they go back and write the beginning.

This order of preparing the text is helpful in several ways. It helps get the important points and their support lined up. In turn, the process provides an overall picture of the importance and significance of the presentation. That kind of information must be included in the introduction, so speakers write the introduction last. When they know what they want to say and how they want to say it, they have a better idea of how to begin it. A first draft makes the point clearer to the speaker; by the end the speaker knows what to say. But a first draft is inappropriate for listeners. What appeared at the end to the writer must appear *first* to the listeners. The main point must be evident early in the talk.

Some people begin with anecdotes—little stories that illustrate the nature and significance of what they want to say later. Some begin starkly with facts and figures meant to startle the listeners, to grab their attention, and to define the context. Others begin with short histories of the problem, maybe also given in anecdotal form.

Leah had tried all these ways and usually had some success, although she found out that using only one way, because it had worked once, was not necessarily the way to go. Telling the story of Jimmy, who was coming to school high on coke, who could not pay attention to what was going on in his classes, who used to go into deep funks by the end of the day, was impressive for parents attending PTA meetings, who may be worried about their own children's behavior in and out of school. But it didn't do much for the kind of people she would be talking to next week.

They would be more impressed with some facts and figures. They knew about the Jimmys, or at least they thought they did, and would be impatient with such an approach. If they were to have an anecdote, it would have to be based on how EDUCARE's program had grown and thrived, even on limited funds, and over a relatively short period of time. Then they would be prepared, perhaps, for the main body of the presentation—the ways and means by which EDUCARE had increased and improved its services to its clients and to the community.

With this in mind Leah prepared two visual aids. The first, shown in Figure 12.3, is an article that appeared in a local newspaper on the success of the EDUCARE program. With this article Leah can show her audience that EDU-CARE has public recognition. The second visual aid, shown in Figure 12.4, consists of a line graph showing the growth of client enrollment and an outline of her presentation. As introductory visuals, both direct the attention of the audience to the specifics of the programmatic success enjoyed by EDUCARE. Leah knows that while the newspaper article is quite general and was written for the lay reader, it will provide a good anecdotal opening to the statistical information that she will want to address immediately.

Figure 12.3
Leah Feldstein's first visual aid

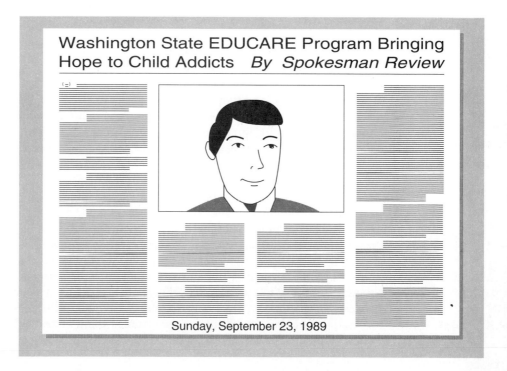

Washington State EDUCARE Program Bringing Hope to Child Addicts *By Spokesman Review*

Sunday, September 23, 1989

Figure 12.4
*Leah's second
visual aid*

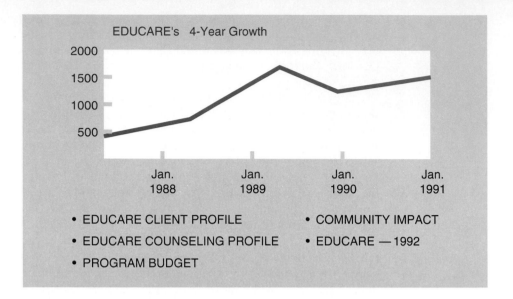

To sum up, the beginning of any talk is probably the most important part. The audience's interest must be engaged from the outset or it is likely that it never will be. Speakers who have not started strongly have to work extra hard to bring the audience around, so that they are paying attention and at least appear interested in what the speaker is saying. There is no substitute for good beginnings, and the time spent to make them good is time well spent.

The Body (or the Main Course)

Our earlier discussion about the need for speakers to discriminate among pieces of information in order to present that which is most important and convincing applies here as well. But we can add at this point the notion of relevance, which suggests another matter of audience analysis. Speakers must decide not only what is important and convincing, but also what is relevant to their audience. Relevant information, that is, information that an audience can easily identify as part of their personal or professional lives, is also important information, and it will almost certainly be convincing. The three requirements for determining the body of the presentation are thus bound up together: the information to be presented must be *important, convincing, and relevant*. Logical development with good illustrations and examples—the basic main course of the meal—will satisfy all three requirements.

Leah knew this to be true in her preparations for different kinds of presentations. For the PTAs of various schools she relied on a good deal of specific, anecdotal information. She knew that she could grab the attention of her audience in her introduction as she laid out the troubles Jimmy faced every day he came to school high on coke. But to keep their interest she would have to talk about what steps in education and counseling had seemed to work and how they were likely to work again to get Jimmy and those like him back on track. This kind of audience was less interested in how the program of education and counseling had expanded than it was in how successful individual efforts to get students off drugs had been.

Leah's PTA audiences are afraid. They want their children to succeed, to be helpful and productive, happy in the rather traditional forms they believe happiness takes. But they also know that the difficulties of the drug culture among teenagers are not easy to solve and that they themselves are probably not capable of solving them. They have come to rely on professionals like Leah, people whose work helps solve the drug problem among youths, and so they look to evaluate the tangible results of their efforts. They are interested in specific information about other children, so that they might be able to help out in the education and counseling of their own.

What is important, convincing, and relevant for an audience like the assessment team, Leah knew, would be quite different. The team would want to know how the program had worked in different terms: the number of clients served, the length of their association with the program, the number who could be identified as having passed successfully through the program. It would also want to know some of those hard figures on client-counselor ratios, areas of potential dispute with EDUCARE.

The body of the presentation should be carefully planned, including appropriately placed and constructed graphic aids. Discussion outlines, summaries, charts, graphs, tables, illustrations, and photographs can all be helpful if they are relevant to an audience's backgrounds, interests, and needs. Simply drawn but vivid flowcharts of counseling procedures would probably appeal to the PTA audience, whereas the assessment team would find them unnecessary. It would be more interested in graphs or tables that show expenditure of resources in relation to general client relations and services.

Figures 12.5, 12.6, and 12.7 show three visual aids that Leah could incorporate into her presentation. Following her introduction of the history of client participation, Leah could use the table and line graph in Figure 12.5 to give the audience a closer description of clients. She could use the overhead shown in Figure 12.6 to clarify her discussion of how the increase in contact hours in both group and individual counseling sessions has resulted in an increase in the percentage of clients who have successfully completed the program. Knowing that the assessment is an economic one, Leah wants to show the breakdown of the program costs, focusing specifically on the portion allocated for counselors' salaries. The pie charts shown in Figure 12.7 would serve this purpose well. These three visual aids help focus the audience's attention on the counselors' roles and their impact on the clients, the basis of the need for maintaining EDUCARE's current counseling programs.

As Leah prepared the body of the text for her presentation, including the visual aids she would use, she had to keep in mind that the success of this portion of the presentation depends on three essential ingredients: what is important, what is convincing, and what is relevant.

Figure 12.5
*Client profile
visual aid*

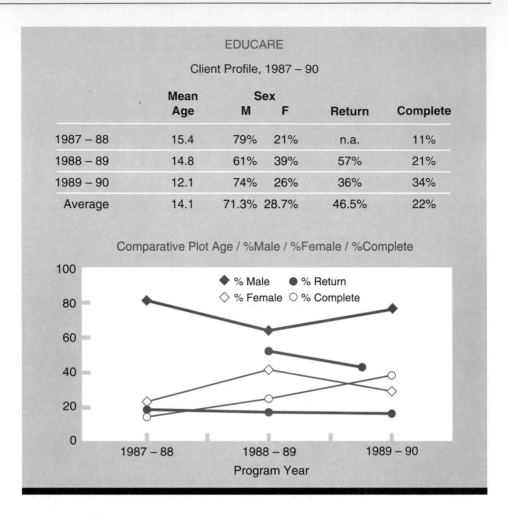

EDUCARE

Client Profile, 1987 – 90

	Mean Age	Sex		Return	Complete
		M	F		
1987 – 88	15.4	79%	21%	n.a.	11%
1988 – 89	14.8	61%	39%	57%	21%
1989 – 90	12.1	74%	26%	36%	34%
Average	14.1	71.3%	28.7%	46.5%	22%

Comparative Plot Age / %Male / %Female / %Complete

◆ % Male ● % Return
◇ % Female ○ % Complete

Program Year

The Conclusion (or the Dessert)

Speakers are often deceived into thinking that conclusions are the easiest part of a presentation to write. They think that if they just summarize everything that has gone before, that's all that's necessary: they are finally done. They believe the cliché that first you tell them what you're going to tell them, then you tell them, then you tell them what you just told them. But it is not so simple as that. Good conclusions are as important as good beginnings. They complement the rest of the talk by both satisfying the audience with a point of closure, and leaving them with thoughts that should go beyond the confines of the presentation. A strong conclusion will consider implications of the talk.

Sometimes conclusions are meant to move the audience to action or to make some kind of decision: strong conclusions of political speeches often send audiences to the polls; boards of directors are often moved to decide policy based on good presentations with strong conclusions. The point is that the meal is not

Figure 12.6
Counseling profile
visual aid

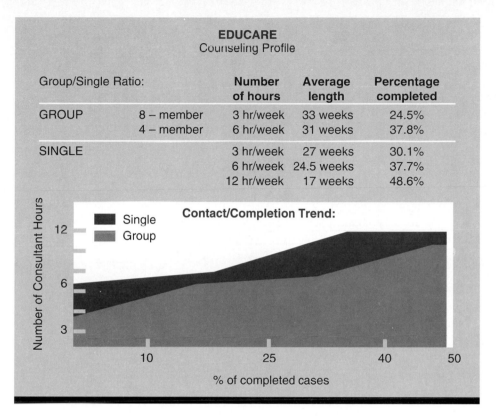

EDUCARE
Counseling Profile

Group/Single Ratio:		Number of hours	Average length	Percentage completed
GROUP	8 – member	3 hr/week	33 weeks	24.5%
	4 – member	6 hr/week	31 weeks	37.8%
SINGLE		3 hr/week	27 weeks	30.1%
		6 hr/week	24.5 weeks	37.7%
		12 hr/week	17 weeks	48.6%

Contact/Completion Trend:

Single
Group

Number of Consultant Hours

% of completed cases

complete without the dessert—and one that is appropriate to all that has been served before.

Leah knew the importance of effective conclusions from her college experience, when on some occasions, mainly because she had not timed her presentation well, she had ended with, "Well, I guess that's it; are there any questions?" The deafening silence threw her. She thought she had flopped entirely. But people often are not prepared to ask questions unless the conclusion challenges them in some way. Audiences want to test what they think they have heard and understood, and they can do that only if they have a prompt from a well-planned and well-executed conclusion.

In the PTA talks, for instance, Leah wanted to leave her audiences with some hope that through their own efforts in concert with EDUCARE's, their children might be helped to bring themselves out of the bind of drug abuse. She would always conclude with some practical steps that parents could take and with reminders that those steps had worked before and could work again. She wanted the audience not only to think positively about the future, but also to take some action that might help ensure that the future would be positive.

For the upcoming presentation to the assessment team Leah's conclusion would be different, because it wouldn't appeal to the audience on any emotional level, but would call for some action, or at least for a decision from her audience.

Figure 12.7
EDUCARE
budget visual aid

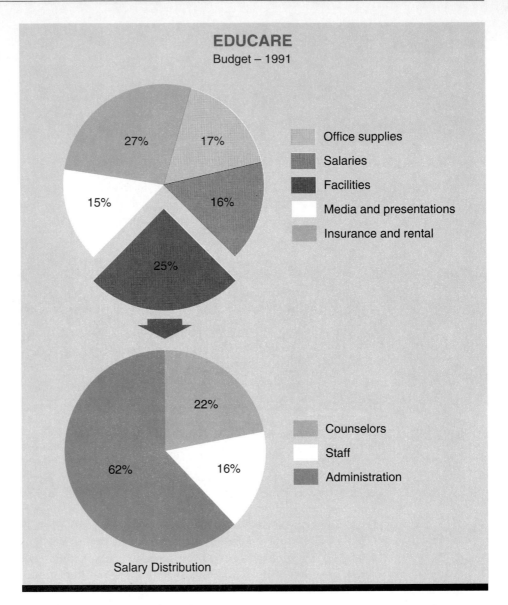

EDUCARE
Budget – 1991

27% 17%

15% 16%

25%

- Office supplies
- Salaries
- Facilities
- Media and presentations
- Insurance and rental

22%

62% 16%

- Counselors
- Staff
- Administration

Salary Distribution

In that way her conclusion would be similar to those given for PTA groups. The need for the presentation, but for the conclusion in particular, was simple: she wanted the assessment team to recommend continued funding of EDUCARE's program at least at present levels. If that couldn't happen, she wanted its recommendation to specify only minimal cuts, especially in the outreach segment of the program, so that EDUCARE could continue its work without major interruption. With this in mind, she would conclude her presentation with a recap of the accomplishments of the program, emphasizing how well the present organization matches the current funding. Leah decided to use the graphic shown in Figure 12.8 as a concluding visual to illustrate the interrelationships among all areas of the

Figure 12.8
EDUCARE task network visual aid

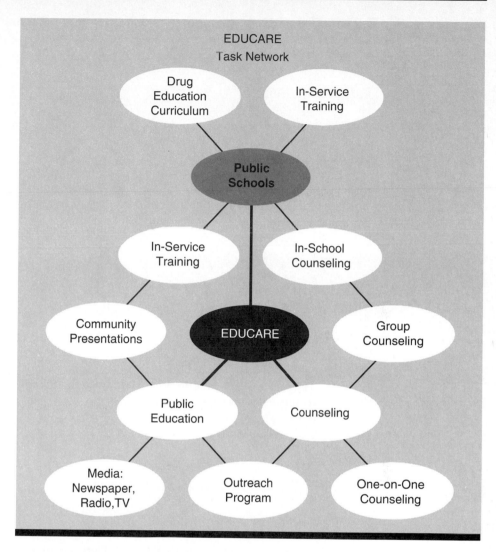

program and to show that this network was effective both administratively and economically.

Leah understood well now, much better than she did when she was in college, how important strong conclusions are. They tie things together, they give a sense of completion, but most important, they make people think about the future, and about what decisions or actions they may have to take.

THE MECHANICS OF EFFECTIVE PUBLIC SPEAKING

After analyzing the rhetorical situation, attending to all additional considerations, and preparing the text and visuals, Leah felt ready for her presentation. She remembered her instructor's tips on how to speak well in front of groups. In the years since college she was able to add a few of her own. She tried her best, whenever she spoke publicly, to keep all of them in mind.

Relax

Leah knew that this was easier said than done. But she also understood the basis for this advice. In any talk before any audience the speaker is the expert—or at least should be the expert, given the purpose and scope that have been set, and the research he or she has had to do. Thus there is no better way to gain confidence and be able to relax than to know the material thoroughly and to anticipate questions the audience might have. Although realistically, some speaking situations would be more stressful than others (the upcoming presentation before the assessment team was a good example), none should be completely daunting if the speaker is thoroughly prepared.

Speak Loudly Enough to Be Heard

This may seem obvious, but many beginning speakers often don't realize, given the size and acoustics of the room, how difficult it is for an audience to hear if speakers don't speak up. There is no need to shout, but clearly one must be heard. In many large rooms and auditoriums, microphones are provided that permit speakers to speak at conversational levels. But again, speakers should test the equipment for quality and working order before the presentation. In smaller rooms, seating twenty-five or so, a good strong delivery is all that is needed.

Maintain Eye Contact with the Audience

A very important ingredient of good speaking is keeping in touch with the audience through eye contact. No one likes to feel left out, and it is a simple fact of being a part of an audience that as the numbers of listeners increase, the chances of feeling like just one of a crowd also increase. So it is incumbent upon the speaker to look at people in the eyes.

The problem that many beginning speakers (and some veterans as well) find is that the self-consciousness they feel, for whatever reason, causes them to look anywhere but in their audience's eyes. They look at the ceiling or at the floor, or they bury their noses in their notes. The result is that they cut themselves off from their audience, and their message doesn't get through.

Some speakers have another problem. Remembering that they should maintain eye contact, at the beginning of the talk they find a friendly, accepting face, or perhaps several in a group, and keep addressing that person or group to the exclusion of the others. That may be fine for those who are favored, but the others pick up on it fast, and actually begin to resent the speaker for excluding them.

Instead of listening to what is being said, they start to think only about why they are being left out and why the other people are being favored. This can have an even worse effect on the success of the talk than speakers' eyes averted to ceilings, floors, or notes. In the latter case, at least, personalities are not involved, and no one feels like the object of exclusion.

The problem in general is made easier when speaking to large groups. The distance between speaker and audience is increased, and generalized looks at various parts of the audience will usually be enough to keep everyone in touch.

Keep the Body Poised and Vibrant

Many people speak and have written about the importance of body language and its effect on how messages are sent and received. More than one might think is communicated by the way a person stands, sits, or moves: feelings of discomfort, insecurity, and hostility, or on the more positive side, warmth, friendliness, and affection all can be transmitted through postures of the body.

Speakers, therefore, should be careful about how they move and hold themselves. If they stand rigidly, audiences may interpret this posture as evidence of insecurity or maybe even inflexibility of thinking—certainly nothing that speakers want to project. On the other hand, if speakers slouch or lean against the podium, they may be seen as not taking their subject or their audience seriously, an equally undesirable effect of body language.

Speakers want to try for something in between. They should want to appear energetic, but poised and relaxed. Occasional turns of the body from right to left to right, thus complementing eye contact with their audience, and occasional gestures of hands and head to punctuate points they are trying to make all contribute to an image of confidence. And a sense of confidence is what all speakers should want most to project.

Something should be said here about idiosyncrasies. Most speakers have them, and depending on how pronounced they are, they will be more or less distracting. The most common idiosyncrasy is pacing. Many speakers, usually to release nervous energy, will pace back and forth behind the speaker's podium, stopping only occasionally at the podium to glance at their notes. Although it may be impressive that they need to stop only occasionally to check their notes, the pacing itself is usually a distraction. The audience begins to concentrate on the pacing and not on the speaking. They begin to think about how many miles the speaker will walk today, not about how many ideas they can take away from the presentation. On the other hand, a compelling speaker can overshadow the pacing, so that it becomes part of a unique style, adding dramatic tension to the talk.

There are other kinds of idiosyncrasies, most the result of nervousness. Some speakers tap their feet, or beat little rhythms with their fingers or hands on the podium. It doesn't matter what the habit is. If it takes over the speaker's presentation, it needs to be eliminated, because the basic message of the talk is thrown off course; people go away thinking more of the peculiarities of the speaker's presentation than they do of its substance.

A short footnote to this: most of us have speaking idiosyncrasies, some more pronounced than others. Although it's good to try to control them, if the result is artificial or stilted speech, the message will still be blurred. In this case, however, the message is blurred because it is not being delivered comfortably.

Talk—Don't Read

Leah remembered this instruction well. She got it directly from her college instructor, who insisted that his students speak from notes and not read their presentations. Listening to reading, unless it is a dramatic reading of poetry or prose, is boring, he used to say. People soon stop listening and start thinking of other matters: where they will have to be in an hour, what they will have to do tomorrow or the next day.

No matter how painful it was, he made students talk the presentation rather than read it. Before their presentations he had them turn in to him their written scripts (if they had one) and their outline of notes. The outline was supposed to cover the main elements of the talk and points of reinforcement, like the use of graphics—overhead transparencies, posters, handouts, slides, and the like. He would then give them back their outlines, and they were to speak from them, and from them only.

Although Leah struggled through this, she did not realize what good instruction and practice it was until later, when she started giving presentations in which she would read the texts, as a way of protecting herself, she thought, from forgetting points she needed to make. She soon saw that the audiences got restless, easily distracted, and generally inattentive. As a result, they also responded less well, or not at all, in the question and answer period that usually followed her presentations.

Leah's experience told her that, if at all possible, she should speak from her notes, not read a script. In that way she could engage her audience more surely, she could show the confidence necessary for an audience to take her more seriously, and she could deliver her message more directly. Showing confidence and keeping her audience with her were, as she found out, the most important elements of good speaking.

Don't Take the "Sleepers" Personally

Leah always remembered this bit of advice with a smile. At the time she thought it was kind of funny, but it wasn't until she started giving talks more frequently out of school that she realized what good advice it was.

This tip, she found out, is related to all the other tips on good speaking: knowing the material, being well organized, speaking loudly enough, maintaining eye contact, and the like. If speakers keep all these elements in mind and try their best to achieve them, most people in an audience will pay attention. Depending on the subject of the talk and the speaker's position on it, the audience's attention can range from polite to riveted, but at least they will be paying attention.

But there may be someone, sometimes a few, who will appear bored or occupied with some extraneous matter. One or two may actually be sleeping. Speakers, especially if they are maintaining good eye contact, will find these people very fast. Although their discovery is disturbing even to veterans, beginning speakers are almost invariably thrown off stride. They think they are doing something terribly wrong, that all their preparation has been for naught. But the worse effect is that they get flustered and begin to lose their train of thought, sometimes stumbling and having to stop to regain their footing.

The tendency for this to happen is once again a function of the size of the audience. As the size of the audience increases, so does the variety of the people who come to listen. Even though they think they have an interest in the subject of the talk, the degree or nature of the interest of each person cannot be known, and therefore specific responses cannot be precisely predicted. Some may be there only because someone has told them to be; others attend with misconceptions, perhaps, about what will be discussed and why. And some turn up with other more personal problems: inexperience in attending public lectures, an inability or an unwillingness to pay attention, and yes, finally, a lack of sleep.

The smaller the audience, the greater the chance the whole group will have similar interests and expectations. Responses are, therefore, easier to predict, and the smaller size of the group also helps to act as a check on what in larger groups becomes anonymous behavior. People are less inclined to drift away, at least visibly, because the purposes for being there seem clearer and more focused. And they feel a certain pressure, both self-imposed and from those around them, to pay attention to what the speaker is saying so that they can respond intelligently.

But the important thing to remember is that if you have addressed the technical and rhetorical problems of the presentation seriously and thoroughly, have planned and practiced carefully, and have created an effective text to highlight what is important, convincing, and relevant, the presentation will work well—may even be a resounding success. You may still have a couple of sleepers, but don't take them personally: they have problems you don't want to know about.

 ## TIPS FOR GIVING ORAL PRESENTATIONS TO SPECIFIC GROUPS

All oral presentations, whether to be given to large or small groups, require that the speaker attend to the concerns of technical and rhetorical problem solving: the additional considerations of research, discrimination, planning, and practice; the organization of an effective text; and the mechanics of public speaking. In addition, other specific elements come into play depending on the type of group the speaker is addressing. Following are discussions of factors to consider when giving oral presentations to three types of groups—committees, civic or special interest groups, and boards of directors.

Committees

The purpose speakers have for speaking at committee meetings depends on their positions with regard to the committee: they can be guests, presenting information the committee has requested or that they themselves asked to present; they can be committee members, reporting on specific assignments they have received from the committee; or they can be chairs of committees, who are responsible for managing the flow of information that committees generate and for reporting on what has happened as a result of committee actions.

When the Speaker Is a Guest

In the position of guest, speakers must worry about the same elements that Leah would have to worry about in talking to the assessment team from Washington. They must make sure that the background to the problem is clearly understood; that the evidence they present is pertinent, relevant, and timely; and that they conclude in a way that will leave the committee with a clear path to enable them to make a decision or take some action. Since guests are not privy to the workings of the committee, they have to present their information more formally, and plan their presentations more carefully.

Leah had this experience when, soon after EDUCARE got started, she had to speak to the Seattle school district's secondary curriculum committee. Made up of some fifteen teachers and administrators, the committee is responsible for overseeing the workings of the curriculum in place as well as its future development. Leah knew she would be speaking to professionals who understood how to assess the effectiveness of already existing curricula and how to gauge the likely success of new curricula being proposed. She had to keep in mind not only the philosophical underpinnings of EDUCARE's program, but also its practical applications: how teachers would be trained, how students would be engaged and then tracked in the program, and what kinds of assessments of student progress could be made. Clearly, these were all elements that required thoughtful, thorough preparation and formal presentation.

When the Speaker Is a Committee Member

As committee members, speakers can be less concerned with formality than they would be as a guest, though no less concerned with the pertinence, relevance, and timeliness of their presentations. Normally, they are responding to specific assignments from the committee. The committee wants to hear specifically about the matter assigned, and so there is no need for formal introductions or conclusions. On occasion, speakers may need to present their information with special visual aids, like overhead projections or handouts, but generally other committee members rely and take notes on only what is said.

Leah's experience as a member of the Greater Seattle Task Force on Drug Education and Rehabilitation serves as an example. Leah's responsibility on that committee is very specific: to report on the general progress of EDUCARE's program both within the schools and in outreach, but especially with regard to how EDUCARE's efforts are coordinated with those of other social service agencies in Seattle. To that end, Leah reports regularly (the committee meets once a month) on what teachers are doing in their classrooms, how many students have been identified as needing special help outside of school, how many of those have been referred to other agencies, and what kind of services and relationships have resulted from those referrals.

Reports to committees are no less guided or determined by time than any other presentation. The length is normally limited by the meeting's agenda—the other items that will be covered, their importance and place on the agenda, whether they are old or new items, and so forth. Members' presentations should not take any longer than experience dictates, given the other business of the committee and the relative importance of the information the member is presenting.

When the Speaker Is the Committee Chair

Chairs of committees are usually responsible for three things: agendas of meetings; the flow of information, both within and beyond the committee; and final reports on actions the committee has taken or recommended. Presentations, then, are of two kinds: those to the committee itself about the business that it has to undertake or on the results of work it has already undertaken, and those to groups outside the committee that rely on information the committee has generated: upper management, boards of directors, or the larger constituency of the organization of which the committee is a part. The latter can often mean presentations to sales conventions or stockholders meetings, which have to take on the more formal trappings of presentations to larger groups.

Presentations generally respond to particular items that have already been introduced and are under discussion. Detailed introductions concerning background or intentions are unnecessary, unless a new item has been presented to the committee for its consideration. For new items, chairs have to start from the beginning—or almost from the beginning. Since they know their committee members, and everyone understands the purposes the committee has for meeting, chairs can take some shortcuts and present the new problem in terms that the committee will already be familiar with, making sure, however, they define specifically what role the committee will have to take to address the problem.

Conclusions for this kind of presentation can be similarly abbreviated. They are not normally couched in philosophical terms, but usually take the form of specific instructions to committee members about what and when tasks have to be performed.

Civic or Special Interest Groups

Civic or special interest groups are generally friendly groups. The members volunteer their time and work, and genuinely believe that they can be of help in solving the problems their groups confront. Thus the Lions, the Rotary Club, the

Chamber of Commerce, the Friends of the Library, the Friends of the Earth, MADD (Mothers Against Drunk Driving), or even the local PTA of Franklin School all meet regularly to decide how their projects are progressing and what more they can do to see them along to successful conclusions.

Professionals from all areas are often called upon to speak to these groups' meetings, and depending on the community and the circumstances of the problems they are confronting, their presentations can mean a great deal. Presentations to these groups can also build good will and enhance the public image of the organization that the speaker represents. For these reasons, then, speakers should take their jobs of presenting seriously.

Understanding the Goals of the Group

The backgrounds of members of civic and special interest groups vary. Members may be retired executives, line workers, active members of the business community, teachers; the one thing they have in common is interest and commitment to the goals of the groups to which they belong. Therefore, speakers must keep those goals in mind when preparing their presentations. Since the topics of the presentations are almost always specified, either by the group if it has invited the presentation or certainly by the speaker if he or she has volunteered the presentation, the job of focusing the presentation is much easier. But speakers must also connect the ideas they present to the general purposes of the group to which they are speaking: for the Friends of the Earth, how does Acme Incorporated help meet the standards for a clean environment? For MADD or the local PTA, how does EDUCARE address the problems of drinking and drugs in a controlled, educational environment?

Meeting the Informational Needs of the Group

Although presentations to groups like these need to be specific and pertinent to the general interests of the group, they should not be terribly technical. Only a few members of the audience are likely to appreciate or be able to digest technical information, and even they, because they understand the diversity of the group they have joined, don't expect or want to hear about all the technical details of a problem. They, like the other members, want to hear about basic issues, approaches, solutions, and not about the minutiae that constitute them.

Groups like these also need fairly vivid graphic support of the words they are hearing; maps, illustrations, simple charts and tables, posters, and discussion outlines can be useful, presented either through overhead projection or in print. But graphic support shouldn't be overwhelming—too many things to read, consider, or react to will confuse and drown out the presenter's basic message. The graphics help enormously, however, to reinforce basic points. It is generally more difficult to hear a presentation than to read one. People retain less of the essential message by listening than by reading. It's often a good idea, then, to supply backup print copies of overhead projections. Audiences can use them to refer to and consider after the presentation.

The general tips for presentations to civic and special interest groups are simple and sensible: keep the presentation focused, simple but not simplistic, pertinent to the problems the group is interested in, graphic, and short—but not too short (8- or 10-minute presentations are often seen as slights to the group or to the principles for which they are organized). Unless otherwise specified, 20- to 25-minute presentations are generally long enough. Speakers can make their points; listeners can absorb the points; and no one gets too restless.

Boards of Directors

Understanding the Purposes of Board Meetings

Boards of directors, as is true of most small groups, have very specific purposes for meeting, usually to do with establishing and evaluating the policies and directions an organization is operating under. Thus, boards of directors meet specifically to make decisions—decisions that normally will have a significant, global impact on the conduct of the business of the organization.

The board of directors of the Chrysler Corporation, for example, must decide on such major issues as whether to expand or contract the corporation's operations, whether certain investments of capital should be made and where, whether the general corporate image needs to be changed and in what way. It also makes decisions on changes in top management practices and personnel, which clearly have a significant impact on the operations of the corporation. Board members do not make decisions about how changes or new initiatives in the operations will be implemented; those are left to lower-echelon personnel, although the results of the implementation can become the subject of future discussion.

To help them make these decisions, boards often call for oral presentations from people in various divisions of the corporation. This saves them time, since they don't have to read through pages of proposals, reports, or position papers. Since saving time is part of the purpose of calling for presentations, boards expect that they will be clearly, concisely, straightforwardly, and efficiently rendered.

Providing Information to Enable Decision Making

The guiding principle, then, in preparing an oral presentation for a board meeting is to give the members information that will enable them to make a decision; this means presenting the information in a compelling way, one that is clearly intended to recommend a course of action. The board is not interested in the technical details that so fascinate the professional in the trenches. All the board wants, in the tritest of terms, is the big picture, presented with background, implications, and focus filled in.

Presenters must center specifically on the problem, what it means for the organization if it is unsolved, and what is likely to happen if the speakers' recommendations are agreed to and implemented. Presentations of this kind must be specific, concrete, down to earth, and precisely timed. Since boards meet only occasionally (the schedule of meetings varies with each board), their agendas are usually rigidly set, and the members don't like rambling, unfocused, apparently endless presentations. Such presentations waste everyone's time.

Presentations to boards of directors are more successful if they are enhanced with graphic aids: simple flowcharts, tables, and illustrations presented through overhead transparencies or handouts. It's often a good idea to provide backup handouts of overhead projections, so that members of the board can have them to refer to when they deliberate and finally make their decisions.

Presentations to boards of directors are clearly understood to be performances. They require careful definition of the problem at hand, research and analysis, synthesis, planning, practice, and finally, stage presence. Presenters need to understand why they have been asked to present information, to whom, and how it will be used. They also need to know when to get off stage. These are not essentially different from demands of any writing or speaking task, but if they are not taken seriously, the effects can be dramatic.

CONCLUSIONS

Although the techniques of giving oral presentations are different from those of writing, the basic principles for preparing them are the same: careful analysis of the problem or problems to be discussed, the purpose of the presentation, the intended audience, and, finally, the speaker's position—his or her stance on the importance of the problem and how it might be solved. Thus, the same steps discussed and outlined earlier in this book on solving technical and rhetorical problems in writing apply to speaking. The only difference—and it is significant—is that oral presentations elicit immediate, even palpable, responses from those who hear them. Speakers know very quickly the impact they've made, whereas writers must wait much longer. A speaking situation, for this reason and for others we've spoken about in this chapter, is often more intimidating—maybe just scarier—for most people than a writing situation. That's understandable. Our advice is simple, though it may not be simple to follow. Consider the steps for giving oral presentations we have discussed in this chapter, and don't take the sleepers personally.

EXERCISE

1.   Imagine that you have an entry-level job in the kind of firm you have always wanted to work for, doing what you have been educated and trained to do. You get in your mail a memo from your immediate superior asking you to present a 20-minute talk to high school seniors during their Career Week activities about what you do and why it is important.

Here are some of the specifics:
   a.   You will be speaking to a class of twenty-five honors students, all of whom will be going off to college in the fall.

b. A major purpose of the Career Week activities is to give students an idea of what people in the working world do so that their choices of majors in college might be made easier.

c. The company you work for is thinking of offering several scholarships to promising high school seniors to cover most of their college expenses. The company sees this not only as a civic duty but also as a means of encouraging the development of better employees for the future.

Plan your presentation by writing out a thorough rhetorical analysis: consider purpose, audience, context, and ethical stance. Then decide what you are going to say, in how much detail, and what kinds of aids you will need to support your presentation. A descriptive outline of your presentation should be the result of your work.

ASSIGNMENT

1. Present a 15-minute talk to your classmates on research you either have worked on or are presently working on.

TERM PROJECT OPTION

Present a 15-minute talk to your classmates on the research you performed for your proposal and completion report. Remember to focus your talk appropriately so that you make a specific, overriding point. Mere overviews will come across as vague and pointless.

Your instructor may want to assign two students per talk to act as respondents. They will ask the speaker one pertinent question apiece. They will also evaluate the speaker's focus, appeal, and effectiveness on a form like the one in Figure 12.9. Note that the form asks for substantive comments that both describe and judge the talk. The evaluations should be signed and returned to the instructor.

Figure 12.9
Respondent's evaluation form

RESPONDENT'S EVALUATION

Speaker: ————————————————————————

Topic: ——————————————————————————

1. What was the focus of the talk?

   Difficulties?

   Suggestions?

2. Did the speaker appeal well to the audience?

   Techniques used:

   Difficulties?

   Suggestions?

3. Was the presentation effective?

   Techniques used:

   Difficulties?

   Suggestions?

4. Overall evaluation

Respondent's signature: ———————————————————

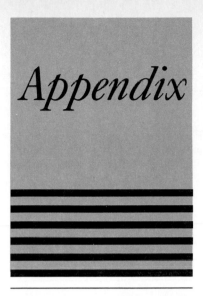

Appendix

SELECTED PROBLEMS

OF USAGE AND STYLE

 ## PROBLEMS WITH THE PASSIVE VOICE

Identifying Passive Voice and Passive Constructions

Voice is a function of grammar that shows the relation of the subject of a verb to the action the verb expresses; changes in the form of the verb help express this relation. The following examples illustrate the difference between active and passive voice.

This statement is in the active voice:

(subject)   *(verb)*
Medical researchers from Johns Hopkins University discovered new
         (object)
gene-splitting techniques last month.

The voice in this case is defined as *active* because the subject of the verb, *medical researchers*, is the performer of the action the verb expresses, *discovered*. The object of the verb, *gene-splitting techniques*, is the recipient of the action of the verb.

Following is the statement recast in the passive voice:

(subject)   *(verb)*   *(object)*

```
New gene-splitting techniques were discovered by medical researchers from
Johns Hopkins University last month.
```

This statement is in the passive voice, because the original object of the verb, *gene-splitting techniques,* still receives the action, but has now taken the subject position in the sentence. Whereas formerly it was the object, *gene-splitting techniques* becomes the subject in a passive construction.

The relation of the subject to the action the verb expresses is *active* when the subject *performs* the action. But the relation of the subject to the action of the verb is *passive* when the subject *receives* the action. A few more simple examples, illustrate the contrast between active and passive constructions:

```
  Active: The dog chased the cat.
 Passive: The cat was chased by the dog.

  Active: The boss complimented Joan.
 Passive: Joan was complimented by the boss.
```

Note the transformations a sentence undergoes to become passive. First, the object of the active construction *(cat, Joan)* becomes the subject in a passive construction. Second, the subject of the active construction *(dog, boss)* becomes the object of the prepositional phrase *(by the dog, by the boss)* in the passive construction. Finally, the verb form requires the addition of an auxiliary (helping) verb *(was).* Remember that the prepositional phrase may not appear because it is understood, as in this sentence:

```
His chest was then opened with forceps.
```

In this statement the prepositional phrase *by the surgeon* is understood.

Recognizing When It Is Appropriate to Use the Passive Voice

Some authorities advise against ever using passive constructions. They claim passives sap the strength of a person's writing and require unnecessary additional words. But this advice ignores the point that the passive voice is sometimes required, for instance, when the subject that performs the action is unknown, as in this sentence:

```
The Christian sectors of Beirut were bombed last night for the fifth time in two
months.
```

This sentence was written in the passive voice because terrorist factions in the Middle East are numerous and their actions cannot always be specifically attributed. Moreover, in corporate work an agent often can't be singled out since myriad employees may have worked on the same project. This reason explains the following passive:

The new waste container was produced ahead of schedule and under budget.

It would be absurd to name all the individual participants in this one statement.

Matters of emphasis may determine the use of a passive construction. Depending on the subject and the context established, writers may choose to emphasize the results of the action rather than the action itself, or in terms of this discussion, they may want to emphasize the *recipients* of action rather than the *performers* of it. Thus, given the context of the discussion, if the newness of the gene-splitting techniques mentioned above was more important than the discoverers or the action of discovery, then the writer does well to cast the statement in the passive voice, so that *gene-splitting techniques* becomes the subject of the sentence.

The question finally comes down to a matter of thoughtful choice. The passive voice is not in itself bad style; in fact, its judicious use can enhance the effectiveness of a document. Only when it is overused or used specifically to diminish authorial presence does it become a problem.

Furthermore, mindless passives that ignore common sense to please convention are no longer required of writers. For example, when writing a periodic report, an author need not write *research was performed* in lieu of *I researched*. Some "authorities" in business, the social sciences, and other technical and scientific areas have said that a writer should never use the first-person pronoun *I*, because doing so adds subjectivity to a document. Writers, instead, should strive for objectivity—a detachment of the author from the written piece—to show no personal bias or prejudice. Supposedly, the passive voice achieves this sense of detachment and objectivity. Unfortunately, that produces such awkward constructions as the following:

In reviewing the installation for approval, it was discovered that a concrete foundation has been installed within the Utility District's easement area.

This easement, which was on file and made known to all subsequent landowners purchasing the property, was required per the National Safety Code for the protection and safeguarding of the public while ensuring the maintenance of the electric system.

The report was pointed out by the manager as one in which the writer reported more than was necessary.

The notion of professional objectivity is good, but the suggestion that it can be achieved through writing in the passive voice is bad. Objectivity, both philosophically and practically, has to do with the way professionals carry out their work. It means collecting data and analyzing them without bias, without preconceived ideas of what the data will show, or what people want them to show. But objectivity cannot be achieved merely through the forms of writing. It depends fundamentally on how work is performed, whether a research design, for instance, has accounted for all variables, or whether the variables have been accounted for and treated in the same way. Objectivity in writing is violated only when writers

461

decide purposefully to slant the interpretation and discussion of the findings to favor their particular biases; there is nothing inherent in the forms of language themselves that establishes objectivity.

Variations of Passive Constructions

A variation of the problems of passive constructions comes with the use of the adverb *there* as a dummy subject of a statement connected to auxiliary verbs of being, as in this sentence:

There have been many ups and down in the stock market this year.

This can be more easily and concisely stated as follows:

The stock market saw many ups and downs this year.

The revision places a logical subject, *the stock market*, in the subject position of the sentence instead of in an object position, and adds the active verb *saw* to make the statement active and more concise. Here are some other examples of wordy, basically passive constructions, with revisions:

Original: In the tart cherry industry, there have been no new products developed in the last 60 years, and there have never been any industry advertisement or promotion programs.

Revision: The tart cherry industry has developed no new products in the last 60 years, and it has never advertised or promoted its products.

Original: Since the beginning of marketing in the industry, there have been large fluctuations in production, causing large fluctuations in prices of up to 39 cents per pound.

Revision: Since the beginning of marketing in the industry, large production fluctuations have caused wide price fluctuations, sometimes as much as 39 cents per pound in any 2 years.

EXERCISES

1. Transform the following passives into active sentence structure:
   a. The mission was flown successfully until the radio was dropped on the floor.
   b. The car was hit at 65 mph by the truck.
   c. That principle is kept in mind by all of us.
   d. The executive summary was written by S. Johnson and myself.
   e. The two teams were beaten by the Bengals.
   f. We are exposed to radiation from radioactive elements contained in fallout from nuclear explosives testing and unavoidable discharges from nuclear installations.

g. However, if alpha-emitting materials are taken into the body by inhalation or along with food or water, they can expose internal tissues directly and may therefore represent a hazard.

h. There has always been a desire by the tart cherry producers for formal organization.

2. Go back through a paper you have written either for this class or for another and underline all the passive constructions. Then decide in each case whether passivity was necessary. Defend it if it was; change it to active voice if it wasn't.

3. Identify and evaluate passive constructions in someone else's writing. You may choose a published or unpublished piece or one in draft form. Be clear about how your changes would improve the piece of writing. (Peer reviews of classmates' writing are good opportunities for doing this work.)

PROBLEMS WITH NOMINALIZATION

Identifying Nominalizations

Nominalization refers to the process by which a writer casts what could be an active verb into a noun and attaches another auxiliary verb to make one longer predicate. An easy example is the following:

    The task force carried out an investigation of the failure of the conveyor
    system.

A good revision of this is also easy:

    The task force investigated the conveyor system failure.

The writer had turned the verb *investigated* into the noun *investigation,* and so had to add the less vivid verb *carried out,* the article *an,* and the preposition *of,* so that the statement makes sense. Actually, the single verb *investigated* vividly describes the action, and the writer has eliminated four unnecessary words.

The following example presents an interesting case:

    Gas utilization should follow company guidelines.

This sentence could be revised as follows:

    Use gas according to company guidelines.

The nominalization here is twice removed from the real verb, *use,* which we reach through *utilize.* There is no difference in meaning between *utilize* and *use,* although people assume *utilize* is more formal or technical or scientific. They assume this based on the sound of the word's latinate ending, *-ize,* and the extra prepositions that get thrown in. This makes a real mouthful out of the very simple verb *use.*

The problems with nominalization are wordiness and awkwardness; eliminating them makes writing clearer. The deeper problems again arise from writers' mistaken beliefs that their writing will sound more formal, official, or important if they use more words with more syllables. But two of the primary goals in good technical and professional writing are economy and clarity. Writers can achieve a more formal tone through other means, such as diction (word choice) and syntax (sentence structure). They should not attempt it simply by padding words.

Nominalizations can sometimes be complicated by passive constructions, as is the case in this sentence:

    The Twin Trade Towers have experienced a complete renovation as to access to
    fire exits done by the Acme Company.

The statement could be revised as follows:

    The Acme Company has completely renovated access routes to fire exits at the
    Twin Trade Towers.

In this case the writer has made two good changes. She has put the Acme Company, which was in the object position of a passive construction, into the subject position in an active construction. She has rewritten the nominalization *experienced a complete renovation* to read *has completely renovated*. She has also tossed out the phrase *as to access*, which didn't make much sense in the original anyway. The revision is clear and concise—something that certainly could not be said of the original.

The only question that the revision doesn't answer is whether the Twin Trade Towers need to be emphasized in the subject position of the sentence, perhaps because they have been the focus of the piece all along. If that's the case, then the preceding revision won't do. But the following revision might work:

    The Twin Trade Towers's access routes to fire exits have been completely
    renovated by the Acme Company.

Here the passive construction remains, because it is important to emphasize the Twin Trade Towers and not the Acme Company. But the nominalization is gone—*have experienced a complete renovation* has become *have been completely renovated*—still a distinct improvement over the original.

Using too many words when fewer will do is true of this example:

    Researchers at the Northwest Institute for Environmental Improvement have
    begun to take on a study of the spotted owl's habitat.

This could be more easily written as

    Researchers at the Northwest Institute for Environmental Improvement have
    begun to study the spotted owl's habitat.

To take on a study and *to study* mean essentially the same thing, but somehow this writer thinks that *to take on a study* sounds better. If it does, it does so only at the expense of the clarity and conciseness of the statement. And the better sound, if indeed it is better, isn't worth it.

Some final examples should help make the point.

The lack of detail about the fire at Unit Three provided by the Clean-Up Team created a disturbance in the management sector.

Rewritten, this statement might read as follows:

Management was disturbed by how little detail the Clean-Up Team provided about the fire at Unit Three.

Once again the problems here are wordiness and awkwardness. The revision places *management* in the subject position of the sentence, and although it retains a passive construction, *was disturbed by*, it eliminates the nominalization *created a disturbance in*. It also turns the passive construction *provided by the Clean-Up Team* into an active construction, *the Clean-Up Team provided*. In all, the revision is clearer, more concise, and more effective.

Here is a short list of common nominalizations that can be eliminated to make writing or speaking more concise and straightfoward:

Wordy: The Committee has made the determination that . . .
Concise: The Committee has determined that . . .

Wordy: The manager made the point that . . .
Concise: The manager pointed out that . . .

Wordy: It was the thinking of the President that . . .
Concise: The President thought that . . .

Wordy: The contractor is in the continuation phase of making deliveries . . .
Concise: The contractor continues to deliver . . .

Recognizing When a Revision Will Alter Meaning

Just as writers should be careful about when to use the passive voice, so should they be careful about when to change nominalizations. Not every change will retain the meaning of the original. Here is an example:

The police have produced a report on the activities of teenage drug pushers.

An energetic searcher for nominalizations might be tempted to revise this as follows:

The police have reported on the activities of teenage drug pushers.

But the revision could change the sense of the original. *Producing a report* implies the five basic steps of solving or addressing problems: definition, research, analysis, resolution and synthesis, and implementation. It also implies a written product—a report—that has gone through all the stages of production: writing, revising, editing, proofreading, and printing and binding.

The revision might mean something much less. *Reporting* can be done orally at police department briefings, at city council meetings, or at press conferences; it need not mean a formally produced report. Therefore, the appropriateness of nominalizations will depend on what actually took place, and on the writer's intentions.

By using almost the same example, however, we can see where a nominalization should be removed to make matters simpler. The original might read as follows:

```
The police made a report on the activities of teenage drug pushers.
```

The revision would be the same as the earlier example:

```
The police reported on the activities of teenage drug pushers.
```

Making a report is different from *producing* a report. Making a report, in fact, implies the same informal activity as reporting. There is no sense in the original sentence of production—of all the steps necessary to submit a formal report. The police can present their information orally, or in short written forms, and the process of making a report might stop there. Or it could take off from there into the more complex process of producing a report, but the point is that the writer doesn't imply anything more than simple reporting. Therefore, the writer would do better to use *reported* and not *made a report*, eliminating the problem of nominalization—using too many words where only a few will do.

EXERCISES

1. Eliminate the nominalizations from the following sentences:
    a. One worker does the assembly; the other checks the proper procedure step by step in the Poulex Final Assembly Safety Manual.
    b. The use of nuclear energy for electricity production is inevitably connected with the production of large amounts of radioactive material that must and can be controlled.
    c. One of the objectives of the IAEA (International Atomic Energy Association) is to "seek to accelerate and enlarge the contribution of atomic energy to peace, health, and prosperity throughout the world."
    d. We don't have anything to do here with the actual fabrication of weapons.

2. Go back through a paper you have written either for this class or for another and underline all the nominalizations. Decide whether a revision will alter the meaning. In most cases you will want to change the nominalizations so that active verbs do the work more concisely.

3. Identify and evaluate nominalizations in someone else's writing. You may choose a published or unpublished piece or one in draft form. Be clear about how your changes would improve the piece of writing. (Peer reviews of classmates' writing are good opportunities for doing this work.)

PROBLEMS WITH DICTION AND JARGON

Diction means word choice; any choice a writer or speaker makes in the use of words has to do with diction. *Jargon* refers to word choice (or diction) that is specialized or appropriate to a particular group. Jargon is often used pejoratively as coded word choice, to appeal to a particular group; often it is used to exclude those outside of the group. But jargon, as the vocabulary (diction) of a particular group, shouldn't be thought of as necessarily negative. If jargon can make communication easier within a group, then it should be used. It's only when the jargon of one group starts to leak into the vocabulary of another, or when one group starts to appropriate the jargon of another, that misunderstanding may arise.

For example, when some groups start to talk about *interfacing* with one another, they are using language to obscure the actual activity: talking about ideas with other people. *Interfacing* comes from computer science, in which bringing one function of a computer program into contact with another constitutes an interface. *Interfacing* seems all right to use as the name of a technical activity in computer technology, because it has a specific meaning, and everyone involved in the technology knows immediately what it means. But when others use the term to mean something as simple as discussing ideas and problems with other people, it assumes a falsely official or technical tone—an attempt to make something sound more important than it really is—the same problem that nominalization tends to foster.

A final situation that encourages jargon, which sometimes may jar notions of conventional diction, comes from changes in cultural conditions. The verb *to parent* is an example. In this case, the noun *parent* has been made into a verb, *to parent*, which means, in more conventional terms, to rear children. The verb most likely was created to reflect a new cultural emphasis on child-rearing practices that results, in part, from the greater demands put upon households with two working parents. Also, other cultural complications for children, such as drug use and early sexual activity, focused the modern difficulties of raising children, and both mothers and fathers have had to assume more active and thoughtful roles as parents.

Creating *to parent*, in turn, has created the verbal *parenting*, which is used more often than the verb, both as a noun and as an adjective.

```
Parenting, we find, is often more complicated today than it was 25 years ago.
```

```
We have found that developing parenting skills is the most important part of our program.
```

Ultimately, the point is that changes in language accommodate changes in culture, but it often takes a long time before the changes in language are fully accepted. Until that time the changes may appear forced or artificial, or which is worse to some, trendy. Always thoughtful of their audiences, good writers are careful not to offend their readers by using terms that have not been fully accepted into the language.

Following are some terms, both nouns and verbs, that qualify as questionable uses of diction. Because they are inappropriately borrowed jargon or have been coined to create a tone of officialdom or importance, they have not yet been fully accepted by many speakers and writers of Standard American English.

Some Questionable Nouns

The Bottom Line

As used in business, finance, or accounting, *the bottom line* refers to the last line of the ledger, which reveals the final figures of revenue, expenditures, or profit and loss. But it has come to be used in other areas to mean the final consideration, or what has to be done given all the information that has been presented already. And so we hear comments like the following:

> The bottom line is that we cannot accept the Finance Committee's decision to reject the City Manager's proposal for recycling in all neighborhoods.

As used by those outside of business, the rather trendy term *the bottom line* has been substituted for simpler but more dignified wording. The careful writer or speaker would use *in the end* or *finally* instead of *the bottom line is that*.

Perception Check

It is hard to say what the origin of *perception check* is, although it may have come from business and industry as a variant of *quality control check*. It means, roughly, an attempt to review what someone thinks he or she understands of a discussion or of a written document; it is a recapitulation. We hear someone say the following, then, in the midst of long discussions of changes in zoning policy at city council meetings:

> Let's stop for a minute; I think we need a perception check on what has gone on so far.

A better statement would be this:

> I think we need to make sure we understand what has gone on so far.

Again, the easier, more straightforward expression fits the situation better: it is clear and unpretentious, and it does not confuse or cloud the need for action.

Quality Time

The use of *quality* as an adjective to modify any noun, as in *quality products* or *quality service*, got started in advertising jargon and is used to mean high quality, clearly different from low quality, even though the possibility of something of low quality still exists. The problem is that those who use the noun *quality* as an adjective to modify other nouns have unnecessarily shortened otherwise meaningful expressions to gain what they think is greater efficiency, or even elegance of expression.

Thus we get *quality time*, which is used frequently in talk of child rearing just as *quality parenting* is, to mean especially concentrated, thoughtful attention given to children in the course of their growing up. We read in articles in parents' magazines about the need to spend quality time with children, and we may hear a parent saying something like this after a busy week at the office:

> I need to spend some quality time with Hannah this weekend; I've been so busy with the contract negotiations that I've barely seen her.

It has also been appropriated by others to refer to times of particular productivity, as in this statement:

> I spent some quality time writing this proposal.

More meaningful ways of expressing the ideas in these two sentences are as follows:

> I need to do something special with Hannah this weekend; I've been so busy with the contract negotiations that I've barely seen her.

> I spent some concentrated, productive time writing this proposal.

Reality Check

This term falls into the same category as *perception check*, in that it attempts to dress up an otherwise plain need: to determine whether an issue, idea, or plan of action coincides with or reflects what people think of as the reality of a situation. In a discussion of a recycling plan presented by the City Manager, in which she presents figures on how much garbage residents produce, and on the capacity of the local landfill to receive it, a participant might say this:

> We've heard a lot of suggestions. It's time for a reality check.

What the person means, in clearer terms, is this:

> Let's review our plans for recycling and decide how they will help solve what we know as problems of waste disposal.

Some Questionable Verbs and Verbals

The verbs and verbals discussed below have all been created out of nouns commonly used in Standard American English, which in most cases express the activity in question as precisely and efficiently as these newly created ones.

To Access, Accessing

Clearly an unnecessary borrowing, *to access* comes directly from computer science, but it was originally expressed *to gain access*, and it was specifically used to mean to get into a program or a file. Now it is has been appropriated by other groups to mean simply to get to or into, or to see anything. People now want or need to access databases, library archives, files of any organization; some people want even to access people: the general manager, the executive vice president, or the president of an organization. The simpler and more understandable verbs *to get into*, *to look at*, or when referring to people, *to talk to*, are preferred.

To Conference, Conferencing

These terms were created out of the noun *conference*. The difference between creating *to conference* and *conferencing* and creating *to parent* and *parenting* is that we already have a perfectly clear and useful verb, *to confer*, commonly used to express the idea of meeting with people to discuss something. Had the new words *to conference* and *conferencing* been coined to describe an activity like attending conferences, for which we have no convenient, commonly understood descriptor, then it would be easier to understand how the words have come into use.

But that is not the case here. *To conference* and *conferencing* are used primarily among teachers (but their use is not limited to them) to describe the same small-group interaction that *to confer* describes. Thus we may hear or read this:

> I will be conferencing individually with my students during the eighth week of the semester. Individual conferencing plays a big role in my teaching.

These constructions add unnecessary weight to what can be clearly expressed by saying or writing this:

> I will be conferring individually with my students during the eighth week of the semester. Individual conferences play a big role in my teaching.

To Fast-Track, Fast-Tracking

In the world of racing (of any kind—car, horse, human) the term *fast track* is used to describe a track that has ideal conditions to produce the fastest times in competition. But it has been turned into a verb, *to fast-track*, which means to push ahead or promote someone or something.

If students in school are particularly bright and promising, they may be fast-tracked into a program, which is designed to challenge and test them. A teacher can be heard saying the following to a parent:

> I think you should consider fast-tracking Priscilla, since she's done so well on the last battery of achievement tests.

In business or government, some change in policy or procedure may be fast-tracked to get it going or past bureaucratic hurdles, so that the measure can be implemented immediately:

> Let's fast-track Plan B, so that we can get this product to market in time for Christmas.

Clearer, more understandable expressions would be as follows:

> I think you should consider moving Priscilla into a more challenging program, since she's done so well on the last battery of achievement tests.

> Let's push ahead with Plan B, so that we can get this product to market in time for Christmas.

Again, writers and speakers need to think about the need for the new verb. If there are already perfectly useful, understandable verbs such as *to promote, to move along,* even *to push,* is there need for yet another verb that expresses essentially the same idea?

To Impact, Impacting

Again, we have a perfectly clear and useful verb, *to affect,* which is all that *to impact* means. Impacts on anything—budgets, government programs, teaching, the conduct of business—appear somehow to have become more remarkable, and people feel the need, unnecessarily, to create a new verb out of the noun. And so we hear and read the following:

> The budget cuts ordered by Washington will impact us greatly.

> How do you think the new procedures and operations manual will impact line workers?

> How do you think the new directives from the Executive Office will be impacting our operations in the future?

All these statements can be simplified by using the verb *to affect* or the present participle, *affecting.* Writers and speakers should consider carefully the need to create a new verb or verbal when one already exists that conveys the meaning as well, without risking offense to more conventional users of the language.

To Mainstream, Mainstreaming

To mainstream and *mainstreaming* fall into a similar category as *to fast-track* and *fast-tracking.* Used almost exclusively in education and social work circles at present, to mainstream someone means to move someone from a peripheral or special position into a central position.

Some see the need, then, to mainstream students or clients into general programs and out of special programs, so that they can better adapt to more usual social, cultural, and educational conditions. Thus we may hear the following:

> The purpose of the second tier of our learning disabled program is to prepare students so that we can mainstream them into the general program.

A clearer statement would be this:

> The second phase of our learning disabled program is designed to prepare students to move into the general program.

To Network, Networking

To network, or *networking*, comes from the term *network*, which designates a structure or fabric of interconnecting items, such as threads, cords, or wires that meet or cross at certain places or junctures. But to network has come to mean to get in touch with people one knows in her or his professional field, or in some other area of interest. The goal may be getting a bill passed in a legislature, or establishing a referendum to be voted upon, or getting a friend, colleague, or protege hired in a position that he or she wants.

Networking can happen both within and outside organizations: all that is required is contacts who are in a position to get something done that needs to be done. Thus we may hear someone say this:

    I'll network with Joe and Mary to see what they can do.

The statement simply means this:

    I'll call Joe and Mary to see what they can do.

To Transition, Transitioning

We are beginning to hear more often *to transition* to mean something as simple as to move from one stage or condition to another, or to make a transition. In this case, the new word seems completely unnecessary: no cultural change appears to require it, and no real economy is gained by using it.

The logically attendant verbal, *transitioning*, appears in such phrases as the following:

    We are now transitioning from theory to implementation in Plan B of the 4-Year
    Plan.

The careful speaker or writer will use *moving* or *making a transition* rather than *transitioning*.

Other Problems with Diction

Two expressions—one a phrase, the other a clause—that have become overused and abused are *in terms of* and *as far as . . . is (are) concerned*. Speakers and writers, probably in an attempt to sound more formal, have peppered their language with them, but have wound up misusing them so that they no longer add anything but unnecessary weight.

In Terms Of

The phrase *in terms of* is correctly used when it connects one idea or set of conditions with another idea or set of conditions defined differently. Earlier in this chapter, in the discussion of the passive voice, this sentence appears:

> Depending on the subject and the context established, writers may choose to emphasize the results of the action rather than the action itself, or in terms of this discussion, they may want to emphasize the recipients of action rather than the performers of it.

In this case *in terms of* is used to remind readers that the function of the passive voice has already been defined in certain terms they are familiar with: "the recipients of action rather than the performers of it." But now that new terms have been introduced, "results of the action rather than the action itself," those should be spoken of in words that readers already know. The phrase *in terms of* helps make the connection.

Another example of the correct use of *in terms of* will help illustrate the point:

> Now that we have discussed the logistical difficulties of deploying troops to the Persian Gulf, we should talk about other difficulties in terms of funding.

There are two sets of difficulties here: one of logistics and one of funding, and they are defined differently. But if a writer wants to express a connection between the two, the phrase *in terms of* will do the job, if it is used in this way.

The phrase will not do the job, however, in the following example, written by an engineer working for a western public utility district:

> In terms of the excavating, the Utility District will resurvey the existing ground conditions to assess the work that will be required to reestablish and ensure the integrity of our transmission line structures.

There are other problems with this sentence, but the main problem is that *in terms of* just hangs out there with no sensible function. It is used incorrectly to get the sentence going, perhaps to make it sound more formal. But the result is just additional words that mean little, if anything. A more efficient and meaningful revision would be this:

> The Utility District will resurvey the ground conditions to determine what needs to be done to reestablish and ensure the integrity of our transmission line structures.

This final example was written by a clinical psychologist about one of his patients:

> Jon also has a great fear of trusting people and has mistrusted others for at least the past ten years, probably longer. When I asked Jon if he were to feel more comfortable in terms of decreased fear, how he would feel about getting help about working again, he replied that he would consider it if he could feel more comfortable. He emphasized that he hates feeling nervous and so upset and does not like himself that way.

Again there are several problems here, but the most troublesome is that the writer's use of *in terms of* and the clause in which it appears make very little sense. The writer seems to be saying something like this:

> I asked Jon if he felt less afraid, would he accept some help in finding work again.

Or maybe the writer is saying this:

> I asked Jon if he felt more comfortable about trusting others, would he be willing to look for work again.

Either revision is less awkward and makes better sense than the original.

As Far As . . . Is (Are) Concerned

The misuse of the clause *as far as . . . is (are) concerned* is at once easier to identify and harder to explain. The phrase is used correctly in the following examples:

> As far as excavating is concerned, resurveying the ground conditions to ensure the integrity of the Utility District's transmission lines will be necessary.

> The deployment of troops to the Persian Gulf has become increasingly difficult as far as funding is concerned.

The clause *as far as . . . is (are) concerned* is adverbial; that is, it modifies the verbs or predicates in question. But increasingly, speakers and writers have begun to lop off the words *is (are) concerned*, making the clause a phrase that has no grammatical function, making it in grammatical terms an absolute that has no meaning. Thus we hear and read statements like the following:

> As far as excavating, resurveying the ground conditions will be necessary.

> The deployment of troops to the Persian Gulf has become increasingly difficult as far as funding.

It is hard to explain why speakers and writers have made this change, but until it is fully accepted and no longer seen as an error by most writers and speakers, it stands out and draws negative attention to a person's writing or speaking.

EXERCISES

1. Take an inventory of the jargon used in your own area of study, and decide whether it is used intelligently and with purpose. Also decide whether the jargon is particularly germane to the field and therefore makes communication more efficient, or whether it has been appropriated from other fields simply because it is popular. How much of the jargon of your field has been appropriated by or has leaked into the vocabularies of other fields, or perhaps into people's everyday or nonprofessional language?

Write a short article for a professional newsletter that analyzes the use of diction (particularly jargon) in your field.

2. As you did in the exercise on passive constructions, go over a recent piece of your own writing and evaluate your diction. Do any of the terms and uses of terms we have defined here as "questionable" show up? Can you defend your use of them? If not, change them so that the piece in general becomes clearer and more readable.

Using the same piece, do the same for "there is or are," "in terms of," and "as far as" constructions.

PROBLEMS WITH EMBEDDED PROSE

Identifying Embedded Prose

Embedding is both a common and very serious problem of technical and professional writing. That the prose is embedded means that the writer's main point is buried within the words of the text. There are a number of ways to bury points: write them in the middle of a long paragraph; separate them with commas in a subordinate part of a sentence; omit them from the introduction to a report; write a descriptive executive summary that lists topics instead of a conclusive one that states conclusions, results, and recommendations.

For example, the following contains some embedding:

> It is hoped that future conferences will be planned in order to avoid repetition of some of the problems of this one. The Executive Committee, while working efficiently itself, was not wholly supported by the Transportation Committee and the Proceedings Committee.

For whatever reason, the author chose to waffle around the main point:

> The Transportation Committee and the Proceedings Committee must work within the deadlines given them by the Executive Committee.

It is more efficient and truthful to deliver this message directly and explicitly instead of embedding it. While the author may be concerned about wounded feelings, they may be assuaged by equally concrete recommendations to help these committees get their work done.

Why Embedded Prose Is a Common Problem

Embedded prose is so common for a number of reasons. First, people often don't think through what they have to write before they start writing. Thus, the text such writers deliver is really their attempt to figure out what they want to say. And because such writers often don't rewrite, the reader has to do what should be the writer's work to figure out the main point. If we remember the model of the harried reader, we understand that such embedded prose is extremely frustrating to read.

Another reason people write embedded prose is that they want to back off a bit from what they have figured out to say. They want to distance themselves from the bad news they must tell, or perhaps they want to try to protect the reader from a less than flattering conclusion. At any rate, these circumstances amount to the writer's trying to sneak the unwelcome news into a document. In fact, students are quite open about using this strategy when asked to explain how they approach a particularly difficult point. This strategy may not even be conscious; most of us are uncomfortable with any situation that demands we confront something.

Why the Strategy of Embedding Is a Bad Policy

The "sneak-it-in" strategy is a bad one, though, and very often does not work. It is a bad policy ethically because writers find themselves in the position of trying to lie or, to use a euphemism, trying to suppress some aspect of the truth. It is also a bad policy practically because, once caught, writers lose a great deal of credibility. Neither is it a strategy management appreciates. The only way to fix problems efficiently is to have a clear notion of them to begin with. If the problem is defined vaguely or hazily, or if the mere existence of a problem is hidden, then it is virtually impossible for management to summon the resources necessary to fix it. Moreover, managers want to hear about problems in their groups as soon as possible; they find it humiliating to be told about their own problems by someone else.

A noteworthy situation has called our attention to the problem of embedding in technical and professional writing. A Bill Moyers special included a memo from the space shuttle case. This memo reveals that the O-ring problem indeed was called to the attention of management. But the problem was mentioned in the middle of a middle paragraph in a rather long, single-spaced memo. Someone skimming the memo would not necessarily have caught the problem. Granted, the problem was also discussed among engineers and upper management; but it is very hard for people to listen in stressful situations, and it is even harder for people to remember what they heard after they have listened. When information is written down, it can have a powerful impact. But it must be written down so that the reader can't miss it or skip it. Writers of procedures are also notorious for burying material that operators need immediate access to; and accident reports often do a good job of obscuring instead of clarifying the events involved. Situations such as these can result in unsafe practices and insufficient knowledge to correct a problem.

The Writer's Commitments to Avoid Embedded Prose

The antidote for embedded prose is explicit prose. Explicit prose calls for intellectual, rhetorical, and ethical commitments from the writer.

The Intellectual Commitment

The intellectual commitment is to think carefully through the message before sending it. Writers need to understand that the first draft of a text—the draft that searches for the writer's point—is never sufficient for any audience; the writer must always take the extra step to revise the original so that the main point appears up front in the text. The conclusion, main point, thesis—whatever you want to call it—should appear in the first or second paragraph of a letter or memo and in the first or second page of a report. Technical and professional writing is the opposite of a good detective story, which announces the perpetrator on the last page. The harried reader wants no surprises, no red herrings, no suspense.

The Rhetorical Commitment

The rhetorical commitment to be explicit is the contract the reader has with the writer. In this contract the writer promises to deliver a professional discussion about certain topics, in a certain order, for certain reasons. Once writers set the contract, they must abide by it. If they do not, they will confuse the readers, who will expect certain topics, in the order promised to them, for the reasons given.

The rhetorical commitment appears throughout a text, not just in a clear thesis statement. It is seen in a sentence of division, for example, that signals the reader about the number of secondary arguments a writer will cover: "There are two important reasons for this decision." The reader then knows what to expect: "Ah! I must read through *two* arguments." The commitment shows in topic sentences to paragraphs. A good test of this level of explicitness is to read through a report from one topic sentence to another, picking one's way through the document as if walking from clear patch to clear patch on an icy sidewalk. If the sense of the document doesn't hold together on a reading of topic sentences, then the chances are good that additional or clearer topic sentences need to be written. We also see the rhetorical commitment in explicit transitional words and phrases, like *because, first, on the other hand.* Not only do these transitions make the prose flow, but they also specify the logic of the text for the reader. For example, instead of requiring the reader to keep track of the argument the writer is concentrating on, the writer reminds the reader very simply through the use of phrases such as *"the final point,"* and the like.

Two other expressions of rhetorical commitment are the conclusive abstract and the conclusive summary (see Chapter 2). Instead of just describing what kind of material appears in a text, the conclusive abstract tells what the author's main point is. The conclusive summary tells what the main point and supporting points are and even what the report's recommendations are. These important technical and professional forms, the abstract and the summary, must give the reader the essence of the text. Having read the abstract or summary, the reader can decide whether the text is necessary to read and even decide which particular parts of the text to delve into in more depth. These forms are not teases to try to entice the reader to start reading. Remember that technical and professional writers don't need to entice their readers, except to read journal articles; their readers have a professional responsibility to read the material and they very often have a need to know the contents. All this writing answers a specific purpose, most often assigned. While unsolicited proposals are certainly not assigned, they are professional documents. No one is reading such documents for fun; professionals read them to get their work done. So, the writer is giving nothing away by making abstracts and summaries as explicit as they can be. In fact, such explicitness often motivates readers to delve more closely into the body of the report. The clarity of explicit writing gives the reader some hope that the details will be equally clear and purposeful, and experienced readers know that this clarity is a rare enough commodity in the technical and professional world.

Compare, for example, these two versions of an abstract:

Version 1: This report covers the accident to the silicon-controlled rectifier (SCR) that occurred 10/94. The report describes the likely cause, responsive measures, and lessons learned.

Version 2: October 1994's silicon-controlled rectifier (SCR) accident was most likely caused by a fire in the control house. That fire's cause is as yet to be determined. Response was somewhat inadequate, which may have contributed to the extensive damage. The SCR casing should be protected with a double-layered steel cover.

The first version gives the reader virtually no information. The second version is very conclusive, providing the investigators' findings about the fire.

The Ethical Commitment

The ethical commitment the writer takes on is to make the truth explicit. There is a good deal of pressure on people in professional situations to interpret events in the most flattering light. And it is true that events must be interpreted; the facts do not always speak for themselves, nor do the facts always cooperate in getting to the heart of an issue. So, given a certain audience, a writer will choose language that best reveals the truth to that group. For example, there are ways of revealing that mistakes were made in previous estimates that are clearer and more productive than other ways would be. And we have been saying all through this textbook that the writer must take the needs of the audience into account. However, the writer should not change the truth depending on the audience.

The writer should adjust a text's language for jargon, level of technicality, and insider-outsider factors so that the text's truth will be as clear as possible. For example, insiders in an organization might already know that a certain facility is still on the drawing board, but that it is useful to speculate about the impact of that facility once it's built. Outsiders, however, may not know that the facility has not been built yet. Therefore, a problem exists if the writer uses present tense, which would give the impression that the facility is already built and functioning. In the following sentence it is impossible to say whether or not an existing facility is being discussed:

The level of pollutants from Steam Closet II may well significantly decrease.

It is better to refer to *the proposed Steam Closet II* or *the still-to-be-built Steam Closet II* to make Steam Closet II's status clear to the lay audience. The ethical commitment means more than agreeing not to lie; it means writing specifically to prevent reader misunderstandings and false assumptions.

One often reads advice to technical and professional writers that sounds like this: be concise. In fact, many people try to use conciseness as a kind of defining characteristic of technical and professional writing. It may well be that such advice is a confused plea for explicitness. Concise prose that is not conclusive, not explicit, is still relatively worthless as technical and professional writing. The demand on the writer is to get to the point, not to limit the number of words on a page. If a writer knows the point and gets there efficiently, then a page can read as quickly as a paragraph that contains an embedded point.

Embedding has been called the most serious problem in technical and professional writing. While this section concentrates on embedding as a discrete problem, it actually pervades all documents. Writers should read their own and others' writing specifically with an eye to ferreting out embedding.

EXERCISES

1.   Find the embedded points in the following passage; then rewrite the passage to make the points explicit.

I have some experience fixing motors of all kinds. These are DC motors and motor-generators. I also have worked in customer service for 15 years. Customer service means taking complaints and suggestions. Then, there were 5 years when I did some accounting and some sales. The sales were mostly trailer hitches and special features. My school experience was also in motors and dynamics, with the usual math and humanities courses that might interest a company like yours.

2.   Review the interview report you wrote for your instructor in Chapter 3 for any sign of embedding. Revise the report to make your essential points explicit.

3.   Rewrite a piece of writing you find, or one supplied by your instructor, that suffers from embedded prose. Bring important ideas, conclusions, or implied recommendations to prominent structural positions so that readers won't miss them. Then write a short analysis of your rewrite, suggesting why you think the original was written the way it was, and how you think your rewrite improves it.

PROBLEMS WITH SENTENCE STRUCTURE

Sentence Fragments

Sentence fragments are incomplete sentences; they are missing either a subject or a predicate, or both. They are considered a problem in writing because they confuse the reader. For example, if I leave this as a sentence. You will be tripped up in your reading because the previous sentence is not complete, but a fragment missing both subject and predicate (or noun phrase and verb phrase). Some other examples of fragments follow:

The engine, running at 350 rpms and catching on the clutch.

After hours of discussion, the group came to a consensus. That the best course was to follow the procedure.

In the first example the sentence fragment is lacking a predicate. The phrases that follow the noun, *engine*, all modify the noun; they do not describe any action or current state of the engine. In fact, if we deleted them, the fact that we have only a modified noun in that fragment would become absolutely clear. If the engine's current state is being described by the modifying phrases, then we need only add the word *is*:

The engine is running at 350 rpms and catching on the clutch.

In the second example we see a common sort of sentence fragment that results from incorrect punctuation, although chances are that the writer is also confused about the grammar of a complete sentence. The second sentence is obviously supposed to be a part of the first, the complete sentence. Because of worries over sentence length, the writer punctuated too soon. Notice that the fragment contains neither a subject nor a predicate. The corrected version shows that the fragment's whole function is to explain what the consensus was:

After hours of discussion, the group came to a consensus that the best course was to follow the procedure.

When your instructor has marked sentence fragments in your work, you need to note the pattern the fragments take. Perhaps you regularly forget the verb phrase, or perhaps you include it but punctuate it as a fragment. Usually students' fragments contain a pattern of some sort, so you should become familiar with your own grammatical pattern. Then, when you edit your work, you can read through once specifically for that pattern of error.

You should also either work in your school's writing laboratory or learn basic grammar with the help of a tutor. Students in college today have not necessarily received any grammatical training. If you are one of these students, then you must make up the slack in your education. Grammar provides the language necessary to talk about sentences; it is very difficult to correct your own prose without this basic understanding. While it is not anyone's idea of fun to learn grammar, the fact is that the technical and professional world expects standard written English from its workers. Whereas you could write several drafts of one paper in your composition class, you must write more efficiently in your professional life. As a professional, you will be expected to deliver standard written English fairly promptly. Reviewers will catch the errors that they see, but they will expect you to deliver the basics, and complete sentence structure is a basic.

Run-On Sentences and Comma Splices

A comma splice occurs when two sentences that could stand on their own are joined with a comma. The resulting sentence is called a run-on sentence. The following is such a sentence:

```
The engine ran well for the first trial, for the second it performed poorly.
```

Often the comma seems sufficient to the writer, because the writer sees it as a full stop, a full break in the flow of the sentence. But a conventional reader will see the comma as a slight stop, not the full stop we are accustomed to seeing at the end of a sentence.

There are at least three ways to correct a comma splice:

1. Put a period between the two complete sentences:

```
The engine ran well for the first trial. For the second it performed poorly.
```

2. Put a semicolon between the two complete sentences:

```
The engine ran well for the first trial; for the second it performed poorly.
```

3. Add the necessary coordinating conjunction after the comma:

```
The engine ran well for the first trial, but for the second it performed poorly.
```

The coordinating conjunctions are *and, but, or,* and *nor.*

In order to catch comma splices and run-on sentences, you must first realize that you tend to write them. If your instructor has marked them in your work, then you know that you write in that pattern and can edit for comma splices particularly. You need to understand that while some will defend sentence fragments as stylistic flourishes, none will defend run-on sentences. They are difficult to read.

Fused Sentences

As their name indicates, fused sentences are fusions of more than one sentence without any punctuation like the example of this sentence that we're working on here this first sentence is a fused sentence. You should have no doubt that fused sentences impede reading.

Since we are concerned with technical and professional writing and not experimental novels in this discussion, we must reject fused sentences for their nonstandard structure. The obvious correction is to punctuate them coherently:

```
As their name indicates, fused sentences are fusions of more than one sentence
without any punctuation. This first sentence is a fused sentence.
```

We have edited and punctuated the fused sentence so that it is grammatically correct, although now nonsensical.

Again, if you see that you tend to write fused sentences, you must read through all your work one extra time, focusing specifically on finding fused sentences. It may help you to read your work aloud, since fused sentences will require you to take a deep breath in the middle of the sentence.

EXERCISES

1. Write a brief paragraph summarizing the patterns of error your instructor has marked in your work. You will need to go back through your papers to find these

patterns. Patterns of error certainly extend beyond our discussion here of sentence structure problems. You may find that your patterns include chronic difficulties like subject-verb agreement, noun-pronoun agreement, faulty diction, undeveloped introductions, or undeveloped conclusions. Include embedded prose and the other topics discussed in this appendix as part of your analysis.

2. Correct the errors in the following sentences. If a sentence is correct, mark it with a *C*.

    a. The validation phase has gone smoothly so far, the results are as predicted.

    b. Our recommendations, based on study of your numbers over the past 2 years.

    c. Without actually going into the details of the program.

    d. Sinking the second pilot hole proved the most difficult because the slurry from the first threatened to swamp the stabilizers.

    e. The tests require rework, not one of them validated our predictions.

    f. When Sales decides to run another contest like this one, we suggest that the work of the rest of the staff be considered more carefully because the past few weeks have brought continued disruption to our operation from the start we were worried about this possibility.

    g. Continuing the project simply is not feasible now, no one knows exactly when we should resume it, but we should stop it immediately.

SELECTED BIBLIOGRAPHY

Alley, Michael. *The Craft of Scientific Writing*. Englewood Cliffs, NJ: Prentice-Hall, 1987.

Anderson, Paul V. *Technical Writing: A Reader-Centered Approach*. New York: Harcourt Brace Jovanovich, 1987.

Anderson, Paul V., John R. Brockman and Carolyn R. Miller, eds. *New Essays in Technical and Scientific Communication*. Farmingdale, NY: Baywood, 1983.

Blicq, Ron S. *Technically Write! Communicating in a Technological Era*. 2nd ed. Englewood Cliffs, NJ: Prentice—Hall, 1981.

Blyler, Nancy Roundy. "The Heuristics of Pedagogy: Approaches to Teaching Technical Writing." *The Technical Writing Teacher 13* (1986): 101–111.

Bolles, Richard N. *What Color Is Your Parachute?* Berkeley, CA: Ten Speed Press, 1992.

The Chicago Manual of Style. 13th ed. Chicago: University of Chicago Press, 1982.

Cunningham, Donald H., and Herman A. Estrin. eds. *The Teaching of Technical Writing*. Urbana, IL: NCTE 1987.

Dobrin, David N. "Is Technical Writing Particularly Objective?" *College English 47*, No. 3 (March 1985): 237–251.

———. "What's Technical about Teaching Technical Writing?" in *New Essays in Technical and Scientific Communication*. Paul V. Anderson, R. John Brockman, and Carolyn R. Miller, eds. Farmingdale, NY: Baywood, 1983.

———. "What's Difficult about Teaching Technical Writing." *College English 44*, No. 2 (February 1982): 135–140.

Feinberg, Susan. *Components of Technical Writing*. NY: Holt, Rinehart and Winston, 1988.

Flower, Linda. "Writer-Based Prose: A Cognitive Basis for Problems in Writing." *College English 41*, No. 1 (September 1979): 19–37.

———. *Problem-Solving Strategies for Writing*. 2nd ed. NY: Harcourt Brace Jovanovich, 1985.

Flower, Linda, and John R. Hayes. "The Cognition of Discovery: Defining a Rhetorical Problem." *College Composition and Communication 31*, No. 1 (February 1980): 21–32.

———. "Problem-Solving Strategies and the Writing Process." *College English 39*, No. 4 (December 1977): 449–461.

Forbes, Chris J., and Tracy T. Montgomery. "Towards Advanced Instruction in Academics and Industry."

Paper delivered at the 34th International Technical Communication Conference, May 11–14, 1987. Denver, CO.

Glasstetter, S. R., T. T. Montgomery, and D. L. Plung. "Flow Charting: A Logical Approach to Procedure Writing." Paper delivered at the International Professional Communication Conference, October 22–24, 1986. Charlotte, NC.

Hairston, Maxine. "The Winds of Change: Thomas Kuhn and the Revolution in the Teaching of Writing." *College Composition and Communication 33*. No. 1 (February 1982), 76–88.

Harkins, C., and D. L. Plung. *A Guide for Writing Better Technical Papers*. New York: IEEE Press, 1982.

Harmon, Joseph E. "The Structure of Scientific and Engineering Papers: A Historical Perspective." *IEEE Transactions on Professional Communication 32*, No. 3 (September 1989): 132–138.

Harris, Elizabeth. "Applications of Kinneavy's *Theory of Discourse* to Technical Writing." *College English 40* (1979): 627.

———. "In Defense of the Liberal Arts Approach to

Technical Writing." *College English 44* (1982): 625–632.

Harty, Kevin J., and John Keenan. *Writing for Business and Industry: Process and Product.* NY: Macmillan, 1987.

Hayes, John R., and Linda S. Flower. "Writing as Problem Solving." *Visible Language 14,* No. 4 (1980): 388–399.

Keene, Michael L. *Effective Professional Writing.* Lexington, MA: D. C. Heath, 1987.

Kennedy, George E. "Teaching Formal Proposals: A Versatile Minicourse in Technical Writing." *Journal of Technical Writing and Communication 13,* No. 2 (1983): 123–137.

Lannon, John M. *Technical Writing.* Boston: Little, Brown, 1979.

Marder, Daniel. "Technical Reporting is Technical Rhetoric," *Technical Communication 26,* No. 4 (1978): 11.

Markel, Michael H. *Technical Writing: Situations and Strategies.* NY: St. Martin's Press, 1984.

Miller, Carolyn R. "A Humanistic Rationale for Technical Writing." *College English 40* (February 1979): 613.

Mills, Gordon H., and John H. Walter. *Technical Writing.* NY: Holt, Rinehart and Winston. 1986.

Montgomery, Tracy T. "Bad Company: Why Technology Is a Problem for Technical Writers." *Rendezvous 26,* No. 2 (Spring 1991): 99–105.

———. "Beyond the Stereotype: Teaching the Complexities of Audience Analysis." Paper presented at the International Technical Communication Conference. May 1989, Chicago, IL.

———. "A Method-Oriented, Dramatic Technical and Professional Writing Course."

(Proceedings of the International Professional Communication Conference, October 29–November 1, 1992, Orlando, FL.) NY: IEEE Press, 1991, 84–88.

———. "Negotiating Corporate Culture: An Exercise in Documentation. *The Technical Writing Teacher 18,* No. 1 (Winter 1991): 75–80.

Montgomery, Tracy T., and Daniel Plung. "When Engineers Talk to Management: Writing Effective Material for Progress Reports." Paper delivered at the International Professional Communication Conference, October 13–16, 1987, Winnipeg, MB, Canada.

———. "A Definition and Illustrated Taxonomy of Technical Writing." (Proceedings of the International Professional Communication Conference. October 1988, Seattle, WA.) NY: IEEE Press, 1988, 141–146.

Montgomery, Tracy T., Susan R. Glasstetter, and D. L. Plung. "The Professional Imperative: Redefining the Boundaries of Editorial Responsibility." Paper delivered at the 34th International Technical Communication Conference, May 11–14, 1987, Denver. CO.

Moran, Michael G., and Debra Journet, eds. *Research in Technical Communication: A Bibliographic Sourcebook.* Westport, CT: Greenwood Press, 1985.

Pearsall, Thomas E., and Donald H. Cunningham. *How to Write for the World of Work.* New York: Holt, Rinehart and Winston, 1978.

Philosophical Transactions of the Royal Society. Vols. 1 and 65. London: The Royal Society.

Plung, Daniel L., Tracy T. Montgomery, and Susan R.

Glasstetter. "WIPP Documentation Plan." Poster session at the Waste Management '86 Conference, March 1986, Tucson, AZ.

Randolph, W. Alan, and Barry Z. Posner. "What Every Manager Needs to Know about Project Management." *Sloan Management Review* (Summer 1988): 65–73.

Sawyer, Thomas M., ed. *Technical and Professional Communication: Teaching in the Two-Year College, Four-Year College, and Professional School.* Ann Arbor: Professional Communication Press, 1977.

Schindler, George E. "Why Engineers and Scientists Write as They Do—Twelve Characteristics of Their Prose." *IEEE Transactions in Professional Communication 10* (1967): 27.

Selzer, Jack. "The Composing Processes of an Engineer." *College Composition and Communication 34,* No. 2 (May 1983): 178–187.

Shimberg, H. Lee. "Ethics and Rhetoric in Technical Writing." *Technical Communication 26,* No. 4 (1978): 16–18.

Smith, D. B. "Axioms for English in a Technical Age." *College English 48,* No. 6 (October 1986): 567–579.

Smith, Terry C. "What Bugs Engineers Most about Report Writing." *Technical Communication 24,* No. 4 (1976): 185–187.

Stephenson, Dwight W., ed. *Courses, Components, and Exercises in Technical Communication.* Urbana, IL: NCTE Press, 1981.

Stratton, Charles R. "Technical Writing: What It Is and What It Isn't." *Journal of Technical Writing and Communication 9,* No. 1 (1979), 9–16.

U.S. Government Printing Office

Style Manual. Washington, DC: U.S. Government Prinring Office, 1984.

Walzer, Arthur E. "The Ethics of False *Implicature* in Technical and Professional Writing Courses." *Journal of Technical Writing and Communication 19,* No. 2 (1989), 149–160.

Weisman, Herman M. *Basic Technical Writing.* 5th ed. Columbus, OH: Charles E. Merrill, 1985.

Zappen, James P. "The Discourse Community in Scientific and Technical Communication: Institutional and Social Views." *Journal of Technical Writing and Communication 19,* No. 1 (1989), 1–11.

INDEX

Abstracts, 102
Active voice, 459–462
Administrative procedure,
    309–314, 317–320
Administrative writing, 325–353
    conventions, 333–334
    efficiency, 329
    errors in, 337, 339
    process, 341–344
    tasks, defined, 7
Alignment (see Justification)
Amenities in oral presentations,
    437–438
Analogies, 31
Analysis, 38–41
Andreini, Kay, 133–143
Anecdotes, 440–441
Annotated bibliographies, 37–38
Annotated texts, for instruction:
    memo report, 68
    problem-solving memo, 69
    professional completion report,
        185–206
    professional periodic report,
        164–168
    professional trip report,
        233–239
    standard letter (block format),
        330
    standard memo, 331–332
Annotation, 37
Antonyms, 30
Appendix, 459–481
Area format, 419–420
Audience, 53, 58–65, 79–80,
    429–434, 437, 447–451
Audience analysis, 58–60, 91–94,
    372–373, 432–434
    in cover letters, 372–373
    first level, 59–60
    in job search, 359–362
    second level, 60

Audience profiles, 60–65

Block text, 412
Boards of directors, 444, 455–456
Bullets, 415–416

Carbon copies (see Copy notation)
Case studies:
    Allen, Rick, 294–295
    Cox, Mary Anne, 50–51
    Dalton, Jay, 326, 344–348
    Ersting, Kevin, 404–405,
        421–425
    Feldstein, Leah, 156, 428
    Gutierrez, Alfred, 394–395
    Hanley, Bob, 293
    James, Susan, 2, 22
    Kennewick, Bruce, 228,
        233–239
    Loomis, John, 358, 367,
        370–371, 376, 379–380
    Robinson, Al, 241
    Warner, Ruth, 292
    Wynjenek, Patricia, 292
Chalkboards, 437
Charts, 415
    Flow, 307–309
    GANTT, 105
    milestone, 107
    PERT, 106
    pie, 417
Checklist for research process, 39
Civil groups, 453–455
Collaboration, 393–402
    overview, 395–396
Collaboration process, 396–401
    distribution and document con-
        trol, 401
    drafting, 398
    establishment of tracking sys-
        tem, 398

Collaboration process (cont.):
    final revision and product
        preparation, 401
    initial planning, 396–398
    organization and assignment of
        tasks, 396–398
    review and comment, 398–401
    sample review and comment
        sheet, 399
Columns, 412–413
Comma splices, 480–481
Committees, to present to,
    452–453
Comparison and contrast, for de-
    fining, 27
Completion reports, 170–225
    format, 175–185
        academic, research-oriented
            audience, 181–185
        nonacademic audience,
            175–181
    fundamentals, 171
    purpose and rationale, 171
    questions they answer,
        172–174
    sample professional completion
        report, 185–206
    sample student completion
        report, 208–225
Conciseness, 465
Conclusiveness, 37
Conference rooms, 437
Context, 53, 65–66, 434
Contracts, format, 408
Conventions, v. creativity in
    writing, 408–409, 424
Conventions of administrative
    writing, 329, 333–334
    length, 333–334
    structure and content, 333
Copy editing, 401
Copy notation, 340, 349–350

Correspondence (*see* Administrative writing; Letters; Memoranda)
Courtesy copies (*see* Copy notation)
Cover letters, 363, 372–378
   adaptation for audience, 372–373
   informing through summary, 373
   persuasion in, 373
   sample, for an advertised position, 374, 376
   sample, for an unadvertised position (unsolicited application), 378–380
   synthesis in, 373
Cover pages, 102, 104
Creativity, as opposed to convention, 424

Decision making, oral presentations for, 455–466
Definition process, summary, 32
   analogies, 31
   comparison and contrast in, 27
   etymology, 29
   metaphors, 30
   process description, 27–28
   similes, 30
   synonyms, 30
Design of research, 33
Desselle, Diane, 145–153
Diagrams, 415
   (*See also* Graphs; Illustrations)
Diction, 467–474
Dictionaries, format, 408
Direct beneficiaries, 91
Displaced text, 415–416
Document analysis worksheet, 79–80
Document design, 403–426
   elements, 407–421
      graphics, 414–421
         bar graphs, 417–419
         displaced text, 415–416
         illustrations and drawings, 420–421
         line graphs, 419–420
         photographs, 420
         pie charts, 417
         tables, 416–417
      text, 409–414
      white space, 408–409

Document design (*cont.*):
   creativity versus convention in, 424
   functions, 406
   justification, 413–414
   presentation, 405–407
   sample professional document design, 421–425
   successful design, 406
Documentation through memos and letters, 327–328
   via transmittal letters, 349
   of problems, 401
Drawings, 420–421

Editing, 398–401
Effective communication, 52
Efficiency in administrative writing, 329
Embedded prose, 475–479
Engineering Feasibility of a 150-kW Irrigation Pumping Plant Using Shallow Solar Ponds, 245–271
Environmental factors, 53
   (*See also* Context)
Errors:
   in administrative writing, 337, 339
   in job application process, 360–362
Ethical constraints, 78, 80
Ethical stance, 53–54, 66, 434
Ethics, of embedded prose, 478
Etymology, analogical, 29
Examples, 28–29
Executive summaries, 37, 102
Explicitness, 38

Feasibility studies, 240–271
   fundamentals, 240
   purpose and rationale, 240, 242
   questions they answer, 243
   sample engineering feasibility study, 244–271
   sample outline for, 243–244
      abstract, 243–244
      analysis, 244
      conclusion and recommendation, 244
      description of the problem and summary of testing, 244
      discussion, 244
      future needs, 244

Figures, 417
   bar graphs, 417–418
   illustrations and drawings, 420–421
   line graphs, 419–420
   stack graphs, 418–419
   (*See also* Graphics)
Flowcharts, 307–309
Format:
   of a completion report, 175–185
   of dictionaries, 408
   of glossaries, 408
   of letters, 328–330
   of manuals, 301–302
   of memos, 328–329
   multicolumn, 412–413
   note, marginal, 413
   of newsletters, 421–424
   of periodic reports, 163
   of procedures, 307–309
   of proposals, 100–107
   of résumés, 365–372
   of scientific reports, 275
   single-column, 412–413
   of textbooks, 408
   of trip reports, 232
Full justification, 413–414
   (*See also* Justification)
Fused sentences, 481

GANTT chart, 105
Ghost writing, 70, 339–340, 350, 353
Glasstetter, Susan, 307
Glossaries, format, 408
Grammar (*see* Appendix)
Graphics, 414–421, 441–447, 454, 456
Graphs:
   bar, 417–418
   line, 419–420
   stack, 418–419
GSOPs (General Standard Operating Procedures), 229

Handouts, 437
Headings, 419–411
History of discovery or development, 31

Illustrations, 420–421
Implementation, in technical problem solving, 44–46

Interview process, in the job search, 386–389
  guidelines, 386–389
  interviewers, 386
Interviewing an expert, in research, 81–82

Jargon, 467
Job application errors, 360–362
Job search (*See* Professional job search)
Justification, in document design, 413–414

Lab reports (*see* Scientific writing)
Lead role, in collaboration, 395–397
Length, 369
Letters, 327–344, 348–351
Lions clubs (*see* Civil groups)
LSOPs (Local Standard Operating Procedures), 229

Manuals, 293, 296–299, 301–304
  appendixes and attachments, 303
  formatting, 301–301
  organization, 302
  readability, 302
  sample outline for, 303–304
Margins, in document design, 409
Memo, interoffice, sample, annotated, 69
Memo, with no apparent purpose, 335
  revised, 338
Memo report, sample, annotated, 68
Memoranda, general discussion, 327–348
Metaphors, in definition, 30
Methods section, in proposals, 96–98
Milestone chart, 107
Multicolumn format, in document design, 412–413

Narratives (*see* Case studies)
Negative space (*see* White space)
Newsletters, 415, 421–424
Newton, Sir Isaac, 272
Nominalization, 463–466

Nominals (*see* Nominalization)
Note marginal format, 413

Objectives statement, in résumés, 363, 368
Objectivity, 461–462
Operations procedure, 314–316
Optiks, 272
Oral communication, 429–430
Oral presentations, 430–447, 451–456
  as meal, 439–447
Oral reports (*see* Oral presentations)
Otis, Susan, 133–143
Outlines, 410
Overhead projectors, 437

Palatino, 369
Passive voice, 459–462, 464
Patterns of error, 481–482
Peer review worksheet for proposals, 110–111
Periodic reports, 156–169
  format, 163
  fundamentals, 157–158
  purpose and rationale, 157–158
  questions they answer, 158–163
  sample professional periodic report, 164–168
PERT chart, 106
Photographs, 420
Physical descriptions, 27
Physical setting, for oral presentations, 429–430, 437–438
Placement file, 363–364
Platt, E. A., 245–271
Plung, D. L., Dr., 307
Policy statements, 292, 296–301
  guidelines, 299–300
  sample, 300
Position descriptions, 363, 365
  sample, 374–375
Posters, 437
Practical proposals, 88
Practice, for oral presentations, 438–439
Presentation, in document design, 405–407
Presentations (*see* Oral presentations)
Private sector (*see* Proposal writing process, review process)

Problem, 5
  defined, 5
  rhetorical elements, 5
  technical elements, 5
Problem solving, 52
  rhetorical, 52
  technical, 52
Procedures, 294–299, 303–320
  essential characteristics, 305–307
  guidelines, 303, 305
  model, 307–309
    flowchart components, 308–309
    action step, 308
    cross reference, 308–309
    decision step, 308
    note, 309
    warning, 308
  sample administrative procedure, 309–314
  analysis of, 317–320
  sample operations procedure, 314–316
Process description, 27–28
Professional activity, 5–7
Professional collaboration, 395–397
  role of lead, 395–397
Professional job search, 357–389
  fundamentals, 359–362
  guidelines, 386–389
    honesty, 389
    preparedness, 387–388
    responsiveness, 387
    trick and hostile questions, 388
  interviewers, 386
  job search process, 362–378
  shaping up a student résumé, 382–386
Professional profiles, 7–16
  chief chemist (Elizabeth J. Frederickson), 9–10
  director of catering (Bruce K. Kennewick), 14–15
  director of client relations (Leah S. Feldstein), 10–11
  director of marketing (James R. Brookings), 13–14
  director, university art museum (Victoria P. Wilson), 12–13

Professional profiles (*cont.*):
highlights, 15–16
operations engineer (Joseph T. Brown), 7–9
time spent on writing-related tasks, 9–11, 13–15
Professional writing continuum, 273–274
Professional writing samples:
block letter, 330
professional memo, 331, 345–346
professional transmittal letter, 351–352
professional trip report, 232–239
rejected job application letter, 361
review and comment sheet, for collaboration, 399
Professionalism, 3–5
defined, 3
examples of its lack, 4–5
Professionals, defined, 3
Progress reports (*see* Periodic reports)
Proofing, 353
Proposal writing process, 88–100
audience analysis, 91–94
budget and schedule, 99–100
expected results and evaluation plan, 100
facilities, 98
methods, 96–98
personnel, 98–99
review of literature and previous work, 95–96
review process, 92–94
private organizations, 93–94
public organizations, 92–93
statement of objectives, 94–95
statement of problem, 88, 90
Proposals, 83–153
format, 100–107
basic, 101
expanded, 101–107
abstract or executive summary, 102
cover page, 102, 104
graphic depictions of schedule, 105–107
reference cited, 106–107
table of contents, 105
transmittal letter, 102, 103

Proposals (*cont.*):
purpose and rationale, 85
student samples, 113–153
types, 85–88
Public sector (*see* Proposal writing process, review process)
Public speaking, 447–451
Punctuation (*see* Appendix)
Purpose, 53, 56–58
primary, 57
secondary, 57–58

Questions:
completion reports answer, 172–174
feasibility studies answer, 243
periodic reports answer, 158–163
proposals answer, 89
rhetorical problem solving answers, 55
for solving problems, 16–18
for technical problem solving, 24
Readability, 302
Reading professionally, 334–341
implicit level, 339–341
identity of author, 339–340
writer's tone, 339
indication of a ghostwriter, 340
to interpret recipients of copies, 340–341
literal level, 334–339
Recipients of copies, 340–341
Recommendation report (*see* Feasibility studies)
Recommenders, 363–364
References cited section, of a proposal, 106–107
Reports (*see* Completion reports; Feasibility studies; Memo reports; Oral presentations; Periodic reports; Trip reports)
Request for bid (RFB), 86
Request for proposal (REP), 86, 92–94
Request for quote (RFQ), 86
Research, 32–38, 363, 365
annotated bibliography, 37–38
complex primary research with fieldwork, 33–35
of prosective empoyers, 363, 365

Research (*cont.*):
secondary, 35–37
straightforward primary research, 33
Research design, 33–35
Research proposals, 87–88
Resolution and synthesis, in technical problem solving, 41–44
Respondent evaluation form, oral presentations, 457–458
Résumés, 363, 365–372
basics, 365–366
arrangement, 366
audience, 366
purpose, 365–366
readability, 369
length, 369
typography, 369
white space, 369
revision of, 368–369
sample college résumé, 366–367
revision plan, 366, 368
sample professional résumé, 369–372
Review and editing tasks, defined, 7
Review of literature and previous work section, in proposals, 85–96
Reviewing audiences, 92
RFB (*see* Request for Bid)
RFP (*see* Request for Proposal)
RFQ (*see* Request for Quote)
Rhetoric, 52
Rhetorical analysis, 430–434
Rhetorical problem solving, 49–82, 343–344, 430–434
audience, 53
context, 53
ethical stance, 53–54
overview, 51–56
purpose, 53
a recursive process, 66–67
Right justification, 414
Run-on sentences, 480–481

Samples:
block letter, 330
professional memo, 331, 345–346
professional trip report, 232–239

Samples (*cont.*):
  professional transmittal letter, 351–352
  rejected job application letter, 361
  review and comment sheet, for collaboration, 399
  student completion report, 208–225
  student proposals, 113–153
  student résumés, 367, 383, 385
  student scientific article, 277–290
Sans serif, 412
Schedule, graphics, 105–107
Scientific report, format, 275
Scientific writing, 272–290
  evolution of, 272–273
  fundamentals, 272
  in professional writing continuum, 273–274
Sentence fragments, 479–480
Sentence structure (*see* Comma splices: Fused sentences; Run-on sentences; Sentence fragments)
Serif, 412
Setting, in oral presentations (*see* Physical setting)
Similes, in definition, 30
Single-column format, 412–413
Soderstrom, Sheryl. 113–132, 208–225
Solicited proposals, 86–87, 90
Solving problems, by asking and answering questions, 16–18
SOPs (Standard Operating Procedures) (*see* Procedures)
Stand-out quotes, 415–416
Statement of objectives, in proposals, 94–95
Statement of problem, in proposals, 88, 90
Student authors:
  Andreini, Kay, 133–143
  Desselle, Diane, 145–153

Student authors (*cont.*):
  Otis, Susan, 133–143
  Soderstrom, Sheryl, 113–132, 208–225
  Sutter, Jon, 277–290
  Wheeler, Eric, 133–143
Student writing samples:
  completion report, 208–225
  proposals, 113–153
  résumés, 367, 383, 385
  scientific articles, 277–290
Summaries, 37
Summary of the research process, 38–39
Sutter, Jon, 277–290
Synonyms, in definition, 30

Table of contents, in proposal format, 105
Tables, 416–417
Technical and professional writing tasks, defined, 7
Technical manual (*see* Manuals)
Technical problem solving, 21–48
  analysis, 23
  conclusions, 46
  defined, 23
  defining multiple problems, 25–27
  definition in, 23
  implementation, 23
  overview, 23
  research, 23
  resolution and synthesis, 23
  techniques of definition, 27–31
    lay audience, 29–31
    well-informed audience, 27–29
Technical writing (*see* Professional writing continuum)
Technological breakdown, 71
Template, 424–425
Term project option, 18–19, 47–48, 81–82, 112, 169, 207, 240, 356, 390, 426, 457

Textbooks, format, 408
Thomas, Lewis, 31, 76–77
Thumbnail sketches, 406, 422–423
Timing, in oral presentations, 439
Title page (*see* Cover page)
Tone, 60
Transmittal letters, 102–103, 348–352
Trip reports, 228–239
  format, 232
  fundamentals, 229
  parts of, 230–232
    conclusions and recommendations, 232
    introduction, 230
    overall assessment, 230–231
    problems and solutions, 231–232
  purpose and rationale, 229
  questions they answer, 229–230
  sample professional trip report, 232–239
Typefaces, 411–412
Typography, 369

Unsolicited proposals, 87, 90–91
Utilization, 463

Visual aids (*see* Graphics)
Voice, grammatical (*see* Active voice; Passive voice)

Wheeler, Eric, 133–143
White space, 369, 407–409
Wood, R. L., 245–271
Wordiness, 465
Writer's tone, 339
Writing to address problems, 6–7
  (*See also* Documentation)
Writing for someone else's signature, 70
  (*See also* Ghost writing)